BASIC CRIMINAL PROCEDURE

JYOUNG UBS 3-27-95

Officer Jonathan Young
206-684-8499
206-917-0574

[ii]

BASIC CRIMINAL PROCEDURE

By

STEPHEN A. SALTZBURG

Howrey Professor of Trial Advocacy,
Litigation and Professional Responsibility
George Washington University National Law Center

DANIEL J. CAPRA

Professor of Law
Fordham University School of Law

CATHERINE HANCOCK

Associate Professor of Law
Tulane Law School

BLACK LETTER SERIES®

WEST PUBLISHING CO.
ST. PAUL, MINN.
1994

Black Letter Series and Black Letter Series design appearing on the front cover are registered trademarks of West Publishing Co. Registered in the U.S. Patent and Trademark Office.
COPYRIGHT © 1994 By WEST PUBLISHING CO.

      610 Opperman Drive
      P.O. Box 64526
      St. Paul, MN 55164–0526
      1–800–328–9352

Library of Congress Cataloging-in-Publication Data
Saltzburg, Stephen A.
    Basic criminal procedure / Stephen A. Saltzburg, Daniel J. Capra, Catherine Hancock.
      p.   cm. — (Black letter series)
    Includes index.
    ISBN 0–314–02734–3
    1. Criminal procedure—United States—Outlines, syllabi, etc.
I. Capra, Daniel, 1953–   . II. Hancock, Catherine, 1951–   .
III. Title. IV. Series.
KF9619.3.S25 1994
345.73′05—dc20
[347.3055]   93–45340
                      CIP

ISBN 0–314–02734–3

(S., C. & H.) Crim.Proc. BLS

 TEXT IS PRINTED ON 10% POST CONSUMER RECYCLED PAPER   

PUBLISHER'S PREFACE

This "Black Letter" is designed to help a law student recognize and understand the basic principles and issues of law covered in a law school course. It can be used both as a study aid when preparing for classes and as a review of the subject matter when studying for an examination.

Each "Black Letter" is written by experienced law school teachers who are recognized national authorities in the subject covered.

The law is succinctly stated by the author of this "Black Letter." In addition, the exceptions to the rules are stated in the text. The rules and exceptions have purposely been condensed to facilitate quick review and easy recollection. For an in-depth study of a point of law, citations to major student texts are given. In addition, a **Text Correlation Chart** provides a convenient means of relating material contained in the Black Letter to appropriate sections of the casebook the student is using in his or her law school course.

If the subject covered by this text is a code or code-related course, the code section or rule is set forth and discussed wherever applicable.

FORMAT

The format of this "Black Letter" is specially designed for review. (1) **Text.** First, it is recommended that the entire text be studied, and, if deemed necessary, supplemented by the student texts cited. (2) **Capsule Summary.** The Capsule Summary is an abbreviated review of the subject matter which can be used both before and after studying the main body of the text. The headings in the Capsule Summary follow the main text of the "Black Letter." (3) **Table of Contents.** The Table of Contents is in outline form to help you organize the details of the subject and the Summary of Contents gives you a final overview of the materials. (4) **Practice**

Examination. The Practice Examination in Appendix B gives you the opportunity of testing yourself with the type of question asked on an exam, and comparing your answer with a model answer.

In addition, a number of other features are included to help you understand the subject matter and prepare for examinations:

Short Questions and Answers: This feature is designed to help you spot and recognize issues in the examination. We feel that issue recognition is a major ingredient in successfully writing an examination.

Perspective: In this feature, the authors discuss their approach to the topic, the approach used in preparing the materials, and any tips on studying for and writing examinations.

Analysis: This feature, at the beginning of each section, is designed to give a quick summary of a particular section to help you recall the subject matter and to help you determine which areas need the most extensive review.

Examples: This feature is designed to illustrate, through fact situations, the law just stated. This, we believe, should help you analytically approach a question on the examination.

Glossary: This feature is designed to refamiliarize you with the meaning of a particular legal term. We believe that the recognition of words of art used in an examination helps you to better analyze the question. In addition, when writing an examination you should know the precise definition of a word of art you intend to use.

We believe that the materials in this "Black Letter" will facilitate your study of a law school course and assure success in writing examinations not only for the course but for the bar examination. We wish you success.

THE PUBLISHER

SUMMARY OF CONTENTS

APPENDICES

*

TABLE OF CONTENTS

APPENDICES

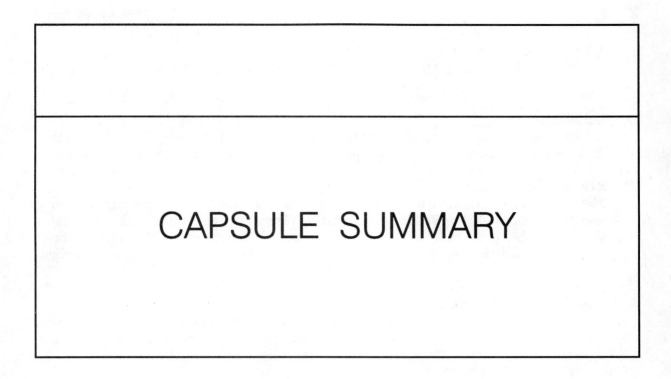

CAPSULE SUMMARY

INTRODUCTORY CONCEPTS

I. INCORPORATION
Virtually all of the protections granted under the Bill of Rights are granted in equal measure against the states through the Fourteenth Amendment's Due Process Clause.

II. RETROACTIVITY
A *new rule* is applicable retroactively to all cases on or before direct appeal. However, a new rule cannot generally be used to obtain relief in a habeas corpus petition after a conviction has become final.

A. Exceptions
The limited *exceptions* to the general rule of non-retroactivity on habeas are where:

1. Fundamental
The rule is so fundamental to the judicial system that it is likely that the old rule caused a miscarriage of justice in the defendant's trial; or

2. Prohibits Conviction or Punishment
The new rule prohibits the conviction or punishment of a class of defendants because of their status or offense.

B. Definition
A *new rule* is one not dictated by existing precedent. If reasonable minds could differ on a question of law, then the result reached by the court is a new rule.

III. STATE COURT ACTIVISM
The Supreme Court determines the minimum amount of protection granted to individuals through the Federal Constitution. State courts cannot grant defendants *less* protection than that provided by the Federal Constitution. However, a state court can construe its state constitution to give *greater* protection to a defendant.

A. Clear Statement Requirement
There is a *presumption* that the state constitution provides *coextensive* protection with the Federal, *unless* the state court makes a *clear statement* that its decision is based solely on the state constitution, regardless of what the Federal constitution may provide.

FOURTH AMENDMENT

I. INTRODUCTION
The Fourth Amendment represents a compromise between the need of government officials to gather evidence and the right of citizens to be free from governmental intrusion. Fourth Amendment limitations on governmental investigations are equally applicable to the state and federal governments.

A. Basics of the Fourth Amendment
1. Does Not Apply to Private Activity
The Fourth Amendment regulates state action, but does not limit private individuals acting on their own initiative. Thus, no matter how unreasonable a search may be, the Fourth Amendment is not implicated if the search is conducted by private actors not acting as agents of the government.

a. Applies to All Government Agents, Not Just Police Officers
The Amendment applies to the acts of all government officials, not just to law enforcement officers.

2. Protects "Persons, Houses, Papers and Effects"
Although the Fourth Amendment does not facially distinguish between the existence or scope of protection of a person, his property, or his home, the courts have developed a general hierarchy of protection wherein the greatest

protection is given to the house, then to the person's property, then to the person himself.

3. **Two Clauses**
    The Fourth Amendment has two clauses. The first clause, the reasonableness clause, provides a general standard that all searches and seizures must be reasonable. The second clause imposes requirements for obtaining warrants.

    a. **Which Clause Predominates?**
        The Supreme Court has read the warrant clause to predominate, or to define presumptively whether official conduct is "reasonable". A search or seizure is presumed unreasonable in the absence of a warrant based upon probable cause.

4. **The Theory of the Warrant Clause**
    The preeminence of the warrant clause was the result of early Supreme Court decisions which stressed the importance of imposing an unbiased factfinder as a buffer between the citizen suspected of crime and the officer engaged in the competitive enterprise of ferreting out crime.

    a. **Prior Record of Probable Cause**
        A subsidiary benefit of the warrant requirement is that it requires the officer to establish, on the record, the facts allegedly constituting probable cause *before* the search is conducted. Thus, the warrant requirement prevents post hoc submissions on probable cause.

    b. **Limitation on the Scope of a Search**
        Another benefit of the warrant requirement lies in the language of the amendment which requires that the warrant must *particularly describe* the place to be searched and the things to be seized. A warrant defines the scope of a search and thereby limits the discretion of the officers conducting the search.

5. **The Rise of the Reasonableness Clause**
    Even though the warrant clause is still considered the first reference point for the legality of a search or seizure, the Supreme Court has gradually moved to the point where most searches and seizures are in fact governed by a general standard of reasonableness. A general overview of the Supreme Court's Fourth Amendment cases shows that the dual requirement of *a warrant and probable cause are not needed in the following situations:*

    a. Where a warrant is *impracticable* to obtain. See the exigent circumstances exception. (Exception to warrant requirement but not an exception to the probable cause requirement).

Where the police conduct a *limited* seizure to investigate possible criminal activity and a *limited* search for weapons to protect the investigating officer. See the *Terry* Doctrine. (Exception to both warrant and probable cause requirements).

c.   Where the official is searching for evidence, but the search is conducted for purposes *other than criminal law enforcement*. See administrative and other "special needs" searches. (Exception to both warrant and probable cause requirements).

d.   Where a search is conducted *incident to a valid arrest*. (Exception to both warrant and probable cause requirements).

e.   Where there is *voluntary consent*. (Exception to both warrant and probable cause requirements).

f.   Where the citizen is *arrested in public*. (Arrest warrant not required, but police must have probable cause).

g.   Where an incriminating object is in *plain view or plain touch*, it may be seized without a warrant. (Probable cause required).

h.   Where the officer searches an *automobile* or other form of transportation. (Exception to warrant requirement but not to probable cause requirement).

II.   THRESHOLD REQUIREMENTS FOR FOURTH AMENDMENT PROTECTIONS; "SEARCH AND SEIZURE"

The Fourth Amendment prohibits unreasonable searches and seizures. Unless the government activity is either a "search" or a "seizure" it is not regulated by the Fourth Amendment, and therefore it does not have to be reasonable. In contrast, if the Court holds activity to be a search or a seizure, it does not mean that the activity is prohibited, but only that it must be reasonable.

A.   The *Katz* Test

In *Katz v. United States,* 389 U.S. 347, 88 S.Ct. 507, 19 L.Ed.2d 576 (1967), the Supreme Court rejected a literal interpretation of the Fourth Amendment, and held that the amendment was designed to protect *legitimate expectations* of privacy, personal security, and possessory interests in property. "The Fourth Amendment protects people, not places."

1.   Modern Definitions of "Search" and "Seizure"

After *Katz,* the term "search" is triggered whenever the state intrudes in any way upon the individual's protected interest in privacy. The term "seizure" is triggered whenever the state intrudes in any way on a protectable interest in property or security.

2.

2. Concurring Opinion of Justice Harlan

Justice Harlan's concurring opinion in *Katz* set forth a two-pronged test to determine whether a search has occurred:

a. Manifestation

First, has the citizen *manifested a subjective expectation of privacy?*

b. Reasonable Expectation

Second, is the interest one that *society is prepared to accept as reasonable?*

B. Interests Protected by the Fourth Amendment After *Katz*

1. "Legitimate" Interests

The Fourth Amendment protects only reasonable and legitimate interests in privacy. Thus, the Court has held on several occasions after *Katz* that there is no legitimate privacy interest in illegal activity. However, to protect innocent people with legitimate privacy and security expectations from mistaken assumptions by Government officials, certain interests must be presumed and protected before the intrusion takes place.

a. Physical Disruption and Inconvenience

All citizens have an interest in being free from physical disruption, inconvenience, or terrorization by Government officials.

b. Interest in Secrecy

Citizens have a right to secrecy—a right of protection against disclosure of information which, although not incriminating, may be embarrassing, sensitive, or extremely private.

c. Possessory Interests

The Fourth Amendment regulates not only invasions of privacy and security interests, but also invasions of possessory interests. The Fourth Amendment prohibits unreasonable *seizures* as well as searches.

C. Manifestation of a Subjective Interest in Privacy

How far must a citizen go to protect his privacy interests?

1. Strict Application

Generally speaking, the courts have required citizens to take vigorous measures to protect their claimed privacy interests.

2. Abandonment

Abandonment of property is inconsistent with the retention of any privacy or possessory interests.

D. Legitimacy of the Expectation of Privacy; Access by Members of the Public
After *Katz,* if an aspect of a person's life (such as his trash or public movement) is subject to scrutiny by members of the public, then that person has no legitimate expectation in denying equivalent access to the police. *There is no search if the police obtain information that members of the public could obtain.*

E. Investigation Which Can *Only* Uncover Illegal Activity Is Not a Search
There is no legitimate privacy interest in illegal activity.

    1. Dog Sniffs
    A dog sniff of a place or container is not a search as it can only tell the officer whether or not contraband is located therein, and there is no legitimate expectation of privacy in contraband.

    2. Chemical Tests
    If a chemical test merely discloses whether or not a substance is contraband, the test is not a search.

F. Reopening of Packages by Government Officials
If a package has once been opened consistently with the Fourth Amendment, it will not be a search if it is reopened by a Government official, unless there is a substantial probability that the contents of the package have been changed since the original opening. However, if the subsequent official investigation of the package or its contents exceeds the scope of the original search, it may trigger Fourth Amendment protection to the extent that a further intrusion is made.

G. Sensory Enhancement Devices
Generally speaking, the use by officials of devices which aid their investigation by enhancing the senses does not constitute a search, so long as the devices do no more than aid the police in obtaining information that they could have obtained through their own sensory perception.

H. Prisoners and Jail Cells
A prisoner has no legitimate property or privacy interests in his or her belongings kept in the prison cell that would trigger Fourth Amendment protections.

I. Open Fields
A person has no legitimate expectation of privacy in property that lies beyond his house and curtilage. The Fourth Amendment does not protect such "open fields."

    1. Curtilage Remains Protected
    If the property investigated is within the "curtilage", then the open fields doctrine does not apply, and a state intrusion into the curtilage will be a search if the citizen has manifested an expectation of privacy. Structures appurtenant to the home, such as porches and decks, are part of the

curtilage, at least so long as the structure is not shared with other homeowners and is restricted from public access.

J. Public School Students

High school students have an expectation of privacy while in school. However, the high state interest in promoting school discipline allows searches of students' belongings without first obtaining a warrant, and on the basis of reasonable suspicion rather than the higher standard of probable cause.

K. Government Employees

Intrusions into the private areas of Government employees, such as a desk or file cabinet, are searches covered by the Fourth Amendment. However, the search may be made without a warrant, and on the basis of reasonable suspicion.

III. THE PROBABLE CAUSE REQUIREMENT

Probable cause is a standard of proof of criminal activity that justifies a search or seizure. The probable cause standard strikes a balance between the rights of innocent citizens to privacy and security, and the interest of the state in investigating and prosecuting crime.

A. Standard of Proof Required for Probable Cause to Exist

The standard of proof required for probable cause is: enough particularized facts to lead a common sense person of reasonable caution to believe that there is a *fair probability* of criminal activity. Proof beyond a reasonable doubt is not required; neither is proof by a preponderance of the evidence.

1. Officers Are Allowed to Make Reasonable Mistakes

Because the probable cause standard is lower than a preponderance, it follows that officers need not be correct in their assessment of the facts. Arrests of the wrong person, and searches which uncover no incriminating evidence, are nonetheless permissible if the officer's mistake was reasonable.

2. Totality of the Circumstances

The analysis of probable cause requires a cumulative look at all pertinent factors.

3. Deference to Police Officer's Expertise

The experience and expertise of the officer is also taken into account. A fact which does not look suspicious at all to the untrained eye may be indicative of criminal activity to a person versed in how criminals operate.

4. Collective Knowledge

The particular officer who conducts an arrest or search need not have personal knowledge of all the facts on which probable cause is based. Probable cause can be based on the *collective knowledge* of the police department.

B. Generally Required for All Searches and Seizures
A search or seizure is presumptively unreasonable unless it is supported by probable cause and a warrant. But even if a search or seizure is conducted pursuant to an exception to the warrant requirement, it generally must still be supported by probable cause.

1. Exceptions
The Court has found three exceptional situations where a nonconsensual search or seizure may be conducted in the absence of probable cause:

a. Seizures of Persons or Things Which Constitute a Limited Intrusion
Temporary and minimally invasive detentions of persons and things, which are necessary to conduct a preliminary investigation, are allowed upon a showing of reasonable suspicion—which is a less demanding standard of proof than probable cause.

b. Limited Searches to Protect the Officer From Harm
An officer can, on reasonable suspicion instead of probable cause, conduct a limited search of a person, thing, or premises in order to protect himself from bodily harm while he is conducting a legitimate investigation.

c. Search or Seizure Conducted for Special Needs Beyond Criminal Law Enforcement
If the search or seizure is not conducted for purposes of criminal law enforcement but rather to effectuate some other governmental objective such as a regulatory interest, it can in most cases be conducted on less than probable cause.

2. All Searches for Criminal Law Enforcement Purposes Require Probable Cause
None of the above exceptions apply to a search conducted by law enforcement officers for the very purpose of enforcing the criminal law.

C. Questions of Identity
Probable cause as to identity must be based on specific information which ties a suspect to a crime. Probable cause requires a case-by-case approach; nonetheless, since the standard is only one of fair probability, a suspect's correspondence to a relatively specific description will go far toward a showing of probable cause. Furthermore, the state's case on probable cause as to identity is made significantly stronger if the suspect who fits a general description also has a prior criminal record.

D. Equivocal Conduct
A probable cause question arises where it is unclear whether a crime has been committed or is being committed at all.

1. **Innocent Explanations**
    Most courts will find probable cause if there is some conduct which a reasonable person would think highly suspect, even though an innocent explanation for the conduct is also plausible. The real question is whether plausible innocent explanations substantially outweigh the likelihood of criminality.

2. **First Amendment Considerations**
    First Amendment considerations do not require a standard of proof higher than probable cause before a search may be conducted of speech-related material.

E. Location

A probable cause question arises where officials suspect that a person to be arrested, or evidence of a crime, is located in a particular place. If investigation of such a place would be a search, the officers must have probable cause to believe that the person to be arrested or the evidence to be seized is located in the place to be searched.

1. **Staleness**
    The question of staleness arises when the information on which probable cause is based was discovered significantly earlier than when the search is actually conducted. Whether the information has grown stale is dependent upon such facts as the nature of the crime, the type of evidence, and the length of time that has passed.

2. **One of Several Locations**
    When a piece of evidence could be located in one of several places, but could not be in two locations at the same time, there is probable cause to search in each place, even though the locations are mutually exclusive, so long as there is a *logical nexus* between the crime and the location.

F. The Use of Hearsay

An officer is relying upon *hearsay* information when the officer does not have personal knowledge of the facts, but is instead using information obtained from other parties. A question then arises as to whether the "facts" related by such third parties are reliable enough to be credited in the probable cause determination.

1. **Former Two–Pronged Test**
    To ensure that the magistrate had some way to make an independent determination of the reliability of hearsay information, the Court in *Aguilar v. Texas,* 378 U.S. 108, 84 S.Ct. 1509, 12 L.Ed.2d 723 (1964), and *Spinelli v. United States,* 393 U.S. 410, 89 S.Ct. 584, 21 L.Ed.2d 637 (1969) imposed what came to be known as the *Aguilar–Spinelli two-pronged test* for structuring the magistrate's analysis of probable cause. The two prongs

assessed: (1) the informant's *reliability*, and (2) the *source* of the informant's information. The Supreme Court later rejected the two-pronged test in favor of a less structured *totality of the circumstances* approach. See *Illinois v. Gates,* 462 U.S. 213, 103 S.Ct. 2317, 76 L.Ed.2d 527 (1983). However, lower courts still use the two-pronged test as a helpful means by which to evaluate an informant's hearsay.

2. Impact of *Gates* Totality of Circumstances Approach

If *Aguilar–Spinelli* is satisfied, it follows that *Gates* is as well, since the *Gates* test is avowedly more permissive than the former test. Moreover, under the new approach, if a tip is especially strong on one prong, and not absolutely deficient on the other, probable cause may be found. More importantly, after *Gates,* if the tip is insufficient to establish probable cause, some corroboration of the tip by police investigation will ordinarily suffice to establish probable cause, even if the activity corroborated could be considered completely innocent.

IV. OBTAINING A VALID SEARCH WARRANT

Generally speaking, the Fourth Amendment requires every search or seizure to be made pursuant to a warrant issued upon probable cause. A warrant is a document issued by a judicial officer, usually a magistrate, authorizing a law enforcement official to make a search or seizure.

A. Neutral and Detached Magistrate

The magistrate must be a neutral official, who will make an unbiased determination of whether probable cause exists. There is no requirement that a magistrate give reasons for finding probable cause or for rejecting a warrant application. There is no requirement that the person who issues the warrant must be legally trained.

B. Probable Cause Based Only on Facts Presented to the Magistrate

The warrant requirement forces the officer to establish a record supporting probable cause *before* a search occurs. Probable cause must be judged solely by the information presented to the magistrate in the warrant application.

1. Affidavits

A warrant is ordinarily obtained by submitting an affidavit to the magistrate of all the facts supporting probable cause.

2. Telephone Warrants

A warrant may be obtained upon oral testimony communicated by telephone or other means. However, the officer must prepare a written "duplicate original warrant," and then read that warrant verbatim to the magistrate.

C. Particular Description of Place to Be Searched

Even if there is probable cause to search a certain location, a search warrant provides no authority to search it if the location is not described with *reasonable particularity*.

1. Reasonable Particularity

The degree of particularity which is reasonable depends on the nature of the place to be searched, and on the information that an officer could reasonably obtain about the location. Technical precision is not required in all cases.

2. Applicability to More Than One Location

If the warrant contains information as particularized as the officer could reasonably be expected to obtain, then it is sufficiently particular even though the warrant could actually apply to more than one location. The Fourth Amendment allows for reasonable mistakes of fact.

3. Incorrect Address

Variances between the actual address and the address specified in the warrant do not per se invalidate the warrant. The warrant remains valid so long as there is sufficient information therein for the executing officer to know where to execute the warrant despite the specification of a wrong address.

D. Particular Description of Things to Be Seized

The things to be seized must be particularly described in the warrant.

1. Reasonable Particularity

The test of whether a description of things to be seized is sufficiently particular is one of reasonableness, determined by the information that police could reasonably be expected to know prior to the search.

2. Catch–All Clauses

When the warrant describes some items in detail, and then includes a catch-all clause—e.g., allowing the seizure of "any other evidence of the crime"—courts will generally find such clauses to be overbroad unless they are somehow qualified by the particular descriptions that precede the catch-all clause in the warrant.

3. Severability

If some clauses in a warrant are sufficiently particular and other clauses are not, the overbroad clauses can be *severed* from those that are sufficiently particular. The warrant, and the search conducted pursuant to it, will then be evaluated on the basis of the valid clauses.

E. Warrant Can Authorize the Seizure of "Mere Evidence"
A warrant may be issued to search for and seize all evidence of a crime. An officer's search power is not limited to the actual fruits and instrumentalities of the crime.

F. Issuing Warrants Against Non-suspects
Searches can be made on the premises of non-suspects, either pursuant to a warrant or to an appropriate exception to the warrant requirement, so long as there is probable cause to believe that evidence will be found therein. Nothing in the language of the Fourth Amendment limits its scope to the premises of criminals.

1. No Special First Amendment Protection
The fact that the non-suspect is protected by the First Amendment creates no special protection against a search of the premises for evidence.

2. Statutory Protection
Congress has provided protections for journalists and others in the Privacy Protection Act of 1980.

EXCEPTIONS TO THE GENERAL FOURTH AMENDMENT REQUIREMENTS OF PROBABLE CAUSE AND A WARRANT

I. INTRODUCTION
A search or seizure is *presumptively unreasonable* in the absence of a warrant based upon probable cause and particularly describing the place to be searched and the things to be seized. However, the Supreme Court has established many exceptions to those general requirements.

II. THE PLAIN VIEW DOCTRINE
A. Seizure Without a Warrant
The plain view doctrine allows an officer, during the course of lawful police activity, to seize an object without a warrant if there is probable cause that it is evidence of criminal activity.

B. Limitations
1. Scope of Lawful Activity
The officer must be lawfully located in a place from which the object can be seen, and must also have a lawful right of access to the object.

2. Warrantless Seizures
The plain view doctrine allows a seizure if there is probable cause to believe that there is contraband or evidence in a container. However, the officer must generally obtain a search warrant to *open* the container.

3. **Probable Cause**
   There must be probable cause that the object in plain view is evidence of a crime.

4. **Probable Cause Must Be Immediately Apparent**
   If the item must be searched and investigated in order to determine whether there is probable cause to seize it, such an investigation is itself a search which requires probable cause.

C. **Plain Touch Exception to the Warrant Requirement**
   The police may seize evidence lawfully discovered through the sense of touch.

III. WARRANTLESS ARRESTS

A. **No Warrant Required for a Public Arrest**
   The Fourth Amendment does not require an officer to obtain a warrant before making a public arrest. This is so even if the officer could easily have obtained the warrant without jeopardizing the arrest.

1. **Post–Arrest Determination of Probable Cause**
   If a citizen is arrested without a warrant, he has the right to a prompt post-arrest determination of probable cause by a magistrate or judge.

   a. **Prompt Hearing Is Required**
      A 48 hour delay between arrest and hearing is presumed reasonable. The hearing need not be held at the first practicable opportunity; the state is allowed some flexibility to create efficient pre-trial procedures. However, any delay beyond 48 hours is presumed unreasonable, and the state has to present compelling circumstances to explain the delay.

B. **Warrant Required for an In–Home Arrest**
   The Fourth Amendment prohibits the police from arresting a defendant in his home without a warrant, in the absence of exigent circumstances.

1. **Violation Constitutes Illegal Search, Not an Illegal Arrest**
   When an officer has probable cause and arrests the defendant in his home without exigent circumstances, the officer has conducted an illegal *search* of the home by entering it to seize the arrestee. But the arrest itself is not illegal presuming it was made with probable cause.

C. **Search Warrant Required for an Arrest in the Home of a Third Party**
   An arrest warrant is insufficient to authorize the arrest of a suspect in the home of another person. In the absence of exigent circumstances or consent, a search warrant must be obtained to look for the suspect in the home of a third party. It is important to determine whether the suspect lives at the premises (in which case an arrest warrant is sufficient), or whether he is merely visiting there (in which case a search warrant is required).

IV.   EXIGENT CIRCUMSTANCES

A.   Introduction

Police are not required to obtain a warrant if exigent circumstances exist. However, officers operating under this exception must still satisfy the probable cause requirement. Generally speaking, the risks that trigger the exigent circumstances doctrine include those stemming from *hot pursuit* of a suspect, risks to *public safety*, and the risk of *destruction or loss of evidence*.

B.   Hot Pursuit

If officers are in hot pursuit of a suspect, this will excuse an arrest warrant where one is otherwise required, and it will also excuse a search warrant where a search of an area must be conducted in order to find and apprehend the suspect. The "hot pursuit" exception cannot apply where the suspect is unaware that he is being pursued by police officers.

C.   Risk to Public or Police Safety

If circumstances exist in which the police or the public would be harmed in the time it takes to obtain a warrant, officers are not required to obtain a warrant before entering a private area.

D.   Destruction or Loss of Evidence

The ground of exigency most often invoked is that in the time it would take to obtain a warrant there is an imminent risk of destruction or loss of evidence.

1.   Relevant Factors

The following is a non-exclusive list of factors courts take into account in determining whether the risk of destruction or loss of evidence is sufficient to excuse the warrant requirement. All of the factors are relevant and none are necessarily dispositive.

—The *degree of urgency* involved and the *amount of time* necessary to obtain a warrant.

—A reasonable belief that contraband or evidence is *about to be removed*.

—The *possibility of danger* to police officers guarding the premises while a search warrant is sought.

—Information indicating that suspects *know that the police are on their trail*.

—The ready *destructibility* of the evidence.

—The *gravity of the offense* of which the suspects are to be charged.

—Whether the suspects are reasonably believed to have *firearms* in their possession.

—Whether *probable cause is clear* or is rather a close question.

—The *likelihood that suspects may escape* in the absence of an immediate entry.

—The *peaceful circumstances* of the entry.

—The *amount of time* it would take to obtain a warrant. If a *telephone warrant* is available in the jurisdiction, then the time it would take to obtain such a warrant is the benchmark. Telephone warrants are available under Federal practice.

2. Narcotics Cases
Most lower courts liberally apply the exigent circumstances exception in drug cases.

a. Need Not Be in the Process of Destruction
Courts generally do not require narcotics to be in the actual process of destruction before a warrantless entry can be justified.

3. Murder Scene Searches
While the gravity of the crime is a factor in determining exigent circumstances, there is not a per se exigent circumstances exception for the search of a murder scene.

4. Minor Crimes
It is more difficult to establish exigency if the crime is a minor one.

E. Impermissible Creation of Exigent Circumstances
The warrant requirement will not be excused where the exigency has been impermissibly created by the police.

F. Prior Opportunity to Obtain a Warrant
If the officers had probable cause and a clear opportunity to obtain a warrant for a significant time before an exigency arose, they are not excused from the warrant requirement.

G. Securing Premises While Waiting for the Warrant
Even in the absence of exigent circumstances, officers can protect against the destruction of evidence by securing a premises for the reasonable time it takes to obtain a warrant.

V.   STOP AND FRISK

A.   *Terry* and the Court's Reliance on the Reasonableness Clause of the Fourth Amendment

In *Terry v. Ohio,* 392 U.S. 1, 88 S.Ct. 1868, 20 L.Ed.2d 889 (1968), the Court held that a *stop* can be conducted if an officer has *reasonable suspicion* to believe that crime is afoot. The *Terry* Court further held that an officer who makes a legal stop can conduct a *protective frisk* of a suspect if the officer has *reasonable suspicion to fear* that the suspect is armed and dangerous.

1.   Three Categories of Police–Citizen Contacts

After *Terry,* there are three categories of police-citizen contact:

a.   Arrest and Incident Search

The most serious intrusion is an arrest, and the standard of proof required to justify an arrest is probable cause. An arrest allows a complete search incident to the arrest, for self-protection and to protect against the destruction of evidence.

b.   Stop and Frisk

A less serious intrusion is a stop, which is permitted on the lesser standard of proof of reasonable suspicion. Incident to a stop is a frisk, which is a limited search for weapons, *not for evidence.*

c.   Encounter

If an officer merely engages the citizen in an encounter, this is not considered an intrusion at all. Since an *encounter is not a seizure*, it does not implicate the Fourth Amendment, and therefore the officer need not satisfy any standard of proof before conducting an encounter.

B.   What Is a "Stop"?: The Line Between Stop and Encounter

If an officer "stops" a citizen, he must have reasonable suspicion, because a stop is a seizure which requires a justification; but an officer can "encounter" a citizen for any reason or no reason, as an encounter is not a seizure.

1.   The *Mendenhall* Reasonable Person Test

In *United States v. Mendenhall,* 446 U.S. 544, 100 S.Ct. 1870, 64 L.Ed.2d 497 (1980), Justice Stewart proposed a definition for "stop" which was later adopted by the Court with certain modifications: if, in view of all the circumstances, a *reasonable innocent person would have believed that he was not free to leave,* then a stop has occurred.

2.   Active Coercion Prohibited

Under the *Mendenhall* test, an officer who affirmatively employs *coercive* tactics will be held to have conducted a seizure, requiring (at least) reasonable suspicion. If, instead, the officer acts politely and the citizen merely responds to the fact that the questioning is conducted by an officer, then the contact will be deemed an encounter.

3. **Informing the Citizen of the Right to Terminate an Encounter or to Refuse Consent**
An officer is not obligated to tell the citizen that he has the right to refuse to answer questions or consent to a search. However, if the officer does inform the citizen of these rights, this will go far toward establishing a consensual encounter.

4. **Two Recent Modifications to the *Mendenhall* "Free to Leave" Test**
   a. **Not Free to Leave Because of the Suspect's Own Circumstances**
   If the citizen is confined because of his own circumstances (e.g., the citizen is in a bus, a subway, or an elevator), the question is whether *the police conduct would have communicated to a reasonable person that the person was not free to decline the officers' requests or otherwise terminate the encounter*. The fact that the citizen is not physically free to leave is essentially irrelevant where the condition is not created by the police but by the suspect's own circumstances.

   b. **If Coercive Tactics are Non-physical, There Is No Stop Until the Suspect Submits**
   In *California v. Hodari D.,* 499 U.S. 621, 111 S.Ct. 1547, 113 L.Ed.2d 690 (1991), the Court separated "seizures" into two types: those in which the officer has *physically touched* the suspect, and those in which the officer has used a non-physical *show of authority* (such as drawing a gun, ordering the suspect to stop, etc.). A stop *automatically* occurs when an officer physically touches a suspect with the intent of restraining him. Where the officer employs a non-physical show of authority, it must be such that a reasonable innocent person would not feel free to leave, *and the citizen must actually submit to the show of authority*.

5. **Officer is Not Required to Use an Encounter as a "Less Intrusive Alternative"**
If an officer has reasonable suspicion to support a stop, she can seize the suspect even though an encounter may be equally productive. The officer is not required to employ the less intrusive alternative.

C. **What Is Reasonable Suspicion? Similar Analysis to Probable Cause**
The analysis used to determine whether reasonable suspicion exists to support a stop is similar to that employed in assessing probable cause. The following analytical concepts are applicable to both standards:

—A *common sense* analysis of the facts presented.

—*Deference* to the *expertise* of law enforcement officers.

—The *totality of circumstances* must be assessed.

—Reasonable mistakes of fact are permitted.

1. **Difference in Quantity and Quality of Proof**
   The difference between reasonable suspicion and probable cause is that reasonable suspicion is a *less demanding* standard of proof—a stop is permissible upon something less than the fair probability standard which defines probable cause. Reasonable suspicion can be usefully referred to as *possible cause*.

2. **Questions of Identity of a Perpetrator**
   Stops are permissible where it is clear that a crime has occurred, and the officer has an articulable suspicion that a particular person is the perpetrator.

3. **Suspicious Conduct**
   A stop is permitted if, considering all the circumstances, an officer could find it reasonably possible that "criminal activity is afoot." The fact that an innocent explanation for the suspect's conduct can be hypothesized does not preclude a finding of reasonable suspicion.

   a. **Non-cooperation During an Encounter**
      The mere fact that a person acts somewhat nervously in the presence of a police officer is not suspicious. Further, a suspect's mere failure to consent to requests by a police officer during an encounter can not be a factor which contributes to reasonable suspicion, as a person who is merely encountered has the absolute right to refuse cooperation and terminate the encounter. However, certain out-of-the-ordinary activity designed to avoid or terminate conduct with the police may be considered suspicious.

4. **Use of Profiles**
   A profile is a list of characteristics compiled by a law enforcement agency which have been found through experience to be common to those engaged in a certain type of criminal activity. The most common example is a drug courier profile.

   a. **Match With Profile Is Not Dispositive**
      A suspect's correlation with a profile is no guarantee that there is reasonable suspicion to justify a stop; the reasonableness of a stop must be assessed in light of the *particular circumstances*.

   b. **Officers' Use of Profile Does Not Render the Stop Illegal**
      On the other hand, the officer's use of a drug courier profile does not somehow taint the stop, assuming reasonable suspicion exists on the facts.

5.   Relevance of Suspect's Race

Courts have traditionally considered racial "incongruity" (i.e., that a person of a certain race is unlikely to be in a certain neighborhood or area) as relevant in assessing reasonable suspicion—although such incongruity is not ordinarily dispositive. However, there is a recent trend to prohibit reliance on racial incongruity.

6.   Use of Informants

An officer's assessment of reasonable suspicion is often based in whole or in part on information from an informant. However, the *Aguilar–Spinelli* reliability and credibility factors, and even the less demanding *Gates* test for probable cause, are considered unnecessarily rigorous for the standard of reasonable suspicion. Reasonable suspicion is not only a less demanding standard, it is also less rigorous in the types of information that can be used as proof.

a.   Reasonably Correct Prediction of Future Activity Is Crucial

An informant's tip will be an important consideration towards reasonable suspicion if it correctly predicts future activity. In contrast, corroboration of contemporaneous conditions (e.g. that the suspect is driving a certain car) indicates little about the reliability of the informant's assessment of criminal conduct, since such conditions could be easily observed by one who has no inside information about criminal activity.

D.   The Right to Frisk Incident to a Stop

A stop is a seizure. A frisk is a search, which is an independent intrusion that must be separately justified. There are two critical determinations that must be made in judging the legality of a frisk: 1) whether the officer's action was justified at its *inception*, and 2) whether it was reasonably related in *scope* to the circumstances which justified the interference in the first place.

1.   Frisk Is Not a Search for Evidence

Terry does not permit a search for evidence. A search for evidence, in the absence of a need to protect the officer, requires probable cause.

2.   Inception of a Frisk; Reasonable Suspicion of Bodily Harm

Terry requires "reasonable, individualized suspicion before a search for weapons can be conducted." Assuming that a stop is justified, the question upon which the legality of a frisk depends is whether there is reasonable suspicion to believe that the suspect is armed and dangerous. The following is a list of relevant factors which may support a frisk:

—Reasonable suspicion that a person is involved in a *crime of violence*.

—Suspicion of *large-scale drug distribution*.

—A *bulge* on the suspect that appears to be a weapon.

—A *sudden movement* by the suspect toward a place where a weapon might be hidden.

—*Previous violent activity* on the part of the suspect, which activity is known to the officer.

—*Aggressive or violent behavior* on the part of the suspect.

—The *number of suspects compared to the number of police officers.*

—The *nature of the surroundings* and the *time of day.*

3. **Self-protective Frisk of Those Not Suspected of a Crime**
   A person cannot be frisked merely because he or she is at a location where criminal activity exists. However, if an officer can point to articulable facts linking that person to the criminal activity, then a protective frisk will be permitted.

4. **Ordering a Suspect Out of a Car for Self–Protection**
   An officer has an *automatic* right to order a person to step out of a vehicle where that vehicle has been lawfully stopped.

5. **Limitations on the Scope of a Frisk**
   In conducting a frisk, an officer can be *no more intrusive than is necessary* to protect against the risk of harm posed by the suspect. A detailed touching of all areas of the suspect's body is beyond the scope of a *Terry* frisk.

   a. **Probable Cause**
      If an officer feels a soft package, it cannot be taken out and inspected under the *Terry* doctrine; but the fact that the suspect was carrying a soft package may, together with other factors, constitute probable cause that the suspect is carrying contraband. If this is so, then the suspect may be arrested and the package may be searched incident to the arrest.

   b. **Containers on the Suspect's Person**
      If the officer reasonably takes a hard object from the suspect's person and it turns out to be a container, generally the officer may open the container.

6. **Right to Protective Search Beyond the Suspect's Person**
   Officers are permitted to conduct protective searches of containers carried by the suspect or within the suspect's grab area, if there is a reasonable risk that an accessible weapon could be located in that area.

a.   Protective Search of Automobiles
Cursory inspections of the accessible areas of the passenger compartment of an automobile are permitted whenever there is reasonable suspicion to believe that the suspect poses a threat of harm.

b.   Protective Sweep
A "protective sweep" is a quick and limited search of a premises, incident to an arrest and conducted to protect the safety of police officers or others. A protective sweep can be conducted if officers have articulable facts that give rise to reasonable suspicion; probable cause is not required. A protective sweep can only be conducted for safety purposes, and not to prevent the destruction of evidence.

E.   Brief and Limited Detentions: The Line Between Stop and Arrest
Stops are permitted upon a showing of reasonable suspicion because stops are more limited intrusions than arrests. Using a totality of the circumstances approach, courts generally look at the following factors to determine whether a police intrusion constitutes a stop requiring reasonable suspicion or an arrest requiring probable cause:

1.   Forced Movement of the Suspect to a Custodial Area
Generally, the forced movement of suspects for investigative purposes is beyond the scope of *Terry,* and thus requires probable cause. However, if reasonable suspicion exists, it is often permissible to transport the suspect a short distance so that eyewitnesses may attempt to make an identification. Also, a suspect may be moved from one location to another for purposes of safety or security.

2.   Investigative Techniques
While an officer conducting a *Terry* stop can engage in preliminary investigation designed to clear up or to further develop reasonable suspicion, some investigative techniques are themselves so intrusive as to require probable cause (e.g., body cavity searches).

3.   Time Limits on *Terry* Stops
There is no absolute time limit at which point a stop will automatically become an arrest. While the question of whether the police "diligently pursued" a quick means of investigation is a *factor* in determining the level of seizure that took place, officers are generally given the benefit of the doubt if they are acting reasonably and not wasting time.

a.   Suspect's Refusal to Consent to a Search
A suspect's refusal to consent to a search cannot be used as a justification for prolonging a stop. However, a detention can be prolonged if the suspect acts *improperly* to subvert the officer's investigation (e.g., by running away).

b.   Detention of Household Occupants During Execution of a Search Warrant
Police officers with a valid search warrant may order persons on the premises to remain there while a search warrant is being executed—even if the length of the detention exceeds that ordinarily associated with a *Terry* stop.

4.   Show of Force or Use of Restraint
The use of forceful, coercive tactics—such as the use of handcuffs or a drawn gun—does not automatically transform a stop into an arrest. Stops may be accompanied by force when the circumstances indicate such means are reasonably necessary to insure the safety of the officers. The following factors are relevant in determining whether an officer, in the course of a *Terry* stop, permissibly employed custodial tactics:

—The *number of officers* involved.

—The *nature of the crime* for which reasonable suspicion exists.

—Whether there is *reasonable suspicion to believe the suspect might be armed*.

—The *strength of the officers' articulable suspicions*.

—Whether the *suspect is cooperative*.

—The *need for immediate action* by the officers and the lack of opportunity for them to have made the stop in *less threatening circumstances*.

F.   Detentions of Property Under *Terry*
Terry applies both to seizures of property and persons. There are three types of police contact with personal property which require correspondingly increasing standards of proof:

—*Non-material interference* which does *not implicate Fourth Amendment concerns*.

—*Temporary detentions* interfering with possessory or liberty interests which require at least *reasonable suspicion*.

—Detentions *so lengthy and intrusive* that they require *probable cause*.

1.   Relevant Factors
The following factors are relevant in determining whether the detention of property is so prolonged as to require probable cause, or sufficiently limited as to be permissible upon reasonable suspicion:

—The *length* of the detention and whether *liberty interests as well as possessory interests are at stake.*

—*Information conveyed to the suspect* concerning the seizure—e.g., when the property can be retrieved.

G. Roadblocks
While stops of vehicles ordinarily require reasonable suspicion, there are certain circumstances in which roadblock seizures at fixed checkpoints are allowed without any suspicion of criminal activity.

VI. ADMINISTRATIVE AND REGULATORY SEARCHES AND SEIZURES
If a search or seizure is justified by *special needs beyond criminal law enforcement*, the Court will balance the state interest in conducting the search against the individual privacy interest at stake, under the *reasonableness clause* of the Fourth Amendment. These searches and seizures, unlike those conducted under the *Terry* doctrine, can be directed towards uncovering evidence.

A. Safety Inspections of Homes
A home inspection, arising from an established inspection policy, can be conducted without probable cause but, except in emergency situations or with the homeowner's consent, the inspection does require a search warrant.

B. Administrative Inspections of Businesses
Administrative inspections of businesses usually can be conducted without probable cause. Furthermore, heavily regulated businesses may be searched without a warrant, due to the significant state interest involved as well as the diminished expectation of privacy attendant to participation in a heavily regulated business. However, such warrantless inspections must *necessarily further a substantial governmental interest*, and statutes must provide *constitutionally adequate substitutes for a warrant* (i.e. notification, scope, and limitation of the inspectors' discretion). Investigations of areas open to the general public are not considered searches covered by Fourth Amendment protections.

C. Civil–Based Searches of Individuals Pursuant to "Special Needs"
A special needs balancing analysis is used to uphold civil-based searches of individuals in the absence of a warrant and probable cause. Any evidence uncovered from such searches may be used in traditional criminal law proceedings, so long as the search itself was conducted for a regulatory objective.

1. Searches Directed at Students, Government Employees, Parolees, and Probationers
Searches of the belongings of students (at school), Government employees (at the workplace), parolees, and probationers may be conducted without a warrant and on the basis of reasonable suspicion.

   2. **Security Searches at Airports, Courthouses, Military Installations, Prisons, etc.**
       In order to provide safety and security for the public in various locales where a security risk has been demonstrated, checkpoint security searches are allowed at airports, courthouses, jails, military installations, etc. without warrants or individualized suspicion. People must be given the option to avoid a search by leaving the premises.

   3. **Drug Testing of Government Employees**
       As public employers have a regulatory interest in both public safety and job performance, *drug testing of Government employees* may be conducted without use of warrants and, in certain circumstances, without a finding of reasonable suspicion. Even in the absence of a documented problem of drug abuse, *neutral, non-discretionary, suspicionless testing* may be allowed if undetected drug use would impair a *substantial governmental interest*.

D. **Border Searches and Seizures**
    Border searches, or searches at the functional equivalent of the border, are generally allowed without warrants, and often without any suspicion at all, due to the Government's interest in protecting the American borders and regulating goods flowing in *and out* of the country (i.e. communicable diseases, narcotics, explosives, illegal aliens). Particularly intrusive searches, such as body cavity or full strip searches, require a finding of individualized suspicion.

VII. **SEARCH INCIDENT TO ARREST**
    The search incident to arrest exception—also known as the "arrest power rule"—automatically allows police officers during a lawful custodial arrest to secure the suspect and his grab area without reasonable suspicion or probable cause, and without a warrant. This right is based on two grounds: 1) to *protect the officers making the arrest* and 2) to *protect against the destruction of evidence*.

A. **Relevant Factors to Determine Arrestee's "Grab Area"**
    A suspect's grab area is determined on a case-by-case basis, but certain factors are helpful in these determinations:

    —Whether the suspect is *cuffed or restrained*.

    —The *physical characteristics* of the particular suspect.

    —The *ratio of police officers to suspects*.

    —Whether the item searched is *reasonably accessible to the suspect*.

B.   Circumstances Which Justify Searches Beyond the Grab Area
While a search incident to arrest is subject to spacial limitations, other exceptions might apply during or after an arrest which may permit officers to conduct searches or seizures *beyond* the area within the arrestee's immediate control.

1.   Moving Grab Area
If an arrestee moves to a different location during a lawful arrest, the *grab area automatically moves along with the suspect*; police officers need not show a case-by-case risk of danger to follow the suspect and inspect the suspect's grab area.

2.   Exigent Circumstances
When a person is arrested, a risk may arise that the arrestee's associates will destroy evidence before a warrant can be obtained.

3.   Protective Sweep
The fact of arrest may create a risk of harm to the arresting officers from the arrestee's associates, which could justify a *protective sweep* of the premises.

4.   Securing Premises
There may be a need to *secure the premises* during the time it takes to obtain a search warrant after a suspect is arrested.

C.   Temporal Limitations
Searches "incident to arrest" are allowed slightly before the formal arrest process, as long as the probable cause to arrest is present *before* such a search is conducted. Also, searches and seizures that *could* be made at the time of the arrest are allowed slightly *later* in time as long as the arrest process is not yet complete. A search is ordinarily no longer incident to arrest if the suspect has been removed from the arrest scene.

D.   Searches of the Person
Police officers have the *automatic* right to conduct a *complete body frisk*, and to pull out and search all objects *on an arrestee's person*, even if there is no factual risk of harm to the officer or likelihood of destruction of evidence. Generally, police may search, as well as seize, all items that are "immediately associated" with the arrestee (e.g., wallets and purses).

1.   Objects in the Grab Area
Most courts allow searches, as well as seizures, of items *not* immediately associated with the arrestee, but within the arrestee's grab area (e.g., briefcases and book bags). But there is a split in the courts on this point—some courts allow the automatic *seizure* of such items, but preclude a search of these items in the absence of warrant and probable cause, or some other exception to the warrant requirement.

E. Searches of Automobiles

When the occupant of a car is lawfully arrested, the arrest power rule allows an *automatic* search of the passenger compartment of the car without a warrant or probable cause. The passenger compartment of a car is *always* in the "grab area", even if the arrestee does not have reasonable access to this area. Generally, anything accessible from the interior of the car encompasses the passenger compartment. The police may search and open all containers found in the passenger compartment.

VIII. PRETEXTUAL SEARCHES AND SEIZURES

Generally, if an officer has an *objective* right to make a stop or arrest for a minor infraction, the stop is legal and it makes no difference that the officer might have "subjectively" used the stop or arrest as a pretext to obtain evidence of a more serious crime. Nor does it matter that a reasonable officer would not, under the circumstances presented, have stopped or arrested the defendant for the minor crime. A minority of courts, however, hold that a stop or arrest for a minor offense is invalid if a reasonable officer would not have intervened absent a pretextual motive to obtain evidence of a more serious crime.

IX. SEARCHES AND SEIZURES OF AUTOMOBILES AND OTHER MOVABLE PROPERTY

A. Automobile Exception

The automobile exception allows the police to search a car without obtaining a warrant if there is probable cause to believe that the car contains evidence of criminal activity. A warrant will be required only if the police have a reasonable opportunity to obtain a warrant before seizing the car. The automobile exception may also be applied to airplanes and mobile homes.

    1. Distinguishing the Automobile Exception From a Search Incident to Arrest

    The search of an automobile incident to arrest does not depend on the existence of exigent circumstances or probable cause to search, but rather it focuses on the *legality of the underlying arrest* and the *area in which the search occurred*.

    2. Which Exception Is Preferred?

    The state prefers to invoke the *arrest power rule* because once the arrest of a suspect is found lawful, the right to search the passenger compartment of a car is *automatic*. In contrast, searches pursuant to the automobile exception are not permissible unless officers have probable cause to believe that evidence will be found in the car. However, there are at least three situations in which the arrest power rule will not apply and then the state may find it necessary to resort to the automobile exception:

    —The arrest is *not* made *in or near a car*.

—The search of the car is *too far removed* from the arrest so that it can *no longer be deemed incident to the arrest.*

—Officers wish to search the *trunk* of the car.

B. Movable Property—In and Out of Cars
If a car is subject to a warrantless search under the automobile exception, then the police may search any container located in the car, without a warrant, so long as they have probable cause to believe that the container holds evidence of criminal activity. However, in the absence of exigent circumstances, a warrant is required to search a container that is located outside a car; there is no analogy to the automobile exception for movable containers, such as luggage, which are found outside a car.

C. Car Searches and Seizures Pursuant to the Community Caretaking Function
If officers are performing duties *apart* from those associated with traditional law enforcement, the officers may conduct warrantless searches of vehicles so long as the searches are reasonably conducted for safety purposes. Similarly, the police do not need probable cause or a warrant to impound a car for caretaking purposes.

1. Inventory Exception
Automobiles that are lawfully held in police custody may be searched without a warrant or suspicion under the inventory exception to the warrant requirement, so long as standardized inventory regulations are in place to control the discretion of the searching officer. Inventory searches are administrative searches conducted for safety purposes, and to protect vehicles from theft or vandalism.

2. Purpose
Police officers may also conduct inventory searches of property carried by a person at the time of his arrest, unless a suspect is being charged with an immediately bailable offense.

X. CONSENT SEARCHES
If a suspect *voluntarily* consents to a search, the search is permissible even in the absence of a warrant or any articulable suspicion. Consenting to a search is *not* considered a *waiver* of a constitutional right—which must be intelligent, voluntary, and knowing. Rather, a search made pursuant to voluntary consent is considered a *reasonable* search under the Fourth Amendment. The Government must show by a preponderance of the evidence that the consent was *voluntary under the totality of circumstances.*

A. Factors Relevant to Voluntariness
No single factor is dispositive, but the following factors are relevant in assessing whether a consent was voluntarily obtained:

—Whether the person consenting is *in custody.*

—The presence of *coercive police procedures*.

—The extent and level of the person's *cooperation* with the police.

—The person's *awareness of his right to refuse consent*. Note that the police are *not* obligated to inform a person of his right to refuse consent. Furthermore, a person's lack of knowledge regarding this right does *not* preclude a finding of consent. On the other hand, if a person is informed that he has a right to refuse consent, a subsequent consent is likely to be found voluntary.

—The person's *education and intelligence*.

—The person's *belief that no incriminating evidence will be found*.

B. Third Party Consent

If a third party has access to or control over a private area, he or she is considered to have an *independent privacy interest*, and the suspect is considered to have *assumed the risk* that the third party may lawfully consent to a search of that area. A third party's access may be limited or conditional, depending on the circumstances.

1. Marital Relationships

Generally, there is a presumption of *common authority* over premises jointly occupied by both spouses.

2. Defendant's Refusal to Consent May Effect Validity of Third Party Consent

Generally, if both the defendant and third party are present, the third party may not validly consent to a search if the defendant simultaneously objects. However, some courts will allow a search over a defendant's refusal if a third party subsequently consents.

3. The Third Party Must Possess Actual or Apparent Authority

Third party consent is valid if the third party possesses *actual or apparent authority*. Apparent authority results when police officers *reasonably believe* that the third party has authority to consent. This reasonable belief does not arise merely from a third party's assertion of common authority; police officers have a *duty* to make *reasonable inquiries* regarding the third party's claim of authority.

C. Scope of Consent

A consenting party may place limitations on the *scope* of the consent. A search is not a valid consent search if a *reasonable person* would conclude that it exceeds the limitations established by the consenting party.

1. **Ambiguity Regarding Scope of Consent Is Construed Against the Suspect**
    If an officer's interpretation of a general or ambiguous consent is a reasonable one, the resulting search will be considered within the scope of the consent—even if the scope is not crystal clear. It is up to the *suspect* to clarify the scope of an ambiguous consent. However, a search which requires mutilation or destruction of property or premises is considered beyond the reasonable scope of a general consent.

D. **Revocation of Consent**
    A suspect has the right to revoke consent, although it cannot be revoked retroactively after an officer has found incriminating evidence. The mere withdrawal or limitation of a consent cannot be considered a factor in an officer's determination of reasonable suspicion or probable cause.

REMEDIES FOR FOURTH AMENDMENT VIOLATIONS

I. **THE EXCLUSIONARY RULE**
    The *exclusionary rule* provides that evidence obtained in violation of a defendant's Fourth Amendment rights must be excluded from trial in both federal and state courts. The exclusionary rule is a *court-made rule* designed to deter future violations of the Fourth Amendment, and a court is *not constitutionally required* to exclude illegally obtained evidence. The Supreme Court has created exceptions to the exclusionary rule for situations where the rule's costs significantly outweigh the deterrent value of the rule.

II. **STANDING TO INVOKE THE EXCLUSIONARY RULE**
    The standing requirement provides that a defendant cannot obtain exclusion of evidence unless his *own personal Fourth Amendment rights* are violated.

A. **Reasonable Expectation of Privacy**
    Standing questions are resolved by determining whether a person has a *legitimate expectation of privacy* in the area or thing that was searched, or a legitimate possessory interest in the thing seized.

    1. **Burden on Defendant**
        The *defendant* bears the burden of proving that he had a legitimate expectation of privacy that was violated by the challenged search and seizure.

    2. **Possessory Interest in Items Seized Is Insufficient**
        A defendant does not automatically have standing to contest the *search* of an area merely because the items *seized* are owned by the defendant. However, he generally does have a right to object to the *seizure* of such property, even if it is being held by a third party. A seizure would implicate a suspect's *personal* Fourth Amendment possessory interest in the item seized.

3.   **Disassociation With the Object of the Search**
     Where a defendant disavows any knowledge of or interest in property that is
     being searched or seized, such an action is inconsistent with a reasonable
     expectation of privacy, and the defendant will not have standing to object to
     the police activity.

4.   **Co-conspirator Status**
     The mere fact that a search or seizure has occurred with respect to property
     controlled by a conspiracy does not mean that each co-conspirator has
     standing to object. There is no joint venture exception to the principle that
     standing is dependent on a violation of one's own personal Fourth
     Amendment rights.

III. **EXCLUSION OF "THE FRUIT OF THE POISONOUS TREE"**
A.   **Introduction**
     A defendant often seeks exclusion of the *very evidence* that was found in an
     illegal search or seizure. Such evidence is termed the "direct" or "primary"
     evidence of the illegal search. However, the defendant may also challenge the
     admission of evidence which was *derived from* an initial illegality. Such evidence
     is termed "derivative" evidence, or "fruit of the poisonous tree." The exclusionary
     rule generally applies to *all evidence derived* from the evidence obtained in the
     illegal search—i.e. to all fruits of the illegality. But there are exceptions to this
     exclusionary principle.

B.   **Attenuation**
     In some cases, the link between the illegal search or seizure and the evidence
     obtained is *so attenuated* that the evidence can no longer be meaningfully
     considered "tainted" or the "fruit of the poisonous tree." Under those
     circumstances, the deterrent effect of the exclusionary rule is considered equally
     attenuated and, therefore, the cost of excluding reliable evidence outweighs the
     negligible benefit of deterrence. Attenuation is determined on a case-by-case basis.

     1.   **Test of Causation**
          The Court has rejected a "but for" test for determining whether evidence has
          been tainted by, or rather is attenuated from, an illegality. Instead, the test
          to determine whether there is a sufficient connection between the illegality
          and the derivative evidence so as to justify exclusion is as follows: whether,
          under the totality of circumstances, the evidence has been come at by
          exploitation of the illegality or instead by means *sufficiently distinguishable* to be
          purged of the primary taint.

     2.   **Relevant Factors in Determining Attenuation**
          Once an illegal search or seizure is established, the *Government has the
          burden* of proving that the causal chain is sufficiently attenuated to dissipate
          the taint of the illegality. Several factors are deemed relevant in this
          determination:

—The giving of *Miranda warnings*. Note that *Miranda* warnings will *not* per se break the chain of causation, but they are relevant to dissipating the taint of an illegal search or seizure.

—The *time* between the *arrest and the confession*.

—The presence of *intervening circumstances*.

—The *purpose and flagrancy of the official misconduct*.

3. **Abandonment During the Course of an Illegal Search or Seizure**
   A suspect's decision to abandon property subsequent to an illegal search or seizure may or may not be tainted by that illegality. Courts determine if abandoned evidence is tainted by looking at whether a defendant had *sufficient time and opportunity* to make a *calculated* decision to abandon the property, or whether the decision to abandon the property was a *spontaneous reaction* to the illegal activity.

4. **Testimony of Live Witnesses**
   An illegal search or seizure may lead to the discovery of a witness who can give testimony against the defendant. Generally, a witness' voluntary decision to testify against the defendant will mean that the testimony is attenuated from the illegality.

C. **Independent Source**
   Evidence will not be excluded as the fruit of the poisonous tree if the Government can show that it was derived from an *independent legal source*. The independent source exception admits the fruits of illegally obtained evidence when such fruits are also found by *legal means unrelated to the original illegal conduct*. Under those circumstances, application of the exclusionary rule would impermissibly place the officers in a *worse* position than they would have been absent any violation.

D. **Inevitable Discovery**
   The *inevitable discovery* exception to the exclusionary rule allows the fruits of illegal activity to be admitted at trial if the Government can show that the challenged evidence would *inevitably* have been discovered through means completely independent of the illegal activity. In essence, the inevitable discovery exception is a "hypothetical" independent source exception.

1. **Inevitability Must Be Shown by a Preponderance**
   The exception is applicable if the Government proves by a *preponderance of the evidence* that the discovery would have inevitably occurred through legal means.

2.   Focus on What Would, Not Could, Have Been Done
For the inevitable discovery exception to apply, the question is *not* what the police *could* or *should* have done, but what they actually *would* have done to reach the evidence by independent legal means.

3.   Active Pursuit
Some courts require the police to be *actively pursuing* lawful means *at the time* the illegal search is conducted in order to invoke the inevitable discovery exception. Under the majority view, active pursuit is one way, but not the only way, to meet the state's burden of proof on inevitability.

IV.   "COLLATERAL USE" EXCEPTIONS TO THE EXCLUSIONARY RULE
A.   Introduction
Use of illegally obtained evidence outside the context of the Government's case-in-chief is generally permitted, though there are some exceptions where the deterrent effect of the rule has been found to outweigh the cost of exclusion.

B.   Grand Jury
The exclusionary rule does not apply to grand jury proceedings.

C.   Sentencing, Parole or Probation Revocation
The exclusionary rule is generally inapplicable to the consideration of evidence for purposes of sentencing, parole or probation revocation proceedings. However, if a search or seizure is made to *harass* a defendant, or if it has been conducted *expressly for the purpose of obtaining evidence for a parole or probation revocation, or to enhance a sentence*, then the exclusionary rule may apply.

D.   Forfeiture Proceedings
The exclusionary rule is applicable to forfeiture proceedings if the property is not *intrinsically illegal in character*. Illegally seized *contraband per se* need not be returned to the owner.

E.   Deportation Proceedings
The exclusionary rule is inapplicable in civil deportation proceedings.

F.   Civil Proceedings
The exclusionary rule is inapplicable in a civil proceeding brought by the Government (e.g. a tax collection action), at least where the proceeding falls outside the offending officer's zone of primary interest.

G.   Habeas Corpus Proceedings
A habeas petitioner cannot invoke the exclusionary rule to challenge evidence seized in violation of the Fourth Amendment unless the petitioner was not given a "full and fair opportunity" to litigate the Fourth Amendment claim during his state court proceeding. If a petitioner loses a Fourth Amendment claim in the state courts because of *ineffective assistance of counsel*, habeas review may be

allowed, as a violation of the standards of effective assistance is considered a separate constitutional issue.

H. Impeachment
1. Direct Testimony
The exclusionary rule does not prevent the prosecution from using illegally obtained evidence to *impeach* the defendant's direct testimony.

2. Cross–Examination
Moreover, the prosecutor may use illegally obtained evidence to impeach a defendant's answer to a question put to him on cross-examination, so long as the question is within the scope of the direct examination.

3. Defense Witnesses
However, the exclusionary rule does prohibit the use of illegally obtained evidence to impeach the defendant's *witnesses*. See the full outline for the reasoning behind the distinction.

V. THE "GOOD FAITH" EXCEPTION TO THE EXCLUSIONARY RULE
Where an officer, acting in objective good faith, has obtained a search warrant from a judge or magistrate that is ultimately found to be unsupported by probable cause, any evidence obtained from the resultant search or seizure may generally be used in the Government's case-in-chief, despite the fact that it is illegally obtained. This is because the error was made by the magistrate, not the officer, who reasonably relied on the magistrate's action. The exclusionary rule is considered to have deterrent effect on the conduct of police officers in the competitive enterprise of ferreting out crime, but to have no deterrent effect on the activity of magistrates, who are judicial officers.

A. Reasonably Unreasonable
An officer can "reasonably" rely on an invalid warrant as long as reasonable minds can differ as to whether a particular warrant is valid. Where all reasonable people would agree that a warrant is invalid, then the officer will be in error in relying on that warrant; in those circumstances, the exclusionary rule is presumed to have some deterrent effect in assuring future compliance.

B. Exceptions to the Good Faith Exception
There are *four situations* in which an officer's reliance on a warrant is considered unreasonable:

1. Misleading Information
If the magistrate who issued the warrant was misled by information in an affidavit that the affiant *knew or would have known* was false except for his *reckless disregard* of the truth, then the error in issuing the warrant was that of the officer, not the magistrate, and the exclusionary sanction will apply.

2. Abandonment of Judicial Role

Where the issuing magistrate wholly abandons his judicial role, then no reasonably well-trained officer should rely on the warrant. The officer's reliance on such a warrant is not fatal, however, unless the officer *knew or had reason to know* of this abandonment.

3. Affidavit Clearly Insufficient to Establish Probable Cause

If all reasonable minds would agree that the information set forth in the affidavit did not constitute probable cause, then the officer cannot reasonably rely on the magistrate's issuance of the warrant.

4. Facially Deficient Warrant

If a warrant is *so egregiously deficient* in its particularization, or in comporting with other procedural requirements, that all reasonable people would find it invalid, then an officer who relies on it is in error and the exclusionary rule will apply.

C. Unreasonable Execution of the Warrant

Improper execution of a valid warrant is an error attributable to the officer rather than to the magistrate, and is therefore subject to the exclusionary rule.

D. Reliance on Unconstitutional Legislation

Where the officer reasonably relies on a statute which is subsequently held unconstitutional, the officer has not committed a wrong, and the exclusionary rule will not apply. The exclusionary rule is considered to have no effect on the conduct of legislators.

1. Unreasonable Reliance on Unconstitutional Legislation

If the legislature wholly abandons its responsibility to enact constitutional laws or if a statute is clearly unconstitutional, it would be objectively unreasonable for an officer to rely on such legislation.

2. Misinterpretation of Legislation

The good faith exception does not apply to a police officer's reasonable though mistaken interpretation of the *scope* of a statute permitting a search. Such a mistake is one that is made by the *officer*, not by the legislature, and the exclusionary rule would apply to this misconduct—assuming that the search itself is in violation of the Fourth Amendment.

E. Does Not Apply to Warrantless Searches

Currently, the exclusionary rule applies if an officer conducts an illegal warrantless search, even if the officer had an objective good faith belief that the warrantless search was legal. The good faith exception only applies where an officer has reasonably relied on a magistrate or a legislative act.

THE PRIVILEGE AGAINST SELF–INCRIMINATION

I. INTRODUCTION

The Fifth Amendment's privilege against compelled self-incrimination prohibits the Government from compelling individuals to provide incriminating testimony in *any proceeding* if their answers might incriminate them in an *ongoing or future* criminal proceeding. A statement can tend to incriminate even if the offense admitted is rarely, if ever, prosecuted. The state may compel disclosure of information for use in civil or other non-criminal proceedings. Generally, a proceeding is "civil" in nature when incarceration is not a possible penalty. Also, as a general rule, the Fifth Amendment does not protect against the risk of foreign prosecution.

II. WHAT IS COMPULSION?

A. Use of Contempt Power

The state's *use of the contempt power* is *compulsion* because it imposes substantial punishment on a witness who claims the privilege, and presents the witness with the classic *"cruel trilemma"* of choosing between *self-accusation, contempt, and perjury*—each of which could lead to imprisonment.

B. Other State–Imposed Sanctions Which May Create Compulsion

1. Custodial Interrogation

See the *Miranda* doctrine, infra.

2. The Threat of Economic Sanctions

If a person suffers a Government-imposed economic sanction for invoking his Fifth Amendment right to silence, the sanction is considered compulsion because it punishes the person for invoking his right. Examples of such compulsion are disbarment, and depriving the person of the right to bid on public contracts.

3. Comment by the Prosecutor or Judge on a Defendant's Failure to Testify

Adverse comment to the jury on the defendant's election not to testify constitutes punishment for the invocation of silence and violates the Fifth Amendment.

III. IDENTIFYING THE HOLDER OF THE PRIVILEGE

A. The Privilege Is Personal

The privilege against self-incrimination belongs only to the person who has incriminated himself by his own testimony.

B. Business Entities; Collective Entity Rule
The Fifth Amendment does not protect partnerships or corporations.

C. Sole Proprietorships
The Fifth Amendment protects a sole proprietorship as it is not an entity that is legally separate from the individual.

IV. INFORMATION PROTECTED BY THE PRIVILEGE
A. Testimonial Evidence
The Fifth Amendment only protects against compelled disclosure of *testimonial* evidence. If evidence is non-testimonial, the Government can compel its production.

   1. The Cruel Trilemma
   Evidence is testimonial when it contains an express or implied assertion of fact which can be either true or false; it is only this type of evidence which may subject an individual to the cruel trilemma of truth, falsity and silence that is at the heart of Fifth Amendment protection. In contrast, physical evidence cannot be either true or false, and thus a defendant cannot commit perjury by its compelled production. So for example, the Government can compel the defendant to provide a blood sample or a handwriting exemplar, even though the evidence could incriminate the defendant.

   2. Refusal to Supply Physical Evidence
   An individual's refusal to supply the state with physical evidence may be used against him at trial.

B. Documents
Generally, the contents of both business and personal documents are not protected by the Fifth Amendment if they were prepared before a Government subpoena was ever served. This is because the *preparation* of such documents is "wholly voluntary" and an act completely independent from the compelled act of *producing* the documents for use by the Government.

   1. Act of Production
   The act of producing documents communicates that documents *exist*; that they are under the *control and in the possession* of the person producing the documents; and that the documents are *authentic* (i.e. that they are in fact the documents described by the subpoena). Thus, the act of production could have certain testimonial aspects triggering Fifth Amendment protection, independent of the content of the documents, which are not protected by the Fifth Amendment. While *incriminating* acts of production are generally protected, the privilege will not apply if existence, control, and authentication can be proven through *independent evidence*. In such cases, the act of production, in context, is not sufficiently incriminating to trigger the privilege.

2. **Compelling Agents of Business Entities to Produce Documents: The Collective Entity Rule**
    If an agent of a business entity produces compelled documents, the act of production may incriminate the agent. However, the agent produces such documents *not* in a personal capacity, but as a representative of a corporation, and so his act of production is not protected by the Fifth Amendment. The collective entity rule does not allow the Government to force a corporate agent to give personally incriminating *oral* testimony.

C. Required Records Exception
If the Government *requires* documents to be kept for a *legitimate administrative purpose*, neither the content nor the act of production of these documents are protected by the Fifth Amendment. However, if the recordkeeping requirement is directed to a class that is inherently suspected of committing criminal activity (e.g. marijuana growers), the required records exception does not apply.

V.   PROCEDURAL ASPECTS OF SELF–INCRIMINATION CLAIMS
A. Assertion of the Privilege
Whenever a person is compelled to answer questions that might tend to incriminate him, he has the right to refuse to answer. If he does answer, the privilege is lost with respect to the answer and the answer can be used as evidence.

B. Immunity
Even assuming the testimony tends to incriminate a witness, the Government may compel testimony when the witness has received immunity. There are *two types* of immunity: *transactional immunity* and *use immunity*.

1. **Transactional Immunity**
    Transactional immunity protects an individual from prosecution for *any transaction* described in his testimony. Transactional immunity gives *greater* protection than is constitutionally required.

2. **Use and Derivative Use Immunity**
    Use and derivative use immunity prevent the use of testimony or other information obtained from a person, or any information directly or indirectly derived from such testimony. A grant of use and derivative use immunity is *coextensive* with the Fifth Amendment privilege, and therefore a person who receives such immunity has no right to refuse to testify.

    a. **Prosecution Is Still Possible**
        The Government may grant use immunity and yet still prosecute the witness for the transaction admitted to if there is evidence *independent of* such testimony and the fruits of such testimony.

b.   Government's Burden
The burden is on the Government to prove that the evidence it proposes to offer against the witness at trial is derived from a source independent of the immunized testimony.

C.   Waiver of the Privilege
Individuals can *explicitly waive* the privilege against self-incrimination, and can also *implicitly waive* the privilege by giving testimony that is inconsistent with the retention of the privilege. If a witness testifies or supplies information as to part of a story, he cannot, under a claim of the privilege, refuse to testify about *related* subject matter.

SELF–INCRIMINATION AND CONFESSIONS

I.   CONFESSIONS AND DUE PROCESS
A.   A Confession Must Be "Voluntary" in Order to Be Admissible at Trial
The Due Process Clause of the Fifth and Fourteenth Amendments prohibits the admission of "involuntary" confessions, generally defined as confessions obtained by *physical force* or *psychological coercion*. A court determines the "voluntariness" of a confession under the totality of circumstances by focusing on *three main factors:* the *actions of the police*, the *personality of the defendant*, and the *circumstances surrounding the confession*.

B.   Judicial Interpretations of "Voluntariness" and "Coercion"
1.   Actual Violence Not Required
A *credible threat of physical violence* is ordinarily sufficient to support a finding of coercion. Police practices that fall short of threats of violence or actual physical force are less likely to establish a claim of "coercion" under the Due Process Clause. In particular, a misrepresentation of fact—e.g., that the suspect's fingerprints were found at the scene when that is not the case—is ordinarily insufficient in itself to render a subsequent confession involuntary.

2.   Some Police Coercion Required
The Due Process Clause is not implicated unless there is some police conduct which is causally related to a confession.

3.   An Involuntary Confession Is Not Admissible at Trial for Any Purpose
A coerced confession may not be admitted either in the state's case-in-chief, or during the state's cross-examination of a defendant whom the state wishes to impeach.

4.   The Harmless Error Doctrine and Involuntary Confessions
The erroneous admission of an involuntary confession is *not* per se reversible error but, instead, is reviewed under the "harmless error" standard for

constitutional violations—i.e., whether the erroneous admission of the involuntary confession was harmless beyond a reasonable doubt.

II. CONFESSIONS AND THE FIFTH AMENDMENT
A. *Miranda v. Arizona*
Intimidating police techniques may produce a confession that is not "involuntary" under Due Process standards, but is nonetheless obtained in violation of the privilege against self-incrimination. In *Miranda v. Arizona,* 384 U.S. 436, 86 S.Ct. 1602, 16 L.Ed.2d 694 (1966), the Court established *prophylactic safeguards* to protect a suspect's Fifth Amendment right to remain silent from the *inherently coercive pressures of custodial interrogation*. The need for such safeguards exists in all arrests, whether for felony or misdemeanor offenses.

1. The *Miranda* Safeguards
a. The Warnings
A suspect must be warned that he has the right to remain silent, and that anything he says can and will be used against him in court. The suspect must also be informed that he has the right to consult with a lawyer and to have the lawyer with him during interrogation; and that if he is indigent, a lawyer will be appointed to represent him.

b. Custodial Interrogation
The warnings about the rights to silence and counsel are *absolute prerequisites to custodial interrogation*. However, the warnings are not required if the police interrogate a suspect who is not in custody, or if the police place a suspect in custody but do not interrogate him. It is the interplay between custody and interrogation that creates the inherent Fifth Amendment compulsion that the warnings are designed to alleviate.

c. The *Miranda* Right to Counsel Distinguished From the Sixth Amendment Right to Counsel
The *Miranda* right to counsel is not constitutionally guaranteed. Rather, it is a *procedural safeguard* designed to provide protection for a defendant's right to remain silent during custodial interrogation as long as the suspect affirmatively *invokes* the right to counsel. In contrast, the Sixth Amendment right to counsel applies *automatically*, whenever a defendant who is formally charged (e.g., by indictment) is subject to *deliberate elicitation* by a Government agent.

d. Counsel Has No Independent Role to Play
Under *Miranda* the right to counsel must be invoked by the suspect. In the absence of an invocation, counsel has no independent authority to control police interrogation.

2. *Miranda* Is Not a "Constitutional Straightjacket"

Congress and the states may create alternatives for protecting the privilege, so long as they are as effective as the *Miranda* rules. But in the absence of *equally effective* procedures for protecting the rights of suspects, *Miranda* safeguards must be observed. Consequently, the Court has held that the *Miranda* safeguards are not constitutionally mandated, but are rather prophylactic, court-made rules designed to protect the suspect's Fifth Amendment rights. It follows that a confession obtained in the absence of *Miranda* warnings need not be excluded as a constitutional matter.

B. Impeaching the Defendant–Witness at Trial

Since *Miranda* rights are not constitutional requirements, the failure of an officer either to give warnings or to abide by them does not prevent the use of the *Miranda* -defective statements to impeach a defendant at trial. However, the post-arrest statements can only be considered in judging the defendant's "credibility," and not as evidence of guilt.

1. Defense Witnesses

Statements obtained in violation of *Miranda* cannot be used to impeach a defendant's witnesses.

2. Invocation of the Right to Silence

A reference to a defendant's post-warning silence at trial violates the defendant's constitutional right to Due Process and, therefore, may not be used for any reason at trial. A prosecutor *may* impeach a defendant about inconsistent *omissions* in post-warnings statements as those omissions are not "silences" protected by Due Process.

3. Silence Before *Miranda* Warnings Are Given May Be Used for Impeachment Purposes

There is no constitutional bar to the prosecution's reference on cross-examination to a defendant's pre-arrest or post-arrest silence *before* receiving *Miranda* warnings, as no governmental action "implicitly induced" the defendant to remain silent.

C. The Fruit of the Poisonous Tree, and the Non–Constitutional Nature of the *Miranda* Safeguards

The "fruit of the poisonous tree" doctrine—under which all evidence derived from a constitutional violation is excluded—does not generally apply to *Miranda* violations, because a violation of *Miranda* is not a violation of the Constitution.

1. Subsequent Confessions

Where a defendant makes a *Miranda*-defective confession and subsequently makes a confession pursuant to *Miranda* warnings, the subsequent confession is ordinarily admissible even though it may be considered the "fruit" of the original, *Miranda*-defective confession.

2. **The Fruits of Involuntary Confessions Are Excluded**
Even when police officers give proper *Miranda* warnings, an involuntary confession, and any fruits of such a confession, are excluded from trial.

3. **Physical Evidence as the Fruit of a *Miranda* Violation**
Physical evidence obtained as a fruit of a *Miranda* violation is not excluded from trial.

D. **The "Voluntary, Knowing, and Intelligent" Waiver of *Miranda* Rights**
Police must seek a "voluntary, knowing, and intelligent" waiver of rights before interrogating a suspect in the absence of an attorney. A "voluntary, knowing, and intelligent" waiver must be the product of *free and deliberate choice*, and must be made with a *full awareness* both of the nature of the right being abandoned and the consequences of the decision to abandon it. No waiver can be considered knowing and intelligent in the absence of *Miranda* warnings.

1. **The State Has the Burden of Proving Waiver**
The state must prove a waiver by a preponderance of the evidence. The state must make an *affirmative* showing of free choice, and must show that the defendant both had the capacity to understand the warnings and, in fact, *did* understand the warnings imparted by the officer. The suspect's capacity for understanding is a factor independent from police wrongdoing.

2. **A "Conditional" Waiver May Be "Knowing and Intelligent"**
If a defendant makes a conditional waiver of *Miranda* rights, a subsequent confession is admissible so long as police comply with the suspect's condition.

3. **A Waiver Is Valid Even When a Suspect Is Not Informed of Matters That Would Be Useful in Making an Informed Decision**
Miranda warnings encompass the sum and substance of all the information required for a defendant to make a knowing and intelligent waiver. The police need not impart further "useful" information to a suspect that goes beyond the general *Miranda* structure. For example, the police need not inform a suspect that his lawyer wants to speak with him. Even affirmative deception by the officer (e.g., that the victim died, even though that is not the case) does not *automatically* render a subsequent waiver or confession involuntary; it is only one relevant factor in a totality of circumstances inquiry.

4. **Revoking a Waiver**
A suspect may invoke his rights *after* answering some questions, and thereby withdraw any waiver given at the outset.

E. **Waiver and the Resumption of Questioning After Invocation of Rights**
The state has a more difficult case to make on waiver if a defendant first *invokes* either his right to silence or right to counsel, and then later decides to *waive* his

rights. Under these circumstances, the state must show that the defendant's rights were given the proper respect, and that no police pressure was responsible for the defendant's change of heart.

1. **Police May Obtain a Waiver From a Suspect Following His Invocation of the Right to Remain Silent**
    Miranda did not create a blanket prohibition of or permanent immunity from police interrogation following a suspect's invocation of the right to remain silent. Instead, *Miranda* requires only that the right to cut off questioning be "scrupulously honored" by the police. This "scrupulous honor" requirement is generally met by giving the suspect a "cooling off" period, after which the suspect can be given fresh warnings and asked whether he has changed his mind about remaining silent. The "scrupulous honor" requirement is a requirement *in addition to* the suspect knowingly and voluntarily waiving his *Miranda* rights.

2. **Waiver Following the Invocation of the Right to Counsel**
    If a suspect invokes his right to counsel, police officers may not further interrogate the defendant unless the defendant's attorney is present, or unless the *defendant* initiates at least a generalized discussion of the investigation. This rule applies even after a suspect has consulted with an attorney.

    a. **Bright Line Rule**
        A confession is *automatically* excluded if the police initiate reinterrogation of the suspect after he has invoked his right to counsel—even if the state can make a convincing argument that the defendant knew his rights and voluntarily waived them.

    b. **Definition of "Initiation"**
        Generally, a defendant "initiates" discussion by making an inquiry or statement relating directly or indirectly to the investigation. An inquiry or statement that merely relates to "routine" incidents of the custodial relationship does not constitute initiation.

    c. **Knowing and Voluntary Waiver Must Still Be Found**
        The bright-line initiation or presence of counsel requirement is in addition to the general requirement that all *Miranda* waivers must be knowing and voluntary.

3. **Right to Counsel Is Not "Offense–Specific"**
    A suspect's invocation of the right to counsel under *Miranda* is not *offense-specific*. Thus, when a suspect invokes the right to counsel, the police are barred from initiating an interrogation even about a crime different from that for which the suspect was arrested.

a. Distinction From a Defendant's Sixth Amendment Right to Counsel

If a defendant requests counsel at the start of *formal* proceedings, the defendant is invoking his offense-specific, Sixth Amendment right to counsel. If only the Sixth Amendment right to counsel is involved, officers may subsequently obtain a voluntary waiver from the defendant for a separate investigation, without the presence of counsel or initiation by the defendant.

b. Formal Proceedings

An invocation of counsel during a formal proceeding such as an arraignment is considered an invocation of the Sixth Amendment right to counsel, and not the offense-general right to counsel under *Miranda*. This is because no custodial interrogation occurs at a formal proceeding, and *Miranda* rights cannot be invoked in *anticipation* of a future custodial interrogation.

4. Ambiguous Invocations

If a defendant makes an ambiguous invocation of his right to silence or counsel, police officers must cease interrogation of the suspect, and are generally only allowed to ask clarifying questions regarding the possible invocation. Officers may not take a clear invocation and, through questioning the suspect, render it ambiguous.

F. Incomplete or Ambiguous *Miranda* Warnings

The *Miranda* warnings merely have to reasonably convey the *Miranda* rights to a suspect; they need not be a verbatim recital of the *Miranda* opinion. However, an officer may not *affirmatively mislead* a suspect through ambiguous wording of the *Miranda* rights.

G. The Meaning of "Custody"

Miranda protections only apply when a defendant is *both* in custody and under interrogation by the police. A defendant is in *custody* when, under the totality of circumstances, he is either under arrest or his freedom of movement is restrained to the degree associated with arrest. A *stop* will never trigger *Miranda* rights because, by definition, a defendant is not under arrest.

1. Questioning a Suspect at the Stationhouse

Questioning a suspect at the stationhouse does not *per se* constitute custody. With stationhouse interrogation, the question of custody will generally depend on whether the suspect came to the stationhouse voluntarily or not. Custody will ordinarily not be found in the former case and ordinarily it will be found in the latter.

2. Relevant Factors

The determination of custody focuses on *objective* factors of police coercion. Some of the relevant factors are:

—The *purpose* of the police investigation.

—The *place and length* of the interrogation.

—The suspect's *awareness of his freedom to leave*.

—The suspect's *actual freedom from restraint*.

—The *source of initiation* of the contact with the suspect.

—The use of *"coercive stratagems"* by the police.

—The similarity of the setting to the *"police-dominated"* atmosphere of the stationhouse.

H. The Meaning of "Interrogation"
Interrogation by police under *Miranda* is defined as express questioning or its functional equivalent.

1. Functional Equivalent
The "functional equivalent" of express questioning includes words or actions that police should have known are *reasonably likely to elicit an incriminating response* from an *average suspect*.

2. Intent of the Officer
Although the definition of interrogation focuses *primarily* upon the perceptions of the suspect, the intent of the police officers to obtain incriminating information, or the lack of such intent, is an important, though not dispositive, factor in this determination. This is because if an officer intends to obtain information, the tactics that he will employ are more likely to elicit information from an average suspect than if the officer had no such intent.

3. Peculiar Susceptibility
If officers know or have reason to know that a defendant has a peculiar susceptibility, exploitation of that weakness will generally constitute interrogation.

4. Police Procedures
Questions attendant to legitimate police procedures (such as whether the suspect understands what he is supposed to do during a sobriety test) do not fall within the *Miranda* definition of interrogation.

5. Confrontation With Incriminating Evidence May Be a Form of Interrogation
Confronting a suspect with incriminating evidence is ordinarily likely to elicit an incriminating response from the average suspect.

6. Routine Booking Questions Are an Exception

Booking questions for legitimate administrative purposes are an exception to *Miranda*'s interrogation prong. A question will not come within the booking question exception if it is designed to elicit incriminating admissions.

I. The Application of *Miranda* to Undercover Police Activity

Miranda warnings are not required when a suspect is unaware that he is speaking to a law enforcement officer, as the "coercive atmosphere" of police interrogation does not exist in these circumstances. Therefore, an undercover agent may validly elicit incriminating statements from a suspect under *Miranda*.

J. The "Public Safety Exception" to *Miranda*

Police may ask questions reasonably prompted by a concern for public safety without first advising a suspect in custody of the *Miranda* warnings. The validity of this "exception" to *Miranda* does not depend upon the motivation of the individual officers involved. Generally, the public safety exception is analogous to the exigent circumstances exception to the Fourth Amendment warrant requirement.

1. Involuntary Confessions Not Admitted

If a confession is *involuntary*, it is inadmissible even if obtained in response to a public safety problem. The introduction of an involuntary confession at trial violates the Due Process Clause at the time of admission and, thus, exclusion is constitutionally required.

III. CONFESSIONS AND THE SIXTH AMENDMENT AFTER *MIRANDA*

The Sixth Amendment right to counsel prohibits the police or secret Government agents from "deliberately eliciting" incriminating statements from suspects in the absence of counsel during or after the initiation of adversary judicial proceedings. Deliberate elicitation does not focus on the subjective intent of the officer but, rather, on whether a *reasonable person would find it likely* that a planned course of conduct would lead to the elicitation of incriminating information from a formally charged defendant. Unlike Fifth Amendment protections which focus upon *police coercion*, the Sixth Amendment focusses on whether the state acted *unethically* by interposing itself between the accused and his counsel after the commencement of adversarial proceedings.

A. Sixth Amendment Waiver

The Sixth Amendment right to counsel *automatically* attaches upon the start of adversarial judicial proceedings. Police officers must then obtain a "voluntary, knowing, and intelligent" waiver from a defendant before an officer's deliberate elicitation of information. A waiver of the Sixth Amendment right to counsel will not be found merely because a defendant was warned of his rights and subsequently confessed. The state must *affirmatively* show that the defendant knowingly and voluntarily waived his rights and confessed.

1. **Sixth Amendment Warnings**
    The *Miranda* warnings generally provide the sum and substance of Sixth Amendment rights. No extra warnings are ordinarily necessary to support a knowing and intelligent waiver of the Sixth Amendment right to counsel.

2. **Sixth Amendment "Initiation" Rule**
    Police officers may seek a waiver of a defendant's Sixth Amendment right to counsel unless the defendant *invokes* his right to counsel. After an invocation of his rights, officers may only approach the defendant absent counsel if the *defendant* "initiates" a generalized discussion regarding the pending charges. Initiation is a bright-line rule that requires exclusion of any statement in the absence of counsel from a defendant who did not seek discussion with officers following an invocation of his rights.

3. **Offense–Specific Invocation**
    The Sixth Amendment right to counsel is *offense-specific*. After an accused has invoked his Sixth Amendment right to counsel, an officer may validly approach the accused and seek a waiver regarding crimes different from that with which the defendant is formally charged. This is so even if the defendant has not initiated further interrogation.

4. **Impeachment**
    The Sixth Amendment bright-line initiation rule is considered a prophylactic safeguard of the right to counsel and, thus, while statements obtained in violation of the rule are excluded from the prosecution's case-in-chief, they may still be used to impeach the credibility of the defendant. It is unclear whether involuntary statements from a defendant obtained absent counsel or invocation are direct constitutional violations requiring total exclusion from trial.

5. **Lawyer Trying to Reach an Indicted Defendant**
    The Sixth Amendment right to counsel is concerned with the state placing a bar between attorney and client once formal proceedings have begun. Therefore, if police know that an indicted defendant's lawyer is trying to contact him, the police must inform the defendant of that fact before there can be a knowing waiver of Sixth Amendment rights.

B. **"Deliberate Elicitation" and the Passive Ear**
    If a Government informer "passively listens" to an accused without any affirmative attempt to "elicit" incriminating information, there is no Sixth Amendment violation and the statements may be introduced in court. Similarly, if a private individual obtains information from an indicted defendant, and then unilaterally refers it to the Government, the information is admissible because there is no improper "elicitation" by the Government.

C.   Deliberate Elicitation and Continuing Investigations
Statements pertaining to pending charges are inadmissible when obtained absent
counsel or waiver of counsel—even if the purpose of the investigation was to
obtain information about *uncharged* crimes. However, statements concerning
uncharged crimes, obtained in the absence of counsel, are admissible in
subsequent prosecutions for those crimes, at least insofar as the Sixth Amendment
is concerned.

CONSTITUTIONAL LIMITATIONS ON IDENTIFICATION EVIDENCE

I.   POST–INDICTMENT IDENTIFICATIONS
A corporeal, post-indictment line-up conducted without notice to and in the
absence of defense counsel, and without a valid waiver of such counsel, violates
the Sixth Amendment's right to counsel which applies during *critical pre-trial
stages* as well as at trial.

A.   "Per Se" Exclusion
Post-indictment, out-of-court identifications that take place absent counsel are
"per se" excluded from trial. Exclusion is required even if the state can show that
the identification is in fact reliable.

1.   In–Court Identification and Independent Source
The same witness whose out-of-court identification is excluded from trial may
make an *in-court identification* if the prosecution proves that, under the
totality of circumstances, the in-court identification stems from an
independent source sufficiently distinguishable from the previous, illegal
line-up.

2.   Relevant Factors
Certain factors are relevant to a determination of whether an in-court
identification is based on a source *independent* from an illegal pre-trial
identification:

—The extent of the *prior opportunity to view* the defendant other than at the
illegal line-up.

—*Discrepancies*, if any, between the witnesses' description of the suspect
before the line-up was conducted, and the defendant's actual appearance.

—The *certainty* of the witness' identification at the line-up or, conversely, the
witness' failure to identify the defendant on prior occasions.

—The *lapse of time* between the criminal act and the line-up identification.

—The *degree of suggestiveness* employed in the tainted pre-trial lineup.

II. PRE–INDICTMENT IDENTIFICATIONS

The Sixth Amendment does not apply to counsel-free, out-of-court identifications that occur *prior* to indictment or formal charge. However, if adversary proceedings are *deliberately delayed* in order to evade the post-indictment rule, the resulting counsel-free identification will be invalidated.

A. Charge–Specific

It is permissible to hold a counsel-free line-up for an indicted defendant as to a different charge, since being indicted on one charge is not a "criminal prosecution" as to any other.

B. Photographic Identification

A defendant has *no right to counsel at a photographic identification* conducted either pre- or post-indictment.

III. DUE PROCESS LIMITATIONS ON SUGGESTIVE IDENTIFICATIONS

Where the Sixth Amendment right to counsel does not apply to an identification procedure, the identification must still satisfy the Due Process Clause, which requires exclusion if *police suggestiveness creates a substantial risk of mistaken identification.*

A. Two–Step Test

The defendant has the burden of proving a due process violation through a two-step test. First, the defendant must show that the identification procedure was *impermissibly suggestive.* If so, the defendant must then show the identification was *unreliable* under the *totality of circumstances.*

1. Exigent Circumstances

Certain exigent or extraordinary circumstances can make suggestive police procedure necessary and, thus, *permissible.* However, courts rarely find the circumstances so exigent as to allow the state to conduct a suggestive identification.

2. The Linchpin of Reliability

An identification may be reliable *despite* police suggestiveness. Suggestive procedures are considered in light of all the circumstances to determine whether an *independent source* exists for a reliable identification. Certain *factors* are relevant in a totality of circumstances determination of the reliability of an identification, although none are dispositive:

—The degree and nature of *police suggestiveness.*

—The extent of the witness' *opportunity to view* the suspect prior to the challenged identification (e.g., at the scene of the crime).

—The witness' degree of *attention* to the suspect prior to the challenged identification.

—The *accuracy of the description* of the perpetrator given by the witness before the identification.

—The witness' *level of certainty* at the time of making the identification.

—The time between the pre-identification opportunity to view the suspect and the identification itself.

B. If Pre-trial Identification Is Excluded, At–Trial Identification Is Impermissible
If the pre-trial identification is unreliable because it is caused by police suggestiveness, then the Due Process Clause prohibits an at-trial identification as well. This is because if the prior identification was caused by police suggestiveness, there can *by definition* be no independent legal source for the in-court identification.

THE RIGHT TO COUNSEL

I. TWO SOURCES FOR COUNSEL RIGHTS: THE SIXTH AMENDMENT AND THE FOURTEENTH AMENDMENT
A. The Sixth Amendment
The Sixth Amendment provides that "[i]n all criminal prosecutions, the accused shall enjoy the right . . . to have the Assistance of Counsel for his defense." The Sixth Amendment applies directly to the Federal Government, and applies to the states through the incorporation doctrine of the Fourteenth Amendment. However, the scope of the Sixth Amendment's right to counsel is more limited in state courts than in federal courts.

B. The Fourteenth Amendment
The Fourteenth Amendment provides additional assistance of counsel in cases where the Sixth Amendment does not apply. The Amendment's Due Process Clause, and the parallel provision in the Fifth Amendment, prevents the states and the Federal Government from "depriv[ing] any person of life, liberty, or property, without due process of law." One prominent example of a Due Process right is the right to counsel on appeal. Additionally, the Fourteenth Amendment's Equal Protection Clause bolsters counsel rights—such as the rights to appellate counsel and transcripts—applicable through the Due Process Clause.

II. BASICS OF THE SIXTH AMENDMENT RIGHT TO COUNSEL
The Sixth Amendment's guarantee of *assistance of counsel* encompasses the right of indigent defendants to receive appointed counsel, as well as the qualified right of a non-indigent defendant to use retained counsel of choice. Counsel must provide "effective" assistance, and generally must not labor under conflicts of

interest. The right to assistance of counsel and to "effective" assistance may be waived, and the right to self-representation invoked in its stead. These rights apply only at trial or at "critical" pre-trial stages.

A. The Right to Appointed Counsel for Indigent Defendants

Indigent defendants have the right to appointed counsel in *all federal criminal prosecutions*, and in all *state felony* prosecutions. In *misdemeanor* or petty offense cases, counsel must be provided only if the defendant receives an actual *jail sentence*. There is no constitutional right to appointed counsel of choice. Trial courts have broad discretion to decide whether to accept a defendant's preferred choice of counsel.

B. Collateral Consequences of Uncounselled Convictions

An *uncounselled* misdemeanor conviction may not elevate a second conviction to a felony with an enhanced penalty if *all* of the following circumstances are present: 1) a subsequent misdemeanor is *automatically* converted by statute, 2) into a *felony,* and 3) the defendant receives a jail term which he would not otherwise receive, solely *because* of the prior uncounselled conviction.

C. The Right to "Effective Assistance" of Counsel

The right to counsel means the right to *effective assistance* of either appointed or retained counsel. Conversely, if there is no right to counsel, there is no right to effective assistance of counsel.

1. Ineffective Assistance Based on Deficient Performance

A defendant's right to effective assistance of counsel is violated when counsel's performance falls below "prevailing professional norms," and when this performance causes "prejudice" because there is a reasonable probability it affected the outcome (i.e. *but for* the attorney's errors, there is a reasonable probability that the case result would be different.) Counsel must render effective assistance during the plea bargaining process, as well as during the process of trial preparation and the trial itself. Claims of ineffective assistance are ordinarily assessed on a case-by-case basis.

2. Per Se Prejudice

There are certain very limited circumstances in which ineffectiveness and prejudice are *presumed*, because the likelihood that any lawyer, even a fully competent one, could provide effective assistance of counsel is so minimal that a presumption of prejudice is appropriate *without inquiry into the actual conduct of the trial*.

3. Ineffective Assistance Based on Conflict of Interest

Multiple representation of criminal clients is not a "per se" violation of the clients' right to effective assistance. Rather, there is a *limited and conditional presumption of prejudice* if the defendant establishes that counsel "actively represented conflicting interests," *and* that "an actual conflict of interest adversely affected" the lawyer's performance. A defendant may waive his right to conflict-free counsel by making a knowing, intelligent, voluntary, clear and unequivocal waiver. A trial court has discretion whether to accept the waiver.

D. The Right to Self–Representation

In *Faretta v. California,* 422 U.S. 806, 95 S.Ct. 2525, 45 L.Ed.2d 562 (1975), the Court held that a defendant has a right to self-representation which is derived by implication from the text of the Sixth Amendment. The option of self-representation respects the personal autonomy of the defendant.

1. Self–Representation Requires a Waiver of the Right to Counsel

The right to counsel and the right to self-representation are mutually exclusive. A defendant who is "literate, competent and understanding" may waive the right to counsel, and thereby invoke the right to self-representation. The waiver must be *unequivocal* to ensure that the defendant does not *inadvertently* waive the right to counsel, and to prevent the defendant from taking advantage of the mutual exclusivity of the two rights. A defendant's technical legal knowledge is not relevant to an assessment of his knowing exercise of the right to defend himself.

2. Limitations on the Right of Self–Representation

The right of self-representation is not absolute. A state may impose certain conditions on the defendant's right to proceed pro se, where such conditions are necessary to further legitimate state interests. These conditions include the court's option to appoint standby counsel to assist the pro se defendant—even over the defendant's objections. Self-representation may be precluded altogether if the defendant makes an untimely request to represent himself, or if the defendant is disrupting courtroom proceedings.

3. The Role of Standby Counsel

A "pro se" defendant *may* be given standby counsel to assist him at trial or to take over the defense if necessary. There is no constitutional right to receive such counsel; nor may a defendant object to the appointment of standby counsel. Standby counsel violates the *Faretta* right when he deprives the defendant of actual control over the case, or destroys the jury's perception that the defendant represents himself. A defendant has the right to claim that standby counsel was ineffective.

4. *Faretta* Violation Cannot Be Harmless

A *Faretta* violation cannot constitute harmless error. A violation of *Faretta* means that the defendant has been deprived of his *choice* to represent himself; thus, a state may not argue that the counsel imposed upon the defendant against his will did a better job than the defendant could have done.

E. **The Definition of a "Criminal Prosecution" Where Counsel Rights Apply**

Right to counsel protections attach after "adversarial judicial proceedings" have begun, and the trial process has reached a "critical stage". A stage in the trial process is considered "critical" if substantial potential prejudice to a defendant's rights inhere in a confrontation, and the presence of counsel may help to avoid that prejudice. Critical stages include a preliminary hearing, a post-indictment lineup, and a sentencing hearing. Non-critical stages include photographic identification procedures, handwriting exemplar procedures, probation revocation hearings, and administrative detention of inmates.

III. **THE RIGHT TO COUNSEL IN PROCEEDINGS THAT ARE NOT PART OF A CRIMINAL PROSECUTION**

Due Process precedents establish the right to a hearing and fair procedures whenever a person's "liberty" is at stake. A jail sentence is only one kind of liberty loss faced by indigents, as physical confinement in state institutions could result from determinations made at hearings in a variety of "civil" proceedings. Thus, there is a right to appointed counsel in such civil proceedings if the proceeding contains a threat of physical confinement by the state.

IV. **BASICS OF THE FOURTEENTH AMENDMENT**

A. **Due Process Rights to Counsel at Trial**

Defendants in state misdemeanor and lesser offense cases do not have a Sixth Amendment right to appointed counsel, unless they receive a sentence of imprisonment. Such defendants may, however, have a right to appointed counsel under the Due Process Clause if they can show that a totality of special circumstances establishes the need for counsel.

B. **The Right to Counsel on Appeal**

There is a per se Due Process right to effective counsel on the first appeal. But there is no such right for later appeals, for the certiorari process, or for collateral attack. Thus, even if counsel is representing a defendant past the first appeal, there is no Due Process right to effective assistance of counsel.

C. **Due Process Right to Tools With Which to Prepare an Effective Case at Trial and on Appeal**

Besides the right to counsel, there are some circumstances in which the state must provide technical support for counsel so that an effective case can be prepared.

1. **The Right to a Trial Transcript**

In order for an indigent defendant to have adequate access to the appellate process, a trial transcript must be provided by the state.

2. The Right to Obtain Expert Witnesses for Trial
Due Process requires that indigent defendants receive the basic tools of an adequate defense at trial, including expert witnesses where necessary for an effective presentation of the case.

D. Equal Protection Rights of Indigents in the Appellate Process
States cannot grant appellate review in a way that discriminates against defendants on account of their poverty. This means that states must give indigents "meaningful access" to the appellate process.

1. The Right to Counsel on Appeal
The right to counsel for the first appeal is supported by the Equal Protection Clause, as well as the Due Process Clause. However, neither Clause supports a right to counsel on later appeals.

2. No Right to Appointed Counsel in Discretionary Appeals
An indigent has no equal protection or due process right to appointed counsel for discretionary appeals.

3. The Right to Transcripts and Filing Fee Waivers
Defendants have a right to receive trial transcripts from all state trials, as a matter of Equal Protection and Due Process. Transcripts of state habeas hearings must also be provided. Indigent defendants cannot be required to pay filing fees for appeals or post-conviction proceedings.

4. The Right to Be Free From Special Penalties Resulting From Indigency
Indigents who are unable to pay fines cannot be incarcerated beyond statutory maximum terms, or incarcerated at all when a statute prescribes only a fine as a penalty. Nor may such indigents be subjected to the automatic revocation of probation.

*

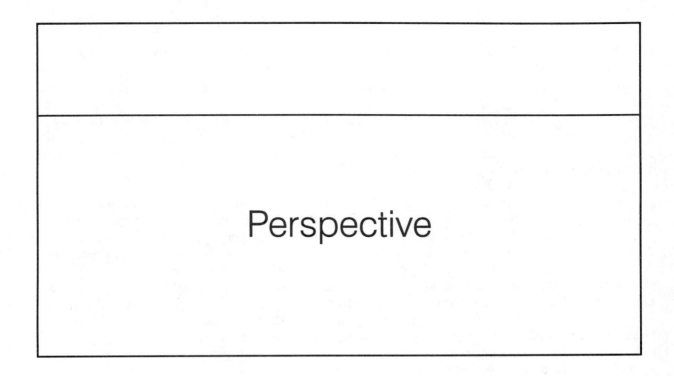

Perspective

THE STUDY OF BASIC CRIMINAL PROCEDURE

The basic course in Criminal Procedure concerns the limitations imposed on the State and Federal Governments in investigating and prosecuting crime. These limitations are mainly grounded in the Fourth, Fifth, Sixth and Fourteenth Amendments of the United States Constitution. This outline is intended to provide comprehensive coverage of the scope of constitutional protections ordinarily considered in a basic course in Criminal Procedure.

The Fourth Amendment requires generally that before the police conduct a search or seizure, they must obtain a warrant based upon probable cause that the search or seizure will uncover criminal activity or evidence thereof. As will be seen in the outline, there are many exceptions to this general rule, as the Supreme Court has sought to balance the needs of law enforcement against the privacy rights of the people.

The Fifth Amendment prohibits the state from compelling a citizen to be a witness against himself. This prohibition now comes into play when the police seek to obtain a confession from a suspect. As will be seen in the outline, the Supreme Court in the landmark *Miranda* case sought to protect Fifth Amendment rights by imposing procedural safeguards, such as warnings, when a suspect is subject to custodial interrogation.

The Fifth Amendment also contains a due process clause, which generally protects criminal defendants from the introduction of evidence that is unreliable, or which was obtained by egregious methods. As in other areas of constitutional adjudication, due process protection is applied in a case-by-case approach, with the court looking at the totality of circumstances. The Fifth Amendment also provides protections which are not ordinarily considered in the basic course on Criminal Procedure (and hence are not treated here) such as the right to be free from double jeopardy and the right to grand jury indictment.

The Sixth Amendment guarantees certain fundamental rights to an "accused" in a "criminal prosecution." These terms imply that the Sixth Amendment protections apply only when the state has proceeded from an investigatory stage to an accusatory stage. The Supreme Court has held that the protections of the Sixth Amendment do not attach until the state has begun formal proceedings against the citizen. Usually this is done by way of indictment. Once the Sixth Amendment has attached it provides several protections to a criminal defendant. Most importantly it guarantees a right to effective counsel. This right is applicable not only at trial, but also at certain other critical stages after indictment. For instance, the Supreme Court has held that the accused has an automatic right to counsel whenever the state deliberately elicits a confession from him concerning a charge for which he has been indicted. Also, if the state conducts a line-up post-indictment, the defendant has the right to have counsel present.

The Sixth Amendment also contains important trial rights, such as the right to confrontation, the right to compulsory process, and the right to a jury based on a fair cross-section of the community. These rights are ordinarily not treated in the basic Criminal Procedure course, and hence they are not treated here.

The limitations on Government contained in the Fourth, Fifth and Sixth Amendments were not originally applicable to the states. However, the Fourteenth Amendment's Due Process Clause has been held to incorporate all the protections in these amendments, (with the exception of the right to grand jury indictment) so that they are equally applicable to state and federal actors.

The basic course in Criminal Procedure is generally concerned with Supreme Court jurisprudence interpreting and applying the Fourth, Fifth and Sixth Amendments. A cursory review of any Supreme Court term in the last thirty years will show that the Court has devoted a major part of its docket to Criminal Procedure cases. It is no secret that the area of Criminal Procedure has been largely constitutionalized by the Supreme Court, beginning with the Warren Court in the 1960's. However, non-constitutional standards are also pertinent to criminal investigation and prosecution, most notably the Federal Rules of Criminal Procedure and many state counterparts. The obvious thrust of the outline is to provide an understanding of the constitutional standards affecting Criminal Procedure; but non-constitutional standards will be discussed as well.

GENERAL PRINCIPLES

The course in basic Criminal Procedure highlights the tension between the Government's interest in investigating and prosecuting crime, and the individual's interest in privacy, dignity, autonomy and fair treatment. A balance inevitably must be struck between these competing interests. On the one hand, it is costly to impose procedural limitations on the state: some crimes may go unpunished if the state is too constricted. On the other hand, if the state is not constricted at all, the rights of all individuals could be in peril. In deciding any issue of constitutional criminal procedure, this general tension is at the heart of Supreme Court decisionmaking. Speaking very generally, the Court in the 1960's incorporated many rights to apply to the states, and expanded procedural protections owed to criminal defendants. Later, the Burger and Rehnquist Courts expanded fewer rights, limited some earlier holdings, and often struck the balance in favor of prosecution of the factually guilty. While there are many exceptions to this general rule, one of the most fascinating aspects of the course in Criminal Procedure is its jurisprudential component: how, within the confines of *stare decisis,* the Supreme Court first recognized and then limited the reach of particular constitutional provisions.

Amidst this tension between claims of individual liberty and the need to prosecute the guilty, there are several factors that influence members of the Court. Each justice establishes his or her own balance on the basis of these factors. The relevant factors include:

1. **THE PERCEIVED ROLE OF THE COURT IN PROTECTING CIVIL LIBERTIES**
   Our democratic state and federal governments rely heavily on the electoral process and majoritarian rule. In theory, if there is a problem, it can be addressed through the ballot box where the legislative and executive branches are elected. The theory works best when those effected by legislative action or inaction have sufficient political clout to make their voices heard.

   The Warren Court decisions of the 1960's, dealing with civil rights issues generally and criminal procedure issues specifically, were based on the proposition that the majoritarian model breaks down when those who suffer from the acts of Government officials are politically powerless. Such is often the case with an individual who claims to be the subject of overreaching investigative or prosecutorial activity. Criminal suspects have no lobbyist in the legislature; they are a highly unpopular minority. Moreover, criminal suspects are often members of minority groups and poor, possessing little political influence outside the criminal justice system. The Warren Court exercised a counter-majoritarian influence to address problems that it felt could not be fairly addressed by the majoritarian legislative and executive bodies. In so doing, it frequently took an expansive view of the rights of criminal defendants in the justice system.

   In contrast, the Burger and Rehnquist Courts have tended to look at the counter-majoritarian nature of the Supreme Court to be something of a danger to democratic principles. Hence, the Court has in recent years been more willing to defer to legislative and executive action or inaction, and has intervened less often to protect those highly unpopular minorities who would seem to need court protection. This trend is less clear in criminal procedure than in some other areas, however, since in the ordinary criminal procedure case, the Court is analyzing an ad hoc action by a police officer, rather than the constitutionality of legislation or standard executive practice. Judicial deference to the legislative and executive process is not as easily translated to the random act of a police officer.

2. EMPHASIS ON RELIABILITY AS OPPOSED TO PROTECTION OF THE GUILTY

To some justices, the main goal of the criminal justice system is to assure that all verdicts are reliable. Some constitutional provisions are specifically designed to assure that a verdict will be reliable. An example is the right to effective assistance of counsel at trial. Without that right, there can be no assurance that the adversary system will work properly to achieve a correct result. However, other constitutional provisions focus on other interests and have little to do with reliability. In fact, they may be responsible for the exclusion of reliable evidence, and make it more likely that an incorrect result will be reached. An example is the Fourth Amendment, which protects the privacy and security rights of innocent and guilty alike.

Some justices believe that the interest in reliable verdicts is paramount, and take the position that a higher priority should be given to those protections which ensure reliable fact-finding. These justices concomitantly think that less emphasis should be given to those protections which serve to exclude reliable evidence and protect the factually guilty.

Other justices take the position that all constitutional provisions bearing on the criminal justice system are to be given high priority. These justices assert that provisions which protect the guilty in a particular case also serve to protect society at large. For example, the Fourth Amendment might protect a guilty defendant in an individual case, but it also protects the innocent by discouraging the police from making unreasonable searches and seizures against anyone. Thus, the criminal defendant may essentially be a class action plaintiff (though an odious one) protecting the rights of all. Moreover, these justices argue that even constitutional provisions which protect only the guilty are important, because a society is judged by the way it treats those suspected and charged with crime.

In recent years, the Court has tended to give greater emphasis to reliability in fact-finding as opposed to protection of the factually guilty. This has especially occurred where the issue is not whether the constitution has been violated, but rather whether exclusion of evidence is the appropriate remedy for the constitutional violation.

3. BRIGHT LINE RULES AS OPPOSED TO CASE–BY–CASE ADJUDICATION

The Supreme Court takes cases, and thus decides the applicability of a constitutional protection to a specific fact situation. A case-by-case approach to constitutional adjudication can sometimes lead to unacceptable results, however. It is possible that lower courts may be reluctant to provide the scope of protection intended by the Supreme Court, and may thus seek to distinguish cases on their facts. Another deleterious effect of the case-by-case approach is that officials may be hard-pressed to apply Supreme Court precedent to different fact situations. Arguably, the officer in the field needs clear guidance in how to follow the law: telling him to be reasonable under the circumstances tells him little. A third cost of a case-by-case approach is that it imposes a burden on the lower courts in having to struggle to apply vague law to the factual circumstances of every case.

On the other hand, establishment of a bright line rule for a generally worded constitutional provision is both overinclusive and underinclusive. For instance, the Fourth Amendment demands that a search be reasonable. Reasonableness obviously depends on the facts. If the Court establishes a bright line rule as to what is reasonable in a particular situation (as it has done in some cases) the rule by definition will result in upholding some searches that are in fact unreasonable and in invalidating some searches that are reasonable.

The question, then, is whether a bright line rule can be established which will reach the correct result in the vast majority of circumstances. If so, the cost of over- and under-inclusiveness will be outweighed by the benefits of clear conduct guidance and ease of administration. The Court has adopted several bright-line rules, (such as with custodial confessions in *Miranda* and search incident to arrest in *New York v. Belton*) with varying success. In other situations (such as with the *Terry* stop and frisk doctrine) the Court has usually employed a case-by-case approach.

4. BURDENS ON THE STATE

Rulings which give constitutional protection to criminal defendants are, to a greater or lesser degree, burdensome on the state. There is considerable disagreement among the justices as to whether and how to consider the burdens imposed on the state by a proposed constitutional ruling. At one end of the spectrum, some justices argue that if a guarantee is constitutionally mandated, then the burdens it imposes on the state are irrelevant, since the Framers have already considered those burdens in establishing the constitutional guarantee. This argument is more compelling when the constitution clearly provides a protection than when the constitutional language is ambiguous. Where there is ambiguity, the argument that burdens are irrelevant is somewhat question-begging, since the very question is whether the Constitution requires such protection.

At the other end of the spectrum, some justices believe that burdens on the state should always be considered in determining whether a right should be recognized, and further that in some cases the burdens on the state can be so compelling as to deny the right entirely. This was the thrust of the Court's opinion in *Scott v. Illinois,* where the Court held that an indigent has no Sixth Amendment right to counsel in misdemeanor cases, unless he receives a prison sentence; the Court largely focussed on the burdens which would be imposed upon the state if it had to provide counsel to all indigents in all misdemeanor cases. Justices who find administrative burdens to be especially relevant may be prone to find substantial burdens on law enforcement where there is a dispute between the Government and an individual as to the extent of the actual burden. For instance, those justices who oppose the exclusionary rule argue that the rule imposes substantial burdens on law enforcement; in fact, the evidence that the exclusionary rule imposes substantial burdens is equivocal at best.

AN APPROACH TO THIS BOOK

The primary goal of this book is to give comprehensive treatment to Supreme Court cases setting forth the scope of individual rights under the Fourth, Fifth and Sixth Amendments. Reference is also made where appropriate to important lower court cases, different approaches taken by state courts, and non-judicial sources such as the Federal Rules of Criminal Procedure. To understand current rules, it is usually necessary to trace the progression from Warren Court rulings to modifications by the Burger and Rehnquist Courts. Therefore, we have tried, where appropriate, to discuss an entire line of cases leading up to the latest Supreme Court ruling. We feel that this will aid an understanding of current law, and raise the important question of whether current law provides an approach which is preferable to its immediate antecedents.

We have found that more than any other course, Basic Criminal Procedure generates heated discussion and debate. The issues brought up in the course go to the heart of how we think about individual rights in America. The issues and the fact situations that generate them are as up-to-date as today's newspaper. Because the cases are controversial, Basic Criminal Procedure runs a danger of confusion of legal and "political" viewpoints. It is a risk, therefore, to discuss the rationale of a case as well as the rule it establishes. But, we believe it is a risk worth taking. We have attempted to provide the rationale for many leading cases, a critique of that rationale, and an analysis of the likely scope of the decision. Our goal is not to persuade anyone to adopt a particular point of view, but is rather to provide some perspective which will help the reader to participate in classroom discussion and to give more full-bodied answers on the examination. In the end, we believe that a reader who thinks about the issues will settle on his or her own view, and that such a view will benefit from the analysis we offer.

EXAMINATIONS IN BASIC CRIMINAL PROCEDURE

Like other examinations, an exam in Criminal Procedure requires you to spot the issues. For this process, there are standard exam-taking techniques that are obvious but helpful.

First, read the entire examination through quickly before you start to write. You may think you spot an issue hidden in question one, but if you read question four, it is clearly the main issue. It is rare that a professor wants the same issue discussed fully in two separate questions. Consequently, by reading the entire exam, you can give the issue its due at the place where the professor intended.

Second, answer only the question that is asked. For instance, if the question is whether evidence should be excluded, you must answer both whether a right has been violated and whether exclusion is the appropriate remedy. In contrast, if the question is whether the search is illegal, a thorough discussion of the exclusionary rule is probably not mandated (and thus not credited), since the exclusionary rule presumes that the search is illegal.

Third, avoid long preparatory discussion of lines of precedent. Thus, if the question is whether the exclusionary rule should apply, a long discussion of the history of Supreme Court jurisprudence concerning the exclusionary rule is interesting, but not likely to be given much credit.

Fourth, it is crucial to apply law to fact. Discussing the law of search incident to arrest, the validity of current Supreme Court doctrine, and the scope of that doctrine is fine, but ultimately you must tell the professor in detail how that doctrine is applied to the facts set forth in the exam. While the goal of every exam-taker is to demonstrate how well he or she knows the law, this can be accomplished only by applying the correct law to the fact situation provided. Legal concepts mean little in the abstract on an exam.

Fifth, to apply law to fact, you must be clear on what the facts are. The fact situations in Criminal Procedure exams can be more complex and convoluted than in other exams. Mastery of the facts is crucial. Thus, if the agent took the defendant's airplane ticket before he asked the defendant to accompany him to another room, that is a fact that cannot be overlooked. If you miss that fact, your entire analysis may be altered, and may be irrelevant because the pertinence of later facts and questions often depends on what has gone before. Some professors are merciful about such an error if your analysis of the facts as you have misinterpreted them is sound. Other professors believe that mercy is for sentencing, not for grading.

Sixth, if you are stumped, or if you think you have more to say but are just not sure what it will be, move on and come back later. But make sure you leave room in your exam. Arrows, directions like "continued at end of exam," writing in margins, etc. are the bane of law professors. No matter how fairly a professor tries to grade, it stands to reason that you do not want to make your exam an ordeal for any professor if that can be avoided. A disorganized paper might suggest a disorganized mind, and that can never reflect well on the test-taker.

Seventh, if the question asks you to, be sure to come to a conclusion and to justify it. It is of course necessary and appropriate to discuss both sides of an argument. But sometimes one argument is more compelling than another, and the two do not deserve equal weight. Other times, the law clearly favors one position over the other, even though you might believe the favored position is wrong. We have seen students, consumed with the need to discuss both sides of an issue, reach out to set forth specious arguments for one side or the other. This wastes time and suggests that you are unable to determine which arguments are strong and which are weak.

Eighth, in preparing for an examination, focus primarily on those issues which have been left open by the courts, or in which there has been recent action. If an issue has been closed by a clear and long-standing Supreme Court ruling, it is less likely to be tested than is newer, developing material. It is also important, of course, to attend classes and note where the professor thinks the most interesting issues are. A review of the professor's prior examinations can give you a clue as to the nature of the questions you may face.

The above "tips" are pretty universal. But there is one more that we give in the belief that it is especially important in many Criminal Procedure courses. We suggest that you pay close attention in class to whether the professor spends time analyzing and critiquing Supreme Court decisions in Constitutional Criminal Procedure. When you read cases, is your professor content when you know the holding? Or, does the professor question the holdings and ask you to think about them? Some thoughts the professor might seek to encourage are: 1. Are the cases well-reasoned? 2. Do they ignore, reject, or improperly distinguish prior precedent? 3. Do they give too much discretion to the police? 4. Do they create intractable problems for law enforcement? 5. Do they do what they set out to do?

While it is hard to generalize, we feel that professors who ask you to think about these questions in class may develop exams that invite and indeed call for a broader approach than merely issue spotting and discussing what the law is. Rather, just as in the classroom, the professor may want to know whether you think a rule is well-reasoned, problematic, insupportable, etc. This requires a deeper understanding of the cases and reasoning than can be provided by hornbook law. It is our hope that, even though this is called a "Black Letter Outline," we can give you some perspective on the deeper questions underlying Supreme Court cases in Criminal Procedure.

<table>
<tr><td></td><td>**I**</td></tr>
</table>

INTRODUCTORY CONCEPTS: DETERMINING THE EFFECT OF A SUPREME COURT DECISION ON CRIMINAL PROCEDURE

Analysis

I. *Application of Bill of Rights Protections to the States—Incorporation.*
  A. *Bill of Rights and Fourteenth Amendment.*
  B. *Advantages and Disadvantages of Equal Application on Federal and State Level.*
  C. *Non-constitutional Protections.*
II. *Retroactive Applicaton of Supreme Court Rulings Establishing Constitutional Protections.*
  A. *Retroactivity Options.*
  B. *Adoption of the Harlan Approach.*
  C. *Complete Retroactivity if the Rule Is Not "New" but Is an Application of Old Law to a Different Fact Situation.*
III. *State Court Activism: Providing Greater Rights to Criminal Defendants by Relying on the State Constitution.*
  A. *Greater Protection Under State Law.*
  B. *Two–Step Process.*
  C. *Limitations on Activism.*

Before addressing the constitutional protection afforded criminal defendants, most courses in basic Criminal Procedure consider three general doctrines which help to put the Supreme Court's Criminal Procedure decisions, and their effects, into context.

1. The first is the *incorporation* doctrine, which established that Supreme Court decisions construing constitutional protections apply on both the state and federal level.

2. The second is the *retroactivity* doctrine, which determines to what extent a Supreme Court decision will apply to cases and activities which pre-date the decision.

3. The third doctrine is that of *state court independence,* which means that Supreme Court decisions favoring the Government may not be the last word as a matter of state law.

I. APPLICATION OF BILL OF RIGHTS PROTECTIONS TO THE STATES—INCORPORATION

A. BILL OF RIGHTS AND FOURTEENTH AMENDMENT
The Bill of Rights, as originally enacted, imposed limits only on the Federal Government, not on the states. *Barron v. Mayor of Baltimore,* 32 U.S. (7 Pet.) 243, 8 L.Ed. 672 (1833). The Fourteenth Amendment was enacted in 1868, and specifically prevents the states from depriving any person of life, liberty or property without due process of law.

1. Scope of Protection
Thus, it is clear that the Fourteenth Amendment's Due Process Clause imposes some limitations on state criminal procedures. The question is whether the limitations imposed by the Fourteenth Amendment on the states is different in any way from those imposed by the Bill of Rights upon the Federal Government.

2. Incorporating the Bill of Rights
The Supreme Court, in a series of cases, has held that almost all of the protections granted under the Bill of Rights are granted in equal measure against the states through the Fourteenth Amendment's Due Process Clause. In the Court's own terminology, the Fourteenth Amendment *incorporates* most of the Bill of Rights protections. *Duncan v. Louisiana,* 391 U.S. 145, 88 S.Ct. 1444, 20 L.Ed.2d 491 (1968) (Sixth Amendment right to jury trial applies to states through the Fourteenth Amendment).

3. Analysis Employed
The analytical process by which Bill of Rights protections have become applicable to the states has been tortuous at best. At one time or another,

three views have been espoused by various members of the Court on the incorporation question.

a. **Fundamental Rights Approach**

   The fundamental rights approach was the predominant way of looking at the Fourteenth Amendment up until the 1960's. This approach views the Fourteenth Amendment as prohibiting only those practices which are inconsistent with the concept of "ordered liberty". *Palko v. Connecticut,* 302 U.S. 319, 58 S.Ct. 149, 82 L.Ed. 288 (1937). According to this view, the Due Process Clause requires a case-by-case, totality of circumstances approach to determine whether a particular state practice so *shocks the conscience* that it is unacceptable in the Anglo–American legal system. Under this view, the Bill of Rights protections are relevant indicators of fundamental rights, but they do not necessarily apply to the states. An action may be prohibited by the Bill of Rights and yet still be consistent with fundamental concepts of ordered liberty. It may be inconsistent with the Bill of Rights and yet not shock the conscience. For example, in *Betts v. Brady,* 316 U.S. 455, 62 S.Ct. 1252, 86 L.Ed. 1595 (1942) (overruled by *Gideon v. Wainright, infra*), the Court held that the "shock the conscience" test did not require the State to appoint counsel to an indigent felony defendant, even though it had previously held that the Sixth Amendment required such an appointment at the Federal level.

b. **Criticism of Case-by-Case Approach**

   Critics of the fundamental rights approach argued that the test imposed few meaningful limitations on the states. They contended that Supreme Court overview of criminal justice rendered by the states is all but impossible if the applicability of a right such as the right to jury trial turns on all the conditions of a case. The result of the fundamental rights approach was that the limitations imposed upon state governments were significantly less than those imposed upon the Federal Government. Critics also asserted that the fundamental rights approach allowed the judiciary to make largely personal judgments about what is or is not implicit in the concept of ordered liberty.

c. **Total Incorporation Approach**

   This view, primarily espoused by Justice Black, holds that the Fourteenth Amendment incorporates the entire Bill of Rights, and makes all Bill of Rights protections applicable to the states. Under this view, the terms "privileges and immunities" and "due process" are convenient shorthand devices used in the Fourteenth Amendment as substitutes for an entire restatement of the Bill of Rights. See *Duncan v. Louisiana, supra* (concurring opinion of Justice Black).

d.   Total Incorporation "Plus"

Some justices went even further than Justice Black, and argued that the Due Process Clause not only incorporated all Bill of Rights protections, but also included any unenumerated rights which were essential to ordered liberty. This is known as the "total incorporation plus" theory. See *Adamson v. California,* 332 U.S. 46, 67 S.Ct. 1672, 91 L.Ed. 1903 (1947) (dissenting opinion of Justice Murphy).

e.   Criticism of Total Incorporation Approach

Critics of the total incorporation view argued that there is little in the legislative history of the Fourteenth Amendment which shows that the drafters intended to incorporate all Bill of Rights protections through the terms "privileges and immunities" and "due process." If that were the intent, it could have been clearly stated by providing that "The Bill of Rights protections are hereby applicable to the states." Critics also pointed out that the Bill of Rights protections are as susceptible to judicial subjectivity as is the Due Process Clause. For instance, the term "reasonable" in the Fourth Amendment is no more limiting of judicial subjectivity than is the term "due process."

f.   Effect of Total Incorporation View

The total incorporation approach never gained the support of a majority of the Court. Nonetheless, the views espoused by Justice Black and others had a great influence on the ultimate incorporation of most Bill of Rights guarantees under the selective incorporation approach.

4.   The Selective Incorporation Approach

This view, originally espoused by Justice Brennan, is a hybrid of the fundamental rights and the selective incorporation theory. Selective incorporation theorists agree that the Due Process Clause encompasses rights that are necessary to "ordered liberty" and that the Bill of Rights protections are neither the required nor the exclusive fundamental protections. However, the selective incorporation approach rejects the totality of circumstances, case-by-case analysis of that fundamental rights approach as impermissibly subjective, formless and inefficient.

a.   Generalized Approach

To determine whether a Bill of Rights protection is "fundamental" the selective incorporation approach requires that the Court look at the total right guaranteed by the Bill of Rights provision, not just a single aspect of that right, and not as applied to particular factual circumstances. If a particular Bill of Rights provision is *fundamental to the Anglo–American system of jurisprudence,* it is incorporated into the Fourteenth Amendment *in its entirety.* For example, if the right to jury trial is fundamental (as it is) then it must be applied in every state case to the same extent that it applies to the Federal Government under the Bill of

Rights. And that includes "accoutrements" such as the number of jurors, whether they must be unanimous, etc.

b. Criticism of Selective Incorporation

The selective incorporation approach has been criticized as being an artificial compromise between the fundamental rights and the total incorporation approaches, and as having no basis in the language or history of the Fourteenth Amendment. See *Duncan v. Louisiana, supra* (dissenting opinion of Justice Harlan). It has also been criticized as being contrary to basic notions of federalism. Critics argue that it is inappropriate to impose nationwide solutions on local problems, and that placing a constitutional strait-jacket on the states will prevent them from experimenting with local solutions. Finally, some Justices have attacked the proposition that all aspects of a Bill of Rights protection are equally fundamental. For instance, in *Apodaca v. Oregon,* 406 U.S. 404, 92 S.Ct. 1628, 32 L.Ed.2d 184 (1972), Justice Powell argued that while the Sixth Amendment right to jury trial was fundamental, the unanimity requirement of the Sixth Amendment was not. (His vote was the deciding vote because the eight other justices divided evenly on whether the Sixth Amendment required a unanimous jury).

5. Selective Incorporation Predominates

The selective incorporation approach has been predominant since the 1960's, and is unlikely to be rejected by a majority of the Court at this point. Using selective incorporation, the Court has held that the following Bill of Rights protections are applicable to the states to the same extent as they are applicable to the Federal Government:

a. The Fourth Amendment right to be free from unreasonable searches and seizures. *Mapp v. Ohio,* 367 U.S. 643, 81 S.Ct. 1684, 6 L.Ed.2d 1081 (1961).

b. The Eighth Amendment prohibiton against cruel and unusual punishment. *Robinson v. California,* 370 U.S. 660, 82 S.Ct. 1417, 8 L.Ed.2d 758 (1962).

c. The Sixth Amendment right to counsel. *Gideon v. Wainwright,* 372 U.S. 335, 83 S.Ct. 792, 9 L.Ed.2d 799 (1963).

d. The Fifth Amendment privilege against compelled self-incrimination. *Malloy v. Hogan,* 378 U.S. 1, 84 S.Ct. 1489, 12 L.Ed.2d 653 (1964).

e. The Sixth Amendment right to confrontation. *Pointer v. Texas,* 380 U.S. 400, 85 S.Ct. 1065, 13 L.Ed.2d 923 (1965).

f.   The Sixth Amendment right to a speedy trial. *Klopfer v. North Carolina,* 386 U.S. 213, 87 S.Ct. 988, 18 L.Ed.2d 1 (1967).

g.   The Sixth Amendment right of compulsory process for obtaining favorable witnesses. *Washington v. Texas,* 388 U.S. 14, 87 S.Ct. 1920, 18 L.Ed.2d 1019 (1967).

h.   The Sixth Amendment right to jury trial. *Duncan v. Louisiana, supra.*

i.   The Fifth Amendment protection against double jeopardy. *Benton v. Maryland,* 395 U.S. 784, 89 S.Ct. 2056, 23 L.Ed.2d 707 (1969).

j.   The Sixth Amendment rights to a public trial and to notice of the nature and cause of the accusation. *Gannett Co., Inc. v. DePasquale,* 443 U.S. 368, 99 S.Ct. 2898, 61 L.Ed.2d 608 (1979) (interpreting prior cases as selectively incorporating these rights).

6. Rights Not Selectively Incorporated

Only two Bill of Rights protections bearing upon criminal procedure have not been incorporated through the Fourteenth Amendment. They are the Fifth Amendment requirement of a grand jury indictment in felony cases, and the Eighth Amendment limitation on excessive bail. The Supreme Court has not directly ruled on the bail clause, but has implied that it is fundamental. See *Schilb v. Kuebel,* 404 U.S. 357, 92 S.Ct. 479, 30 L.Ed.2d 502 (1971). Prosecution by grand jury indictment was found not to be fundamental in *Hurtado v. California,* 110 U.S. 516, 4 S.Ct. 111, 28 L.Ed. 232 (1884), and the Court has continued to follow *Hurtado.* See *Gerstein v. Pugh,* 420 U.S. 103, 95 S.Ct. 854, 43 L.Ed.2d 54 (1975).

B. ADVANTAGES AND DISADVANTAGES OF EQUAL APPLICATION ON FEDERAL AND STATE LEVEL

A central point of incorporation is that once the right is considered fundamental, it is applied to the states in exactly the same way as it is applied to the Federal Government. Thus, if the Fourth Amendment applies to the states, as it does, then the same tests for probable cause, particularity of a warrant, and validity of an arrest, apply on a Federal and state level. Supreme Court cases construing the amendment apply equally at both levels.

1. Efficiency

Incorporation is efficient in terms of case management. The Court does not have to decide both a Federal and a state case—either one will do.

2. Possible Erosion of Federal Protections

However, the incorporation approach, which was originally designed to upgrade state standards by tying them to Federal standards, may in fact erode Federal protections in cases where the Court decides that the states should be allowed to experiment with alternative forms of procedure. The only way to allow the states to experiment with lesser protections, within the confines of incorporation, is to dilute the Federal standard as well.

> *Example:* An example of possible dilution of Federal protection due to incorporation is *Williams v. Florida,* 399 U.S. 78, 90 S.Ct. 1893, 26 L.Ed.2d 446 (1970), where the Court held that the Sixth Amendment did not require twelve jurors in a criminal case. If not for incorporation, the Court may well have allowed the state to experiment with the number of jurors, up to the bounds of "shocking the conscience", while continuing to insist that the Federal Sixth Amendment standard required twelve jurors.

C. NON-CONSTITUTIONAL PROTECTIONS

It should be noted that even while the Bill of Rights protections generally apply against the states, there remain some non-constitutional limitations which apply only against the Federal Government and its agents. For example, the Federal Rules of Criminal Procedure continue to require twelve jurors, even though the Sixth Amendment does not after *Williams.*

1. Supervisory Power

Federal courts may in some limited circumstances impose standards on the Federal system pursuant to their supervisory power. See *McNabb v. United States,* 318 U.S. 332, 63 S.Ct. 608, 87 L.Ed. 819 (1943) (excluding confessions obtained if arraignment delayed).

2. Limitations

The Court has, however, recently restricted the use of the supervisory power. A Federal court cannot use its supervisory power simply because it believes that a current constitutional protection is insufficient. *United States v. Payner,* 447 U.S. 727, 100 S.Ct. 2439, 65 L.Ed.2d 468 (1980) (court cannot use supervisory power to exclude evidence otherwise admissible under the Fourth Amendment); *United States v. Williams,* __ U.S. __, 112 S.Ct. 1735, 118 L.Ed.2d 352 (1992) (Federal court has no supervisory authority to dismiss an indictment on the ground that the prosecutor refused to present exculpatory evidence to the grand jury).

II. RETROACTIVE APPLICATION OF SUPREME COURT RULINGS ESTABLISHING CONSTITUTIONAL PROTECTIONS

Whenever the Supreme Court establishes a new constitutional protection—for example, that counsel must be present at a line-up, or that a warrant is required for an in-home arrest—the question will arise as to who gets the benefit of the new rule. Of course the rule will apply to future events. But some people will already have been affected by an action which is subsequently held to be unconstitutional. Whether and how to apply a new rule to past events are questions with which the Supreme Court has struggled.

A.   RETROACTIVITY OPTIONS
Some of the options with respect to retroactive application of a new rule are:

1.   Full Retroactivity
Under this view, every criminal suspect or defendant, whether awaiting trial or already convicted, would get the benefit of the new rule. The result might be the exclusion of evidence, the dismissal of the case, or a new trial, depending on the stage of the proceedings.

a.   Criticism of Full Retroactivity
Obviously, fully retroactive application of all new rules would impose severe limitations on the notion of finality, especially as to individuals who were tried and convicted, and who unsuccessfully appealed. Given the inevitable loss and deterioration of evidence, the granting of a new trial in these finalized cases is at best very costly, and at worst tantamount to acquittal. Critics of full retroactivity also point out that before a new decision is published, the police, prosecutors, and courts were acting correctly under the law as it existed at the time. These authorities will undoubtedly feel unfairly penalized for following the law as it was then understood.

b.   Argument in Favor of Full Retroactivity
Proponents of full retroactivity argue that if past conduct is now found to have been wrong, then under the rule of law, all similarly situated claimants should obtain the same relief.

2.   Total Prospectivity
Under this alternative, the new rule would be applicable only to conduct occurring after the date of the Supreme Court decision. Obviously, this would limit the costs of the new rule.

a.   Advantage of Prospective Approach
Some have argued that prospective-only application of new rules might encourage the development of rules which would not otherwise be promulgated by a cost-conscious court. See *Jenkins v. Delaware,* 395 U.S. 213, 89 S.Ct. 1677, 23 L.Ed.2d 253 (1969) (non-retroactivity provides an impetus for the "implementation of long overdue reforms which otherwise could not be practicably effected.").

b.   Criticism of Prospective Approach
Critics argue that total prospectivity is a virtual impossibility because the conduct in the very case in which a court announces a new rule occurred, by definition, before the date of the decision. For example,

Ernesto Miranda's confession was obviously obtained before the Court's decision in *Miranda v. Arizona,* 384 U.S. 436, 86 S.Ct. 1602, 16 L.Ed.2d 694 (1966). The application of the *Miranda* rule to Miranda himself is an example of retroactive application. Critics point out that retroactive application, at least in the case before the court, is necessary as a practical matter. Otherwise there may not even be a case or controversy before the Court; nor would there be an incentive for defendants to establish new rules which would not benefit them.

3. Almost Wholly Prospective

This is a compromise position under which the new rule would be applied retroactively only to one person: the defendant in whose case the rule was changed. This option satisfies the case and controversy requirement, provides an incentive for defendants to establish new rules, and yet avoids most of the costs of retroactive application.

a. Criticism

Critics argue that the "almost wholly prospective" approach is unfair because similarly situated people are not treated similarly. For instance, when *Miranda* was decided, there were many lower court cases and appeals that involved unwarned and uncounselled confessions. To some extent, it was pure happenstance that Miranda's case was chosen by the Court instead of that of a similarly situated defendant.

b. Supreme Court's Initial View of Retroactivity

For many years, the Court viewed the almost wholly prospective approach as a permissible option. Justice Harlan strenuously argued that it resulted in unequal treatment and was tantamount to judicial legislation. See *Desist v. United States,* 394 U.S. 244, 89 S.Ct. 1030, 22 L.Ed.2d 248 (1969) (dissenting opinion of Justice Harlan).

4. The Harlan Approach

Justice Harlan, in his dissenting opinion in *Desist,* laid out a different approach toward retroactive application of new rules—an approach which was eventually adopted, almost in its entirety, by the Supreme Court. Justice Harlan argued that a new rule should be applied to all those whose appellate rights had not run out as of the date of the decision. That is, the new rule should apply to cases not yet final on the date of the new ruling.

a. Finalized Conviction

Under the Harlan view, a case is finalized (and thus not generally entitled to retroactive application of new rules) if, on the date of the new ruling, the defendant has been convicted, the availability of appeal has been exhausted, and the time for petition for certiorari has elapsed or a petition for certiorari has been finally denied.

b.   Collateral Attack

The fact that a case is final does not end the possibility of review. The defendant can *collaterally attack* his conviction, for example by seeking a writ of habeas corpus. Habeas corpus (or a motion by a federal defendant under 28 U.S.C.A. § 2255, which is the substantial equivalent of habeas corpus) is the most common device by which a person challenges the lawfulness of his custody after his appeals have been exhausted. It allows the Federal district court to review the constitutional validity of convictions; most collateral attacks brought in the Federal court seek to challenge the constitutional validity of convictions rendered in the state courts. The procedure is called a collateral attack, since it is a new proceeding, brought to attack the results of a completed proceeding. This is in contrast to a direct attack on a trial court judgment by way of an appeal. If a Federal district judge finds that a conviction was obtained through a denial of a defendant's constitutional rights, the judge will order the petitioner-defendant's release unless he is retried within a certain period of time. Appeal from denial of the writ can be taken to the appropriate Federal circuit court, and a petition for certiorari from a negative decision of the circuit court can thereafter be filed in the Supreme Court.

c.   Generally No Retroactive Application to Habeas Cases

Justice Harlan reasoned that, as a general matter, a new rule should not be applied to a case on collateral review, i.e. to habeas corpus cases. Thus, Justice Harlan's retroactivity analysis is dependent upon a distinction between those cases which are final and those which are not—a distinction between those cases on direct appeal and those on collateral review.

d.   Rationale for the Harlan Approach

Justice Harlan objected to non-retroactivity on the ground that it was inequitable and arbitrary. He argued that a new rule must apply to all those whose cases were not final when the rule was announced; otherwise similarly situated people would not be treated similarly. Justice Harlan reasoned that a distinction between direct and collateral review could be justified, because of the purpose behind the writ of habeas corpus. According to Justice Harlan, habeas corpus was an extraordinary remedy, the purpose of which was not to allow defendants to retry every issue in light of intervening decisions. Justice Harlan saw the purpose of habeas corpus as assuring that courts apply constitutional law properly, *as it exists at the time that a case is decided on direct review*. In his view, the writ was designed solely to prevent courts from making incorrect applications of then-prevailing constitutional standards. Justice Harlan did not see habeas corpus as designed to assure a trial free from all constitutional error. At some point, he concluded, there must be finality to litigation.

Consequently, Justice Harlan concluded that a new rule should not generally be applied in habeas corpus cases, since the issue in such cases is whether the courts applied the old rule properly. He proposed exceptions to the general rule of non-retroactivity, however. These exceptions are considered infra.

B. ADOPTION OF THE HARLAN APPROACH

In a series of cases culminating with *Teague v. Lane,* 489 U.S. 288, 109 S.Ct. 1060, 103 L.Ed.2d 334 (1989), the Supreme Court adopted the Harlan approach to retroactivity virtually in its entirety, thus rejecting its earlier adherence to the almost wholly prospective approach. After *Teague,* the following rules determine the retroactivity of a new Supreme Court rule.

1. Retroactive Application to All Cases Which Have Not Been Finalized

The general rule is now that a new rule must be applied to all those defendants who are currently being tried, or who are to be tried, and to all those whose appeals have not been finalized. Finalization of appellate review occurs with the Supreme Court's denial of certiorari, or where the time to file such a petition has run out. See *Griffith v. Kentucky,* 479 U.S. 314, 107 S.Ct. 708, 93 L.Ed.2d 649 (1987).

a. No Exception For Reasonable Reliance By Authorities

A defendant whose appeal has not been finalized gets the benefit of a new rule even if nobody could have anticipated that the then current rule was wrong, and even if the new rule explicitly and suddenly overrules a prior decision which was relied on in good faith. Thus, at least as applied to defendants whose appeals have not been finalized, the Court no longer considers it relevant that the authorities properly relied on existing law, as it had under its prior approach to retroactivity, which balanced reliance interests against fairness concerns for defendants.

Example: For example, in *Griffith v. Kentucky, supra,* the Court held that, though authorities were clearly acting correctly under prior law, the new rule would apply to all defendants whose appeals had not been finalized. The Court reasoned that the principle that similarly situated people should get the same rule of law outweighed any reliance interest that the authorities had in the old law.

2. As a General Rule, There Is No Retroactive Application of New Rules to Finalized Convictions

A new rule cannot generally be argued as a basis for obtaining habeas corpus relief, since the purpose of habeas corpus is to determine whether the defendant was properly tried under the law as it existed at the time of trial.

a. Criticism

It can be argued that the line drawn by Justice Harlan and by the Court in recent cases is just as arbitrary as the almost wholly prospective approach. For example, a defendant who is in a state with an efficient appellate system will have his conviction more quickly finalized than a defendant in a state with a backlogged appellate system. The former defendant would not get the benefit of a new rule, whereas the latter would, even though the defendants may have been subjected to the same unconstitutional activity at the same time.

b. Response

A possible response to the above criticism is that the line between direct and collateral review does roughly correspond to the recency of the crime. So the cost of a new rule is not as great as it would be if convictions that have long been final could be overturned. It can be argued that while the Harlan approach does not establish total equality, it does give the benefit of a new rule to a greater number of similarly situated people than the former balancing approach, which permitted almost wholly prospective application.

3. Limited Exceptions to Non-retroactivity in Habeas Corpus Cases

Justice Harlan saw two situations in which the presumption of non-retroactivity of new rules for habeas corpus cases could be overcome. He stated that these exceptions would be limited to egregious cases, where the need for retroactivity was so great that it outweighed both finality principles and the fact that the state court properly applied the law as it existed at the time. The Supreme Court, in adopting Justice Harlan's view of retroactivity, also adopted his exceptions to the general rule of non-retroactivity in habeas corpus cases, with one minor change to make one of the exceptions even more limited than Justice Harlan intended. The Court has stressed that the exceptions to non-retroactivity in habeas cases are extremely limited. See *Teague v. Lane, supra.*

a. Total Retroactivity for Rules Which Go to the Integrity of the Criminal Justice System

One of Justice Harlan's exceptions was that habeas corpus petitioners should get the benefit of a new rule if it is so fundamental that it bears upon the integrity of the criminal justice system. In *Teague,* the Court narrowed the concept of fundamentality, and limited new rules qualifying under this exception to those *"watershed rules of criminal procedure"* which raise a substantial possibility that without the rule, a factually innocent person may have been unfairly convicted. Here, the interest in finality is outweighed by the fact that a possibly innocent person was deprived of a crucial protection for maintaining that innocence.

Example: The right to counsel (see *Gideon v. Wainright, supra*), and the right to have every element of an offense proven beyond a reasonable doubt (see *In re Winship,* 397 U.S. 358, 90 S.Ct. 1068, 25 L.Ed.2d 368 (1970)) are rules which are given full retroactivity, since without such rules there is a risk that an innocent person could be convicted. See *Saffle v. Parks,* 494 U.S. 484, 110 S.Ct. 1257, 108 L.Ed.2d 415 (1990) (noting *Gideon* as the benchmark case for this limited exception to non-retroactivity for habeas cases).

Example Not Within the Exception: The right stated in *Edwards v. Arizona,* 451 U.S. 477, 101 S.Ct. 1880, 68 L.Ed.2d 378 (1981), to have counsel present at an interrogation, has nothing to do with the reliability of the resulting confession, or with whether the defendant is factually guilty. A rule excluding a reliable confession is not intended to further accurate decisionmaking. Hence it will not be retroactively applied to habeas corpus cases. See *Butler v. McKellar,* 494 U.S. 407, 110 S.Ct. 1212, 108 L.Ed.2d 347 (1990).

b. **"Watershed Rule" Exception Not Likely to Arise in the Future**
As the Court has recently stated, the exception to non-retroactivity in habeas corpus cases for "fundamental" rules is intended to apply only to truly watershed rules of criminal procedure, such as the Court does not anticipate ever promulgating again. See *Teague v. Lane, supra* ("Because we operate from the premise that such procedures would be so central to an accurate determination of innocence or guilt, we believe it unlikely that many such components of basic due process have yet to emerge."). See also *Sawyer v. Smith,* 497 U.S. 227, 110 S.Ct. 2822, 111 L.Ed.2d 193 (1990) (rule preventing a prosecutor from telling the jury in a death penalty case that any error they made could be corrected on review was not to be retroactively applied to a habeas case; while the rule was designed to assure accuracy in capital sentencing, it was not a "watershed" rule necessary to assure fundamental fairness).

c. **Total Retroactivity if Defendant Should Never Have Been Tried at All**
Another exception to non-retroactivity in habeas corpus cases, similarly based on an outweighing of the principles behind the general rule, is that full retroactivity is required for new rules which show that the defendant should not have been tried at all, or that he was not subject to the penalties that were imposed in his case.

Example: Defendant is convicted of burning the flag. His appeals and his petition for certiorari have been denied. Then, the Supreme Court holds that flag-burning is protected by the First Amendment. This rule applies retroactively even in habeas cases, since the new rule means that the defendant's conduct could not be constitutionally proscribed, and thus he should never have been tried. Another rule, applicable to the penalty phase rather than the trial phase, would be a rule holding that the execution of a certain class of defendants is constitutionally prohibited. This rule would be retroactively applied to habeas cases since the Court would have held that the state has no authority to execute such defendants. See *Penry v. Lynaugh*, 492 U.S. 302, 109 S.Ct. 2934, 106 L.Ed.2d 256 (1989) (a rule providing that the Eighth Amendment prohibits the execution of mentally retarded defendants would be applicable to habeas cases).

d. Limited Costs

Note that there will be no retrial in the "never should have been tried at all" situation, and therefore the Government cannot readily complain when a defendant who should not have been tried is freed, or when a defendant who cannot be executed is given a life sentence.

4. Petitioners Generally Cannot Seek to Establish a New Rule of Law in a Habeas Corpus Petition

Since a new rule of law cannot be applied on habeas corpus as a general rule, it follows that a habeas corpus petitioner cannot argue for the *adoption* of a new rule in his case. Habeas corpus petitioners cannot seek to establish new rules of law, unless such a rule could be applied retroactively to all habeas petitioners. This will only be the case if the new rule fits within one of the two very limited exceptions discussed above. Since a new rule could not generally be applied to anyone else on habeas if promulgated in petitioner's case, it would be inequitable to apply it to the petitioner himself. See *Teague v. Lane, supra* ("Habeas corpus cannot be used as a vehicle to create new constitutional rules of criminal procedure unless those rules would be applied retroactively to all defendants on collateral review.").

a. Retroactivity Question Is Considered in the Petitioner's Case

Consequently, not only are habeas claimants deprived of the benefit of a new rule decided in another case, they are deprived of the opportunity to argue for the adoption of a new rule in their own case. Retroactive effect is now considered in the very case in which the new rule is sought to be adopted.

b. Limit on Habeas Corpus

The ruling in *Teague* significantly limits the efficacy of the writ of habeas corpus, since if the petitioner needs to persuade the court that new law should be adopted in order for the writ to be granted, the petition will be dismissed without consideration of the merits of the argument.

C. COMPLETE RETROACTIVITY IF THE RULE IS NOT "NEW" BUT IS AN APPLICATION OF OLD LAW TO A DIFFERENT FACT SITUATION

As discussed above, new rules are generally inapplicable to those whose convictions have been finalized. But while Justice Harlan believed that most collateral attacks on final judgments should be resolved under the law as it existed at the time, he also emphasized that some "new" holdings are not "new" at all. Rather, some "new" cases are merely applications of well-settled principles to different fact situations. To take an obvious example, a rule is not "new" merely because it is applied to a defendant with a different name, or to a search of a different house. In these simple cases, a court applies an old rule to a virtually identical set of facts.

1. Settled Precedent

The Court, following Justice Harlan's approach, has mandated that when a decision merely applies settled precedent to a similar fact situation it is not a "new" rule at all, and is thus completely retroactive. This is consistent with the purpose of habeas corpus, since if the rule is not "new", it was the law as it existed at the time of conviction, and it should have been applied at the time of the defendant's trial. See *Yates v. Aiken,* 484 U.S. 211, 108 S.Ct. 534, 98 L.Ed.2d 546 (1988).

2. Definition of "New" Rule

The Supreme Court has recognized that it is "often difficult" to determine when a case announces a new rule. The Court has stated that a case announces a new rule when it breaks new ground or imposes a new obligation on the Government; this will occur if the result was *not dictated by existing precedent.* See *Teague v. Lane, supra.*

a. *Butler*

In *Butler v. McKellar,* 494 U.S. 407, 110 S.Ct. 1212, 108 L.Ed.2d 347 (1990), the Court adopted a narrow test for determining whether a rule was dictated by existing precedent and hence not "new". The result is that most Supreme Court decisions will be deemed new rules not applicable on habeas, rather than old rules applied to similar fact situations. The Court in *Butler* stated that *if reasonable minds could have differed* about the outcome of a Supreme Court case before it was rendered, then the rule ultimately adopted is "new" and thus generally non-retroactive in habeas cases.

Example: In *Edwards v. Arizona, supra,* the Court held that a confession could not be obtained from a defendant who had invoked his right to counsel, unless counsel was present or the defendant initiated later contact with the police on his own. In *Arizona v. Roberson,* 486 U.S. 675, 108 S.Ct. 2093, 100 L.Ed.2d 704 (1988), the defendant invoked his right to counsel, and the police then interrogated him about an offense that was *unrelated* to the subject of the initial interrogation. The Court in *Roberson* refused to establish an "exception" to *Edwards* for interrogation about a different offense. The habeas petitioner in *Butler v. McKellar* argued that the rule in *Roberson* should be completely retroactive, on the ground that the Court itself stated in *Roberson* that it was not making a new rule but rather was merely applying *Edwards* to a different fact situation. The Court in *Butler* rejected petitioner's argument on the ground that lower courts before *Roberson* had differed about whether *Edwards* would apply to questioning about unrelated investigations. The fact that the majority in *Roberson* characterized its decision as indistinguishable from *Edwards,* and had refused to create an "exception" to *Edwards,* was not dispositive. According to Chief Justice Rehnquist, "courts frequently view their decisions as being 'controlled' or 'governed' by prior opinions even when aware of reasonable contrary conclusions reached by lower courts."

b.   Implications of *Butler*

The test in *Butler* for whether a rule is new effectively means that all Supreme Court decisions will be "new" and hence non-retroactive to habeas cases. Almost by definition, the Supreme Court does not take a case unless reasonable minds could differ about its resolution. The major ground for granting certiorari is a split in the lower courts. This is exactly what Chief Justice Rehnquist refers to as a reasonable difference of opinion in the lower courts, making a Supreme Court decision on the point a "new" rule. The *Butler* test may also mean that if a Supreme Court decision is non-unanimous, it will not be retroactively applied to habeas cases. Such a decision should be, by definition, the announcement of a new rule, since reasonable minds (i.e. the Justices of the Supreme Court) differed about the result.

c.   Recent Retroactivity Cases Severely Limit the Habeas Corpus Remedy

When *Butler* is combined with *Teague,* which held that "new" rules generally may not be *adopted* on collateral review, the effect is to substantially limit the utility of habeas corpus. For example, a Federal court reviewing a state court decision cannot grant the petition for habeas corpus if reasonable minds could differ about the correctness of the state court result. Granting the petition where reasonable minds could differ would be tantamount to applying a new rule on habeas, which is prohibited by *Teague.* Consequently, the petition will only be granted if the state court was so incorrect as to be completely unreasonable; or, to put it another way, the petition will only be granted if the state court misapplied *clearly established law,* such as by holding that there is no right to counsel in felony trials. See *Butler v. McKellar, supra* (dissenting opinion of Justice Brennan) (arguing that the test in *Butler* effectively adopts a clearly erroneous standard of review in habeas cases).

III. STATE COURT ACTIVISM: PROVIDING GREATER RIGHTS TO CRIMINAL DEFENDANTS BY RELYING ON THE STATE CONSTITUTION

As the Supreme Court in the 1970's and 1980's began to retreat from earlier decisions which provided significant constitutional rights to criminal suspects, many state courts retained the earlier rules. They did so by providing greater protection under their state constitutions than the Supreme Court provided under the federal constitution. The states in the forefront of relying on their own constitutions are Alaska, Connecticut, Hawaii, Mississippi, New York, Oregon, and Washington; many other state courts have invoked their state constitution to protect criminal defendants from time to time. In the 1970's, California's Supreme Court was the best example of a tribunal willing to rely on its state constitution to expand the rights of criminal defendants. The political backlash against some of its decisions resulted in the transformation of that court.

A. GREATER PROTECTION UNDER STATE LAW
There can be no disagreement about the scope of a federal constitutional protection once the Supreme Court has spoken. However, a state court can construe its state constitution to give greater protection to a defendant than is granted by the Federal Constitution.

1. No Federal Question
As to state law, the highest court of the state is the supreme arbiter. The United States Supreme Court cannot even review a state court's construction of its state constitution, because such a case does not invoke a federal question. If the Court were to take such case and hold that the result was not mandated by federal law, its ruling would have no effect, since the state court's decision would still be mandated by *state* law. Thus, while a state cannot give a suspect less protection than the Federal Constitution provides, it can give more.

B. TWO–STEP PROCESS
State courts have generally used a two-step process to determine whether the state constitution gives more protection than the Federal.

1. Different Language
The first step is to determine if there is specific language in the state constitution, different from the Federal, which would show some indication of special protection.

Example: In Washington, Article I, section 7 of the state constitution is analogous to the Fourth Amendment. However, the drafters of the Washington State Constitution rejected the language of the Fourth Amendment, in favor of language which specifically protected a citizen's private affairs. This specific mention of privacy has been relied on by the Washington Supreme Court to provide more protection than that given to citizens under the Fourth Amendment. See *State v. Gunwall,* 106 Wash.2d 54, 720 P.2d 808 (1986) (rejecting Supreme Court decision which held that the monitoring of telephone calls by a pen register was not a search).

2. Independent Policy Determination

The second step, when the language of the state provision is identical, is for a state court to make its own policy determination and its own balance of interests. While there is a presumption that the state constitution is coextensive with the Federal, that presumption can be overcome.

Example: The New York Court of Appeals has rejected Supreme Court cases as unsound, insufficiently protective of citizens, and in conflict with the clear common law and political history of the utmost respect for personal rights in New York. See *People v. Johnson,* 66 N.Y.2d 398, 497 N.Y.S.2d 618, 488 N.E.2d 439 (1985) and *People v. Bigelow,* 66 N.Y.2d 417, 497 N.Y.S.2d 630, 488 N.E.2d 451 (1985) (rejecting the totality of circumstances approach to informant hearsay and the good faith exception to the exclusionary rule).

C. LIMITATIONS ON ACTIVISM

There have been *two recent developments* which have dampened state court activism somewhat.

1. Amendments to State Constitutions

A few states have amended their constitutions in an attempt to prevent greater rights being given on the state level.

Example: The Florida constitution now states that United States Supreme Court decisions provide the full extent of protection from search and seizure. After this amendment, the state constitution cannot provide greater protection, ending a trend of several cases in which the Florida courts had granted greater rights against searches and seizures than those provided by the Fourth Amendment.

2. Plain Statement Rule

The Supreme Court has held that it can review state court cases unless the state court makes a *clear statement* that its decision is based solely on the state constitution. See *Michigan v. Long,* 463 U.S. 1032, 103 S.Ct. 3469, 77 L.Ed.2d 1201 (1983). Thus, in the absence of a clear indication that the state court has decided the case solely on state grounds, the Supreme Court *presumes* that the state court decided the case on Federal constitutional grounds and hence that it can review the decision.

a. Decision on Both Federal and State Grounds

To avoid review under *Long,* a state court must make a clear statement that the state constitution requires a certain protection *regardless* of what the Federal Constitution may provide. A state court which bases a ruling on *both* Federal and state law does not satisfy the clear statement rule of *Long* and its ruling can be reviewed by the Supreme Court. When the state court relies on Federal and state law simultaneously, it may be saying that the state constitution requires a protection because the Federal Constitution does. This is not a clear statement that the state constitution grants a right regardless of the limitations of Federal law.

b. Remand to State Court

If there is no clear statement and the Supreme Court decides that a state court erred in giving the defendant too much protection, the state court can nonetheless have the final word on remand. For example, the New York Court of Appeals in several cases held that the state and Federal constitutions were violated. These cases were reversed by the Supreme Court. That Court reached the merits because the New York court had not made a clear statement that it was relying solely on state law. But on remand, the New York court adhered to its views that state law required the protection the court had previously mandated, and thus the defendant eventually prevailed. See *New York v. P.J. Video,* 68 N.Y.2d 296, 508 N.Y.S.2d 907, 501 N.E.2d 556 (1986).

*

II

THE FOURTH AMENDMENT

Analysis

83

I. INTRODUCTION

The Fourth Amendment represents a compromise between the need of Government officials to gather evidence and the right of citizens to be free from governmental intrusion. The Amendment provides that "The right of the people to be secure in their persons, houses, papers, and effects, against unreasonable searches and seizures, shall not be violated, and no Warrants shall issue, but upon probable cause, supported by Oath or affirmation, and particularly describing the place to be searched and the persons or things to be seized." Fourth Amendment limitations on governmental investigations are equally applicable to the state and Federal governments. *Mapp v. Ohio,* 367 U.S. 643, 81 S.Ct. 1684, 6 L.Ed.2d 1081 (1961).

A. BASICS OF THE FOURTH AMENDMENT

From a reading of the Amendment itself and an understanding of general constitutional principles, some basic points can be derived which will apply generally to all Fourth Amendment questions.

1. Does Not Apply to Private Activity

The Fourth Amendment, like other protections in the Bill of Rights and the Due Process Clause, is a limit on state action, but does not limit private actors acting on their own. See *United States v. Jacobsen,* 466 U.S. 109, 104 S.Ct. 1652, 80 L.Ed.2d 85 (1984) (no Fourth Amendment protection where package was opened by Federal Express employees acting on their own). Thus, no matter how unreasonable a search is, the Fourth Amendment is not implicated if the search is conducted by private actors not acting as agents of the Government.

a. Government Can Use the Fruits of a Private Search

If a private party conducts a search and uncovers evidence, the Fourth Amendment does not prohibit the Government from using that evidence in a criminal trial or in any other way. This is because the subsequent Government conduct is not itself a search or seizure—that has already been done by the private party. See *Burdeau v. McDowell,* 256 U.S. 465, 41 S.Ct. 574, 65 L.Ed. 1048 (1921).

b. Not Acting in an Official Capacity

Generally speaking, anyone who is not employed by the Government, and who is acting in the course of their private employment or private life, is a private actor to whom the Fourth Amendment does not apply. Thus, even Government employees are private actors if they are not acting while in the course of employment. See *United States v. McGreevy,* 652 F.2d 849 (9th Cir.1981) (police officer working at second job as security officer is not governed by Fourth Amendment).

c. **Private Actors as Government Agents**
    If the private actor is making a search at the behest of a state actor or
    is encouraged to act by a Government official, then state action may be
    found and the Fourth Amendment will apply. See *United States v.
    Walther,* 652 F.2d 788 (9th Cir.1981) (airline employee acted as
    Government agent when he expected a DEA reward for his actions and
    the agency had encouraged him). Otherwise, Government officials could
    too easily avoid the strictures of the Fourth Amendment by "deputizing"
    private actors to do their work for them. The Government need not
    require or mandate a private party to conduct a search in order for state
    action to be found. If the facts show significant Government
    encouragement, endorsement and participation at the outset, then state
    action will be found and the private party's search will trigger the
    Fourth Amendment.

    Example: Government regulations applicable to railroads require them
    to conduct drug-testing of railroad employees under certain
    circumstances, and authorize such testing in other
    circumstances even if there is a collective bargaining
    provision to the contrary. Where testing is authorized but
    not required, Government regulations make plain a strong
    preference for testing to fulfil the railroad's nondelegable
    duty to promote public safety, and the regulations further
    authorize a Federal agency to have access to the test
    samples. Under these circumstances, the Supreme Court
    unanimously found that private testing pursuant to the
    regulations was state action subject to the Fourth
    Amendment. The provisions requiring drug testing clearly
    made the railroad an instrument of the Government; and
    even the regulations which merely authorized drug testing
    were so invasive that a private actor acting pursuant to the
    regulations was fairly treated as a Government agent. See
    Skinner v. Railway Labor Executives' Assoc., 489 U.S. 602,
    109 S.Ct. 1402, 103 L.Ed.2d 639 (1989).

d. **Applies to All Government Agents, Not Just Police Officers**
    The Court has rejected the argument that the Fourth Amendment
    regulates only searches and seizures by law enforcement officers. The
    Amendment applies to the acts of Government officials generally. *New
    Jersey v. T.L.O.,* 469 U.S. 325, 105 S.Ct. 733, 83 L.Ed.2d 720 (1985)
    (school principal governed by Fourth Amendment). However, as will be
    discussed later in this outline, a search or seizure undertaken by non-law
    enforcement personnel may be considered reasonable where the same
    conduct by a police officer enforcing criminal law objectives may not.

2. Protects "the People"

The Fourth Amendment ascribes the right provided to the people, not to a "person" as the Fifth and Sixth Amendments do. This language lends support to the position that the Fourth Amendment can be employed to deter future violations of privacy and security, and that a court enforcing the Fourth Amendment is not necessarily limited to remedying an individual violation.

a.   Protects Innocent and Guilty Alike

Most Fourth Amendment questions arise in the context of a criminal proceeding, in which a person who appears to be factually guilty seeks to suppress probative evidence. Courts have recognized that the Fourth Amendment protects innocent "people" as well as the guilty person before the court. Much evidence that is seized is neither contraband nor the fruits of crime and is taken from individuals who are presumed innocent until convicted.

b.   Does Not Protect Aliens When the Search Is Conducted Abroad

In *United States v. Verdugo–Urquidez,* 494 U.S. 259, 110 S.Ct. 1056, 108 L.Ed.2d 222 (1990), the Supreme Court held that the Fourth Amendment does not apply to a search of property which is owned by an alien and located in a foreign country. The Court stated that the Fourth Amendment's reference to "the people," as opposed to a particular person, was a "term of art" intended to refer to a class of persons "who are part of a national community or who have otherwise developed sufficient connection with this country to be considered a part of that community." Thus, the Court looked at the term "the people" as a limiting term. The Court held that the defendant, who had been involuntarily transported to the United States three days before the foreign search was conducted, lacked sufficient connection with the United States to be one of "the people" protected by the Fourth Amendment.

c.   Dissent

Dissenting in *Verdugo–Urquidez,* Justice Brennan argued that it was anomalous for the Federal Government to require aliens residing outside the United States to obey Federal laws (through extraterritorial application), and yet for the Government to refuse to obey its own laws in investigating the very extraterritorial activity that it has criminalized. According to Justice Brennan, such a lack of mutuality is inconsistent with basic notions of fundamental fairness: if the Government has the power to enforce the criminal law, the Fourth Amendment is an "unavoidable correlative."

Justice Brennan also contended that the Court's construction of "the people" as a limiting term had no basis. He asserted that if the Framers had wanted to, they could have limited the protection of the Fourth Amendment to a specific class of people (e.g. "citizens" or "the American people"). He concluded that in context, the term "the people" refers to everyone to whom American governmental power extends: to the governed. Applying these arguments to the facts, Justice Brennan stated that an alien defendant subject to criminal prosecution in the United States is one of the governed, since the Government treats him as a member of the community by prosecuting him.

d. **Open Question: Does the Fourth Amendment Apply To Searches Conducted of Illegal Aliens and Their Property In the United States?**
In *Verdugo–Urquidez,* the Court specifically refused to decide whether an illegal alien who lived in the United States would be one of "the people" protected by the Fourth Amendment. Presumably, however, the Fourth Amendment would apply, since an illegal alien living in the United States would seem to have the "connection" with this country required to be one of "the people". Five members of the Court in various opinions in *Verdugo–Urquidez* indicated that they would hold the Fourth Amendment applicable to searches of illegal aliens conducted within the United States. See the opinions of Justice Stevens, Justice Kennedy, Justice Blackmun, and Justice Brennan joined by Justice Marshall. Note, however, that two of these Justices have since left the Court.

e. **Abduction Does Not Deprive the Government of Jurisdiction to Try the Alien Defendant**
Verdugo–Urquidez had been abducted from Mexico, and was tried in the United States despite formal objection from the Mexican Government. Mexico argued that forced abduction of a Mexican national for trial in the United States was in violation of the extradition treaty between the two countries. On remand from the Supreme Court, the Ninth Circuit agreed with the Mexican Government and held that the forced abduction of a Mexican national deprived United States courts of jurisdiction to try him. In a related case, the Supreme Court rejected the Ninth Circuit position. See *United States v. Alvarez–Machain,* __ U.S. __, 112 S.Ct. 2188, 119 L.Ed.2d 441 (1992). The Court held that there was nothing in the extradition treaty which specifically prohibited forced abduction, and therefore that the treaty was not violated when the defendant was kidnapped in Mexico by DEA agents and brought to the United States for trial. Since the extradition treaty did not prohibit the abduction, the Court relied on its prior case law, particularly *Ker v. Illinois,* 119 U.S. 436, 7 S.Ct. 225, 30 L.Ed. 421 (1886), where the Court had held that an illegal arrest of a person did not deprive a court of jurisdiction.

3. **Protects "Persons, Houses, Papers and Effects"**
At least on its face, the Fourth Amendment does not draw a distinction in the existence or the scope of protection between a person, his property, or his

house. In fact, however, the courts have frequently distinguished between these various interests. In descending order, courts give the greatest protection to the house, then to the person's property, then to the person himself. See *United States v. United States District Court*, 407 U.S. 297, 92 S.Ct. 2125, 32 L.Ed.2d 752 (1972) ("Entry into the home is the chief evil against which the wording of the Fourth Amendment is directed."); *United States v. Chadwick*, 433 U.S. 1, 97 S.Ct. 2476, 53 L.Ed.2d 538 (1977) (providing greater protection to defendant's property than to his person in a search incident to arrest).

4. Two Clauses

The Fourth Amendment has two clauses. The first clause, the reasonableness clause, provides a general standard that all searches and seizures must be reasonable. The second clause imposes requirements for obtaining warrants.

a. Which Clause Predominates?

A quick reading of the Amendment would indicate that the reasonableness clause should set the standard for most Government searches and seizures, and that the text of the Fourth Amendment does not require all or even any searches to be made pursuant to a warrant. The warrant clause seems merely to impose limitations on a warrant should a police officer decide to obtain one. These expressed limitations on the warrant process are consistent with the intent of the Framers to control the possibility of officials obtaining a *general warrant* to conduct arbitrary searches.

b. Historical Basis

It was the use of general warrants by British officials that spurred the inclusion of the Fourth Amendment in the Bill of Rights. See *United States v. Verdugo–Urquidez, supra* ("The driving force behind the adoption of the Amendment, as suggested by Madison's advocacy, was widespread hostility among the former Colonists to the issuance of writs of assistance * * * and general search warrants."). It may seem anomalous that a warrant requirement would be the touchstone of an amendment designed to limit warrants.

c. Predominance of the Warrant Clause

Despite the way the Amendment reads, the Supreme Court has read the warrant clause to predominate, or to define presumptively whether official conduct is "reasonable". That is, a search or seizure is presumed unreasonable in the absence of a warrant based upon probable cause.

d. Rationale

The Court has concluded that the warrant clause must provide the yardstick against which searches and seizures are measured. The rationale is that without the content and specific limitation which the warrant clause provides, the Fourth Amendment's general command that a search be "reasonable" would be devoid of meaning, and subject to case-by-case balancing approaches of shifting judicial majorities. The Court has asserted that the only principled way to limit searches and seizures, and protect the rights of the people in the way intended by the Fourth Amendment, is to require the Government to adhere as a general rule to the specific requirements of warrant and probable cause. To the extent that the Framers were concerned with the threat of arbitrary police activity, the warrant clause addresses that concern by requiring the official to obtain authorization from a neutral magistrate before conducting a search.

e. Common Law Approach

There is another method of construing Fourth Amendment protections, that is to some people truer to the plain language and historical context of the Amendment, and yet is arguably not susceptible to result-orientation by shifting judicial majorities. This method is to consider the Fourth Amendment as codifying the protections provided by the common law at the time the Amendment was adopted. The main proponent of this historical approach is Justice Scalia. See *California v. Acevedo,* ___ U.S. ___, 111 S.Ct. 1982, 114 L.Ed.2d 619 (1991) (concurring opinion). Under Justice Scalia's view, if a warrant was not required for a police practice under common law, it is not generally required by the Fourth Amendment. Justice Scalia does recognize that certain police activities, such as wiretapping and automobile searches, were unheard of in 1791. But he maintains that common law principles can be translated to these activities as well. While Justice Scalia's view has persuaded the Court in only one case (*California v. Hodari D.,* discussed below), it will not be surprising if his historical approach becomes more influential in the coming years.

5. The Theory of the Warrant Clause

The preeminence of the warrant clause was the result of early Supreme Court decisions which stressed the importance of imposing an unbiased factfinder as a buffer between the citizen suspected of crime and the officer engaged in the competitive enterprise of ferreting out crime. The thought was that if the question of probable cause was left to the officer, the officer's natural bias may lead him to find that sufficient cause existed and that a search could be conducted. According to this view, the warrant requirement prevents questionable searches from being conducted, and assures that only those as to whom probable cause exists will be subject to an intrusion. See *Johnson v. United States,* 333 U.S. 10, 68 S.Ct. 367, 92 L.Ed. 436 (1948) (Fourth Amendment requires that probable cause must be determined by a neutral and detached magistrate rather than "by the officer engaged in the often competitive enterprise of ferreting out crime").

a. Prior Record of Probable Cause

A subsidiary benefit of the warrant requirement is that it requires the officer to establish, on the record, the facts allegedly constituting probable cause, before the search is conducted. Without an antecedent warrant requirement, an officer questioned about probable cause could work backwards from the search, and fill in the facts as if he knew them before the search was conducted. Thus, the warrant requirement prevents post hoc submissions on probable cause. Some justices feel, however, that the risk of post hoc recreation of the facts is overstated.

b. Limitation on the Scope of a Search

Another benefit of the warrant requirement lies in the language of the Amendment which requires that the warrant must particularly describe the place to be searched and the things to be seized. A warrant therefore defines the scope of a search and thereby limits the discretion of the officers conducting the search.

6. The Rise of the Reasonableness Clause

Even though the warrant clause is still considered the first reference point for the legality of a search or seizure, the Supreme Court has gradually moved to the point where most searches and seizures are in fact governed by a general standard of reasonableness. The strict requirement of a warrant based upon probable cause can be dispensed with in a variety of situations. While each situation will be discussed in detail later in this Outline, a general overview of the Supreme Court's Fourth Amendment cases shows that the dual requirement of *a warrant and probable cause are not needed in the following situations:*

—Where a warrant is impracticable to obtain. See the exigent circumstances exception.

—Where the police conduct a *limited* seizure to investigate possible criminal activity and a *limited* search for weapons to protect the investigating officer. See the *Terry* Doctrine.

—Where the official is searching for evidence, but the search is conducted for purposes *other than criminal law enforcement*. See administrative and other "special needs" searches.

—Where a search is conducted *incident to a valid arrest*.

—Where there is *voluntary consent*.

—Where the citizen is *arrested in public*.

—Where an incriminating object is in *plain view*.

—Where the officer searches an *automobile* or other form of transportation.

Some of these exceptions still require probable cause for the search or seizure to be reasonable. Others do not. For a full discussion of each of these exceptions, see the discussion below.

II. THRESHOLD REQUIREMENTS FOR FOURTH AMENDMENT PROTECTIONS; "SEARCH" AND "SEIZURE"

The Fourth Amendment prohibits unreasonable searches and seizures. Unless the Government activity is either a "search" or a "seizure" it is not regulated by the Fourth Amendment, and therefore it does not have to be reasonable. So when the Court holds that a police activity is neither a search nor a seizure, it means that it is not subject to restriction, and the officer has no obligation to explain it. See *Florida v. Riley,* 488 U.S. 445, 109 S.Ct. 693, 102 L.Ed.2d 835 (1989) (aerial surveillance need not be based on any suspicion and does not require a warrant). In contrast, if the Court holds activity to be a search or a seizure, it does not mean that the activity is prohibited, but only that it must be reasonable.

Commentators have argued that in determining whether an invasion is a search or seizure, it is appropriate to err on the side of triggering the Fourth Amendment: since the consequence is that the officer is merely required to act reasonably, whereas if it is not a search or seizure, the officer can act unreasonably and arbitrarily. See Amsterdam, "Perspectives on the Fourth Amendment," 58 Minn.L.Rev. 349 (1974). In fact, however, the Court in recent years has often held that a certain challenged police activity is neither a search nor a seizure, and is thus free from the strictures of the Fourth Amendment.

A. THE *KATZ* TEST
1. Government Contentions in *Katz*
In *Katz v. United States,* 389 U.S. 347, 88 S.Ct. 507, 19 L.Ed.2d 576 (1967), Government officials intercepted Katz's telephone conversations by use of an electronic listening and recording device attached to the outside of the public telephone booth from which Katz placed his calls. The Government, relying on *Olmstead v. United States,* 277 U.S. 438, 48 S.Ct. 564, 72 L.Ed. 944 (1928), argued that there was no search of a person, house, paper or effect, as those terms are used in the Fourth Amendment. The Government also contended that there was no seizure, since it was impossible to seize an intangible conversation. The Government argued further that there was no search or seizure because there was no physical intrusion into a private area: Katz was at a public telephone booth when he placed his calls.

2. Court's Response in *Katz*
In *Katz,* the Court rejected the Government's literal interpretation of the Fourth Amendment. Essentially, the Court looked beyond the words of the

Fourth Amendment to determine what it thought the Amendment was designed to protect. The Court's answer was that the Fourth Amendment was designed to protect the *legitimate expectations of the people to privacy and security.* After *Katz,* the Fourth Amendment is not to be read literally as protecting only against a physical invasion of certain protected areas.

3. Modern Definition of "Search" and "Seizure"

After *Katz,* the term "search" is triggered whenever the state intrudes in any way upon the individual's protected interest in privacy. And the term "seizure" is triggered whenever the state intrudes in any way on a protectible individual interest in property or security. See *United States v. Mendenhall,* 446 U.S. 544, 100 S.Ct. 1870, 64 L.Ed.2d 497 (1980) (a person is seized by an officer when a reasonable person in his position would not feel free to leave). Thus, if Katz is entitled to assume that his telephone conversation would remain private, the intrusion into that privacy by electronic surveillance is a search: even though the invasion is not physical, and even though Katz is in public. As the Court in *Katz* stated: "The Fourth Amendment protects people, not places."

4. Concurring Opinion of Justice Harlan

Justice Harlan's concurring opinion in *Katz* is often quoted and has had as much influence as the majority opinion. Justice Harlan set forth a two-pronged test to determine whether a search has occurred:

—First, has the citizen manifested a subjective expectation of privacy?

—Second, is the interest one that society is prepared to accept as reasonable?

Even though Justice Harlan later expressed reservations about his own test (see his opinion in *United States v. White,* 401 U.S. 745, 91 S.Ct. 1122, 28 L.Ed.2d 453 (1971)), the Supreme Court has adopted the two-pronged test to determine whether a search has occurred. See *California v. Greenwood,* 486 U.S. 35, 108 S.Ct. 1625, 100 L.Ed.2d 30 (1988).

B. INTERESTS PROTECTED BY THE FOURTH AMENDMENT AFTER *KATZ*

If the Fourth Amendment protects only reasonable and legitimate interests in privacy, one could question why Katz was entitled to protection. Katz was not talking about his private thoughts; he was engaging in illegal betting transactions.

1. The Fourth Amendment Protects "Legitimate" Interests

The Court has held on several occasions after *Katz* that there is no legitimate privacy interest in illegal activity. See *United States v. Place,* 462 U.S. 696, 103 S.Ct. 2637, 77 L.Ed.2d 110 (1983) (no privacy interest in possession of contraband). However, people such as Katz receive Fourth Amendment protection nonetheless, since it is usually not possible to know in advance of the search that their activity is illegal. To protect innocent people with legitimate privacy and security expectations from mistaken assumptions by Government officials, certain interests must be presumed and protected before the intrusion takes place.

2. If It Is Legitimate, What Is There to Hide?

It could be argued that if the Fourth Amendment is designed to protect legitimate expectations, then the Amendment is unnecessary, since a person engaged in legitimate activity has nothing to hide. In fact this is not true. An innocent person can indeed be harmed by a Government intrusion. The courts after *Katz* have found three separate interests of innocent persons which can be affected by a Government intrusion.

a. Physical Disruption and Inconvenience

All citizens have an interest in being free from physical disruption, inconvenience, or terrorization by Government officials. For the official to say, after an arrest and body search, "no harm done" because nothing was found or seized is not acceptable. Such an "explanation" fails to consider the privacy and security interests of innocent individuals.

b. Interest in Secrecy

Another protectible interest of innocent citizens, one implicated in *Katz,* is the right to secrecy—a right of protection against disclosure of information which, although not incriminating, may be embarrassing, sensitive, or extremely private. Without the Fourth Amendment's protection of innocent people, the state could listen to a private conversation which may disclose illness, love, suffering, and many other types of non-incriminating but nonetheless sensitive, information.

c. Possessory Interests

The Fourth Amendment regulates not only invasions of privacy and security interests, but also invasions of possessory interests. The Fourth Amendment prohibits unreasonable seizures as well as searches.

3. Different Intrusions

A seizure may occur without a search, and a search may occur without a seizure.

Examples: A police officer detains a suspect's luggage pending a canine sniff or the obtaining of a warrant. This is a seizure of the luggage, and triggers the Fourth Amendment even if the luggage is never opened. See *United States v. Place, infra.*

In *Katz,* the Government did not seize the defendant or his property. But a search occurred because the Government intruded upon a private conversation.

C. APPLICATION OF THE *KATZ* PRINCIPLE: MANIFESTATION OF A SUBJECTIVE INTEREST IN PRIVACY

If Katz had been shouting into a telephone, so that his conversation could be heard down the block, officers who heard him would not be engaged in a search since Katz would not have manifested any interest in keeping the conversation private. The question is, how far must the citizen go to protect his privacy interests?

1. Strict Application

Generally speaking, the courts have required citizens to be extremely protective of their claimed privacy interests.

> *Example:*   Defendant's barn has no windows. The door of the barn is six feet high. Above the door is a heavy mesh fabric, which cannot be seen through from any distance. However, if one were to jump up on the door and press one's face to the mesh, one could see inside the barn. The officer did this. The Supreme Court held that this was not a search, since defendant had not sufficiently manifested an expectation of privacy in the interior of the barn, even presuming that society was prepared to accept such an expectation as legitimate. *United States v. Dunn,* 480 U.S. 294, 107 S.Ct. 1134, 94 L.Ed.2d 326 (1987).

2. Abandonment

Abandonment of property is inconsistent with the retention of any privacy or possessory interests. Courts have held that if a person is questioned by the police and denies that certain property is his (e.g. an unidentified suitcase in the baggage claim area of an airport), he thereby abandons any interest in the property. See *United States v. McBean,* 861 F.2d 1570 (11th Cir.1988).

3. Sufficient Manifestation Found Under Some Circumstances

There are some cases, however, where the police conduct has been especially energetic, and the courts have held that the citizen has sufficiently manifested a protected interest.

> *Example:*   An officer climbs to the top of a building and peers through louvers of a vented fan in the ceiling. The court found that this was a search, explaining that a citizen does not need to deprive himself of all ventilation in order to retain a privacy interest. *United States v. Amuny,* 767 F.2d 1113 (5th Cir.1985).

D. APPLICATION OF THE *KATZ* PRINCIPLE: LEGITIMACY OF THE EXPECTATION OF PRIVACY; ACCESS BY MEMBERS OF THE PUBLIC

Even if a citizen tries to keep information private (thus having a subjective expectation), it is sometimes the case in society that the citizen will not get her wish. Sometimes we do not get all the privacy we want. One person cannot tell another not to look at him as he walks down the street. Nor can a homeowner demand that planes not fly overhead. Society is not prepared to accept such demands as reasonable and legitimate. After *Katz* the Supreme Court has held in a series of cases that if an aspect of a person's life (such as his trash or public movements), is subject to scrutiny by members of the public, then that person has no legitimate expectation in denying equivalent access to the police. *There is no search if the police obtain information accessible to members of the public.*

1.   Bank Records

In *United States v. Miller,* 425 U.S. 435, 96 S.Ct. 1619, 48 L.Ed.2d 71 (1976), the Government served a subpoena on Miller's bank to obtain checks, deposit slips and financial statements. The Court held that this activity was not a search (and therefore the Government did not have to obtain a warrant and did not have to have any suspicion of wrongdoing), since Miller had no reasonable expectation of privacy in information which he had conveyed to his bank. Since the bank had access to the information, Miller could not reasonably seek to prevent the Government from equivalent access.

2.   Telephone Pen Registers

In *Smith v. Maryland,* 442 U.S. 735, 99 S.Ct. 2577, 61 L.Ed.2d 220 (1979), the police installed a pen register device in the phone company offices. This device recorded the numbers called by the defendant on his home telephone. The Court held that the use of the pen register was not a search, and therefore the Fourth Amendment did not apply, since Smith had no right to expect that the phone numbers he called would remain private. In making the call, Smith gave this information to the phone company; therefore equivalent access by the Government could not be denied.

a.   Recordkeeping By Third Party Not Required

In *Smith,* the Government obtained the numbers of local calls, which were not itemized on Smith's monthly bill, and which were not recorded by the phone company as a general matter. The Court found it irrelevant that the phone company kept no records of local phone numbers called. The Court found it controlling that the phone company was given the information by Smith, and that the company could have kept the records if it so desired.

b.   Secrecy Interest at Stake?

The Court in *Smith* seemed to recognize that there was a privacy interest at stake in the numbers dialed. The numbers themselves contain content: private and embarrassing affiliations, and even the substance of the conversation itself can often be inferred merely because a certain number is called. Thus, the holding in *Smith* does not stand for the proposition that no secrecy interest was invaded. Rather, the Court held that Smith had no reasonable expectation that the information would remain private.

c.   **Dissents in *Smith* and *Miller***

The dissenters in *Smith* and *Miller* attacked the rationale that if members of the public have access to information, the Government cannot reasonably be excluded. While not objecting in principle to such a broad statement, the dissenters found that *as applied*, the results in the cases were harsh and unrealistic. The release of information by the citizens in *Smith* and *Miller* was very circumscribed. The defendants in these cases did not grant access to all members of the public and then unreasonably seek to exclude the police. Even though a citizen is aware that the phone company knows the numbers he dials, it does not follow that he should expect the Government to know as well. The dissenters pointed out that the grant of access to information in these cases was not the product of free choice. It is hard to do without a phone and a bank account.

d.   **Response**

The majority in these cases responded that free choice is not the issue. The issue is whether society is prepared to accept a privacy expectation as reasonable where members of the public have access to the information. Whether the citizen likes it or not, it is not always possible in today's society to keep all information totally private. The majority found no reason to create a distinction between access to members of the public and access by the police. Thus, if information is exposed to a third party, it is exposed in equal measure to the police.

3.   **Trash**

In *California v. Greenwood,* 486 U.S. 35, 108 S.Ct. 1625, 100 L.Ed.2d 30 (1988), the police over a two month period rummaged through trash left by the defendant for the local garbage service. Defendant left the trash in opaque bags at the curb in front of his house. The Court held that such rummaging was not a search. It reasoned that since passersby, snoops, scavengers, the trash service, and animals have access to trash left out at the curb, the trash is exposed in equal measure to the police. Hence there is no legitimate expectation of privacy.

a.   **Lack of Choice Irrelevant**

Greenwood was prohibited by city ordinance from disposing of his trash in any way other than leaving it for the trash service. Greenwood argued that he did not voluntarily waive any right to privacy he had in the trash. The Court found, however, that lack of choice was irrelevant to whether defendant's expectation of privacy was reasonable, just as it had been in *Smith* and *Miller.* For good or ill, society does force the citizen to put some information at risk of public access; the question is not whether a waiver has occurred, but whether one can reasonably expect to keep information from members of the public. If members of the public could obtain access, the police have equivalent access to the

information, because it is unreasonable to expect that the police would
be excluded when members of the public are not.

b. Efforts at Concealment

It did not matter in *Greenwood* that the trash was in an opaque bag.
Nor would it matter if the trash was mingled with the trash of others in
a dumpster, because if the public has access, the defendant would be
engaged in the futile activity of trying to manifest a privacy interest that
does not in fact exist.

c. Dissent

Dissenting in *Greenwood,* Justice Brennan argued that society is
prepared to accept a citizen's expectation of privacy in trash as
reasonable. According to Justice Brennan, most members of society
would be appalled at the prospect that others would search through their
trash to obtain intimate details of how they lead their personal lives.

Justice Brennan further argued that the *mere possibility* that some
member of the public may rummage through trash should not preclude
a legitimate expectation of privacy. In *Greenwood,* there was no
indication that local residents routinely, or ever, had their trash
investigated by members of the public. Justice Brennan contended that
if the mere possibility of public access is enough to destroy a privacy
interest, then there is little privacy left. For example, the mere
possibility that a house could be broken into by burglars cannot mean
that the homeowner has no expectation of privacy in his home. Yet
Justice Brennan found it difficult to draw a principled line between the
Greenwood ''mere possibility'' analysis and this hypothetical.

d. Societal Expectations

Part of the dispute in *Greenwood* is based on the individual justices'
views of American society. The *Katz* test is very susceptible to the
subjective views of individual justices and judges, who determine what
society is prepared to accept as reasonable. The Supreme Court has
provided little guidance as to how it goes about making a judgment
about societal expectations.

e. Limitations on *Greenwood*

The majority in *Greenwood* relied on the fact that Greenwood left his
trash out on a public street. *Greenwood* does not apply when the police
officer enters an area from which the public is excluded in order to
obtain the trash. This is because, in the process of obtaining the trash,
the officer will have conducted a search of a private area. See *New York
v. Class,* 475 U.S. 106, 106 S.Ct. 960, 89 L.Ed.2d 81 (1986) (there is no
privacy interest in a vehicle identification number, but an officer who
entered the automobile to find the number conducted a search of a

private area). However, while the police cannot enter a private area to obtain trash, they can certainly wait until the trash collector does so, and then obtain the trash from him. That would not be a search.

f. Homeless Persons

At least one court has found the *Greenwood* analysis inapplicable to homeless persons. That court found that a homeless person had a reasonable expectation of privacy in a duffel bag and a cardboard box kept on public property. The court reasoned that a contrary result would mean that millions of Americans would be unable to assert a privacy interest in their personal belongings. See *State v. Mooney,* 218 Conn. 85, 588 A.2d 145 (1991).

4. Aerial Surveillance

The Court has applied the public access rationale of *Smith* and *Miller* to aerial surveillance of private areas. In *California v. Ciraolo,* 476 U.S. 207, 106 S.Ct. 1809, 90 L.Ed.2d 210 (1986), police officers used an airplane to conduct aerial surveillance of defendant's backyard, and found marijuana growing there. The police had no warrant or probable cause to conduct the aerial surveillance. The airplane flew over the defendant's yard in navigable airspace at a height of 1,000 feet. The Court held that the Fourth Amendment did not apply to the police conduct because the aerial overflight was not a search.

a. Rationale

As in *Smith* and *Miller,* the Court reasoned that since members of the public could fly over the defendant's yard and view the activity therein, Ciraolo could not reasonably expect to exclude the police from doing so. Thus, the fact that the area was viewed by the use of a police plane rather than a commercial airliner was irrelevant: if two planes pass over, the effect on the privacy interest is the same even though one is being used for investigatory purposes and one is not.

b. Dissent

Justice Powell, dissenting in *Ciraolo,* argued that the majority's reasoning was unsound for at least two reasons. First, the majority basically required a property owner to put a dome on his backyard in order to have a legitimate expectation of privacy there. Justice Powell complained that the Court thereby deprived citizens of the very thing that makes a backyard worthwhile—light and air. Second, the fact that a commercial airliner could fly overhead did not in Justice Powell's view mean that police airplane surveillance ought to be free from Fourth Amendment constraints. *Smith* and *Miller* allow the police *equivalent* access to information disclosed to the public. But Justice Powell contended that aerial surveillance by police is of a different character from that obtained by commercial aircraft. Passengers in a commercial airplane do not generally circle continually over a particular backyard to inspect activity in detail; and even if they do, they do not connect any discovered activity with a specific person, so that the property owner effectively retains a secrecy interest.

c.   Low–Flying Helicopters
The Court extended *Ciraolo* in *Florida v. Riley,* 488 U.S. 445, 109 S.Ct. 693, 102 L.Ed.2d 835 (1988), and held that surveillance of a backyard from a helicopter hovering at 400 feet was not a search. The crucial question in *Riley* was whether the public indeed had access to the information in Riley's backyard by way of aerial surveillance. All members of the Court agreed that if there was sufficient public access to Riley's backyard by way of a helicopter overflight, then the use of a helicopter by police would not be a search. Yet there was significant disagreement as to whether there was sufficient public access in *Riley.*

d.   Legally Permissible Access
Justice White wrote a plurality opinion in *Riley* (joined by Justices Kennedy and Scalia and Chief Justice Rehnquist) which reasoned that since the public *could legally* hover over Riley's property in a helicopter at 400 feet, the police could do so as well. Justice White relied on FAA regulations which allow helicopters to be operated at virtually any altitude so long as they do not pose a safety hazard. Thus, according to Justice White, since the police helicopter was flying where a private helicopter could legally fly, there was no search.

e.   Actual Access
Justice O'Connor's opinion concurring in the result in *Riley* disagreed with Justice White's analysis and in fact agreed with the four dissenting justices as to the appropriate test for determining whether helicopter surveillance is a search. A majority of the court therefore was of the view that the test for a search was whether members of the public *in fact ordinarily hovered* over Riley's yard at 400 feet in helicopters—if so, it would be unreasonable to expect that the police could not do so. According to five justices, the mere fact that it would be legal under FAA regulations for a member of the public to hover in a helicopter at 400 feet did not preclude a legitimate expectation of privacy from such activity. These justices reasoned that FAA regulations have nothing to do with privacy or with what a person can reasonably expect from the rest of society.

f.   Burden of Proof
Justice O'Connor nonetheless concurred in the result in *Riley.* While agreeing with the dissenters as to the appropriate test, Justice O'Connor was of the view that the *burden was on the defendant* to show that members of the public did not regularly hover over his property in helicopters at 400 feet. Since Riley offered no proof on this point in the

lower court, she concluded that a search was not shown on the facts in *Riley*. The four dissenters in *Riley* argued that the burden should be on the Government to show that the defendant's Fourth Amendment rights were not violated. They found support in the fact that it is the Government which is moving to admit the evidence. They expressed dismay that the Court did not allow Riley an opportunity to prove that members of the public did not hover in helicopters above his yard, especially since it seemed so unlikely that citizens in helicopters routinely hovered over Riley's yard.

g.   Implications From *Riley*

The actual rule to be derived from *Riley* is not as drastic as the result in the case would make it appear. A majority of the court focussed on whether the public would *ordinarily have access* to the defendant's information, not on whether it was physically and legally possible to get the information as a theoretical matter. On this point, *Riley* may actually signal a retreat from the views of the Court in the trash search case, *California v. Greenwood*. In *Greenwood*, Justice White for the majority found that there was no search of trash because members of the public *could have* rummaged through Greenwood's trash. There was no showing that members of the public in fact regularly did so. After *Riley*, a case like *Greenwood* might be decided differently if the defendant could show that members of the public did not ordinarily rummage through his trash.

h.   Routine Nature of Government Surveillance

In *Riley*, the state argued among other things that Riley had no expectation of privacy because police surveillance helicopters routinely circled the area. A majority of justices held that the pervasiveness of police surveillance was irrelevant to a person's expectation of privacy. Otherwise, the Government could anomalously evade the requirements of the Fourth Amendment by engaging in pervasive investigative activity. The Government could destroy privacy interests by ignoring them, while ordinary members of the public respected them. Such a dichotomy was found not consistent with the public access theory of cases such as *Smith, Miller* and *Greenwood*.

i.   Dust, Injury and Intimate Details

Justice White, for the plurality in *Riley*, implied that a search would have been found if the helicopter surveillance had caused undue noise, dust or threat of injury, or if it had uncovered "intimate details". The dissenters found it difficult to understand why activity which is not a search becomes a search when it creates dust and noise.

5.   Limitations on Public Access Theory
From time to time the Court finds the Fourth Amendment applicable and
rejects the Government's argument that members of the public had access to
the information uncovered by police officers. The reasoning in these cases is
not always consistent with that of *Smith, Miller,* and *Greenwood,* and the
cases seem to indicate that the Court is not prepared to hold that a person
surrenders his privacy interests in all cases where some member of the public
has technical access to an area.

a.   Hotel Room Searches
In *Stoner v. California,* 376 U.S. 483, 84 S.Ct. 889, 11 L.Ed.2d 856
(1964), the Supreme Court found that a paying guest had a reasonable
expectation of privacy in a motel room. The Court concluded that such
a person pays for the right to privacy and has the right to exclude
others, even management. It found that the Fourth Amendment applied
even though a hotel tenant implicitly authorizes maids, janitors and
repair personnel to enter his room. The implied grant of public access
did not mean that the police were granted equivalent access.

b.   Distinction from *Smith* and *Miller*
The distinction between *Stoner* and *Smith* and *Miller* is elusive. In all
these cases, the citizen grants access to one or two discrete parties. Yet
in *Smith* and *Miller* that limited grant of access renders unreasonable
the expectation of excluding the Government. One possible distinction is
that in *Smith* and *Miller,* the records were actually the property of the
third parties who had access to them, whereas in *Stoner,* the hotel
tenant, by paying the bill, is the holder of property and associated
privacy rights. A more important distinction is that in *Smith* and *Miller,*
the Government access was *equivalent* to that granted to the third party,
whereas the access granted in *Stoner* was *more limited in nature* than the
actual search conducted by the Government authorities. That is, in
Smith and *Miller,* the bank and the telephone company had an absolute
right to inspect the subject information, so the police officer could do so
as well. In contrast, in *Stoner,* the maid had the right to enter the hotel
room to clean it, but the police officer entered the hotel room to inspect
it. Thus, the grant of access in *Stoner* was more limited than that sought
to be used by the police officer.

c.   Must Have a Current Right to Reside in the Room
Of course, to trigger an expectation of privacy in a hotel room, the
tenant must have paid for the right to exclude management, other
guests, and hence the police. So for example, if checkout time has
passed, and the tenant has not paid for the next day, the tenant loses
his expectation of privacy. A subsequent inspection of the room by police
officers will not invade the privacy rights of a person who is no longer
the tenant. Courts have held that an expectation of privacy in the room

is lost even if the defendant has been arrested and thus is unable to keep his hotel bill current. See *United States v. Rahme,* 813 F.2d 31 (2d Cir.1987).

d. Property in the Room

If the bill is not current, the police can search the room without being restricted by the Fourth Amendment. But what about the defendant's property, such as closed suitcases, that are located in the room? If the tenant does not pay the bill, management in most states has the right to take custody of the property in the room under the state innkeeper's lien law. If management may open the property pursuant to the lien law, such property may be freely turned over to the police, who may open it as well. If management may only hold the property but may not open it, then a search will occur if the property is opened by the police. See *Walter v. United States,* 447 U.S. 649, 100 S.Ct. 2395, 65 L.Ed.2d 410 (1980) (police officer's opening of a container constitutes a search when the container was turned over by a third party who had no right to open it).

E. APPLICATION OF *KATZ*: INVESTIGATION WHICH CAN *ONLY* UNCOVER ILLEGAL ACTIVITY IS NOT A SEARCH

There is no legitimate privacy interest in illegal activity. Those engaged in illegal activity are ordinarily protected by the Fourth Amendment only because there is no way to tell beforehand whether or not the activity is illegal. However, if a certain mode of investigation can only uncover *whether or not* illegal activity exists, and cannot disclose innocent activity, then the investigation is not a search because it does not implicate any secrecy interest protected by the Fourth Amendment.

1. Dog Sniffs

In *United States v. Place,* 462 U.S. 696, 103 S.Ct. 2637, 77 L.Ed.2d 110 (1983), the Court held that a dog sniff of closed luggage was not a search, and thus not controlled by the reasonableness requirement of the Fourth Amendment. A dog sniff can only tell the officer whether the luggage contains contraband or not. There is no protectible privacy interest in contraband, and through the sniff, the officer learns nothing about any personal, innocent information contained in the luggage. Consequently, the canine sniff is not a search because it can never disclose a protected Fourth Amendment secrecy interest.

a. Implications From *Place*

If a canine sniff is not a search, it means that there are no reasonableness limitations imposed upon it. It follows from *Place* that officers could arbitrarily use dogs to sniff any piece of luggage, or indeed to roam through a neighborhood without justification.

b. Seizure of Luggage in Order to Conduct the Canine Sniff Triggers Fourth Amendment Protections

While the dog sniff in *Place* was not a search, the Court nonetheless held that the cocaine found in Place's luggage had to be suppressed. This was because before conducting the sniff, the police detained the luggage for 90 minutes. This detention was an exercise of dominion and control over Place's property, which implicated the Fourth Amendment because it was a *seizure*. As such, the Fourth Amendment standards were triggered, and the seizure had to be reasonable. The Court in *Place* found that the deprivation of Place's possessory interest in the luggage was lengthy and severe, and that the length of the seizure could have been minimized if the officers had acted with reasonable diligence. Under the circumstances, the Court found that the seizure could only be reasonable if the officers had probable cause to detain the luggage; and probable cause did not exist before the canine sniff on the facts of *Place*. See the further discussion of *Place* in the stop and frisk section, *infra*.

c. Different Analysis for Searches and Seizures

The decision in *Place* indicates that the Fourth Amendment protects property interests as well as privacy interests, and that Fourth Amendment analysis may differ depending on whether a possessory or privacy interest is involved.

d. Positive Result Does Not Allow Opening the Luggage

Even if a dog sniff of luggage is positive, and the seizure giving rise to the sniff is reasonable, it does not follow that the officers can open the luggage. Even with a positive alert, there may be legitimate secrecy interests contained in the luggage. So, while the sniff is not a search, and the information from the sniff is legally obtained, the *opening is a search*, which triggers the Fourth Amendment and requires a warrant or some exception. The advantage to the sniff, however, is that the information therefrom can be freely used for the probable cause determination by either the magistrate or the officer who searches pursuant to an exception to the warrant requirement.

A positive result from a canine sniff can also be used as justification to detain the bag pending a warrant. The detention of the bag would of course be a seizure, but it would be reasonable given the positive alert. Unlike *Place,* there would be probable cause to detain the bag pending a warrant.

e. Dog Sniffs of People

The Supreme Court has never considered whether a canine sniff of a person is a search. The fact that innocent secret information would be free from detection does not necessarily mean that the Fourth Amendment is inapplicable. The Fourth Amendment guarantees personal security as well as privacy. There was no threat to personal security in *Place* because the dog sniff was conducted without Place even being present. It is probable, then, that a dog sniff of a person implicates the Fourth Amendment.

f. Dog Sniffs of Rooms and Residences

The lower courts are split as to whether the reasoning of *Place* applies to dog sniffs outside residences as well as to luggage. The Second Circuit has held that a dog sniff of a house, from the outside, is a search because the area intruded upon is more private than that involved in *Place*. See *United States v. Thomas,* 757 F.2d 1359 (2d Cir.1985). The District of Columbia Circuit disagrees, reasoning that while a privacy interest in a dwelling is more profound than that in luggage, in neither case does a dog sniff intrude upon a legitimate privacy interest. The sniff uncovers no innocent secret information, regardless of where the sniff occurs. See *United States v. Colyer,* 878 F.2d 469 (D.C.Cir.1989) (permitting a canine sniff of an Amtrak sleeper compartment in the absence of articulable suspicion). The reasoning of *Place* appears to support the view of the District of Columbia Circuit. It must be remembered, however, that houses have been treated differently from other objects and areas in Fourth Amendment cases. See, e.g., *Payton v. New York,* 445 U.S. 573, 100 S.Ct. 1371, 63 L.Ed.2d 639 (1980) (arrest warrant needed to arrest felony suspect at home).

2. Chemical Tests

If a chemical test merely discloses whether or not a substance is contraband, the test is not a search. There is no legitimate expectation of privacy in the information uncovered by such a test if a positive result shows only the existence of contraband (as to which there is no legitimate expectation of privacy) and a negative result uncovers no secret, innocent information. In *United States v. Jacobsen,* 466 U.S. 109, 104 S.Ct. 1652, 80 L.Ed.2d 85 (1984), the Court relied on its rationale in *Place* to hold that a chemical field test of a white powder was not a search, since the test would only indicate whether the powder was contraband or not.

a. Possible Limitation on Pervasive Police Activity

Justice Stevens, for the majority in *Jacobsen,* addressed the dissenters' concerns that if the Fourth Amendment did not apply, field tests could be conducted arbitrarily and pervasively. In a footnote, Justice Stevens stated that if the police, for instance, indiscriminately field test sugar bowls throughout a neighborhood, such a practice may be sufficiently pervasive and disquieting to trigger the Fourth Amendment. But the Court set forth no standards as to when such activity would be so pervasive as to constitute a search.

b.   Not All Chemical Tests Are Free From Fourth Amendment Scrutiny

The Court in *Jacobsen* stated that if a chemical test could only uncover contraband, and not innocent, secret information, it is not a search. This limited statement does not free all chemical tests from the constraints of the Fourth Amendment. Some chemical tests uncover not only contraband but also innocent private information. For example, a drug test of a urine sample indicates whether or not the subject has taken illegal drugs, but it also may uncover the existence of epilepsy, pregnancy, or the use of prescription drugs. Since such a test can convey innocent, secret information, a drug test of urine was unanimously held by the Supreme Court to be a search in *Skinner v. Railway Labor Executives' Assoc.*, 489 U.S. 602, 109 S.Ct. 1402, 103 L.Ed.2d 639 (1989). See also *United States v. Mulder*, 889 F.2d 239 (9th Cir.1989) (sophisticated chemical test of white powder, which was used to determine the components of the powder, constituted a search).

c.   Seizure to Do the Test

As in *Place*, the investigative activity in *Jacobsen* was *not a search* because it could only uncover the existence of contraband, but a *seizure* was still necessary in order to conduct the test. Arguably, the seizure in *Jacobsen* was more intrusive than that in *Place*, because it was necessary to *destroy* the substance in order to do the field test. However, the Court in *Jacobsen* found that the seizure was reasonable (unlike in *Place*) because only a de minimis amount of property was destroyed, and because the officer had probable cause to believe the substance was cocaine *before he did the field test*.

F.   APPLICATION OF *KATZ:* RE-OPENING OF PACKAGES BY GOVERNMENT OFFICIALS

If a package has once been opened consistently with the Fourth Amendment, it will not be a search if it is reopened by a Government official, unless there is a substantial probability that the contents of the package have been changed since the original opening.

1.   Rationale

The Court has reasoned that if the original opening of a container was legal, the owner's privacy interest in the package has been lost. The secrecy interest in the contents of the package has already been disclosed; it does not reattach to the very contents already viewed, since once a privacy interest has been lost, it does not return. However, if the contents have been changed, a secrecy interest does re-attach. Otherwise, a suitcase once legally opened in, say, a customs search could be re-opened years later without a warrant or probable cause.

2.   **Re-opening After Private Search**

In *United States v. Jacobsen, supra,* a Federal Express employee opened a package, and notified authorities of his suspicion that it contained contraband. He then sealed the package. Then a DEA agent reopened the package while it was still in the custody of Federal Express. The Court held that the DEA agent's re-opening of the package was not a search, since the package had by that time already been legally opened; the original opening was not prohibited by the Fourth Amendment since it was done by a private party; and the contents of the package had obviously not been changed since the original opening.

a.   **Dissent**

Justice White, dissenting in *Jacobsen,* could not see the difference between a package opened by a private party, and a house entered by a private party. He argued that if the *Jacobsen* rationale were taken to its logical extreme, police could enter a home after a private party did so, even if the private party entered the home illegally, and the subsequent police entry would not be a search. Justice White thus found *Jacobsen* to be a dangerous precedent. As previously stated, however, the *Jacobsen* rule does not inevitably allow the police to enter a house previously entered by a private person, since the Court has often treated the house as deserving of special Fourth Amendment protection.

b.   **Later Activity Can Be a Search to the Extent That It Exceeds the Scope of the Original Legal Search**

If the subsequent official investigation of the package or its contents exceeds the scope of the original search, it may trigger Fourth Amendment protection to the extent that a further intrusion is made. For instance, in *Walter v. United States, supra,* a private party opened a package and found that it contained films. Police officers then viewed the films through a projector. The Court held that the viewing of the films was a search, since it exceeded the scope of the private search. If the private parties had viewed the films originally, then the police activity probably would not have been a search, since the privacy interest attaching to the films would already have been lost.

c.   **Field Test Exceeds the Scope of the Original Intrusion**

In *Jacobsen,* the DEA agent did exceed the scope of the private party search when he conducted a chemical test on the substance in the package; the private party had not conducted such a test. But this extra step was not itself a search because, as discussed above, the chemical test could only discover contraband; therefore, it did not trigger the Fourth Amendment anyway, even though the officer went beyond the private party's conduct.

3. Controlled Delivery

The proposition that a privacy interest, once invaded, does not return, has been applied to validate controlled deliveries of packages. In a controlled delivery, a package is sent by mail or delivery service, and is legally opened while in transit—for instance, by a customs search or in a search by a private party. The package is then resealed and the police track it to its ultimate destination. When it arrives, the recipient is arrested and the police reopen the package. Reopening a package pursuant to a controlled delivery is *not a search*, provided that the privacy interest in the contents has already been legally disclosed. *Illinois v. Andreas,* 463 U.S. 765, 103 S.Ct. 3319, 77 L.Ed.2d 1003 (1983).

a. Lapse in "Control"

Even if the police conducting a controlled delivery temporarily lose sight of the package, their subsequent re-opening of the package will not be a search, so long as there is a substantial likelihood that the contents of the package have been unchanged since the original opening.

> *Example:* In *Andreas,* police officers, posing as deliverymen, delivered a package which had originally been legally opened. The package contained a table with contraband inside. The officers lost sight of the package when it was brought into the defendant's apartment for 35 minutes. Then the defendant exited his apartment, carrying the package. The police then arrested defendant, seized the package, and reopened it. The Court held that the re-opening was not a search. The unusual size of the package, its non-generic purpose, and the relatively limited time period of lapsed control, all indicated that there was a substantial likelihood that the contents of the package had not been changed.

b. Dissent

Justice Brennan in dissent complained that the Court had gone a long way in *Andreas* to hold that the police activity was not a search. Ordinarily, when police activity is not a search, it does not have to be justified by any explanation or any standard of proof. But in *Andreas,* the Court found the reopening not to be a search only if the state could satisfy a standard of proof—a substantial probability that the contents remained unchanged. Justice Brennan attacked the majority decision as analytically confusing, and proposed that "a reasonable expectation of privacy should re-attach if the person has unobserved access to the package and any opportunity to change its contents."

G. APPLICATION OF *KATZ*: SENSORY ENHANCEMENT DEVICES

Generally speaking, the use by officials of devices which aid their investigation by enhancing the senses does not constitute a search, so long as the devices do no more than aid the police in obtaining information that they could have obtained through their own sensory perception.

1. Beepers

In *United States v. Knotts,* 460 U.S. 276, 103 S.Ct. 1081, 75 L.Ed.2d 55 (1983), police officers tracked the movements of the defendant's vehicle by using an electronic device which sent out radio "beeping" signals. The Court held that the use of the beeper was not a search in these circumstances. The information obtained consisted only of the defendant's public movements, as to which he had no reasonable expectation of privacy. (See the *Smith* and *Miller* "public access" doctrine, *supra*). The fact that the police tracked the defendant's public movements through an electronic beeper rather than through sensory perception was held immaterial. The Court reasoned that the beeper did no more than what could be done through ordinary sensory perception—i.e. the police could themselves have tracked the defendant's public movements. In essence, the defendant suffered "no prejudice" through the use of an electronic device.

a. Sale of Merchandise Containing a Beeper

The fact that the police have installed a beeper device in merchandise later purchased by a citizen does not itself constitute a search or seizure. This is because the installation of the device does not invade a privacy interest. No information is obtained by the installation. The Fourth Amendment only becomes applicable when the beeper begins to transmit information, and then only if the information transmitted concerns private activity. Nor is the installation of a beeper tantamount to a seizure of the merchandise. It does not significantly change the character of the merchandise, nor does it deprive the owner of the right to possession or control. *United States v. Karo,* 468 U.S. 705, 104 S.Ct. 3296, 82 L.Ed.2d 530 (1984) ("Although the can may have contained an unknown and unwanted foreign object, it cannot be said that anyone's possessory interest was interfered with in a meaningful way.").

b. Dissent

The dissenters in *Knotts* and *Karo* complained that the Court ignored the broader concerns that may arise through the pervasive use of sophisticated investigative devices. Whether or not a beeper conveys private information in particular circumstances, the dissenters found it unsettling to think that the police can use electronic and other investigative devices in a pervasive and arbitrary manner. For example, after *Karo,* police officers can install a "bug" on any piece of merchandise before it is sold; they need no justification, and the Fourth Amendment will not come into play unless and until private information is thereafter obtained. As Justice Stevens argued in his dissent in *Karo,* the Court's assertion that a beeper is not harmful until it is turned on is equivalent to having a plumber in the bathroom while you are taking a bath: little comfort is derived by the plumber's assurance that his back is turned.

c. Response

The majority's response in these cases is that if the defendant has not been prejudiced by a police activity, he or she has no right to complain of the broader societal implications of that activity. Moreover, the Court has not foreclosed the possibility that use of beepers and other enhancement devices could be regulated by the Fourth Amendment should they be used indiscriminately.

d. Entering a Private Area to Install a Beeper

While the use of a beeper is not a search if it conveys public information, police installation of the beeper may itself be a search under certain circumstances. For example, if the police open a car door to place a beeper inside, the entry into the car will be a search. See *New York v. Class, supra* (there is no privacy interest in a vehicle identification number, but an officer who entered the automobile to uncover the number conducted a search of a private area). There was no search on these grounds in either *Knotts* or *Karo*. In both cases, the beeper was installed on merchandise before it was sold. See *Karo* ("The can into which the beeper was placed belonged at the time to the DEA, and by no stretch of the imagination could it be said that the respondents then had any legitimate expectation of privacy in it.").

e. Obtaining Private Information Through Use of a Beeper

If the police use a beeper to obtain private information that they could not obtain through their own sensory perception, the use of the beeper is a search. This occurred in *United States v. Karo* when officers installed a beeper in a can of ether, and then tracked the movement of the can into the defendant's house. The Court held that the defendant had a reasonable expectation of privacy in movements inside the house; and the beeper gave the officers information about the location of the can in the house which they could not have obtained through their own sensory perception.

f. Result in *Karo*

The tracking of the can into Karo's house was held to be a search. Since it was not conducted pursuant to a warrant and probable cause, that search was illegal. Yet the search that ultimately resulted in the seizure of the can and other incriminating evidence was upheld. This was because the defendant moved the can from his house into a car, and then to a storage area. The police tracked the movements of the can, and thereafter obtained a warrant to search the storage area. The Court held that the police, by tracking the can's *public movements into the storage area, obtained probable cause independent of the information* gained in the in-house tracking. In other words, the police were not allowed to track the can into the house, but they were allowed to track it up to the house and thereafter to its ultimate destination. Obviously, the ruling in *Karo* provides little protection against the use of beepers, even inside the home.

2. Flashlights

The use of a flashlight to aid an officer in an inspection is not itself a search. The flashlight aids the officer's perception, but it does not provide the officer with information beyond what could be obtained from unaided sensory perception. Essentially, the use of a flashlight does not prejudice the defendant in any way. See *Texas v. Brown,* 460 U.S. 730, 103 S.Ct. 1535, 75 L.Ed.2d 502 (1983) ("The use of artificial means to illuminate a darkened area simply does not constitute a search, and thus triggers no Fourth Amendment protection.").

3. Binoculars

If police use binoculars to see what could otherwise have been seen through the naked eye, then the use of binoculars as a sensory aid is not a search under *Knotts,* because it results in exposure only of that information which is otherwise visible. On the other hand, if police use binoculars to discover minute details located in a private area, which information could not otherwise be seen through the naked eye (such as the lettering on bottles on the bedroom bureau) the use of binoculars will be a search under *Karo.* See *United States v. Taborda,* 635 F.2d 131 (2d Cir.1980) (agents invaded a reasonable expectation of privacy when they used a telescope to see into an apartment at a distance from which the activities viewed would not be visible with the naked eye).

4. Microphones

The use of microphones for auditory enhancement is comparable to the use of binoculars for visual enhancement. If a conversation could be heard with the naked ear, then the use of microphones is not a search. If it could not be heard by ordinary sensory perception, then the use of microphones is a search.

5. Other Enhancement Devices

In *Dow Chemical Co. v. United States,* 476 U.S. 227, 106 S.Ct. 1819, 90 L.Ed.2d 226 (1986), Government officials flew over Dow's commercial property, and used a $22,000 camera to take pictures of the areas between the defendant's buildings. The photographs could be enlarged so that objects one-half inch in diameter could be seen. The Court held that the use of the camera was not a search. Relying on the rationale of *Knotts,* the Court stated that Dow had no legitimate expectation of privacy in the area between its buildings—at least not with respect to aerial surveillance. Therefore, aerial surveillance of that area could not be a search. Since no private information was obtained, the mode of investigation could not be of concern to Dow; it was not prejudiced by the use of the camera.

a. Limitations on *Dow*

Dow is most fairly read as holding that if the defendant has no privacy interest in information to begin with, the use of an enhancement device is not a search, even if it gives the officer information he could not otherwise gain through personal perception. The mode of investigation can make no difference to the citizen if he or she has no right to privacy protection in the first place. This doctrine carries its own limitation. If the camera in *Dow* could pierce through walls and obtain *private* information that could not be obtained through sensory perception, then the use of such an enhancement device would be a search. See *Dow* ("an electronic device to penetrate walls or windows so as to hear and record confidential discussions ＊ ＊ ＊ would raise very different and far more serious questions").

H. APPLICATION OF *KATZ*: PRISONERS AND JAIL CELLS

In *Hudson v. Palmer*, 468 U.S. 517, 104 S.Ct. 3194, 82 L.Ed.2d 393 (1984), the Court held that a prisoner has no legitimate property or privacy interests in his or her belongings kept in the prison cell. Consequently, the Fourth Amendment did not apply to an officer's intentional destruction of this property. Nor would the officer's arbitrary inspection of such property implicate the Fourth Amendment. Police are not required to be reasonable if their conduct is neither a search nor a seizure.

1. Rationale

The Court analyzed the legitimacy of a prisoner's expectation by considering the societal interests furthered by prison cell searches, and by balancing these interests against the prisoner's privacy and property interests. The Court concluded that the state interests in maintaining prison discipline and controlling crime outweighed the obviously limited privacy and property interests that a prisoner could expect to have. It held that society was not prepared to accept *any* expectation of privacy or use of property as reasonable.

2. Dissent

The dissenters in *Hudson* argued that by balancing interests, the majority had ignored the explicit language of the Fourth Amendment, which is triggered upon the search or seizure of a person, house, *paper or effect.* They found it inconsistent with the plain language of the Fourth Amendment to hold that an officer's rummage through a prison cell and destruction of personal property is neither a search nor a seizure of papers or effects. The dissenters contended that the majority's balancing analysis was more appropriately applied to determine whether a search is *reasonable,* but that it should be used to conclude that conduct which appears in ordinary parlance to be a search is not in fact a search at all. The dissenters pointed out that an application of the balancing analysis to whether a search is reasonable, as opposed to whether the conduct is a search at all, would not impose substantial burdens on law enforcement in the prison context. Given the state interests at stake in prison searches, most searches of prison cells would probably be found to be reasonable under the circumstances. The dissenters found it probable that a reasonableness test would prohibit only those searches conducted for purposes of harassment or in violation of prison regulations, and thus not effectuating a state interest. Ironically, these were the very types of searches—conducted for harassment and in violation of prison regulations—at issue in *Hudson;* they are now beyond the reach of the Fourth Amendment.

3.   Response

The majority in *Hudson* responded that a prisoner ordinarily has a remedy under state law for the arbitrary destruction of his or her property. *If* (and only if) the state provides no remedy, the prisoner has a claim that he was deprived of a property interest without due process accorded by the state. Under these circumstances, the prisoner can sue for damages under the Federal civil rights statute, 42 U.S.C.A. § 1983. The prisoner in *Hudson* sought to resort to the Fourth Amendment because the state provided a tort remedy for his claims of property loss. The existence of this state law remedy extinguished the prisoner's Federal due process claim, since the state, in authorizing a tort claim in the state court, had provided the prisoner adequate process. By bringing a Fourth Amendment claim in the Federal court, the prisoner was viewed as having attempted to evade the limitations imposed upon Federal actions which allege a violation of due process. This the Court would not let him do.

4.   Searches of Persons

Even after *Hudson,* the Fourth Amendment probably applies to searches of prisoners, as opposed to their cells. In *Bell v. Wolfish,* 441 U.S. 520, 99 S.Ct. 1861, 60 L.Ed.2d 447 (1979), the Court implicitly held that the Fourth Amendment applied to searches of pretrial detainees, though it found the searches there conducted (body inspections after contact with visitors) to be reasonable. The same result should apply for prisoners as applies to detainees—though whether a search is reasonable under the circumstances may depend in part on the status of the incarcerated person. A search which may be reasonable as applied to a death-row inmate may not be reasonable as applied to a suspected misdemeanant who is about to post bail.

I.   APPLICATION OF *KATZ:* OPEN FIELDS

In *Oliver v. United States,* 466 U.S. 170, 104 S.Ct. 1735, 80 L.Ed.2d 214 (1984), the Court held that a property owner's fields which lay beyond the house and its curtilage were not protected by the Fourth Amendment. The rule that the Fourth Amendment has no applicability beyond the curtilage has been termed the "open fields" doctrine. But as the Court recognized in *Oliver*, this term is somewhat of a misnomer, since the doctrine permits the search of all property beyond the curtilage, whether or not it is open, and whether or not it is a field. For instance, in *Oliver*, the property searched could not in any way be called "open". It was set back behind fences and gates, "no trespassing" signs were posted, and the area could not be seen from any public vantage point.

1. Rationale

The Court in *Oliver* first looked at the literal language of the Fourth Amendment, found that it only covered "persons, houses, papers and effects," and reasoned that a field outside the curtilage was none of these. The Court also contended that society was not prepared to accept as legitimate an expectation of privacy in the area outside the curtilage. The Court claimed that open fields are not usually the settings for intimate activity, and that they are usually open to public scrutiny.

a. No Case by Case Approach

Responding to the majority's analysis of privacy interests in *Oliver*, the defendant argued that while open fields are *normally* subject to public scrutiny, that may not be so in an individual case—as the facts in *Oliver* demonstrate. The majority rejected the defendant's argument for a case-by-case determination of whether property really is open or closed and private. The Court stated that a case-by-case approach to the problem would be unworkable, because police officers would have to guess in every case whether the citizen had sufficiently closed the field from public scrutiny to establish a right of privacy. The Court's rejection of a case-by-case approach means that there can never be an expectation of privacy in an open field, no matter what the property owner has done to deny public access. Such a property owner would be demonstrating a subjective expectation of privacy which is not reasonable after *Oliver*.

b. Violation of State Trespass Laws Irrelevant

In *Oliver*, the officers violated the state law of trespass in order to investigate Oliver's property. But the Court found that to be of no consequence. The Court held that state protection of a property right did not indicate that expectations of privacy on that property were legitimate. The Government did not challenge Oliver's right of ownership, but rather his right to expect privacy on the property he owned. The consequence of the holding in *Oliver* is that state officials can arbitrarily enter property beyond the curtilage, and violate their own state's law, free from Fourth Amendment scrutiny.

2. Dissent

The dissenters in *Oliver* complained that the majority's literal construction of the Fourth Amendment was without support after *Katz*. In *Katz*, the Court found that wiretapping was a search, even though it was not literally a search of a person, house, paper or effect. The Court's literal approach in *Oliver* was also criticized as inconsistent with *Hudson v. Palmer,* where the Court took a non-literal approach to find that the officer's rummaging through and destroying personal property was *not a search of effects.* Finally, the dissent argued that the Court's analysis in *Oliver* failed on its own terms, because it purported to construe the Fourth Amendment literally, while admitting that the curtilage around the house is protected by the Fourth Amendment. The language of the Fourth Amendment does not specifically refer to curtilage, however. There is nothing on the face of the Amendment which protects curtilage but not the property beyond it.

3.   Curtilage Remains Protected

If the property investigated is within the "curtilage", then the open fields doctrine of *Oliver* does not apply, and a state intrusion into the curtilage will be a search if the citizen has manifested an expectation of privacy. The scope of curtilage must be resolved through a case-by-case approach. The Supreme Court has stated that four factors are pertinent to this determination (see *United States v. Dunn, supra*):

(1)   The *distance* between the home and the area claimed to be curtilage;

(2)   Whether the area is within a *fence or enclosure* that surrounds the home;

(3)   Whether the *uses to which the area is put* correspond to those ordinarily conducted in a home or not; and

(4)   The *steps taken by the citizen to protect the area* from public view.

Example: In *Dunn,* an entire ranch was enclosed by a perimeter fence, and an interior fence circled the farmhouse alone. A barn was sixty yards from the farmhouse, outside the interior fence. To get to the barn, the officers had to cross the perimeter fence and two other fences. The Court held that the barn was not within the curtilage, and therefore that the officer's action of pressing his face above the gate to the barn to see through mesh material into the interior of the barn was not a search. The Court stated that the distance between the barn and the house was "substantial;" that the house was enclosed by an interior fence which did not include the barn; that the officers possessed objective data that the barn was being used as a place for manufacturing drugs, and thus was not being used for activities associated with the home; and that Dunn did not sufficiently manifest an expectation of keeping the barn private from those standing in the open fields.

a. **Implications From *Dunn***

The Court's strict construction of curtilage in *Dunn* means that many outlying buildings will be in the open field, and thus beyond the scope of Fourth Amendment protection. It should be noted, however, that *the Court did not hold that the officers could freely enter the barn.* Rather, they could peer into the barn as could any member of the public in the open field. Thus, the owner of a building in an open field (like the owner of a car parked out on the street) retains an expectation of privacy in all areas within the building that cannot be viewed from the outside.

b. **Porches, Decks, etc. as Curtilage**

Courts applying the *Dunn* factors have generally held that structures appurtenant to the home, such as porches and decks, are part of the curtilage, at least so long as the structure is not shared with other homeowners and is restricted from public access. See *State v. Santiago,* 27 Conn.App. 741, 610 A.2d 666 (1992) ("A sheltered porch, attached to a home, is an area intimately tied to the home itself, and an area in which domestic activity commonly occurs").

c. **Aerial Surveillance**

As discussed above, a homeowner's curtilage is not free from aerial observation if members of the public routinely fly overhead and can see into the curtilage. See *Florida v. Riley, supra.*

d. **Industrial Property**

In *Dow Chemical Co. v. United States, supra,* the Court held that the area surrounding a commercial or industrial building is not entitled to the same Fourth Amendment protection as the area immediately surrounding the home. Areas outside commercial and industrial buildings have some of the characteristics of open fields, and some of the characteristics of curtilage. The Court concluded that such an area could not be entered from ground level so long as fences excluded the public (as if it were curtilage), but that it could be viewed from the air (as if it were an open field). Thus, the Fourth Amendment does not recognize the concept of industrial curtilage, at least with respect to aerial surveillance.

e. **Other Property**

In *Dunn,* the Court implicitly rejected the notion that the barn itself could have curtilage surrounding it. Even though the barn had a fence around it, the Court held that it was permissible for the officer to jump that fence and peer into the barn. Apparently, the barn was neither commercial enough to warrant protection of the areas surrounding it as "industrial curtilage" (protected from ground inspection under *Dow, supra*), nor domestic enough for the area to be treated as curtilage surrounding a home. See *United States v. Pace,* 950 F.2d 961 (5th

Cir.1991) ("Whatever *Dow Chemical* may have left open concerning the concept of a curtilage surrounding a business or commercial establishment, *Dunn* indicates that there is no business curtilage surrounding a barn lying within an open field.").

f. Underground Searches

In *Husband v. Bryan,* 946 F.2d 27 (5th Cir.1991), the court held that the open fields doctrine supports only visual inspections. It therefore concluded that the property owner's Fourth Amendment rights were violated when officers, looking for a buried body, used bulldozers to dig up three acres of his pasture. It is unclear whether the Supreme Court would agree with the analysis of the court of appeals. In *Oliver,* the Court relied on the assertions that a field is not protected by the language of the Fourth Amendment, and that private activities are not ordinarily conducted in an open field. The same assertions apply to the area beneath an open field.

J. APPLICATION OF *KATZ:* PUBLIC SCHOOL STUDENTS

In *New Jersey v. T.L.O.,* 469 U.S. 325, 105 S.Ct. 733, 83 L.Ed.2d 720 (1985), the Court rejected a state's argument that high school students have no reasonable expectation of privacy while attending school. It declined the invitation to apply the prison case, *Hudson v. Palmer,* to the school context. The Court stated that schools could not yet be equated to prisons in terms of expectation of privacy. Thus, a student does not lose all rights to privacy by bringing personal property into the school.

1. Search Is Reasonable

Finding that state investigative activity is a search only begins the analysis. The Court in *T.L.O.* held that while the school official's opening of a student's purse was a search, it was conducted consistently with the Fourth Amendment because the search was reasonable under the circumstances. The high state interest in regulating school discipline, even when balanced against a student's expectation of privacy, led the Court to conclude that the search was reasonable even though conducted without a warrant, and on the basis of reasonable suspicion rather than the higher standard of probable cause.

K. APPLICATION OF *KATZ:* GOVERNMENT EMPLOYEES

In *O'Connor v. Ortega,* 480 U.S. 709, 107 S.Ct. 1492, 94 L.Ed.2d 714 (1987), the Court rejected the state's argument that Government employees can never have an expectation of privacy in their place of work. While there was no opinion for the Court, all Justices agreed that where the employee keeps a private area such as a desk or a file cabinet, a Government intrusion into that area will constitute a search. A majority of the Court further held that an employee's office itself would be protected by the Fourth Amendment, unless the office was subject to unrestricted public access. Four members of the Court found it unnecessary to determine whether an employee could have a reasonable expectation of privacy in his office, as distinct from the close containers therein.

1. Search Is Reasonable
Like *T.L.O.*, the finding that the conduct in *O'Connor* was a search was only the beginning of the analysis. A majority of the Court balanced the state and the individual interests at stake and found the search of the employee's desk and file cabinets to be reasonable, even though it was conducted without a warrant, and was made with only reasonable suspicion as opposed to probable cause to believe the employee had engaged in misconduct.

III. THE PROBABLE CAUSE REQUIREMENT

Probable cause is a standard of proof of criminal activity, which justifies a search or seizure. Even though a citizen may be innocent of wrongdoing, a showing of probable cause is sufficient to permit intrusions into the citizen's interests in privacy and security. The legitimate state interests in investigating and prosecuting crime could be impaired if a standard of proof higher than that of probable cause were required before a search or seizure could even be conducted. Thus, the probable cause standard strikes a balance between the rights of innocent citizens to privacy and security, and the interest of the state in investigating and prosecuting crime.

A. STANDARD OF PROOF REQUIRED FOR PROBABLE CAUSE TO EXIST
The standard of proof required for probable cause is: enough particularized facts to lead a common sense person of reasonable caution to believe that there is a *fair probability* of criminal activity. See *Illinois v. Gates*, 462 U.S. 213, 103 S.Ct. 2317, 76 L.Ed.2d 527 (1983).

1. No Requirement of Certainty
The Court in *Gates* emphasized that the "fair probability" standard is not especially strenuous. Proof beyond a reasonable doubt is not required; neither is proof by a preponderance of the evidence. Probable cause is a standard which permits investigations of suspects, and investigations are needed to allow the state to obtain proof beyond a reasonable doubt.

2. Plausible, Innocent Explanations Are Not Dispositive
Because the term "fair probability" is intentionally meant to be less than a preponderance, the fact that a citizen has plausible explanations for his activity does not preclude a finding of probable cause. It is only where the plausible explanations substantially outweigh the probability of criminal activity that probable cause will not be met.

Example: A person sends a small package by way of an airline's "express overnight" service. The package is mailed in November, and on the package is written the message "Do not open until

Christmas." The sender exhibits nervousness when arranging for the transport of the package. The sender tells the airline clerk that the package contains watches. But when the agent passes the package through the magnetometer, there is no indication that it contains anything metallic. The airline clerk notifies a law enforcement officer of all this information. The officer opens the package and finds narcotics. The court held that under the totality of circumstances, there was probable cause to open the package. Even though the package may well have contained a fruitcake, or a book, there were suspicious facts which, taken in their entirety, indicated a fair probability that the package was evidence of some criminal activity. These facts included: the nervousness of the sender; the sender's untruthful description of the contents of the package; and the implausibility of sending a package in November by overnight service if it truly was a Christmas present. See *United States v. Sullivan,* 544 F.Supp. 701 (D.Me.1982).

3. Officers Are Allowed to Make Reasonable Mistakes

Because the probable cause standard requires only a fair probability, it follows that officers need not be correct in their assessment of the facts. Arrests of the wrong person, and searches which uncover no incriminating evidence, are nonetheless permissible if the officer's mistake was reasonable.

Example: In *Hill v. California,* 401 U.S. 797, 91 S.Ct. 1106, 28 L.Ed.2d 484 (1971), two men driving Hill's car admitted that they and Hill had committed a robbery. Based upon the description the two gave of Hill, and verified by police records, police went to Hill's apartment and arrested a man who fit the description, but who claimed to be Miller. The arrestee was in fact Miller and not Hill. The Court nonetheless held that there was probable cause to arrest Miller even though he was the wrong man, and even though he protested his innocence. Miller's protestations did not preclude a finding of probable cause, since criminals commonly use aliases, and commonly protest their innocence. The Court stated that "sufficient probability, not certainty, is the touchstone of reasonableness under the Fourth Amendment." See also *United States v. Philibert,* 947 F.2d 1467 (11th Cir.1991) (probable cause existed to arrest the defendant for assaulting a federal officer, even though police were mistaken in their belief that the defendant attacked a United States attorney; the United States attorney was in fact out of town at the time, but "we are concerned with what the arresting officers could reasonably have believed at the time.").

4. Totality of Circumstances

The analysis of probable cause requires a cumulative look at all pertinent factors. Perhaps the defendant could come up with an innocent explanation for each factor, taken individually. But that will not suffice if all the factors taken together are indicative of criminal activity. Probable cause takes into account the cumulative effect of suspicious factors, since each may color the other.

Example: There are many legal reasons for a person to buy dry ice, acetone and a beaker; and there are many reasons for a substantial increase in the electrical bill of that person's house; and it is no crime for that person to associate with one who has been convicted in the past of manufacturing methamphetamines. No single one of these factors is enough in itself to constitute a fair probability of criminal activity. But if all the factors are considered together, the entire submission is suspicious enough that probable cause will be found. Isolating acts which in themselves are innocent fails to admit the force that converging details have in creating probability.

5. Deference to Police Officer's Expertise

The Supreme Court has stated that probable cause is a common sense standard. But while the Court looks at how a common sense person would evaluate the evidence, the experience and expertise of the officer is also taken into account. A fact which does not look suspicious at all to the untrained eye may be indicative of criminal activity to a person versed in how criminals operate. For instance, if the officer knows that a certain chemical or a certain smell is often associated with the manufacture of an illegal drug, that fact may be taken into account when probable cause is assessed by the officer, even though it is beyond the experience of the common person.

6. Collective Knowledge

The particular officer who conducts an arrest or search need not have personal knowledge of all the facts on which probable cause is based. Probable cause can be based on the *collective knowledge* of the police department. Thus, an officer who executes an arrest warrant supported by probable cause is acting legally even if he or she has no personal knowledge of the facts upon which the warrant is based. On the other hand, in order to be relied upon, the collective knowledge of the police must equal probable cause. An officer can thus violate the Fourth Amendment by serving as an arresting or searching functionary, when the collective information of the department as a whole does not constitute probable cause. See *Whiteley v. Warden,* 401 U.S. 560, 91 S.Ct. 1031, 28 L.Ed.2d 306 (1971).

7. **Probable Cause Standard Factors in the Propriety of Further Investigation**
    A determination of probable cause may involve an examination of whether further investigation would easily remove or increase suspicion. If further investigation could easily be conducted, and would significantly aid the officer's determination of whether criminal conduct was afoot, then such investigation will be demanded by the courts before probable cause can be found.

Examples: (1) An officer is called to a restaurant. The owner tells him that one of the customers failed to pay his bill and left the restaurant. The police proceed to the customer's home and arrest him after he admits to having been at the restaurant that evening. No further questions are asked. Under these circumstances, one court found that there was an insufficient showing for probable cause. Whatever suspicious circumstances may have existed could have been largely resolved, one way or the other, by merely asking the customer to explain his conduct. Such questioning would not have required extensive and burdensome investigation, and would have gone far to clarifying the situation. Therefore, such investigation could be reasonably demanded of the officer, and his failure to conduct it meant that probable cause did not exist. See *Moore v. Marketplace Restaurant, Inc.*, 754 F.2d 1336 (7th Cir.1985) ("it is incumbent upon law enforcement officials to make a thorough investigation and exercise reasonable judgment before invoking the awesome power of arrest and detention").

(2) An officer is called to a department store. The security guard has detained a customer. The guard tells the officer that he caught the customer shoplifting. The officer asks the customer his side of the story. The customer explains that he was returning items to their proper place when he was accosted by the security guard, at which point there was a heated dispute, which led to the customer's detention. The officer then arrested the customer for shoplifting. The court held that the arrest was supported by probable cause. Unlike *Moore, supra,* the officer heard both sides of a disputed story. He was entitled to rely on the story of an apparently sober security guard, since it could reasonably be presumed that the guard would not lightly bring charges against customers and expose himself and the store to civil liability. Most important, further investigation would have required the officer to obtain information from third parties. This would be burdensome, and uncertain to yield results. Therefore, the arrest was supported by probable cause. See *Gramenos v. Jewel Companies, Inc.*, 797 F.2d 432 (7th Cir.1986).

B. GENERALLY REQUIRED FOR ALL SEARCHES AND SEIZURES

A search or seizure is presumptively unreasonable unless it is supported by probable cause and a warrant. But even if a search or seizure is conducted pursuant to an exception to the warrant requirement—such as the exigent circumstances exception—it must still be supported by probable cause, as a general rule. Otherwise, the officer would have an incentive to invoke an exception to the warrant requirement, and the Fourth Amendment's preference for warrants would be undermined. To deter the incentive to invoke exceptions to the warrant requirement, the Court has intimated that a showing of probable cause will be *more strictly scrutinized* if the search or seizure is conducted without a warrant.

1. Exceptions

The Court has found three exceptional situations where the Fourth Amendment does not require probable cause. (All these exceptions will be discussed in detail later in this Outline).

a. Seizures of Persons or Things Which Constitute a Limited Intrusion

Temporary and minimally invasive detentions of persons and things, which are necessary to conduct a preliminary investigation, are allowed upon a showing of reasonable suspicion, which is a lesser standard of proof than probable cause. *Terry v. Ohio, infra* (seizure of person); *United States v. Van Leeuwen, infra* (detention of package). The rationale is that the limited nature of the intrusion, and the legitimate law enforcement objective for making the intrusion, justify the police action on less than probable cause.

b. Limited Searches to Protect the Officer From Harm

An officer can, on reasonable suspicion instead of probable cause, conduct a limited search of a person, thing or premises in order to protect himself from bodily harm while he is conducting a legitimate investigation. See *Terry v. Ohio, infra* (frisk of person while conducting stop); *Michigan v. Long, infra* (cursory weapons check of automobile passenger compartment pursuant to traffic stop); *Maryland v. Buie, infra* (protective sweep of premises to search for persons who could injure police officers who are making a legal arrest).

c. Search or Seizure Conducted for Special Needs Beyond Criminal Law Enforcement

If the search or seizure is not conducted for purposes of criminal law enforcement but rather to effectuate some other governmental objective such as a regulatory interest, it can in most cases be conducted on less than probable cause. See *New Jersey v. T.L.O., infra* (search of students to maintain school discipline); *Michigan v. Tyler, infra* (administrative warrant may issue on less than probable cause to investigate the origin of a fire, but an ordinary warrant based upon probable cause is required for a criminal investigation).

2. All Searches for Criminal Law Enforcement Purposes Require Probable Cause

None of the above exceptions apply to a search conducted by law enforcement officers for the very purpose of enforcing the criminal law. The Supreme Court has consistently held that such searches must be supported by probable cause. It has rejected arguments, for instance, that a search by law enforcement officers for evidence of a crime could be conducted on less than probable cause so long as it was minimally intrusive. See *Arizona v. Hicks,* 480 U.S. 321, 107 S.Ct. 1149, 94 L.Ed.2d 347 (1987) (lifting turntable to check serial numbers is a search which must be supported by probable cause). Some lower courts have, however, failed to follow what appears to be a clear statement from the Court in *Hicks.* See *United States v. Concepcion,* 942 F.2d 1170 (7th Cir.1991) (officers took a key found on the defendant, and inserted it into a lock on a door to an apartment in which drugs had been found; while this was a search, it could be conducted on less than probable cause, because the search was minimally intrusive and the information uncovered— that the defendant had a key to the apartment—was not intensely private).

C. APPLICATION OF THE PROBABLE CAUSE STANDARD TO QUESTIONS OF IDENTITY

One circumstance in which a question of probable cause arises is where a crime has been committed, but it is unclear whether the suspect to be arrested is the perpetrator.

1. Particularized Information Required

Probable cause as to identity must be based on specific information which ties a suspect to a crime. A pure statistical analysis is not determinative of probable cause. For example, statistics may indicate that one out of five people in a certain area is a criminal; but this does not allow the police to randomly arrest every fifth person in the area. See *Wong Sun v. United States,* 371 U.S. 471, 83 S.Ct. 407, 9 L.Ed.2d 441 (1963) (person cannot be arrested on a pure statistical probability). The question is, how particularized must the information be?

2. Fitting a Description

Probable cause requires a case by case approach, and as such it is difficult to draw conclusions as to the facts necessary to justify an arrest of a person on the ground that he was identified as the perpetrator of a crime. Nonetheless, since the standard is only one of fair probability, a suspect's correspondence to a relatively specific description will go far toward a showing of probable cause.

Example: An officer reports a drug transaction in the area of 48th Street and Ninth Avenue in Manhattan. This is an area known for drug trafficking, and the residents are predominantly Hispanic. The officer describes one of the perpetrators as "Hispanic male in his 20's, black leather jacket, grey pants with a comb in back pocket, and a white v-neck shirt." Ten minutes later, another officer arrests Valez, who is walking in the area. Valez fits the description, and the arresting officer searches Valez and finds cocaine. The officer who originally reported the drug transaction later comes by and states that Valez is not the perpetrator: Valez had facial hair while the perpetrator did not. The court held that the arrest and the resulting search were valid, because the arrest was supported by probable cause. The suspect fit a description that was not impermissibly general, and he was found in the area. *United States v. Valez,* 796 F.2d 24 (2d Cir.1986).

3.   Prior Criminal Record

The state's case on probable cause as to identity is made significantly stronger if the suspect who fits a general description also has a prior criminal record. This information adds to the fair probability that the suspect was the perpetrator, especially if the defendant has been previously convicted of a crime similar to that currently being investigated. Rules of evidence (such as the rule excluding from trial some prior crimes of a criminal defendant) do not apply to a probable cause determination.

D.   APPLICATION OF PROBABLE CAUSE STANDARD TO EQUIVOCAL CONDUCT

Another circumstance in which a probable cause question arises is where it is unclear whether a crime has been committed or is being committed at all. In these instances, the officer has a specific person in mind as a perpetrator, but is not certain whether there is any criminal activity afoot. For example, suppose that an officer on patrol sees a person at 2:00 a.m., in a high crime area, pushing a shopping cart which contains a television and a stereo. The question is not the identity of the perpetrator; the question is whether there has been a crime.

1.   Innocent Explanations for Equivocal Activity

While each case of equivocal conduct depends on a common sense view of the particular facts, this much can be said: the presence of an innocent explanation for the conduct is clearly not enough to eliminate probable cause. Most courts will find probable cause if there is some conduct which a common sense person would think highly suspect, even though an innocent explanation for the conduct is also plausible. The real question is whether plausible innocent explanations substantially outweigh the likelihood of criminality.

Example: Acting on a tip, officers investigated a secluded farmhouse. They detected the odor of phenylacetic acid and of ether, two chemicals commonly used in the manufacture of amphetamines. The next day, they found that the farmhouse had been boarded up, and the only opening other than the doors was a large vent equipped with a fan. A pickup truck entered the driveway of the farmhouse, its driver honked the horn, and the vehicle remained there for five minutes before someone came from the farmhouse and entered the passenger side of the truck. The officers followed the pickup truck for several miles, to a point where it appeared to be leaving the area. They stopped the truck and placed the driver and passenger under arrest. The driver challenged the arrest as lacking probable cause. The court rejected the driver's argument. While there is no probable cause to arrest someone merely because he associates with a criminal, the court found more than mere association in this case. The farmhouse was in an isolated location. The driver drove directly up to the farmhouse in a manner that indicated he knew his destination and was not lost. He did not appear to be seeking directions, or to be engaged in an innocent errand like delivering milk. He blew the truck's horn as if he were expected, and someone came from the house in response. The truck appeared to be leaving the area, and the officer could fairly presume that the truck was loaded with drugs. *United States v. Raborn,* 872 F.2d 589 (5th Cir.1989).

2.   First Amendment Considerations

In *People v. P.J. Video, Inc.,* 475 U.S. 868, 106 S.Ct. 1610, 89 L.Ed.2d 871 (1986), the Court held that First Amendment considerations do not require a standard of proof higher than probable cause before a search may be conducted of speech-related material. The warrants at issue in *P.J. Video* authorized the seizure of certain films that were allegedly obscene. The affidavits on which the warrants were based described sex acts occurring in excerpted scenes of the films. The defendant argued that the affidavits merely described the sex scenes, but did not establish probable cause that the film as a whole lacked artistic merit. The defendant contended that while the affidavits were pervaded with sexually explicit acts, the state had failed to show that this was true of the films as a whole. The Court rejected this argument, reasoning that since so many sex scenes were described in films that lasted from sixty to ninety minutes, there was a fair probability that there was little other than sex scenes in the films, and that the films therefore as a whole lacked artistic value. An actual assertion in the warrant application as to the lack of artistic value was held not required, given the minimal standard of the "fair probability" test.

E. PROBABLE CAUSE AS APPLIED TO LOCATION

A third situation in which the probable cause question arises is where officials suspect that a person to be arrested, or evidence of a crime, is located in a particular place. If investigation of such a place would be a search, the officers must have probable cause to believe that the person to be arrested or the evidence to be seized is located in the place to be searched.

1. Staleness

One problem that can arise with location is that there may have been probable cause at one point to believe that evidence or a person to be arrested would be found therein, but the search is actually conducted at a point significantly later in time. This is a question of staleness. For example, the day after a bank robbery, there may be probable cause to believe that the money from the robbery will be located in the robber's house. But that probability is significantly diminished a year after the robbery. Whether the information on which probable cause was originally based has grown stale is dependent upon such facts as the nature of the crime, the type of evidence, and the length of time that has passed.

Example: The police have probable cause to believe that the suspect ordered and accepted magazines showing sex acts conducted with children. The magazines were, however delivered to defendant's home six months prior to the time the officers obtained a warrant. The defendant argues that the information is stale—that there is no probable cause to believe that the magazines are still in his home at the time the warrant is issued. However, in the affidavit supporting the warrant, the officers included a statement from a psychiatrist who concluded that the facts indicated that the defendant was a pedophile, and that pedophiles are likely to retain such magazines for a long time, rather than destroy or distribute them. Consequently, the court found that the information upon which probable cause was based had not grown stale—there was a fair probability that the magazines were still in the defendant's home. *United States v. Rabe,* 848 F.2d 994 (9th Cir.1988). See also *United States v. Ponce,* 947 F.2d 646 (2d Cir.1991) (information that was two weeks old was not stale where it indicated that the premises were used for an ongoing narcotics trafficking operation).

2. One of Several Locations

Another problem that arises in determining whether there is probable cause to search a certain location is where a piece of evidence could be located in one of several places, but could not be in two locations at the same time. For example, the suspect's murder weapon could be in his car, his office, or his home. But it cannot be in all three places. In this situation, the courts have held that there is probable cause to search in each location, even though they are mutually exclusive, so long as there is a *logical nexus* between the crime and the location. This nexus need not be based on direct observation, but can be based on the type of crime, the nature of the items, and logical inferences as to where evidence would be located. So for example, in a fraud case, where the suspect is a stockbroker, there will generally be probable cause to search for a "smoking gun" document in the suspect's office, home, and briefcase, as well as in other places which have a logical nexus with the fraud.

F. THE USE OF HEARSAY IN THE PROBABLE CAUSE DETERMINATION

Where probable cause is based solely on an officer's observation and the inferences derived therefrom, the only question is whether all the facts known lead to a fair probability of criminal activity. However, where officers do not have personal knowledge of the facts, but are instead relying upon information from other parties, there is also a question of whether the "facts" related by such third parties are reliable enough to be credited in the probable cause determination. Probable cause does not exist if the "facts" related are actually false. An officer who must rely on an informant is in no position to know whether the facts related are true or not. Nor does the magistrate know whether the informant is telling the truth; and it is the magistrate who must make an independent determination of the facts. If the officer relies on other sources, he or she is relying on hearsay information. As in the course on Evidence, hearsay statements, to be credited, must be evaluated to determine whether they are reliable.

1. Former Two–Pronged Test for Evaluating Hearsay

To insure that the magistrate—or the reviewing court if a warrant was not obtained—had some way to make an independent determination of the reliability of hearsay information, the court in *Aguilar v. Texas,* 378 U.S. 108, 84 S.Ct. 1509, 12 L.Ed.2d 723 (1964) and *Spinelli v. United States,* 393 U.S. 410, 89 S.Ct. 584, 21 L.Ed.2d 637 (1969) imposed what came to be known as the *Aguilar–Spinelli two-pronged test* for structuring the magistrate's analysis of probable cause. The Supreme Court later rejected the two-pronged test in favor of a less structured totality of circumstances approach. See *Illinois v. Gates,* 462 U.S. 213, 103 S.Ct. 2317, 76 L.Ed.2d 527 (1983). However, as the Court in *Gates* recognized, the two-pronged test is still a helpful means by which to evaluate an informant's hearsay, and lower courts have used the structure as a means of evaluation, though not as a dispositive test. Consequently, it is necessary to understand the structure set forth in *Aguilar* and *Spinelli.*

2. First Prong: Reliable Informant

Under *Aguilar–Spinelli,* the person providing the information upon which the warrant is based must be reliable and credible. The person providing information could be found reliable on one of several grounds:

a. Police Officers

Under *Aguilar–Spinelli,* police officers were presumed to be telling the truth when reporting facts to other officers or to the magistrate.

b. Citizen–informants

Where police obtain information from non-criminal sources, such as ordinary citizens, or victims or witnesses of crimes, these sources are presumed reliable. It is a reasonable presumption that a law-abiding citizen would tell the truth to a police officer.

c. Informants With Track Records

Criminals and ex-criminals working as police informants are not presumed reliable under either *Aguilar–Spinelli* or the later test of *Gates.* Under *Aguilar–Spinelli,* the presumption was that such an informant was prone to lie, and hence was not credible. However, this presumption could be overcome by a showing that the informant had given reliable information on numerous occasions in the past. An inference of truthfulness in the current case could be drawn from a past record of truthfulness.

d. Declarations Against Interest

Under *Aguilar–Spinelli,* the informant could overcome the presumption of untruthfulness by describing criminal activity in which he participated, which if true would subject him to penal liability. Under these circumstances, courts draw an inference that the informant would not have related such self-inculpatory facts unless they were true. Thus, in *United States v. Harris,* 403 U.S. 573, 91 S.Ct. 2075, 29 L.Ed.2d 723 (1971), the informant stated that he had purchased illegal liquor from Harris. A majority of the Court found that this declaration could be weighed in deciding whether the veracity prong of *Aguilar–Spinelli* had been satisfied, since the informant by describing Harris' activity had also implicated himself in a crime.

e. Anonymous Informants

Under both *Aguilar–Spinelli* and *Gates,* if the informant is anonymous, reliability cannot be presumed. There is no way to know whether an anonymous informant is an ordinary citizen, or a person steeped in criminality. Even if the informant is an ordinary citizen, anonymity is a protection against any sanction for lying to the police, and consequently the anonymous informant may tell a lie.

3. Second Prong: Personal Knowledge

Even if the information comes from a reliable source, that source may not have personal knowledge of the facts attested to. Under the *Aguilar–Spinelli* test, a warrant could not be issued if the informant based his information on unreliable sources, such as "barroom rumor."

a. Direct Statement of Personal Knowledge

If the informant stated to the police officer that he heard or saw the information he was relating, such a direct statement of knowledge satisfies the personal knowledge prong of *Aguilar–Spinelli,* and goes far toward establishing probable cause under the *Gates* totality of circumstances test.

b. Self–Verifying Detail

Even if there is no direct statement of personal knowledge, a statement containing a wealth of detail can create an inference of personal knowledge. For example, an informant might say: "Joe keeps his drugs in a striped suitcase inside a secret compartment behind his bookshelf, which is opened by pulling out the third book on the top left shelf." The informant has not stated how he came by his information. However, the wealth of detail creates a fair inference of "inside information"— knowledge either from personal observation or from the defendant himself. As stated in *Spinelli,* in order for detail to be considered "self-verifying" and thus to satisfy the personal knowledge prong, the detail must be such as would not be imparted by "barroom rumor."

4. Independent Prongs

Under *Aguilar–Spinelli,* the veracity prong and the personal knowledge prong were analyzed as totally separate and independent from each other. Thus, even if an informant had a previous track record of truthfulness, his information could not be credited for a warrant application unless he was speaking from a proper basis of knowledge. Conversely, a statement clearly based on personal knowledge could not be credited if the source of the information was unreliable.

5. Corroboration

Under *Aguilar–Spinelli,* a defect in one or both prongs could be remedied if the police obtained significant independent evidence corroborating that the facts related by the informant were true. However, the corroborative evidence had to be *substantial*, or corroborative of *suspicious facts* in order to shore up a defect in one of the prongs.

Example: In *Spinelli,* the officer sought a warrant to search Spinelli's apartment for evidence of a bookmaking operation. The application was based in major part on a tip from an informant, who related that Spinelli was a gambler who had two phone lines in his apartment; the informant gave the phone number for each line. The warrant application did not state how the informant came upon this information, or on what basis the informant concluded that Spinelli was a gambler. Nor was there a showing that the informant had a previous track record of reliable tips. However, the police determined through independent investigation that the informant was correct as to the two phones and separate phone numbers. The Court, however, found this information to be insufficient corroboration for either prong. The information corroborated was neither substantial nor in any way suspicious or incriminating. The Court contrasted its prior decision of *Draper v. United States,* 358 U.S. 307, 79 S.Ct. 329, 3 L.Ed.2d 327 (1959), in which a reliable informant stated that Draper would be arriving on a certain train wearing distinct clothing; the officers met that train and saw a person disembark with the exact unique clothing that the informant had described in advance. In *Spinelli,* the Court found that the corroboration in *Draper* was substantial enough to shore up a defect in the basis of knowledge prong.

a. Explanation

The Court in *Spinelli* reasoned that, without *substantial* corroboration of a defective tip, no real inference could be drawn that the declarant had personal knowledge or was reliable as to his conclusion that the defendant was involved in criminal conduct. Minimal corroboration of some facts in the tip was considered not sufficient to assure that the tip was reliable. For example, the fact that the informant in *Spinelli* was correct about the phone numbers and that Spinelli had two phones did not create an inference that the informant knew that Spinelli was involved in illegal gambling or that the informant was reliable.

G. REJECTION OF THE TWO-PRONGED TEST AND ADOPTION OF THE TOTALITY OF CIRCUMSTANCES APPROACH

In *Illinois v. Gates, supra,* the Court rejected the *Aguilar–Spinelli* test as a controlling framework for evaluating hearsay information in determining probable cause. The *Aguilar–Spinelli* two-pronged approach is still used by courts after *Gates* to analyze a hearsay problem, and according to *Gates* the two-pronged test is still relevant. But the Court in *Gates* rejected the notion that the *Aguilar–Spinelli* test had to be satisfied before a hearsay statement could be credited toward probable cause. The Court stated that the correct approach is whether the judge, using common sense, and taking into account the fact that there is a hearsay problem, could find under the totality of circumstances that probable cause exists.

1. Facts of *Gates*

Police in *Gates* received an anonymous letter that Lance and Sue Gates were drug traffickers. The letter alleged that the Gates' were about to obtain drugs in Florida and bring them home to Illinois, and it described their itinerary: Sue would drive their car down to Florida on a certain day, Lance would take a certain flight down to meet her; Lance then would drive back with drugs in the trunk, and Sue would fly back. The police checked out this information. They found that Lance had booked a flight to West Palm Beach.

Lance was followed to a hotel room registered in Sue's name. The next morning, Lance and a woman (later identified as Sue) began to drive northbound on the freeway, in a car registered to Lance. Based upon the above information, the officer obtained a warrant from the magistrate to search the Gates' house and car. When the Gates' returned to Illinois, their house and car were searched pursuant to the warrant, and drugs were found in both places.

2. Lower Court Analysis

The Illinois courts excluded the evidence on the ground that the informant's tip, even though corroborated to some extent, failed under *Aguilar–Spinelli*. The informant was anonymous, and so there was no presumption of reliability. Nor did the informant's letter indicate that it was based on personal knowledge. Thus the tip on its face failed both prongs of the *Aguilar–Spinelli* test. The lower courts rejected the Government's argument that the corroboration of the Gates' travel plans was sufficient to shore up the defects in the tip itself. According to the Illinois courts, the corroboration was not substantial, since it merely concerned the Gates' itinerary, and was not even completely correct as to that: the tip stated that Sue would fly back when in fact she did not. Nor were the facts corroborated sufficiently suspicious to shore up the prongs.

3. Analysis in *Gates*

The Court in *Gates* rejected the *Aguilar–Spinelli* two-pronged test on the ground that it imposed an unduly rigid, technical and legalistic structure on what ought to be a common sense evaluation. Justice Rehnquist, writing for the majority, began from the well-accepted proposition that probable cause is a standard to be applied in light of a common sense evaluation of the totality of the circumstances. To Justice Rehnquist, it followed that information supporting probable cause—even hearsay information—should be evaluated the way that a common sense person would. A common sense person looking at an informant's hearsay information would not separate it out neatly into "prongs"; would not evaluate the sufficiency of corroboration in the same manner as a schooled appellate court; and would not disregard the hearsay upon the mere fact that there was a technical defect in one or the other prong. Rather, a common sense person would look at the totality of information, considering the fact that some of it was hearsay, and make a common sense determination of the reliability and sufficiency of the information supporting probable cause. Thus, the question after *Gates* for informant's hearsay is not "does it satisfy the two-pronged test?", but rather "how would it strike a common sense person?"

4. Dissent in *Gates*

Justice Brennan's dissenting opinion in *Gates* recognized that many lower courts prior to *Gates* had applied excessively strict scrutiny to warrant applications. However, he argued that this was not reason enough to dispense with the *Aguilar–Spinelli* test. Justice Brennan contended that the majority had confused the relevant standard of proof—probable cause, which requires a common sense evaluation of the facts—with the *permissible sources* of proof, i.e. whether certain information is even reliable enough to count as a fact toward probable cause. Justice Brennan asserted that there is no "common sense" way to evaluate the reliability of hearsay; rather, legal standards were needed so that the magistrate could properly assess whether the hearsay was sufficiently reliable to count toward probable cause. He complained that a common sense approach would credit even unreliable hearsay, and noted that at trial, the judge is obligated to exclude hearsay, precisely because a jury of common sense persons is unable to evaluate it. Justice Brennan concluded that *Aguilar–Spinelli* gave the magistrate and reviewing court a proper structure for resolving the hearsay problem, but that the *Gates* standard, which consists largely of an instruction to use common sense, and to find probable cause in all but the most egregious situations, gives little if any guidance to magistrates or reviewing courts.

H.   IMPACT OF *GATES*
To determine the effect of *Gates* on probable cause determinations it is necessary to apply the two-pronged test and see how it differs from the *Gates* test in concrete cases. Most courts still apply the two-pronged test as a non-dispositive guideline to evaluating hearsay from informants.

1.   No Change in Many Cases
In many cases since *Gates,* probable cause would be found even under the *Aguilar–Spinelli* two-pronged test. If *Aguilar–Spinelli* is satisfied, it follows that *Gates* is as well, since the *Gates* test is avowedly more permissive than the former test.

> *Example:*   An informant whose information has led to convictions on four past occasions tells the officer that "Little Mike" will be carrying illegal weapons to a meeting of the Hells Angels. The informant provides a detailed description of the car, of the weapons in the car, and of "Little Mike's" itinerary. Under these circumstances, probable cause would be found under *Aguilar–Spinelli.* The informant has a track record of reliability, and has given a wealth of detail which creates an inference of personal knowledge. Accordingly, the more permissive common sense standard of *Gates* is automatically satisfied. See *United States v. Lessard,* 720 F.2d 1000 (8th Cir.1983).

2.   A Tip Which Fails Both Prongs Cannot Itself Constitute Probable Cause
If an informant's tip fails both of the *Aguilar–Spinelli* prongs, *and there is no police corroboration of the information*, then the tip is insufficient for probable cause even under the more permissive *Gates* standard.

Example: This is shown by the facts and analysis in *Gates*. The tip was from an anonymous informant, and thus did not of itself satisfy the *Aguilar–Spinelli* veracity prong. Nor did the informant relate his basis of knowledge, and the detail in the tip was not sufficient to be deemed self-verifying. Justice Rehnquist stated that the tip itself would not satisfy probable cause even under the common sense, totality of the circumstances approach mandated by *Gates*. Justice Rehnquist also gave another example of a tip failing both of the *Aguilar–Spinelli* prongs which would be insufficient under *Gates*: the *barebones affidavit*. An affidavit such as "a reliable informant told me that Joe Smith was selling illegal drugs" provides the magistrate with absolutely no way to determine whether the information is reliable, and consequently fails both *Aguilar–Spinelli* and *Gates*. See *Nathanson v. United States,* 290 U.S. 41, 54 S.Ct. 11, 78 L.Ed. 159 (1933).

3. Strong Showing on One Prong Can Make up for a Weak Showing on the Other

The Court in *Gates* stated that a common sense approach would not separate the prongs and require that each be satisfied in all cases; a common sense person could believe hearsay as itself sufficient for probable cause when one prong is especially strong and the other prong is somewhat weak. The strength in one could make up for the weakness in the other. Thus, if the informant has been unusually reliable in the past, his failure to set forth the specific basis for his knowledge or to give minute detail should not necessarily preclude a finding of probable cause. Conversely, even if there is some reason to doubt the informant's reliability, that doubt can be overcome by an especially strong showing that the informant observed the event first-hand. Thus, *even without corroboration,* a tip which is especially strong on one prong, and not absolutely deficient on the other, can itself satisfy probable cause.

Examples: Phillips' estranged wife goes to the police and tells them, in specific and copious detail, about Phillips' drug transaction, including where exactly in the home the drugs are stored. The wife admits that she has "an axe to grind" against Phillips, and it would please her to see him get in trouble with the law. A court after *Gates* found this tip sufficient in itself to constitute probable cause. The court recognized that the informant's reliability was somewhat suspect given her motives for vengeance. However, her credibility was not as questionable as a criminal paid informant, so the tip was found not completely lacking on the veracity prong. To the extent the wife did not satisfy the veracity prong, the court found that the defect was more than offset by the strong showing on the basis of knowledge prong. See *United States v. Phillips,* 727 F.2d 392 (5th Cir.1984).

An informant with a track record of reliable tips informs the police that marijuana is growing on Carter's property. The informant gives the general locations and dimensions of the field, but does not say how he came by his information. After *Gates,* a reviewing court found that this tip, standing alone, established probable cause. The court noted that there was a minor defect in the basis of knowledge prong, since the informant did not say that he had visited the field. However, the informant did give some detail about the field, though perhaps not enough to constitute "self-verifying" detail under *Aguilar–Spinelli*. Still, the court reasoned that any defect in the basis of knowledge prong was overcome by the strong showing of the informant's veracity. The court concluded that a common sense person would credit the informant's tip as true. See *Carter v. United States,* 729 F.2d 935 (8th Cir.1984).

4. The Expanded Role of Corroboration

After *Gates,* even if the tip is insufficient to establish probable cause, some corroboration of the tip by police investigation will ordinarily allow a common sense person to believe the informant's report of criminal activity. This is where *Gates* has had its largest impact. Under *Aguilar–Spinelli,* corroboration could shore up a defective tip, but only if the corroboration was itself substantial (not just phone numbers as in *Spinelli*) or if the corroborated facts were themselves highly suspicious. Moreover, if there were discrepancies between the tip and the corroborated facts (e.g. the tip indicated travel plans different from the travel which actually occurred) this would count heavily against crediting the tip. After *Gates,* the function of corroboration is simply to help a common sense person determine, without regard to specific defects in specific prongs, whether the informant is telling the truth. The question under *Gates* is: how does the tip strike a common sense person, knowing that it has been checked out and supported in some particulars? Would the common sense person, suspicious of the tip because it is hearsay, feel sufficiently assured by the fact that police investigation found that the tip was true in at least some respects? The answer to that question after *Gates* is ordinarily "yes".

Example: In *Gates,* the police checked out the travel plans of the Gates'. They found that the informant correctly related some aspects of the travel plans: that Sue would drive to Florida by herself and rent a room, and that Lance would fly down to meet her on a certain day, and drive the car back immediately. But the investigation also showed that the tip was incorrect in at least one respect: the informant said that Sue would fly back when in fact she did not. The corroboration in *Gates* would probably not have been sufficient under *Spinelli,* since it did not deal with any obviously suspicious activity, (as the dissenters pointed out, at the time the warrant was issued, the police did not know that the Gates' were driving immediately back to their home), nor did it corroborate a significant portion of the facts related in the tip. Also under *Spinelli,* the discrepancies would weigh heavily against both the veracity and basis of the informant. Nonetheless, in *Gates* the Court concluded that a common sense person, evaluating the tip together with the corroboration, would conclude that the informant knew basically what was going on, and appeared to be telling the truth. The corroboration in *Gates* sufficiently reduced the risk of a total untruth, since, in common sense, the fact that the informant knew some facts made it more likely that he knew the important incriminating fact—that Lance and Sue were transporting drugs.

a.   Corroboration of Innocent Activity

The Court in *Gates* held that corroboration could be sufficient to support a tip even though the activity corroborated could be considered completely innocent. According to the Court, the innocent nature of the corroborated facts would not prevent a common sense person from concluding that the informant was correct in his assertion about criminal activity. Thus in *Gates* it did not matter that the travel plans corroborated by police officers could well have been made by tourists rather than drug dealers. The function of corroboration is to provide some assurance that the informant is telling the truth and knows what he is talking about; and the *Gates* Court reasoned that this function could be satisfied even if the facts corroborated give no hint that criminal activity is afoot. The tip itself can then explain why the facts, though apparently innocent, are indicative of criminality.

5.   Strict Scrutiny of the Magistrate's Determination Is No Longer Permitted

According to *Gates,* one of the defects of the *Aguilar–Spinelli* approach was that reviewing courts reviewed magistrates' determinations in an excessively legalistic and rigid manner. In response, the Court in *Gates* held that a reviewing court is not allowed to strictly scrutinize a magistrate's determination of probable cause. The Court reasoned that probable cause is a common sense approach, and concluded that a legalistic, excessively strict review was inconsistent with that approach. The standard of review after *Gates* is deferential: the reviewing court determines only whether the magistrate had a *substantial basis* for finding probable cause, and for crediting an informant's hearsay. Put another way, the question for the reviewing court is: could any reasonable person have found that the hearsay was reliable and that the facts indicated a fair probability of criminal activity?

6. **Deferential Review in Warrantless Search Cases**

Lower courts have read *Gates* to mean that the same deferential standard of review of magistrates' determinations should also apply to a court's review of a police officer's assessment of probable cause, in cases where the officer acts pursuant to an exception to the warrant requirement (e.g. if there are exigent circumstances). Thus, the courts will not second-guess an officer's reliance on an informant's tip, so long as the officer had a substantial basis for crediting the hearsay.

I. *GATES* REJECTED BY A NUMBER OF STATE COURTS

At least eight states have rejected *Gates* as a matter of state law, concluding that its treatment of hearsay is unacceptably shapeless and permissive. These courts argue that the *Spinelli* test, if not applied hypertechnically, is a good structure for solving the legal problem presented when hearsay information is offered to show probable cause. See e.g. *People v. Johnson,* 66 N.Y.2d 398, 497 N.Y.S.2d 618, 488 N.E.2d 439 (1985). Remember that a state court, construing its own state's constitution, can provide for more protections than are granted by the Federal Constitution.

J. DISCLOSURE OF INFORMANT'S IDENTITY

Where probable cause is based in whole or in part on an informant's information, the defendant will often seek disclosure of the informant's identity at a suppression hearing. Defendants claim that such disclosure is required in order to assure that the informer was in fact reliable (for instance, that he could have witnessed what he said he did), and indeed to assure that the officer is not just *inventing an informant*.

1. **Disclosure Is Not Generally Required**

In *McCray v. Illinois,* 386 U.S. 300, 87 S.Ct. 1056, 18 L.Ed.2d 62 (1967), the Court held that disclosure of an informant's identity at a suppression hearing is ordinarily not required. The Court reasoned that it did not matter whether the informant was actually telling the truth to the police officer. The relevant question for probable cause was whether the officer could reasonably believe that the informant was telling the truth. The *McCray* Court concluded that disclosure of the informant's identity was not needed to determine whether the officer reasonably believed the informant. The Court also noted that the state had a legitimate interest in protecting the confidentiality of its informants.

2. **Where Officer's Testimony Is Not Credible**

If it appears that the officer is not being truthful about whether an informant even existed, the court may in its discretion compel production of the informant. This discretionary power is designed to assure that officers will not simply manufacture probable cause by creating fictional informants.

3. *In camera* Proceedings

Many courts protect against the problem of police perjury by requiring disclosure of the informant's identity at an *in camera* proceeding. The *in camera* proceeding is conducted outside the presence of defendant and his counsel; however, the judge is given access to the informant. In this way, police perjury can be uncovered, while the state's interest in confidentiality is preserved. A court will generally order an *in camera* proceeding only upon a substantial showing by the defendant that the existence of an informant is in doubt.

K. POLICE MISREPRESENTATION OF FACTS CONSTITUTING PROBABLE CAUSE

Besides creating informants, some police officers may try to create facts in order to make a showing of probable cause to obtain a warrant. Even if an affidavit submitted by police officers to the magistrate states facts sufficient to constitute probable cause, there may be a question of whether the "facts" in the affidavit are true or false.

1. *Franks* Hearing

If the defendant makes a substantial showing that a false statement was included in the affidavit, *and that the officer included the information with knowledge or reckless disregard of its falsity*, then the defendant is entitled to a hearing to prove his allegations. If at the hearing, the defendant proves his allegations by a preponderance of the evidence, then the misstatements must be struck from the affidavit, and the court must determine whether the remaining information in the affidavit establishes probable cause. See *Franks v. Delaware,* 438 U.S. 154, 98 S.Ct. 2674, 57 L.Ed.2d 667 (1978).

2. No Relief for Negligent Misstatements

The Supreme Court in *Franks* held that if the misstatement in the affidavit was the result of mere negligence, the defendant is not entitled to relief. Consequently, *Franks* gives a very limited remedy to defendants: they must show not only that a fact in the affidavit is untrue, but also that the officer included it in the affidavit knowing or having reckless disregard for its falsity.

3. Remaining Information May Still Constitute Probable Cause

Even if there are intentional or reckless misstatements in the affidavit, the resulting warrant may still be valid. So long as the remaining information constitutes probable cause, the Fourth Amendment is not violated. In other words, the Court in *Franks* gave protection only as to *material* misstatements. See *United States v. Ferra,* 948 F.2d 352 (7th Cir.1991) (warrant which led to seizure of cocaine was not invalid despite the detective's false representation in the warrant application that a reliable informant bought cocaine from the defendant; probable cause was independently established by what the detective learned during a visit to the premises). Compare *United States v. DeLeon,* 979 F.2d 761 (9th Cir.1992) (if officer had included the informant's statement that he had denied seeing marijuana growing on

(S., C. & H.) Crim.Proc. BLS—7

defendant's premises, then "no reasonable person could have found probable cause to issue the warrant"; the only information left in the warrant application was from another informant to the effect that he had smelled marijuana on the defendant's property, and there was no indication that the other informant was qualified to recognize the odor of growing marijuana).

IV. OBTAINING A VALID SEARCH WARRANT

Generally speaking, the Fourth Amendment requires every search or seizure to be made pursuant to a warrant issued upon probable cause. A warrant is a document issued by a judicial officer, authorizing a law enforcement official to make a search or seizure. The judicial officer is usually a magistrate, and we will use that term here generically to refer to any judicial officer who issues a warrant. The following section describes the procedural prerequisites for obtaining a valid search warrant.

A. NEUTRAL AND DETACHED MAGISTRATE
The rationale of the warrant requirement is to interpose an unbiased judicial official between the citizen and the police officer who is in the competitive enterprise of ferreting out crime. Accordingly, the magistrate must indeed be a neutral official, who will make an unbiased determination of whether probable cause exists.

1. Cannot Be a Law Enforcement Official
In *Coolidge v. New Hampshire,* 403 U.S. 443, 91 S.Ct. 2022, 29 L.Ed.2d 564 (1971), the state Attorney General issued a search warrant, as authorized by state law. The state Attorney General is the highest law enforcement official in the state, and was in fact conducting the investigation at issue in *Coolidge.* The Court held that the warrant was invalid since the state Attorney General could not be considered neutral and detached.

2. Conducting the Search Destroys Neutrality
In *Lo-Ji Sales, Inc. v. New York,* 442 U.S. 319, 99 S.Ct. 2319, 60 L.Ed.2d 920 (1979), the magistrate issued a warrant to seize pornographic books from a store. Then the magistrate accompanied law enforcement officers to the store, and actively participated in the search by examining items in the store to determine whether they should be seized. The Court held that the active participation of the magistrate destroyed his neutrality and thus resulted in an illegal seizure.

3. Contingent Fee Destroys Neutrality
In *Connally v. Georgia,* 429 U.S. 245, 97 S.Ct. 546, 50 L.Ed.2d 444 (1977), a magistrate received $5 for every warrant he issued, but received nothing for any warrant application he denied. The Court held that such a magistrate was not neutral and detached as required by the Fourth Amendment: his salary was contingent upon issuing warrants, and such a pecuniary interest

could impermissibly affect his impartial judgment. Therefore, the warrant issued by the magistrate in *Connally* was invalid, and the evidence obtained pursuant to the warrant had to be suppressed.

4. "Rubber Stamp"
A magistrate who issues a warrant without reading the warrant or the supporting application is not considered neutral and detached as required by the Fourth Amendment. Such a magistrate has become nothing more than a rubber stamp for law enforcement. See *United States v. Decker*, 956 F.2d 773 (8th Cir.1992) (magistrate loses neutral and detached status when he fails to read a warrant because he was "intrigued" by the manner in which the officer became suspicious of the defendant). However, the burden of showing that a magistrate is a rubber stamp is a heavy one. For example, in *United States v. Brown*, 832 F.2d 991 (7th Cir.1987), the defendant submitted to the court several thousand warrant applications approved by a particular magistrate. All of the applications contained the same boilerplate language; all had been approved. The magistrate had issued many more warrants than other magistrates in the area. The court held that the defendant's proof was insufficient to show that the magistrate had become a rubber stamp. Rather, the court found to the contrary that the evidence showed that the magistrate had extensive expertise in issuing warrants.

5. Need Not Be Lawyers
In *Shadwick v. City of Tampa*, 407 U.S. 345, 92 S.Ct. 2119, 32 L.Ed.2d 783 (1972), the Court held that a municipal court clerk, who was authorized by state law to issue warrants but who was not a lawyer, could constitutionally issue arrest warrants for municipal violations.

a. Federal Courts
The ruling in *Shadwick* authorizing non-lawyers to issue warrants has no bearing on Federal practice. In the Federal courts, magistrates are lawyers who are appointed by the district courts under 18 U.S.C.A. § 3060.

6. Must Be Competent to Determine Probable Cause
The magistrate must have the intellectual ability to determine probable cause. However, since probable cause is a common sense standard, there would appear to be no intellectual prerequisite or educational credential that is required as a matter of constitutional law. While *Shadwick* dealt with arrest warrants for minor offenses, the Court in *Illinois v. Gates, supra*, assumed that non-lawyers may issue search warrants for major crimes as well.

7. Magistrate Decisions
There is no requirement that a magistrate give reasons for finding probable cause or for rejecting a warrant application.

B. PROBABLE CAUSE BASED ONLY ON FACTS PRESENTED TO THE MAGISTRATE

One rationale behind the warrant requirement is that it forces the officer to establish a record supporting probable cause *before* a search occurs. This prevents the officer from "working backward": the danger is that, having found the evidence, an unscrupulous officer will construct a factual scenario by which one could have obtained probable cause before the search. To protect against this danger, probable cause must be judged solely by the information presented to the magistrate in the warrant application. The officer is not allowed to rely on information not included in the application, since the warrant requirement mandates that probable cause be determined by the magistrate, not by the officer.

1. Affidavits

A warrant is ordinarily obtained by submitting, to the magistrate, an affidavit of all the facts supporting probable cause. Some courts have held that probable cause must be determined solely on the basis of the information submitted in the affidavit. See Federal Rule of Criminal Procedure 41(c). Other courts have held that the affidavit can be supplemented by sworn oral testimony before the magistrate.

2. Telephone Warrants

Federal Rule of Criminal Procedure 41(c) authorizes a warrant to be obtained upon oral testimony communicated by telephone or other means, "if the circumstances make it reasonable to dispense with an affidavit." However, a warrant cannot be obtained by mere telephone conversation. The officer must prepare a written "duplicate original warrant," and then read that warrant verbatim to the magistrate. The magistrate then must transcribe what is read in order to prepare an original warrant. A record must be made of the telephone conversation. Those who give testimony over the telephone are sworn by the magistrate.

3. Warrant Is Obtained *ex parte*

The defendant is not present at a warrant application, and does not at that point get an opportunity to challenge the police officer's submission on probable cause. However, the validity of the warrant can be attacked at a suppression hearing before trial.

C. PARTICULAR DESCRIPTION OF PLACE TO BE SEARCHED

Even if there is probable cause to search a certain location, a warrant authorizing a search is invalid if the location is not described with reasonable particularity.

1. Rationale

The Colonial experience with general warrants was the major reason for including the Fourth Amendment in the Bill of Rights. The particularity requirement is designed to protect against the use of a warrant as a general warrant. The protection of the particularity requirement operates in three ways. First, if the executing officer has no knowledge of the underlying facts, the particular description of the premises in the warrant operates as a "map"; without such a description, the officer may conduct a search in every place which fits a general description such as "a blue house on the West Side." Second, even if the executing officer knows the place he wants to search, the particular description in the warrant establishes a specific record of probable cause as to location prior to search. Finally, the particularity requirement prevents the investigating/executing officer from using the warrant as a blank check to expand a search by relying on an overly general description of the place to be searched.

2. Reasonable Particularity

The Fourth Amendment requires that the warrant must set forth the location of the place to be searched with *reasonable particularity*. Technical precision is not required in all cases. The degree of particularity which is reasonable depends on the nature of the place to be searched, and on the information that an officer could reasonably obtain about the location.

Example: In urban areas, a street address and, if applicable, an apartment number reasonably limit the discretion of the executing officer, and are reasonable to obtain. If the officer has probable cause to search a certain apartment as opposed to all apartments on the floor, the warrant should be restricted to the single apartment. If the officer cannot identify a particular apartment, then it is unlikely that there is probable cause to search the apartment in the first place. If the search is to be conducted in a rural area, courts necessarily take a more flexible view of whether a description is sufficiently particular. For instance, "a blue house with a trailer, with a broken mailbox, on highway 23A two miles from Tannersville" would be reasonably particular, whereas "a house two miles from Tannersville" would not be.

3. Applicability to More Than One Location

If the warrant describes a location with information as specific as one could reasonably expect to obtain, then it is sufficiently particular even though the warrant could actually apply to more than one location.

Example: In *Maryland v. Garrison,* 480 U.S. 79, 107 S.Ct. 1013, 94 L.Ed.2d 72 (1987), the warrant authorized a search of the entire third floor of an apartment building. Officers had probable cause to believe that illegal activity was being conducted in an apartment on the third floor, and they undertook an investigation to determine whether there was more than one apartment on the floor. An officer obtained information from the utility company and telephone company which appeared to indicate that the entire third floor consisted of one apartment. A look at the door buzzers outside the apartment building did not indicate how many apartments were on any particular floor. There were seven apartments listed in the four-story building. After entering the apartment building, the officers eventually found that there were two apartments on the third floor, with one door to both apartments, and a shared entryway. The Court held that the warrant was sufficiently particular as issued, even though as it turned out it authorized the search of two apartments rather than one. This factual overbreadth did not invalidate the warrant because the officer who obtained the warrant could not have been reasonably expected to know at the time of issuance that there were two apartments on the floor. The Fourth Amendment requires *reasonable* particularity, and accordingly allows for reasonable mistakes of fact. As the Court stated, "the validity of the warrant must be assessed on the basis of the information that the officers disclosed, or had a duty to discover and disclose, to the issuing magistrate."

4.   Problems of Execution

In executing the warrant, the police may commit error if it is clear that the warrant, even though sufficiently particular when issued, was not intended to cover a certain area. Thus, in *Garrison,* the officer could not execute the warrant if it was readily apparent before the search that there were two apartments on the floor instead of one. See *Kreines v. United States,* 959 F.2d 834 (9th Cir.1992) (warrant to search a house cannot cover an internally separate living area, marked with a different number, and leased out to a third party). However, under the circumstances of *Garrison,* where there was only one door to enter both apartments, the police could not have reasonably known that there were two apartments until both had been entered, and separate kitchens were found in each living area off the common entryway. Up to that point, the warrant was being properly executed since the Fourth Amendment allows for reasonable mistakes of fact. The Court in *Garrison* therefore held that evidence seen in plain view in the apartment not intended to be covered by the warrant was seized consistently with the Fourth Amendment. It concluded that the reasonableness of a searching officer's conduct depends on the information that becomes available as the search proceeds.

5.   Incorrect Address

One problem that arises with respect to particularity of location, especially in urban areas, is where the warrant gives the wrong address for the premises to be searched. For example, assume that there is probable cause to search an apartment in a building on the corner of Maple and Elm. The building's entryway faces Maple, and the officer who prepares the affidavit gives the address as Maple Street. But the actual mailing address is Elm Street. Can the warrant satisfy the particularity requirement even though it sets forth the wrong address?

a.   Technical Accuracy Not Required

Variances between the actual address and the address specified in the warrant do not per se invalidate the warrant. The warrant remains valid so long as there is sufficient information therein for the executing officer to know where to execute the warrant despite the wrong address; that is, so long as the executing officer's discretion is reasonably limited. Thus, if the warrant gives the wrong address, but describes the corner, the building, the color of the building, etc. sufficiently to distinguish it from other buildings, then there is no risk of an official's abuse of discretion, and the warrant will be deemed sufficiently particular as to location.

Example: A warrant authorized the search of defendant's home, and gave the street address as 1601 Marsh. "The premises were described as a light green house trailer, which faces north and has a concrete step and porch structure leading to the front door." The residence to be searched was actually 8300 Karleen. While facially these addresses seem widely disparate, on closer examination they are not. Karleen and Marsh Streets intersect. The defendant's business was on the southeast corner of the intersection, with the street address of 1601 Marsh. The business was located in a single story, cinder block building. Immediately behind and to the east of the business was the defendant's residence, a light green house trailer with a concrete step and porch structure leading to the front door. Thus, while the warrant misdescribed the address, the actual address described in the warrant was contiguous to the trailer, and both the trailer and the business at 1601 Marsh were owned by the defendant. Moreover, nobody could have mistaken the defendant's business for the premises to be searched. Any officer coming to that address would know that the warrant authorized the search of the trailer and not of the business. In light of the physical arrangement of the properties and the particular description of the defendant's home, the court upheld the warrant as sufficiently particular. *United States v. Ridinger*, 805 F.2d 818 (8th Cir.1986).

D. PARTICULAR DESCRIPTION OF THINGS TO BE SEIZED

The things to be seized, like the place to be searched, must be particularly described in the warrant. As with location, the rationale of the particularity requirement respecting things to be seized is to control the discretion of the executing officer. A general rummaging could occur unless the officer's goals are specifically delineated in the warrant. Without a particular description of the things to be seized, there is a risk that the officer will use the warrant as a general warrant to search a particular location, which is no less problematic than a general warrant to search several locations.

1. Reasonable Particularity

As with other particularity issues, the test of whether a description of things to be seized is sufficiently particular is one of reasonableness, determined by the information that police could reasonably be expected to know prior to the search. In order to have probable cause to seize something, there must ordinarily be some information which reasonably identifies it, although the degree of precision will depend on the facts and circumstances of each case.

Example: In theft cases, the courts have required that the warrant contain detailed descriptions of the property to be seized, including brand names. The rationale is that in order to obtain probable cause to believe something is stolen, the police must have developed a description of the property in their investigation, oftentimes particularized down to the serial number. This prior information must be used to limit the discretion of the officers who execute the warrant. For example, a warrant to seize "stolen clothing" from a clothing warehouse was held overbroad since it could be construed to authorize the seizure of every piece of clothing in the warehouse. The court reasoned that the police, in the course of their investigation leading up to probable cause, must necessarily have obtained a much more precise description of the clothing. *United States v. Fuccillo,* 808 F.2d 173 (1st Cir.1987).

2. Documents

Assuming probable cause to seize documents, a warrant allowing the seizure of "all documents, books and records" is obviously overbroad, since there is no limitation on the executing officer's discretion. On the other hand, especially with complex fraud cases, it is difficult for police to specifically describe all pertinent documents before the search. As a result, courts will generally find a warrant to be sufficiently particular if police have done all they reasonably could to limit the discretion of the officer who executes the warrant. The warrant must contain a substantive, subject matter limitation sufficient to control the discretion of the executing officer.

Examples: Officers have probable cause to believe that metamphetamines are being manufactured at a certain house. Documents and papers are in the house, which would tend to prove who resided there—thus implicating the residents in the crime. Examples of such papers would include utility bills, addressed letters, lease agreements, and the like. The warrant authorizes seizure of all "papers reflecting proof of residency, such as utility and telephone bills." This warrant is sufficiently particular since it is limited by subject matter, gives some examples, and sets forth a standard that a reasonable executing officer can evaluate.

Police officers have probable cause to believe that a doctor has been prescribing quaaludes to patients without a proper medical purpose. A warrant authorizing the seizure of "all patient records" is overbroad, since it would cover the doctor's entire medical practice. However, a warrant authorizing seizure of "all patient records where quaaludes were prescribed" is as particular as can be expected under the circumstances, and gives a clear standard for evaluation, thus limiting the discretion of the executing officer. The officers who obtained the warrant could not be expected to know in advance exactly which patients received quaaludes for proper medical reasons and which did not.

a. Document Searches Will Usually Be Extensive

Even if a search of documents is reasonably limited by a subject matter description in the warrant, the search will often require the inspection of thousands of documents to determine whether they fit the subject matter described. But this is not a problem under the Fourth Amendment so long as there is probable cause to search the files, and the officer's discretion to search and seize is as limited as reasonably possible. See e.g. *United States v. Hayes,* 794 F.2d 1348 (9th Cir.1986) (the fact that officers looked through 10,000 patient files is not problematic, since there was probable cause to search for distribution of controlled substances, and officers were allowed to seize only those records concerned with such substances).

b. Pervasive Criminal Activity

Ordinarily, a warrant authorizing the seizure of "all documents and records" or "all property" is patently overbroad. This will not be the case, however, if criminal activity on the premises to be searched is so pervasive that every document or piece of property is in fact connected to a crime. If a business is "permeated with fraud" so that no document is prepared for a legal purpose, a warrant authorizing the seizure of all documents on such premises will be found sufficiently particular. In such cases there is probable cause to seize every document, and no risk that the executing officer will abuse his or her discretion.

3.   Catch–All Clauses in the Warrant

The most difficult particularity problems arise where the warrant describes some items in detail, and then includes a catch-all clause—for example, a clause allowing the seizure of "any other evidence of the crime". These clauses become relevant at a suppression hearing when the Government attempts to uphold the seizure of items not specifically described in the warrant by arguing that the items were covered by the catch-all clause.

a.   Catch–Alls Must Be Qualified by Preceding Descriptions

Looked at independently, a catch-all clause in a warrant is no better at controlling police discretion than a warrant which is overbroad in its entirety. The mere fact that a catch-all clause is included within the same warrant as particular descriptions does not make a catch-all clause sufficiently particular. Consequently, courts find catch-all clauses to be overbroad unless they are somehow qualified by the particular descriptions that are set forth together with the catch-all clause in the warrant.

b.   Qualification by Reference to a General Crime Is Insufficient

Catch–alls are not made sufficiently particular by merely referring to the specific crime for which there is probable cause. Evidence of that crime can be far-ranging, and difficult for the executing officer to determine. The executing officer would essentially be left to his or her own devices to determine the scope and meaning of the relevant criminal statute. This leaves the officer too much discretion and is inconsistent with the particularity requirement of the Fourth Amendment.

Example: Catch-all clauses allowing the seizure of "other stolen property", other evidence of "narcotics trafficking" and other "misbranded drugs" have been struck down as overbroad.

c.   Must Be Qualified by Previously Described Property

To be sufficiently particular, a catch-all clause must be related to and qualified by previously described property, as opposed to a generalized criminal offense.

Examples: A warrant authorized the seizure of certain specified drugs that were cocaine substitutes. The court held that a catch-all clause allowing the seizure of "other cocaine substitutes" would be sufficiently particular, whereas a clause applying to "misbranded drugs" would not. The term "misbranded drugs" could apply to any drug, including, presumably, penicillin. *United States v. Storage Spaces,* 777 F.2d 1363 (9th Cir.1985).

A warrant authorized the seizure of a long list of documents which were pertinent to the fraudulent sale of a particular real estate lot. The warrant also included a catch-all clause covering "fruits and instrumentalities." The Supreme Court found the catch-all to be sufficiently particular, but only because it construed the clause as referring to the particular crime and particular lot previously mentioned in the warrant. *Andresen v. Maryland,* 427 U.S. 463, 96 S.Ct. 2737, 49 L.Ed.2d 627 (1976).

4. Severability

If some clauses in a warrant are sufficiently particular and other clauses are not, the overbroad clauses can be *severed* from those that are sufficiently particular. The warrant, and the search conducted pursuant to it, will then be evaluated on the basis of the valid clauses. If an item is covered by one of the valid clauses, then it is properly seized pursuant to the warrant even if the item is also covered by an overbroad clause such as a catch-all.

Example: Officers investigated a credit card fraud scheme and obtained a warrant to search the motel rooms of the suspects. The warrant described certain items to be seized with particularity, including "credit cards under miscellaneous names", and "bonds and notes." The warrant also contained a catch-all clause allowing the seizure of "any property or devices used or obtained through fraud operations." The officers seized many United States Savings Bonds with forged endorsements. The court held that the catch-all clause was impermissibly general, since it provided the searching officers "no reasonable guidance": the language did not limit the search to items readily identifiable with a particular transaction. Nonetheless, the search for and the seizure of the bonds was upheld, because that search and seizure did not depend on the catch-all for its validity. The warrant specifically described "bonds" in a prior clause. The court held that the particular descriptions in the warrant retained their validity and that the overbroad catch-all could be severed. *United States v. Holzman,* 871 F.2d 1496 (9th Cir.1989).

E. WARRANT CAN AUTHORIZE THE SEIZURE OF "MERE EVIDENCE"

It has always been the case that a warrant could authorize the seizure of the instrumentalities of a crime (such as a gun used for an armed robbery), the fruits of a crime (such as the money obtained in an armed robbery) and contraband (materials whose possession is prohibited by law, such as illegal narcotics). However, before 1967, the Court did not permit the seizure of items which were of evidentiary value only, such as a diary containing incriminating information. The rationale was that the Government had no valid property interest in such "mere evidence." See *Gouled v. United States,* 255 U.S. 298, 41 S.Ct. 261, 65

L.Ed. 647 (1921). In *Warden v. Hayden,* 387 U.S. 294, 87 S.Ct. 1642, 18 L.Ed.2d 782 (1967), the Court discarded the "mere evidence" rule, holding that the right to seize evidence did not rest on the Government's property interest, but rather on the Government's legitimate interest in solving crime. The Court also noted that nothing in the nature of property seized as evidence rendered it more private than property seized as a fruit or instrumentality of a crime. Consequently, the seizure of a robbery suspect's clothing, which had been identified by an eyewitness, was upheld. Federal Rule of Criminal Procedure 41(b) now specifically states that a warrant may be issued to search for and seize all evidence of a crime.

F. ISSUING WARRANTS AGAINST NON-SUSPECTS

Searches can be made on the premises of non-suspects, either pursuant to a warrant or an appropriate exception to the warrant requirement, so long as there is probable cause to believe that evidence will be found therein. This principle is a natural outgrowth from *Warden v. Hayden,* the case allowing the search for and seizure of "mere evidence". The state's interest in enforcing the criminal law and recovering evidence is the same whether the third party is culpable or not. Nothing in the language of the Fourth Amendment limits its scope to the premises of criminals. *Steagald v. United States,* 451 U.S. 204, 101 S.Ct. 1642, 68 L.Ed.2d 38 (1981) (police can search a non-suspect's home after obtaining a warrant to search for a suspect); *United States v. Ponce,* 947 F.2d 646 (2d Cir.1991) (if there is probable cause to believe that evidence of a crime is located on particular property, then a warrant may be issued and it is not necessary that the owner of the property be suspected of crime).

1.   No Special First Amendment Protection
The fact that the non-suspect is protected by the First Amendment creates no special protection against a search of the premises for evidence. For example, officers had probable cause to believe that pictures indicating the identity of certain persons involved in a crime would be located in the files of the Stanford Daily, a student newspaper. The officers obtained a warrant to search the files and conducted a search pursuant to that warrant. The Court upheld the search as supported by a warrant and probable cause, and rejected the newspaper's argument that the search was prohibited by the First Amendment. *Zurcher v. Stanford Daily,* 436 U.S. 547, 98 S.Ct. 1970, 56 L.Ed.2d 525 (1978).

2.   Statutory Protections for the Media
In response to *Zurcher,* Congress provided protection for the press in the Privacy Protection Act of 1980, which limits the Government's authority to conduct a search of journalists and news organizations. 42 U.S.C.A. § 200aa. Government agents may not search for the work product of the media, unless the newsgatherer is involved in the crime, or unless an immediate search is necessary to prevent the death or serious bodily injury of a human being. Documents are subject to search under similar circumstances and also when

there is reason to believe that serving notice by subpoena would result in the destruction of the documents, or when the newsgatherer has defied a court order to produce the documents. The statute also requires the Attorney General to promulgate regulations governing other sensitive searches which may intrude upon privileged relationships—such as law office searches.

V. EXECUTION OF SEARCH WARRANTS

The Fourth Amendment does not contain specific language directing law enforcement agents on the correct procedure with which to execute a warrant. However, the general clauses requiring probable cause and reasonableness have been interpreted as placing constitutional limitations on the manner in which agents perform those duties. The following section describes the constitutional and other limitations on time, manner, and scope for validly executing a search warrant.

A. TIME OF EXECUTION

Many jurisdictions have statutes or court rules providing that a search warrant must be executed within a fixed period of time (e.g. ten days). If law enforcement officers execute the warrant after that set time, the prevailing view requires evidence found in that search to be suppressed. *Sgro v. United States,* 287 U.S. 206, 53 S.Ct. 138, 77 L.Ed. 260 (1932); *Commonwealth v. Cromer,* 365 Mass. 519, 313 N.E.2d 557 (1974). Suppression as a result of violating a rule may not be constitutionally necessary. However, a constitutional violation may occur when the probable cause that gave rise to the search warrant has dissipated before the warrant is executed. See *United States v. Nepstead,* 424 F.2d 269 (9th Cir.1970). If there is no constitutional violation, some courts will not suppress evidence. Thus, in *State v. Miller,* 429 N.W.2d 26 (S.D.1988), the court held that evidence found in a search after the statutory 10 day rule need not be suppressed because probable cause still existed at the time the search was conducted and therefore "the letter, not the spirit, of the law was broken."

1. New Information

As stated above, a delay in executing the warrant may mean that the probable cause which existed when the warrant was *issued* is gone by the time the warrant is *executed.*

Example: In *United States v. Bowling,* 900 F.2d 926 (6th Cir.1990), the police conducted a search of premises pursuant to a warrant. Between the time the warrant was issued and the search conducted, the police had already searched the premises pursuant to the consent of the owner. That search had not uncovered any evidence. The court concluded that "where an initial fruitless consent search dissipates the probable cause that justified a warrant, new indicia of probable cause must exist to repeat a search of the same premises pursuant to the warrant." The court further stated that the question of whether "new indicia of probable cause" exists, absent exigent circumstances, is one for a neutral magistrate, rather than police officers, to decide. Compare *Wicks v. State,* 552 A.2d 462 (Del.1988) (although defendant informed police prior to search for a stolen gun that he had sold the evidence, probable cause remained as police were "simply not required to believe this statement").

2. Staleness

Sometimes a defendant may attempt to show that the separation in time between the issuance of the warrant and its execution has resulted in the information upon which probable cause was based to turn "stale." The argument is that the conditions which supported probable cause no longer exist at the time the warrant is executed. Such an argument is often difficult to make, however, because courts have held that a search warrant issued with a fixed time limit retains a presumption of validity throughout that period. *State v. Evans,* 815 S.W.2d 503 (Tenn.1991); *Williams v. United States,* 576 A.2d 700 (D.C.App.1990).

a. Relevant Factors

In assesssing whether probable cause has grown stale, the court will consider factors such as the nature of the evidence, and the type of alleged criminal activity in which the defendant is involved. Search warrants based on ongoing criminal activity are likely to survive a staleness claim, because the relevant facts will not ordinarily have changed between the date of issuance and the date of execution of the warrant. See *United States v. Allen,* 960 F.2d 1055 (D.C.Cir.1992) (warrant executed approximately 12 days following a controlled drug sale upheld as it was "reasonable for the police to assume * * * the house would continue to serve as a fixed and secure location for drug sales"); *State v. Germano,* 559 A.2d 1031 (R.I.1989) (probable cause does not grow stale during nine-day delay between informant's sighting of drugs and the execution of the warrant, because the drug operation had a "lengthy, if not indefinite, duration").

3. Anticipatory Search Warrants

Some lower courts have upheld search warrants based on "anticipatory" probable cause. The search warrant in such cases is grounded in the magistrate's determination that, if certain expected events happen in the future, probable cause will then exist to execute the warrant. Thus, in *United States v. Garcia,* 882 F.2d 699 (2d Cir.1989), the court upheld a warrant based on a future delivery of cocaine to a specific location. Noting that the warrant contained explicit conditions under which probable cause could be triggered, thus limiting the discretion of the police officers involved, the *Garcia* court found that the objectives of the Fourth Amendment would be better served by this initial judicial determination. The alternative was to

require the officers to wait for the delivery, at which point they would
probably conduct a warrantless search (due to exigent circumstances, consent,
etc.) that might later be overturned by a finding of insufficient cause.

4. Execution in the Nighttime

Slightly less than half the states restrict execution of searches to "daylight"
hours absent special circumstances; Fed.R.Crim. 41 restricts such searches to
daytime unless "reasonable cause" is shown. "Daylight" is generally defined
by specific hours in the state statutes; it encompasses the hours of 6:00 a.m.
to 10:00 p.m. according to local time in the Federal rule. The lower courts
have further delineated day and nighttime searches by distinguishing when
the search has actually begun. For example, in *State v. Valenzuela,* 130 N.H.
175, 536 A.2d 1252 (1987), the court upheld a search that began in the
daytime but continued long into the night. "It is the *entry* of the police in
the nighttime, *not* their mere presence, that is thought to call for particular
judicial authorization." See also *United States v. Young,* 877 F.2d 1099 (1st
Cir.1989).

a.   Constitutional Concerns

In *Gooding v. United States,* 416 U.S. 430, 94 S.Ct. 1780, 40 L.Ed.2d 250
(1974), the majority found it unnecessary to determine whether the
Fourth Amendment imposed any limitations on nighttime searches. The
Court held that a Federal statute relating to searches for controlled
substances, rather than a District of Columbia provision, governed the
search, and, thus, the District's requirement of a special showing of
"need" to search at night was not applicable. The constitutional issue
was not argued to the Court in *Gooding.*

b.   Dissent

The three dissenting judges in *Gooding* argued that the majority's
interpretation of the Federal statute, as imposing no special limitations
on nighttime searches, might actually conflict with the Fourth
Amendment. The dissenters argued that nighttime searches should be
subject to more substantial Fourth Amendment limitations than daytime
searches because nighttime searches are significantly more intrusive.
Using a balancing approach to satisfy what they believed was likely a
"constitutional imperative", the dissenters preferred a test of greater
showing of need—over and above the ordinary showing of probable
cause—to counter the greater intrusion of privacy.

c.   Lower Courts

Although the Supreme Court has never held that the Fourth Amendment
imposes special restraints on nighttime searches, lower courts have given
a certain amount of credence to the *Gooding* dissent when interpreting
statutory provisions concerning nighttime searches. Many courts require
a showing of some form of exigent circumstances before a nighttime

search can be authorized. See e.g., *United States v. Morehead,* 959 F.2d 1489 (10th Cir.1992) (noting that nighttime searches are related to the "reasonableness" issue of the Fourth Amendment but upholding the search as the evidence could have been destroyed during the night). But see *State v. Lewis,* 107 Idaho 616, 691 P.2d 1231 (1984) (Federal Constitution does not require a more rigorous showing of cause to justify the execution of a warrant at night).

5. Execution in the Absence of the Occupant

Although the Supreme Court has not spoken directly on the subject, it has indicated in dictum that a search is permissible in the absence of the occupant. *Alderman v. United States,* 394 U.S. 165, 89 S.Ct. 961, 22 L.Ed.2d 176 (1969). The lower courts have almost unanimously followed this position; a few courts have found it relevant to consider whether officers made any effort to locate the occupants of the premises before conducting a search in their absence. See *Commonwealth v. Prokopchak,* 279 Pa.Super. 284, 420 A.2d 1335 (1980) (noting that officers both notified a number of people to admit them into house, and also waited an additional 15 minutes past the time the occupants should have returned to the house before forcibly entering the premises under the reasonable assumption that no one was planning to arrive and voluntarily let the officers inside).

6. Covert and Surreptitious Entries

Officers sometimes may wish to enter a premises surreptitiously, so as not to notify the suspects that a search is being or has been conducted. A warrant issued to conduct a surreptitious search has been referred to as a "sneak and peek" warrant. In *United States v. Freitas,* 800 F.2d 1451 (9th Cir.1986), the court held that a warrant allowing surreptitious entry to scrutinize a drug lab operation, without any provision for post-search notice to the occupants, was constitutionally defective. The *Freitas* court reasoned that surreptitious entries should not be authorized except in circumstances of the greatest necessity, because such searches are unusually intrusive: "the mere thought of strangers walking through and visually examining the center of our privacy interest, our home, arouses our passion for freedom as does nothing else."

B. NOTICE REQUIREMENT

18 U.S.C.A. § 3109 provides that a law enforcement officer may break into premises to execute a search warrant "if, after notice of his authority and purpose, he is refused admittance or when necessary to liberate himself or a person aiding him in the execution of the warrant." This Federal "knock and announce" statute, as well as similar state statutes, codifies the longstanding common law rule of notice conditioning official entry to premises absent exigent circumstances.

1. **Rationale**
    The concept of requiring law enforcement officers to give notice before entering private premises is grounded in practical realities. Notice decreases the potential for violence as occupants are made aware of law officers' official purpose and presence. Prior announcement decreases the possibility of police mistakenly entering the wrong premises thereby subjecting innocent individuals to the shock and embarrassment of unannounced police entry. Notice allows for at least a minimal amount of time to prepare for official entry into the home. Lastly, notice provides occupants with the opportunity to voluntarily admit officers into their home, facilitating and speeding up the search process while, at the same time, minimizing the privacy intrusion and the possibility of property damage. See generally *Ker v. California,* 374 U.S. 23, 83 S.Ct. 1623, 10 L.Ed.2d 726 (1963).

2. **Constitutional Basis**
    In *Ker, supra,* police officers broke into the defendant's home without prior notice to make a warrantless arrest based upon the suspect's possession of marijuana. The state successfully argued in the California state courts that an entry without notice was permissible under a state statute that provided for exceptions to notice because of exigent circumstances. In a plurality opinion, four Justices found the officer's method of entry to be reasonable under the Constitution. Pointing both to the easy destruction of the narcotics, and to the possibility that the defendant knew the police were coming, thus making notice a useless gesture, the plurality held that the officers' actions were reasonable "in the particular circumstances in the case." Justice Harlan concurred in the result because he, alone on the Court, did not believe that the Fourth Amendment bound the states.

    a. **Dissent**
        The four dissenting judges in *Ker* explicitly stated that the Fourth Amendment was violated by police entries into private homes without notice unless one of three specific circumstances are shown: (1) the occupants are already aware of the officers' authority and purpose, or (2) the officers have a justifiable belief in imminent bodily harm, or (3) the officers have a justifiable belief that the suspects are attempting to escape or destroy evidence. The dissenters argued that the particular facts of *Ker* did *not* fall into any of the exceptions to the notice requirement and, thus, the officers' conduct was not reasonable under the Fourth Amendment.

    b. **Lower Courts**
        The lower courts generally agree that the *Ker* decision controls the execution of both search and arrest warrants. However, the courts split on whether the opinion actually established a constitutional requirement of notice before entering private premises absent exigent circumstances. While the dissent explicitly relied on the Fourth Amendment, the

plurality narrowly, and somewhat ambiguously, based its decision on the reasonableness of the officers' actions in following state law in that particular case. Thus, some courts have concluded that a majority of the *Ker* Justices did not address the issue of whether notice was constitutionally required prior to entering private dwellings. See *Commonwealth v. Goggin,* 412 Mass. 200, 587 N.E.2d 785 (1992) ("our knock and announce rule is one of common law which is not constitutionally compelled"); *State v. Anonymous,* 34 Conn.Sup. 531, 375 A.2d 417 (1977) ("[e]ntry without prior announcement does not render a search reasonable under the Fourth Amendment"). Other courts find that the Court assumed that the Fourth Amendment restricted entries without notice. See *United States v. Mueller,* 902 F.2d 336 (5th Cir.1990) ("Since *Ker,* most of the circuits have followed * * * the four-Justice dissent * * * that a violation of the "knock and announce" rule of section 3109 should also be a violation of the Fourth Amendment"); *United States v. Price,* 441 F.Supp. 814 (E.D.Ark.1977) (*Ker* establishes constitutionally required notice rule with exceptions).

c. **Section 3109**
    Federal courts disagree on whether a violation of the Federal "knock and announce" statute, 18 U.S.C.A. § 3109, is also a violation of the Fourth Amendment. Since the Federal statute does not govern the activities of state officers, the question whether evidence acquired by state officers who do not follow § 3109 should be excluded in Federal prosecutions turns on a constitutional analysis.

    Example: In *United States v. Moore,* 956 F.2d 843 (8th Cir.1992), the court upheld a no-knock search conducted by state officers using a state-authorized no-knock search warrant. The officers obtained the warrant based on a reliable informant's information that the suspect was involved in ongoing sales of "street-packaged" narcotics from his home, as well as from the officers' past experience with suspects' easily destroying similar evidence when the police announced their presence before entering premises. The court concluded that Federal law does *not* govern *all* aspects of state-acquired evidence presented in Federal prosecutions. Describing § 3109 as a statute "*more* restrictive than the Fourth Amendment", the court declined to suppress the evidence. But see *United States v. Mueller,* 902 F.2d 336 (5th Cir.1990) (court contends in dictum that a violation of § 3109 knock-and-announce rule is a violation of the Fourth Amendment, although it never reaches the constitutional issue as defendant failed to establish a prima facie claim that the notice rule was violated).

3. Manner of Entry

The notice requirement, whether mandated by statute or constitutionally required, generally is triggered when law enforcement officers forcibly enter private premises. The Federal statute requires that notice must be given before an officer can "break open any outer or inner door or window of a house." The Supreme Court has stated that the Federal statute is triggered whenever "officers break down a door, force open a chain lock on a partially open door, open a locked door by use of a passkey, or, as here, open a closed but unlocked door." *Sabbath v. United States,* 391 U.S. 585, 88 S.Ct. 1755, 20 L.Ed.2d 828 (1968). Most lower courts follow this comprehensive definition of forcible entry, some basing their analysis on Fourth Amendment grounds. See e.g., *People v. Gifford,* 782 P.2d 795 (Colo.1989). The courts do, however, allow a certain amount of leeway so that officers are capable of efficiently carrying out their duties. For example, in *Commonwealth v. McDonnell,* 512 Pa. 172, 516 A.2d 329 (1986), the court upheld the officers' entry through an unoccupied porch before making an announcement at the dwelling's inner door. The court reasoned that the policies of the notice requirement were better met if the officers made their announcement at a point where the inner occupants were more likely to hear them.

a. Open Doors

The courts are split on whether entry through an open door is a "breaking" that requires prior notice by police officers. Although the majority view is that an open door does not trigger the statutory requirement, see *United States v. Remigio,* 767 F.2d 730 (10th Cir.1985), some courts have required notice in particular cases. See *People v. Bradley,* 1 Cal.3d 80, 81 Cal.Rptr. 457, 460 P.2d 129 (1969) (although not every entry through an open door will require notice, an officer's entry through an open door at night when the occupant is apparently asleep violates the California statutory requirement).

b. Entry by Ruse

Courts generally agree that an officer's entry by ruse does not constitute a "breaking" requiring prior notice. See e.g., *United States v. Leung,* 929 F.2d 1204 (7th Cir.1991) (police acted reasonably when posing as hotel personnel to gain entry to defendant's room as they did not exceed scope of consent). Most of the concerns underlying the notice requirement are not present when officers are voluntarily admitted into a private dwelling. If trickery employed by the police is unsuccessful, then, absent exigent circumstances, the police remain subject to the notice requirement, which is *not* excused simply because their ruse failed. See *State v. Bates,* 120 Ariz. 561, 587 P.2d 747 (1978).

4. Compliance With the Notice Requirement

Assuming that an officer is preparing to enter premises in a manner that requires prior notice, the general common law procedure, codified in most jurisdictions, is that an officer must "give appropriate notice of his authority and purpose to the person * * * in apparent control of the premises to be searched." Model Code of Pre–Arraignment Procedure § 220.3(2) (1975). As one court noted, the proper focus is not on "magic words" spoken by the police but, rather, on how the policemen's actions are perceived by the occupants. *United States v. One Parcel of Real Property,* 873 F.2d 7 (1st Cir.1989) (officers' pounding on door and yelling out "police" sufficiently informs the occupants that the officers wish to enter either for purposes of search or arrest).

a.   Response by Occupants

Once the officers have knocked, and announced their identity and purpose, they are then required to wait for voluntary admittance or constructive refusal of admittance. Courts generally defer to the police assessment as to the amount of time they should wait before reasonably assuming that they are being refused admittance; in some cases, a delay of from 5–10 seconds has been found sufficient to permit police to forcibly enter the premises. See *People v. Saechao,* 129 Ill.2d 522, 136 Ill.Dec. 59, 544 N.E.2d 745 (1989) (court upholds search conducted when officer waited for 5–10 seconds after knocking and requesting admission; court notes the mid-morning timing of the entry); *United States v. Bonner,* 874 F.2d 822 (D.C.Dir.1989) (10 seconds sufficient when warrant was executed in a small apartment in the early evening). Sounds from inside the premises are frequently factored into the court's holding that occupants are preparing to keep the officers out. See, e.g., *State v. Ruscoe,* 212 Conn. 223, 563 A.2d 267 (1989) (clicking sound as officers approach reasonably assumed to be occupants locking the front door).

5.   Destruction of Evidence Exception

Police officers need not "knock and announce" their presence when they are acting to prevent the imminent destruction of evidence. But there is sharp disagreement as to what proof is necessary to satisfy this exception.

a.   "Blanket" Approach

Some courts are satisfied with a showing that the *type* of crime and evidence involved—e.g. gambling records or "street-package" narcotics— are easily and readily disposable. See *State v. Spisak,* 520 P.2d 561 (Utah 1974). The *Spisak* court points to the facts in *Ker* to bolster its argument that a "blanket rule" is all that is required. See also *United States v. Moore,* 956 F.2d 843 (8th Cir.1992) (*Ker* court adopted an exigent circumstances requirement but "was evenly divided on the question whether it can be satisfied by the general experience of law enforcement officers").

b. **Case-by-Case Approach**

However, there is resistance by some courts to the use of a "blanket rule" which does not take into account whether an emergency situation sufficient to excuse the knock and announce requirement exists on the particular facts of a case. For example, in *Commonwealth v. McCloskey*, 217 Pa.Super. 432, 272 A.2d 271 (1970), the court refused to uphold a supposedly exigent, unannounced entry to search a fifth floor college dorm room for five pounds of marijuana, where the room contained no toilet or other means for destruction of evidence, and there was no clandestine way in which to exit the dormitory. See *Moore, supra* ("a blanket rule * * * in all drug cases, regardless of whether the forms and quantities suspected to be present can be readily destroyed, is patently unjustifiable and would invite unnecessarily violent and intrusive execution of many search[es]").

6. **Danger of Bodily Harm Exception**

Officers are excused from the knock and announce announcement requirement when they reasonably believe that notice would put themselves or third parties in danger of bodily harm. See Model Code of Pre–Arraignment Procedure § 220.3(3) (1975). In order to trigger the exception, the courts generally require more than just the knowledge that an occupant possesses a gun. See *People v. Dumas*, 9 Cal.3d 871, 109 Cal.Rptr. 304, 512 P.2d 1208 (1973). The *Dumas* court pointed out that the concerns for safety which support the notice requirement are strengthened, rather than diminished, when officers are aware that a home owner possesses a firearm. A legally armed yet "startled and fearful householder" with no true intention of shooting a police officer might inadvertently harm a person supposedly breaking into his home. Although the court upheld the unannounced entry because of the particular facts of the case, it stressed that notice should be excused "only where the officers reasonably believe the weapon will be used against them if they proceed with the ordinary announcements." Other courts accept the *Dumas* rationale, allowing unannounced entry only when presented with facts more substantial than the mere knowledge that the occupant owns a gun. See e.g., *United States v. Nabors*, 901 F.2d 1351 (6th Cir.1990) (knock and announce requirement excused when the officers had suspicion of large-scale drug trafficking and were aware that the defendant owned an "array of firearms" and "habitually wore a bulletproof vest").

7. **Useless Gesture Exception**

The notice requirement is excused if officers reasonably believe that the occupants are already aware of their presence, authority, and purpose. See *United States v. James*, 764 F.2d 885 (D.C.Cir.1985) (sound of running feet following announcement of "police" justified officers' reasonable belief that stating purpose of visit would be a useless gesture). While the Justices in *Ker* disagreed on their interpretation of the specific facts in the case, the majority and dissent both agreed that prior knowledge by the occupants of the officers' presence and purpose would excuse the "knock and announce" requirement.

8. No–Knock Search Warrants

A minority of jurisdictions have statutory provisions for "no-knock" search warrants which are warrants that pre-determine the necessity of entering premises without notice. A federal "no-knock" statute, enacted to combat escalating criminal drug activity, was repealed in 1974 due to concerns over violations of privacy rights. The Supreme Court has not ruled on whether no-knock warrants are constitutionally permissible, and the lower courts are divided on the question. Compare *Parsley v. Superior Court,* 9 Cal.3d 934, 109 Cal.Rptr. 563, 513 P.2d 611 (1973) ("Unannounced entry is excused only on the basis of exigent circumstances existing at the time an officer approaches a site to make an arrest or execute a warrant.") with *State v. Meyer,* 209 Neb. 757, 311 N.W.2d 520 (1981) (no-knock warrant permissible "under the Fourth Amendment as construed in *Ker v. California*").

C. USE OF EXTRAORDINARY FORCE

It is sometimes necessary for police officers to use extraordinary force in order to enter the premises of certain types of suspected criminal enterprises. When officers use such force, questions arise of how much force is permissible, and who is to determine whether such force may be employed. In *Langford v. Superior Court,* 43 Cal.3d 21, 233 Cal.Rptr. 387, 729 P.2d 822 (1987), the court addressed both of these issues when it was confronted with the possibility of enjoining the Los Angeles Police Department from using certain destructive devices to gain entrance to what the police contended were "fortress-like" buildings where drugs were being prepared and sold. The court found that police guidelines were sufficient to control the discretion of officers' employing "flashbangs," described as low-impact explosive devices, concluding that such devices caused suspects only momentary disorientation and a minimal risk of physical injury. However, it held that the use of motorized battering rams posed a serious risk of physical injury and excessive property damage, and that battering rams could only be employed when prior judicial authorization is combined with exigent circumstances arising contemporaneously with an attempt to search the premises. See also *United States v. Stewart,* 867 F.2d 581 (10th Cir.1989) (court finds use of steel battering ram unreasonable under the circumstances).

D. SCOPE AND INTENSITY OF THE SEARCH

As previously discussed, the discretion of an officer operating pursuant to a warrant is limited by the constitutional requirement of particularity relating both to location and to the items to be seized. Similarly, the scope and duration of a search relate directly to the neutral magistrate's previous determination of probable cause, thus limiting the officers' discretion throughout the search.

1. **Search of the "Premises" Described in the Warrant**

   A warrant which authorizes a search of "premises" or a particular street number is generally deemed to cover, not only the basic residence, but also the grounds and other structures that are found within the curtilage of the house. "Curtilage" is defined as "the area to which extends the intimate activity associated with the sanctity of a man's home and the privacies of life." *Oliver v. United States,* 466 U.S. 170, 104 S.Ct. 1735, 80 L.Ed.2d 214 (1984). Courts commonly interpret this definition to include backyards, courtyards, and the acreage and associated buildings of farms and ranches as long as there is some indicia that such outer area is connected to the main dwelling named in the warrant. For example, in *Arnett v. State,* 532 So.2d 1003 (Miss.1988), the court upheld the search of a shed approximately 150–175 feet from the main house described in the warrant as within the curtilage of the home. In *United States v. Griffin,* 827 F.2d 1108 (7th Cir.1987), the court held that a warrant authorizing the search of the premises covered "the yards generally, both above and below the ground."

   a. **Scope of Curtilage After *Dunn***

      Justice Brennan's dissent in *United States v. Dunn,* 480 U.S. 294, 107 S.Ct. 1134, 94 L.Ed.2d 326 (1987), questioned the continued validity of searches of outlying buildings following the *Dunn* Court's narrowed definition of curtilage. In *Dunn,* the Court held that the search of a barn about fifty yards from a farm house—separated by inner fences but connected by a "well walked" and "well driven" path—was outside the constitutionally protected curtilage of the house and, instead, was subject to the "open fields" exception to the Fourth Amendment. Justice Brennan, writing for the dissent, argued that by "narrowing the meaning given to the concept of curtilage, the Court also narrows the scope of searches permissible under a warrant authorizing a search of building premises." Some courts have not found *Dunn* to be very restrictive. See *United States v. Sturmoski,* 971 F.2d 452 (10th Cir.1992) (court upholds search of trailer connected by path to building described in warrant as within curtilage); but see *State v. Townsend,* 186 W.Va. 283, 412 S.E.2d 477 (1991) (*Dunn* holding prohibits search of hog house no longer considered within curtilage of residence).

2. **Vehicles Within Curtilage of Described Premises**

   A vehicle may be searched if a warrant either authorizes a search of the vehicle alone, or describes both the vehicle and the premises on which the vehicle is located. *United States v. Motz,* 936 F.2d 1021 (9th Cir.1991). If the warrant merely authorizes a search of premises, the scope of the search will include any vehicles within the curtilage. *United States v. Gottschalk,* 915 F.2d 1459 (10th Cir.1990). But, the reverse is not true. If a warrant limits a search to a car alone, "authority to search a vehicle [will] not include authority to enter private premises to effect a search of a vehicle within those premises." *People v. Sciacca,* 45 N.Y.2d 122, 408 N.Y.S.2d 22, 379 N.E.2d 1153 (1978).

a.   Control by the Owner of the Premises
Some courts require that for vehicles to be covered by search warrants for the premises, they must not only be within the curtilage of the dwelling, but must also reasonably appear to be under the "control and dominion of the premises' owner." *United States v. Gottschalk,* 915 F.2d 1459 (10th Cir.1990). Thus, a car that does not appear to be under the owner's control, but is fortuitously parked in a suspect's driveway when a search takes place, is outside the scope of such a search. See *Dunn v. State,* 292 So.2d 435 (Fla.App.1974).

3.   Scope of Search Inside the Premises
"A lawful search of fixed premises generally extends to the entire area in which the object of the search may be found and is not limited by the possibility that separate acts of entry or entry or opening may be required to complete the search." *United States v. Ross,* 456 U.S. 798, 102 S.Ct. 2157, 72 L.Ed.2d 572 (1982). Thus, a valid search warrant need not (and likely could not) particularly describe every room, cabinet, or piece of furniture to be searched. Rather, the search of a house authorizes smaller, separate entries into rooms and containers that might feasibly contain the item(s) sought in order to "promptly and efficiently" complete the "task at hand." *Id.* See also *Miller v. State,* 751 P.2d 733 (Okl.Crim.1988) (search warrant extends to locked rooms on premises). Of course, a warrant may restrict a search to certain areas in the house; however, officers are entitled to walk through unnamed parts of a residence if reasonably necessary to gain access to the areas to be searched. See, e.g., *Commonwealth v. Young,* 6 Mass.App.Ct. 953, 383 N.E.2d 515 (1978) (reasonable for officers to walk through first floor apartment in order to reach basement apartment when the only outer entrance to basement was locked and barricaded).

4.   Personal Effects in Described Premises
"In general, a warrant authorizing a search of a premises justifies a search of the occupant's personal effects that are plausible repositories for the objects specified in the warrant." *State v. White,* 13 Wash.App. 949, 538 P.2d 860 (1975). This rule parallels the broader concept that the scope of a search extends to where the items described in the warrant may reasonably be concealed. See *United States v. Hughes,* 940 F.2d 1125 (8th Cir.1991) (a search of a coat pocket for a necklace is within the scope of a warrant authorizing the seizure of the necklace).

5.   Property of Visitors
There is a split in the courts as to whether the search of personal items of visitors are covered by a warrant which generally authorizes the search of a premises. Some courts have held that such items are subject to search so long

as they could contain the items described in the warrant. *United States v. Gonzalez,* 940 F.2d 1413 (11th Cir.1991) (court upholds search of a visitor's briefcase capable of concealing evidence sought in the warrant). Many courts, however, will not sustain a search based on the mere fact that the property could hold the items to be seized in the warrant. These courts hold that people not mentioned in a search warrant—and, by extension, personal effects worn or held or owned by those individuals—may not be searched absent exigent circumstances or a separate showing of probable cause. *State v. Worth,* 37 Wash.App. 889, 683 P.2d 622 (1984). See generally *Ybarra v. Illinois,* 444 U.S. 85, 100 S.Ct. 338, 62 L.Ed.2d 238 (1979) (police executing a search warrant cannot automatically frisk persons found on the premises to be searched).

a. Assessment of Ownership

Even the courts which require a stricter standard for searching the personal belongings of visitors do not require police officers to curtail or postpone searches in order to determine whether certain personal effects belong to the occupant or to a visitor. Instead, the courts generally hold that "the police are entitled to assume that all objects within premises lawfully subject to search under a warrant are part of those premises for the purpose of executing the warrant." *State v. Nabarro,* 55 Haw. 583, 525 P.2d 573 (1974); *State v. Kurtz,* 46 Or.App. 617, 612 P.2d 749 (1980) (no "duty of inquiry" as to ownership of an unidentified bag). The limitation on searching the personal effects of visitors becomes relevant only if the police "knew or should have known" that the items belonged to a "mere visitor". *State v. Thomas,* 818 S.W.2d 350 (Tenn.Crim.App.1991) (search of purse invalid when police *knew* that the purse belonged to visitor and had no facts upon which to believe that the visitor hid evidence in the purse).

b. Probable Cause and Exigent Circumstances

Even if a visitor's property is not covered by the warrant, a search of that property is permissible if there is probable cause to search the property and exigent circumstances to support a warrantless search. *United States v. Johnson,* 475 F.2d 977 (D.C.Cir.1973) (search of visitor's purse upheld when noises and delay preceding officers' entrance into apartment reasonably led officers to believe that the visitor was attempting to destroy or conceal evidence).

6. Search of Person Described in Warrant

A warrant may validly authorize the search of a person either exclusively or jointly with a search of a particular location. See *United States v. Ward,* 682 F.2d 876 (10th Cir.1982). If the search warrant authorizes a joint search, courts generally require that the search of the person take place on the premises contemporaneously with the search of the residence. In *People v. Kerrigan,* 49 A.D.2d 857, 374 N.Y.S.2d 22 (1975), the court refused to uphold the search of an individual the day after officers searched the suspect's place of employment. See also *Commonwealth v. Santiago,* 410 Mass. 737, 575 N.E.2d 350 (1991) (search warrant for both person and apartment does not authorize search "whenever and wherever the defendant was found"). On the other hand, search warrants issued exclusively to search individuals do not limit the location where such a search may take place. *United States v. O'Connor,* 658 F.2d 688 (9th Cir.1981).

7. Search of Person Includes Things Carried by the Person

A warrant authorizing the search of an individual extends to property carried by the individual at the time of the search. *State v. Worth,* 37 Wash.App. 889, 683 P.2d 622 (1984) (purse considered "readily recognizable personal effect" of the defendant such that it became "an extension of her person"). In *United States v. Graham,* 638 F.2d 1111 (7th Cir.1981), the court upheld the search of a suspect's shoulder bag conducted pursuant to a personal search warrant. The court reasoned that the human body does not contain convenient pockets in which to conceal personal items, and therefore people are compelled to carry such items both in the pockets of clothing and in larger containers such as pocketbooks and shoulder bags. It concluded that if such containers were not "identified with and included within the concept of one's person," the scope of a personal search would be so limited as to lose all practical meaning.

8. Search of Person Not Described in Warrant

"A warrant to search premises does not authorize officers to conduct a personal search of individuals found at the site but not described in the warrant." *State v. Worth,* 37 Wash.App. 889, 683 P.2d 622 (1984). The Supreme Court, in *United States v. Di Re,* 332 U.S. 581, 68 S.Ct. 222, 92 L.Ed. 210 (1948), stated in dictum that a search of a house or car pursuant to a warrant would not permit a search of its occupants. Thereafter, in *Ybarra v. Illinois,* 444 U.S. 85, 100 S.Ct. 338, 62 L.Ed.2d 238 (1979), the Court concluded that an individual's mere presence at premises being searched pursuant to a warrant should not automatically subject the individual to a search of his person.

a. Probable Cause

The *Ybarra* holding precludes officers from searching individuals who happen to be on the premises in which a warrant-based search is being conducted. However, an individual may be searched if the officers can show "additional independent factors" tying the suspect "to the illegal activities being investigated such that probable cause exists that evidence being sought is on the person of that individual." *State v. Broadnax,* 98 Wash.2d 289, 654 P.2d 96 (1982).

9. **Detention of Individuals While the Premises Is Searched**

It is generally accepted that officers can prevent individuals from leaving the premises "until the officer[s] can be certain that the detainee is not engaged in removing the property specified in the warrant", assuming that the evidence sought is of a nature to be "easily removed or concealed". *United States v. Festa,* 192 F.Supp. 160 (D.Mass.1960). In *Michigan v. Summers,* 452 U.S. 692, 101 S.Ct. 2587, 69 L.Ed.2d 340 (1981), the Court held that police could seize and detain an *occupant* of premises during the time it takes to properly execute a search warrant. The Court identified three important governmental interests in detaining such individuals: 1) preventing the possible flight of the individual if incriminating evidence is discovered; 2) minimizing the risk of harm to officers as the suspect might leave and then return with the intention of thwarting the success of the search; and 3) facilitating the orderly completion of the search by "open[ing] locked doors or locked containers to avoid the use of force that is not only damaging to property but may also delay the completion of the task at hand." The Court also pointed out that this type of detention was substantially less intrusive than a full-fledged arrest, and only minimally added to the public stigma of the search itself.

10. **Arrival While Search Is Conducted**

Some courts restrict the officers' ability to search individuals not specifically covered in a warrant by requiring a showing that the individuals had an opportunity at the commencement of the search to hide or conceal the evidence sought on their person. Thus, an individual under constant surveillance or who enters after the search has begun would be outside the permissible scope of such searches. See *Smith v. State,* 292 Ala. 120, 289 So.2d 816 (1974). However, under some circumstances, courts allow searches of individuals who arrive subsequent to the execution of the warrant. See *Logan v. State,* 135 Ga.App. 879, 219 S.E.2d 615 (1975) (search for gambling paraphernalia allows "search of individuals entering while the search of the house was going on").

11. **Intensity of Search**

The scope of a search is limited to places in which items described in the warrant may reasonably be concealed. Thus, it would be unreasonable to search for a handgun nine inches long "inside a utility bill or bank statement envelope, in a flat notebook, or inside any other container too small to hold the weapon." *Miles v. State,* 742 P.2d 1150 (Okl.Crim.1987). Within the permissible physical boundaries of a search, the type of procedure utilized is largely left to the discretion of the officers; warrants do not contain specific guidelines that the officers must follow when executing a search warrant.

12. **Length of Search and Damage to Premises**

Courts generally follow the longstanding common law rules that officers may remain on the premises only as long as is reasonably necessary to quickly and efficiently complete the search, and that officers must refrain from committing unnecessary property damage during the course of a search. See Model Code of Pre–Arraignment Procedure § 220(3), (5) (1975) (the scope of a search under a warrant is "only such as is authorized by the warrant and is reasonably necessary to discover the individuals or things specified therein"); *Tarpley v. Greene,* 684 F.2d 1 (D.C.Cir.1982) (officers must avoid unnecessary damage to premises). Although the courts generally give officers a certain amount of latitude as to how a search is conducted, deliberate attempts to widen the scope of a search may result in suppression of the evidence. *Purcell v. State,* 325 So.2d 83 (Fla.App.1976) (fruits of search suppressed when officers almost immediately saw the container mentioned in the warrant but nonetheless proceeded to thoroughly search the rest of the premises before seizing the container). However, if the warrant authorizes a search for an undisclosed amount of evidence such as "narcotics," the police are allowed to search through the entire premises, even if a large amount of contraband has already been found. *Hagler v. State,* 726 P.2d 1181 (Okl.Crim.1986) (police allowed to search for more drugs after finding a large amount of drugs, because the "scope of the warrant authorized a seizure of marijuana in general").

a. Assistance by Occupant
While the direction of an occupant might be helpful to the authorities, officers are not *required* to limit the scope of their search on the basis of where an occupant claims the contraband can be found. *United States v. Hughes,* 940 F.2d 1125 (8th Cir.1991) (although the occupant informed police that the necklace described in the warrant was in a jewelry box, the search of the bedroom was upheld as "the officers were not required to accept the word of [the defendant] and alter the sequence of their search").

b. Assistance of Private Individuals
Courts will sometimes permit officers to be accompanied by private citizens during a search in order to more quickly and efficiently execute the warrant. For example, in *United States v. Clouston,* 623 F.2d 485 (6th Cir.1980), the court upheld a search conducted with the assistance of two telephone company employees where the warrant authorized seizure of certain electronic devices used in surreptitious interception of wire communications. Warrants may even authorize outside assistance in the execution of a warrant from experts in a particular field. *People v. Noble,* 635 P.2d 203 (Colo.1981) (warrant authorizes observations by an expert on child abuse).

13. Flagrant Disregard of Warrant Limitations
If officers legally seize evidence pursuant to a warrant, but then continue the search beyond the limitations of the warrant, a question arises whether the previously obtained evidence should be excluded. For example, in *Waller v.*

Georgia, 467 U.S. 39, 104 S.Ct. 2210, 81 L.Ed.2d 31 (1984), the defendant objected to the introduction of wiretap evidence, claiming that the officers flagrantly disregarded the scope of the warrants. He argued that because the search so exceeded the warrant limitations, all of the evidence obtained by the officers should be excluded—even the evidence which was admittedly obtained within the scope of the warrant. In rejecting the defendant's claim, the Court distinguished between the conduct of an officer which exceeded the scope of a warrant "in place searched" from that which exceeded the scope of the warrant in the evidence to be seized. Noting that the officer's conduct in *Waller* fell into the latter category, the Court concluded that the lawfully seized evidence should not be suppressed—even presuming that the officers flagrantly disregarded the warrant limitations. Similarly, in *United States v. Decker,* 956 F.2d 773 (8th Cir.1992), the court held that although over 300 items were improperly seized, under *Waller,* the lawfully seized items were still admissible as the officers merely indulged in "excessive seizures".

*

III

EXCEPTIONS TO THE GENERAL FOURTH AMENDMENT REQUIREMENTS OF PROBABLE CAUSE AND A WARRANT

Analysis

I. INTRODUCTION

A. PRESUMPTIVELY UNREASONABLE
A search or seizure is presumptively unreasonable in the absence of a warrant based upon probable cause and particularly describing the place to be searched and the things to be seized. However, the Supreme Court has established many exceptions to those general requirements.

B. DIFFERENT REQUIREMENTS FOR EACH EXCEPTION
In the discussion of exceptions which follow, you must keep in mind which requirements are being excused by the particular exceptions. Some exceptions, like those for automobiles and for exigent circumstances, excuse the warrant requirement but still require the officer to have probable cause. Other exceptions, such as the stop and frisk doctrine, excuse both probable cause and a warrant. Some exceptions, such as the plain view exception, authorize warrantless seizures but not warrantless searches.

II. THE PLAIN VIEW DOCTRINE

A. SEIZURE WITHOUT A WARRANT
The plain view doctrine is an exception to the warrant requirement, which arises whenever the police are engaged in a legitimate investigative activity, and come across evidence not covered by any warrant. The plain view doctrine allows the police to seize an object in these circumstances if there is probable cause that it is evidence of criminal activity.

Examples: In executing a warrant to search for and seize guns, the officer walks through a house and sees a bag of white powder on top of the television. The officer can seize this white powder because he is operating in the course of legal activity, the powder is in plain sight, and there is probable cause to believe that the bag of white powder is narcotics.

While making a lawful traffic stop, the officer looks into the defendant's car and sees a sawed-off shotgun on the seat. A warrantless seizure of the gun is permitted under the plain view doctrine.

1. Justification
A warrant is not needed to make these seizures because the heart of the Fourth Amendment is already complied with: the officer came upon the incriminating object while within the scope of legal activity. Moreover, if the object is incriminating and in plain view, the extra intrusion of seizing it is not that great, and there is little to be gained from a warrant requirement at that point.

(S., C. & H.) Crim.Proc. BLS—8

B. LIMITATIONS ON THE PLAIN VIEW DOCTRINE

The justifications for the plain view doctrine—that the officer is already acting within the scope of permissible police activity and that there is probable cause to seize an object in plain view—suggest the limitations on the scope of the doctrine.

1. Officer Must Be Within the Scope of Lawful Activity

The plain view doctrine can apply to seizures in the course of both warrantless searches and searches conducted pursuant to a warrant. However, the officer must be lawfully located in a place from which the object can be seen, and must also have a lawful right of access to the object in order to seize it. So even though an officer sees contraband through a house window, he is not allowed to enter the house to seize it, unless there is an independent lawful means of access into the house.

Example: Officers enter an apartment in response to a call that a fight is going on and neighbors heard a shot. When they enter the apartment, they see a large brick of white powder on a table in the foyer. They seize the brick without a warrant. This seizure is permissible under the plain view doctrine since the officers were in the course of legal activity when they came upon the brick; the imminent risk to public safety allowed the initial intrusion under the exigent circumstances exception to the warrant requirement. However, if the officers entered the apartment, arrested the two occupants who were fighting in the foyer, and then searched the upstairs bedroom and discovered a large brick of white powder, then the plain view doctrine could not apply. The intrusion into the bedroom would not be justified by a warrant or an exception to the warrant requirement.

2. Plain View Doctrine Allows Warrantless Seizures, Not Warrantless Searches

Just because a briefcase is in "plain view" does not mean it can be *searched* without a warrant—even if there is probable cause to open it. The plain view doctrine does, however, allow a *seizure* if there is probable cause to believe that there is contraband or evidence in the container. Then the officer must obtain a search warrant to open the container. The term "seizure" refers to a deprivation of dominion or control over property while the term "search" refers to an invasion of privacy. The plain view justification for an exception to the warrant requirement is addressed to the concerns implicated by seizures rather than searches.

Example: Officers investigating the defendant on suspicion of drug dealing, and acting in the course of legitimate activity, come upon a leather camera lens case. They have probable cause to believe that the lens case contains cocaine. Under these circumstances, the plain view doctrine authorizes the *seizure* of the lens case, but not the search. See *United States v. Donnes,* 947 F.2d 1430

(10th Cir.1991) ("In cases involving closed containers * * * the plain view doctrine may support the warrantless *seizure* of a container believed to contain contraband but any subsequent *search* of the concealed contents of the container must be accompanied by a warrant or justified by one of the exceptions to the warrant requirement.").

a. Exception for Containers Which "Bespeak" Their Contents

A search of a container will be permissible under the plain view doctrine where the contents of the container are a "foregone conclusion" because the container "bespeaks its contents." For example, the configuration or the labelling of a container may be so distinctive as to indicate that contraband or an instrumentality of crime is contained therein. See *United States v. Eschweiler*, 745 F.2d 435 (7th Cir.1984) (police may open envelope that clearly contained a key which incriminated the defendant); *United States v. Morgan*, 744 F.2d 1215 (6th Cir.1984) (police may, without a warrant, open a bottle where the label on the bottle made it apparent that the bottle contained contraband).

3. Probable Cause Required for a Plain View Seizure

A third limitation on the plain view doctrine is that there must be probable cause that the object in plain view is evidence of a crime. The question of whether probable cause exists has already been considered in this outline, and the "fair probability" test discussed in that section is fully applicable to the question of whether an object in plain view can be seized.

a. Nexus to Criminal Activity

In some contexts, objects which would otherwise seem innocent may provide a fair probability of a connection to criminal activity. For example, assume that officers searching through a house used as a narcotics distribution center come upon twenty fur coats hanging in a closet. While there is nothing inherently incriminating in having fur coats, there is a fair probability under these circumstances that the coats are the fruits of drug proceeds, and therefore the coats can be seized without a warrant under the plain view doctrine.

4. Probable Cause Must Be Immediately Apparent, Without the Necessity of a Further Search

If the item must be searched and investigated in order to determine whether there is probable cause to seize it, such an investigation is itself a search which requires probable cause.

a. *Hicks*

An example of the requirement that probable cause must be immediately apparent without the necessity of a further search is found in the important case of *Arizona v. Hicks,* 480 U.S. 321, 107 S.Ct. 1149, 94

L.Ed.2d 347 (1987). In *Hicks,* Arizona police entered Hicks' apartment after a bullet was fired through its floor into the apartment below, injuring a man. The officers looked for the shooter, other victims and weapons. The apartment was in squalid condition. The officers noticed two new sets of stereo components in the apartment. Suspecting that the components were stolen, one officer moved a turntable in order to read its serial number. This led to information that the turntable had been taken in an armed robbery. The state conceded that there was no probable cause to seize the stereo components without first looking at the serial number. But it argued that the components could nonetheless be seized under the plain view doctrine.

b.   Ruling in *Hicks*

The Supreme Court rejected the state's argument and found the plain view doctrine inapplicable because the officers engaged in a search to determine whether there was probable cause to seize the stereo, and that search was beyond the permissible scope of the initial intrusion into the apartment. The Court held that such a search could not be conducted in the absence of probable cause. The fact that there was some suspicion, short of probable cause, that the stereos were stolen, did not justify the search of the turntable. Thus, the plain view doctrine does not permit an officer to search or seize an object in the absence of probable cause; probable cause is necessary to justify a search that precedes a plain view seizure.

c.   Immediately Apparent

The result in *Hicks* means that in order to seize something under the plain view doctrine, probable cause must be *apparent upon visual inspection*—no search, no matter how cursory, is allowed in order to determine whether probable cause exists. Courts refer to this as a further requirement of the plain view doctrine—that probable cause must be "immediately apparent". This might have been the case in *Hicks* if there had been several brand new stereos in boxes in the squalid apartment. Then there may well have been probable cause to believe that all the stereos were stolen.

C.   NO REQUIREMENT THAT THE PLAIN VIEW DISCOVERY BE INADVERTENT

In *Coolidge v. New Hampshire,* 403 U.S. 443, 91 S.Ct. 2022, 29 L.Ed.2d 564 (1971), a plurality of the Supreme Court stated that the plain view doctrine could not apply unless the officer's discovery of the object in plain view was "inadvertent". Apparently this meant that if the officer anticipated, before the intrusion, that he would find the object in the course of his search, then he could not rely on the plain view doctrine when he subsequently discovered the object. The "inadvertence" requirement was, however, rejected by the Supreme Court in the recent case of *Horton v. California,* 496 U.S. 128, 110 S.Ct. 2301, 110 L.Ed.2d 112 (1990).

1. **Facts of *Horton***

    The warrant in *Horton* authorized the search of Horton's house and the seizure of the proceeds of a robbery. The officer also had probable cause to believe that the weapons used in the robbery would be found in the search, but he did not seek a warrant for the weapons, and the warrant therefore did not authorize their seizure. In the course of the search for the proceeds, the officer, as he had expected, saw the weapons in plain view. The State admitted that this discovery was not inadvertent. The Court held that the weapons were properly seized under the plain view doctrine.

2. **Rationale of *Horton***

    The Court in *Horton* found the inadvertence requirement to be unsound on two grounds. First, the standard of inadvertence employed in *Coolidge* was impermissibly subjective. It invalidated a seizure based on the state of mind of the officer. But the *Horton* Court found that the officer's state of mind is irrelevant, because the question under the Fourth Amendment is whether the search or the seizure is objectively "reasonable".

    Second, the Court found unpersuasive Justice Stewart's reasoning in *Coolidge* that an inadvertence requirement was necessary to prevent warrantless general searches. The Court in *Horton* reasoned that an inadvertence requirement would do nothing to reduce the scope of a search or the number of places in which the officer could look for an item specified in a warrant or pursuant to an exception to the warrant requirement. In order to trigger the plain view doctrine, the officer must be in a lawful place to find the items which are described in a warrant or in the proper scope of warrantless activity. So rejecting the inadvertence requirement would not allow the officer to look in any more places or with any more intensity than he would otherwise be able to do. In fact, the officer would want to include all seizable materials in a warrant, since that could serve to expand the scope of a lawful search.

3. **Dissent in *Horton***

    Justice Brennan, in dissent in *Horton*, argued that the inadvertence requirement was necessary to guarantee that a warrant will control the things to be seized by the officer. He was concerned that, without an inadvertence requirement, an officer could deliberately omit certain items from the warrant application, secure in the knowledge that those items would later be found in plain view. Essentially, Justice Brennan thought that the warrant process would be made too easy if the officer only had to justify the seizure of one item as opposed to many. His concern was that the officer, if freed from the inadvertence requirement, would act with uncontrolled discretion in determining the things to be seized.

D. PLAIN TOUCH

If an officer, acting in the course of lawful activity, can determine by touch that an object is evidence or contraband, can he seize the object? In the recent case of *Minnesota v. Dickerson,* ___ U.S. ___, 113 S.Ct. 2130, 124 L.Ed.2d 334 (1993), the Court answered this question in the affirmative. In *Dickerson,* an officer, in the course of a stop and frisk permitted by the *Terry* doctrine, frisked the suspect and felt a small, hard, pea-shaped object in the suspect's shirt pocket. At the suppression hearing, the officer testified that when he patted Dickerson down, he examined the object with his fingers "and it slid and it felt to be a lump of crack cocaine in cellophane." Since the suspect had left a house known to be a place for drug activity, the officer concluded that there was probable cause to believe that the pea-shaped object was crack cocaine, and pulled the object (which was indeed crack) from the suspect's pocket. This seizure would not have been permitted under the *Terry* doctrine itself, because a *Terry* frisk is only permitted to the extent necessary to uncover weapons.

1. Rationale

The Court in *Dickerson* stated that the plain view doctrine "has an obvious application by analogy to cases in which an officer discovers contraband through the sence of touch during an otherwise lawful search." Like the plain view doctrine, if an officer determines probable cause by sense of touch while within the scope of lawful activity, the seizure of the object should be permissible because "there has been no invasion of the suspect's privacy beyond that already authorized by the officer's search". The Court rejected the reasoning of the lower court which distinguished plain touch from plain view on the ground that touch was less reliable than sight. The Court stated: "Even if it were true that the sense of touch is generally less reliable than the sense of sight, that only suggests that officers will less often be able to justify seizures of unseen contraband. Regardless of whether the officer detects the contraband by sight or touch, however, the Fourth Amendment's requirement that the officer have probable cause to believe that the item is contraband before seizing it ensures against excessively speculative seizures."

2. Touch Cannot Be Beyond the Scope of Legal Activity

Even though there is now a plain touch exception to the warrant requirement, it must be remembered that the touching must be within the scope of lawful activity. While the Court in *Dickerson* validated the plain touch exception, it also found that the exception was not applicable under the facts presented. This was because the officer did more than merely touch the object in the course of a lawful *Terry* frisk. Rather, he pushed and prodded the object in order to determine whether it was contraband. Such an aggressive procedure was held to be beyond the limited frisk authorized by *Terry.* Accordingly, the incriminating nature of the object was not immediately apparent under *Hicks, supra,* and the Court therefore found that the cocaine was illegally obtained.

III. WARRANTLESS ARRESTS

A. NO WARRANT REQUIRED FOR A PUBLIC ARREST

In *United States v. Watson,* 423 U.S. 411, 96 S.Ct. 820, 46 L.Ed.2d 598 (1976), the Court held that the Fourth Amendment did not require an officer to obtain a warrant before making a public arrest. This was so even if the officer could easily have obtained the warrant without jeopardizing the arrest. Thus, for public arrests, the officer can determine for himself whether probable cause exists to support the arrest.

1. What Is at Stake

In a case like *Watson,* the defendant has little incentive to contend that his arrest was illegal and therefore he cannot be tried. An illegal arrest does not preclude a prosecution. See *United States v. Crews,* 445 U.S. 463, 100 S.Ct. 1244, 63 L.Ed.2d 537 (1980). Rather, the defendant is arguing that because of the illegal arrest, the evidence that was obtained as a result of the arrest should be excluded as the fruit of the poisonous tree. For example, in *Watson,* the defendant sought to suppress evidence that was obtained from him in a search incident to the arrest. Watson's argument was unsuccessful because the Court held that there was no poisonous tree—that the arrest was permissible without a warrant.

2. Rationale of *Watson*

The majority in *Watson* relied heavily on the premise that warrantless arrests were permissible under the common law. The Court also used a utilitarian analysis and concluded that the benefits of a warrant requirement (i.e. the protection of citizens' privacy interests) were outweighed by the costs to law enforcement of having to obtain warrants for public arrests.

3. Dissent

Justice Marshall, joined by Justice Brennan, asserted that the majority's reference to practice under the common law was flawed, because, while the common law permitted warrantless felony arrests, only the most serious crimes were considered felonies. Justice Marshall therefore argued that common law practice could not be automatically transposed to the much broader category of modern felonies. Justice Marshall was also unimpressed with the burdens that would be imposed by a warrant requirement for public arrests.

4. Post–Arrest Determination of Probable Cause

While a warrantless public arrest is permissible upon an officer's determination that probable cause exists, the Supreme Court has recognized that the officer's determination of probable cause may be erroneous because the officer is in "the competitive enterprise of ferreting out crime". Therefore, the Court in *Gerstein v. Pugh,* 420 U.S. 103, 95 S.Ct. 854, 43 L.Ed.2d 54 (1975), held that if a citizen is arrested without a warrant, he has the right to a prompt post-arrest determination of probable cause by a magistrate or judge.

a. **Much Like a Pre-Arrest Warrant Procedure**
The Court in *Gerstein* stressed that the Government was not required to provide a full-blown adversary hearing for a post-arrest determination of probable cause. Thus, protections such as the right to counsel or the right to confrontation are not required. The intent in *Gerstein* is to provide the citizen with essentially the same protection after an arrest as the citizen would have received if the officer had obtained an arrest warrant.

b. **Prompt Hearing Is Required**
The role of a post-arrest determination of probable cause is to keep the damage from an erroneous arrest to a minimum. The Court in *Gerstein* therefore held that a citizen is entitled to a "prompt" post-arrest determination of probable cause if the citizen was arrested without a warrant. In *County of Riverside v. McLaughlin,* __ U.S. __, 111 S.Ct. 1661, 114 L.Ed.2d 49 (1991), the Court defined "prompt" as "reasonably prompt." The Court stated that a 48 hour delay between arrest and a *Gerstein* hearing would be presumed reasonable. Any delay beyond 48 hours would be presumed unreasonable, and the state would have to present compelling circumstances to explain the delay. The Court specifically held that the state could delay a *Gerstein* hearing—so long as it was provided within the presumptively reasonable 48 hour period—in order to consolidate such a hearing with other preliminary proceedings such as a bail hearing or an arraignment. In other words, the *Gerstein* hearing need not be held at the first practicable opportunity; the state is allowed some flexibility to create efficient pre-trial procedures.

B. WARRANT REQUIRED FOR AN IN–HOME ARREST
In *Payton v. New York,* 445 U.S. 573, 100 S.Ct. 1371, 63 L.Ed.2d 639 (1980), the Court held that the Fourth Amendment prohibited the police from arresting the defendant in his home without a warrant, in the absence of exigent circumstances.

1. **Distinguished From *Watson***
The essential distinction between *Payton* and *Watson* is that an in-home arrest is a greater intrusion on privacy than a public arrest. In the course of making an in-home arrest, the officer must enter into an area which has traditionally been accorded the highest protection. As the Court has stated, entry into the home is the "chief evil" at which the Fourth Amendment is directed. The warrant requirement in *Payton* is not intended to protect the citizen from being wrongly arrested; rather, it is intended to protect the citizen from having his home searched in the absence of probable cause to arrest him.

2. ***Payton* Violation Constitutes Illegal Search, Not an Illegal Arrest**
It follows that when an officer has probable cause and arrests the defendant in his home without exigent circumstances, the officer has conducted an illegal search of the home by entering it to seize the arrestee. But the arrest itself is not illegal presuming it was made with probable cause. This was made plain in *New York v. Harris,* 495 U.S. 14, 110 S.Ct. 1640, 109 L.Ed.2d 13 (1990), where the officer arrested the defendant in his home without a warrant. Harris was subsequently taken down to the police station, where he confessed. He moved to suppress the confession as "the fruit of the poisonous tree". But the Supreme Court held that the confession was properly admitted, because there was no connection between the *Payton* violation and the subsequent confession. The Court stated that "the rule in *Payton* was designed to protect the physical integrity of the home". It was not intended to protect defendants who are arrested with probable cause.

a. **Consequences of an Illegal *Payton* Search**
While a violation of *Payton* does not result in an illegal arrest, it does result in an illegal search of the home. Therefore, any information that the officer discovers during such a search is illegally obtained and subject to exclusion from trial. Moreover, in a case like *Harris,* if the officers used evidence obtained from the house during a warrantless arrest as a means by which to obtain a subsequent confession, then the confession would probably be subject to exclusion as the "fruit of the poisonous tree". That was not the case under the facts of *Harris* however.

3. **When Is an Arrest Made in the "Home"?**
Given the bright-line distinction between home arrests, which require a warrant, and public arrests, which do not, it becomes important to determine whether an arrest is made in the home or in public.

a. **Doorway Arrests**
Where the defendant is arrested upon answering the door to his home, courts have split on whether the arrest occurs in the home or in public. Some courts have stated that if the defendant is ordered to open the door under a lawful claim of authority, and is arrested upon opening the door, then the arrest occurs in the home and a warrant is required. See *United States v. Winsor,* 846 F.2d 1569 (9th Cir.1988). Other courts hold that if the officers remain outside the doorway and inform the defendant that he is under arrest, then the arrest is made in public. This view leads to difficult fact questions where the officer subsequently enters the home; if the arrest was made before the physical entry, then the entry can be justified as incident to the arrest and information discovered during the incident search will be considered legally obtained. However, if the arrest is made after the entry, then there has been a *Payton* violation, and the information discovered during the entry is illegally obtained. See *United States v. Berkowitz,* 927 F.2d 1376 (7th Cir.1991)

(remanding to determine whether the officers informed the defendant that he was under arrest before or after entering his home). The courts which hold that a doorway arrest constitutes an arrest in the home do not have to deal with such fine-line distinctions.

b. Common Hallways
If the arrest is made in a common hallway outside the defendant's apartment, then the arrest is treated as a public arrest which does not require a warrant. See *United States v. Holland,* 755 F.2d 253 (2d Cir.1985) (public arrest where the defendant answers the buzzer at the outside door to his apartment building, while standing in a common hallway).

c. Homeless Persons
Some courts have held that the arrest of a homeless person cannot violate *Payton,* even if the arrest occurs in a place which the person calls "home". See *United States v. Ruckman,* 806 F.2d 1471 (10th Cir.1986) (warrantless arrest of defendant in a cave on Government-owned property did not violate *Payton*). Increasingly, however, courts have been sympathetic to the privacy interests of homeless persons, and have begun to hold that the term "home" must be flexibly applied to include a public area in which a homeless person has established a living space. See e.g. *Community for Creative Non–Violence v. Unknown Agents of U.S. Marshals Service,* 797 F.Supp. 7 (D.D.C.1992) (*Payton* applies to arrests conducted in a homeless shelter).

d. Hotels and Motels
The protections against warrantless intrusions into the home announced in *Payton* apply with equal force to a properly rented hotel or motel room during the rental period. *United States v. Morales,* 737 F.2d 761 (8th Cir.1984). However, this is only the case so long as the person has rightful possession of the room. If the rental period has terminated, or if the person has been rightfully rejected from the premises, then the premises can no longer be considered a "home". *United States v. Larson,* 760 F.2d 852 (8th Cir.1985).

e. Houseboats, Mobile Homes, etc.
Relying on cases dealing with searches of motor vehicles and boats, the courts have held that *Payton* does not require officers to obtain an arrest warrant before entering a houseboat, car, or motor home to effectuate an arrest. *United States v. Hill,* 855 F.2d 664 (10th Cir.1988).

4. Arrest in the Course of Executing a Search Warrant
If an officer has a valid search warrant, an arrest of the defendant in his home during the course of that search is valid even though the officer does not also have an arrest warrant. The rationale is that the evil with which

Payton is concerned (the warrantless search of the home in the course of effectuating an arrest) is nullified by the officer having obtained a valid search warrant. See *Mahlberg v. Mentzer,* 968 F.2d 772 (8th Cir.1992).

C.   SEARCH WARRANT IS REQUIRED FOR AN ARREST IN THE HOME OF A THIRD PARTY

An arrest warrant authorizes an arrest of a particular person, but it does not specify the particular places in which the arrest can be effectuated. In *Payton,* the Court noted that an arrest warrant affords less protection than a search warrant, because a search warrant must describe a particular place in which the search is to be conducted. The Court did hold, however, that officers armed with an arrest warrant could only enter the suspect's home if "there is reason to believe that the suspect is within". But this factual standard need not be demonstrated to a magistrate; *Payton* leaves it to the officer executing the arrest warrant to determine whether there is "reason to believe the suspect within the home".

1.   Arrest Warrant Not Sufficient if the Suspect Is in the Home of Another

In *Steagald v. United States,* 451 U.S. 204, 101 S.Ct. 1642, 68 L.Ed.2d 38 (1981), the Court held that an arrest warrant was insufficient to authorize the arrest of a suspect in the home of another person. The Court stated that in the absence of exigent circumstances or consent, a search warrant must be obtained to look for the suspect in the home of a third party. That is, a magistrate must determine whether there is probable cause to believe that the suspected is located in the home of a third party.

2.   Rationale of *Steagald*

The Court reasoned that an arrest warrant could not protect the privacy interests of a third party homeowner, since the arrest warrant was not based on any judicial determination that there was probable cause to search for the suspect in the third-party's home. The Court was concerned that a contrary rule would invite abuse: "Armed solely with an arrest warrant for a single person, the police could search all the homes of that individual's friends and acquaintances."

3.   Distinction From *Payton*

In a case like *Payton,* there is a risk of error in the execution of an arrest warrant, i.e. that the officers may determine that there is reason to believe Payton is at home when in fact he is not. The Court determined that this risk of error did not justify review by a magistrate. In *Steagald,* there was the same risk of error—that officers may determine there is probable cause that the suspect is in the home of a third party when in fact he is not. However, the risk of error is more grave in *Steagald* because the error could be made in any and every house that the officer chooses to search. In *Payton,* the risk of erroneous entry is limited to a discrete number of places; in *Steagald,* there is a risk that an arrest warrant can be used as a general warrant to search any house in the community. Consequently, this much greater and more pervasive risk of erroneous entry required a magistrate's review.

4.   Is the Suspect Living at or Visiting the Premises?
After *Steagald,* it is important to determine whether the suspect lives at the premises (in which case an arrest warrant is sufficient), or whether he is merely visiting there (in which case a search warrant is required). Courts have looked to how long and how consistently the suspect has stayed at the premises, whether the suspect is responsible for utilities, and other indicia of permanent residence. See e.g. *Perez v. Simmons,* 859 F.2d 1411 (9th Cir.1988) (staying over at the premises a few days a month does not indicate that it is the suspect's home).

5.   Who Has Standing to Object to the Lack of a Search Warrant?
In *Steagald,* the officers entered Steagald's home with a warrant to arrest the suspect Lyons. In the course of effectuating the arrest, the officers discovered evidence which was used against Steagald at trial. The Court held that the evidence should have been suppressed because Steagald's Fourth Amendment rights were violated in the absence of a search warrant. It follows from this reasoning that Lyons, the suspect, would have no standing to object to the lack of a search warrant, since *Steagald* was concerned with the privacy rights of the third-party homeowner. See *United States v. Underwood,* 717 F.2d 482 (9th Cir.1983) (*Steagald* addressed only the right of a third party not named in the arrest warrant to the privacy of his or her home; this right is personal and cannot be asserted vicariously by the person named in the arrest warrant).

a.   Anomaly
It would be anomalous to allow the suspect to challenge the lack of a search warrant when he is arrested in a third party's home. Such a rule would mean that the suspect would be entitled to demand a search warrant when arrested in the home of another, while he could only demand an arrest warrant when arrested in his own home. It would also be anomalous in that the suspect would be entitled to greater protection from arrest in the third party's home (a search warrant) than the third party would have if arrested in his own home (an arrest warrant). For these reasons, the courts have held that the suspect has no right to challenge the lack of a search warrant when he is arrested in the home of a third party. See *United States v. Kaylor,* 877 F.2d 658 (8th Cir.1989) ("Kaylor cannot claim any greater Fourth Amendment protection in the Lindgren home than he possessed in his own home.").

b.   Can a Visitor Object to the Lack of an Arrest Warrant When Arrested in a Third Party's Home?
In *Minnesota v. Olson,* 495 U.S. 91, 110 S.Ct. 1684, 109 L.Ed.2d 85 (1990), the Court held that a defendant had standing to object to his

warrantless arrest where it occurred in an apartment in which he was an overnight guest. However, what if the suspect is not an overnight guest, but is rather merely temporarily visiting the premises of a third party? Can he object to a warrantless arrest under *Payton,* or is it as if he is being arrested in a public place, wherein he has no expectation of privacy? Courts have recently held that a temporary visitor has no standing to object to the lack of an arrest warrant when arrested in a third party's home. See *United States v. McNeal,* 955 F.2d 1067 (6th Cir.1992) (since the defendant was not even an overnight guest, his arrest in the home of another occurs in what amounts to a public place, and therefore no arrest warrant is required).

c.   **Third Party Has Standing, but What Is the Remedy?**
Of course, if the officers enter a third party's home to arrest the suspect, and they have no search warrant, the arrestee has no complaint, but the homeowner does have standing to claim a Fourth Amendment violation. But if the officers neither obtain evidence against the third party homeowner, nor are concerned with doing so, the only remedy that the homeowner will have is a civil action. Thus, the *Steagald* search warrant requirement is subject to evasion by officers who are focussing on the suspect rather than on the homeowner.

IV. EXIGENT CIRCUMSTANCES

A.   INTRODUCTION
Police are not required to obtain a warrant if exigent circumstances exist. However, while exigent circumstances provide an exception to the warrant requirement, officers operating under this exception must still satisfy the probable cause requirement. For example, if exigent circumstances exist, officers can enter a person's home to arrest him without a warrant. But the officers still must have probable cause for the arrest.

1.   **Rationale**
The exigent circumstances exception is based on the fact that it takes time to obtain a warrant, and in some cases, imminent risks will be created during the delay caused by the warrant process. Certain risks resulting from the delay in obtaining a warrant are so severe that in order to avoid them, the Fourth Amendment's preference for obtaining a warrant is excused.

2.   **Types of Risks Which Excuse the Warrant**
Generally speaking, the risks that trigger the exigent circumstances doctrine include those stemming from *hot pursuit* of a suspect, risks to *public safety,* and the risk of *destruction or loss of evidence.*

B. HOT PURSUIT

If officers are in hot pursuit of a suspect, this will excuse an arrest warrant where one is otherwise required, and it will also excuse a search warrant where a search of an area must be conducted in order to find and apprehend the suspect. The rationale is that it is unrealistic to expect police officers to stop in the middle of a chase and resort to the warrant process. To do so could allow the suspect to get away and thus render the warrant meaningless. The delay of obtaining a warrant could also allow the suspect to destroy evidence or to create a dangerous situation for police officers or members of the public.

> *Example:* The leading hot pursuit case in the Supreme Court is *Warden v. Hayden,* 387 U.S. 294, 87 S.Ct. 1642, 18 L.Ed.2d 782 (1967). Officers pursued a robbery suspect into what was subsequently determined to be the suspect's house. The suspect's wife answered the door, and the police entered the house to search for the suspect. In the course of looking for him, they also looked for weapons which he might have concealed during the pursuit. The officers found incriminating clothing in a washing machine. The Court held that the warrantless search was justified by the "hot pursuit" exception. The fact that the officers found clothing as opposed to weapons in the washing machine was not problematic, since the officers had the right, in these emergency circumstances, to search the washing machine to look for weapons, and thus the seizure of the clothing was permissible under the plain view doctrine.

1. Suspect Must Be Aware of Pursuit

The "hot pursuit" exception is based on the fact that the suspect, knowing that he is being pursued, may seek to escape, or to destroy evidence or create a threat to public safety. It follows that the "hot pursuit" exception cannot apply where the suspect is unaware that he is being pursued by police officers. If the "hot pursuit" exception were based only on how "hotly" the officers were "pursuing" a suspect, then it could apply in virtually every case.

> *Example:* In *Welsh v. Wisconsin,* 466 U.S. 740, 104 S.Ct. 2091, 80 L.Ed.2d 732 (1984), officers were called to the scene of a car which had been driven into a ditch. Eyewitnesses told the officers that the driver had been driving erratically, and had walked away from the scene. The officers expeditiously went to the address listed on the vehicle registration, and arrested Welsh in his home for driving while intoxicated. The Court held that the "hot pursuit" exception could not apply in these circumstances, since Welsh was never aware until he was arrested that he was being pursued by police officers. There was no semblance of a chase.

C. RISK TO PUBLIC OR POLICE SAFETY

Even in the absence of hot pursuit of a suspect, there may be circumstances in which the police or the public would be harmed in the time it takes to obtain a warrant. If so, the police are excused from obtaining one. For example, if officers hear screams and shooting from an apartment, or if officers have reason to believe that the health and safety of a child is in imminent danger, they are not required to obtain a warrant before entering the premises. See e.g. *State v. Boggess,* 115 Wis.2d 443, 340 N.W.2d 516 (1983) (warrantless entry permitted to investigate reliable report of child abuse).

1. Government Must Show an Imminent Risk to Public Safety

The warrant requirement will not be excused unless the Government can establish facts which indicate that the officers faced an imminent risk to public or police safety. The Government must show that the risk was substantial, and was likely to arise during the delay attendant to obtaining a warrant. Broad, conceptual arguments that "public safety" was at stake will not do.

Example: In *Welsh v. Wisconsin, supra,* the State argued that the officers' warrantless arrest of Welsh in his home was required because Welsh represented a threat to public safety, in that he was intoxicated and had recently left his car in a ditch. Essentially, the State made the broad argument that intoxicated drivers present a risk to public safety, which should excuse the warrant requirement. The Court rejected this broad argument and noted that on the facts, Welsh presented no *imminent risk* to public safety. At the time of his arrest, he was sitting in his home and there was no indication that he was going out to drive while intoxicated.

2. Fire Scenes

When a building is on fire, firefighters may enter without a warrant in the name of public safety. In *Michigan v. Tyler,* 436 U.S. 499, 98 S.Ct. 1942, 56 L.Ed.2d 486 (1978), the Court extended this principle and held that firefighters and inspectors could remain on the premises for a reasonable time in order to investigate the cause of the fire. However, the Court held that subsequent entries made days and weeks after the fire required a warrant, because these entries were "detached from the initial exigency".

D. DESTRUCTION OR LOSS OF EVIDENCE

The ground of exigency most often invoked is that in the time it would take to obtain a warrant, there is an imminent risk of destruction or loss of evidence.

Example: In *United States v. Riley,* 968 F.2d 422 (5th Cir.1992), officers were aware that a drug deal had been arranged from a certain house. They placed the house under surveillance. They observed a person leaving the house carrying a white bag. Two officers followed this person as he drove to a hotel where the drug deal was to be consummated. The person who was followed, subsequently determined to be Terry Moore, was arrested on a drug charge. The white bag contained cocaine. Moore informed the officers that there was a large sum of money, a gun, and another person at the house from which he came. Officers also discovered that Moore was carrying a cellular phone. The commanding officer then dispatched nine officers to the house. They forced open the door, and discovered Riley, and incriminating evidence, in the house. The court held that the warrantless entry was justified. It stated that "the presence of a cellular phone indicated to the officers that Moore was going to report back and failure to call back or return would alert the other occupant that something had gone wrong." The court also emphasized that the evidence, narcotics, was easily destructible.

1. Factors Relevant to Whether an Imminent Risk of Destruction of Evidence Exists

Courts have set forth several factors which are considered relevant to whether the officers faced an imminent risk of destruction of evidence. None of these factors are dispositive and the list is not exclusive. As the courts have stated, the essential question is whether officers were faced with an *"urgent need"* to take action. In determining whether this "urgent need" existed, the following factors are relevant:

—The *degree of urgency* involved and the *amount of time* necessary to obtain a warrant. For example, in *Riley, supra,* the court took account of the fact that the arrest of the drug dealer took place on a Sunday night, and concluded that "the warrant would not be fast coming". The degree of urgency may be dependent on whether a telephone warrant is available. See the discussion of telephone warrants in this section, *infra.*

—A reasonable belief that contraband or evidence is *about to be removed*. For example, if officers become aware that the suspect is about to wash clothing that may contain incriminating forensic evidence, this may be a reason to enter the premises in the absence of a warrant.

—The *possibility of danger* to police officers guarding the premises while a search warrant is sought.

—Information indicating that suspects *know that the police are on their trail*. See *United States v. Miles,* 889 F.2d 382 (2d Cir.1989) (undercover agent's failure to return to the scene of a drug transaction after a drug buy "would create a substantial risk of alerting [the defendants] to the imminence of an arrest").

—The ready *destructibility* of the evidence. This is obviously an important factor in drug cases. See *Riley, supra* ("The need to invoke the exigent circumstances exception is particularly compelling in narcotics cases because of the ease with which they may be destroyed."). Compare *United States v. Holzman,* 871 F.2d 1496 (9th Cir.1989) (no exigency where, among other things, the evidence of stolen credit cards was not easily destructible).

—The *gravity of the offense* of which the suspects are to be charged. See the discussion of minor offenses, and searches of a murder scene, below.

—Whether the suspects are reasonably believed to have *firearms* in their possession. If so, it may be necessary to enter immediately before the suspects become aware of police surveillance and decide to arm themselves. See *United States v. MacDonald,* 916 F.2d 766 (2d Cir.1990) (exigent circumstances to search an apartment used as a distribution center for narcotics was found in part because "the defendant and at least one of his associates were armed with loaded, semi-automatic weapons").

—Whether *probable cause is clear* or is rather a close question. The stronger the showing of probable cause, the less crucial the need to obtain a magistrate's review, and the more likely it is that a court will accept the argument that emergency circumstances excused the failure to bring the facts before a magistrate.

—The *likelihood that suspects may escape* in the absence of an immediate entry.

—The *peaceful circumstances* of the entry.

2. Narcotics Cases

Relying upon the seriousness of a narcotics offense and the ready destructibility of narcotics, most lower courts liberally apply the exigent circumstances exception in drug cases. See *Riley, supra.* This is despite the Supreme Court's ruling in *Vale v. Louisiana,* 399 U.S. 30, 90 S.Ct. 1969, 26 L.Ed.2d 409 (1970). Officers arrested Vale outside his home after they had seen him engage in a narcotics sale. The officers then entered Vale's home to prevent the destruction of evidence. The Court held that the exigent circumstances exception did not apply, because there was no indication that Vale's accomplices were *in the process of destroying evidence.*

a. Need Not Be in the Process of Destruction

Most courts after *Vale* have not required narcotics to be in the actual process of destruction before a warrantless entry can be justified. Thus, there may be an imminent risk of destruction of evidence even though no evidence has yet been destroyed. See *United States v. MacDonald,* 916 F.2d 766 (2d Cir.1990) (risk of destruction of evidence found after undercover officer made a drug buy, even though the suspects were not aware that the buyer was an undercover agent and there was no indication that police surveillance has been discovered). The court in *MacDonald* noted that due to the severity of the crime and the destructibility of the evidence, "ongoing retail narcotics operations often confront law enforcement agents with exigent circumstances".

3. Murder Scene Searches
While the gravity of the crime is a factor in determining exigent circumstances, it is not a per se factor. In *Mincey v. Arizona,* 437 U.S. 385, 98 S.Ct. 2408, 57 L.Ed.2d 290 (1978), the Court held that there is no per se exigent circumstances exception for the search of a murder scene. A police officer was shot and killed in Mincey's apartment. Mincey was arrested and detectives undertook an extensive search of the apartment. The search lasted four days, during which Mincey was in the hospital and no person other than police officers attempted to enter the apartment. The officers never tried to obtain a warrant. The Court held that an immediate warrantless search of a murder scene is permissible to determine whether perpetrators or victims remain at the scene. However, the Court concluded that the extensive four-day search of Mincey's apartment was illegal, because there was no factual indication that there was an imminent risk of destruction of evidence during that time.

4. Minor Crimes
Since the gravity of the crime is a factor in determining exigent circumstances, it follows that it is more difficult to establish exigency if the crime is a minor one. This principle was applied in *Welsh v. Wisconsin, supra.* Officers arrested Welsh in his home without a warrant. They had probable cause to believe that Welsh had been driving while intoxicated. Under Wisconsin law, this was a noncriminal, civil forfeiture offense for which no imprisonment was possible. The Court recognized that in the time it would have taken to obtain an arrest warrant, evidence of Welsh's intoxication probably would have been lost. But it held that in light of the state's expression of minimal interest in the substantive offense, "a warrantless in-home arrest cannot be upheld simply because evidence of the petitioner's blood-alcohol level might have dissipated while the police obtained a warrant". The Court concluded that application of the exigent circumstances exception "should rarely be sanctioned when there is probable cause to believe that only a minor offense, such as the kind at issue in this case, has been committed".

a. No Misdemeanor/Felony Distinction
The Court in *Welsh* specifically rejected the suggestion that an offense is "minor" (and thus an insufficient basis for excusing the warrant requirement on the ground that evidence of the crime is at risk) merely because it is classified as a misdemeanor. It appears that after *Welsh,* the

exigent circumstances doctrine will be unavailable only when the evidence at risk pertains to offenses similar to that in *Welsh:* noncriminal offenses for which no imprisonment is authorized.

E. IMPERMISSIBLE CREATION OF EXIGENT CIRCUMSTANCES

All courts agree that even if an exigency exists, the warrant requirement will not be excused where the exigency has been impermissibly created by the police. For example, officers cannot goad a suspect into running away in order to engage in a "hot pursuit". See *United States v. Munoz–Guerra,* 788 F.2d 295 (5th Cir.1986) (no exigent circumstances where an officer, ostensibly conducting surveillance, presses his nose up to the front window of the premises, and the suspects thereupon begin to destroy evidence). However, as the courts have noted, "in some sense the police always create the exigent circumstances that justify warrantless entries and arrests." For example, by arresting one member of a drug conspiracy, other members may become aware that something is wrong and may begin to destroy evidence. It is important to distinguish police activity which constitutes *impermissible* creation of exigent circumstances from police activity which is legitimate. There is substantial disagreement as to how to distinguish impermissible creation of exigency from legitimate police activity.

1. One View—No Impermissible Creation of Exigency Where Officers Act Lawfully

Some courts refuse to find impermissible creation of exigent circumstances where the officers' activity is objectively lawful—even if it is apparent that the officers acted with the intent to create a situation in which the suspects would attempt to destroy evidence. For example, in *United States v. Acosta,* 965 F.2d 1248 (3d Cir.1992), officers entered an apartment building to execute an arrest warrant for Carlos Santiago, who had previously lived in the building. Officers began knocking on the doors of the apartments in the building, and announced that they were the police and that they had a warrant, and ordered the occupants to open the door. When they conducted this procedure at Acosta's apartment door, officers heard scuffling and commotion, and toilets flushing. Officers stationed in the back of the building informed the officers at the door that the people in the apartment were throwing "stuff" out the back window. At that point, the officers at the front door broke down the door and entered the apartment. A search of the premises revealed contraband and related items. Acosta argued that while there may have been an imminent risk of destruction of evidence at the time the officers entered the apartment, the exigency was impermissibly created by the officers having knocked on the door and announced their presence. The Court held, however, that the officers' act of simply knocking on the door and ordering it to be opened was not itself unlawful: such conduct was not itself a search or seizure, and therefore it did not matter that the officers had no search warrant for Acosta's apartment and no probable cause to believe that Santiago was in the apartment. The court in *Acosta* concluded that "exigent circumstances are not to be disregarded simply because the suspects chose to respond to the agents' lawful conduct by attempting to escape, destroy evidence, or engage in any other unlawful activity."

Ironically, if Acosta had *opened the door* pursuant to the officers' claim of authority, and the officers had then entered the apartment, the search of the apartment would have been illegal; it would have been a non-consensual search in the absence of probable cause and without exigent circumstances. See *United States v. Winsor*, 846 F.2d 1569 (9th Cir.1988) (illegal search where occupant of a motel room opened the door after officers ordered him to open it, and officers had no probable cause to search the room). But there was no illegal search or seizure (and thus no impermissible creation of exigency) in simply knocking on the door. See also *United States v. MacDonald*, 916 F.2d 766 (2d Cir.1990) (exigency was not impermissibly created where officers knocked on the door of an apartment used for an ongoing drug operation, and announced their presence, ostensibly to seek consent to search the apartment; the court found it irrelevant that the officers were carrying a battering ram with them when they were seeking "consent").

a. Initial Search or Seizure Must Itself Be Illegal for "Impermissible Creation" Doctrine to Be Applicable

In the view of the Second and Third Circuits, discussed above, there is no such thing as impermissible creation of exigency if the officer's activity which creates the exigency is not itself an illegal search or seizure. Under this view, the doctrine of impermissible creation of exigency is no different from the standard rule that evidence which is the fruit of an illegal search or seizure is generally excluded from trial. As the dissenter in *Acosta* noted, the Third Circuit's position may create "a substantial danger to the constitutional rights of apartment dwellers who simply happen to live in a multi-unit dwelling in which the subject of an arrest warrant may once have lived." The police can knock on any door and announce their presence in the hopes of creating exigent circumstances.

2. Another View—Impermissible Creation Is Found When the Officer's Sole Intent Is to Create Exigent Circumstances

Other courts have held more broadly that police activity which is not illegal in itself can nonetheless constitute impermissible creation of exigent circumstances. According to these courts: "even when the conduct of Government agents may be termed lawful, we must not countenance deliberate efforts to circumvent the warrant requirement". These courts equate "deliberate" creation of exigency with "impermissible" creation of exigency. For example in *United States v. Timberlake*, 896 F.2d 592 (D.C.Cir.1990), officers, who had no warrant, knocked on the door to an apartment and shouted "police, open up." They then heard sounds which made it apparent that evidence was being destroyed in the apartment; they broke down the door and entered. The court held that the exigent circumstances exception could not apply, because the officers had "deliberately" created exigent circumstances. The court explained that there was "no evidence that the police, when they knocked on the door, intended anything other than a warrantless search of the apartment." Compare *United States v. Socey*, 846 F.2d 1439 (D.C.Cir.1988) (no "deliberate" creation of exigency where officers staking out a retail drug operation arrested one of the drug dealers when he came outside); *United States v. Duchi*, 906 F.2d 1278 (8th Cir.1990) ("deliberate" and thus impermissible creation of exigency where police drastically altered a package of drugs being sent to the defendant and then conducted a controlled delivery to the defendant's home).

a. Intent–Based Test

Under the "deliberate creation" view, the exigent circumstances may be impermissibly created (and a warrantless search found illegal) even though the officer's conduct leading up to the emergency situation was legal and objectively reasonable. Some have criticized this approach as inconsistent with the Fourth Amendment's emphasis on objective reasonableness. See *Scott v. United States*, 436 U.S. 128, 98 S.Ct. 1717, 56 L.Ed.2d 168 (1978) ("subjective intent alone does not make otherwise lawful conduct illegal or unconstitutional").

F. PRIOR OPPORTUNITY TO OBTAIN A WARRANT

If the officers had probable cause and an opportunity to obtain a warrant for a significant time before an exigency arose, they are not excused from the warrant requirement. To take an easy example, assume that on Monday morning, officers obtain reliable information that stolen goods are being stored in a warehouse, and that the goods will be sold on Thursday afternoon. On Thursday afternoon, there is a risk of loss of evidence because the buyers will be taking delivery of the stolen goods. But the exigent circumstances exception does not permit a warrantless entry into the warehouse on Thursday afternoon. This is because the officers had three days to obtain a warrant before the exigency arose, and this exigency was foreseeable.

1. Probable Cause and Opportunity to Obtain a Warrant Must Be Clear

Officers are not required to go to the magistrate for a warrant immediately upon determining that probable cause could arguably exist. Officers are permitted to strengthen doubtful cases on probable cause by taking more time and conducting further investigation. Moreover, even if there is a strong case on probable cause, officers may find that reporting to the magistrate could interrupt the flow of a continuing investigation. Therefore, courts have held that a prior opportunity to obtain a warrant will be found (and hence the exigent circumstances exception will be inapplicable) only if the officers had *clear probable cause* and an *obvious opportunity* to obtain a warrant. See *United States v. Hultgren*, 713 F.2d 79 (5th Cir.1983) ("the fluidity of an ongoing investigation of the distribution of narcotics makes the obtaining of an adequate search warrant more difficult to time in the flow of events").

Example: In *United States v. Miles*, 889 F.2d 382 (2d Cir.1989), a reliable informant arranged a cocaine buy in Miles' apartment. Officers monitored a telephone call between Miles and the informant indicating Miles' willingness to make the deal later that day. The officers did not obtain a warrant. Subsequently, they entered Miles' apartment after the transaction was consummated between Miles, the informant, and the drug supplier, and after the informant had left the apartment ostensibly to obtain money for the buy. At that point, exigent circumstances existed because the informant's absence "for an extended period of time while the agents sought a warrant would create a substantial risk of alerting" the suspects to the imminence of an arrest. Miles argued that the officers should not have been allowed to take advantage of that exigency because they had an opportunity to obtain a warrant at any time after they monitored the telephone call. But the court responded that "law enforcement officers may delay obtaining a warrant until events have proceeded to a point where agents are reasonably certain that the evidence would ultimately support a conviction" and that it was not until the transaction actually took place that such a reasonable certainty existed.

2. Litigation Anomaly

Note that at a suppression hearing the issue of whether the officers had a prior opportunity to obtain a warrant before an exigency arose leads the parties to make arguments that appear contrary to arguments that they would make in other contexts. Thus, it is the defendant who must argue that the officers had a clear case of probable cause, and it is the State which must argue that the officers had no probable cause or at best a weak case before the exigent circumstances arose.

G. TELEPHONE WARRANTS

The doctrine of exigent circumstances is invoked when deleterious consequences would occur within the time it takes to obtain a warrant. The length of time necessary to obtain a warrant is thus crucial to the inquiry. Federal Rule of Criminal Procedure 41 authorizes officers to obtain warrants by telephone, and such warrants are available in many states as well. Courts have accordingly held that where one is available, exigent circumstances must be determined in light of the time it takes to obtain a telephone warrant. See *United States v. Cuaron*, 700 F.2d 582 (10th Cir.1983) ("courts should consider the amount of time required to obtain a telephone warrant in assessing the urgency of the situation").

1. Telephone Warrants Can Be Time–Consuming

Under Rule 41 and similar telephone warrant requirements in the states, a duplicate original warrant must be prepared by the officer, and must be read verbatim over the phone to the magistrate, who must physically transcribe it and prepare an original warrant for the record. Thus, obtaining a telephone warrant can be a time-consuming process, although it obviously involves less time than that required to obtain a warrant in person. Generally speaking, if an exigency would arise within a few minutes, courts will find the danger to be so imminent as to prevent the officers from obtaining even a telephone warrant. Compare *United States v. Berick,* 710 F.2d 1035 (5th Cir.1983) (risk of destruction of evidence resulting from arrest of drug seller was so immediate as to render it impracticable to obtain a telephone warrant), with *United States v. Patino,* 830 F.2d 1413 (7th Cir.1987) (agent could have obtained a telephone warrant during a 30–minute wait for back-up assistance).

H. SECURING PREMISES WHILE WAITING FOR THE WARRANT

Even in the absence of exigent circumstances, officers can protect against the destruction of evidence by securing a premises for the reasonable time it takes to obtain a warrant. By seizing the premises, officers can prevent people from going in and out, thus eliminating the risk of destruction of evidence by preserving the status quo while a warrant is being sought. In *Segura v. United States,* 468 U.S. 796, 104 S.Ct. 3380, 82 L.Ed.2d 599 (1984), Chief Justice Burger, joined by Justice Stevens, stated that "securing a dwelling, on the basis of probable cause, to prevent the destruction or removal of evidence while a search warrant is being sought is not itself an unreasonable seizure of either the dwelling or its contents". A majority of the Court found it unnecessary to reach the question of whether the seizing of the premises in *Segura* was reasonable. However, the principle established by Chief Justice Burger in *Segura* has become well-accepted in the lower courts. See *United States v. Rodriguez,* 869 F.2d 479 (9th Cir.1989) (seizure of premises for 48 hours during which a warrant was obtained was a reasonable seizure under the Fourth Amendment).

1. Seizure of Premises Distinct From a Search

While courts permit officers to secure premises pending a warrant, they do not permit the officers to enter the premises to secure it from within. This would constitute a warrantless *search* of the premises.

V. STOP AND FRISK

A. *TERRY* AND THE COURT'S RELIANCE ON THE REASONABLENESS CLAUSE OF THE FOURTH AMENDMENT

In *Terry v. Ohio,* 392 U.S. 1, 88 S.Ct. 1868, 20 L.Ed.2d 889 (1968), Terry and two others walked several times back and forth past a store. Officer McFadden, an experienced policeman, saw this activity and suspected that the three men were casing the store in preparation for a robbery. Officer McFadden approached the suspects and identified himself, and asked them to identify themselves and explain their conduct. When the suspects mumbled something that he couldn't hear, Officer McFadden grabbed Terry, patted down the outside of his clothing, felt a pistol in Terry's pocket, and confiscated the pistol. Terry was convicted on charges of carrying a concealed weapon, and he challenged the search and seizure of the pistol. In the Supreme Court it was undisputed that McFadden lacked probable cause when he spun Terry around and frisked him. The question was whether the seizure and search were justifiable on a standard of proof less demanding than that of probable cause.

1. **Stop and Frisk Permissible if Reasonable Suspicion Exists**

   The Court in *Terry* found that Officer McFadden had both seized and searched Terry, and therefore that the Fourth Amendment applied to the officer's conduct. The Court, however, rejected Terry's argument that both a warrant and probable cause were required for a search and seizure such as that conducted by Officer McFadden. The Court held that a *stop* can be conducted if an officer has *reasonable suspicion* to believe that crime is afoot. The *Terry* Court further held that an officer who makes a legal stop can conduct a *protective frisk* of a suspect if the officer has *reasonable suspicion to fear* that the suspect is armed and dangerous. Although the majority in *Terry* never used the term "stop-and-frisk", this term has become a well-recognized description of the intrusions upheld in *Terry*.

2. **Inapplicability of the Warrant Clause**

   In a typical stop and frisk situation, there is no serious argument that the officer should have obtained a warrant. For example, in *Terry,* if Officer McFadden had left the scene to obtain a warrant, the suspects would probably have been gone when he returned. Yet under the Court's warrant clause jurisprudence, probable cause is still required for a search or seizure even if exigent circumstances excuse the warrant requirement. The chief innovation of *Terry* is the Court's holding that the warrant clause (and its concomitant requirement of probable cause) was inapplicable to the stop-and-frisk conducted by Officer McFadden. Rather, Officer McFadden's conduct was reviewed to determine whether it was a *reasonable* search and seizure. Contrary to its previous jurisprudence which held the warrant clause predominant over the reasonableness clause, the Court in *Terry* held that the reasonableness clause provided the benchmark for assessing the constitutionality of a stop and frisk.

3. **Importance of Reasonableness Clause Analysis**

   An analysis based on reasonableness is obviously more flexible than an analysis which assumes that a search or seizure requires probable cause in all circumstances. What is reasonable depends on a balance of interests. In the Fourth Amendment context, reasonableness depends on the nature of the state interest involved in conducting the search or seizure, as balanced against the nature of the intrusion on the individual. It may be that requiring probable cause for a certain intrusion would give too much weight to the individual interest at the expense of the state interest. An analysis based on reasonableness could take account of this and conclude that a certain intrusion could be conducted on a standard of proof less demanding than probable cause. In other words, an analysis based on reasonableness will probably permit many more searches and seizures to be conducted than would the traditional analysis requiring probable cause.

4. **Application of Reasonableness Balancing to Stop and Frisk**
The Court in *Terry* balanced the nature of the intrusion involved in a stop and frisk with the state interest involved in conducting such an intrusion, and concluded that probable cause was not required for a stop and frisk. Rather, a stop and frisk was reasonable if conducted on the lesser standard of proof of reasonable suspicion. The Court's rationale was that the individual interest at stake in a stop and frisk was less serious than that involved when a suspect is arrested and a full-scale search is conducted. Unlike an arrest, a stop is a momentary, small-scale intrusion. And unlike a full-scale search for evidence, a frisk is a cursory inspection for weapons. Balanced against these lesser intrusions was the high state interest in conducting a stop and frisk. A stop is often necessary to investigate crime on a preliminary basis, and is an essential tool of crime prevention as well as detection. A frisk effectuates the strong state interest of protecting the safety of police officers. The Court in *Terry* concluded that if a stop and frisk required probable cause, the interests of the state and the individual would not be in appropriate balance. The state would be forced to wait until probable cause developed before it could engage in the minimal intrusion of a stop and frisk. This would mean that an unacceptable number of crimes would go undetected or unprevented, and also that police officers would face an unacceptably high level of risk.

5. **Application of Reasonable Suspicion Standard to the Facts of *Terry***
The Court concluded that the stop of Terry was reasonable because it would have been "poor police work" to allow the suspicious activity to have gone uninvestigated. The Court further concluded that the frisk of Terry was reasonable because the suspects appeared to be involved in planning an armed robbery and therefore the officer had reasonable suspicion to believe that Terry was armed. The Court also noted that the frisk was no more intrusive than necessary to find and seize a weapon.

6. **Reasonableness Balancing Not Limited to Stop and Frisk**
The Court in *Terry* took pains to note that its rejection of the warrant clause in favor of a reasonableness balancing approach was limited to the unique area of stop and frisk. Justice Douglas, in dissent, was unconvinced, and predicted the demise of the probable cause requirement in favor of a more flexible and more permissive ad hoc balancing approach. For better or worse, Justice Douglas' predictions have come true, at least in part, as the Court

has extended its reasonableness analysis well beyond the context of stop and frisk. Once a reasonableness balancing process was undertaken in one area, it became difficult to prevent its application to other searches and seizures. See the discussion of reasonableness searches, infra in this outline. See also Justice Marshall's dissent in *Skinner v. Railway Labor Executives' Ass'n,* 489 U.S. 602, 109 S.Ct. 1402, 103 L.Ed.2d 639 (1989) (decrying the rejection of the probable cause standard and the employment of reasonableness balancing in a drug-testing case).

7. Rejection of Sliding Scale Approach to Reasonableness

A court assessing the reasonableness of a search or seizure must balance the nature of the intrusion against the state interest involved. One possible way of striking this balance would be to use a sliding scale approach, matching a wide variety of intrusions to an appropriate standard of proof. For example, an intrusion that is more serious than an ordinary stop but less serious than an ordinary arrest could require some standard of proof between reasonable suspicion and probable cause. But the Court in *Terry* and subsequent cases has been critical of such an approach. Given the wide variety of police-citizen contacts, the Court has expressed concern that a sliding scale approach would be so flexible as to be unpredictable and incapable of application on the street or in trial courts.

8. Three Categories of Police–Citizen Contacts

In place of a sliding scale approach, the Court has defined three categories of police-citizen contact, and has set forth the appropriate standard of proof for each:

a. Arrest and Incident Search

The most serious intrusion is an arrest, and the standard of proof required to justify an arrest is probable cause. An arrest allows a complete search incident to the arrest, for self-protection and to protect against the destruction of evidence.

b. Stop and Frisk

A less serious intrusion is a stop, which is permitted on the lesser standard of proof of reasonable suspicion. Incident to a stop is a frisk, which is a limited search for weapons, *not for evidence.* The permissibility and scope of a frisk is limited to its rationale of protecting the officer in the course of a lawful stop. See *Sibron v. New York,* 392 U.S. 40, 88 S.Ct. 1889, 20 L.Ed.2d 917 (1968) (*Terry* does not permit a search for evidence on less than probable cause; frisk must be justified by the need for self-protection).

c. Encounter

If an officer merely engages the citizen in an encounter, this is not considered an intrusion at all. Since an *encounter is not a seizure,* it does not implicate the Fourth Amendment, and therefore the officer need not satisfy any standard of proof before conducting an encounter. Obviously no incident search or frisk is allowed pursuant to an encounter.

9. Standard of Proof Must Accord With the Intrusion

It is crucial for the state to match its intrusion with the correct standard of proof. Otherwise, a subsequent search or seizure is likely to be excluded as the fruit of the poisonous tree. For example, in *Florida v. Royer,* 460 U.S. 491, 103 S.Ct. 1319, 75 L.Ed.2d 229 (1983), the officers obtained consent from Royer to search his luggage. However, this consent was held tainted since Royer had been subjected to such a serious intrusion that the Court found that he was under arrest at the time he gave his consent; and at that time the officers had only reasonable suspicion, and not probable cause, to believe that Royer was involved in drug trafficking. If the officers had had probable cause, Royer's consent would probably have been valid. Likewise, if the officers had not exceeded the limitations of a stop and escalated the intrusion into an arrest without probable cause, the consent would probably have been valid. See *United States v. Taylor,* 956 F.2d 572 (6th Cir.1992) (consensual search of bag held permissible where consent was obtained in an encounter; therefore it did not matter that the officers had no reasonable suspicion to believe that defendant was involved in drug activity).

B. WHAT IS A "STOP"?: THE LINE BETWEEN STOP AND ENCOUNTER

If an officer does not have reasonable suspicion that a citizen is involved in illegal activity, he cannot "stop" the citizen, because a stop is a seizure which requires a justification; but an officer can "encounter" a citizen for any reason or no reason, because an encounter is not a seizure. See *United States v. Taylor,* 956 F.2d 572 (6th Cir.1992) (since officers conducted an encounter rather than a stop, it was irrelevant under the Fourth Amendment that the officers approached the defendant because he was African–American). It is therefore important to delineate stops from encounters. The Court in *Terry* clearly found that a stop occurred when Officer McFadden spun Terry around, but the Court was not specific about whether a stop had occurred prior to this action. In several subsequent cases, the Court has refined the test for determining whether police conduct has crossed the line from "encounter" to "stop".

1. The *Mendenhall* Reasonable Person Test

In *United States v. Mendenhall,* 446 U.S. 544, 100 S.Ct. 1870, 64 L.Ed.2d 497 (1980), Justice Stewart proposed that a stop be defined as follows: if, in view of all the circumstances, a *reasonable innocent person would have believed that he was not free to leave,* then a stop has occurred. While the majority of the Court in *Mendenhall* found it unnecessary to employ this test, the "free to leave" test was subsequently adopted by the Court (see *INS v. Delgado,* 466 U.S. 210, 104 S.Ct. 1758, 80 L.Ed.2d 247 (1984)), though it has subsequently been modified for some situations, as discussed below.

2. **Does a Reasonable Person Ever Feel Free to Leave From an Officer's Presence?**

If the *Mendenhall* test were applied literally, it is arguable that *every* police-citizen contact would constitute a stop. Very few citizens feel free to walk away from an officer who approaches them to ask questions. Even if an officer does not *act* coercively, there is an inherent coercive power in the status of an officer, which renders most citizens reluctant to leave the scene. It is clear, however, that the Court has never intended that the *Mendenhall* test be applied literally, since the Court has specifically held that an officer needs no justification to approach a citizen and ask a few questions. See *INS v. Delgado, supra* ("police questioning, by itself, is unlikely to result in a Fourth Amendment violation. While most citizens will respond to a police request, the fact that people do so * * * hardly eliminates the consensual nature of the response").

3. **Active Coercion Prohibited**

The *Mendenhall* test is an attempt to balance the need of an officer to conduct a preliminary enquiry without having to justify it, and the interests of ordinary citizens in being free from police coercion. Therefore, as applied, the test has come to mean that an officer who affirmatively employs coercive tactics will be held to have conducted a seizure, requiring (at least) reasonable suspicion. If, instead, the officer acts politely and the citizen merely responds to the fact that the questioning is conducted by an officer, then the contact will be deemed an encounter.

4. **Factors Considered Under the *Mendenhall* Test**

While each case varies on its facts, courts have established and applied a variety of factors to determine whether an officer has employed coercive tactics sufficient to constitute a stop. On the one hand, it is clear that simply approaching a citizen and asking a few questions is not a stop. On the other hand, drawing a gun and placing the citizen in the back of a police car is at least a stop. In between these two situations is a gray area, in which the following factors are relevant.

—Physical Obstruction of Movement

If officers block the suspect's forward movement, this will go far toward showing that a stop has occurred. See *Brower v. County of Inyo*, 489 U.S. 593, 109 S.Ct. 1378, 103 L.Ed.2d 628 (1989) (use of roadblock to force a suspect to stop constitutes a seizure).

—Show of Force.

A show of force, such as drawn guns, or other menacing activity, is a strong indication that a stop has occurred.

—Retaining Identification, Airplane Tickets, and the Like

An officer can, without reasonable suspicion, approach a suspect and politely ask him for identification, or for his airplane ticket in an airport situation. The suspect is considered free to reject the request. However, if the suspect complies with the request, the officer is not permitted, in the absence of reasonable suspicion, to retain the identification or the ticket in order to prolong the inquiry. A reasonable person is not likely to feel free to leave when his identification or his airplane ticket would be left behind. See *United States v. Jordan,* 958 F.2d 1085 (D.C.Cir.1992) ("police withholding of a person's identification conveys a definite message that the person is not free to leave"); *Florida v. Royer, supra* (stop occurs where officers retain Royer's airplane ticket).

—Threatening Tones

While polite questioning is permissible, the officer's use of threatening language or tone of voice is relevant to whether a seizure has occurred. In specific, courts have usually found that a stop has occurred if the officer threatened the suspect with detention, or accused the suspect of criminal activity.

—Brevity

Even polite questioning must be brief, otherwise it could appear to the reasonable person that the officer will not be satisfied no matter what answers are given.

—Polite Requests to Consent to Search or to Move the Questioning

If the officer politely asks the citizen whether he would consent to a search of his person or of a piece of luggage or the like, this will be considered a consensual encounter in the absence of other coercive factors. Likewise, if the officer politely asks the citizen to continue the conversation in a different place (such as to move the questioning from an airport concourse to an investigative office), the citizen's compliance with this request will not itself indicate that a stop has occurred.

—Informing the Citizen of the Right to Terminate an Encounter or to Refuse Consent

An officer is not obligated to tell the citizen that he has the right to refuse to answer questions or consent to a search. However, if the officer does inform the citizen of these rights, this will go far toward establishing a consensual encounter.

—Coercive Surroundings

If the police-citizen contact occurs in closed surroundings, that setting may be indicative of coercion, though not dispositive. Thus, in *Florida v. Bostick,* __ U.S. __, 111 S.Ct. 2382, 115 L.Ed.2d 389 (1991), the Court recognized that if questioning occurs in the cramped confines of a bus, it is more likely to be coercive than if it occurs in a more open area such as an airport concourse—though the Court held that a seizure does not *automatically* occur merely because the questioning occurs in close physical surroundings. Likewise, if questioning occurs in an area away from public view, it is more likely to be coercive than if the questioning occurs in an area visible to the public—though again this factor is not dispositive. See *United States v. Ward,* 961 F.2d 1526 (10th Cir.1992) (questioning in train roomette found to constitute a stop, due to cramped confines and the fact that it was conducted out of public view; the court found it "particularly significant" that "defendant was not in an open public place where he was within the view of persons other than law enforcement officers").

5.   Application of the *Mendenhall* Test

The best way to get a command of the *Mendenhall* factors is to apply them to a specific set of facts. *United States v. Taylor,* 956 F.2d 572 (6th Cir.1992) provides typical facts. Taylor flew into the Memphis airport from Miami; he was the only African–American in the initial group of deplaning passengers. He was carrying a shoulder bag. As he exited the jetway and entered the terminal corridor, he was observed by three plainclothes officers of the Memphis police department assigned to drug interdiction. Without consulting each other, the officers—Eldridge, Bevel and Roberts—tracked Taylor as he walked from the gate and down the concourse toward the baggage claim facility. Taylor, walking rapidly, went directly out of the airport building without claiming any baggage, and was going in the direction of a parking lot. Eldridge approached Taylor shortly after Taylor exited the building, identified himself as a police officer and solicited Taylor for an interview. He did not touch Taylor. Bevel joined Eldridge while Roberts proceeded to a position across the roadway adjacent to the parking lot. Eldridge asked Taylor where he lived and where he had been. Taylor responded that he lived across the river and had been in Miami for three weeks; but he could not explain the absence of luggage. In further response to Eldridge's questions, Taylor produced a one-way ticket from Miami to Memphis, purchased with cash, and a driver's license with a name corresponding to that on the ticket. The license and ticket were returned to Taylor. Bevel then asked Taylor if he would permit her to inspect the contents of his shoulder bag. In response to this request, Taylor placed the bag on the sidewalk, unzipped it, riffled through it, and told Bevel and Eldridge that there was nothing in the bag they would be interested in. Bevel asked again if he would mind if she looked in the bag. Taylor said "okay". Bevel's inspection disclosed two large, spherical bundles wrapped in tape. Upon this discovery, the officers directed Taylor to accompany them to the Drug Task Force office inside the terminal. After obtaining further incriminating information pursuant to their inquiries, the officers placed Taylor under arrest. A search of the spherical objects uncovered drugs, and a search of Taylor's person uncovered a large sum of money.

The court held that Taylor was not seized until he was directed to return to the terminal: "a seizure does not occur when officers approach an individual and, after identifying themselves, request an interview and an opportunity to inspect the individual's driver's license and airline ticket." The court also found that Taylor voluntarily consented to a search of his bag. The court concluded that Taylor was seized when he was ordered to return to the terminal, stating that "the one occurrence which seems to separate seizures from casual contacts between police and citizens is when the defendant is asked to accompany the police or agents to a place to which the defendant has not planned to go." However, at that point, the officers had reasonable suspicion (on the basis of the bundles in the bag, among other things), for the seizure.

a. Escalating Intrusions Matched With Escalating Standards of Proof
The facts of *Taylor* show a common method by which officers successfully uncover criminal activity. The officers in *Taylor* used an encounter to obtain enough information to support a stop. Then the stop was used to obtain further information, leading to probable cause, thus permitting the officers to arrest the suspect and conduct a search incident to arrest.

6. Two Recent Modifications to the *Mendenhall* "Free to Leave" Test
Recently, the Court has modified the *Mendenhall* test in two important cases. Both cases expanded the authority of officers to investigate free from the strictures of the Fourth Amendment.

a. *Bostick*: Not Free to Leave Because of the Suspect's Own Circumstances
In *Florida v. Bostick,* __ U.S. __, 111 S.Ct. 2382, 115 L.Ed.2d 389 (1991), two officers boarded an interstate bus on which Bostick was a passenger. They boarded during a stopover in Fort Lauderdale. The officers swept through the bus and, without articulable suspicion, picked out Bostick and asked to inspect his ticket and identification. Bostick complied. Bostick's ticket matched his identification and both were returned to him as unremarkable. The officers then told Bostick that they were on the lookout for illegal drugs and requested Bostick's consent to search his luggage. Bostick agreed and the officers found drugs in his luggage. Bostick argued that he was seized without reasonable suspicion at the time he gave his consent, and that therefore the consent was tainted and the evidence was illegally obtained. He contended that he was not "free to leave" because the bus was soon scheduled to depart.

i. Literal Application Rejected
Justice O'Connor, writing for the majority, concluded that the "free to leave" test could not be applied literally in cases like Bostick's.

She stated that the term "free to leave" should be construed in accordance with "the principle that those words were intended to capture." In this case, Bostick had no desire to leave, because the bus was about to depart. Therefore the "free to leave" test, as applied to these circumstances, was "not an accurate measure of the coercive effect of the encounter" since Bostick would not have felt free to leave even if the police had not been present.

ii. **Freedom to Terminate the Encounter**
The question, therefore, in cases where the citizen is confined because of his own circumstances (such as in a bus, a subway, or an elevator) is whether *the police conduct would have communicated to a reasonable person that the person was not free to decline the officers' requests or otherwise terminate the encounter*. The *Bostick* court remanded the case to determine whether the officers' conduct constituted a seizure under that modified standard.

b. *Hodari* : **If Coercive Tactics Are Non-physical, It Is Not a Stop Until the Suspect Submits**
In *California v. Hodari D.,* 499 U.S. 621, 111 S.Ct. 1547, 113 L.Ed.2d 690 (1991), officers encountered a group of youths who were huddled around a car and who fled when they saw the officers. The officers pursued Hodari. In the course of the chase, Hodari discarded a rocklike object. One officer tackled Hodari and handcuffed him. Subsequently, the officer discovered that the discarded rock was crack cocaine. Hodari argued that the police pursuit was a seizure, since a reasonable person would have considered it so coercive as not to feel free to leave.

i. **Two Types of Seizures**
Justice Scalia, writing for the Court, consulted the common law to define the term "seizure". Based upon his review of the common law, he separated seizures into two types: those in which the officer has *physically touched* the suspect, and those in which the officer has used a non-physical *show of authority* (such as drawing a gun, ordering the suspect to stop, etc.).

ii. **Physical Touching Is a Seizure**
Justice Scalia concluded that a stop *automatically* occurs when an officer physically touches a suspect with the intent of restraining him. He stated that a seizure "is effected by the slightest application of physical force". He noted, however, that such a seizure would not be permanent if the suspect breaks away from the officer's control.

iii. **Non-physical Show of Authority Is Not a Stop Until the Suspect Submits**

The physical touching aspect of the seizure definition was not at issue in *Hodari,* since the parties agreed that Hodari was stopped when he was tackled and handcuffed. The question was whether he was "seized" when he was being pursued. Justice Scalia recognized that the *Mendenhall* test could be construed to apply to coercive activity to which the suspect does not in fact submit. He rejected this construction, however, and concluded that the *Mendenhall* test, when read "carefully", says that a person has been seized "only if", not "whenever" the officer employs a show of authority. Thus, where the officer employs a non-physical show of authority, it must be such that a reasonable person would not feel free to leave, *and the citizen must actually submit to the show of authority*.

iv. **Application to the Facts of *Hodari***

As applied to *Hodari,* there would have been a stop if Hodari had stopped running in response to the police activity; but he did not. Therefore the stop did not occur until Hodari was physically subdued by the officer. The pursuit did not require articulable suspicion because a seizure had not yet occurred.

v. **Dissent's Concern About Risk of Abuse**

Justice Stevens, in dissent in *Hodari,* expressed concern that the majority's "narrow construction" of the word "seizure" would allow officers to employ abusive, coercive tactics, without any articulable suspicion, in the hopes of rattling a citizen into fleeing, dropping objects, or engaging in some other suspicious activity sufficient to support a stop. For example, under *Hodari,* an officer could fire his gun into the air in the hopes of inciting a citizen to suspicious activity.

vi. **Response of Majority**

Justice Scalia concluded that officers were unlikely to try to manufacture reasonable suspicion by engaging in abusive conduct, short of physical touching, in the hope that suspects would react in some suspicious way. According to Justice Scalia, officers do not issue orders expecting them to be ignored. Therefore, an officer would be very unlikely, in the absence of articulable suspicion, to engage in conduct which would constitute a stop if the suspect submitted—a reasonable officer would fully expect a suspect to submit to such coercive activity. If the suspect did submit, the officer would know that the resulting stop would be illegal in the absence of reasonable suspicion. Thus, Justice Scalia found it unlikely that an officer would "gamble" that the suspect would ignore his orders.

7.   Officer Is Not Required to Use an Encounter as a "Less Intrusive Alternative"

In *United States v. Sokolow,* 490 U.S. 1, 109 S.Ct. 1581, 104 L.Ed.2d 1 (1989), officers stopped Sokolow in an airport on suspicion that he was trafficking in narcotics; he gave consent to a search of his luggage and narcotics were found. The Court rejected Sokolow's argument that the officers did not have reasonable suspicion to support the stop. Sokolow argued further, however, that even if the officers had reasonable suspicion, their seizure of Sokolow in the airport was illegal because they could have obtained the same results (consent to search Sokolow's luggage) if they had merely encountered him rather than seized him. The Court held that agents are not obligated to use the least intrusive means available to verify or dispel their suspicions. The Court reasoned that a rule requiring a "least intrusive alternative" approach would unnecessarily penalize the police for making objectively reasonable, on-the-spot decisions. Therefore, if the officers have reasonable suspicion to support a stop, they can seize the suspect even though an encounter may be equally productive.

C.   WHAT IS REASONABLE SUSPICION?

The Court in *Terry* reasoned that, because a stop is less intrusive than an arrest, it could be conducted upon satisfying a less rigorous standard of proof than the probable cause required for an arrest. The degree of suspicion required to make a stop is referred to as "reasonable suspicion" by the courts. Since *Terry,* courts have struggled with the meaning of reasonable suspicion and with how the reasonable suspicion standard differs from that of probable cause. It is clear, however, that the standards are materially different. There are many cases in which the courts have held that reasonable suspicion existed but probable cause did not; the consequence of the distinction would be the exclusion of any evidence obtained if the officer's intrusion constituted an arrest rather than merely a stop. See *Florida v. Royer,* 460 U.S. 491, 103 S.Ct. 1319, 75 L.Ed.2d 229 (1983) (consent tainted where it was obtained while Royer was under arrest and officers had only reasonable suspicion and not probable cause to believe that Royer was involved in drug activity).

1.   Nature of the Analysis Is Similar

The analysis employed by the courts in assessing reasonable suspicion is similar to that employed in assessing probable cause. The following analytical concepts are applicable to both standards:

—A *common sense* analysis is employed to evaluate the facts presented.

—*Deference* is given to the *expertise* of law enforcement officers, who may know through experience that certain facts are indicative of criminal activity (e.g. that drug dealers often carry beepers or cellular phones).

—*The totality of circumstances* must be assessed. While each fact may seem innocent if considered individually, the factors considered in their totality may not be so easily explained away.

—*Reasonable mistakes of fact* do not preclude a finding of either reasonable suspicion or probable cause. Certainty is not required for either standard.

Example: In *United States v. Baker,* 850 F.2d 1365 (9th Cir.1988), the defendant was driving a "hot rod" through a small town. An officer stopped Baker on suspicion that he was violating a local noise ordinance. The ordinance stated that a violation occurred if the vehicle's noise level was more than 92 decibels as measured from 20 feet away. The defendant argued that the stop was illegal because the officer never got a reading from a decibel meter before he stopped Baker, and thus could not have determined that the decibel level was more than 92 from 20 feet away. The court responded that Baker had misconstrued the reasonable suspicion standard. An officer need not be certain that criminal activity is afoot before he or she stops a suspect. All that is required is articulable facts supporting a fair possibility of illegal activity. In this case, the officer did not need a meter to assess the likelihood of a noise violation. The officer's testimony that the "hot rod" was noticeably and significantly louder than ordinary traffic was enough to support a finding of reasonable suspicion.

What Is at Stake: In a case like *Baker,* one might be tempted to conclude that the reasonable suspicion question is of little importance, since Baker's vehicle either violated the noise ordinance or it did not, and that could be determined for trial by the use of a decibel meter. But Baker was not being tried for the noise violation. Rather, he was being tried for the illegal possession of a firearm. The firearm was discovered in the course of the stop for the noise violation. If there was no reasonable suspicion that Baker had violated the noise ordinance, then the stop would have been illegal and the evidence of firearms would have been subject to suppression.

2. Difference in Quantity and Quality of Proof

The difference between reasonable suspicion and probable cause is that reasonable suspicion is a less demanding standard of proof—a stop is permissible upon something less than the fair probability standard which defines probable cause. Some courts have defined reasonable suspicion as a fair *possibility* (as opposed to probability) of criminal activity. Reasonable suspicion can be usefully referred to as *possible cause*.

Example: A probabilistic example of the difference between reasonable suspicion and probable cause is presented by the facts of *United States v. Winsor*, 846 F.2d 1569 (9th Cir.1988). Officers chased suspected bank robbers fleeing from the bank into a hotel. The hotel had approximately 40 guest rooms. The question was whether there was probable cause to search each of the rooms for the suspects. The court found that a one-in-forty probability was too small to establish probable cause, but that it did establish reasonable suspicion: "The odds on discovering the suspect in the first room upon whose door the police knocked were high enough to support a founded suspicion. The odds favoring discovery increase as rooms are searched. At some point, perhaps at the last two or three unsearched rooms, probable cause may be said to exist." Conversely, at some point of improbability, reasonable suspicion would not have existed—for example, if the hotel had 600 rooms, there would clearly have been no reasonable suspicion to believe that the suspects were in any particular room. Because there was only reasonable suspicion and not probable cause in *Winsor*, the court held that the search of the hotel room in which the suspects were found was illegal. A search for law enforcement purposes requires probable cause and cannot be justified under *Terry*.

3.   **Quantum of Suspicion Required for Reasonable Suspicion**
The Supreme Court's definition of the appropriate quantum of suspicion to support a stop was articulated in *United States v. Cortez*, 449 U.S. 411, 101 S.Ct. 690, 66 L.Ed.2d 621 (1981): "Based upon the whole picture the detaining officers must have a particularized and objective basis for suspecting the particular person stopped of criminal activity * * *. The process does not deal with hard certainties, but with probabilities."

4.   **Questions of Identity of a Perpetrator**
The Court in *Terry* and in *Cortez* dealt with questions of reasonable suspicion in the context of an identifiable suspect who was engaged in ambiguous activity. The question was not who did the crime. The question was whether any crime had been or was being committed at all. But stops are also permissible where it is clear that a crime has occurred, and the question for the officer is whether a particular person is the perpetrator. In *United States v. Hensley*, 469 U.S. 221, 105 S.Ct. 675, 83 L.Ed.2d 604 (1985), the Court approved the use of stops where "police have a reasonable suspicion, grounded in specific and articulable facts, that a person they encounter was involved in or is wanted in connection with a completed felony." The

question in these cases is whether the officer has enough articulable facts as to the identity of the perpetrator to match with the suspect.

a. General Description Can Support a Stop

As discussed above, reasonable suspicion is a minimal standard. Therefore, a stop may be justified even though the suspect merely accords with a general description. For example, in the section on probable cause, the case of *United States v. Valez* was discussed. In that case, the description of the perpetrator was "Hispanic male in his 20's, wearing a black leather jacket, grey pants with a comb in the back pocket, and a white or off-white V-neck shirt." This was in an area in which the majority of residents were Hispanic. The *Valez* court held that there was probable cause to arrest a person who fit that description, though there was a spirited dissent. While the facts of *Valez* presented a close case on probable cause, it is quite likely that most courts would have had little problem in finding reasonable suspicion to support a stop of Valez. The following discussion sets forth the factors that courts apply in determining whether reasonable suspicion exists to believe that a certain suspect is the person who was identified as the perpetrator of a crime.

b. Descriptions Can Be Incorrect in Certain Particulars

When there are several points of comparison between the suspect and the description of the perpetrator, it may be permissible to stop the suspect even though there is a discrepancy on some points. Officers may take into account that some of the descriptive factors supplied by witnesses or victims may be in error. The question is whether there are enough specific factors which do match up so that, when weighed against the discrepancies, it is reasonably possible that the suspect is the person described as the perpetrator. For example, in *United States v. Wantland,* 754 F.2d 268 (8th Cir.1985) an eyewitness reported that a bank robber fled in a gold 1971 Dodge Dart with license number 104–819. The officer stopped a Plymouth Duster leaving the town in which the bank robbery occurred; the Duster's license number was 104–849. The court held that there was reasonable suspicion to stop the car, given the similarity of the two vehicles and the license plate numbers, and the fact that an eyewitness description, under the circumstances, could not be expected to be exact.

c. Changed Circumstances May Be Taken Into Account

An officer assessing a description can take into account the fact that circumstances may have changed between the time of the description and the point at which the officer discovers a person whom he suspects as the perpetrator. The concept of reasonable suspicion accommodates the possibility that a perpetrator may try to conceal his identity or avoid detection. For example, if a bank robber is known to have fled in one type of car, it may be permissible to stop a different kind of car driving from the direction of the bank, due to the possibility of a switch. Similarly, if three people are seen leaving a bank robbery, and an officer comes across two people who fit the description of two of the robbers, the officer must obviously be allowed to take into account the fact that the group may have split up—or that some members may be concealed from view. See *Williams v. State,* 261 Ind. 547, 307 N.E.2d 457 (1974) (officer knew that two robbers had fled by car; he stopped a car fitting the general description, even though there was only one person visible in the car; the other robber was found hiding in the rear seat). Likewise, if a perpetrator is described as having a beard, an officer may be permitted to stop a person with no facial hair. The reasonable possibility may exist that the beard was a disguise.

d. Size of the Area Is Relevant

If the description is so general as to cover a large number of persons (such as the description in *Valez*) then it will be important to assess the distance between the stop and the scene of the crime. Of course, the spatial relationship is dispositive if a stop is conducted in an area where the suspect could not have physically transported himself; put another way, the stop must be within the range of possible flight. See *State v. Smith,* 9 Wash.App. 279, 511 P.2d 1032 (1973) (stop held proper in part because it was reasonably within appropriate driving distance from the crime scene, considering the time of the robbery). More importantly, the size of an area also helps to determine the universe of potential suspects. Therefore, a general description (e.g. short white man in a black suit) may support a stop within a two block radius of a shooting incident, but not within a five mile radius.

e. Number of People in the Area Is Relevant

The sufficiency of a description to support a stop can only be assessed by considering the number of people to whom it could apply under the circumstances. It therefore follows that a description must be more particular if the stop is made in a location where there are many people about (such as a crowded urban area) than if it is made in an uncrowded area. See *United States v. Basey,* 816 F.2d 980 (5th Cir.1987) (stop based on description that perpetrator was driving a "1980 yellow Ford Sedan" held permissible; court stresses the minimal number of persons and cars about in a rural area). In fact, there have been cases in which the number of people in the vicinity of a crime was so few that a stop of a person in that area was upheld even though the officer had no description of the perpetrator whatever. See *United States v. Crittendon,* 883 F.2d 326 (4th Cir.1989) (call to police about burglary in progress made at 3 a.m.; defendant and his companion were "the only persons encountered in the vicinity of the reported crime"). Compare *Cauthen v. United States,* 592 A.2d 1021 (D.C.App.1991) (call to police about drug transactions on the street, made at 2 a.m.; stop not permissible without any description, since police response time was 20 minutes and there was much street activity in the area).

f. **Suspicious Activity of a Person Fitting a General Description**
While some descriptions may be too general to support reasonable suspicion (e.g. white male in his 20's), the police, through further investigation, may stop a person fitting that description if the person is in fact acting suspiciously. The suspicious conduct, together with the general description, may make it reasonably possible that the suspect is the perpetrator. It will be relevant, for example, if the suspect is acting as if he is trying to avoid detection, or if he appears inordinately nervous. See *United States v. Danielson,* 728 F.2d 1143 (8th Cir.1984) (suspect was leaving the area at an unusually fast speed, and tried to duck out of sight when police officers approached).

g. **Suspect "Fails" the Encounter**
Recall that a police officer can encounter a citizen, and ask a few preliminary questions, even without reasonable suspicion. Officers working with an overly general description will often encounter, rather than stop a person who fits the description. If the citizen gives implausible answers to the preliminary questions, then this may be sufficiently suspicious to support a stop. See e.g. *United States v. Morgan,* 725 F.2d 56 (7th Cir.1984) (suspect stated that he was travelling alone, though officers knew that he was travelling with a companion); *United States v. Blanco,* 844 F.2d 344 (6th Cir.1988) (suspects state that they drove 1000 miles to Cincinnati to see a Reds baseball game, even though the Reds were at that time on an extended road trip; officer could consider it suspicious that "two gentlemen who had driven from Miami to Cincinnati to take in a baseball game should not have known that the team was going to be out of town").

h. **Prior Record of Criminal Activity**
There may be reasonable suspicion to support a stop if a general description is coupled with the officer's knowledge that a suspect who fits the description has previously engaged in similar crimes. See *United States v. Morgan,* 936 F.2d 1561 (10th Cir.1991) (description of "three black males" as bank robbers held sufficient to stop a car with three black males where, in addition, officer recognized the car as having been reported leaving the scene of a different bank robbery, and recognized one of the men as having previously been charged with bank robbery).

i. **At Some Point, the Totality of Factors Remains Too General to Support a Stop**
The standard of reasonable suspicion is minimal, and the use of a totality of circumstances approach will often lead to a finding that a stop

was permissible on the basis of the suspect's matching a general description together with other relevant factors. Nonetheless, there are cases in which a stop was found invalid due to the lack of suspicious circumstances and the generality of the description.

Example: In *People v. Miller,* 121 A.D.2d 335, 504 N.Y.S.2d 407 (1st Dep't 1986), officers responded to a call stating that a short, black Jamaican man wearing a tan leisure suit had taken a gun out of a case and placed it in his waistband; that he ran with two other black men into the basement of 277 Edgecombe Avenue; that one of the other men was dressed all in grey and was a little taller than the gunman; and that the man carrying the gun looked like he was going to shoot someone. Officers were at the address within a minute. In front of the building, they saw defendant, who was 6'1" tall, wearing an open gray shirt with a black tank top underneath, and black pants; they also saw a man about 5'3" tall, in a brown uniform, sweeping the sidewalk; and a third man was sitting on the stoop of the building with defendant. All three men were black. No one else was on the street. The officers observed the defendant remove his hand from inside the front waistband area of his pants, consistent with either tucking in his shirt or, in the officers' experience, the act of a gun carrier pushing the weapon down to make sure that it does not slip out. The officers seized the defendant, and a subsequent frisk uncovered a gun. Defendant was convicted on a weapons charge and argued on appeal that the officers had no reasonable suspicion to seize him. The appellate court agreed with the defendant. The court noted that the defendant was taller than the description given to the police officers of the gunman's companions, and that the clothes he was wearing did not match the description. The court also emphasized that all three men were acting naturally and calmly in front of the building when the police arrived. The court found the defendant's hand movement to be "innocuous" in light of all the circumstances, and noted that the officers never testified that they saw a bulge or protrusion in the area of the gesture.

5. Suspicious Conduct

A different situation in which the reasonable suspicion standard is applied is where the officer sees or knows about conduct which the officer views as suspicious. This application of reasonable suspicion is different from the questions presented as to identity. As applied to suspicious conduct, the question is not whether a person accords with a sufficiently specific identification and whether other circumstances may tie him to the crime.

Rather, the question is whether any crime has been committed at all. So the focus is on the totality of circumstances bearing upon the suspect's conduct. A stop is permitted if, considering all the circumstances, an officer could find it reasonably possible that, as the Court in *Terry* put it, "criminal activity is afoot". In most cases, an innocent explanation for the suspect's conduct can be hypothesized, but that alone does not preclude a finding of reasonable suspicion. If there is any significant possibility that the conduct is criminal, a stop is justified.

a. Case-by-Case Approach; Relevant Factors

There is obviously a wide variety of circumstances in which an officer might stop a suspect on the basis of suspicious activity. This makes it difficult to state clearly exactly what situations indicate a sufficient level of suspicion to justify a stop. As the Supreme Court stated in *United States v. Sokolow,* 490 U.S. 1, 109 S.Ct. 1581, 104 L.Ed.2d 1 (1989), "the concept of reasonable suspicion, like probable cause, is not readily or even usefully reduced to a neat set of legal rules." However, some factors arise frequently enough in the cases to indicate that they will ordinarily be relevant to a finding of reasonable suspicion. The more these factors accumulate, the stronger the case on reasonable suspicion will be. It must be kept in mind, however, that ordinarily, no single factor is a dispositive indicator of reasonable suspicion. See *Sokolow* (finding reasonable suspicion that defendant was a drug courier, on the basis of several suspicious factors, while recognizing that "any one of these factors is not by itself proof of any illegal conduct and is quite consistent with innocent travel"). Conversely, the fact that several suspicious factors can be individually explained away is not dispositive. As the Court stated in *Sokolow,* the relevant inquiry "is not whether particular conduct is innocent or guilty, but the degree of suspicion that attaches to particular types of noncriminal acts".

Example: In *Sokolow,* the defendant travelled round-trip from Honolulu to Miami, a known source city for drugs, over a 48–hour period. He paid $2100 for two airplane tickets with cash from a roll of $20 bills. He travelled under a name that did not match the name under which his telephone number was listed. He had appeared nervous during the trip. He had not checked any luggage. Each of these factors was consistent with innocent activity. The Court found, however, that these factors taken together made it reasonably possible that the defendant was a drug courier.

b. Patterns of Activity

Activity that appears repetitious may indicate that the suspect may be checking out whether a crime can be successfully completed. For example, if a person looks into the interior of one or two cars in a parking lot, this will not ordinarily seem suspicious. However, if a person walks down a line of thirty cars in a parking lot, and looks into the interior of each one, an inference may be drawn that the person may be looking for a car to break into. Indeed, the suspects in *Terry* were stopped by Officer McFadden because they repeatedly passed back and forth and peered into a store—this activity was suspicious because it was consistent with that of a person "casing" a premises for a robbery.

c. Demonstrated Unfamiliarity

If the suspect's activity indicates that he is unfamiliar with either his surroundings or with the things he is carrying or operating, this may be some indication that crime is afoot. For example, if a person has a set of keys and tries several of them in a door lock, an officer may reasonably suspect that the keys are stolen. Likewise, if a person has difficulty operating a car with a standard transmission, or has difficulty finding the lights or the emergency brake, this demonstrated unfamiliarity is relevant to whether the car has been or is being stolen. Unfamiliarity with the area in which the suspect is found may be suspicious, though it will rarely be dispositive, since it may be that the suspect is, simply and innocently, lost. Compare *United States v. Holland,* 510 F.2d 453 (9th Cir.1975) (reasonable suspicion where, among other things, the suspects were in a car driving slowly in a rural area, as if they were unfamiliar with the areas and looking for a particular residence), with *United States v. Pavelski,* 789 F.2d 485 (7th Cir.1986) (no reasonable suspicion to stop car with out of state license plates, after car took an abrupt turn down a country road; this single factor is not enough to establish reasonable suspicion).

d. Time of Day

Activity which is completely unremarkable at one time of day may be very suspicious at another. For example, it is not suspicious to push a rack of clothing down the street in the Garment District of New York City at midday. But it is very suspicious to do so at 3 a.m. Courts take account of the fact that most criminal activity occurs at night rather than in broad daylight. See *United States v. Kerr,* 817 F.2d 1384 (9th Cir.1987) (no reasonable suspicion where defendant was "loading boxes into a vehicle on residential property at mid-afternoon, a time of day not raising an inference of criminal activity"); *People v. Allen,* 50 Cal.App.3d 896, 123 Cal.Rptr. 80 (1975) (reasonable suspicion found where defendant was standing in a used car lot at 2:35 a.m.). However, the fact that activity occurs at night is not itself sufficient grounds for a stop; there must be some other suspicious circumstances. See e.g. *State v. Phipps,* 429 So.2d 445 (La.1983) (stop not permissible merely because defendants were out on the street at 3 a.m.; Mardi Gras parade had taken place a few hours previously).

e.   Location of Activity; High Crime Area

The location in which an act occurs may have some bearing on whether it is suspicious. For example, an overloaded truck near the border is more suspicious than an overloaded truck on an interstate highway in the middle of the country. Shaking hands and passing a glassine envelope in an area known for drug activity is more suspicious than if the same activity occurred in a suburban backyard. Courts frequently rely on the fact that a suspect's conduct occurred in a high crime area, and that the conduct was consistent with the type of crime pervasive in the area. See *United States v. Garrett*, 959 F.2d 1005 (D.C.Cir.1992) (stop permissible where defendant was observed exchanging money for a small object in an area rife with drug activity). However, as with time of day, the fact that a person is simply found in a high crime area is not itself sufficient to justify a stop. See *Brown v. Texas*, 443 U.S. 47, 99 S.Ct. 2637, 61 L.Ed.2d 357 (1979) ("The fact that appellant was in a neighborhood frequented by drug users, standing alone, is not a basis for concluding that appellant himself was engaged in criminal conduct.").

f.   Known Criminal Record

A suspect's activity may take on a more suspicious color if it is consistent with criminal activity for which the suspect has already been arrested or convicted. See *United States v. Barnes*, 496 A.2d 1040 (D.C.App.1985) (defendant's previous arrest for armed robbery, when considered with the fact that he was loitering outside a store while his companion entered several times, gave rise to reasonable suspicion). Again, however, the mere fact that a person has prior arrests or convictions is not itself sufficient to justify a stop; a seizure may not be based solely on the suspect's past record. See *People v. Johnson*, 64 N.Y.2d 617, 485 N.Y.S.2d 33, 474 N.E.2d 241 (1984) (the fact that defendant had previously been arrested for burglary and was found in an alley looking at houses did not constitute reasonable suspicion: "It can hardly be regarded as unusual that defendant was looking at houses, for there is little else to look at in a residential neighborhood.").

g.   Reaction to Police Officers

When a person sees police officers approach, or notices their presence, his reaction to the officers can sometimes be considered indicative of consciousness of guilt. For example, most courts have held that it is suspicious for a person to run away when he sees police officers approach. See *United States v. Lane*, 909 F.2d 895 (6th Cir.1990) (reasonable suspicion existed when "four males broke into a run when the uniformed officers entered an apartment building" known for drug activity). Likewise, it may be suspicious if a person tries to hide something (or tries to hide himself) when uniformed officers approach. See *United States v. Orozco–Rico*, 589 F.2d 433 (9th Cir.1978) (defendant, after seeing police approach, threw something over a wall).

However, it has not been finally decided whether evasive action can, in and of itself, constitute reasonable suspicion. The Court implied, in *California v. Hodari D., supra,* that a person's flight from approaching police officers could itself constitute reasonable suspicion; but the Court found it unnecessary to decide the issue.

h.   Some Reactions Are Not Evasive

The mere fact that a person acts somewhat nervously in the presence of a police officer is not suspicious. It is an ordinary reaction to the presence of the police. So, for example, if a driver slows down below the speed limit so as not to pass a police car on the road, this will not be considered suspicious. See *State v. Johnson,* 444 N.W.2d 824 (Minn.1989) (no grounds for a stop if a driver "merely appears startled at the sight of a police officer passing him and then slows down a bit"); *United States v. Pavelski, supra* (no reasonable suspicion where driver and occupants of a car stare straight ahead and avoid eye contact with police when being passed by a police car). Also, it is obviously the case that evasive action will not be considered suspicious where the officers are not identifiable as police officers. See *People v. Allen,* 109 A.D.2d 24, 489 N.Y.S.2d 749 (1st Dep't 1985) (no reasonable suspicion where defendant merely stepped back from an elevator and put his hand to his pocket upon seeing eight men step out of the elevator, in a high crime area; defendant had no way of knowing that the men were plainclothes officers). As stated above, however, a person who breaks into a run at the sight of police may be considered suspicious. Such conduct is more than ordinary nervousness.

i.   Failing an Encounter

As with questions of identity, a person whose activity may not be suspicious enough to permit a stop may nonetheless be approached and asked preliminary questions. Then, if the answers to the questions are implausible or demonstrably false, the suspect's "failure" may raise the level of suspicion to that required for a stop. See *United States v. Lanford,* 838 F.2d 1351 (5th Cir.1988) (disheveled-looking driver in a fancy car, driving in New Mexico; when asked what he was doing, he stated that he was "just driving around"; this was implausible because the car had Louisiana license plates; the answer, together with other factors already known, constituted reasonable suspicion to believe that the car was stolen).

j.   Non-cooperation During an Encounter

A suspect's mere failure to consent to requests by a police officer during an encounter cannot be a factor which contributes to reasonable suspicion. For example, if a suspect refuses to produce identification, or refuses to consent to a search of his bag, or refuses to answer questions, such refusals are not relevant to reasonable suspicion. This is because a person who is merely encountered has the absolute right to refuse cooperation and terminate the encounter. It would be anomalous if officers could term the police-citizen contact an encounter because it was completely consensual, and then, in the course of that encounter, consider it suspicious that the citizen refused to cooperate, thereby permitting a stop.

k.   Non-cooperation Distinguished From Evasion

While a citizen has an absolute right to terminate an encounter, it is nonetheless true that certain out-of-the-ordinary activity designed to avoid or terminate conduct with the police may be considered suspicious. It is one thing to walk away from an encounter; it is another to run away at full speed. It is one thing to refuse consent. It is another to slap the officer. See *People v. Vasquez,* 108 A.D.2d 701, 485 N.Y.S.2d 1008 (1st Dep't 1985) (reasonable suspicion found when, together with other suspicious facts, defendant slapped at the officer's hand when he approached: "Ordinarily, a person addressed by a police officer does have an equal right to ignore his interrogator and walk away. This should not, however, be read to mean that one can strike out at an officer in doing so.").

6.   Example of Case in Which Reasonable Suspicion Was Found

The best way to get a handle on the case-by-case analysis of reasonable suspicion is to apply the above factors to a real case. A close case on reasonable suspicion is found in *United States v. Weaver,* 966 F.2d 391 (8th Cir.1992). Officer Hicks was at the Kansas City airport, awaiting the arrival of an early morning flight from Los Angeles. As Weaver disembarked from the flight, he caught the officer's attention because he was a "roughly dressed" young African–American male who was carrying two bags and walking rapidly, almost running, down the concourse toward a door leading to a taxi stand. Hicks was aware that a number of young African–American males from street gangs in Los Angeles frequently brought drugs into the Kansas City area. He also testified that narcotics couriers commonly leave an airport by walking quickly towards a taxi. Hicks approached Weaver and asked Weaver if he would answer some questions. Weaver said "o.k." In response to Hicks, Weaver stated that he had been in Los Angeles trying to find his sister who had been missing for several years. Hicks requested to see Weaver's airline ticket, but after searching his pockets, Weaver said that he must have left it on the plane. Nor could Weaver provide any identification, though he did give his correct name and Kansas City address. Hicks testified that while it is extremely uncommon for adults to be without identification, it is common for drug couriers not to have any. Hicks also testified that Weaver appeared to be very nervous; his voice was unsteady, his speech was rapid, his hands shook, and his body swayed. Hicks testified that although people often became nervous when approached by a police officer, Weaver exhibited "more nervousness than innocent people usually do." Weaver declined Hicks' request to search his bags, and began to walk out of the terminal. At this point, Hicks decided to seize the bags, and so informed Weaver. Weaver nevertheless got into the back seat of the taxi with both bags. Hicks grabbed one of the bags and tried to take it out of the taxi. When Weaver began to hit Hicks' hand in an attempt to pry it loose from the bag, he was placed under arrest. Drugs and money were found on Weaver pursuant to a search incident to the arrest. On the basis of all this information, Hicks obtained a warrant to search the bags. A subsequent search of the bags uncovered more than six pounds of crack cocaine.

The court first held that Weaver was not seized until the point where Hicks decided to seize Weaver's bags. Up to that point, it was a consensual encounter. The question then was whether there was reasonable suspicion to stop Weaver at the time that Officer Hicks seized the bags. If not, the subsequent search of Weaver's person, and even the search of the bags pursuant to a warrant, would be considered "fruit of the poisonous tree" and the evidence could be excluded. The court held that reasonable suspicion existed for a seizure. It relied most heavily on the facts that Weaver was walking briskly, lacked identification, had no plane ticket, and was exceedingly nervous. As the Supreme Court has done, the court in *Weaver* emphasized that while each of the factors could be viewed as innocent, non-suspicious details, a reasonable suspicion was raised when all the factors were considered together.

a. Dissent

Chief Judge Arnold dissented in *Weaver*. He argued that "sometimes innocent people lose their tickets, to say nothing of ticket coupons which may be of no further use to them." He interpreted Weaver's failure to produce identification as a *refusal* to produce identification, and noted that Weaver had an absolute right to refuse to produce identification in the context of an encounter: "we have not yet come to the point in this country when citizens must identify themselves to public employees." Finally, he argued that the court placed too much weight on Weaver's nervousness, noting that such a subjective factor "can be wheeled out for use in almost every airport-stop case." Judge Arnold was particularly taken aback by the Officer's testimony that Weaver was more nervous than an innocent person would be. He stated that "the predicate of this assertion must be that Agent Hicks and his colleagues have questioned many passengers, some of whom are innocent, enough passengers, in fact, to be able to vouchsafe an expert opinion on the relative nervousness of drug-carrying passengers as opposed to law abiding ones."

7. Example of Case in Which Reasonable Suspicion Was Not Found

In *United States v. Rodriguez*, 976 F.2d 592 (9th Cir.1992), officers sitting in a marked car alongside Interstate 8 in California saw Rodriguez drive toward straight, kept both hands on the wheel, and looked straight ahead. He did not "acknowledge" the agents, which they thought suspicious because all the other traffic which went by had acknowledged the presence of the officers. The agents testified that Interstate 8 is a "notorious route for alien smugglers" and that Ford Rancheros have a space behind the seat where illegal aliens can be concealed. The agents followed Rodriguez. They testified that his car responded sluggishly when it went over a bump, as if heavily loaded, rather than with a "crisp, light movement" that was typical of a Ford Ranchero. They also noted that, while being followed, Rodriguez looked often into his rear view mirror and swerved slightly within his lane. On the basis of this information, the officers stopped Rodriguez's vehicle. A subsequent search yielded 168 pounds of marijuana.

The court held that reasonable suspicion did not exist to stop Rodriguez. It first noted that the testimony of the officers was eerily similar to that provided in other cases, so similar that "an inquiring mind may wonder about the recurrence of such fortunate parallelism in the experiences of the arresting agents." The court concluded that it could not accept "what has come to appear to be a prefabricated or recycled profile of suspicious behavior very likely to sweep many ordinary citizens into a generality of suspicious appearance merely on hunch." According to the court, the factors cited by the agents "describe too many individuals to create a reasonable suspicion that this particular defendant was engaged in criminal activity." The court concluded as follows:

> In short, the agents in this case saw a Hispanic man cautiously and attentively driving a 16 year-old Ford with a worn suspension, who glanced in his rear view mirror while being followed by agents in a marked Border Patrol car. This profile could certainly fit hundreds or thousands of law abiding daily users of the highways of Southern California.

8. Use of Profiles

In both *Weaver* and *Rodriguez*, it is apparent that the officers were comparing the activity of the suspect to a profile of a person engaged in criminal activity. Officers often use profiles to determine whether the conduct of citizens is sufficiently suspicious to justify a stop. A profile is a list of characteristics compiled by a law enforcement agency, which characteristics have been found through experience to be common to those engaged in a certain type of criminal activity. The most common example is a drug courier profile, but officers also employ such profiles as gang member profiles.

a. Match With Profile Is Not Dispositive

As shown by the differing results in *Weaver* and *Rodriguez*, it is apparent that the suspect's correlation with a profile is no guarantee that there is reasonable suspicion to justify a stop. Partly this is because the profile used will vary among law enforcement agencies, and partly it is because the courts adhere steadfastly to the principle of *Terry* that the reasonableness of a stop must be assessed in light of the *particular circumstances*. See *United States v. Berry,* 670 F.2d 583 (5th Cir.1982) (because a case-by-case approach is mandated, "a match between certain characteristics listed on the profile and characteristics exhibited by a defendant does not automatically establish reasonable suspicion"). Most importantly, the suspect's correlation with a drug courier profile is not dispositive because many profiles are obviously overinclusive. Profiles have been used to find it suspicious that a person was the first to deplane, that another was among the last to deplane, and that another deplaned in the middle of the crowd. A person who uses one-way tickets can match a profile, while a person who uses round-trip tickets can also match a profile. Correlation with a profile has been found when a person was carrying luggage and when a person was carrying no luggage. Therefore, the courts have generally concluded that "we will assign no characteristic greater or lesser weight merely because the characteristic happens to be present on, or absent from, the profile." *United States v. Berry, supra.*

b. Officers' Use of Profile Does Not Render the Stop Illegal
On the other hand, the officer's use of a drug courier profile does not somehow taint the stop, assuming reasonable suspicion exists on the facts. In *United States v. Sokolow, supra,* the Court concluded that a court "sitting to determine the existence of reasonable suspicion must require the agent to articulate the factors leading to that conclusion, but the fact that these factors may be set forth in a profile does not somehow detract from their evidentiary significance as seen by a trained agent." In other words, a profile can be used as an investigative tool by the officer, but the actual existence of reasonable suspicion must be determined on the facts. The suspect's correlation with a profile is, in itself, irrelevant.

9. Relevance of Suspect's Race
For questions of identity, the suspect's race must obviously be considered relevant. For example, if the perpetrator is described a black male in his 20's, an officer assessing reasonable suspicion must necessarily take into account that the person he decides to stop is black. More difficult questions arise, however, when the suspect's race is taken into account as a suspicious factor, on the ground that a person of the suspect's racial group may be unusual in the place where the stop occurs. For example, is it appropriate to consider it suspicious that an African–American male was walking down the street of an affluent suburb at 11 p.m., where the same conduct from a white male would not be suspicious in the least?

a. Traditional Rule Is That Racial Incongruity Is Relevant

Courts have traditionally considered racial "incongruity" as relevant in assessing reasonable suspicion—although such incongruity is not ordinarily dispositive. See *United States v. Weaver,* 966 F.2d 391 (8th Cir.1992) ("Had Hicks relied solely on Weaver's race as a basis for his suspicions, we would have a different case before us. As it is, however, facts are not to be ignored simply because they may be unpleasant—and the unpleasant fact in this case is that Hicks had knowledge * * * that young black Los Angeles gangs were flooding the Kansas City area with cocaine. To that extent, then, race, when coupled with the other factors Hicks relied upon, was a factor in the decision to approach and ultimately detain Weaver. We wish it were otherwise, but we take the facts as they are presented to us, and not as we would like them to be.") See also *State v. Ruiz,* 19 Ariz.App. 84, 504 P.2d 1307 (1973) (Hispanic person properly stopped where it was officers' experience that it was unusual for other than black people to frequent the area except for the purpose of buying drugs).

b. Recent Trend to Prohibit Reliance on Racial Incongruity

Recently, some courts have invalidated stops which have been based in material part on the fact that it may have been unusual for a person of the suspect's race to be in a certain place at a certain time. One court has referred to a stop on the basis of racial incongruity as "invidious discrimination". See *City of St. Paul v. Uber,* 450 N.W.2d 623 (Minn.App.1990) (invalidating a stop made on the basis that a white male from the suburbs was driving in an area with mostly African–American residents: "We would not tolerate the blatant discriminatory proposition that any member of a minority group found on a public street in [an affluent suburb] had better live there, or be required to stop and justify his or her presence to the authorities."); *State v. Barber,* 118 Wash.2d 335, 823 P.2d 1068 (1992) ("racial incongruity, i.e., a person of any race being allegedly out of place in a particular geographic area, should never constitute a finding of reasonable suspicion of criminal activity").

c. Reliance on Racial Incongruity Where Reasonable Suspicion Exists on Other Grounds

What if the officer stops a person on the basis of racial incongruity, but he is also aware of sufficient suspicious factors to justify a stop independent of the suspect's race? Does the officer's subjective reliance on race—assuming that reliance on racial incongruity is impermissible—render the stop illegal? The answer would appear to be "no" because a court applying *Terry* must assess the *reasonableness* of the officer's conduct. The question is whether the officer acted in an objectively reasonable manner, not whether the officer had a certain offensive state of mind. So for example, in *Barber, supra,* an officer saw three

African–American males walking down the street in an affluent white suburb. One was carrying a duffle bag over his shoulder, and there was obviously something heavy in the bag. Another was carrying a bundled blanket loaded with heavy items. When the officer passed them in his marked car, the three men panicked and the man with the sack threw it into the bushes, where it landed with a thud. The officer stopped the men and stolen goods were recovered. The court assumed, on the basis of the suppression hearing testimony, that the officer relied at least in part on the suspect's racial incongruity to make the stop. But the court refused to invalidate the stop, choosing instead to remand the case to determine whether sufficient information existed to support the stop independent of the suspects' racial incongruity. In other words, if reasonable suspicion existed to support a stop regardless of the race of the suspects, the stop would be objectively reasonable and therefore not illegal. Presumably, an officer would have reasonable suspicion to stop three men of any race, where they are carrying heavy and suspicious bundles, and where one bundle is thrown away when the officer approaches.

10. Officers Can Rely on Collective Knowledge

An officer involved in making a stop need not be personally aware of all the facts justifying the intrusion. The officer may rely on the knowledge of another officer or officers. This "collective knowledge" concept was endorsed by the Supreme Court in *United States v. Hensley,* 469 U.S. 221, 105 S.Ct. 675, 83 L.Ed.2d 604 (1985), where officers who stopped Hensley in Kentucky acted solely in reliance on a flyer issued by Ohio police stating that Hensley was wanted for criminal investigation in connection with a felony committed in Ohio. The Court held that a stop based on such a flyer was permissible so long as the officers who issued the bulletin themselves had an adequate basis for making a stop.

a. Rationale

The principle behind *Hensley* is that law enforcement officers must be allowed to pool and coordinate their information; otherwise law enforcement interests would be unduly impaired in an era where criminal suspects are increasingly mobile.

b. Limitation

If the officers who have personal knowledge do not in fact have sufficient information to support a stop, then the stop is illegal. In other words, the stopping officer is not entitled to plead his lack of personal knowledge as an excuse for stopping a citizen where reasonable suspicion does not in fact exist. The Court in *Hensley* specifically stated that if the Ohio officers who issued the bulletin did not have a sufficient factual basis for requesting the stop, then the stop of Hensley would have been illegal.

11. Use of Informants

As with probable cause, an officer's assessment of reasonable suspicion is often based in whole or in part on information from an informant. In *Illinois v. Gates, supra,* the Court employed a totality of circumstances approach to assess the reliability of an informant's statement that was used by the officers to justify a search as based on probable cause. In *Alabama v. White,* 496 U.S. 325, 110 S.Ct. 2412, 110 L.Ed.2d 301 (1990), the Court held that an anonymous tip which was partially corroborated could constitute reasonable suspicion to support a *Terry* stop.

a. Facts of *White*

Police received an anonymous tip that White would be leaving a particular apartment in a brown Plymouth station wagon with the right taillight lens broken, and would be driving to Dobey's Motel with a brown attache case containing cocaine. The officers went to the apartment, and saw White enter a brown Plymouth station wagon with a broken right taillight. She was not carrying an attache case. The police followed the station wagon as it took the most direct route to Dobey's Motel. White was stopped just short of Dobey's Motel, and consented to the search of a brown attache case that had been placed in the car before police began surveillance. The officers found marijuana in the attache case, and three milligrams of cocaine in White's purse, which was searched during processing at the station. The issue for the Court was whether there was reasonable suspicion to make the stop, given that the tip was from an anonymous informant and that none of the activity corroborated was in any way suspicious.

b. Analysis in *White*

The Court relied on two lines of authority to find that reasonable suspicion existed on the basis, in part, of the tip from an anonymous informant. First, the Court relied heavily on the totality of circumstances approach to informant's tips as supporting probable cause, originally established in *Illinois v. Gates*. As discussed in the section on probable cause, the Court in *Gates* looked to the two traditional "prongs" of veracity and basis of knowledge in assessing the informant's reliability, and also considered the extent to which the officers corroborated the informant's tip. But the fact that a tip has been corroborated receives more consideration under *Gates* than previously.

The second established line of cases used in *White* is that proceeding from *Adams v. Williams,* 407 U.S. 143, 92 S.Ct. 1921, 32 L.Ed.2d 612 (1972), where the Court specifically applied the *Terry* doctrine and upheld a stop based on a known informant's tip, even though the tip was not reliable enough to satisfy the then-applicable *Spinelli* standards. The Court in *Adams* concluded that *Spinelli's* requirements for probable cause were unnecessarily rigorous for the less demanding standard of reasonable suspicion. In other words, reasonable suspicion is not only a less demanding standard of proof, it is also less rigorous in the types of information that can be used as proof.

The majority opinion in *White* applies the reasoning of *Adams v. Williams* to the post-*Gates* era, and to a situation where the informant was anonymous rather than known. The majority found that the factors of basis of knowledge and veracity are also relevant in the reasonable suspicion context. But the Court reasoned that these factors must be applied even more permissively than under the *Gates* approach, since reasonable suspicion is a less rigorous standard of proof than probable cause.

c.   **Application of the More Permissive Standards to the Facts of *White***
Even given the lesser showing required, the majority in *White* acknowledged that the anonymous tip did not itself provide reasonable suspicion, since it did not show that the informant was reliable, nor did it give any indication of the informant's basis for predicting White's activities. However, that did not end the analysis. While the tip did not stand on its own, even for reasonable suspicion, the majority found that as with probable cause, corroboration of the tip could lead to a finding of reasonable suspicion. The crucial question in *White,* then, was whether the corroboration was sufficient to cure the defects in the tip standing alone.

d.   **Corroboration Not as Substantial**
The majority determined that the corroboration in *White* was not as substantial as that in *Gates*. In *Gates,* for instance, the officers corroborated relatively unique travel plans, with more details than those given by the informant in *White*. Also, the defendants in *Gates* were observed to engage in somewhat suspicious travel activity. There was nothing unique, suspicious, or detailed about the travel activity in *White*. White merely got in the car and drove a direct route toward Dobey's Motel; the route could also have taken her to a wide variety of places, and even if she was going to Dobey's Motel, there was nothing inherently incriminating or suspicious about that fact.

However, the fact that the corroboration was less than that necessary to satisfy probable cause was held not fatal in *White*. The Court reasoned, as it had in *Adams,* that since reasonable suspicion is a less stringent standard than probable cause, the degree of corroboration required to support reasonable suspicion could be correspondingly less. The lesser standard is a reduction in both quantity and quality of proof.

e. Corroboration Sufficient to Support a Stop

The Court found that the stop of White was based on reasonable suspicion, even though the corroboration of the tip was not complete, and in fact the tip was not correct in some details. The majority acknowledged that the corroboration of the mere existence of the car was insignificant, since "anyone could have predicted that fact because it was a condition presumably existing at the time of the call." What was important was the caller's ability to predict White's *future behavior*, i.e. the travel plans. According to the Court, the correct prediction of itinerary (incomplete though the itinerary was at the time of the stop) demonstrated that the informant had inside knowledge about White's activity. Unlike the facts about the car, the general public would have had no way of knowing White's future travel plans. The Court found it reasonable for police to believe that a person with access to innocent inside information is likely to also have access to reliable information about that individual's illegal activities—at least it is an inference strong enough to support the minimal, lesser standards of reasonable suspicion.

f. Dissent in *White*

Justice Stevens wrote a short dissenting opinion, joined by Justices Brennan and Marshall. The dissenters argued that the activity predicted by the informant and corroborated by the police (i.e. leaving an apartment and driving toward a motel) was completely innocent, and that any prediction as to criminal activity was a leap of faith that could not reasonably be made. Justice Stevens found it especially dangerous that an anonymous informant, with the barest knowledge of a person's innocent future activity, could generate a police intrusion. He argued that, after *White,* an officer can draw a reasonable inference that the tipster's conclusion of criminal activity is reliable even though it could be patently false and not verifiable. He concluded that "an anonymous neighbor's prediction about somebody's time of departure and probable destination is anything but a reliable basis for assuming that the commuter is in possession of an illegal substance—particularly when the person is not even carrying the attache case described by the tipster."

g. Reasonably Correct Prediction of Future Activity Is Crucial

After *White,* a very important form of corroboration will be evidence showing an informant's substantially correct prediction of future activity. It need only be substantially correct, since reasonable suspicion is such a minimal standard. See *United States v. Thompson,* 906 F.2d 1292 (8th Cir.1990) (where informant predicted defendant would be robbing certain banks, and defendant was parked outside one of the banks, there was reasonable suspicion to make a stop, even though description of car and license plate were wrong). Moreover, the activity corroborated can be completely innocent, again because the minimal reasonable suspicion standard allows an inference to be drawn that an informant's prediction of innocent activity makes it sufficiently likely that the prediction of criminal activity is true.

h. **Corroboration of Contemporaneous Conditions Is Entitled To Little Weight**

On the other hand, the Court in *White* clearly indicated that corroboration is insufficient if all that is confirmed is a condition that existed at the time the tip was made. Such confirmation gives no indication that the informant has inside information. See *Minnesota v. Albrecht,* 465 N.W.2d 107 (Minn.App.1991) (anonymous tip giving general directions to defendant's house, and stating that defendant had a red and white pickup truck, was a drug dealer, and that informant had seen marijuana in defendant's home 6–8 times, and as recently as 5 days before, was not sufficiently corroborated by verification by police of location of defendant's home and of the fact that he owned the pickup truck; the facts corroborated were "easily obtained facts and conditions" and not predictions of future actions).

i. **Reliability of a Tip Is Irrelevant if Police Investigation Uncovers Sufficient Facts**

If the investigation made to corroborate the tip uncovers articulable facts which independently support a reasonable suspicion of criminal activity, then it does not matter whether the tip is reliable or not. For example, in *United States v. Lane,* 909 F.2d 895 (6th Cir.1990), the police received an anonymous tip that drug dealing was going on in an apartment hallway in a building known to police for drug activity. When uniformed officers entered the building, the defendants fled at the sight of them. The court held that the flight, "along with the background facts" supplied the officers with a reasonable basis for conducting an investigative stop and made it "unnecessary to decide whether the anonymous tip in this case was sufficiently corroborated."

D. THE RIGHT TO FRISK INCIDENT TO A STOP

A stop is a seizure. A frisk is a search, which is an independent intrusion that must be separately justified. The justification for a frisk is to protect the officer who is making the stop. In *Terry,* the Court reasoned that if an officer has the right to make a stop, he should be able to protect himself in the course of a lawful seizure. It therefore held that if policer officers are justified in believing that the individuals whose suspicious behavior they are investigating at close range are armed and presently dangerous, they may conduct a limited protective search for weapons. As one court applying *Terry* has stated: "The Fourth Amendment does not require police to allow a suspect to draw first." *United States v. Rideau,* 969 F.2d 1572 (5th Cir.1992).

The Court in *Terry* stated that there were two critical determinations that must be made in judging the legality of a frisk: "whether the officer's action was justified at its *inception*, and whether it was reasonably related in *scope* to the circumstances which justified the interference in the first place."

1. **Frisk Is Not a Search for Evidence**

Since the justification for a frisk is to protect the officer who is making a stop, it follows that *Terry* does not permit a search for evidence. A search for evidence, in the absence of a need to protect the officer, requires *probable cause*. In *Arizona v. Hicks,* 480 U.S. 321, 107 S.Ct. 1149, 94 L.Ed.2d 347 (1987), the Court refused to permit a search for evidence where the officers had only reasonable suspicion and not probable cause to believe that the search would be successful. The Court in *Hicks* squarely rejected the Government's argument that reasonable suspicion was sufficient to justify a search for evidence beneath a stereo turntable; the Government argued that the search was so limited as to be merely a "cursory inspection" rather than a full-blown search. But the Court stated that "a search is a search" and refused to distinguish between extensive searches and cursory inspections. Thus, even cursory inspections for evidence require probable cause. See *Maryland v. Buie,* 494 U.S. 325, 110 S.Ct. 1093, 108 L.Ed.2d 276 (1990) (re-affirming *Hicks* and distinguishing a self-protective search under *Terry* from a search for evidence).

a. **Plain View**

While a search for evidence cannot be conducted as part of a frisk, it will often occur that an officer, in the course of a lawful self-protective frisk, will uncover evidence of crime. For example, an officer who has reasonable suspicion of bodily harm may frisk and pull out a hard object on the suspect's person which may be a weapon. If the object turns out to be a large sum of cash, or tightly bundled drugs, this evidence can be lawfully seized under the plain view doctrine.

2. **Inception of a Frisk; Reasonable Suspicion of Bodily Harm**

Terry requires "reasonable, individualized suspicion before a search for weapons can be conducted." *Maryland v. Buie,* 494 U.S. 325, 334 (1990). Thus, the same standard of proof is required for a frisk as is required for a stop. However, the question to which the standard is applied is somewhat different. The question is not whether there is reasonable suspicion to believe that the suspect has committed or is about to commit a crime. Assuming that this is the case and thus that a stop is justified, the question upon which a frisk depends is whether there is reasonable suspicion to believe that the suspect is armed and dangerous. As stated in *Buie,* such reasonable suspicion must be based on articulable facts specific to the suspect, and not on mere hunches.

a. Automatic, Immediate Right to Frisk a Person Suspected of Violent Crime

If an officer reasonably suspects that a person is involved in a crime of violence, that same reasonable suspicion will ordinarily justify an officer in believing that the suspect may be armed and dangerous. Justice Harlan, in his concurrence in *Terry,* stated that "the right to frisk must be immediate and automatic if the reason for the stop is, as here, an articulable suspicion of a crime of violence." His view was subsequently adopted by a majority of the Court in *Adams v. Williams,* 407 U.S. 143, 92 S.Ct. 1921, 32 L.Ed.2d 612 (1972), where the officer had reasonable suspicion to believe that the suspect was involved in a violent crime, and the Court upheld an immediate protective frisk. Lower courts have held that the right to frisk is automatic for such crimes as robbery, burglary, rape, and assault with a deadly weapon.

b. Drug Distribution

If a person has been stopped on suspicion of large-scale drug distribution, most courts will find that the officer has an automatic right to a self-protective frisk. The rationale is that it is not unreasonable to assume that drug dealers are likely to be armed, even though drug dealing is not per se a crime of violence. See *United States v. Brown,* 913 F.2d 570 (8th Cir.1990) ("since weapons and violence are frequently associated with drug transactions, the officers reasonably believed that the individuals with whom they were dealing were armed and dangerous").

c. Non-violent Crimes

For other types or crimes, such as shoplifting, public drunkenness, prostitution, or bookmaking, there must be articulable circumstances present other than the suspicion of the crime itself, in order to justify a protective frisk. Examples of some common factors include: a *bulge* on the suspect that appears to be a weapon; a *sudden movement* by the suspect toward a place where a weapon might be hidden; *previous violent activity* on the part of the suspect, known to the officer; *aggressive or violent behavior* on the part of the suspect; the *number of suspects compared to the number of police officers*; and *the nature of the surroundings and the time of day.*

Example: In *United States v. Rideau,* 969 F.2d 1572 (5th Cir.1992) officers were patrolling a high crime area, where people often carried weapons and transacted drug deals on the street, and where public drunkenness was a recurring problem. Officer Ellison saw a man wearing dark clothing standing in the road. Ellison flashed his bright lights to see the man better and to encourage him to get out of the road. The man stumbled as he moved toward the shoulder. Ellison suspected he was drunk. He pulled over, got out of the car, and approached the man to investigate. Ellison asked the man his name. The man seemed nervous; when he did not answer but began to back away, Ellison immediately closed the gap and reached out to pat the man's outer clothing. The first place he touched was the man's right front pants pocket, where he felt a firearm. Ellison removed the gun and placed the man under arrest. The man, Rideau, was subsequently charged with illegal possession of a firearm, and he moved to exclude the gun.

The court held that the gun was legally obtained as a result of a permissible *Terry* frisk. The court relied on the following articulable facts: First, Rideau backed away from the officer, so "it was not unreasonable under the circumstances for Ellison to have feared that Rideau was moving back to give himself time and space to draw a weapon". Second, Rideau's moves took place at night. Third, the confrontation occurred in a high crime area. The court recognized that the mere fact that a person is in a high crime area at night is not in itself enough to support either a stop or a frisk. But the court concluded that "when someone engages in *suspicious activity* in a high crime area, where weapons and violence abound, police officers must be particularly cautious in approaching and questioning him."

3. Self-Protective Frisk of Those Not Suspected of a Crime

A question that often arises is whether an officer can frisk a person who is not himself suspected of a crime, but who is in the vicinity of a police officer acting in the course of lawful police activity. For example in *Ybarra v. Illinois,* 444 U.S. 85, 100 S.Ct. 338, 62 L.Ed.2d 238 (1979) officers arrived at a bar to conduct a search pursuant to a search warrant. They decided to frisk everyone who was in the bar. The Supreme Court declared that Ybarra's *mere presence* in the bar was not enough to indicate reasonable suspicion of bodily harm, and therefore that the frisk of Ybarra was illegal. The Court emphasized that *Terry* mandated a *case-by-case* approach, and that an officer cannot conduct a frisk unless he or she has *articulable* facts supporting reasonable suspicion that the suspect presents a risk of harm.

a. Automatic Companion Rule

Some courts have held that an officer who is conducting an arrest has an *automatic right* to conduct a weapons frisk on any companion of the arrestee. The leading case following this view is *United States v. Berryhill,* 445 F.2d 1189 (9th Cir.1971), where the court upheld the frisk of a person who was a passenger in a car driven by the arrestee. The court reasoned that "it is inconceivable that a peace officer effecting a lawful arrest of an occupant of a vehicle must expose himself to a shot in the back from defendant's associate because he cannot, on the spot, make the nice distinction between whether the other is a companion in crime or a social acquaintance." Other courts have rejected the automatic companion rule on the ground that it is inconsistent with the case-by-case approach to reasonable suspicion mandated by *Terry*. In these courts, a companion or associate can only be frisked upon articulable facts establishing reasonable suspicion to believe that the person is armed and dangerous. See *United States v. Whitfield*, 907 F.2d 798 (8th Cir.1990) (rejecting automatic companion rule, but upholding the frisk on the ground that the companion of the arrestee was wearing a bulletproof vest and there was a suspicious bulge underneath the vest).

4.   **Ordering a Suspect Out of a Car For Self–Protection**
In *Pennsylvania v. Mimms*, 434 U.S. 106, 98 S.Ct. 330, 54 L.Ed.2d 331 (1977), an officer stopped a vehicle for the purpose of issuing a traffic citation. The officer lacked grounds to conduct a frisk, but he nonetheless ordered the driver, Mimms, to step out of the car. This was a standard police practice. When Mimms got out of the car, the officer noted a bulge under his jacket, which *then* gave the officer grounds to conduct a frisk, and a gun was uncovered. Mimms did not challenge the stop itself; he argued that the officer acted unreasonably in ordering him out of the car, in the absence of reasonable suspicion to believe that Mimms was armed and dangerous. The Supreme Court balanced the state interest in officer safety against the individual interest in privacy, and held that an officer has an automatic right to order a person to step out of a vehicle where that vehicle has been lawfully stopped. The Court found this to be merely a "de minimus" incremental intrusion which was justified as a "precautionary measure to afford a degree of protection to the officer."

a.   **Bright Line Rule**
The Court implicitly determined that its automatic rule for de minimus intrusions was not prohibited by the case-by-case approach to reasonable suspicion mandated by *Terry*.

b.   **Passengers**
Some courts have extended the automatic rule of *Mimms* to passengers (see *State v. Webster*, 170 Ariz. 372, 824 P.2d 768 (App.1991)), while others have not (see *Cousart v. United States*, 618 A.2d 96 (D.C.App.1992)). The courts which have refused to extend *Mimms* to passengers have reasoned that the intrusion on the passenger's privacy interest is greater than that of a driver, who has been lawfully stopped for some violation.

5. Limitations on the Scope of a Frisk

In conducting a frisk, an officer can be no more intrusive than is necessary to protect against the risk of harm posed by the suspect. Ordinarily, a pat-down is sufficient to determine whether the suspect is carrying weapons which could be used effectively by the suspect during the course of the stop. A detailed touching of all areas of the suspect's body is beyond the scope of a *Terry* frisk. See *Rideau, supra* (touching the suspect's pocket to determine whether there was a weapon "was a limited and tailored response" to the officer's fears for his safety, and was not "the intrusive exploration of a detainee's body" forbidden by *Terry*).

a. Feeling an Object During a Pat–Down

If an officer feels an object during a pat-down, the question is whether the officer can take the object from the suspect's person in order to determine whether it may be a weapon. This depends on whether there is reasonable suspicion to believe that the object could be a weapon. Generally speaking, an inspection of the object is not permissible if it is *soft to the touch*. See *Ellis v. State,* 573 So.2d 724 (Miss.1990) (officer who pulls out object which turns out to be a bag of marijuana has acted beyond the permissible scope of a *Terry* frisk). If the object feels hard to the touch, then the question is whether it could be a weapon in light of its *size or contour*; because the operative standard is reasonable suspicion, the officer need not be certain that the object is a weapon. See *United States v. Quarles,* 955 F.2d 498 (8th Cir.1992) (large hard lump "might have been a firearm").

b. Probable Cause

If an officer feels a soft package, it cannot be taken out and inspected under the *Terry* doctrine; but the fact that the suspect was carrying a soft package may, together with other factors, constitute probable cause that the suspect is carrying contraband. If this is so, then the suspect may be arrested and the package may be searched incident to the arrest. See *United States v. Salazar,* 945 F.2d 47 (2d Cir.1991) (officer who conducts legal pat-down of suspected drug dealer and feels a soft package has probable cause to arrest and search the suspect for drugs). See the discussion of the "plain touch" doctrine, *supra*.

c. Containers on the Suspect's Person

If the officer takes a hard object from the suspect's person and it turns out to be a container, the question arises whether the officer can open the container under *Terry*. Assuming that up to this point there has been and remains reasonable suspicion that the suspect is armed and dangerous, does the need to protect the officer extend to opening a container that the officer is currently holding? Of course a search of the container is impermissible if it could not reasonably contain a dangerous weapon. See *People v. Roth,* 66 N.Y.2d 688, 496 N.Y.S.2d 413, 487

N.E.2d 270 (1985) (where hard object turned out to be a roll of papers, officer was not justified in unwrapping and examining the papers). But even if it could reasonably contain a weapon, one might question whether opening it is necessary in light of the fact that the officer has custody of the container. Most courts, however, have held that the officer may open the container on the ground that the suspect is only being stopped and not arrested. Since the stop is a momentary intrusion, and the suspect must eventually be released (if arrested because probable cause subsequently develops, the container may be searched incident to arrest), the officer will have to return the container to the suspect. Under these circumstances, an officer may reasonably fear the possibility of harm if he returns the container unexamined at the conclusion of the stop—especially considering the fact that the officer's back may be turned after the stop is concluded. See *Michigan v. Long,* 463 U.S. 1032, 103 S.Ct. 3469, 77 L.Ed.2d 1201 (1983) (noting the risk to officers after a stop if the suspect is not arrested and regains access to weapons). Courts have generally been unsympathetic to the argument the risk to the officer is minimal where the suspect has been told that he is free to go. But see *People v. Torres,* 74 N.Y.2d 224, 544 N.Y.S.2d 796, 543 N.E.2d 61 (1989) ("It is unrealistic to assume that having been stopped and questioned without incident, a suspect who is about to be released and permitted to proceed on his way would reach for a concealed weapon and threaten the departing officer's safety.").

6. **Right to Protective Search Beyond the Suspect's Person**
Assuming reasonable suspicion to believe that a suspect is armed and dangerous, the question arises whether the officer can search areas beyond the suspect's person on the grounds of self-protection. For example, can the officer search containers being carried by the suspect, such as briefcases, or containers within the "grab area" of the suspect? As with containers found on the person, most courts have permitted protective searches of containers carried by the suspect or within the suspect's grab area. Again, the courts reason that such a search is permitted even if the suspect is denied access to the container during the course of the stop. Thus, in *United States v. Johnson,* 932 F.2d 1068 (5th Cir.1991), the court upheld a cursory inspection of a pair of overalls located a few feet away from a suspect who appeared to be attempting to burglarize a house. The court reasoned that the mere separation of the suspect from his effects during the stop would not be a sufficient protection, since if the stop was terminated, the officers would have to return the property to the suspect. An officer could reasonably conclude that the property should be examined before returning it to the suspect.

a. **Protective Search of Automobiles**
In *Michigan v. Long,* 463 U.S. 1032, 103 S.Ct. 3469, 77 L.Ed.2d 1201 (1983), the Court upheld a protective search of the passenger compartment of a car during the course of a *Terry* stop. Long was

stopped by officers who saw him drive erratically. Long was out of his car by the time the officers approached, and he appeared to be under the influence of drugs. He failed to respond to requests for license and registration, and then began to walk toward his car. An officer flashed a light into the car and saw a hunting knife. The officers then conducted a protective search of the passenger compartment and discovered marijuana. The Court held that *Terry* permits a limited examination of any area from which a person, who police reasonably suspect is dangerous, might gain a weapon that could be effectively used against the officers. As discussed above, the Court reasoned that the risk of harm to the officers was unabated by the fact that the suspect would only have access to the weapon after the stop was terminated and the suspect was free to leave. The Court found that there could be a risk of harm to the officers where, "if the suspect is not placed under arrest, he will be permitted to reenter his automobile, and he will then have access to any weapons inside." Lower courts after *Long* have permitted cursory inspections of the accessible areas of the passenger compartment of an automobile whenever there is reasonable suspicion to believe that the suspect poses a threat of harm. See *United States v. Holifield,* 956 F.2d 665 (7th Cir.1992) (search of locked glove compartment permissible where keys were in car, suspect was about to re-enter car, and suspect had exhibited "erratic driving and aggressive and boisterous behavior"). However, a search will not be permitted under *Long* if there is no reasonable suspicion in the first place to believe that the suspect poses a risk of harm to the officer or others. See *United States v. Lott,* 870 F.2d 778 (1st Cir.1989) (search of passenger compartment not permitted under *Long* where the police were not in fear for their own safety, as indicated by the fact that the suspects were not frisked upon exiting the car; *Long* does not permit a search for evidence).

b. Protective Sweep

A "protective sweep" is a quick and limited search of a premises, incident to an arrest and conducted to protect the safety of police officers or others. In *Maryland v. Buie,* 494 U.S. 325, 110 S.Ct. 1093, 108 L.Ed.2d 276 (1990), the Court held that a protective sweep could be conducted if officers have reasonable suspicion to believe that it is necessary to protect police officers or the public; probable cause is not required.

i. Facts of *Buie*

Following an armed robbery, police obtained arrest warrants for Buie and his accomplice, and went to Buie's house. Buie was arrested upon emerging from the basement. The officers did a cursory search of the basement to see if anyone else was there, and in the course of that search, they found incriminating evidence in plain view.

ii.   Analysis in *Buie*
      Justice White, writing for the majority, relied most heavily on *Terry*
      and *Michigan v. Long* which held (as discussed above) that in the
      course of a stop, officers could search accessible areas of an
      automobile for a weapon if they had reasonable suspicion to believe
      that the suspect could harm the officers. According to Justice White,
      the reasonable suspicion standard was an appropriate balance
      between the arrestee's remaining privacy interest in the home and
      the officer's safety-based interest in conducting a protective sweep.
      The Court noted that while even a cursory inspection of a home was
      a severe intrusion, the state has a heavy interest in protecting
      officers who are in the course of making an arrest.

iii. Dissent in *Buie*
      Justice Brennan, joined by Justice Marshall, dissented and noted his
      continuing criticism "of the emerging tendency on the part of the
      Court to convert the *Terry* decision from a narrow exception into
      one that swallows the general rule that searches are 'reasonable'
      only if based upon probable cause."

iv.   Reconciling *Buie* with *Hicks*
      A question arises whether the Court's adherence to the probable
      cause standard for searches in *Arizona v. Hicks,* 480 U.S. 321, 107
      S.Ct. 1149, 94 L.Ed.2d 347 (1987) can be justified in light of *Buie.*
      The Court in *Hicks* specifically rejected an approach which would
      balance the nature of the intrusion against the state interest, and
      which would allow cursory inspections for evidence upon reasonable
      suspicion rather than probable cause. In *Buie,* Justice White
      distinguished *Hicks* as involving a search for *evidence*, rather than
      a search for *safety purposes* as in *Terry* and *Long.* Thus, the Court
      has drawn a constitutional distinction between a search for
      protection, which can be justified by reasonable suspicion, and a
      search for evidence for law enforcement purposes, which requires
      probable cause.

v.   Reconciling *Buie* with the Search Incident to Arrest Doctrine
      A question also arises whether the Court's approval of a protective
      sweep during an arrest can be squared with the spatial limitations
      imposed on searches incident to arrest in *Chimel v. California*, 395
      U.S. 752, 89 S.Ct. 2034, 23 L.Ed.2d 685 (1969). In *Chimel*, the
      Court held that the scope of a search incident to arrest was limited
      to the grab area of the arrestee; the protective sweep in *Buie*
      obviously went beyond the grab area. The majority in *Buie* asserted,
      however, that the spatial limitations of *Chimel* were not undermined
      by allowing a protective sweep on reasonable suspicion, since one
      had nothing to do with the other. Unlike a search incident to arrest,

the protective sweep is limited to areas where persons may be hidden; it does not allow the police to thoroughly search an area, as does *Chimel*. Moreover, unlike a search incident to arrest, a protective sweep is not an automatic right of the officer; it is allowed only upon reasonable suspicion of bodily harm. Therefore, the Court's approval of a protective sweep was found to co-exist with the search incident to arrest rule and the spatial limitations of *Chimel* were retained. *Chimel* still prohibits routine, automatic searches of the area beyond the arrestee's reach, and *Buie* is consistent with that prohibition.

vi.   **Protective Sweep Not Permitted to Protect Against Destruction of Evidence**
As emphasized by Justice Stevens in his concurring opinion in *Buie*, a protective sweep can only be conducted for safety purposes, and not to prevent destruction of evidence. The majority in *Buie* specifically refers to protective sweeps as justified to "protect the safety of officers or others." This is consistent with its derivation from *Terry*. A *Terry* search, of which the protective sweep is just an example, can only be supported by interests in self-protection; it cannot be used to search for evidence.

vii.   **Arrests Outside the Home**
In *Buie,* the defendant was arrested in the home. Could a protective sweep of the premises be conducted if the arrest was made just outside the home? Presuming a reasonable fear of bodily harm from someone within the house, courts both before and after *Buie* have answered in the affirmative. See *United States v. Tisdale,* 921 F.2d 1095 (10th Cir.1990); *United States v. Hoyos,* 868 F.2d 1131 (9th Cir.1989) ("If the exigencies to support a protective sweep exist, whether the arrest occurred inside or outside the residence does not affect the reasonableness of the officer's conduct. A bullet fired at an arresting officer standing outside a window is as deadly as one that is projected from one room to another.").

viii.   **Protective Sweep May Be Permissible Upon Any Legal Entry**
Buie dealt with officers acting in the course of a lawful arrest, but there may be other reasons why an officer is lawfully in a residence. An arrest is not a necessary condition to a protective sweep. For example, in *United States v. Flippin,* 924 F.2d 163 (9th Cir.1991) officers entered a motel room after defendant voluntarily consented. They saw a make-up bag in the room. When the officer turned his back, the defendant grabbed the bag and refused to relinquish it. Fearing the defendant was attempting to arm herself, the officer forcibly took the bag from her and opened it. The Ninth Circuit upheld the search, rejecting the argument that *Buie* required an

initial entry with arrest warrant and probable cause before a protective search in the home could occur. The opening of the bag was justified as well as the seizure, because the officer's seizure of it did not dissipate the danger. The defendant, by struggling to retain possession of the bag, made it reasonable to think she might use force to regain possession of it.

ix.   Articulable Facts Must Indicate a Risk of Harm
A protective sweep is not permissible unless the officers have reasonable suspicion that it is necessary to conduct a sweep to neutralize the risk of harm to the officers or others. For example, in *United States v. Akrawi,* 920 F.2d 418, 421 (6th Cir.1990) the court found a protective sweep improper because the agents conducting the sweep "could point to no particular reason to support a reasonable belief that the second floor harbored a dangerous individual. Furthermore, the government has failed to show that the sweep was quick, and occurred at the time of or promptly after the arrest." In *Akrawi,* despite the fact that the person the police came to arrest immediately answered the door and was then arrested, the "agents inexplicably remained in the house for forty-five minutes." The court further held that, after a proper protective sweep has determined that no one else is on the premises, an officer's continued presence or reentry without a warrant is illegal.

E.   BRIEF AND LIMITED DETENTIONS: THE LINE BETWEEN STOP AND ARREST
The Court in *Terry* permitted a stop upon a standard of proof less demanding than that of probable cause required for an arrest, in part because a stop is a more limited intrusion than an arrest. But it is often difficult to distinguish between a stop and an arrest. Both are seizures, and courts have struggled in defining when an intrusion crosses the line and requires probable cause. A totality of the circumstances approach is employed. Generally speaking, the following factors have been considered relevant: whether the suspect has been *forced to move to a custodial area for investigative purposes*; whether investigative techniques employed are *so intrusive as to exceed those identified with a stop*; whether the suspect has been detained for a *lengthy period of time*; and whether the officers employ a *show of force* or a *method of restraint commonly associated with an arrest*. Each of these factors will be discussed below.

1.   Forced Movement of the Suspect to a Custodial Area
In *Florida v. Royer,* 460 U.S. 491, 103 S.Ct. 1319, 75 L.Ed.2d 229 (1983), officers moved Royer from the public area of an airport to a small room, where they sought and obtained Royer's consent to a search of his luggage. The Court held that the consent was invalid because it was obtained during the course of an arrest without probable cause. In determining that Royer had been arrested, as opposed to merely stopped, the Court found it crucial that officers had transferred the site of the encounter from the airport

concourse to a small interrogation room, solely for the purpose of obtaining Royer's consent to a search of his luggage. The Court concluded that "at the time Royer produced the key to his suitcase, the detention to which he was then subjected was a more serious intrusion in his personal liberty than is allowable on mere suspicion of criminal activity."

a. Police Cars

A suspect who is detained in a police car, for purposes of questioning or other investigation, is ordinarily found to be under arrest. See *United States v. Thompson,* 906 F.2d 1292 (8th Cir.1990) (placing suspect in squad car was not within the scope of a *Terry* stop, where it was done to prolong the investigation and not to ensure the safety of the officers).

b. Transporting the Suspect to the Station for Interrogation or Fingerprinting

The Supreme Court has held that a suspect cannot be transported without his consent to the stationhouse for interrogation or fingerprinting in the absence of probable cause. Such conduct exceeds the permissible scope of a *Terry* stop. See *Dunaway v. New York,* 442 U.S. 200, 99 S.Ct. 2248, 60 L.Ed.2d 824 (1979) (noting that "detention for custodial interrogation—regardless of its label—intrudes so severely on interests protected by the Fourth Amendment as necessarily to trigger the traditional safeguards against illegal arrest"); *Hayes v. Florida,* 470 U.S. 811, 105 S.Ct. 1643, 84 L.Ed.2d 705 (1985) (Fourth Amendment violated where officers, acting only upon reasonable suspicion, forcibly brought the defendant to the stationhouse for fingerprinting).

c. Forced Movement in Order to Obtain an Immediate Identification

Despite the Supreme Court cases which have held that the forced movement of suspects for investigative purposes is beyond the scope of *Terry,* many courts have found that, if reasonable suspicion exists, it is permissible to transport the suspect a short distance so that eyewitnesses may attempt to make an identification. Courts reason that the only other alternative would be to bring the witnesses to the suspect, and that this alternative might be so time-consuming as to be even more inconvenient to the suspect. See *People v. Hicks,* 68 N.Y.2d 234, 508 N.Y.S.2d 163, 500 N.E.2d 861 (1986) (noting that "securing the defendant and his companion and securing transportation for the witnesses would have been a more time-consuming process than that chosen"). The court in *Hicks* upheld the police procedure because of "the following particular factors: the authorities knew that a crime had been committed; the total period of detention was less than 10 minutes; the crime scene to which defendant was taken was very close, and eyewitnesses were there; and there is no proof of significantly less intrusive means available to accomplish the same purpose."

d. Forced Movement for Purposes of Safety or Security

The Court in *Royer* recognized that "there are undoubtedly reasons of safety and security that would justify moving a suspect from one location to another during an investigatory detention, such as from an airport concourse to the interrogation room." So for example, a suspect may be placed in a police car, even though the officers are operating on only reasonable suspicion and not probable cause, if the suspect cannot safely be left in his own vehicle and detention outside the car is impractical. See *United States v. Manbeck,* 744 F.2d 360 (4th Cir.1984) (suspect cannot be left in his car for safety reasons, and cannot be detained outside of car due to weather conditions); *United States v. Espinosa–Guerra,* 805 F.2d 1502 (11th Cir.1986) (proper to order suspect to walk 70 feet into airport office so that agent could summon an interpreter). Compare *United States v. Ricardo D.,* 912 F.2d 337 (9th Cir.1990) (taking person by the arm and placing him in squad car for questioning held impermissible under *Terry,* where there was no showing that the police procedure was "necessary for safety or security reasons").

2. Investigative Techniques

It is clear that an officer conducting a *Terry* stop can engage in preliminary investigation designed to clear up or to further develop reasonable suspicion. Some preliminary investigative techniques found permissible under *Terry* include: a request for identification (as well as airplane tickets or vehicle registration, depending on the circumstances); a request for an explanation of the suspicious circumstances giving rise to the stop; and a request for consent to search. See *United States v. Holzman,* 871 F.2d 1496 (9th Cir.1989) (request for identification was a legitimate investigative technique in the course of a *Terry* stop); *United States v. Guzman,* 864 F.2d 1512 (10th Cir.1988) ("An officer conducting a routine traffic stop may request a driver's license and vehicle identification."). The officer may also verify the information obtained from the suspect by communicating with others, or by conducting a vehicle registration check or a computer search for outstanding warrants. See *United States v. Glover,* 957 F.2d 1004 (2d Cir.1992) (permissible within the confines of a *Terry* stop to conduct a computer check to verify the accuracy of the suspect's "rather dubious" proof of identification); *United States v. Lego,* 855 F.2d 542 (8th Cir.1988) (proper within the confines of a *Terry* stop to check for outstanding warrants). Courts have also permitted officers to detain suspects on reasonable suspicion in order to conduct a canine sniff or to conduct a preliminary investigation of other suspicious circumstances. See *United States v. Hardy,* 855 F.2d 753 (11th Cir.1988) (proper to detain suspects while canine brought to scene to sniff vehicle); *People v. Contreras,* 780 P.2d 552 (Colo.1989) (examination of visible portions of a car to see if it had been stripped, as anonymous caller had asserted).

a. Overly Intrusive Investigation Techniques

On the other hand, some investigative techniques are themselves so intrusive as to require probable cause. The most obvious example is a search for evidence, which, as stated above, goes beyond the scope of a *Terry* stop. But other techniques may be overly intrusive even if they cannot be labelled a "search." So for example, some courts have held that a suspect cannot be subjected to a series of demanding physical tests to determine sobriety in the absence of probable cause. See *People v. Carlson,* 677 P.2d 310 (Colo.1984) (holding that the full battery of tests employed was so intrusive as to constitute an arrest). Roadside sobriety tests that are less demanding may be permissible under *Terry,* however. See *State v. Wyatt,* 67 Hawaii 293, 687 P.2d 544 (1984) (limited field sobriety test permissible on reasonable suspicion). Other courts have held that probable cause is required for vigorous questioning beyond the scope of the matter for which the suspect was stopped. See *United States v. Walker,* 933 F.2d 812 (10th Cir.1991) (where the suspect was stopped for speeding and established that he had license and registration, it was improper to detain him further to question him about guns and drugs). Compare *United States v. Rivera,* 906 F.2d 319 (7th Cir.1990) (where car was stopped for traffic offenses, questions outside the scope of traffic offenses were permissible where they were prompted by inconsistent answers given by driver and passengers and where the questions were "not egregious enough to make the scope of the trooper's investigation unconstitutional").

3. Time Limits on *Terry* Stops

In *United States v. Sharpe,* 470 U.S. 675, 105 S.Ct. 1568, 84 L.Ed.2d 605 (1985), the Supreme Court rejected an absolute time limit for *Terry* stops, though it recognized that "if an investigative stop continues indefinitely, at some point it can no longer be justified as an investigative stop." The test for assessing whether the time limits for a stop have been violated is "whether the police diligently pursued a means of investigation that was likely to confirm or dispel their suspicions quickly, during which time it was necessary to detain the defendant."

a. Reasonable Diligence Test

In *Sharpe,* the Court made clear that the officer's "diligence" would be assessed in light of all the circumstances, and that a detention would not be found beyond the scope of a *Terry* stop merely because, in retrospect, the officers could have acted more quickly in their investigation. Thus, in *Sharpe,* a DEA officer trailed two vehicles, one a camper which was riding low, and one a Pontiac. He radioed for help, and a Highway Patrol trooper came to his assistance. The officers motioned for both vehicles to pull over. The driver of the Pontiac obeyed, but the camper sped away. The trooper followed the camper and eventually overtook it several miles down the road. Being unversed in drug interdiction, the trooper decided to detain the camper until the DEA agent arrived. The DEA agent had to wait for local police to arrive to "maintain the situation" where the Pontiac had been stopped. The DEA agent then drove to where the camper had been stopped. He smelled marijuana, opened the rear of the camper and discovered a number of bales of marijuana, then proceeded back to the Pontiac to arrest its occupants.

The occupants of the Pontiac had been detained between 30 and 40 minutes before they were arrested. They argued that, if the officers had been diligent, the DEA officer would have followed the camper, since that was the more likely storage vehicle for the drugs. The Court in *Sharpe* rejected this argument, stating that a court "should not indulge in unrealistic second-guessing" of the officer's conduct. The Court stated that "the question is not simply whether some other alternative was available, but whether the police acted unreasonably in failing to recognize or pursue it". The Court concluded that the officers had acted reasonably and within the confines of a *Terry* stop, because they were confronted with a "swiftly developing situation" and were engaged in reasonably diligent activity designed to clear up or develop the suspicious facts which justified the stop. After *Sharpe,* lower courts have tended to give officers the benefit of the doubt in assessing whether their conduct was "reasonably diligent". See, e.g., *United States v. Davies,* 768 F.2d 893 (7th Cir.1985) (forty minute detention did not exceed limits of *Terry* stop, where officers were inexperienced and were awaiting advice from superiors as to how to proceed).

b. Suspect's Actions May Justify a Lengthier Detention
The Court in *Sharpe* also relied on the fact that the delay in detaining the suspects was caused, at least in part, by their own actions, i.e., by the refusal of the driver of the camper to stop even though he was ordered to do so. So for example, if a suspect gives a fictitious name or address, and this results in an inconclusive warrant or identification check, the consequent delay will not count against the officers. See *United States v. Knox,* 839 F.2d 285 (6th Cir.1988) (two suspected drug couriers were lawfully detained for thirty minutes; investigation took longer than usual because the suspects falsely claimed not to know each other).

c. Suspect's Refusal to Consent to a Search
A person who is stopped (or, for that matter, a person who is arrested), still has the right to refuse the officer's request to search the suspect's house, suitcase, etc. This is because the stop does not give the officer a right to conduct any kind of search for evidence. If the suspect refuses the officer's request for consent, this will obviously mean that the investigation pursuant to the stop will proceed less smoothly. However, the suspect's refusal to consent to a search cannot be used as a

justification for prolonging the stop. A refusal to consent to a search is unlike the activity of the suspects in *Sharpe,* which activity was used as a justification for prolonging the detention. In *Sharpe,* the people in the truck sped away even though they were ordered to stop. They had no right to do so. Thus, a detention can be prolonged if the suspect acts improperly to subvert the officer's investigation, but not if the suspect lawfully invokes his constitutional rights.

d. **Detention Must End if Suspicious Circumstances Are Explained**
If a person is stopped on the basis of suspicion that he has engaged in criminal activity, but the suspect identifies himself and preliminary investigation shows that no crime occurred or that the suspect could not have been the perpetrator, then the suspect must be released. See *United States v. Thomas,* 863 F.2d 622 (9th Cir.1988) (where the suspect came out of the car and the officer could see that he did not match the description of the perpetrator, and the suspect identified himself correctly and gave a plausible explanation for his activities, the officer could not continue the detention in order to question the suspect about a gun). However, it may be that in the course of the detention an officer obtains reasonable suspicion about a crime other than that for which the suspect was initially stopped. If that is the case, then the detention may be continued if it is necessary for a diligent investigation of the other crime. See *United States v. Harris,* 928 F.2d 1113 (11th Cir.1991) (detention, originally for traffic infraction, could be continued for investigation of drugs where reasonable suspicion of drug trafficking developed).

e. **Detention of Household Occupants During Execution of a Search Warrant**
In *Michigan v. Summers,* 452 U.S. 692, 101 S.Ct. 2587, 69 L.Ed.2d 340 (1981), the Court held that police officers with a valid search warrant could order persons on the premises to remain there while a search warrant is being executed—even if the length of the detention exceeded that ordinarily associated with a *Terry* stop. The Court declared that such a detention would always be reasonable even though it may take a significant period of time to execute the warrant. The Court reasoned that the detention of an occupant in his home is less serious than the public stops approved in *Terry,* that the search warrant protected against the risk of overreaching by the officers, and that the state had a legitimate interest in preventing flight and the destruction of evidence.

4. **Show of Force or Use of Restraint**
An arrest is often accompanied by the use of handcuffs and drawn gun. It does not follow, however, that every use of such coercive tactics will constitute an arrest. Courts have upheld the use of handcuffs, drawn guns and similar tactics when the circumstances indicate that they are reasonably

necessary to assure the safety of the officers conducting the stop. See, e.g., *United States v. Jackson,* 918 F.2d 236 (1st Cir.1990) (police did not exceed the scope of a *Terry* stop when they approached a vehicle with weapons drawn, where there was reasonable suspicion that the suspects were armed, and where the defendant was a convicted felon and a suspected drug trafficker); *People v. Allen,* 73 N.Y.2d 378, 540 N.Y.S.2d 971, 538 N.E.2d 323 (1989) (proper, within the confines of a *Terry* stop, for officers to handcuff suspect who matched the description of an armed bank robber, after chasing him down a dark alley in a high crime area). On the other hand, the use of a gun or other forceful tactics (such as ordering the suspects to lie prone on the ground) cannot be justified under *Terry* if the suspects are cooperative and there is no reason to think that such tactics are necessary to protect the officers. See *United States v. Del Vizo,* 918 F.2d 821 (9th Cir.1990) (where defendant was cooperative and not suspected of violent crime, officers effectuated an unlawful arrest when they drew their weapons, ordered defendant to lie prone on the street, and handcuffed him).

a.   Relevant Factors

Factors to consider in determining the reasonableness of the officers' use of a show of force or other restraining activity during the course of a stop include: 1. the *number of officers* involved; 2. the *nature of the crime* for which reasonable suspicion exists; 3. whether there is *reasonable suspicion to believe the suspect might be armed*; 4. the *strength of the officers' articulable suspicions*; 5. whether the *suspect is cooperative*; and 6. the *need for immediate action* by the officers and the lack of opportunity for them to have made the stop in *less threatening circumstances.*

Example: In *United States v. Raino,* 980 F.2d 1148 (8th Cir.1992), officers responded to a report of a drive-by shooting, and reports that other shots had been fired in the area. When they arrived, they observed a group of people mingling on the street and several people fighting in a nearby yard. They saw a BMW double-parked, with two females leaning into the driver's side, talking to the driver. The officers approached with their marked car, and the BMW began to pull away. The officers shined a spotlight on the driver, got quickly out of their car, and one officer pointed his gun at the driver and ordered him to stop. The driver was ordered out of the car, and the officers saw a gun in plain view behind the driver's seat. A subsequent search uncovered drugs. Raino, the driver, contended that the show of force elevated the initial detention into an arrest. The Government conceded that there was no probable cause to arrest Raino at the time his car was stopped, but contended that there was reasonable suspicion and that the show of force was justified in the context of a *Terry* stop. The court held that there was reasonable suspicion and that the officer's show of force was justified under the circumstances. On the latter question, the court noted that the officers were responding to a late night call in an area where several shots had been fired; that there was a considerable amount of activity in the area; that people were fighting; and that only two officers were present on the scene.

F. DETENTIONS OF PROPERTY UNDER *TERRY*

Terry concerned seizures of the person, but its principles have been applied to seizures of property as well. In *United States v. Place,* 462 U.S. 696, 103 S.Ct. 2637, 77 L.Ed.2d 110 (1983), the Court stated that "the limitations applicable to investigative detentions of the person should define the permissible scope of the person's luggage on less than probable cause." So as in *Terry,* there are three types of police contacts with a person's property, just as there are three types of police contacts with a person: that which is so minimal as not to constitute a seizure; that which is short-term and requires reasonable suspicion; and that which is so serious as to require probable cause. And as in *Terry,* the courts balance the interest of the state against the nature and severity of the intrusion to determine the level of suspicion required to justify the detention of the property.

1. Personal Interests at Stake

Where property is detained, an individual obviously has a possessory interest at stake. During the time that the state detains the property, the citizen is deprived of the use of it. But in some cases, the citizen may also have a *personal liberty interest* at stake when his property is detained. For example, in *Place,* supra, officers detained Place's luggage as he deplaned in New York City from Miami. He was told that he was free to leave but that his luggage would remain with the authorities. The Government in *Place* argued that seizures of property are generally less intrusive than seizures of the person. The Court responded that this assertion was "true in some circumstances" but that the Government's premise was "faulty on the facts we address in this case." The Court noted that the seizure of a traveller's property "can effectively restrain the person since he is subjected to the possible disruption of his travel plans in order to remain with his luggage or to arrange for its return." Accordingly, a seizure of property will be more strictly scrutinized when it is tantamount to the seizure of the person as well, and less strictly scrutinized if it results only in the deprivation of a possessory interest. See *United States v. LaFrance,* 879 F.2d 1 (1st Cir.1989) (detention of Federal Express package for over two hours pending a dog sniff was permissible where officers had reasonable suspicion to believe the package contained drugs: "While the police are not free to dispossess an individual at will, they are subject to fewer restraints where they trammel no other recognized interest apart from possession alone"; court contrasts luggage cases which implicate "dual concerns").

2. **No Suspicion Required if There Is No Material Interference With Property.**
   If the officer's detention of the property is so insignificant that there is no meaningful interference with the citizen's possessory or liberty interest, then the detention will not implicate Fourth Amendment concerns and will not constitute a seizure. As such, the police activity need not be justified by any articulable suspicion.

   Example: In *United States v. England,* 971 F.2d 419 (9th Cir.1992), England deposited two packages for Express Mail delivery from California to Alabama. Officers had a hunch that the packages contained narcotics. Each package was set aside and presented to a narcotics-sniffing dog. The dog reacted positively, and the packages were subsequently opened pursuant to a warrant. It was not disputed that had the sniffs been negative, the packages could have been placed on their regularly scheduled flight to Alabama. The court found it unnecessary to determine whether reasonable suspicion existed to detain the packages, because no seizure had occurred. The detention of the packages was meaningless to England, since his possessory interest was not delayed or impaired in any way—until the police obtained probable cause and then had the right to seize the packages. If the dog sniff had been negative, the police would have let the packages continue to their destination, and England would have received his packages at exactly the same time as if the detention had not occurred. See also *United States v. Brown,* 884 F.2d 1309 (9th Cir.1989) (diversion of suitcases to cargo hold to conduct an investigation was not a seizure because the brief detention would have in no way interfered with the defendant's travel or frustrated his expectations with respect to his luggage).

3. **Reasonable Suspicion Is Sufficient for Certain Temporary Detentions of Property**
   Even if a possessory or liberty interest is impaired by a detention of property, the seizure may be permissible upon reasonable suspicion rather than probable cause. Illustrative is *United States v. Van Leeuwen,* 397 U.S. 249, 90 S.Ct. 1029, 25 L.Ed.2d 282 (1970), where postal inspectors detained two packages they believed contained illegally imported coins. Although the inspectors did not have probable cause, they did have a reasonable suspicion that the packages contained contraband. They delayed the packages for nearly thirty hours in order to conduct an investigation. They ultimately obtained a warrant. The Court held that the thirty hour detention on the basis of reasonable suspicion was permissible under *Terry.* The Court noted that the officers conducted their investigation diligently and promptly.

a. Justification for Lengthy Detention of Property

It is extremely unlikely that the Court would uphold a thirty-hour detention of a person if the officer had only reasonable suspicion and not probable cause. See *Place, supra* (noting that the Court had never approved a 90–minute detention of a person under *Terry*). Yet the thirty-hour detention of the mailed package was unanimously upheld in *Van Leeuwen,* even though the police had only reasonable suspicion and not probable cause to believe that the package contained contraband. This result is not inconsistent with the seizure-of-person cases, however, given the differing nature of the interests at stake in *Van Leeuwen.* Van Leeuwen was deprived of a possessory interest in his property; he had no personal liberty interest at stake when the package was seized. Moreover, even the possessory interest was minimal during the time the package was detained. Van Leeuwen was receiving a package through the mails. As such, he had no assurance that his package would arrive precisely on a certain day. The package may well have been delayed independently of a police investigation. As such, the thirty hour delay was not a very substantial intrusion on Van Leeuwen's legitimate possessory interest in the package—only intrusive enough to require reasonable suspicion rather than probable cause. Compare *United States v. LaFrance, supra* (where package is sent by Federal Express and delivery is guaranteed at noon, the individual's possessory interest is implicated precisely at noon).

4. Detentions of Property Which Require Probable Cause

A detention of property may in some circumstances be so lengthy and intrusive as to require probable cause. Illustrative is *United States v. Place, supra*. Officers had reasonable suspicion to believe that Place was a drug courier. They knew he was travelling into LaGuardia Airport in New York City on a flight from Miami. When Place deplaned, his luggage was seized in order for a dog sniff to be conducted. However, there was no narcotics-detecting dog at LaGuardia. It was only after Place's plane arrived that the officers decided to summon a dog from Kennedy Airport. Because of this last-minute decision, Place's luggage was detained for 90 minutes, with only reasonable suspicion and not probable cause to believe that the luggage contained drugs.

a. Holding in *Place*

The Court in *Place* held that the 90–minute detention of the luggage violated the Fourth Amendment. It concluded that the intrusion was severe both in length (it was a long-term deprivation of a possessory interest) and because the seizure of Place's luggage was tantamount to the seizure of Place under these circumstances.

b. Relevance of Notice

The Court in *Place* noted that the seizure was "exacerbated by the failure of the agents to inform the respondent of the place to which they were transporting his luggage, of the length of time he might be dispossessed, and of what arrangements would be made for return of the luggage if the investigation dispelled the suspicion.''

c.   Diligence of the Investigation

Most importantly, the Court in *Place* concluded that the officers *had not diligently pursued the investigation*, because they had not called for a dog until Place's plane had already arrived.

5.   Relevant Factors Determining Whether a Seizure of Property Requires Probable Cause

After *Place,* courts assess three factors to determine whether a seizure of property is so intrusive that it requires probable cause. Some of these factors are analogous to those used by the courts to determine whether a seizure of a person constitutes a stop or an arrest. The inquiry is necessarily different, however, since some factors which might bear upon an arrest have no place in the detention of property; for example, officers seldom find it necessary to draw a gun or use handcuffs in the course of a seizure of property. The relevant factors under *Place* are: 1. *the diligence of the investigation*; 2. *the length of the detention and whether liberty interests as well as possessory interests are at stake*; and 3. *information conveyed to the suspect concerning the seizure.*

a.   Reasonable Diligence Required

As with seizures of the person, officers are not required to be perfect or as efficient as humanly possible in the course of their investigation attendant to the seizure of property. If the officers are *reasonably diligent*, their detention of property for even a lengthy period of time is likely to be held permissible, even though there is only reasonable suspicion and not probable cause to believe that there is anything incriminating with respect to the property. For example, despite *Place,* there is no requirement that officers have a narcotics sniffing dog immediately at hand for every detention of a package. See *United States v. Tavolacci,* 895 F.2d 1423 (D.C.Cir.1990) (15 minute delay while seeking drug-detecting dog at train station proper, even though ''the dog would have been waiting on the platform in a world where the time of dogs and their handlers was cost-free''). The reason why the officers' conduct was unreasonable in *Place* was not because the dog was unavailable at the very first moment, but rather because the officers did not bother to summon the dog until after Place's plane arrived—even though they could have anticipated the need for a dog from the moment Place got on the plane in Miami. Compare *State v. Jerome,* 69 Hawaii 132, 736 P.2d 438 (1987) (30–minute delay in bringing dog to area was not unreasonable where the officers received their tip only 10 minutes before the suspect's arrival at the airport). See also *United States v. Dass,* 849 F.2d 414 (9th Cir.1988) (reasonable suspicion does not justify detention of mail for 7–23 days, where the delay could have been reduced to 32 hours if officers had acted diligently).

b. **Relevance of Notice to the Property Owner**

According to *Place,* an intrusion becomes more serious if the owner is not notified of the fate of his property and the amount of time he will be dispossessed. This is because, without such information, the owner of the property is likely to wish to remain with the property, and therefore the seizure of the property will also be a deprivation of the owner's liberty interest. Also, the deprivation of a possessory interest is more serious if it appears to the owner that the property may never be returned. Accordingly, courts after *Place* have upheld lengthy seizures where the owner has been informed of the relevant detention procedures. See *United States v. Hooper,* 935 F.2d 484 (2d Cir.1991) (thirty-minute detention permissible, in part because "the agents exchanged phone numbers with Hooper so that arrangements could be made for the return of the suitcase in the event their suspicions were not confirmed").

c. **Notice Not Relevant to Mailed Packages**

In *Place,* the Court found it relevant that the officers did not inform the traveller about the procedures attendant to the seizure of his luggage. This factor is not relevant, however, in cases where packages are placed in the mail and then detained by officers during the course of an investigation. For one thing, such notice could serve as a "tip-off" to the prospective recipient that something is awry. Also, to the extent that the notice serves to limit the intrusion on a liberty interest, it has no place where such a liberty interest is not at stake. See *United States v. LaFrance,* 879 F.2d 1 (1st Cir.1989) (concluding that police were not under an obligation "to telephone the parcel's intended recipient and tell him the nature and cause of the delay").

G. ROADBLOCKS

Under *Terry,* the police are ordinarily required to have reasonable suspicion before stopping an automobile. See *Delaware v. Prouse,* 440 U.S. 648, 99 S.Ct. 1391, 59 L.Ed.2d 660 (1979) (holding that an officer's random, suspicionless decision to stop a car for a vehicle registration check violated the Fourth Amendment). However, in two cases the Supreme Court has applied the *Terry* balancing test and upheld roadblock seizures of automobiles even though the officers had no suspicion that the drivers were engaged in criminal activity.

1. **Permanent Fixed Checkpoints**

In *United States v. Martinez–Fuerte,* 428 U.S. 543, 96 S.Ct. 3074, 49 L.Ed.2d 1116 (1976), the Court upheld suspicionless stops of motorists at permanent fixed checkpoints several miles from the U.S. border. These stops could not be justified under the doctrine allowing suspicionless border searches and seizures (see *infra* for a discussion of border searches), since the checkpoint at issue was so far from the border that it was clear that most of the motorists who were stopped at the checkpoint had not recently, if ever, crossed the border.

a. Balance of Interests

Using the *Terry* balancing analysis, the Court in *Martinez–Fuerte* reasoned that the state interest in investigating and deterring the flow of illegal aliens outweighed the interests of the motorists in being free from suspicionless seizures. The Court asserted that if articulable suspicion was required *before* a stop could be made, the effectiveness of the fixed checkpoint system would be nullified. The Court relied heavily on the fact that the individual interest at stake was minimal, because of the nature of the permanent fixed checkpoint: motorists could not be surprised by the checkpoint, the detention was very brief, and all motorists were stopped and thus *none could be singled out for arbitrary treatment* without any individualized suspicion. The risk of unconstrained and standardless police discretion was eliminated by the fact that all cars were stopped at the checkpoint. This made the intrusion significantly less abusive and harassing than was the case with the ad hoc police stops which the Court has held are invalid in the absence of reasonable suspicion. As the Court put it, "the regularized manner in which established checkpoints are operated is visible evidence, reassuring to law-abiding motorists, that the stops are duly authorized and believed to serve the public interest."

b. Location of a Permanent Fixed Checkpoint

In *Martinez–Fuerte,* the Court emphasized that "the location of a fixed checkpoint is not chosen by officers in the field, but by officials responsible for making overall decisions as to the most effective allocation of limited enforcement resources." The Court also noted that the reasonableness of a particular exercise of discretion as to the location of the checkpoint is subject to post-stop judicial review. Presumably, then, it could be the case that the location of a permanent fixed checkpoint could be deemed unreasonable—for example, if it were placed in an area where the expressed state interest could not possibly be implemented (e.g., an "immigration checkpoint" in the middle of Kansas).

2. Temporary Fixed Checkpoints

In *Michigan Department of State Police v. Sitz,* 496 U.S. 444, 110 S.Ct. 2481, 110 L.Ed.2d 412 (1990), the Court, relying heavily on *Martinez–Fuerte,* upheld suspicionless stops of motorists at *temporary*, fixed sobriety checkpoints.

a. Facts of *Sitz*

The Michigan sobriety checkpoint program allowed checkpoints to be set up along state roads according to a list of considerations including "safety of the location," "minimum inconvenience for the driver," and available space "to pull the vehicle off the traveled portion of the roadway for further inquiry if necessary." Under the program, all motorists passing through the checkpoint would be stopped and briefly examined for signs of intoxication. If such signs were detected, the motorist would be directed to another area where license and registration would be checked, and further sobriety tests would be conducted if warranted. The only checkpoint operated under the program resulted in a stop of 126 vehicles, and only one arrest for drunk driving. The challenge in the Supreme Court focussed solely on the original checkpoint detention and associated preliminary investigation of motorists, not on the subsequent use of sobriety tests and the like.

b. Analysis in *Sitz*

Applying the *Terry* balancing test, the Court in *Sitz* concluded that a suspicionless stop at a sobriety checkpoint was a reasonable balance of the state interest at stake and the nature of the intrusion suffered by the motorist. The Court relied upon the fixed (albeit temporary) nature of the checkpoint to conclude that there was no risk of arbitrariness or abuse of authority, no surprise or humiliation in the stop itself and no long-term seizure. The Court emphasized that the checkpoints were selected pursuant to the department guidelines, and that uniformed police officers stopped every car. The Court concluded that "the intrusion resulting from the brief stop at the sobriety checkpoint is for constitutional purposes indistinguishable from the checkpoint stops we upheld in *Martinez–Fuerte*." Crucially, the Court found the temporary check points in *Sitz* no more intrusive than the permanent ones in *Martinez–Fuerte*.

Against this limited intrusion, the Court balanced the heavy state interest in eradicating drunken driving. Respondents in *Sitz* argued that sobriety checkpoints did not effectively advance this undeniable state interest, and that other methods, such as roving patrols, would be more effective. But the Court responded that the *Terry* balance of interests approach was not intended "to transfer from politically accountable officials to the courts the decision as to which among reasonable alternative law enforcement techniques should be employed to deal with a serious public danger." The Court concluded that "the choice among such reasonable alternatives remains with the government officials who have a unique understanding of, and a responsibility for, limited public resources." The majority faulted the lower court for its "searching examination" of the effectiveness of sobriety checkpoints.

c. Dissenting Opinions in *Sitz*

Justice Brennan wrote a dissenting opinion joined by Justice Marshall. Justice Brennan contended that the controls on official discretion imposed by a fixed checkpoint were no substitute for a standard based on articulable suspicion. He feared that allowing suspicionless detentions would subject the public to arbitrary and harassing conduct by police officers.

Justice Stevens wrote a dissenting opinion joined in large part by Justices Brennan and Marshall. Justice Stevens complained that the Court had misapplied the reasonableness balancing test, by overvaluing the law enforcement interest at stake and undervaluing the citizen's interest at stake. He found the majority's reliance on *Martinez–Fuerte* to be unpersuasive. He argued that unlike the permanent, fixed checkpoint, the temporary nature of the sobriety checkpoint gives officers "extremely broad discretion in determining the exact timing and placement of the roadblock." That is, while the discretion *whether* to make a stop is controlled by the fixed checkpoint, the discretion as to *where* to place the checkpoint is not. Justice Stevens also asserted that a temporary checkpoint is more intrusive because of the element of surprise that it presents—unlike a fixed checkpoint, the location of which is known by most motorists, a temporary checkpoint can be set up in various places at various times.

Finally, Justice Stevens criticized the majority's determination that the sobriety checkpoint was sufficiently effective to outweigh its intrusiveness. He argued that the majority ignored the fact that other police methods, such as roving patrols stopping cars based on reasonable suspicion, would be far more effective in combatting the drunk driving problem.

d. **Controls On Locating a Temporary, Fixed Checkpoint**
The Court in *Sitz* imposed no time, place or manner restrictions on the use of a temporary checkpoint. The standards set forth in the Michigan plan, which were approved without discussion by the Court, did not regulate how often a checkpoint could be used, nor did they delimit the neighborhoods in which a checkpoint could be used. So while the stops themselves are free from police discretion, the decisions as to where and how to place the checkpoints are all but free from Fourth Amendment regulation. This is not to say, however, that the decision as to where to place a temporary checkpoint is *totally* beyond judicial review. The Court in *Martinez–Fuerte* emphasized that a particular exercise of discretion as to the location of a permanent checkpoint is subject to post-stop judicial review; there is no reason to think that the result would be different with respect to temporary checkpoints.

Accordingly, some courts after *Sitz* have sought to limit the discretion of field officers in choosing checkpoint sites. For example, in *Hall v. Commonwealth,* 12 Va.App. 972, 406 S.E.2d 674 (1991), the court invalidated a plan which gave field officers discretion to place a checkpoint on any one of 54 sites throughout the county, at any time. The court was concerned that an officer who had already decided to stop a particular person "could do so within these guidelines by ascertaining at what time that person would travel through a particular intersection and set up a roadblock accordingly." On the other hand, while judicial review of the placement of a checkpoint is possible, the clear deference given by the Court to the guidelines in *Sitz* indicates that it is only the rare case in which the decision to place a checkpoint at a certain location will be deemed unreasonable.

3. Suspicionless Seizures, Not Searches, Are Authorized.

It is important to note that both *Martinez–Fuerte* and *Sitz* are *seizure* cases. They do not allow a search for law enforcement purposes on less than probable cause. The Court has permitted searches on less than probable cause in only two circumstances: 1. a search for weapons and dangerous people, not evidence, made for purposes of self-protection (*Terry*); and 2. a search for evidence, where there are special needs beyond mere law enforcement (see the next section).

In contrast, a search by law enforcement officers for evidence of criminal activity has been held not subject to a balance of interests under the Fourth Amendment's reasonableness clause. Rather, such searches must be supported by probable cause, even if they are minimally intrusive. In *Arizona v. Hicks*, 480 U.S. 321, 107 S.Ct. 1149, 94 L.Ed.2d 347 (1987), the Court specifically rejected a reasonableness balancing approach as applied to a search for evidence by law enforcement officials. See also *United States v. Winsor*, 846 F.2d 1569 (9th Cir.1988) (limited visual intrusion into hotel room by law enforcement officers, upon reasonable suspicion, cannot be justified under the reasonableness clause: "we refuse the government's invitation to decide this case by balancing the competing interests at stake. Instead, we adhere to the bright line rule that *Hicks* appears to have announced * * *"). It should be noted, though, that some circuit courts, despite *Hicks*, have upheld searches based only on reasonable suspicion on the ground that the search in issue was a limited intrusion. See, e.g., *United States v. Lyons*, 898 F.2d 210 (1st Cir.1990) (putting key into lock to see if it fits is such a minimal intrusion that it can be done on reasonable suspicion).

4. Longer Detentions and Interrogations Not Permitted Without Suspicion

The detentions upheld in *Martinez–Fuerte* and *Sitz* were momentary intrusions suffered by all motorists at the checkpoint. However, if an officer decides to single out a motorist for a more prolonged detention or for interrogation, the officer must have at least an articulable suspicion to justify this more serious intrusion. See *United States v. Walker*, 941 F.2d 1086 (10th Cir.1991) (*Sitz* distinguished where officer singles out a motorist for prolonged stop and questioning about contraband; "the lack of any constraint on an officer's decision to detain some individuals and to let others go creates a situation ripe for abuse'').

VI. ADMINISTRATIVE AND REGULATORY SEARCHES AND SEIZURES

The Supreme Court has applied the reasonableness clause of the Fourth Amendment to searches and seizures conducted for purposes other than traditional criminal law enforcement. The Court has reasoned that the traditional requirements of a warrant and probable cause, while usefully applied to searches and seizures of evidence by law enforcement officials, are not well-suited to searches made by various officials for a legitimate administrative or regulatory purpose. Therefore, if a search or seizure is justified by *special needs other than traditional criminal law enforcement*, then the Court engages in a balance of interests under the reasonableness clause to assess the minimum requirements for such a search or seizure. Under this reasonableness analysis, as in *Terry,* the Court balances the need for a particular search or seizure against the degree of intrusion upon personal rights which the search or seizure entails. If the probable cause standard and/or the warrant requirement takes insufficient account of the state interests at stake (i.e. subjugates the state interest in light of the intrusion imposed), then the Court will find it reasonable to dispense with such requirements in favor of lesser standards such as reasonable suspicion, area warrants, or other controls on official discretion. If there is no special need beyond law enforcement at stake, then a search to obtain evidence for law enforcement purposes presumptively requires probable cause and a warrant, or another exception to the warrant requirement such as exigent circumstances. See *Arizona v. Hicks,* discussed supra.

A. SAFETY INSPECTIONS OF HOMES
Inspections of homes by housing inspectors, such as for building code violations and other safety conditions, promote special needs beyond criminal law enforcement. The Court balanced the need for such searches against the intrusion suffered by homeowners in *Camara v. Municipal Court,* 387 U.S. 523, 87 S.Ct. 1727, 18 L.Ed.2d 930 (1967).

1. Probable Cause Not Required
If the traditional probable cause requirement were applied to administrative safety inspections, then a right of entry would arise only if there was a fair probability that certain specific conditions constituted a violation of a safety provision in a specific building. The traditional probable cause requirement would thus preclude area-wide safety inspections, or periodic safety inspections. In *Camara,* the Court rejected the homeowner's claim that the right of inspection was limited to instances where there is probable cause to believe that there is a violation in a specific building. The Court held that a valid entry could be made on other grounds, such as the *passage of time,* the

nature of the building, or the fact that an *area-wide inspection* is being conducted.

a. Rationale

The Court in *Camara* reasoned that periodic and area-wide inspections are crucial to the effectiveness of a safety inspection scheme, and that to require probable cause would undermine the legitimate state interest in building safety. The Court noted that many safety hazards "are not observable from outside the building and indeed may not be apparent to the occupant himself"; these hazards would go unremedied if probable cause were required. Against the state's heavy interest in building safety, the Court weighed the individual interests at stake, and found that home safety inspections "involve a relatively limited invasion of the urban citizen's privacy." The Court reasoned that such inspections are not personal in nature and do not involve a full-scale search of the home. Accordingly, the Court concluded that the probable cause standard was not an appropriate balance of the state and individual interests.

2. Search Warrant Required

The Court in *Camara* held that, except in emergency situations or where the homeowner consents, the safety inspector must have a search warrant to enter the home. Again balancing the interests at stake, the Court concluded that the burden of obtaining a warrant was not likely to frustrate the governmental purpose behind the home safety inspection. It reasoned that "in the enforcement of housing codes immediate searches are almost never necessary" because, if the inspector is turned away and then proceeds to get a warrant, no significant state interest will be impaired. At worst, the homeowner will attempt to make "hasty reparation" before a delayed inspection, which reparation will itself fulfill the objectives of the safety inspection. The Court further reasoned that a warrant requirement would impose only a minimal burden on the state because most homeowners would voluntarily comply with an initial request to conduct the inspection without a warrant; the homeowner would have little to gain by triggering the displeasure of the inspector, who would only return with authority to inspect the premises and with the power to cite the homeowner for code violations.

a. Role of the Judicial Officer

In a criminal investigation culminating with a search warrant application, the magistrate weighs the information presented in the affidavit to determine whether there is a fair probability that a crime has been committed and that evidence connected with the crime will be located at a specific place. A judicial officer issuing a warrant for a home safety inspection under *Camara* necessarily performs a different function than the magistrate assessing a search warrant application in a criminal investigation. This is because, as discussed above, the standard of proof required for a home safety inspection is different from the traditional probable cause standard. A home inspection can be conducted on the basis of such generalized facts as passage of time, nature of the building, and as part of an area-wide inspection.

The Court in *Camara* stressed that judicial review of the reasons for a safety inspection should occur "without any reassessment of the basic agency decision to canvass an area." Thus, the magistrate is not charged with evaluating the legislative and administrative policy decisions as to frequency of inspection, resource expenditures, and the like. The magistrate need only decide whether *an established inspection policy exists* and whether the inspection for which a warrant is sought *fits within that program*.

b. Benefit of the Warrant Requirement

The Court in *Camara* assumed that the magistrate, by determining whether the proposed search fits within an established inspection program, would protect the privacy interests of the homeowner. For example, a warrant sought for personal spite, or for purposes of a "shakedown" by administrative inspectors, may well not fit within the frequency limitations of the established inspection policy. Thus, the warrant process in this setting is intended as a limitation upon arbitrary and abusive searches.

c. Post–*Camara* Limitation on the Use of Warrants Without Probable Cause

The *Camara* Court imposed a rather unique requirement for home safety inspections—that a warrant would be required, but that the warrant would be issued upon some objective standard other than probable cause. Subsequently, in *Griffin v. Wisconsin,* 483 U.S. 868, 107 S.Ct. 3164, 97 L.Ed.2d 709 (1987), the Court again addressed the question whether a warrant which is not based upon particularized probable cause can be mandated. Justice Scalia, writing for the Court, contended that the Fourth Amendment could not be read to provide for such a warrant. He reasoned that such a warrant would violate the specific language in the Fourth Amendment that "no warrant shall issue, but upon probable cause." He distinguished *Camara* as a case where the Court "arguably came to permit an exception to that prescription for administrative search warrants, which may but do not necessarily have to be issued by courts." He emphasized that the *general rule for judicial search warrants is that they can only be issued upon particularized probable cause.*

B. ADMINISTRATIVE INSPECTIONS OF BUSINESSES

As with housing safety inspections, safety and regulatory inspections of businesses fulfill a special need beyond ordinary criminal law enforcement. As with housing inspections, there are two questions which are pertinent to Fourth Amendment limitations on administrative inspections of businesses: 1. whether the search may be conducted on some standard less than the particularized probable cause required for a search for evidence by criminal law enforcement; and 2. whether the inspection, in the absence of consent, may be conducted without a warrant.

1. Same Basic Analysis

In *See v. City of Seattle,* 387 U.S. 541, 87 S.Ct. 1737, 18 L.Ed.2d 943 (1967), the Court concluded that the reasoning of *Camara* was equally applicable to administrative inspections of commercial structures. Therefore, See could not be convicted for refusing to permit a warrantless fire inspection of his locked commercial warehouse. The Court reasoned that "a businessman, like the occupant of a residence, has a constitutional right to go about his business free from unreasonable official entries upon his private commercial property."

a. More Searches May Be Permitted

The Court in *See* cautioned that it was not holding that businesses would be treated exactly the same as homes with respect to administrative searches. It merely concluded that the analysis—a balance of the state and individual interests at stake—would be the same. In particular, the Court stated that "we do not in any way imply that business premises may not reasonably be inspected in many more situations than private homes."

2. May Not Be a Search at All

If the inspector enters and investigates an area that is open to the general public, the inspection will not be a search at all and no Fourth Amendment limitations will apply. For example, in *Donovan v. Lone Steer, Inc.,* 464 U.S. 408, 104 S.Ct. 769, 78 L.Ed.2d 567 (1984), the Court held that the Fourth Amendment did not apply to a fire inspection where the inspector walked through a hotel lobby and checked for fire exits. The Court reasoned that the proprietor had no expectation of privacy in an area open to the public.

3. Balance of Interests at Stake

The Court applied the *Camara* protections to businesses in *See,* but it is apparent that administrative searches of businesses often involve different issues and interests than those presented in home safety inspections. An administrative search of a business may implicate more complex regulatory concerns; the state has an interest not only in the safety of a business structure, but also in whether the business itself is being properly, safely and legitimately conducted. Also, it may well be that a businessperson may have a diminished expectation of privacy in the area to be searched, given the nature of the business conducted. This means that the state interest involved in administrative business searches may be stronger than in home safety inspections, and the individual interest may be weaker, and therefore that even the flexible *Camara* requirements would improperly favor individual interests at the expense of legitimate state interests.

4. Heavily Regulated Businesses

In a series of cases, the Court has held that the *See* warrant requirement is not applicable if the business to be searched is part of a "heavily regulated industry". The rationale is that with such businesses, unannounced and frequent inspections are necessary to effectuate the state interest in the proper operation of the business. See *United States v. Biswell,* 406 U.S. 311, 92 S.Ct. 1593, 32 L.Ed.2d 87 (1972) (warrantless inspection of licensed gun dealer's storeroom: "If inspection is to be effective and serve as a credible deterrent, unannounced, even frequent, inspections are essential. In this context, the prerequisite of a warrant could easily frustrate inspection"). The Court also reasons that a businessperson who operates in a heavily regulated industry has a diminished expectation of privacy. See *Biswell* ("It is also plain that inspections for compliance with the Gun Control Act pose only limited threats to the dealer's justifiable expectations of privacy. When a dealer chooses to engage in this pervasively regulated business and to accept a federal license, he does so with the knowledge that his business records, firearms and ammunition will be subject to effective inspection.").

a. Examples of Heavily Regulated Businesses

Some of the industries held by the courts to be pervasively regulated, and thus not entitled to the protections of the warrant requirement, include: *sales of liquor (Colonnade Catering Corp. v. United States,* 397 U.S. 72, 90 S.Ct. 774, 25 L.Ed.2d 60 (1970)); *sales of firearms (Biswell, supra); mining (Donovan v. Dewey,* 452 U.S. 594, 101 S.Ct. 2534, 69 L.Ed.2d 262 (1981)); *trucking (United States v. Dominguez–Prieto,* 923 F.2d 464 (6th Cir.1991)); *horseracing (Shoemaker v. Handel,* 795 F.2d 1136 (3d Cir.1986)); *public utilities (Rushton v. Nebraska Public Power District,* 844 F.2d 562 (8th Cir.1988)); and *railroads (Skinner v. Railway Labor Executives' Ass'n,* 489 U.S. 602, 109 S.Ct. 1402, 103 L.Ed.2d 639 (1989)).

b. OSHA Searches

In *Marshall v. Barlow's, Inc.,* 436 U.S. 307, 98 S.Ct. 1816, 56 L.Ed.2d 305 (1978), the Court considered the constitutionality of a provision of the Occupational Safety and Health Act (OSHA), which permitted inspectors, without a warrant, to enter any business premises subject to OSHA for the purpose of conducting a safety inspection. The Court held that the provision for warrantless searches violated the Fourth Amendment. It rejected the contention that the "heavily regulated industry" exception to the warrant requirement was applicable; it reasoned that OSHA applied *across the board to a wide variety* of industries, rather than to any discrete, pervasively regulated industry.

Relying on *Camara,* the Court in *Barlow's* held that while a warrant was required to search for OSHA violations, particularized probable cause was not; a search could be conducted pursuant to neutral legislative criteria, as determined by the judicial officer. The Court concluded that a "warrant showing that a specific business has been chosen for an OSHA search on the basis of a general administrative plan for the enforcement of the Act derived from neutral sources such as, for example, dispersion of employees in various types of industries across a given area, and the desired frequency of searches in any of the lesser divisions of the area, would protect an employer's Fourth Amendment rights."

5. Recent Expansion of Heavily Regulated Industries Exception

The Court has recently applied the "heavily regulated" industry exception to the warrant requirement more permissively, in a way that is likely to permit warrantless inspections of a large number of businesses. In *New York v. Burger*, 482 U.S. 691, 107 S.Ct. 2636, 96 L.Ed.2d 601 (1987), the Court held that a vehicle dismantling business was pervasively regulated, and thus that the legislative provision for frequent warrantless inspections did not violate the Fourth Amendment. The scope of the regulation at issue in *Burger* consisted of the following: 1. the operator of the business was required to obtain a license and pay a fee; 2. the operator was required to maintain an inventory list; 3. the operator was required to display his registration number prominently at his place of business, on business documentation, and on inventory that passed through the business.

a. Dissent

The regulation held "pervasive" in *Burger* is not as extensive as that applied to businesses such as public utilities or the sale of liquor or firearms. The application of the "heavily regulated" industry exception to the business in *Burger* led Justice Brennan to comment in dissent that "if New York City's administrative scheme renders the vehicle-dismantling business closely regulated, few businesses will escape such a finding." Justice Brennan noted that no regulation governed the condition of the premises, the hours of operation, the personnel employed, or the equipment utilized. See *S & S Pawn Shop Inc. v. City of Del City*, 947 F.2d 432 (10th Cir.1991) (finding pawn shops to be closely regulated under *Burger* criteria).

b. Relevance of Historical Regulation

Many of the industries which have been held to be "heavily regulated" have been subject to a history of regulation, which would tend to diminish the expectation of privacy of any person who chose to enter such an industry. Examples include sales of liquor, sales of firearms, and mining. The Court in *Burger* held, however, that an "ancient history of government oversight" is *not required* for a finding that a particular industry is heavily regulated. Otherwise, such new industries as nuclear power could not be considered heavily regulated for a long period of time, even though the scope of regulations on such an industry may be pervasive and the state interest in surprise warrantless inspections may be critical.

c. Variant of Traditionally Regulated Industry

The Court in *Burger* also noted that a new industry could be considered to have a history of government oversight if it were merely a variant of an industry with a tradition of regulation. For example, while the vehicle dismantling industry is relatively new, the Court in *Burger* found that the automobile dismantling business is much like a regular junkyard or second-hand shop and is therefore "simply a new branch of an industry that has existed, and has been closely regulated, for many years."

6. Regulatory Statute Must Be an Adequate Substitute for a Warrant

The Court in *Burger* held that even in the context of a pervasively regulated business, there must be some substitute for a warrant. The Court stated that the inspection program itself must "provide a constitutionally adequate substitute for a warrant" in order to protect the privacy interests of the businessperson from the risk of arbitrary searches by Government officials who are unconstrained by a warrant requirement. In particular, the Court stated that the regulatory statute must perform "the two basic functions of a warrant." First, it must advise the citizen that the search is being conducted pursuant to the law and that it has a properly defined scope. Second, it must limit the discretion of the officers by carefully controlling the time, place and scope of the search.

Example: The Court held that the inspection scheme in *Burger* provided a constitutionally adequate substitute for a warrant. The Court relied on the following factors: 1. the statute informed the operator that inspections would be made on a regular basis—so that when the inspection did occur, the operator would know that it was being conducted pursuant to a statute and not as a result of "discretionary acts by a government official"; 2. the scope of the inspection was reasonably limited to the records and the inventory; 3. the statute notified the operator as to who is authorized to conduct the inspection; 4. the statute targeted only vehicle-dismantling and related industries; and 5. inspecting officers were allowed to conduct an inspection only during regular business hours.

a. Limitations on Frequency of Inspection

The statutory scheme upheld in *Burger* placed no limitation on the frequency of inspecting any particular vehicle dismantling business. Under the statute, an inspector could theoretically conduct a search of a particular business several times a day for several days or weeks. The defendant in *Burger* argued that the statute therefore left open a significant possibility of harassment and unconstrained discretion by inspecting officers. But the Court rejected the defendant's argument. It recognized that limitations on the frequency of inspection were "a factor in the analysis of the adequacy of a particular statute." However, the existence or lack of limitations on frequency would not be "determinative of the result so long as the statute, as a whole, places adequate limits upon the discretion of the inspecting officers." The Court noted that with some industries, frequent inspections may be required to fully effectuate the state interest in assuring that businesses are properly conducted. Particularly was this true of the vehicle-dismantling industry, where inventory flows in and out very quickly.

7. Searches Must Be Limited to Those Which Effectuate the State Interest at Stake

Even if warrantless administrative inspections of businesses are permitted, it may be the case that the statutory authorization and a search pursuant to it is broader than necessary to effectuate the state interest. If so, the search may violate the Fourth Amendment. For example, in *Rush v. Obledo*, 756 F.2d 713 (9th Cir.1985), the court considered the constitutionality of state statutes and regulations permitting warrantless inspections of family day care homes. The court found that day care homes were pervasively regulated. However, the court also found that the statutes authorizing the searches of day care homes were overbroad. The statutes permitted general searches of any day care home at any time of the day or night, including areas in the home that were not used for day care. The court noted that "a family day care home is a business only when children cared for from other families for compensation are present and at all other times is a private residence," and that even when children are cared for the provider retains expectations of privacy "in those areas to which the day care children are denied access." Accordingly, the court found that the statute was "far broader than necessary to guarantee the effectiveness of the provisions governing family day care" and thus that it did not provide a "constitutionally adequate substitute for a warrant." See also *Serpas v. Schmidt*, 827 F.2d 23 (7th Cir.1987) (even though horse racing is a pervasively regulated industry, it does not follow that all warrantless inspections of dormitory rooms at the racetrack are lawful).

8. Enforcing the Criminal Law

Since *Camara*, administrative inspections have been subject to more flexible standards than those applied to searches for evidence by law enforcement officers. The traditional standards of a warrant issued upon particularized probable cause have been considered ill-suited to searches which effectuate "special needs" beyond ordinary criminal law enforcement.

a. Argument in *Burger*

In *New York v. Burger, supra,* the defendant argued that the statute authorizing searches of vehicle dismantling businesses had no truly administrative purpose but was "designed to give the police an expedient means of enforcing penal sanctions for possession of stolen property." He noted that under the statute, inspecting officers could conduct an inspection for stolen vehicle parts even if an operator failed to produce his records; from this he concluded that the statute was not directed at appropriate recordkeeping, as was, for example, the statute applied to sales of firearms. The defendant therefore asserted that the traditional standards of a warrant and probable cause ought to apply.

b. **Analysis in *Burger***

The Court rejected the defendant's contentions and held that a state can address a social problem (in this case car theft) both by way of an administrative scheme and through penal sanction. The fact that the ultimate goal is to regulate and limit violations of the penal law does not destroy the administrative nature of the search. According to the Court, "administrative statutes and penal laws may have the same *ultimate* purpose of remedying the social problem, but they have different subsidiary purposes and prescribe different methods of addressing the problem." Thus, under *Burger*, a search is administrative if it *uses administrative methodology* (e.g., the officers are inspecting business records and operating conditions, rather than specifically looking for evidence of criminal activity) and if it is used to *enforce regulatory standards* such as proper recordkeeping and maintenance of the business.

c. **Application of Analysis in *Burger***

The Court found that the statute pursuant to which the search was conducted in *Burger* was administrative in nature, because it served the regulatory goals of "seeking to ensure that vehicle dismantlers are legitimate businesspersons and that stolen vehicles and vehicle parts passing through automobile junkyards can be identified." The Court reasoned that these regulatory objectives were met by allowing a search of the inventory as well as the records of the proprietor: the inventory would have to be compared with the records to determine whether the records were properly kept. The fact that the statute allowed a search of the inventory even if the proprietor failed to produce any records was also held properly within an administrative interest; otherwise an illegitimate vehicle dismantler could "thwart the purposes of the administrative scheme" simply by refusing to produce records. See also *United States v. Hernandez,* 901 F.2d 1217 (5th Cir.1990) (search of commercial truck to check whether bill of lading produced by driver was accurate; search uncovered drugs, held valid administrative search).

d. **Administrative Search Can Lead to Evidence of a Criminal Violation**

A search that is properly administrative in its subsidiary objectives does not become a search for law enforcement purposes merely because it uncovers evidence of a criminal violation. As the Court in *Burger* stated:

"The discovery of crimes in the course of an otherwise proper administrative inspection does not render that search illegal or the administrative scheme suspect."

e. **Use of Police Officers to Conduct an Administrative Search**

In *Burger*, the administrative search of the defendant's vehicle dismantling business was in fact conducted by New York City Police officers. The defendant argued that this destroyed the administrative nature of the search and therefore that the search could not be conducted in the absence of a warrant and probable cause. But the Court rejected this contention. The Court noted that police officers have "numerous duties in addition to those associated with traditional police work" and that many states and localities do not have sufficient administrative personnel to enforce a particular administrative scheme. The Court concluded that, "so long as a regulatory scheme is properly administrative, it is not rendered illegal by the fact that the inspecting officer has the power to arrest individuals for violations other than those created by the scheme itself."

C. **CIVIL–BASED SEARCHES OF INDIVIDUALS PURSUANT TO "SPECIAL NEEDS"**

The Supreme Court has used its special needs balancing analysis in a series of cases to uphold civil-based searches of individuals in the absence of a warrant and probable cause.

1. **Searches Directed at Students**

In *New Jersey v. T.L.O.*, 469 U.S. 325, 105 S.Ct. 733, 83 L.Ed.2d 720 (1985), the Court held that a warrantless search of a student's handbag was reasonable where the school administrator had reasonable suspicion, but not probable cause, to believe that the student was carrying cigarettes in the handbag. The Court found that the traditional requirements of a warrant and probable cause did not apply in light of the state's *special need to maintain discipline and an educational environment* in its schools.

a. **Balance of Interests Does Not Justify a Warrant Requirement**

The Court in *T.L.O.* weighed the student's interest in privacy against the state interest in maintaining discipline and an educational environment and concluded that a warrant requirement was not a prerequisite for a search of a student by an administrator. The Court reasoned that the warrant process is ill-suited to the context in which school searches arise. For one thing, school searches are ordinarily conducted by administrators or teachers unfamiliar with the warrant process. The Court also noted that requiring a teacher or administrator to obtain a warrant would "unduly interfere with the swift and informal disciplinary procedures needed in the schools."

b.   **Balance of Interests Allows a Search on the Basis of Reasonable Suspicion**

The Court in *T.L.O.* held that application of the probable cause requirement to the school search at issue would give undue weight to the student's interest at the expense of the state's interest. Essentially, the Court reasoned that, if the school official was required to wait until probable cause developed, then many essential searches could never be conducted (or they would be conducted too late to be useful in correcting a problem), and school discipline and the educational environment would suffer. Searches of suspicious circumstances that did not rise to the level of probable cause were thought by the Court to be necessary to nip potential disciplinary problems in the bud.

c.   **Distinction From *Terry***

Note that the search conducted in *T.L.O.* could not have been conducted under the *Terry* doctrine. It is true that *Terry* allows searches upon reasonable suspicion, but not if those searches are directed toward uncovering evidence. Rather, *Terry* permits only those searches necessary to protect the officers or others. The school administrator in *T.L.O.* was not concerned with his safety. Rather, he had reasonable suspicion that T.L.O.'s purse contained evidence of a violation of school rules against smoking. The reason that the search for evidence could be conducted on the basis of reasonable suspicion was not that *Terry* applied, but because the search was in furtherance of special needs beyond traditional criminal law enforcement.

d.   **More Intrusive Searches**

The Court in *T.L.O.* stressed that in assessing the reasonableness of a search, a court must take into account the intrusiveness of the search employed. It follows that a search which is significantly more intrusive than the handbag search in *T.L.O.* may require a greater justification than the reasonable suspicion standard approved by the Court in *T.L.O.* For example, a strip search of a student, because of its intrusiveness, may well require probable cause. See Comment, 90 Dickinson Law Review 803 (1986).

e.   **Suspicionless Searches**

In *T.L.O.,* the Court noted that it did not have to decide whether individualized suspicion is an essential element of the reasonableness standard as applied to searches of students. The Court implied, however, that a school search without individualized suspicion might be reasonable if the "privacy interests implicated by a search are minimal and where other safeguards are available to assure that the individual's reasonable expectation of privacy is not subject to the discretion of the officer in the field." So, for example, a minimally intrusive search directed at the student body at large may be permissible, since no particular student would be singled out by an officer's discretionary decision. Thus far, courts are split on whether suspicionless searches of the entire student body are permissible. See *Doe v. Renfrow*, 475 F.Supp. 1012 (N.D.Ind.1979) (permitting such searches); *In Interest of Dumas*, 357 Pa.Super. 294, 515 A.2d 984 (1986) (search of student lockers impermissible without reasonable suspicion).

f. Searches by Law Enforcement Officials

In *T.L.O.*, the search was conducted by a school administrator. The Court cautioned that the case did not present "the question of the appropriate standard for assessing the legality of searches conducted by school officials in conjunction with or at the behest of law enforcement agencies." If the search of the student is conducted by law enforcement officials, a strong argument can be made that the traditional Fourth Amendment requirements should apply, since such a search does not effectuate "special needs" beyond ordinary criminal law enforcement. It is true that in *New York v. Burger*, the Court held that a search of a vehicle dismantling business did not lose its administrative character simply because it was conducted by law enforcement officials. But the Court's rationale on this point was that states and localities might not have the resources to employ specialized administrative officials to conduct the searches. This is hardly the case in the school context, where teachers and school administrators are employed for the very purpose of maintaining school discipline and an educational environment. Accordingly, lower courts have generally held that if the police conduct the search of a student, then the traditional requirements of a warrant and probable cause must be met. See *M. v. Board of Education*, 429 F.Supp. 288 (S.D.Ill.1977); *Cason v. Cook*, 810 F.2d 188 (8th Cir.1987) (*T.L.O.* standard applies where the search of the student's purse and locker was conducted by the vice principal, while police officer who was liaison officer with the school was standing by, for at most "this case represents a police officer working in conjunction with school officials").

g. Use of Evidence Obtained

If the search is conducted by a school administrator and is thus a special needs search, any evidence uncovered can later be used for criminal law enforcement and adjudication. For example, in *T.L.O.*, the school official suspected a violation of school rules against smoking; a search of T.L.O.'s handbag uncovered marijuana, which was subsequently used against T.L.O. in a juvenile proceeding. Yet this was permissible, because, as the Court in *Burger* put it, the "discovery of evidence of crimes in the course of an otherwise proper administrative inspection does not render that search illegal or the administrative scheme suspect."

h. Searches of Students in Private Schools

If a search is conducted by a private school official, it is not subject to even the flexible *T.L.O.* requirements. This is because such a search does not constitute state action, and the Fourth Amendment only regulates the conduct of public officials. See *Duarte v. Commonwealth,* 12 Va.App. 1023, 407 S.E.2d 41 (1991) (search by dean of students at private college, even if without articulable suspicion, is not illegal because the "fourth amendment is not implicated").

2. Employer Inspections of Government Offices

The Court applied the *T.L.O.* balancing analysis to a search by a Government employer of the office of one of its employees in *O'Connor v. Ortega,* 480 U.S. 709, 107 S.Ct. 1492, 94 L.Ed.2d 714 (1987). *O'Connor* involved a work-related search for files. The employer had reasonable suspicion, but not probable cause, to believe that the employee had engaged in various acts of mismanagement. No warrant was obtained. As in *T.L.O.,* the Court found that the search was conducted in furtherance of "special needs" beyond ordinary criminal law enforcement, and therefore that the relevant interests could be balanced to determine the reasonableness of the search. The special need at stake in this case was to ensure "that the work of the agency is conducted in a proper and efficient manner."

a. Balance of Interests Does Not Justify a Warrant Requirement

The Court in *O'Connor* held that a warrant is not required for an inspection of a Government employee's office for employment-related purposes. Relying on *T.L.O.,* the Court reasoned that a warrant requirement was ill-suited to the informal searches conducted by Government employers. The Court noted that "employers most frequently need to enter the offices and desks of their employees for legitimate work-related reasons wholly unrelated to illegal conduct." It stated that work-related searches run the gamut from the search of a person's office for a file needed by another worker, to a search conducted to safeguard Government property, and that none of these searches could be efficiently conducted if the "unwieldy" warrant process were imposed. The Court concluded that "requiring an employer to obtain a warrant whenever the employer wished to enter an employee's office, desk or file cabinets for a work-related purpose would seriously disrupt the routine conduct of business and would be unduly burdensome."

b. Dissent in *O'Connor*

The four dissenters in *O'Connor* did not quarrel with the general proposition that a warrant should not be required for most searches by Government employees, such as a search for files sought by a fellow employee. But, in the fairly unique fact situation presented by *O'Connor,* where the search occurred while the employee was on administrative leave and not permitted to enter the office, and where the search was conducted in order to find evidence to support charges of mismanagement, the dissenters argued that the use of a warrant requirement would not be burdensome. Reviewing the fact situation of *O'Connor,* the dissenters concluded that "this seems to be exactly the kind of situation where a neutral magistrate's involvement would have been helpful," because it would have required the Government employer to articulate reasons for the search and to particularize what they sought. The dissenters thus asserted that a warrant requirement "would have prevented the general rummaging through the [employee's] office, desk and filing cabinets."

c.   **Balance of Interests Allows a Search on the Basis of Reasonable Suspicion**
The Court in *O'Connor* examined two types of searches into the effects of a Government employee: 1) a non-investigatory work-related intrusion, and 2) (as occurred in *O'Connor*) an investigatory search for evidence of work-related malfeasance. The Court held that both types of searches could be conducted if there was "reasonable grounds to suspect" that the search is necessary for a civil-based purpose such as to retrieve a file (in the former situation), or to uncover evidence that the employee is guilty of work-related misconduct (in the latter situation).

d.   **Non-investigative Work–Related Searches**
As to searches conducted for non-investigative reasons, the Court stated that the work of Government agencies would suffer "if employers were required to have probable cause before they entered an employee's desk for the purpose of finding a file or piece of office correspondence." The Court reasoned that in fact the concept of probable cause, rooted as it is in the criminal investigatory context, had little meaning when applied to a non-investigatory work-related search.

e.   **Searches to Investigate Suspicion of Work–Related Misconduct**
On the more difficult question of whether investigatory searches to uncover work-related misconduct should require probable cause, the *O'Connor* Court, as in *T.L.O.,* reasoned that governmental interests would be unduly impaired if officials had to wait for probable cause to develop before such a search could be conducted. As the Court put it, "the delay in correcting employee misconduct caused by the need for probable cause rather than reasonable suspicion will be translated into tangible and often irreparable damage to the agency's work, and ultimately to the public interest." As with *T.L.O.,* the Court expressed concern that a probable cause requirement would mean that a search would have to be delayed until it was too late to correct the administrative problem. Under these circumstances, a probable cause requirement would give insufficient consideration to the state interest and undue weight to the individual interest, especially since, according to

the Court in *O'Connor*, an employee may often have a diminished expectation of privacy in an office, desk or file cabinet, due to office procedures and legitimate regulation.

f.   Suspicionless Searches

The Court in *O'Connor* found it unnecessary to determine "whether individualized suspicion is an essential element of the standard of reasonableness that we adopt today." But as with searches directed at students, some lower courts have upheld the use of suspicionless searches of the effects of Government workers, pursuant to neutral criteria, where such a search is necessary to effectuate "special needs" beyond traditional criminal law enforcement. See *United States v. Donato,* 379 F.2d 288 (3d Cir.1967) (upholding suspicionless searches of all employee lockers at the United States Mint).

g.   Search for Evidence of Criminal Activity Which Is Not Work–Related

The Court in *O'Connor* stressed that the "special needs" balancing analysis was being employed for purposes of regulating work-related conduct. The Court pointedly distinguished cases in which the Government conducted the search of an employee to investigate criminal misconduct unrelated to the work environment. Such law enforcement-based searches are outside the "special needs" analysis and must therefore satisfy the traditional requirements of warrant and probable cause, or some other exception to these requirements (such as exigent circumstances). See *United States v. Taketa,* 923 F.2d 665 (9th Cir.1991) (video surveillance of officer "was not an investigation of work-related employee misconduct that could benefit from the reasonableness standard of *O'Connor.* It was, rather, a search for evidence of criminal misconduct.").

3.   Searches Directed at Parolees and Probationers

The *T.L.O.* "special needs" balancing test was again used by the Court in *Griffin v. Wisconsin,* 483 U.S. 868, 107 S.Ct. 3164, 97 L.Ed.2d 709 (1987), to uphold a warrantless search of a probationer's home. The search was conducted by a probation officer, who had reasonable suspicion, but not probable cause, to believe that Griffin had engaged in an act which violated the terms of his probation. The Court held that a state's operation of its probation system, like its operation of a school or Government office, "presents special needs beyond normal law enforcement that may justify departures from the usual warrant and probable cause requirements." The special needs cited were the state's interest in rehabilitation, and the interest in assuring that "the community is not harmed by the probationer's being at large."

a. Balance of Interests Does Not Justify a Warrant Requirement

After finding the special needs necessary to justify resort to a reasonableness balancing test, the Court in *Griffin* balanced the relevant interests at stake and concluded that a warrant requirement would not sufficiently accommodate the state interest in conducting a search of a probationer's home. The Court found the warrant requirement would "interfere to an appreciable degree with the probation system," because it would substitute the magistrate for the probation officer as the judge of how close the supervision of any particular probationer should be. The Court also stated that the delays inherent in the warrant process would make it more difficult for probation officers to quickly intervene where the probationer is encountering difficulty in adjusting to society, and would "reduce the deterrent effect that the possibility of expeditious searches would otherwise create." Against these state interests, the Court balanced the possible protection that a warrant requirement would provide to a probationer. The Court found that the protection was minimized by the fact that a probation officer, while not a magistrate, is charged by law to take account of the welfare of the probationer; therefore, the risk of arbitrariness that might be posed by a police officer in the competitive enterprise of ferreting out crime is lessened when the search is conducted by a probation officer. The Court also found it relevant that the individual privacy interest at stake was minimized because the citizen was a probationer, whose liberty was conditional.

b. Dissent

Justice Blackmun, speaking for three dissenters, found the majority's establishment of an exception to the warrant requirement unjustified. He argued that the flexibility found necessary by the majority could be adequately accommodated in any particular case under the exigent circumstances exception. He therefore asserted that "there is no need to create a separate exception to the warrant requirement for probationers."

c. Balance of Interests Allows Search Upon Reasonable Suspicion

The Court in *Griffin* held that the special needs of a state's probation system justified the replacement of the traditional probable cause requirement with the less demanding standard of reasonable suspicion. As in previous cases, the Court concluded that the probable cause standard would require the state to wait too long before it could intervene to rectify a civil-based problem. As the Court put it in *Griffin,* "the probation agency must be able to act based upon a lesser degree of certainty than the Fourth Amendment would otherwise require in order to intervene before a probationer does damage to himself or to society."

d. Search by Police Officers

The Court in *Griffin* justified its use of the "special needs" analysis (and its rejection of the warrant and probable cause requirements) in large part on the ground that the search was conducted by a probation officer, who is not "the police officer who normally conducts searches against the citizen." The Court also noted that "we deal with a situation in which there is an ongoing supervisory relationship—and one that is not, or at least not entirely, adversarial—between the object of the search and the decisionmaker." In light of this reasoning, it is unlikely that an investigatory search of a probationer, by a police officer and without any participation by probation officers, could be justified as a "special needs" search. Such a search is likely to require a warrant and probable cause, or some traditional exception. See *United States v. Richardson,* 849 F.2d 439 (9th Cir.1988) (if probation officers play no part in the search, there must be probable cause and a warrant or some other traditional exception).

e. Participation by Police Officers

On the other hand, the search in *Griffin* itself was conducted by probation officers who were *accompanied* by three policemen present at the probation officers' request; the Court found nothing improper in this arrangement. See *State v. Burke,* 235 Mont. 165, 766 P.2d 254 (1988) ("Police cooperation with probation officers is to be encouraged as an important aid to effective administration of the probation system"). Likewise, courts have held that if a search is conducted by police officers *at the request* of probation officers, the search does not lose its character as a "special needs" search. See *United States v. Richardson,* 849 F.2d 439 (9th Cir.1988) (the Court in *Griffin* "approved the concept that the decision to authorize the search was more important than who was present when the search was made"). Under some circumstances, however, a court may find that the probation officer is acting as a mere *"stalking horse"* for law enforcement officers. If that is the case, the search will lose its character as a "special needs" search. *Shea v. Smith,* 966 F.2d 127 (3d Cir.1992) (evidence excluded where parole officers conducted a search solely to retrieve evidence for the police).

f. Application to Parolees

Griffin dealt with a search by a probation officer, but its principles apply equally to a search of a parolee conducted by or at the behest of a parole officer to investigate a possible parole violation. Like a search of a probationer, a search of a parolee is conducted at least in part to effectuate state interests in rehabilitation. Like the probationer, the parolee has a diminished expectation of privacy. See *United States v. Cardona,* 903 F.2d 60 (1st Cir.1990) (applying *Griffin* standards to search of parolee's premises); *United States v. Hill,* 967 F.2d 902 (3d Cir.1992) ("there is no constitutional difference between probation and parole for purposes of the fourth amendment").

4. Security Searches at Airports, Courthouses, Military Installations, Prisons, etc.

After an escalation of airplane hijacking in the 1960's, the FAA ordered air carriers to implement a hijacker detection system. The detection system is a preflight screening program which employs magnetometers and other electronic screening devices. All passengers and carry-on items must be electronically screened as a condition to boarding. Signs were and remain posted warning prospective passengers that they and their baggage are subject to search. If the x-ray of a bag detects an object which could be a weapon or explosive, then the passenger may not board unless he allows the bag to be opened for a visual inspection. If a passenger activates the magnetometer while walking through it, the passenger may not proceed until the matter is cleared up. This may occur by allowing the passenger to take out metallic objects from his pockets, or by submitting him to screening from a hand-held magnetometer, or by submitting him to a frisk.

Similar concerns with security have resulted in checkpoint security searches in places such as courthouses, jails, military installations, and even some schools. Some of these searches use electronic screening devices. Others employ visual inspection.

These security searches are conducted without suspicion and are justified as administrative searches which effectuate "special needs" beyond ordinary criminal law enforcement. The special need asserted is the need to provide safety and security for the public in various locales where a safety risk has been demonstrated. See *United States v. Davis,* 482 F.2d 893 (9th Cir.1973) ("Screening searches of airline passengers are conducted as part of a general regulatory scheme in furtherance of an administrative purpose, namely, to prevent the carrying of weapons or explosives aboard aircraft, and thereby to prevent hijackings. The essential purpose of the scheme is not to detect weapons or explosives or to apprehend those who carry them, but to deter persons carrying such material from seeking to board at all.").

a. No Requirement of Particularized Suspicion

Balancing the state interest in promoting security against the individual interest in privacy and the degree of intrusion imposed by the security search, the courts have held that searches with electronic screening devices, as well as other cursory inspections, can be conducted even in the absence of individualized suspicion, so long as four conditions are met: 1) the search is conducted in response to a *documented security problem* or to address a *serious risk of harm* to the public; 2) *all persons who pass the security checkpoint must be searched*, to prevent the risk

(S., C. & H.) Crim.Proc. BLS—11

that, in the absence of particularized suspicion, officers may subject certain people to arbitrary and harassing searches; 3) the security screening search is *no more intrusive than necessary* to satisfy the security interests that justify the search; and 4) people must be given the *option to avoid a search* by leaving the premises.

Example: In the 1970's, the lower courts upheld suspicionless magnetometer searches at airports, and these cases have been cited favorably by the Supreme Court. Suspicionless screening was found permissible because:

1.   The possibility of airplane hijacking or terrorism presents a significant risk to human lives and to property. See *United States v. Edwards,* 498 F.2d 496 (2d Cir.1974) ("When the risk is the jeopardy to hundreds of human lives and millions of dollars of property inherent in the pirating or blowing up of a large airplane, that danger alone meets the test of reasonableness"). Because of the grave consequences of hijacking or terrorism, the courts found that it did not matter that only an infinitesimal fraction of prospective passengers are likely to be hijackers or terrorists. As the Supreme Court has stated, "when the government's interest lies in deterring highly hazardous conduct, a low incidence of such conduct, far from impugning the validity of the scheme for implementing this interest, is more logically viewed as a hallmark of success." *National Treasury Employees Union v. Von Raab,* 489 U.S. 656, 109 S.Ct. 1384, 103 L.Ed.2d 685 (1989).

2.   All prospective passengers are subject to the search procedures. This eliminates the possibility of arbitrary searches, and also makes the searches less intrusive than they would otherwise be. Part of the intrusiveness of a search for law enforcement purposes is that the person who is searched suffers a stigma and perhaps public ridicule. But there is no stigma suffered when all persons must pass through a magnetometer. Airport security searches are also considered less intrusive because they are conducted by airport officials and not by police.

3.   The electronic screening is no more intrusive than necessary to address the security problem. The search does not involve a detailed visual inspection, or a substantial inconvenience, for example. Also, there is no real alternative to suspicionless searches of all prospective travellers. Requiring particularized suspicion would undoubtedly permit some hijackers or terrorists to get through. As the court in *Davis* noted, "there is no foolproof method of confining the search to the few who are potential hijackers." Finally, if something suspicious is found in the electronic screening, a

subsequent search is conducted in a minimally intrusive fashion: in the case of a bag, the passenger is asked to open his bag for a quick visual inspection; in the case of a person, the passenger merely displays the contents of his pockets, or submits to a more specific magnetometer or, when that fails, to a frisk.

4. Passengers are notified that the search will be conducted and are given the option to avoid the search by choosing not to travel. See *United States v. Davis, supra* ("Since a compelled search of persons who elect not to board would not contribute to barring weapons and explosives from the plane, it could serve only the purpose of apprehending violators of * * * some criminal statute. Such searches would be criminal investigations subject to the warrant and probable cause requirements of the Fourth Amendment.").

b. Distortion by Law Enforcement Objectives

If the security inspection system is operated as a screening device for law enforcement purposes, then it may lose its administrative character and thus be subject to the warrant and probable cause requirements. For example, in *United States v. $124,570 U.S. Currency,* 873 F.2d 1240 (9th Cir.1989), the airport security officer operating an x-ray scanner detected a dark mass in a passenger's briefcase, and asked him to open it. He did. It turned out to be a large amount of currency. This information was reported to customs officials. Ordinarily, of course, evidence of a criminal violation which is found in the course of a legitimate administrative search is admissible in a criminal trial (or, in this case, a criminal forfeiture). See *New York v. Burger, supra.* The court held that this principle did not apply in the instant case, however, since the information was turned over to customs officials pursuant to an established practice whereby security agents were paid a reward of $250 whenever they reported discovery of illegal drugs or of money in an amount over $100,000. The court held that the search under these circumstances "plainly falls outside the administrative search rationale." The court reasoned that "the policy of working hand-in-hand with U.S. Customs and Port Police regarding the detection and reporting of drugs and U.S. currency will very likely influence [security] officers to conduct more searches, and more intrusive searches, than if they focus on air safety alone."

5. Drug–Testing of Government Employees

Because of the drug crisis, a growing number of employers are requiring employees to submit to urinalysis testing. Where the testing is conducted by private employers, the Fourth Amendment does not apply. However, when Government employees are tested, or where the Government requires private employees to be tested, Fourth Amendment concerns are implicated. See *Skinner v. Railway Labor Executives' Ass'n,* 489 U.S. 602, 109 S.Ct. 1402,

103 L.Ed.2d 639 (1989) (Fourth Amendment applies to drug-testing by private railroad companies where there are "clear indices of the Government's encouragement, endorsement, and participation" in the testing process).

a. **Drug–Testing Is a Search**

The Court in *Skinner* held that urine-testing was a search because it invaded an employee's legitimate expectation of privacy. The Court noted that a chemical analysis of urine could disclose private information such as whether the employee was pregnant, diabetic, or was taking prescription drugs. The Court also stressed that the testing *procedures* intruded upon privacy interests, because they required either visual or oral monitoring of the obviously private act of urination.

b. **Special Needs Analysis Applies**

In *Skinner* and the companion case of *National Treasury Employees Union v. Von Raab,* 489 U.S. 656, 109 S.Ct. 1384, 103 L.Ed.2d 685 (1989), the Court held that drug-testing by Government employers effectuates special needs beyond ordinary criminal law enforcement, and therefore that such testing schemes are not necessarily regulated by the traditional requirements of a warrant and probable cause. Rather, the relevant interests could be balanced to determine what requirements complied with general Fourth Amendment standards of reasonableness. *Skinner* involved urinalysis of all railroad employees involved in a railroad accident. *Von Raab* concerned drug-testing of all Customs Service employees upon their promotion to or application for various sensitive positions. In each case, the Court found that the employers had a legitimate regulatory interest in assuring that the tested employees remained drug-free. The Court noted that drug use could impair the employee's job performance and put the public at risk. Also, in *Skinner,* the railroads were found to have an interest in testing after an accident to determine whether or not drug use may have been a contributing factor in the accident.

c. **Dissent**

Justice Marshall, joined by Justice Brennan, dissented from the Court's use of "special needs" analysis in *Skinner* and *Von Raab*. He argued that the warrant and probable cause requirements were necessary to provide a benchmark against which to assess the validity of searches and seizures; a balancing test based on reasonableness was, to him, "virtually devoid of meaning, subject to whatever content shifting judicial majorities, concerned about the problems of the day, choose to give to that supple term."

d.   Balance of Interests Does Not Justify a Warrant Requirement

A finding of "special needs" beyond ordinary criminal law enforcement allows a court to depart from the usual Fourth Amendment standards and to determine whether the balance of relevant interests actually justifies the application of a warrant requirement. With drug-testing of Government employees, the courts have uniformly held that a warrant requirement would skew the balancing process in favor of the employee at the expense of the Government. For one thing, the warrant would be sought in an employment context and, as in *O'Connor,* employers who conduct searches for work-related purposes are not law enforcement officers familiar with the warrant process. Also, the formality of the warrant process is inconsistent with the flexibility required in employer-employee relationships. Finally, and most importantly, most drug-testing procedures are implicated by triggering events or are conducted at random. For example, in *Von Raab,* drug-testing was mandated only when the employee sought promotion or transfer to certain jobs; in *Skinner,* drug-testing was mandated after an accident occurred. Many drug-testing plans are random and are implemented at regular intervals. See *Dimeo v. Griffin,* 943 F.2d 679 (7th Cir.1991) (random drug-testing of jockeys and starters at frequent intervals). Where the search is based on a random plan or an obvious triggering event, there is no contestable issue for a magistrate to review. Accordingly, the Court in *Skinner* and *Von Raab* held that a warrant is not required in the context of drug-testing. See *Skinner* ("imposing a warrant requirement in the present context would add little to the assurances of certainty and regularity already afforded by the regulations, while significantly hindering, and in many cases frustrating, the objectives of the Government's testing program.").

e.   Balance of Interests May Allow Suspicionless Drug–Testing in Some Cases

Before *Von Raab* and *Skinner,* the lower courts had regularly held that drug-testing of Government employees could be conducted on reasonable suspicion rather than probable cause. The courts found that the important state interests at stake could not be sufficiently accommodated if the Government had to wait for probable cause to develop—by that time, much of the damage caused by drug use could already have occurred. See *Fraternal Order of Police v. City of Newark,* 216 N.J.Super. 461, 524 A.2d 430 (1987) (upholding drug-testing of police on reasonable suspicion; collecting cases). The question presented by *Von Raab* and *Skinner* was whether drug-testing plans could ever be reasonable *in the absence of individualized suspicion.* In both cases, the Court answered in the affirmative. The Court stated: "In limited circumstances, where the privacy interests implicated by the search are minimal, and where an important Government interest furthered by the intrusion would be placed in jeopardy by a requirement of individualized suspicion, a search may be reasonable despite the absence of such suspicion."

f.   Diminished Expectation of Privacy

The Court in both cases found the privacy interest minimal. While the monitoring of the act of urination was intrusive, the Court noted in both cases that steps were taken to minimize the intrusion as much as possible: the testing was conducted in a medical environment, and aural rather than visual monitoring was employed. Also, the privacy interests of the employees were found diminished in both cases. In *Skinner,* the employees were found to have voluntarily entered into a pervasively regulated industry. In *Von Raab,* the privacy interest of the employees was minimized by the fact that drug-testing only occurred when the employee sought transfer or promotion to a certain position. Thus, as in the airport magnetometer cases, the citizen could control the search to some extent by refusing to submit to it and engaging in some alternative form of conduct (e.g., not asking for promotion). See also *Dimeo v. Griffin,* 943 F.2d 679 (7th Cir.1991) (rule requiring jockeys and other participants in horse races to submit to random, suspicionless drug-testing was reasonable under the Fourth Amendment; the weaker the personal interest asserted, the weaker the level of state justification needed to support suspicionless testing; horse-racing is a heavily regulated industry, thus diminishing the expectation of privacy of those who participate; the privacy interest implicated by urine-testing is minimal when applied to persons who are subject to frequent medical examinations, and horse-race participants voluntarily enter a profession where frequent medical exams are required).

g.   Government Interest Placed in Jeopardy by Requirement of Individualized Suspicion

Before *Skinner* and *Von Raab* the Court used "special needs" analysis to allow searches based on reasonable suspicion on the ground that important state interests would suffer if the Government had to wait for probable cause to develop. In *Skinner* and *Von Raab,* the Court used the same analysis, but determined that the interests at stake were such that the Government need not even wait for reasonable suspicion to develop. Therefore, suspicionless searches were found reasonable. One reason given by the Court in both cases is that it would be *too difficult to obtain reasonable suspicion* in the cases presented. In *Skinner,* the Court noted that the scene after a train accident was chaotic and that it would obviously be difficult to determine in those circumstances whether there was reasonable suspicion to believe that any of the employees to be tested were drug-impaired. In *Von Raab,* the Court noted that the employees subject to testing were generally field employees, *whose activity could not be closely monitored.*

Furthermore, in both cases, the Court found the interest at stake so crucial that, even if suspicious circumstances could be detected, the state interest would be impaired during the time it had to wait for the facts to develop. For example, *Von Raab* dealt with employees who sought transfer or promotion to jobs on the front-line level of narcotics interdiction. The Court reasoned that, by the time reasonable suspicion developed as to such an employee, the employee may already have been compromised, or may have, while impaired, allowed drug dealers to get away.

h. Deterrence Factor Is Relevant

In deciding whether suspicionless testing was reasonable, the Court in *Skinner* and *Von Raab* relied on the fact that a suspicionless testing scheme may be a more effective *deterrent* to drug use than a scheme triggered by individualized suspicion. As the Court put it in *Skinner,* the suspicionless testing was reasonable in part because it was "an effective means of deterring employees engaged in safety-sensitive tasks from using controlled substances in the first place."

i. Documented Problem of Drug Abuse Not Required for Suspicionless Testing

In *Skinner,* the Government justified the need for a suspicionless testing plan in part on the ground that many previous train accidents had been caused by drug-impaired employees. But there was no such record of drug abuse in *Von Raab* as to Customs employees. The Court in *Von Raab* found the lack of a documented drug problem to be not dispositive of whether random, suspicionless drug-testing could be reasonable. The Court held that it was reasonable to impose a suspicionless testing plan, even in the absence of a documented drug problem, if undetected drug use would impair a *substantial Government interest*. In other words, the question is not necessarily whether there is a problem but rather the nature and gravity of the harm that would ensue if a problem eventually arises and goes undetected. The Court relied on the airport magnetometer cases, discussed *supra,* and noted that such searches are reasonable even though the vast majority of persons subject to the searches pose no danger to airline safety. The Court stated that "where the Government's interest lies in deterring highly hazardous conduct, a low incidence of such conduct, far from impugning the validity of the scheme for implementing this interest, is more logically viewed as a hallmark of success." See also *Rushton v. Nebraska Public Power District,* 844 F.2d 562 (8th Cir.1988) (suspicionless testing of nuclear power employees even in the absence of a documented drug problem); *Dimeo v. Griffin,* 943 F.2d 679 (7th Cir.1991) (state interests in drug-testing of jockeys and starters include assuring the safety of participants, and preserving the integrity of parimutuel betting in order to ensure state revenues; the fact that there have been no proven cases of serious horse-racing accidents caused by drug use is not dispositive after *Von Raab*).

j.   Dissent

Justice Scalia dissented in *Von Raab,* though he joined the majority in *Skinner.* The difference, for him, was that in *Von Raab* there was not "even a single instance in which any of the speculated horribles actually occurred: an instance, that is, in which the cause of bribe taking, or of poor aim, or of unsympathetic law enforcement, or of compromise of classified information, was drug use." He distinguished cases allowing suspicionless searches of airplane passengers and nuclear power plant employees as cases where a violation could cause "such catastrophic social harm that no risk whatever is tolerable." He declared that if the majority considered the threat from drug-impaired Customs officials to be equivalent to that presented by drug-impaired nuclear power employees, "then the Fourth Amendment has become frail protection indeed."

k.   Not All Suspicionless Drug–Testing Is Reasonable

The Court in *Von Raab* clearly expanded the circumstances in which random, suspicionless drug-testing could be permissible. Even in the absence of a documented drug problem, suspicionless testing can be reasonable if drug use could cause *some significant social harm* and if having to *wait for individualized suspicion would impair that Government interest.* However, *Von Raab* does *not* support the proposition that all random, suspicionless drug-testing of Government employees will be reasonable. Indeed, the Court in *Von Raab* found itself unable to assess the reasonableness of suspicionless testing as applied to all employees at the Customs Service who have access to "classified" documents. The Court was concerned that some of the employees subject to testing would not in fact have access to truly sensitive information (given the number of Government documents which are routinely labelled "classified"), and therefore that drug use by these employees would not create such a significant risk of harm as to justify suspicionless testing. Courts after *Von Raab* have held that suspicionless testing, in the absence of a documented drug problem in the work force, is not reasonable if drug use by the employees would do no more than effect the generalized efficiency of Government services.

Example: In *Harmon v. Thornburgh,* 878 F.2d 484 (D.C.Cir.1989), the court upheld suspicionless drug-testing of Justice Department employees with top secret security clearances, but also held that other employees, including attorneys, could not be tested in the absence of reasonable suspicion. The risk from drug use as to the former category of employees was found to be substantial, because if such an employee were drug-impaired, he might disclose top secret information either inadvertently or as a result of being compromised by drug activity. In contrast the court found that the risk to the public from drug use by attorneys working generally in the Justice Department was too remote to support suspicionless testing in the absence of a documented drug problem. The court also noted that an individualized suspicion standard could be implemented without much difficulty, since the attorneys were essentially office employees whose conduct was readily visible. So for example, if the attorney is routinely late to work and exhibits erratic behavior, there may well be reasonable suspicion to justify a drug test. See also *Policemen's Benevolent Ass'n v. Township of Washington,* 850 F.2d 133 (3d Cir.1988) (upholding suspicionless testing of police officers, on the ground that they are armed and charged with protecting the public, and that substantial harm could occur if a police officer is drug-impaired).

I. **Suspicionless Drug–Testing Plan Must Be Neutral to Be Reasonable**
Presuming that suspicionless drug-testing can be reasonable, the Fourth Amendment requires that it must be conducted pursuant to some neutral, non-discretionary standard. A neutral standard substitutes for individualized suspicion; otherwise the Government official's decision to test a particular employee would be completely unrestrained and arbitrary. So for example, the drug-testing plan in *Skinner* subjected *every* employee involved in an accident to drug-testing. See also *National Treasury Employees Union v. Yeutter,* 918 F.2d 968 (D.C.Cir.1990) (upholding drug-testing of Government drivers when conducted on a random basis); *Dimeo v. Griffin,* 943 F.2d 679 (7th Cir.1991) (rule requiring jockeys and other participants in horse races to submit to random, suspicionless drug-testing was reasonable under the Fourth Amendment).

D. BORDER SEARCHES AND SEIZURES

Border searches are considered administrative, "special needs" searches. The special need beyond ordinary criminal law enforcement is the interest in protecting American borders, and regulating the goods which flow into the country. As the Court stated in *United States v. Montoya de Hernandez,* 473 U.S. 531, 105 S.Ct. 3304, 87 L.Ed.2d 381 (1985), officials regulating the border "have more than merely an investigative law enforcement role." They are charged with "protecting this Nation from entrants who may bring anything harmful into this country, whether that be communicable diseases, narcotics, or explosives."

Because a border search serves special needs, it is evaluated under the reasonableness clause of the Fourth Amendment. And given the heavy state interest in protecting the border, as well as the diminished expectation of privacy attendant to a border crossing, border searches are ordinarily found reasonable without a warrant and probable cause, and often without any suspicion at all.

1. Routine Border Searches

In *United States v. Ramsey,* 431 U.S. 606, 97 S.Ct. 1972, 52 L.Ed.2d 617 (1977), the Court held that routine border searches "are reasonable simply by virtue of the fact that they occur at the border." So for example, a person wishing to enter the country by international flight may be required to submit to a search of his outer clothing, his pockets, and his luggage, even though the officers have no warrant and no reason to suspect that the person is bringing contraband or some other prohibited item into the country. See *United States v. Charleus,* 871 F.2d 265 (2d Cir.1989) ("routine border searches of the personal belongings and effects of entrants may be conducted without regard to probable cause or reasonable suspicion"). In *Ramsey,* the Court opined that incoming international mail could be opened without a warrant and without any suspicion of a criminal violation. Technically, however, the Court was not required to decide the legality of suspicionless searches of incoming mail, because the governing statute in *Ramsey* required reasonable suspicion.

a. Minimally Intrusive

Courts have upheld suspicionless routine border searches by balancing the previously discussed substantial state interest against the fact that routine border searches are less intrusive than searches by law enforcement officers for evidence of crime. Courts reason that routine border searches are minimally intrusive for two reasons. First, the citizen has *prior notice* that he or she is subject to such a search; this makes the search, when it is conducted, less surprising and humiliating. Also, because the citizen controls the timing of the search, he can limit its intrusiveness by controlling the nature and character of goods which he brings with him. Second, the search is directed at a *class of travelers* as opposed to any person, and thus lacks the quality of insult, humiliation and stigma associated with the search of a particular person for evidence of a criminal violation.

2. Searches Beyond the Routine

Under the reasonableness balancing test, the level of intrusiveness of a search will have an effect on the level of suspicion required to justify the search. That is, the more intrusive the search, the more suspicious the articulable facts must be for the search to be reasonable. It therefore follows, and all courts have held, that searches more intrusive than a "routine" border search must be justified by some level of individualized suspicion.

a. Definition of "Routine"

What factors distinguish routine from non-routine border searches? A good rule of thumb is that if the search is *typical of that conducted at the border*—such as a simple inspection of luggage—then it is a routine search which can be conducted without suspicion. See *United States v. Sandoval Vargas*, 854 F.2d 1132 (9th Cir.1988) (routine search where border officials referred the defendant's car to a secondary inspection area and conducted a thorough search of the passenger compartment and the trunk; the search was "typical of those conducted at the border").

b. Strip Searches

A "strip" search is clearly more intrusive than the routine border search. But the line between a "strip" search and a routine border search is sometimes difficult to draw. Obviously, if the citizen is forced to completely disrobe, then a strip search is being conducted. More difficult questions arise when the defendant is forced to simply lift a piece of clothing, or to take off only one piece of clothing for inspection. Most courts have held, for example, that simply requiring the defendant to lift his shirt, or to take off his shoe, does not constitute a strip search and therefore is within the realm of a routine border search. See *United States v. Charleus*, 871 F.2d 265 (2d Cir.1989) (discussing cases finding such activity as removal of shoes, pulling down a girdle in a private room, and lifting up a skirt to be routine border searches, and concluding that "since the potential indignity resulting from a pat on the back followed by a lifting of one's shirt simply fails to compare with the much greater level of intrusion associated with a body cavity or full strip search, we decline to hold that reasonable suspicion was here required"). Compare *United States v. Sanders*, 663 F.2d 1 (2d Cir.1981) (requiring the defendant to take off his artificial leg for inspection was tantamount to a body cavity search, and therefore more intrusive than a routine border search; reasonable suspicion required).

c. Drilling or Dismantling

If the border official drills into or dismantles the property of the entering citizen, this is considered a search that is more intrusive than a routine border search. Courts have consequently demanded that the official have reasonable suspicion before such a search can be conducted. See *United States v. Puig*, 810 F.2d 1085 (11th Cir.1987) (reasonable suspicion required before Customs Service official may drill a hole into the hull of a boat); *United States v. Carreon*, 872 F.2d 1436 (10th Cir.1989) (agent's use of electric drill to find marijuana within a camper shell installed on a truck was permissible only because agent had reasonable suspicion of drug smuggling).

d. Extended Detentions

A traveller crossing the border who is subject to a search is also, of course, seized during the course of that search. Such a seizure if routine is, like the routine search, permissible without individualized suspicion. However, if a traveller is detained for an extended period of time, then the seizure will require individualized suspicion even if a search is never conducted. Illustrative is *United States v. Montoya de Hernandez*, 473 U.S. 531, 105 S.Ct. 3304, 87 L.Ed.2d 381 (1985), where the defendant was suspected of being an internal carrier of drugs (a balloon swallower), and was detained for 16 hours until she made a bowel movement; eventually she passed 88 balloons containing 528 grams of 80% pure cocaine. The Court in *Hernandez* did not doubt that the long-term detention was far more serious than a routine border seizure, and held that individualized suspicion was required before such a seizure could occur. On the other hand, a momentary detention of a citizen by a border official, so that the official can ask a few questions or inspect identification, travel arrangements and the like, is permissible without individualized suspicion. See *United States v. Pierre*, 958 F.2d 1304 (5th Cir.1992) (seizure for purposes of questioning occupants of a vehicle about citizenship and travel plans was permissible without reasonable suspicion).

3. Search or Seizure Beyond the Routine Requires Reasonable Suspicion; Sliding–Scale Approach Rejected

In *Montoya de Hernandez, supra,* the lower court had found that the extensive delay was so severe that it had to be justified by a "clear indication" of criminal activity. This was a standard of proof somewhere between reasonable suspicion and probable cause. On review, the Supreme Court held that such a sliding scale approach, matching a variety of intrusions to a variety of standards of proof, was not permissible under the Fourth Amendment. The Court reasoned that "subtle verbal gradations may obscure rather than elucidate the meaning" of reasonableness.

a. Reasonable Suspicion Sufficient

The Court in *Montoya de Hernandez* held that the detention of the defendant for 16 hours until she made a bowel movement was permissible because officers had *reasonable suspicion* to believe that she was an internal carrier. The Court rejected a requirement of probable cause under these circumstances, concluding that this more demanding standard of proof would unduly subjugate state interests in controlling the border. The Court noted that alimentary canal smuggling "gives no external signs and inspectors will rarely possess probable cause to arrest or search, yet governmental interests in stopping smuggling at the border are high indeed."

b. Distinction From *Terry*

Of course, a 16–hour detention such as occurred in *Montoya de Hernandez* would be impermissible under the *Terry* doctrine if the officer had only reasonable suspicion and not probable cause to believe that the defendant was smuggling drugs. However, *Montoya de Hernandez* is not a *Terry* case; it is a border seizure case. The Court specifically noted that "alimentary canal smuggling cannot be detected in the amount of time in which other illegal activity may be investigated through brief *Terry*-type stops." The detention was reasonable as a border seizure where it would not have been under *Terry* because of the heavy state interest and diminished expectation of privacy unique to a border crossing.

c. No Warrant Requirement

The Court in *Montoya de Hernandez* held that the Customs officials did not need a warrant to detain the defendant for over 16 hours while waiting for nature to take its course. This has led some lower courts to conclude that no warrant is required for a border detention, regardless of how long that detention may be, until the defendant is actually arrested and then entitled to a post-arrest determination of probable cause. See *United States v. Esieke*, 940 F.2d 29 (2d Cir.1991) (36-hour detention until bowel movement: "an extended border detention of a suspected alimentary canal smuggler does not implicate the Fourth Amendment's warrant clause and, accordingly, does not require judicial approval * * * The length of an extended border detention is governed by the detainee's bodily processes, not by a clock."). Other courts have imposed procedural safeguards requiring judicial supervision of extended detentions, without specifically stating that such safeguards are required by the Fourth Amendment. See *United States v. Adekunle*, 2 F.3d 559 (5th Cir.1993) (concerned with the "incommunicado" nature of a long-term detention, the court held that the Government is required to obtain judicial determination of reasonable suspicion within 48 hours of detention of a suspected alimentary canal smuggler).

4. Two Types of Intrusions

After *Montoya de Hernandez,* there are apparently two types of intrusions which can occur at the border. One is a routine border search or seizure which can be conducted without suspicion. The other is a non-routine border search or seizure which requires reasonable suspicion.

a. Probable Cause Not Required

It could be argued that some intrusions occurring at the border could be so severe as to be permissible only upon probable cause. However, after *Montoya de Hernandez,* and given the substantial state interest in controlling the border, it is unlikely that probable cause is required for any border search or seizure. It is hard to conceive of an intrusion much greater than the long-term detention and monitored bowel movement in *Montoya de Hernandez;* and yet that intrusion did not require probable cause. See *United States v. Adekunle*, 980 F.2d 985 (5th Cir.1992) (probable cause not required where suspect is subject to 100 hour incommunicado detention, forced use of laxatives, and monitored bowel movement); *United States v. Odofin,* 929 F.2d 56 (2d Cir.1991) (24 day detention before bowel movement does not require probable cause).

b. Some Standard Less Than Reasonable Suspicion Is Not Appropriate

The Court in *Montoya de Hernandez* rejected the use of a standard of proof somewhere between reasonable suspicion and probable cause to regulate searches and seizures somewhere between non-routine and extremely intrusive. The Court reasoned that such a sliding scale approach was unacceptably indeterminate. The same reasoning should preclude the use of a standard of proof somewhere between no suspicion and reasonable suspicion for a search or seizure somewhere between a routine border search or seizure and one that is somewhat more intrusive. So, for example, in *United States v. Charleus,* 871 F.2d 265 (2d Cir.1989), the court rejected a proposed standard of "some suspicion" for a search which "straddles the line between the two categories of border search" and concluded that a traveler could be forced to lift his shirt even though the Customs official had no individualized suspicion. The court reasoned that the Supreme Court's rejection in *Montoya de Hernandez* of a standard of proof somewhere between reasonable suspicion and probable cause "applies equally to the creation of new standards based on levels of suspicion between no suspicion and reasonable suspicion." For a contrary view, see *People v. Luna,* 73 N.Y.2d 173, 538 N.Y.S.2d 765, 535 N.E.2d 1305 (1989) ("some" suspicion required before a patdown border search can be conducted).

5. Functional Equivalent of the Border

A search may be considered as a border search (and thus subject to a balance of interests under the reasonableness clause of the Fourth Amendment) even if it is not undertaken at the geographical point at which a border is crossed. The right to search at the border has been extended to searches conducted at the functional equivalent of the border. The Supreme Court has cited, as examples of a functional equivalent, "searches at an established station near the border, at a point marking the confluence of two or more roads that extend from the border" and "a search of the passengers and cargo of an airplane arriving at a St. Louis airport after a non-stop flight from Mexico City."

6. Recent Border Crossings; Extended Border Search

Even if the search or seizure is not conducted at a border checkpoint or other port of entry which can be considered the functional equivalent of the border, an intrusion may be justified as a border search or seizure if it can be established that a border crossing has been made and that no material circumstances have changed since the border crossing. A typical case is *United States v. Moore,* 638 F.2d 1171 (9th Cir.1980), where agents monitoring a radar screen detected a plane crossing the border from Mexico. The plane was tracked by radar, and tower personnel at the airport kept the plane in view as it landed. Even though the airport was far from the border when the officers searched it, the search of the airplane was upheld as an "extended border search" because it was clear that the plane had crossed the border, and that no material conditions had changed since the border crossing.

a. Suspicion Not Required for Routine Extended Border Search or Seizure

In order to justify a search or seizure under the "extended border" doctrine, the Government must establish a clear indication that the person or thing has recently crossed the border and that material conditions have not been changed by the time of the Government intrusion. But if the subsequent search or seizure is routine, then the Government need not have an independent suspicion that a violation of law has occurred. Thus, a search or seizure under the "extended border" doctrine can be conducted under the same standards as if it were made at an actual port of entry. The standard of proof that must be met pertains to whether the border has been crossed, not to whether the search will be successful.

b. Change of Conditions

Obviously, the "extended border" doctrine does not permit a Customs official to search a person's suitcase on the ground that the person travelled abroad with the suitcase three years earlier. The Government must show an absence of changed conditions to justify an extended border search or seizure. See *United States v. Anderson,* 509 F.2d 724 (9th Cir.1974) (search not justified as an extended border search where car stops after crossing border and a passenger gets out of the car, retrieves a package from behind a tree, and re-enters the car).

c. Importance of Continuous Surveillance

Continuous surveillance is obviously important both to establish that the subject of the search or seizure actually crossed the border, and that material conditions have not changed since the border crossing. Compare *United States v. Martinez,* 481 F.2d 214 (5th Cir.1973) (extended border search after continuous surveillance of a car for 300 miles), with *United States v. Petersen,* 473 F.2d 874 (9th Cir.1973) (when officers lost sight of a car for ten minutes, and then saw it again with two more passengers, the search of the car trunk was not a valid border search because the contraband found in the trunk could have been loaded at the same time as the two passengers). Limited breaks in surveillance will not, however, be fatal where other circumstances establish with reasonable certainty that conditions could not have materially changed during the break in surveillance. See *United States v. Mejias,* 452 F.2d

1190 (9th Cir.1971) (lack of constant surveillance of a suitcase checked through customs was not problematic where the search uncovered narcotics sewn into the lining of the suitcase).

7. Roving Patrols in the Interior

In an effort to deal with the flow of illegal aliens into the United States, immigration officials have undertaken investigative techniques at areas removed from the border. One technique is the roving patrol. The constitutionality of roving patrols was first considered by the Supreme Court in *Almeida–Sanchez v. United States,* 413 U.S. 266, 93 S.Ct. 2535, 37 L.Ed.2d 596 (1973), where the defendant's car was stopped 25 miles from the Mexican border. A subsequent search uncovered contraband. No claim was made that there was probable cause to search the car or that there was probable cause to believe that the car had crossed the border. Nonetheless, the Government argued that the search was a routine border search and was therefore reasonable, particularly in light of a statute permitting roving stops within 100 miles of the border. The Court rejected this argument, and stated that the search "by a roving patrol on a California road that lies at all points at least 20 miles north of the Mexican border, was of a wholly different sort" from a border search. Thus, traditional Fourth Amendment standards applied to the search, and it was therefore declared illegal in the absence of probable cause.

a. Reasonable Suspicion

Thereafter, in *United States v. Brignoni–Ponce,* 422 U.S. 873, 95 S.Ct. 2574, 45 L.Ed.2d 607 (1975), the Court considered "whether a roving patrol may stop a vehicle in an area near the border and question its occupants when the only ground for suspicion is that the occupants appear to be of Mexican ancestry." The Court held that the mere fact of Mexican ancestry would not support a stop and that, as in *Almeida–Sanchez,* a stop by an officer on roving patrol could not be justified as a border seizure. However, invoking the *Terry* doctrine, the Court held that an officer on roving patrol *could* stop a person or vehicle if there is reasonable suspicion to believe that the person is an illegal alien or that the vehicle contains illegal aliens. The Court concluded that "except at the border and its functional equivalents, officers on roving patrol may stop vehicles only if they are aware of specific articulable facts, together with rational inferences from those facts, that reasonably warrant suspicion that the vehicles contain aliens who may be illegally in the country." Since the stop was made on the basis of Mexican ancestry alone, the Court concluded that the reasonable suspicion test had not been satisfied. See also *United States v. Leija,* 735 F.Supp. 701 (N.D.Tex.1990) (stop of car travelling on freeway between San Antonio and Houston, where officer suspects that car contains illegal aliens, is not supported by reasonable suspicion; the fact that the car was large and heavily laden, and that the persons in the car were of Hispanic ancestry, is not sufficient to create an articulable suspicion; the fact that the car was travelling 400 miles from the border does not preclude a finding of reasonable suspicion, but certainly makes such a finding more difficult; the fact that the people in the car looked straight ahead as the officer passed is irrelevant; the court rejected the relevance of "opthamalogical" reactions, and rejected the officer's testimony concerning the "ostrich syndrome"). Compare *United States v. Garcia,* 732 F.2d 1221 (5th Cir.1984) (reasonable suspicion found where occupants of overloaded camper, driving near the border, ducked down when a patrolman shined a light into the vehicle).

8.   Fixed Checkpoints in the Interior

Another device to control the influx of illegal aliens is the fixed checkpoint which is removed from the border. An example is the San Clemente checkpoint in California, which is 66 miles from the Mexican border. Officers at the checkpoint screen all northbound traffic, and, if anything about a vehicle arouses suspicion, the occupants are questioned and, if the suspicion remains or is increased, the vehicle is searched. These checkpoint searches and seizures cannot be justified under the extended border doctrine, since there is a high likelihood that most of the vehicles which are stopped have not recently crossed the border. Nor can they be considered the functional equivalent of the border, since they are so far removed from the meaningful point of entry into the United States.

a.   Regulated by *Terry* Principles

While interior checkpoint intrusions cannot be justified as border searches and seizures, they may be reasonable under the *Terry* doctrine, discussed *supra.* In *United States v. Ortiz,* 422 U.S. 891, 95 S.Ct. 2585, 45 L.Ed.2d 623 (1975), and *United States v. Martinez–Fuerte,* 428 U.S. 543, 96 S.Ct. 3074, 49 L.Ed.2d 1116 (1976), the Court essentially applied *Terry* principles to the various intrusions which can occur at an interior checkpoint. The Court in *Ortiz* held that, as in *Terry,* vehicle searches for evidence of illegal aliens could not be conducted in the absence of probable cause. However, in *Martinez–Fuerte,* the Court upheld the use of a checkpoint to stop vehicles and question the occupants even absent individualized suspicion. See the discussion of *Martinez–Fuerte* in the section on roadblocks, *supra.*

9.   "Reverse" Border Searches and Seizures

Courts have unanimously held that border officials have the same broad power to search and seize outgoing persons and things as they have with respect to persons and things entering the country. Thus, a "routine" search of the luggage of a departing traveler is permissible without a warrant and without any suspicion of illegality. As the court explained in *United States v. Berisha,* 925 F.2d 791 (5th Cir.1991), "both incoming and outgoing border searches have several features in common; for example, the government is interested in protecting some interest of United States citizens, there is a likelihood of smuggling attempts at the border, and the individual is on notice that his privacy may be invaded when he crosses the border." The court in *Berisha* upheld a warrantless, suspicionless patdown search of a departing traveler, which uncovered $17,000 of domestic currency. For a dissenting view on the "reverse" border exception, see *United States v. Nates,* 831 F.2d 860 (9th Cir.1987) (Kozinski, J., dissenting) (noting that exit searches are "quite uncommon" and therefore that departing travelers have no diminished expectation of privacy when crossing the border to exit the country; also noting that intrusions are more serious because luggage searches of departing passengers are ordinarily conducted secretly, after the passenger has checked his bags with the airline).

VII.   SEARCH INCIDENT TO ARREST

Police have historically possessed powers incident to arrest that allow them the automatic right to further intrude upon the arrestee. This right is based on two grounds: 1) to *protect the officers making the arrest* and 2) to *protect against the destruction of evidence.* At one time, the search incident to arrest exception, also called the *arrest power rule,* allowed the police to search a suspect's entire house if they arrested the suspect on the premises. *United States v. Rabinowitz,* 339 U.S. 56, 70 S.Ct. 430, 94 L.Ed. 653 (1950). But then the Supreme Court in *Chimel v. California,* 395 U.S. 752, 89 S.Ct. 2034, 23 L.Ed.2d 685 (1969), imposed spatial limitations on a search incident to arrest, to accord with the reasons underlying the exception.

A.   SPATIAL LIMITATIONS

In *Chimel,* the Court limited the geographical scope of the arrest power rule. The Court confined a search incident to arrest to areas which in fact are accessible to the arrestee. Justice Stewart, writing for the Court, stated that "[t]here is ample justification * * * for a search of the arrestee's person and the area within his immediate control—construing the phrase to mean the area from within which he might gain possession of a weapon or destructible evidence." According to *Chimel,* a search incident to arrest is confined to the search of the suspect and the search of his or her "grab area" or "wing span."

1.   Arrest Power Rule Is Automatic

Although *Chimel* limited the scope of a search incident to arrest, it stressed that the police have the *automatic right* to secure everything within the grab area. Therefore, the police may, incident to a lawful arrest, secure the person and the grab area of the arrestee without reasonable suspicion or probable cause and without a warrant. Because the rule is automatic, there is no case-by-case approach as to whether in fact the arrestee poses a risk of harm, or whether in fact there is destructible evidence within the grab area.

2. Determining the Grab Area

Courts use a case-by-case approach to determine whether a certain place or object is within the arrestee's grab area.

Example: In *United States v. Lucas,* 898 F.2d 606 (8th Cir.1990), the defendant and two men were seated at a kitchen table when police officers approached the apartment. As the officers ran to the kitchen, Lucas attempted to rise and reach toward a cabinet door. As one officer arrested and handcuffed Lucas escorting him to the living room, another officer opened the cabinet door and found a gun. Although Lucas claimed that, under *Chimel,* the search violated the Fourth Amendment, the court looked at the totality of the circumstances and held that the search was valid. The court found that "a warrantless search incident to an arrest may be valid even though a court, operating with the benefit of hindsight in an environment well removed from the scene of the arrest, doubts that the defendant could have reached the items seized during the search." Under the circumstances, the officers could reasonably have believed that Lucas could have obtained access to the cabinet.

a. Differing Views of Lower Courts

Post–*Chimel* courts have adopted different views as to what is within the grab area. While some courts define the "grab area" as the area accessible to the defendant *at the time of the search*, other courts focus on where the defendant could have reached *when arrested*.

b. Determination of Grab Area at Time of Arrest

Some courts determine the grab area by focusing on where the defendant could have reached when arrested, even though the search or seizure occurs *after the defendant has been moved*. Such an application, however, seems contrary to *Chimel* and the rationale behind the exception, which is concerned with neutralizing the arrestee. See e.g., *Davis v. Robbs,* 794 F.2d 1129 (6th Cir.1986) (upholding seizure of rifle in close proximity to arrestee at time of arrest although seizure occurred after arrestee was in squad car). For example, in *United States v. Turner,* 926 F.2d 883 (9th Cir.1991), the police searched the defendant's room and closet after the defendant was handcuffed and removed from the room. The court upheld the search under the arrest power rule, reasoning that the evidence was within Turner's immediate control when he was arrested, and noting that subsequent events did not diminish the risks to such an extent as to make the search unreasonable.

c. Determination of Grab Area at Time of Search

Other courts determine the grab area by analyzing where the defendant could have reached at the time of the search. Some of these courts, however, find the grab area to be remarkably broad under the circumstances.

3. Factors Helpful in Defining the Area Within the Immediate Control of the Arrestee

Although a determination of the grab area depends on the facts of the case, some factors that are helpful in determining this area include: 1) whether the suspect is *cuffed or restrained*; 2) the *physical characteristics* of the particular suspect—a young, agile arrestee will have a more expansive grab area than an older, infirm arrestee; 3) the *ratio of police officers to suspects* —the higher the ratio, the less likely it would be for the suspect to leap a long distance to grab a weapon; and 4) whether the item searched is *reasonably accessible* —a locked safe may be very near to the arrestee, but it is not within the grab area under *Chimel*.

4. Movable Grab Area: No Requirement to Show Risk of Danger

To protect the integrity of an arrest, police officers may accompany an arrestee to a different location without having to prove a risk of danger. With post-arrest movement, the grab area moves along with the arrestee.

Example: In *Washington v. Chrisman*, 455 U.S. 1, 102 S.Ct. 812, 70 L.Ed.2d 778 (1982), a police officer approached a student who was carrying liquor and appeared to be underage. The officer placed him under arrest. Chrisman was not carrying identification, so the officer accompanied him to his dormitory room to retrieve it. Upon entering the room, the officer found evidence of marijuana. Although the officer had no fear of bodily harm or destruction of evidence, the Court held that "the absence of an affirmative indication that an arrested person might have a weapon available or might attempt to escape does not diminish the arresting officer's authority to maintain custody over the arrested person." According to the Court, "every arrest must be presumed to present a risk of danger to the arresting officer." Therefore, a police officer may monitor an arrestee's movements and if, during the course of such activity, the officer observes evidence of criminal activity, he may seize it pursuant to the plain view exception.

a. Application of *Chrisman* in the Lower Courts

A question arising after *Chrisman* is whether officers can demand that an arrestee dress in a certain way to go down to the station, and consequently monitor the arrestee's movements while he changes. For example, in *United States v. Butler*, 980 F.2d 619 (10th Cir.1992), the police arrested the defendant in front of his trailer pursuant to an arrest warrant. The ground outside of the trailer was covered with litter and broken glass. Because the defendant was barefoot, the arresting officer requested that the defendant enter the trailer to retrieve his shoes. When the officer entered the trailer to monitor the defendant's movements, he saw a shotgun in plain view in the defendant's bedroom. The court found that the search was a valid exercise of the arrest power, reasoning that "police may conduct a limited entry into an area for the purpose of protecting the health or safety of the arrestee." Here, the broken glass presented a legitimate and significant threat to Butler's safety and there was no evidence that the concern for his health was pretextual. The court noted that this extension of *Chrisman* "in no way creates a blank check for intrusion upon the privacy of the sloppily dressed." See *United States v. Anthon,* 648 F.2d 669 (10th Cir.1981) (holding that entry into the defendant's residence cannot be effected, in the absence of consent or exigent circumstances, solely upon the desire of law enforcement officers to complete the arrestee's wardrobe); *United States v. Titus,* 445 F.2d 577 (2d Cir.1971) (holding that where defendant was naked when arrested, evidence found while police were getting clothing for the defendant was properly admitted at trial); *United States v. Di Stefano,* 555 F.2d 1094 (2d Cir.1977) (holding that where defendant was arrested in a night gown and bathrobe and the police requested that she change, evidence found while defendant was dressing was admissible).

5. Other Exceptions That Justify Searches Beyond the Grab Area

Even though the arrest power rule has spatial limitations, other exceptions could apply during or after the arrest of a defendant that would allow police officers to conduct searches or seizures beyond the area within the arrestee's immediate control. The three possibilities justifying a search or seizure beyond the grab area are: 1) *exigent circumstances* arising due to an arrest, 2) the need to perform a *protective sweep* to protect the safety of the arresting officer, and 3) the need to *secure the premises* during the time it takes to obtain a warrant.

a. Exigent Circumstances

Justice White, dissenting in *Chimel,* argued for a bright line rule allowing the police to search the entire premises upon an arrest because an arrest most often gives rise to exigent circumstances and probable cause to search the premises. This bright line rule was rejected as overbroad because not every arrest gives rise to these factors. But when an arrest situation also leads to probable cause to believe that evidence is in a certain place, and creates a risk of destruction of that evidence by the arrestee's cohorts, then the police may conduct a search of that place even though it is beyond the grab area.

In many cases, the fact of an arrest will create a risk of destruction of evidence by the arrestee's associates and will thus give rise to exigent circumstances. See *e.g. United States v. Socey,* 846 F.2d 1439

(D.C.Cir.1988) (holding that exigent circumstances existed where arrest was made outside a house serving as a large-scale drug operation). In *Socey,* the U.S. Court of Appeals for the D.C. Circuit held that exigent circumstances will exist if police reasonably believe that third persons are inside a private dwelling and that these persons are aware of an arrest of a confederate outside the premises.

b.   Protective Sweeps

Another justification for searching beyond the grab area in an arrest situation is illustrated in *Maryland v. Buie,* 494 U.S. 325, 110 S.Ct. 1093, 108 L.Ed.2d 276 (1990), discussed *supra* in the section on *Terry.* The Court in *Buie* defined a protective sweep as a "quick and limited search of a premises, incident to an arrest and conducted to protect the safety of police officers or others". In *Buie,* the Court held that police may conduct a protective sweep based on reasonable suspicion. Thus, where circumstances justifying a protective sweep are present, the police may search beyond the grab area of the arrestee. While conducting a search pursuant to a protective sweep, the police may seize evidence of criminal activity by invoking the plain view exception.

c.   Seizing the Premises

Although the arrest power rule may not allow the police to search the premises beyond the arrestee's grab area, the police may seize the entire premises under certain conditions. If the police must leave the premises to obtain a warrant but wish to protect against the destruction of evidence during that time, they may secure the premises when they have probable cause to believe it contains evidence of criminal activity. *Segura v. United States,* 468 U.S. 796, 104 S.Ct. 3380, 82 L.Ed.2d 599 (1984). Although securing the premises is a seizure, because it is an exercise of dominion and control over the property, it is reasonable in these circumstances and thus does not violate the Fourth Amendment. See the discussion of *Segura* in the section on exigent circumstances.

B.   TEMPORAL LIMITATIONS

A search incident to arrest usually occurs immediately after the arrest. But it is permissible for the search to precede the arrest, when both are nearly simultaneous and probable cause to arrest existed before the police conducted the search. See *Rawlings v. Kentucky,* 448 U.S. 98, 100 S.Ct. 2556, 65 L.Ed.2d 633 (1980) ("Where the formal arrest followed quickly on the heels of the challenged search of petitioner's person, we do not believe it particularly important that the search preceded the arrest rather than vice versa."). A search, therefore, may immediately precede an arrest. But the police cannot use evidence discovered by the search to provide probable cause to make the arrest. See *Smith v. Ohio,* 494 U.S. 541, 110 S.Ct. 1288, 108 L.Ed.2d 464 (1990) (while the arrest power rule can justify a search which immediately precedes an arrest, that search cannot be used to provide the probable cause necessary to make the arrest).

1. **When Is the Search Too Late to Be Incident to an Arrest?**
   A search "incident to" an arrest implies that a search conducted too long after the arrest will not satisfy the exception. In *Chambers v. Maroney,* 399 U.S. 42, 90 S.Ct. 1975, 26 L.Ed.2d 419 (1970), the police searched an automobile after it was impounded and brought to the police station. The Court stated that "once an accused is under arrest and in custody, then a search made at another place, without a warrant, is simply not incident to the arrest." See also *United States v. Chadwick,* 433 U.S. 1, 97 S.Ct. 2476, 53 L.Ed.2d 538 (1977) (holding that the search of a footlocker at the police station, after the defendant was arrested and incarcerated, "cannot be viewed as incidental to the arrest or as justified by any other exigency.").

2. **Searches the Day After Arrests May Be Upheld Where Arrest Processes Are Not Yet Complete**
   In *United States v. Edwards,* 415 U.S. 800, 94 S.Ct. 1234, 39 L.Ed.2d 771 (1974), however, a suspect was arrested for attempting to break into a post office and was jailed after midnight. The next morning, police seized Edwards' shirt and pants, and subjected them to forensic analysis which linked Edwards to the crime. The Court upheld the search of the clothing as incident to arrest, stating that "searches and seizures that could be made on the spot at the time of arrest may legally be conducted later when the accused arrives at the place of detention." In *Edwards,* Justice White noted that "the normal processes incident to arrest and custody had not yet been completed when Edwards was placed in his cell." Justice Stewart, joined by Justices Douglas, Brennan and Marshall dissented, arguing that "the considerations that typically justify a warrantless search incident to a lawful arrest were wholly absent here."

   a. **Distinction Between *Edwards* and *Chambers***
      Arguably there is a conflict between *Edwards,* where a search was found to be incident to the arrest even though the arrestee had been incarcerated for several hours, and *Chambers,* where the Court held that the search was not incident to the arrest because the defendant was in jail at the time of the search. These cases can be reconciled on two grounds, however. First, the officers in *Edwards* seized the arrestee's clothing, which he was wearing at the time of the arrest and at the time of the seizure; in contrast, the officers in *Chambers* searched the defendant's car, from which he was obviously far removed in both time and place at the time of the search. Second, because of the late hour of Edwards' incarceration, the arrest process—including taking Edwards' clothing and giving him institutional garb—had not yet been completed. In contrast, in *Chambers,* the process of arrest had been fully completed by the time the search of the car was conducted. Thus, *Edwards* does not by any means eliminate all temporal limitations on the arrest power rule.

C. SEARCHES OF THE PERSON INCIDENT TO ARREST

The search incident to arrest exception has always supported a search of the person of the arrestee. In *United States v. Robinson,* 414 U.S. 218, 94 S.Ct. 467, 38 L.Ed.2d 427 (1973), the Supreme Court addressed questions concerning the scope of such a search.

1. *United States v. Robinson*

In *Robinson,* a police officer conducted a body search of the defendant incident to an arrest for a traffic violation. During this search, the officer felt an object on the defendant's person and although he could not identify whether it was evidence of criminal activity, he pulled it out of Robinson's pocket. The object was a crumbled cigarette package. Because its contents did not feel like cigarettes, the officer opened the package and found heroin. The officer had no probable cause or even reasonable suspicion to believe that Robinson was carrying narcotics, nor was the officer concerned with self-protection when he arrested Robinson. The Court held that a valid arrest supplies police officers with the *automatic power* to neutralize an arrestee in order to protect against danger to the officer and destruction of evidence— whether or not such risks exist on the facts. The Court further held that police officers have the automatic right to conduct a complete body frisk, and to pull out and to search all objects on an arrestee's person, even if there is no factual risk of harm to the officer or destruction of evidence. In *Robinson,* there was clearly no likelihood of destruction of evidence, as the defendant committed a traffic violation. The Court found that "[i]t is the fact of the lawful arrest which establishes the authority to search, and * * * in the case of a lawful custodial arrest a full search of the person is not only an exception to the warrant requirement of the Fourth Amendment, but is also a 'reasonable' search under the Amendment." *Robinson* establishes the automatic right to search containers found on an arrestee. Justice Powell, concurring in *Robinson,* noted that "[i]f the arrest is lawful, the privacy interest guarded by the Fourth Amendment is subordinated to a legitimate and overriding governmental concern."

a. Distinguishing a Search of a Person Incident to Arrest From a *Terry* Frisk

The Court in *Robinson* distinguished a search pursuant to the arrest power from a *Terry* frisk. A search incident to arrest allows an officer the automatic right to perform a full body search and to remove, as well as to open, all objects found during such a search. Under *Terry,* on the other hand, the frisk must be based on reasonable suspicion of bodily harm. The difference between a stop and an arrest justifies the distinction in rules. An arrest is a more serious event in which the arrestee may act more desperately than a suspect engaged in a stop. Although the actual facts in an arrest situation may not show a risk of harm or destruction of evidence, arrests in general create an increased possibility that harm to the police officer or destruction of evidence could occur. Therefore, the Court in *Robinson* found that an *automatic rule* in arrest situations was necessary. The Court stated that "[t]he justification or reason for the authority to search incident to a lawful arrest rests quite as much on the need to disarm the suspect in order to take him into custody as it does on the need to preserve evidence on his person for later use at trial. The standards traditionally governing a search incident to lawful arrest are not, therefore, commuted to the stricter *Terry* standards by the absence of probable fruits or further evidence of the particular crime for which the arrest is made."

b.   Dissent in *Robinson*

Justice Marshall, joined by Justices Douglas and Brennan, dissented in *Robinson,* arguing that "[t]he majority's attempt to avoid case-by-case adjudication of Fourth Amendment issues is not only misguided as a matter of principle, but is also doomed to fail as a matter of practical application." Justice Marshall argued that "there was no justification consistent with the Fourth Amendment which would authorize [the officer's] opening the package and looking inside."

c.   Arrests for Traffic Violations: Police Discretion

In *Gustafson v. Florida,* 414 U.S. 260, 94 S.Ct. 488, 38 L.Ed.2d 456 (1973), which was decided along with *Robinson,* a police officer arrested the defendant for driving without a valid driver's license, and then conducted a full scale body search of the defendant. Unlike *Robinson,* however, no police department regulations required the officer to take the defendant into custody. Also unlike *Robinson,* there was no departmental policy establishing the conditions under which a full scale search should be conducted. Gustafson argued that these differences created an unacceptable risk of arbitrary searches and thus distinguished his case from *Robinson.* But the Court held that these distinctions were not "determinative of the constitutional issue." Thus, there is no requirement that a custodial arrest must be mandated, only that it must be authorized.

2.   Search of Objects in the Grab Area

Under *Robinson,* the arrest power rule allows officers to pull out and search objects *on the person* of the arrestee. *Robinson* did not address whether police officers may search, as well as seize, objects in the grab area but not on the arrestee's person, e.g. a briefcase or book bag.

a.   Effect of *Chadwick*

The Supreme Court's decision in *United States v. Chadwick,* 433 U.S. 1, 97 S.Ct. 2476, 53 L.Ed.2d 538 (1977), further clouds this issue. In *Chadwick,* the police officers arrested the defendant at a railroad station, and then brought his footlocker to the Police Station and searched it there without a warrant. Holding that the search could not be justified as a search incident to arrest, the Court noted that "[u]nlike searches of the person, searches of possessions within an arrestee's immediate control cannot be justified by any reduced expectations of privacy caused by the arrest." Because the footlocker was not "immediately associated" with the arrestee, it retained a privacy interest greater than objects associated with his person. The Court also noted, however, as previously discussed, that the search was too far removed in time to be justified as an exercise of the arrest power rule at any rate. That is, the Court in *Chadwick* gave *two* reasons for why the search of the footlocker could not be justified under the arrest power rule. It is therefore unclear from *Chadwick* whether the Court would prohibit a search of an object within the suspect's grab area if the search were to occur contemporaneously with the arrest.

b.   **Searches of Objects "Immediately Associated" With the Arrestee**
Relying on *Robinson* and distinguishing *Chadwick,* almost all lower courts hold that the police may search, as well as seize, items that are immediately associated with the arrestee, such as wallets and purses. For example, in *United States v. Passaro,* 624 F.2d 938 (9th Cir.1980), the court upheld the warrantless seizure of an arrestee's wallet, the search of its contents, and the photocopying of documents contained in the wallet. The court reasoned that the wallet was an element of the defendant's clothing, which is, for a reasonable time following legal arrest, subject to the automatic right of the officer to search the arrestee's person. The court compared the case to *Robinson,* noting that "[j]ust as the police in Robinson could, incident to a lawful arrest, search the defendant's person, including the contents of a cigarette package found in the defendant's pocket, so too could the search incident to Passaro's arrest include an inspection of the contents of his wallet to discover evidence of crime." Distinguishing the case from *Chadwick,* the court in *Passaro* stated that "[u]nlike a double-locked footlocker, which is clearly separate from the person of the arrestee, the wallet found in the pocket of Mr. Passaro was an element of his clothing, his person." See also *United States v. Castro,* 596 F.2d 674 (5th Cir.1979) (holding that search of defendant's person incident to arrest could properly include an inspection of the contents of his wallet).

c.   **Searches of Objects Not "Immediately Associated" With the Person of the Arrestee**
Lower courts differ as to whether police officers can search, as well as seize, items in the grab area that are not immediately associated with the arrestee. Some lower courts have interpreted *Chadwick* 's dictum as forbidding an automatic search of items in the grab area that are not immediately associated with the arrestee. According to these courts, police officers can automatically *seize* these items, to protect against harm to the officer and against the risk of destruction of evidence, but

cannot search them. Thus, these courts would allow the seizure, but not the search, of objects such as bookbags and briefcases, while permitting both the search and seizure of items immediately associated with the arrestee, such as wallets and cigarette packs. See, e.g., *United States v. Gorski,* 852 F.2d 692 (2d Cir.1988) (holding that search of bag during arrest must be justified by exigent circumstances, otherwise seizure is all that is permitted). For example, in *United States v. Six Hundred Thirty–Nine Thousand Five Hundred and Fifty Eight Dollars in United States Currency,* 955 F.2d 712 (D.C.Cir.1992), the court addressed the issue of whether a warrantless search of the arrestee's luggage could be justified as a search incident to arrest. The arrestee was handcuffed to a chair when the officers searched his luggage. Holding that such a search violated the Fourth Amendment, the court stated that "*Chadwick* rejected the argument that because an immediate search without a warrant could have been justified as incident to arrest, that exception would justify a warrantless search of a closed container conducted later, *after the exigency had ended.*" According to these courts, the arrest power rule does not allow the search of items in the grab area. Therefore, the police cannot open these objects without probable cause and a warrant unless another exception permits this type of intrusion, such as exigent circumstances.

Most courts, however, have applied the automatic arrest power rule of *Robinson* to searches of items in the grab area, such as briefcases, etc. See, *e.g., United States v. Morales,* 923 F.2d 621 (8th Cir.1991) (distinguishing *Chadwick* as a case involving a search which occurred too long after the arrest was completed).

D. SEARCH INCIDENT TO ARREST APPLIED TO AUTOMOBILES

In *New York v. Belton,* 453 U.S. 454, 101 S.Ct. 2860, 69 L.Ed.2d 768 (1981), the Supreme Court clarified the application of the arrest power rule to automobiles. The *Belton* rule is distinguishable from the automobile exception. (See the discussion of the automobile exception to the warrant requirement *infra*). Under the automobile exception, the police can search a car without a warrant, but they must have *probable cause* to believe that there is evidence of criminal activity in the car. In contrast, the arrest power rule as applied to cars allows an *automatic intrusion* into the grab area, without probable cause or a warrant, so long as there is probable cause to make a custodial arrest. The distinction between probable cause to arrest (the relevant issue under the arrest power rule) and probable cause to search (the relevant issue under the automobile exception) is most pronounced when the defendant is arrested for a traffic offense. In such a case, there is probable cause to arrest, but no probable cause to believe that evidence will be found in the car. This was the factual situation in *Belton.*

1. *New York v. Belton*

In *Belton,* the Supreme Court determined the scope of the arrest power rule when an occupant of an automobile is subjected to a lawful arrest.

a.   Passenger Compartments of Cars Are Always in the Grab Area

The Court held that "when a policeman has made a lawful custodial arrest of the occupant of an automobile, he may, as a contemporaneous incident of that arrest, search the passenger compartment of the automobile." The Court determined held that the passenger compartment of a car is *always* within the grab area, even if the arrestee does not have access to this area at the time of the search. The Court thus rejected the case-by-case determination of an arrestee's grab area that was established in *Chimel.* The *Belton* Court reasoned that a bright-line rule was appropriate because the passenger compartment of an automobile "is generally, even if not inevitably, within the area into which an arrestee might reach in order to grab a weapon or evidentiary item." See *United States v. Karlin,* 852 F.2d 968 (7th Cir.1988) (passenger compartment is within the arrestee's grab area even if he is in the squad car and handcuffed).

b.   Does Not Apply to the Trunk

The Court in *Belton* specifically stated that the automatic grab area rule applied only to the passenger compartment of the car, and not to the trunk. Presumably, the trunk could be within the arrestee's grab area, but the state would have to show this to be the case *on the facts.* Thus, wherever the *Belton* bright-line rule does not apply, the court must resort to the *Chimel* case-by-case approach to determine whether a certain place is within the arrestee's grab area.

c.   The Police May Search All Containers Found in the Passenger Compartment

The Court in *Belton* further held that "the police may also examine the contents of any containers found within the passenger compartment, for if the passenger compartment is within reach of the arrestee, so also will containers in it be within his reach." The Court noted that a rule giving the officer an automatic right to open containers in the grab area was consistent with *Robinson.*

d.   Dissent in *Belton*

Justice Brennan, joined by Justice Marshall, dissented in *Belton,* arguing that in "its attempt to formulate a single, familiar standard * * * to guide police officers, who have only limited time and expertise to reflect on and balance the social and individual interests involved in the specific circumstances they confront, the Court today disregards these principles, and instead adopts a fiction—that the interior of a car is *always* within the immediate control of an arrestee who has recently been in the car."

2.   Aftermath of *Belton*
Although *Belton* established some bright-line rules, some questions remain unanswered.

a.   Temporal Limitations
One question concerns the amount of time that can occur between the arrest of the defendant and the search of the passenger compartment. For example, if a search of the compartment occurs one hour after the arrest of the defendant, the defendant may argue that such a search is not "incident to" the arrest. Some post-*Belton* courts have held that searches pursuant to the *Belton* rule are valid so long as the defendant remains at the scene, irrespective of the amount of time between the search and the arrest. For example, in *United States v. Fiala,* 929 F.2d 285 (7th Cir.1991), officers detained a driver at the roadside for 90 minutes, until a drug-sniffing dog was brought to the scene and alerted to drugs in the passenger compartment and in the trunk. The court found that the police acted properly because the defendant was already subject to custodial arrest for a traffic violation, and an officer has an automatic right to search the passenger compartment incident to a custodial arrest. Although the search conducted after the dog sniff occurred 90 minutes after the car was stopped for a traffic infraction, the court found that this search was still incident to the arrest. But see *United States v. Vasey,* 834 F.2d 782 (9th Cir.1987) (holding that a search conducted between thirty and forty-five minutes after the arrest of the defendant lacked the "contemporaneity" requirement of a search incident to arrest). The Supreme Court has focused both on the location and the time interval of the search to determine whether the search is still incident to arrest. See *United States v. Chadwick,* 433 U.S. 1, 97 S.Ct. 2476, 53 L.Ed.2d 538 (1977) (search cannot be justified as incident to arrest "either if the search is remote in time or place from the arrest").

b.   When Arrestee Is Not an Occupant of a Vehicle
In *United States v. Strahan,* 984 F.2d 155 (6th Cir.1993), police officers apprehended the defendant after he had left his car and walked towards a bar. The officers arrested the defendant as he neared the bar, then proceeded to the defendant's car and searched it, and found a gun. Although the court noted that *Belton* allows the search of a passenger compartment after an arrestee is removed from the car, the court found that *Belton* "clearly limits its application to only those settings where an officer makes a custodial arrest of the *occupant* of an automobile." Because the police did not make an arrest of an occupant of a vehicle, the court held that the *Chimel* test for determining the grab area, rather than *Belton*'s bright-line rules, must be applied. The court concluded that "because the passenger compartment of the vehicle was not within

Strahan's immediate control at the time of the arrest, the search was not incident to a lawful arrest."

A case that can be usefully compared with *Strahan* is *United States v. Arango,* 879 F.2d 1501 (7th Cir.1989). Arango was leaving his car, when he was approached by two officers who made inquiries about Arango's suspected drug activity. Arango pushed Officer Martin to the ground, breaking his kneecap, and ran away. Officer Berti gave chase, apprehended Arango a block from the car, arrested him for assaulting an officer, and returned with Arango to the scene of the assault on Officer Martin. Officer Berti then conducted a search of the passenger compartment, and discovered drugs. The court held that the *Belton* bright-line rules applied even though the defendant was arrested a block from the car. The court noted, however, that "nothing in the record indicates that the decision to return Arango to the scene of the assault was for the purpose of supporting a warrantless search of the vehicle." It stressed that Officer Berti had a "legitimate reason and a pressing need to return to the scene of the assault immediately." The court stated that its holding was not intended to "give arresting officers unlimited discretion to search any vehicle, by merely transporting the arrestee to the vehicle's location."

c. **What Is the "Passenger Compartment"?**
The Court in *Belton* noted that the passenger compartment includes only the interior of the car and does not encompass the trunk of the automobile. But with some vehicles it is difficult to determine whether a certain area is within the passenger compartment or the trunk. Most courts have held that anything *accessible from the interior of the car* encompasses the passenger compartment. See *United States v. Thompson,* 906 F.2d 1292 (8th Cir.1990) (holding that the back seat of a car constituted the passenger compartment and noting that the term "passenger compartment" has been interpreted broadly by most courts); *United States v. Pino,* 855 F.2d 357, 364 (6th Cir.1988) (holding that the rear section of a mid-size station wagon was part of the passenger compartment); *United States v. Russell,* 670 F.2d 323 (D.C.Cir.1982) (holding that the hatchback area of a car was part of the passenger compartment).

Example: In *United States v. Chapman,* 954 F.2d 1352 (7th Cir.1992) the court held that where the defendant was hiding in the back of a truck, a money bag found in the back of the truck and handguns found underneath the carpet at the front of the truck bed were properly obtained under *Belton*. The court noted in *Chapman* that "[a]lthough the compartment in which Mr. Chapman was hiding might not be a conventional passenger compartment, he can take no solace from the fact that the *Belton* Court noted that its holding did not extend to the trunk of an automobile. Under the circumstances of this case, it is abundantly clear that the rear of the trunk functioned as a passenger compartment at the time of the arrest."

d. Containers in the Passenger Compartment

The Court in *Belton* specifically held that the police can automatically open all containers in the passenger compartment. This raises the question of what is a container? Are the door panels considered containers because they have an empty space in which something can be stored? Lower courts have limited searches under *Belton* to areas in the passenger compartment that can be investigated *without causing serious damage to the vehicle.* See, e.g., *United States v. Diaz–Lizaraza,* 981 F.2d 1216 (11th Cir.1993) (holding search of defendant's truck as within the scope allowed by *Belton* where police officer "looked under the seats on floor of the truck, but did not rip the upholstery, look under the hood, or damage the trunk in any way."). As the *Belton* Court noted in a footnote that a container found within the passenger compartment "includes closed or open glove compartments," the courts have held that *Belton* allows the search of a locked glove compartment. See *United States v. Holifield,* 956 F.2d 665 (7th Cir.1992).

e. Searching Containers That Arrestee Has Removed From the Car

What if the police arrest an occupant in a car but he steps outside of the car carrying a container, such as a briefcase? As discussed earlier, some lower courts extend *Robinson* to allow the automatic search of all items in a suspect's grab area. These courts would therefore allow the automatic search of containers removed from the car by the arrestee. But other courts only permit the seizure, and not the search, of items within the grab area unless such items are immediately associated with the arrestee. These courts therefore must address whether *Belton* allows the search, as well as the seizure, of such containers. In *State v. Evans,* 181 N.J.Super. 455, 438 A.2d 340 (1981), a New Jersey court allowed the automatic search of a briefcase carried out of the car by the arrestee, relying on *Belton* to hold that it was a valid search incident to arrest. The court noted that "[h]ad the briefcase been left in the car, it would have been proper for the police to remove it and search it under the holding of *New York v. Belton* * * *. If [such a search is] permissible we find no arrogance or overreaching on the part of the police officers in the circumstances of this case." But see *United States v. Vaughan,* 718 F.2d 332 (9th Cir.1983) (holding that search of briefcase carried out of car by passenger was not authorized by *Belton* as "Vaughan did not leave the briefcase in the car, nor was he in the car when his companions were arrested" and noting that "[i]f he had left the briefcase in the car, admittedly it could have been searched.").

f.   Are the Belton Bright–Line Rules Applicable Outside of the Automobile Context?

The Court in *Belton* took pains to note that its bright-line rules were applicable only to the "particular and problematic" context of the search of an automobile incident to arrest, and that its decision "in no way alters the fundamental principles established in the *Chimel* case regarding the basic scope of searches incident to lawful custodial arrests." Nonetheless, some courts have applied *Belton*'s bright line rules in other areas. For example, in *United States v. Palumbo,* 735 F.2d 1095 (8th Cir.1984), the court held that a search of a drawer in a motel room was within the arrestee's control area, even though the arrestee was handcuffed. Relying on *Belton,* the court found that the arrest power rule "is not constrained because the arrestee is unlikely at the time of the arrest to actually reach into an area." See also *United States v. Johnson,* 846 F.2d 279 (5th Cir.1988) (relying on *Belton* to hold that containers within the grab area could be immediately searched, even though the arrest did not occur in or near a car).

VIII.   PRETEXTUAL SEARCHES AND SEIZURES

The arrest-power rule, as we have seen, allows an officer considerable search powers upon the making of a custodial arrest. The *Terry* doctrine allows the officer more limited, but still significant, investigatory power upon the making of a stop. The Supreme Court has never held that the arrest-power rule or the *Terry* doctrine can only be invoked with respect to serious crimes. In fact, a leading case on the arrest-power rule, *United States v. Robinson, supra,* involved the search of a person incident to arrest for a traffic violation. Therefore, the current state of the law is that these search powers can be used to investigate even minor crimes.

A.   THE PRETEXT PROBLEM

Every court agrees that an officer should not and cannot be sanctioned for bad thoughts. So if an officer encounters a situation and responds to it as a reasonable officer would, the fact that the officer secretly welcomes the situation does not invalidate the officer's conduct. For example, if an officer sees a car travelling 95 miles per hour in a 55 mile per hour zone, and a reasonable police officer would stop that car and arrest the driver, it does not matter that the officer is secretly happy because of the opportunity to search the person and passenger compartment of the car for drugs in the course of the arrest.

It may be possible, however, for an officer to invoke the arrest-power rule or *Terry* as to a minor crime, in order to stop or arrest the suspect in circumstances in which a reasonable officer would not have made the stop or arrest for a minor offense. For example, if the same driver is driving at 60 miles an hour instead of

55, he is breaking the laws against speeding, and is technically subject to a stop or arrest; but in reality most officers would not stop or arrest the driver for this conduct. But what if the officer wishes to use such a stop or arrest to search for drugs, in the absence of probable cause or reasonable suspicion as to a drug offense? For example, assume that an officer has merely an inarticulable hunch that a driver is a drug courier, and decides to follow the driver for miles in the hope that the driver will commit a traffic violation. When the driver exceeds the speed limit by even a few miles per hour, the officer places the driver under arrest and conducts an automatic search of the passenger compartment of the car under *Belton*. If the officer has a legal right to stop or arrest the driver, as he has in this example, does it make a difference that no reasonable officer would exercise that right if the speeding violation were the only issue?

This is the pretext problem. Remember that it is assumed that the officer has probable cause to effectuate the arrest (or reasonable suspicion to effectuate the stop) on the minor offense. How can the officer's conduct be illegal if the officer had the right to stop or arrest the defendant, and invoked that right?

1. Supreme Court View

The Supreme Court has never decided whether the Fourth Amendment prevents an officer from using *Terry* or the arrest-power for a minor crime as a pretext to investigate a more serious crime. The Court has from time to time threatened to invalidate searches if they were justified on one ground but were simply a pretext to search on another. For example, in *Skinner v. Railway Executives'*, discussed in the section on administrative searches, the Court upheld suspicionless drug-testing of railroad employees on the ground that the testing scheme effectuated special needs beyond ordinary criminal law enforcement. The Court stated that it would "leave for another day the question whether routine use in criminal prosecutions of evidence obtained pursuant to the administrative scheme would give rise to an inference of pretext." The Court thus suggested that if "administrative" drug-testing was being used as a pretext for criminal law enforcement, it would be invalidated. But this is a suggestion only, and as stated above, the Supreme Court has never actually invalidated an objectively reasonable search on the ground that it was pretextual. See also *United States v. Robinson, supra* (leaving for "another day" whether it would be permissible to use the traffic violation arrest as a pretext for a narcotics search, but stating that "it is sufficient for purposes of our decision that respondent was lawfully arrested for an offense, and that placing him in custody following that arrest was not a departure from established police department practice"). See *Enrique–Nevarez v. United States,* ___ U.S. ___, 112 S.Ct. 428, 116 L.Ed.2d 448 (1991) (White, J., dissenting from denial of certiorari in consolidated Fifth and Seventh Circuit cases presenting pretext issues, arguing that certiorari should be granted "to address this recurring issue and to resolve the split in the Courts of Appeals").

B. MAJORITY VIEW—PRETEXTUAL MOTIVE DOES NOT INVALIDATE A SEARCH OR SEIZURE

Most courts have held that if an officer has an objective right to make a stop or arrest for a minor infraction, the stop is legal and it makes no difference that the officer subjectively used the stop or arrest as a pretext to obtain evidence of a more serious crime. Nor, to these courts, does it matter that a reasonable officer would not, under the circumstances presented, have stopped or arrested the defendant for the minor crime. The only question is whether the officer had the *legal right* to do what he did.

1. Rationale

The rationale for this view is expressed by the majority opinion in the leading case of *United States v. Causey,* 834 F.2d 1179 (5th Cir.1987). The court stated that "it is hard to see what police conduct is sought to be deterred" by a rule invalidating an otherwise legal stop or arrest on the ground that it was pretextual. The court found it inappropriate to "inject a new constitutional issue of subjective police intent into every case in which a suspect is arrested for one offense" and subsequently charged with a more serious offense on the basis of evidence uncovered in the investigation. Essentially, the majority of courts find that if the officer had the legal right to make a stop or arrest on a minor offense, and a legal right to conduct a subsequent investigation of the minor offense, then the citizen has not been prejudiced when evidence is obtained as to a more serious offense—nothing objectively "wrong" has happened to him.

2. Response

Critics of the majority rule argue that in a world in which police do not stop or arrest every individual as to whom they have reasonable suspicion or probable cause, an individual who is stopped or arrested has a legitimate complaint if reasonable officers would not have done the same to others under similar circumstances.

Example: An example of the majority approach is found in *United States v. Kordosky,* 878 F.2d 991 (7th Cir.1989), where an officer suspected Kordosky of drug activity, but had neither reasonable suspicion nor probable cause to justify a search for drugs. So the officer conducted surveillance of Kordosky for over a month in an attempt to uncover evidence that Kordosky was a drug dealer. No suspicious facts were found. Frustrated in his attempts to pin a drug charge on Kordosky, the officer stopped and arrested him on an outstanding traffic ticket. The arrest occurred while Kordosky was driving, and the officer conducted an automatic search of the passenger compartment pursuant to *New York v. Belton, supra.* Drugs were found, and then Kordosky was charged with and convicted for drug violations. The court held that the evidence was legally obtained, since the officer had "a legitimate reason—the traffic violation" for stopping and arresting Kordosky, "and that is the end of our inquiry." See also *United States v. Gallo,* 927 F.2d 815 (5th Cir.1991) (stop and arrest for minor traffic offense was not pretextual even if officers had the motive to search for drugs; traffic violations provided a legitimate reason for defendant's stop and arrest); *United States v. Colin,* 928 F.2d 676 (5th Cir.1991) (stop for a seatbelt offense was valid, even if officers had a motivation to search for evidence).

C. MINORITY VIEW—SEARCH AND SEIZURE IS ILLEGAL IF IT WOULD NOT HAVE BEEN MADE BY A REASONABLE OFFICER IN THE ABSENCE OF PRETEXT

A minority of courts hold that evidence of a serious crime is illegally obtained if the officer purports to act on the basis of a minor offense, and a reasonable officer would not have intervened absent the motivation to obtain evidence on the more serious crime.

1. Rationale

Courts which invalidate searches and seizures as pretextual argue that allowing such intrusions would give rise to arbitrariness and abuse. As Judge Rubin stated in his dissent in *Causey,* "few persons have a life so blameless that some reason to arrest them cannot be found, whether it be for entering an intersection when the light is on caution, or for violating a zoning regulation, or for having an expired brake tag." Thus, the concern is that almost all citizens could be subject to a stop or arrest, and then be investigated for a serious crime as to which neither reasonable suspicion nor probable cause exists. As Judge Rubin stated, "police who desire to arrest [or search] an individual without probable cause may merely leaf through the files or turn to the computer to determine whether they can find some reasons to arrest a suspect for whose arrest they otherwise lack probable cause."

The courts taking the minority view reject the argument that it is contrary to Fourth Amendment standards of objective reasonableness. They note that a pretextual search is not invalidated because the officer had a subjective, bad faith motivation. Rather, it is invalidated because a "reasonable officer" would not have made the stop or arrest absent the motivation to search for evidence of a more serious crime. So for example, if an officer arrests a driver for going 95 miles per hour on the freeway, the subsequent search incident to the arrest will be legal under the minority view, even if the officer harbored a subjective bad faith intention to search for drugs in the absence of probable cause. This is because a reasonable officer would have stopped and arrested a driver going 40 miles over the speed limit even in the absence of a motivation to search for drugs. Consequently, the minority view does not expressly invalidate a search because the officer has bad thoughts.

2. Criticism

Critics of the minority view argue that it is a misplaced attack on Supreme Court cases such as *Robinson, Belton* and *Terry,* which permit extensive investigatory powers to be employed even for minor offenses. Critics conclude that so long as those cases remain on the books, there is nothing wrong with a police officer relying on them. Critics also contend that the reference in the minority view to what a reasonable officer would have done in the absence of improper motivation "is far more pernicious than even a required inquiry into the officer's motives would be, for the standard *presumes* unconstitutional intent from a failure to satisfy its objective element." See *United States v. Rusher,* 966 F.2d 868 (4th Cir.1992) (Luttig, J., concurring). Thus, even if an officer could prove that his motives were not pretextual (e.g. that he would have stopped a person for making an illegal u-turn because he thinks it is important for the u-turn rule to be strictly enforced), his stop or arrest would still be held illegal under the minority view if the other officers on his force might not have effectuated a stop or arrest in those circumstances. Supporters of the minority rule would respond that an officer's conduct should generally be measured by how a reasonable officer would act.

> *Example:* An example of the minority approach to the pretext question is *United States v. Miller,* 821 F.2d 546 (11th Cir.1987). Miller was driving a car on a freeway. A state trooper suspected that Miller was a drug courier, but did not have reasonable suspicion to stop Miller for that offense. The trooper followed Miller and eventually stopped him when Miller drove his wheels across the lane for six seconds. In the course of the stop, the officer found narcotics. The court held that the narcotics were illegally obtained, because a reasonable officer would not have stopped Miller for going over the lane marker for six seconds, absent motivation to search for drugs. See also *United States v. Morales–Zamora,* 974 F.2d 149 (10th Cir.1992) (roadblock check, ostensibly to check driver's license and vehicle registration, was pretextual where officers had drug-sniffing dogs walk around the vehicles stopped at the roadblock).

D. STOP OR ARREST FOR MINOR OFFENSE MUST ITSELF BE LEGAL

While most courts allow officers to stop or arrest a person for a minor infraction and then use the detention to obtain evidence of a more serious crime, this option is open to officers only if they have reasonable suspicion to stop or probable cause to arrest the suspect for the minor crime. Otherwise, the stop or arrest is itself illegal, regardless of pretext. For example, in *United States v. Sanders,* 954 F.2d 227 (4th Cir.1992), officers suspected Sanders of bank robbery, but had insufficient articulable suspicion to justify a search or seizure as to that crime. They found Sanders' car in a parking lot. Then they saw Sanders get into his car, start it and back it up to the other side of the parking lot. They arrested him for

PROBABLE CAUSE AND A WARRANT

having an expired license tag, and an uninsured vehicle. A subsequent search uncovered evidence of a bank robbery. The court held that the arrest was illegal and the evidence inadmissible, because the traffic offenses for which Sanders was arrested required the operation of a vehicle upon the state's highways, and the officers "lacked any evidence that Sanders' car was driven on a public road." The arrest on the minor offenses was illegal and therefore the court did not have to inquire into whether it was a pretextual use of a legal arrest on a minor offense to obtain information as to a more serious offense.

1. Search Must Be Within Confines of Minor Offense

It follows from the above that if the officer ostensibly investigating a minor offense goes beyond the *scope* of a permissible search for that offense, the search will be illegal without regard to the question of pretext. For example, assume that an officer suspects that a driver is a drug courier, but that his suspicion does not rise to the level of probable cause. The officer follows the driver, who changes lanes without signalling, and the officer arrests him for a traffic violation. If the officer searches the passenger compartment and finds drugs, this evidence is legally obtained under the majority view even if the officer used the traffic arrest as a pretext to search for drugs. However, if the officer searches the *trunk* and finds drugs, this evidence is *illegally* obtained even under the majority view. This is because the officer, by searching the trunk, exceeded the scope of the search permitted for the traffic violation; *New York v. Belton* allows a search of the passenger compartment incident to a traffic arrest, but does not allow a search of the trunk. The majority view on pretext thus assumes that the officer is acting in accordance with the Fourth Amendment when conducting a search and seizure with respect to a minor offense.

E. MISTAKEN, SUBJECTIVE BELIEF OF LACK OF AUTHORITY TO SEARCH FOR EVIDENCE OF A SERIOUS CRIME

The question addressed thus far is whether officers can use reasonable suspicion or probable cause of a minor infraction as a pretext to obtain evidence of a serious crime for which the officer has no reasonable suspicion or probable cause. But what if the officer *has* sufficient proof to justify a search for evidence of the serious crime, but just doesn't *believe* that he has sufficient proof? In other words, what if the officer acts pretextually when he doesn't need to? In such a case, a search for evidence of the serious crime will not be invalidated even in the minority of courts which find pretextual searches illegal.

Under the minority view, an officer is not sanctioned for bad faith, subjective beliefs. Rather, the evidence is considered illegally obtained because the officer acts unreasonably in relationship to how other officers would have treated the minor offense absent an impermissible motive. So if an officer actually has probable cause to believe that the defendant has committed a murder, but doesn't think he has it, the officer's search for evidence of murder is objectively reasonable and does not violate the Fourth Amendment. See *United States v.*

Guzman, 864 F.2d 1512 (10th Cir.1988) ("a pretextual stop occurs when the police use a legal justification to make a stop in order to search a person or his vehicle, or interrogate him, for an unrelated and more serious crime *for which they do not have the reasonable suspicion necessary to support a stop* ").

IX. SEARCHES AND SEIZURES OF AUTOMOBILES AND OTHER MOVABLE PROPERTY

A. THE AUTOMOBILE EXCEPTION TO THE WARRANT REQUIREMENT

The automobile exception allows the police to search an automobile without obtaining a warrant if they have probable cause to believe that the car contains evidence of criminal activity. *Carroll v. United States,* 267 U.S. 132, 45 S.Ct. 280, 69 L.Ed. 543 (1925). This exception does not depend upon probable cause to arrest the driver or any particular individual. It applies to all vehicles and is an independent source of authority to search.

1. The *Carroll* Doctrine

In *Carroll,* the Supreme Court created the automobile exception, upholding a search of a car where the police had probable cause to search the car but had no time to obtain a warrant. The Court emphasized that, in the time it would have taken to obtain a warrant, the car could easily have been moved out of the area. In the majority opinion, Chief Justice Taft concluded that "the guaranty of freedom from unreasonable searches and seizures by the Fourth Amendment has been construed, practically since the beginning of the Government, as recognizing a necessary difference between a search of a store, dwelling house or other structure in respect of which a proper official warrant readily may be obtained, and a search of a ship, motor boat, wagon or automobile, for contraband goods, where it is not practicable to secure a warrant because the vehicle can be quickly moved out of the locality or jurisdiction in which the warrant may be sought."

2. Distinguishing *Carroll* From Search Incident to Arrest

The automobile exception is distinct from the search incident to arrest exception as applied to automobiles. *See New York v. Belton,* discussed *supra.* Under the automobile exception, courts must look at whether the police had probable cause to believe that the car contained evidence of criminal activity. See Moylan, *The Automobile Exception: What It Is and What It Is Not—A Rationale in Search of a Clearer Label,* 27 Mercer L.Rev. 987 (1976). In contrast, the search incident to arrest exception, also referred to as the arrest-power rule, does not depend on the existence of probable cause to search but focuses on the legality of the underlying arrest and the area in which the search occurred.

a. **When the Automobile Exception Is Used**

The arrest power-rule is preferred by the state over the automobile exception, because the state must only establish that there was probable cause to arrest the defendant—at that point the right to search the passenger compartment of the car is automatic. In contrast, the automobile exception will not apply unless there is probable cause that evidence will be found in a particular place in the car. Especially with respect to minor offenses such as traffic arrests, the arrest-power rule is easier for the state to invoke than is the automobile exception.

However, there are at least three situations in which the arrest-power rule will not apply and then the state must resort to the automobile exception: 1) Where the arrest is *not made in or near a car*; 2) Where the search of the car is *too far removed* from the arrest so that it can no longer be deemed incident to the arrest; and 3) Where the officers wish to search the *trunk* of the car.

3. **Warrantless Searches and Seizures of Automobiles**

After *Carroll*, most cases applying the automobile exception focused on the existence of probable cause rather than the existence of exigent circumstances. Some courts, however, held that the *Carroll* doctrine did not apply to searches of cars after the driver's arrest. These courts rejected the application of the car exception in these circumstances because no exigency would exist where the driver and the car were in police custody. According to these courts, the police could seize the car without a warrant but could not search it until they obtained a warrant.

a. *Chambers v. Maroney*

The Supreme Court in *Chambers v. Maroney,* 399 U.S. 42, 90 S.Ct. 1975, 26 L.Ed.2d 419 (1970) rejected this limitation on the automobile exception, holding that no difference exists between the search and seizure of a car. Thus, where the police have probable cause to search a car, a warrant is not required. In *Chambers,* the Court upheld the warrantless search at the police station of a car that was seized upon the arrest of the occupants. The Court found that as far as the Fourth Amendment was concerned, there was "no difference between on the one hand seizing and holding a car before presenting the probable cause issue to a magistrate and on the other hand carrying out an immediate search without a warrant." Justice Harlan, concurring in part and dissenting in part, disagreed with the majority's approval of the removal of the car to the station and the subsequent warrantless search of the vehicle "at the convenience of the police."

b. **Justification for the Automobile Exception**

The Court in *Chambers* shed new light on the justification for the automobile exception. As the Court in *Carroll* pointed out, the mobility of a car renders it impracticable to obtain a warrant before any Fourth Amendment intrusion can be made. However, the car's mobility is not enough to justify an immediate warrantless search, because it could be argued that the police should instead be required to *seize* the car pending the issuance of a warrant. The Court in *Chambers,* proceeding from the unassailable assumption that the mobility of the car justifies a warrantless *seizure,* reasoned as follows: If a warrantless seizure is justified, then a warrantless search is equally justifiable so long as it is no more intrusive than a warrantless seizure would be. The Court concluded that in many cases, the delay involved in seizing a car pending a warrant would be even more intrusive than an immediate search—as to which, if no evidence were uncovered, the citizens could immediately proceed on their way. Therefore, the Court found no reason for police to have to choose between a warrantless seizure and a warrantless search of the car. Since they were basically equal intrusions, the fact that one was justified by the car's mobility meant that either could be done.

c.   Dissent

Justice Harlan in dissent stated that "a warrantless search involves the greater sacrifice of Fourth Amendment values * * * [because] in the circumstances in which this problem is likely to occur, the lesser intrusion will almost always be the simple seizure of the car for the period—perhaps a day—necessary to enable the officers to obtain a search warrant." Thus, in his view, a warrantless search would ordinarily be more intrusive than a seizure, and therefore could not be justified by the fact that a warrantless seizure of the car is permissible. He argued that in most cases where probable cause existed to search the car, the driver would be arrested, and would therefore suffer "minimal further inconvenience from the temporary immobilization" of the car pending a warrant. Justice Harlan also found it ironic that "the Court, unable to decide whether search or temporary seizure is the lesser intrusion, in this case authorizes both."

d.   Difference Between Searches and Seizures

Searches and seizures invade different interests. Searches invade privacy interests while seizures invade possessory interests. Thus, in most cases, one would think that a search of a car would be a greater intrusion than the temporary detention of the car pending a warrant—especially since, as Justice Harlan noted, the owner of the car is often incarcerated and cannot use the car at any rate. However, after *Chambers,* the Court explained its equation of automobile searches and seizures by asserting that the search of a car was not in fact a very serious intrusion, due to the fact that a citizen has a *diminished expectation of privacy in a car.* As a result, the search and seizure are equally intrusive, since neither is considered very serious. See *United States v. Chadwick,* 433 U.S. 1, 97 S.Ct. 2476, 53 L.Ed.2d 538 (1977).

e. Reasons for Diminished Expectation of Privacy in Cars

According to the Court, individuals have a lesser privacy interest in cars than in other personal belongings, such as containers, for three reasons. First, a car is a means of *transportation,* in contrast to containers which are used to keep things private. Second, an individual *drives a car in plain view* and other people can see inside of the car. Third, a car is *heavily regulated.* Thus, because the search of a car causes a lesser intrusion than, for example, a search of a house or a suitcase, this minimal intrusion is equivalent to that caused by a seizure of the car pending a warrant. The automobile exception therefore allows both the warrantless search and the warrantless seizure of a car, if there is probable cause to believe that there is evidence in the car.

4. The Role of Exigency in the Automobile Exception

Although the Supreme Court in *Coolidge v. New Hampshire,* 403 U.S. 443, 91 S.Ct. 2022, 29 L.Ed.2d 564 (1971), focused on the presence or absence of exigent circumstances in determining the applicability of the automobile exception, later Court decisions have limited *Coolidge* to its facts. In *Coolidge,* the police arrested the defendant in his home and searched his car at the police station, two days after it was seized from the defendant's driveway. The seizure of the car occurred after an extensive investigation, and after the police had obtained a warrant to search the car. The warrant was declared invalid, however, and so the state sought to resort to the automobile exception to justify what amounted to a warrantless search of the car. In a plurality opinion, the Court held that the automobile exception did not apply because of the absence of exigency. The Court stated that "[t]he word 'automobile' is not a talisman in whose presence the Fourth Amendment fades away and disappears."

a. No Exigency in *Coolidge*

Under the facts present in *Coolidge,* there was "nothing * * * to invoke the meaning and purpose of the rule of *Carroll v. United States*—no alerted criminal bent on flight, no fleeting opportunity on an open highway after a hazardous chase, no contraband or stolen goods or weapons, no confederates waiting to move the evidence, not even the inconvenience of a special police detail to guard the immobilized automobile." Thus, the Court stated that "by no possible stretch of the legal imagination can this be made into a case where 'it is not practicable to secure a warrant.'"

b. Post–*Coolidge* Cases Interpreting the Necessity of Exigency

Lower courts, interpreting *Coolidge,* have held that a warrant is required to search a car only if the police had a *reasonable opportunity to obtain a warrant before seizing the car.* Thus if the police could have obtained a warrant before the original seizure of the car, the automobile exception does not apply. Clearly, there was such a reasonable opportunity in

Coolidge, since the officers in fact obtained a warrant (though it was later determined to be invalid) before seizing Coolidge's car. On the other hand, if the officers come upon a car and had no prior opportunity to obtain a warrant, then they can conduct an immediate seizure of the car, and, under *Chambers,* an immediate or delayed warrantless search as well. The car need not be mobile, nor need there be exigent circumstances, at the time of the seizure, so long as the officers had no reasonable opportunity to obtain a warrant before approaching the car. See *Michigan v. Thomas,* 458 U.S. 259, 102 S.Ct. 3079, 73 L.Ed.2d 750 (1982) ("the justification to conduct such a warrantless search does not vanish once the car has been immobilized"). *Chambers* is based on the rationale that due to its mobility, a car can be seized pending the obtaining of a warrant; and a search without a warrant is permitted because the search of a car is no more intrusive than would be the seizure of the car pending a warrant. But if the original seizure itself could have been preceded by a warrant, then the premise of *Chambers* is missing and the automobile exception ought not to apply.

Example: In *United States v. Lasanta,* 978 F.2d 1300 (2d Cir.1992), the court held that a warrantless seizure and search of a car could not be justified under the automobile exception. Because the car was parked in the defendant's driveway, the police did not have a realistic fear that the car might be removed and the evidence within destroyed if they took the time to obtain a warrant. In addition, the Court found that it was not impracticable for the police to obtain a warrant to seize the defendant's car. The court noted that previous surveillance revealed the presence of the vehicle to the police and thus they could have obtained a warrant prior to the seizure. Compare *United States v. Moscatiello,* 771 F.2d 589 (1st Cir.1985) (*Coolidge* distinguished where officers seized a car after pursuing it in a rapidly developing situation).

5.   Dual Justification for the Automobile Exception

The Supreme Court clarified the basis for the automobile exception in *California v. Carney,* 471 U.S. 386, 105 S.Ct. 2066, 85 L.Ed.2d 406 (1985). The Court in *Carney* stated that there are *two justifications* for the automobile exception. Although the mobility of the automobile, as expressed in *Carroll,* remains a basis for the exception, the Court found that the automobile exception is also justified by the diminished expectation of privacy in automobiles. The Court noted that "[e]ven in cases where an automobile was not immediately mobile, the lesser expectation of privacy resulting from its use as a readily mobile vehicle justified application of the vehicular exception." See *United States v. Chadwick,* 433 U.S. 1, 97 S.Ct. 2476, 53 L.Ed.2d 538 (1977) (noting that the Court has upheld warrantless searches of cars "in cases in which the possibilities of the vehicle's being removed or evidence in it destroyed were remote, if not non-existent.").

6. Application of the Automobile Exception to Mobile Homes

In *Carney,* the Court held that the automobile exception justified a warrantless search of a mobile home. Rejecting the argument that mobile homes are necessarily different from other vehicles, the Court reasoned that such a distinction "would require that [the Court] apply the exception depending on the size of the vehicle and the quality of its appointments." The Court did not address whether the automobile exception would apply to a mobile home "that is situated in a way or place that objectively indicates that it is being used as a residence." In *Carney,* this was clearly not the case, since the mobile home was parked in a parking lot and was not hooked up to utilities or plumbing. It was thus more like a car than a house. In dissent, Justice Stevens, joined by Justice Brennan and Marshall, argued that the decision "accorded priority to an exception rather than to the general rule" by failing to apply the warrant requirement in close cases.

7. The Automobile Exception as Applied to Airplanes

In *United States v. Nigro,* 727 F.2d 100 (6th Cir.1984), the court extended the automobile exception to airplanes. Although the plane was immobilized when the search occurred, the court held that "[t]he automobile exception has always depended on the inherent mobility of the vehicle to be searched, not on whether it could in fact be used immediately to effect a removal of evidence once existing officers have determined that they have probable cause to search it and have taken steps to prevent its departure."

B. MOVABLE PROPERTY—IN AND OUT OF CARS

Because the automobile exception is based on the diminished expectation of privacy in vehicles as well as their mobility, the exception does not permit warrantless searches of other containers, even if these containers are mobile. The Supreme Court distinguished between cars and other containers in *United States v. Chadwick,* 433 U.S. 1, 97 S.Ct. 2476, 53 L.Ed.2d 538 (1977).

1. *Chadwick*

In *Chadwick,* the police, having probable cause but no warrant, seized a footlocker, brought it to the police station, and then searched it and discovered drugs. Although the footlocker was found in the trunk of a defendant's car, the Government did not argue that the footlocker's brief contact with the car made it part of an automobile search. Rather, the Government argued that since the container was mobile, it should be treated the same as a car. The Supreme Court held that the mobility of the footlocker permitted a *seizure* pending a warrant, but that the police needed a warrant to *search* the footlocker unless exigent circumstances were present (such as if the footlocker contained an explosive).

Distinguishing between cars and other containers, the Court stated that "[t]he factors which diminish the privacy aspects of an automobile do not apply to respondents' footlocker." According to the Court, luggage and other similar containers are not open to public view, in contrast to a car. In addition, luggage functions to keep things private, while cars are a means of transportation. Thus, expectations of privacy are substantially greater in luggage than in an automobile. Because of the diminished expectation of privacy in a car, the Court in *Chambers* considered a warrantless search to be no more intrusive than a seizure pending a warrant. But the same could not be said of a container. The Court in *Chadwick* could not equate a search of a container with its seizure, because the search would invade a significant expectation of privacy in the contents of the container. The Court therefore held that the police must obtain a warrant before searching containers, in the absence of exigent circumstances requiring an immediate search. Under *Chadwick,* the police may seize containers if they have probable cause to believe the container holds evidence of criminal activity but they must generally obtain a warrant before searching them.

2. **Rejection of the Worthy Container Doctrine**
In *Carney,* discussed *supra,* the Court declined "to distinguish between 'worthy' or 'unworthy' vehicles." Some courts had previously held that some containers deserved more protection than other containers. For example, these courts had posited that an old paper bag deserves less protection than other more "worthy" containers. Such a distinction, however, may discriminate against indigents. In *United States v. Ross,* discussed *infra,* the Government argued that a paper bag was not a worthy container and thus not subject to the warrant requirement. The Court rejected this argument, stating that "the central purpose of the Fourth Amendment forecloses such a distinction. For just as the most frail cottage in the kingdom is absolutely entitled to the same guarantees of privacy as the most majestic mansion, so also may a traveler who carries a toothbrush and a few articles of clothing in a paper bag or knotted scarf claim an equal right to conceal his possessions from official inspection as the sophisticated executive with the locked attache case." *United States v. Ross,* 456 U.S. 798, 102 S.Ct. 2157, 72 L.Ed.2d 572 (1982).

3. **Containers in Cars**
Because a warrant is required to search a container but not a car, it was unclear after *Chadwick* whether the container rule or the car rule applied to containers found in cars.

a. **Clash Between Container Rule and Car Rule in *Sanders* and *Ross***
In *Arkansas v. Sanders,* 442 U.S. 753, 99 S.Ct. 2586, 61 L.Ed.2d 235 (1979), the police observed Sanders exit an airport carrying a green suitcase after they received an informant's tip that he would do so and that the suitcase would contain marijuana. Sanders' companion placed

the suitcase in a trunk of the taxi. In *Sanders,* the Court held that the police needed a warrant to search the suitcase found in the trunk of the taxi. In *United States v. Ross,* 456 U.S. 798, 102 S.Ct. 2157, 72 L.Ed.2d 572 (1982), however, the Court held that the warrantless search of a bag found during the search of a car did not violate the Fourth Amendment.

b. **The *Ross* Rule**

The Court in *Ross* stated that if probable cause is focused particularly on a container within the car but no probable cause exists to search the car generally, the container rule applies and the police must obtain a warrant before searching the container. This was the case in *Sanders,* where the officers had probable cause to search the suitcase but not the taxi. But the Court in *Ross* further stated that if the police have probable to search the car and, in the course of the search, discover a container, the police may search the container. This type of probable cause was called "car-wide" probable cause. Because the officers in *Ross* had probable cause to search the car, the Court found that "the practical consequences of the *Carroll* decision would be largely nullified if the permissible scope of a warrantless search of an automobile did not include containers and packages found inside the vehicle * * * [as] [c]ontraband goods rarely are strewn across the trunk or floor of a car." The Court in *Ross* distinguished *Sanders* as a case in which there was no car-wide probable cause, and refused to overrule *Sanders.*

c. **Dissent in *Ross***

Dissenting in *Ross,* Justice Marshall, joined by Justice Brennan, stated that anomalous results could occur due to the *Ross* and *Sanders* decisions. Justice Marshall stated that "this rule plainly has peculiar and unworkable consequences: the Government must show that the investigating officer knew enough but not too much, that he had sufficient knowledge to establish probable cause but insufficient knowledge to know exactly where the contraband was located." Thus, under *Ross,* if the officer received a reliable tip that the suspect was dealing drugs out of his car, the officer could search the car without a warrant and he could open all the containers in the car which could contain drugs. However, if the officer received a reliable tip that the defendant had a suitcase full of drugs in his car, then the officer would need a warrant to open the suitcase, because the probable cause would be specific to the suitcase rather than car-wide.

d. ***California v. Acevedo:* Resolving the Anomalies**

The Supreme Court in *California v. Acevedo,* __ U.S. __, 111 S.Ct. 1982, 114 L.Ed.2d 619 (1991), found that the *Ross* distinction of *Sanders* (i.e., the distinction between car-wide and particularized probable cause) was unsupportable in logic and practice. Thus, the Court overruled *Sanders* and held that the police may search any container located in a car, without a warrant, so long as they have probable cause to believe that it holds evidence of criminal activity. Agreeing with the dissenters in *Ross* that the *Sanders–Ross* distinction created anomalous results, the majority in *Acevedo* held that "the Fourth Amendment does not compel separate treatment for an automobile search that extends only to a container within the vehicle." Thus, the Court concluded that "it is better to adopt one clear-cut rule to govern automobile searches and eliminate the warrant requirement for closed containers set forth in *Sanders.*"

e.   Dissent in *Acevedo*

Justice Stevens, joined by Justice Marshall, dissented, stating that "[t]o the extent there was any anomaly in our prior jurisprudence, the Court has cured it at the expense of creating a more serious paradox. For, surely it is anomalous to prohibit a search of a briefcase while the owner is carrying it exposed on a public street yet to permit a search once the owner has placed the briefcase in the locked trunk of his car." Thus, after *Acevedo,* an officer needs a warrant to open a container—until the container is placed in a car.

C.   SEARCHES AND SEIZURES OF AUTOMOBILES PURSUANT TO THE COMMUNITY CARETAKING FUNCTION

The community caretaking function of police officers focuses on the policeman's role as "jack-of-all-emergencies." The doctrine encompasses the wide range of responsibilities that police officers must discharge aside from law enforcement duties. See *Cady v. Dombrowski,* 413 U.S. 433, 441, 93 S.Ct. 2523, 2528, 37 L.Ed.2d 706 (1973). Thus, if such caretaking activities are justified "either in terms of state law or sound police procedure," they do not violate the Fourth Amendment.

1.   Justifying Searches

In performing searches pursuant to their community caretaking function, the police do not have to possess a warrant. The search, however, must be performed pursuant to a community caretaking duty. In *Cady v. Dombrowski,* 413 U.S. 433, 93 S.Ct. 2523, 37 L.Ed.2d 706 (1973), the police searched a car of a police officer that was towed to a garage after the officer was involved in a car accident. The police claimed that they conducted the search because they believed the car contained the officer's gun. The Supreme Court held that the search was reasonable as a community caretaking function "to protect the public from the possibility that a revolver would fall into untrained or perhaps malicious hands."

a.   Must Be a Public Safety Interest

To justify a search under the community caretaking function, the Government must show that the police conducted the search for safety purposes. For example, in *United States v. Lugo,* 978 F.2d 631 (10th

Cir.1992), a police officer, during a search of a car, bent back the corner of a vent in a door panel and reached inside the cavity between the door panel and door to retrieve a paper sack. Because the defendant had told the officer where a weapon in the car was located and the officer had already found that weapon and did not suspect the presence of any other, the court held that the search was not within the community caretaking function and was thus illegal. The officer did not testify that he conducted the search pursuant to public safety interests.

2. Justifying Seizures of Vehicles

The community caretaking function also justifies the initial seizure of vehicles in a variety of circumstances. Thus, the police do not need probable cause or a warrant to impound a car if done for caretaking purposes.

Example: In *United States v. Rodriguez–Morales,* 929 F.2d 780 (1st Cir.1991), the defendants claimed that they were arrested without probable cause which thus tainted the evidence that was found in the car after it was impounded. The police stopped the defendants' car on the highway for reckless driving. Due to the failure of the driver to produce accurate identification, the police transported the defendants to the police barracks for further questioning. The police then impounded the vehicle and allowed a narcotics trained dog to perform a canine sniff around the perimeter of the car. The court found that the seizure of the car was reasonable under the "community caretaking function." The court noted that "it is important to recognize that the community caretaking function is 'totally divorced from the detection, investigation, or acquisition of evidence relating to the violation of a criminal statute.'" Thus, as long as the police act reasonably in carrying out their community caretaking duties, the police may impound a vehicle even though they do not have probable cause to search the car or probable cause to arrest the driver.

D. IMPOUNDMENT OF VEHICLES AND THE INVENTORY EXCEPTION TO THE WARRANT REQUIREMENT

If automobiles are lawfully held in police custody, the police may inventory the contents of the automobiles pursuant to established standardized procedures. Inventory searches are not searches for law enforcement or evidentiary purposes. These searches are based on special needs beyond law enforcement and thus are justified as *administrative searches.* See the chapter on administrative searches, discussed *supra.*

1. When Impoundment Is Justified

To conduct an inventory search, the car must lawfully be in police custody. The police may impound a car to protect it from theft or vandalism, provided they make their impoundment decision "according to standard criteria and on the basis of something other than suspicion of evidence of criminal activity." *Colorado v. Bertine,* 479 U.S. 367, 375, 107 S.Ct. 738, 743, 93 L.Ed.2d 739 (1987). Authority to impound is provided by statute in most states.

a.   Relevance of Location of the Car to the Impoundment Decision
The necessity of impoundment may appear questionable when a parked car would have remained on a residential street near the defendant's claimed residence. In *United States v. Ramos–Morales,* 981 F.2d 625 (1st Cir.1992), the defendant claimed that D.E.A. agents unlawfully impounded his car after his arrest. He argued that he parked his car off the street in a private parking place just outside of his home. The court credited the Government's witnesses who stated that the car was left "on the edge" of the road outside of an unknown building. Thus, the court upheld the impoundment. The court found that the residential quality of the neighborhood did not render the impoundment unnecessary. "[T]he significant risk that an abandoned car will be stolen or damaged does not seem confined to busy streets, 'high crime' neighborhoods, or commercial parking lots." The court stressed that the agents followed standardized D.E.A. procedures in assessing the need for impoundment.

b.   Impoundment Not Linked to Inventory Search
Impoundment of a vehicle may be less intrusive when it is not linked to a subsequent inventory search. In *United States v. Rodriguez–Morales,* 929 F.2d 780 (1st Cir.1991), the police impounded a vehicle and conducted a canine sniff by a narcotics-trained dog around the perimeter of the car. The court noted that a canine sniff is not a search and thus is a police procedure, in contrast to inventory searches, that is not dependent upon the impoundment for its constitutional validity. See *United States v. Place,* 462 U.S. 696, 103 S.Ct. 2637, 77 L.Ed.2d 110 (1983), discussed *supra.* In such a situation, the court found that "the impoundment itself is considerably less intrusive than an impoundment linked to an inventory search."

2.   Requirements for Inventory Searches
Assuming a car is lawfully impounded, the police may conduct inventory searches without suspicion and without a warrant. But regulations must exist which control police discretion.

a.   Must Balance State Interest Against the Nature of the Intrusion
In determining whether to perform an inventory search, the state interests served by the search must be balanced against the nature of the intrusion. In *South Dakota v. Opperman,* 428 U.S. 364, 96 S.Ct. 3092, 49 L.Ed.2d 1000 (1976), the Court upheld an inventory search of an impounded vehicle conducted pursuant to establish standardized

procedures. The court emphasized the diminished expectation of privacy attendant to automobiles, and concluded that inventory searches are reasonable when performed to protect certain state interests.

b. **Special Needs Beyond Law Enforcement That Are Effectuated by Inventory Searches**
The Court in *Opperman* identified three interests that are furthered by a proper inventory search. First, the owner of the vehicle needs protection against the *threat of theft or damage* to the vehicle. Second, the police need protection from *claims of lost or stolen property*. Third, the police and the public need protection from the *potential danger* that the vehicle or its contents may cause. Inventory searches of vehicles protect against these risks and are valid, therefore, when properly conducted, even in the absence of a warrant or suspicion of criminal activity.

c. **Dissent in *Opperman***
Justice Marshall, joined by Justices Brennan and Stewart, dissented in *Opperman,* arguing that an "undifferentiated possibility of harm" should not serve as a basis for an inventory search. He also argued that inventory searches did not protect police against false claims of lost or stolen property. Individuals may merely claim that the police knowingly left an item off an inventory list; thus an inventory is not much protection against theft claims.

3. **Warrant Not Required**
The Court in *Opperman,* held that where inventory searches are performed according to departmental procedures, a warrant is not required. Because inventory searches are conducted pursuant to standardized procedures and not for purposes of a criminal investigation, there are no facts for a neutral magistrate to review.

4. **Must Conduct Inventory Search Pursuant to Standardized Regulations**
For an inventory search to be valid, the police must act pursuant to standardized regulations. In *Colorado v. Bertine,* 479 U.S. 367, 107 S.Ct. 738, 93 L.Ed.2d 739 (1987), the Supreme Court upheld the inventory search of a van which included the search of a backpack, a nylon bag, and other containers within the van. The Court found that "reasonable police regulations relating to inventory procedures administered in good faith satisfy the Fourth Amendment, even though courts might as a matter of hindsight be able to devise equally reasonable rules requiring a different procedure." In *Bertine,* the regulations gave the police discretion to determine whether public safety required the impoundment of a vehicle. In addition, the regulations required the police to open every container found in a car during an inventory search. Dissenting in *Bertine,* Justice Marshall, joined by Justice

Brennan, argued that the officers did not act according to standards that sufficiently controlled their discretion.

a. **Regulations Concerning Treatment of Containers Found in Cars During the Course of an Inventory Search**

In *Florida v. Wells,* 495 U.S. 1, 110 S.Ct. 1632, 109 L.Ed.2d 1 (1990), an officer opened a locked suitcase in a car after impounding the car and arresting the driver. The police department, however, had promulgated no regulations concerning whether a container could be opened in an inventory search. The Court invalidated the search, stating that it could not be classified as an inventory search in the absence of inventory regulations which control the discretion of the officer. Since inventory searches can be conducted without suspicion, the Court noted that there must be some substitute for a standard of articulable suspicion, which will prevent the officer from conducting arbitrary searches. Inventory regulations are thus a necessary substitute for a standard of articulable suspicion.

b. **Some Discretion Permitted**

Although the Court in *Wells* found the search to be insufficiently regulated, the Court disagreed with the Florida Supreme Court's finding that "the police under *Bertine* must mandate either that all containers will be opened during an inventory search, or that no containers will be opened." Chief Justice Rehnquist, writing for the majority, stated that police standards controlling inventory searches could give officers some discretion to decide whether or not to open impounded containers. An all-or-nothing rule was not required. For example, a standard could require police officers to open only containers that reasonably appear to contain valuables.

c. **Police Must Follow Regulations**

When conducting an inventory search, the police must follow the standardized regulations for such searches. If they do not, the search is deemed a search for evidence and not an inventory search. Inventory searches will only pass Fourth Amendment scrutiny if they are performed to protect property, not to search for evidence. If officers comply with the regulations, however, the existence of law enforcement motives becomes irrelevant. Thus, courts will uphold searches performed by officers with pretextual motives if the search is objectively reasonable. So for example, if an officer purports to conduct an inventory search of a car, and discovers drugs, the drugs are subject to exclusion if the officer violated inventory regulations, or failed to file an inventory form, or seized the drugs but left other valuables in the car. On the other hand, the drugs would be admissible if the officer follows all the inventory rules and makes the search look like an inventory search, even if the officer's dominant intent is to search for evidence.

5. Alternative "Less Intrusive" Means

As in other areas of Fourth Amendment analysis, officers are not required to employ the least intrusive means to effectuate the state interests involved in an impoundment or an inventory search. Rather, the question is whether the actions taken are reasonable under the Fourth Amendment. So for example, it could be argued that instead of opening a container to inventory its contents, the officer could merely seal the container. Arguably, this would protect the property from theft and protect the police from false claims, and yet would be less intrusive of the defendant's privacy interest in the contents of the container. However, in *Illinois v. Lafayette,* 462 U.S. 640, 103 S.Ct. 2605, 77 L.Ed.2d 65 (1983), the Court squarely rejected the notion that this less onerous alternative was constitutionally required. The Court stated that "even if less intrusive means existed of protecting some particular types of property, it would be unreasonable to expect police officers in the everyday course of business to make fine and subtle distinctions in deciding which containers or items may be searched and which must be sealed as a unit." Likewise, in *Bertine,* the Court rejected the defendant's claim that the police violated the Fourth Amendment by impounding his car instead of permitting Bertine to make alternative arrangements for its disposition. The Court found that "while giving Bertine an opportunity to make alternative arrangements would have undoubtedly have been possible * * * the reasonableness of any particular governmental activity does not necessarily or invariably turn on the existence of alternative less intrusive means." Thus, defendants cannot prevail by arguing that the police could have protected property interests and public safety interests in ways other than through impoundment of their vehicle. Defendants could claim, however, that impoundment of the vehicle was unreasonable because it was unnecessary. See e.g., *Sammons v. Taylor,* 967 F.2d 1533 (11th Cir.1992) (noting that although appellant cannot argue that the police should have employed alternative means, appellant can claim that the impoundment and inventory search of his car was unreasonable).

6. Inventory Searches of Other Property

In *Illinois v. Lafayette,* 462 U.S. 640, 103 S.Ct. 2605, 77 L.Ed.2d 65 (1983), the Supreme Court upheld the inventory search of a shoulder bag of a suspect arrested for disturbing the peace. The Court stated that the police need to protect the property of arrestees, to protect themselves against claims of lost or stolen property and to remove dangerous instrumentalities from arrestees.

7. Immediately Bailable Offenses

In *Lafayette,* the Court stated that an inventory search may be unreasonable if the defendant is not going to be incarcerated. If, for example, the defendant can and will immediately post bail after being booked, there is no legitimate state interest in inventorying his property; there is, under these circumstances, no risk of loss of property or false claims. See *United States*

v. *Mills,* 472 F.2d 1231 (D.C.Cir.1972) (inventory not permissible where the arrestee has a right to release without incarceration).

X.   CONSENT SEARCHES

When police officers obtain consent to search, they need not possess a warrant or any articulable suspicion. A search based on valid consent is reasonable and thus does not violate the Fourth Amendment.

A.   CONSENT MUST BE VOLUNTARY
In order to be reasonable, consent to search must be voluntarily obtained. The Supreme Court addressed this issue in *Schneckloth v. Bustamonte,* 412 U.S. 218, 93 S.Ct. 2041, 36 L.Ed.2d 854 (1973).

1.   *Schneckloth v. Bustamonte*
In *Bustamonte,* a police officer stopped a car due to a traffic infraction. Six people were in the car. The officer asked an occupant if he could search the car. The man agreed and opened the trunk for the officer. Later, he objected that his consent was involuntary because he never knew that he had a right to refuse the officer's request.

a.   Test for Voluntariness of Consent
The Court in *Bustamonte* stated that "the question whether a consent to search was in fact voluntary or was the product of duress or coercion, express or implied, is a question of fact to be determined from the totality of the circumstances." The Court distinguished the traditional concept of waiver of "the safeguards of a fair criminal trial" from consent to search. The question of waiver is determined by whether the defendant knew his right, and, knowing the consequences of a waiver, voluntarily decided to forego his right. A waiver cannot be obtained in the absence of knowledge of the right. In contrast, where the issue is consent to search, the proper test focuses not on whether the defendant waived his Fourth Amendment rights but instead whether the consent to search was voluntary under the totality of the circumstances. The Court concluded that "[w]hile knowledge of the right to refuse consent is one factor to be taken into account, the government *need not establish such knowledge* as the sine qua non of an effective consent." Although defendants need not know of their right to refuse in order for consent to be voluntary, such consent cannot be "coerced, by explicit or implicit means, by implied threat or covert force."

2.   Dissent in *Bustamonte*
Justices Douglas, Brennan and Marshall filed separate dissenting opinions in *Bustamonte.* All three opinions stressed the importance of the knowledge of the right to refuse consent. Justice Brennan stated that "it wholly escapes

me how our citizens can meaningfully be said to have waived something as precious as a constitutional guarantee without ever being aware of its existence." In addition, Justice Marshall dissented, stating that "[i]f consent to search means that a person has chosen to forego his right to exclude the police from the place they seek to search, it follows that his consent cannot be considered a meaningful choice unless he knew that he could in fact exclude the police." These criticisms, however, miss the majority's point, which is that a search pursuant to a voluntary consent is *reasonable* under the Fourth Amendment, not that the suspect has in some manner waived his Fourth Amendment rights by consenting.

3. Burden of Proof

The state has the burden of showing that consent was voluntary by a preponderance of the evidence. *United States v. Matlock,* 415 U.S. 164, 94 S.Ct. 988, 39 L.Ed.2d 242 (1974). See *Bumper v. North Carolina,* 391 U.S. 543, 88 S.Ct. 1788, 20 L.Ed.2d 797 (1968) (holding that the burden of proving that consent was "freely and voluntarily given" rests with the prosecution and "[t]his burden cannot be discharged by showing no more than acquiescence to a claim of lawful authority.").

4. Factors Relevant to Voluntariness

According to *Bustamonte,* consent need not be knowing or intelligent but must only be voluntary to support a valid search. To determine whether such consent is voluntary, courts must analyze whether a person's free will to refuse consent was overborne by police coercion. In *United States v. Gonzalez–Basulto,* 898 F.2d 1011 (5th Cir.1990), the Fifth Circuit listed some factors that may be relevant in determining whether consent is voluntarily obtained. Such factors include: 1) the voluntariness of the defendant's *custodial status*; 2) the presence of *coercive police procedures*; 3) the extent and level of the defendant's *cooperation* with the police; 4) the defendant's *awareness of his right to refuse consent*; 5) the defendant's *education and intelligence;* and 6) the defendant's *belief that no incriminating evidence will be found*. No single factor is dispositive. See e.g., *United States v. Watson,* 423 U.S. 411, 96 S.Ct. 820, 46 L.Ed.2d 598 (1976) (finding consent voluntary even though the defendant was under arrest). The court in *Gonzalez–Basulto* found that the defendant voluntarily consented to the search of his trailer by relying on the following facts: the border patrol agents did not use any force or threaten the defendant; the defendant was not under arrest when the consent was obtained; the evidence was well-hidden so the defendant may have expected that it would not be found; and the defendant cooperated with the agents when they requested his consent.

a. The Right to Refuse Consent

The police do not have to inform the suspect of his right to refuse consent and the suspect's lack of knowledge regarding this right does not in itself vitiate consent. *Schneckloth v. Bustamonte,* 412 U.S. 218, 93

S.Ct. 2041, 36 L.Ed.2d 854 (1973). The lack of a warning informing the suspect that he may refuse consent is simply a factor to be considered in the "totality of the circumstances." Although such a warning is not required, the presence of a warning strongly indicates that the consent was voluntarily obtained.

5. Threat of a Warrant

Sometimes police officers inform suspects that, if they do not consent to a search, the officers simply will obtain a warrant. Whether such a threat renders the consent involuntary depends on the facts of the case.

a. False Statement Concerning the Possession of a Warrant Renders the Consent Involuntary

In *Bumper v. North Carolina,* 391 U.S. 543, 88 S.Ct. 1788, 20 L.Ed.2d 797 (1968), the police told the defendant's grandmother that they had a warrant to search her home although they did not possess one. The grandmother subsequently consented to the search. The Supreme Court reasoned as follows: "[w]hen a law enforcement officer claims authority to search a home under a warrant, he announces in effect that the occupant has no right to resist the search. The situation is instinct with coercion. Where there is coercion there cannot be consent." Thus, where the police falsely claim that they have a search warrant and the person consents to the search because of this claim, the evidence must be suppressed because the police have actively misinformed the person as to his situation. A similar result must also occur where the police received consent after incorrectly asserting or intimating that they have the right to make a warrantless search under the circumstances.

b. Genuine Expressions of Intent to Obtain a Warrant Do Not Render Consent Involuntary

If the threat to obtain a warrant is factually correct as opposed to an empty threat, then it does not render the consent involuntary. For example, in *United States v. White,* 979 F.2d 539 (7th Cir.1992), the police sought consent from the defendant's wife to search their home and threatened to obtain a search warrant if she refused to agree to the search. Noting that "[b]aseless threats to obtain a search warrant may render consent involuntary," the court found that the expressed intention to obtain a warrant does not vitiate consent when it is genuine, and not merely a pretext to induce submission. The court found that White's wife freely consented to the search, as the police had probable cause to search the premises and there was no indication that they were making an empty threat. In addition, the court stated that "[a]lthough no warning of her right to refuse consent was given, the promise that the police would obtain a search warrant if she refused implicitly communicated the option to her." Similarly, in *United States v. Duran,* 957 F.2d 499 (7th Cir.1992), the police told the defendant's wife that they would obtain a warrant if she did not consent to a search. The court found that this threat was not coercive. Although the court noted that empty threats to obtain a warrant may render a subsequent consent invalid, it concluded that the threat in *Duran* was firmly grounded because the officers had probable cause with which to obtain a warrant.

6. Use of Force

If the police use force while requesting consent, citizens may legitimately feel that they do not have a right to refuse. But whether use of force vitiates the voluntariness of consent is determined on a case by case basis. For example, in *United States v. Kelley,* 953 F.2d 562 (9th Cir.1992), an armed F.B.I. agent ordered a woman to lie prone on the ground while her children were crying and running about nearby. The court found her subsequent consent to be voluntary because the police requested her consent after she was allowed to stand up, she was informed that she was not under arrest, and her children had stopped crying. On the other hand, if the officer beats the suspect in order to obtain consent, the court will of course determine the consent to be involuntary.

7. When the Suspect Is in Custody

The fact that a person is in custody and under police control is relevant but not determinative of the voluntariness of consent. In *United States v. Watson,* 423 U.S. 411, 96 S.Ct. 820, 46 L.Ed.2d 598 (1976), the Supreme Court applied the principles of *Bustamonte* and held that the fact of custody alone is not enough to demonstrate that consent was coerced. The Court in *Watson* found consent to be voluntary where the defendant "had been arrested and was in custody, but his consent was given while on a public street, not in the confines of a police station." According to the Court, "to hold that illegal coercion is made out from the fact of arrest and the failure to inform the arrestee that he could withhold consent would not be consistent with *Schneckloth.*" The Court noted that Watson was given *Miranda* warnings and was cautioned that the results of the search could be used against him. *Watson* has been extended to permit consent searches that are obtained at the police station—so long as there is no other indication that the suspect's will was overborne, the mere fact that the consent was obtained at the police station does not render the consent involuntary. See, e.g., *United States v. Smith,* 543 F.2d 1141 (5th Cir.1976) (holding that "[t]he fact that Smith gave his consent when he was in custody at the police station, while another factor in the overall judgment, does not justify a departure from the totality of circumstances approach established in *Schneckloth* and *Watson.*").

> *Example:* In *United States v. Duran,* 957 F.2d 499, 503 (7th Cir.1992), the defendant's wife consented to a search of their property while she was at the police station. The court held that the consent given by Duran's wife was voluntary despite police threats to obtain a warrant and despite the fact that she

was in custody at the time of consent. Upon her arrest in a mall, Karen Duran was transported to the police station with her two children. The court found that the coercive effect of her custody was mitigated by the following circumstances: she was held without a showing of force such as handcuffs, was not kept under close restraint at the station, was not subject to an aggressive display of weaponry and was not harshly interrogated. The defendant also claimed that his wife's consent was involuntary because the police did not supply her with a diaper when her younger child soiled one during interrogation. The court rejected this argument, concluding that "[w]hile the child's condition probably made Karen's stay at the police department distinctly more unpleasant, the officers did all they had to under the circumstances: their refusal to leave the station and procure a diaper, or to permit Karen to do the same, was not coercive."

8. Requests for Consent

Requests by police officers are less coercive than demands. Thus, whether the police request or demand consent is a relevant factor in determining the voluntariness of consent. In *United States v. Mendenhall,* 446 U.S. 544, 100 S.Ct. 1870, 64 L.Ed.2d 497 (1980), the defendant agreed to accompany police officers to their airport office and to allow them to search her purse and her person. Holding that the consent was voluntary, the Court noted that the police simply asked her to accompany them to the office and she was not threatened or physically forced. Also, she was informed twice that she was free to decline consent.

9. The Manner in Which the Suspect Consents

The way in which suspects supply their consent may be relevant to whether the consent was voluntarily obtained. For example, when a suspect volunteers to aid the officers in their search, this factor supports a finding of voluntary consent. This was the case in *Schneckloth.* In contrast, in *United States v. Shaibu,* 920 F.2d 1423 (9th Cir.1990), the defendant did not verbally respond when police officers at his door asked if a certain suspect was in the apartment. Instead, the defendant walked back into his apartment, leaving the door open. The court found that these actions did not show consent to enter the apartment. According to the court, "[i]t is one thing to infer consent from actions responding to a police request * * * [but] is quite another to sanction the police walking in to a person's home without stopping at the door to ask permission." But cf. *United States v. Griffin,* 530 F.2d 739 (7th Cir.1976) (holding that individual voluntarily consented to entry where he left the door open when police knocked on the door even after individual initially refused police entry).

10. The Character and Emotional State of the Suspect
The character of an individual and his susceptibility to police coercion may help determine whether his consent was voluntary.

a. Suspect's Lack of Education Relevant to Involuntariness
For example, in *United States v. Jones,* 846 F.2d 358 (6th Cir.1988), the court held that the defendant, who was a convicted felon, did not voluntarily consent to a search of his home when he was stopped by three police cars, was not informed of his right to refuse consent, and had no formal education. In holding the consent involuntary, the court stressed that the defendant only possessed a fourth grade education. Judge Ryan dissented, stating that a court "should not be quick to ignore the distinction between a defendant's general intelligence and formal schooling and his familiarity, rooted in experience, with police practices."

b. Suspect's Impaired Mental or Emotional Condition Does Not Necessarily Render Consent Involuntary
In *United States v. Hall,* 969 F.2d 1102 (D.C.Cir.1992), the defendant claimed that she did not voluntarily consent to the search of her bag because she possessed an IQ which, according to her expert witness, placed her in the borderline range between low-average and mild retardation. In addition, the defendant testified that she only received a ninth grade education, she attended special education programs from the fourth through the ninth grades, and she received counseling for certain psychological problems during that time period. She also stated that the police did not inform her of her right to refuse consent. The court stated that the "voluntariness inquiry turns not on whether a reasonable person in the defendant's position would have felt compelled to consent to a police officer's request to search, but, rather, on whether the *accused herself* actually felt compelled to consent." Therefore, it was relevant that the defendant was mentally impaired. But the court stressed that the defendant's mental impairment did not preclude her from giving voluntary consent.

Reviewing the "totality of the circumstances," the court noted that the level of pressure applied to the defendant by the officers was minimal and that the defendant demonstrated a capacity to make autonomous decisions in the face of police questioning. The court thus found that the defendant's consent was voluntarily obtained. See also *Duran,* 957 F.2d at 503 (holding that although Karen Duran had failed to take medicine prescribed for a nervous disorder for about a week prior to her arrest, "the fact that a consenting party is extremely upset at the time she consents is not dispositive.").

11. The Suspect's Belief That Evidence Would Be Found

Defendants sometimes argue that their consent could not have been voluntarily obtained because they knew that the police officers would find incriminating evidence. They argue that no person could voluntarily consent to a search which would uncover incriminating evidence. But acceptance of such an argument would result in suppression of any evidence found in most consent searches. In *Mendenhall,* discussed *supra,* the Court categorically rejected such an argument, stating that although a suspect may later regret having given consent, "the question is not whether she acted in her ultimate self-interest, but whether she acted voluntarily."

12. When Evidence Is Well–Hidden

Conversely, the fact that evidence was well-hidden has been considered by most courts to be relevant to the voluntariness of the consent. The rationale is that the suspect is more likely to consent voluntarily if he has the expectation that evidence is so well-hidden that it will not be found. See, e.g., *United States v. Gonzalez–Basulto,* 898 F.2d 1011 (5th Cir.1990), (finding that "Gonzalez may well have believed that no drugs would be found because the cocaine was hidden in boxes toward the front of the trailer and there was little crawl space in the trailer.").

13. Use of Trickery

The police may not obtain consent by trickery. A consent obtained solely as a result of trickery will not be considered voluntary. Courts determine on a case by case basis whether police conduct constituted trickery. See e.g., *Graves v. Beto,* 424 F.2d 524 (5th Cir.1970) (defendant's blood sample cannot be used to establish identity in a rape case, where he had initially refused to give a blood sample and consented after being told that the sample would be used only to determine the alcohol content of his blood).

B. THIRD PARTY CONSENT

A third party may consent to the search of an area in which a suspect has an expectation of privacy if the third party voluntarily consents to the search and has authority to consent to the search of the area. *United States v. Matlock,* 415 U.S. 164, 94 S.Ct. 988, 39 L.Ed.2d 242 (1974).

1. Rationales for Allowing Third Party Consent

Third party consent is justified on two grounds. First, if third parties have access or control over a private area, they have an *independent privacy interest* in that area and an independent right to forego such interests. Second, because the suspect has granted a third party access to a private area, the suspect has *assumed the risk* that the third party may consent to a search.

Example: In *Frazier v. Cupp,* 394 U.S. 731, 89 S.Ct. 1420, 22 L.Ed.2d 684 (1969), the Supreme Court upheld the search of the defendant's bag when his cousin consented to the search. The defendant's cousin was a joint user of the bag. Although the cousin possessed authority to use only one compartment of the bag, the Court upheld the search of the remainder, stating that it would not "engage in such metaphysical subtleties." The Court stated that by allowing his cousin to use the bag, the defendant assumed the risk that his cousin would consent to a search.

2. Limited Access May Restrict Authority to Consent to a Search

In some circumstances, a third party's access to an area may be limited or conditional. For example, a maid usually only has access to the premises to clean the house. When access is granted for such limited purposes, the third party may not possess the authority to consent to a search, or the grant of access may restrict the authority to consent. For example, in *United States v. Brown,* 961 F.2d 1039 (2d Cir.1992), the defendant's landlady had access to his apartment to turn off the electricity when the power would short-circuit. Noting that "authority granted for a limited purpose does not translate into a general authority to authorize a search," the court held that the evidence obtained as a result of the landlady's consent should have been suppressed. See *United States v. Warner,* 843 F.2d 401, 403 (9th Cir.1988) (holding that landlord who was authorized to enter property inhabited by tenant "for the limited purposes of making specified repairs and occasionally mowing the lawn" could not consent, on behalf of tenant, to a search of the premises).

a. Areas of Access

A third party's access may also be limited by location. If a third party possesses common authority as to only part of the premises, this factor does not imply authority to consent to the search of the entire premises. For example, roommates in a shared apartment or house may have areas of exclusive control, as to which the other person may not consent.

b. Marital Relationships

In marital relationships, most courts have held that there is a presumption of common authority over premises jointly occupied by both spouses. See *United States v. Harrison,* 679 F.2d 942, 947 (D.C.Cir.1982) (upholding consent of defendant's wife as the wife had full "common authority" over storage area in the basement); *United States v. Stone,* 471 F.2d 170, 173 (7th Cir.1972) (holding that where husband and wife have equal rights to the use of the premises, wife's voluntary consent to search is binding on husband). According to these courts, where a defendant's spouse consented to a search of a particular area, the burden is on the defendant to show that the consenting spouse was denied access to that area. See *United States v. Duran,* 957 F.2d 499 (7th Cir.1992).

Example: In *Duran,* discussed *supra,* the defendant's wife consented to
a search of an old farmhouse on their property. The
defendant argued that his wife did not have joint access to
or control of the farmhouse and thus had no authority to
consent to its search. Leaving open the possibility that one
spouse may maintain exclusive control over certain portions
of the family homestead, the court held that "a spouse
presumptively has authority to consent to a search of all
areas of the homestead; the nonconsenting spouse may rebut
this presumption only by showing that the consenting spouse
was denied access to the particular area searched." Applying
this standard to the facts in *Duran,* the court held that the
defendant failed to rebut the presumption of common
authority. The wife's testimony indicated that although she
never entered the barn, she *could have entered* the barn if
she had desired. According to the court, "[o]ne can have
access to a building or a room but choose not to enter."

c.   **Consent by Parents and Children**
Cases involving third party consent by parents and children raise the
issue of whether the parent or child possessed the authority to consent
to a search of a particular private area. Some courts have held that
parents with control over the entire premises may validly consent to a
search of the premises, unless there is a part of the premises which is
clearly and exclusively reserved for a child. See, e.g., *United States v.
Peterson,* 524 F.2d 167 (4th Cir.1975) (holding that mother of one
defendant was vested with sufficient authority to consent to a search of
a bedroom occupied by that defendant and his two brothers in his
mother's home); *In re Scott K.,* 24 Cal.3d 395, 155 Cal.Rptr. 671, 595
P.2d 105 (1979) (holding that where locked toolbox belonged to minor
and minor refused to consent, consent obtained from minor's father
violated the Fourth Amendment). But courts have been reluctant to
allow minor children to consent to searches of homes. See, e.g., *Padron
v. State,* 328 So.2d 216 (Fla.App. 4th Dist.1976) (holding that defendant's
16 year old son did not share common authority with defendant over the
premises to consent to a search).

3.   **Retention of Ownership Interest**
Authority to consent to a search may stem from an ownership interest in the
property. For example, in *United States v. Davis,* 967 F.2d 84 (2d Cir.1992),
police officers received consent to search a footlocker from defendant's friend,
Cleare, who told the officers that he had given the defendant a key to his
apartment and that the defendant had left some belongings in Cleare's
footlocker. Holding the third party consent valid, the court noted that Cleare
obviously had access to the trunk as he lived in the apartment and kept the
trunk, which belonged to him, in his own bedroom. Although Cleare allowed

the defendant to store items in the footlocker, they never agreed that Cleare could not look inside. In addition, Cleare had a substantial interest in the footlocker as he owned the trunk and kept many of his possessions there. According to the court, Cleare possessed common authority over the footlocker even though the defendant had the only key that opened it. See also *United States v. Wright,* 971 F.2d 176 (8th Cir.1992) (holding that "Smith possessed authority to consent to a search of his own home, including the guest bedroom where [the defendant] spent the evening.").

4. Presence of Defendant and Defendant's Refusal to Consent May Effect Validity of Third Party Consent

If the defendant is present and objects when the police ask for consent to search, many courts have held that any third party consent obtained by the police is invalid. See, e.g., *United States v. Impink,* 728 F.2d 1228 (9th Cir.1984) (holding no third party consent is possible where the defendant is present and objecting). Other courts have held, however, that one party may consent to the search even where the other party is present when the consent is sought, and objects to such a search. See *People v. Cosme,* 48 N.Y.2d 286, 422 N.Y.S.2d 652, 397 N.E.2d 1319 (1979) (holding search reasonable upon third party consent even though defendant is present and objecting).

a. Absence of the Third Party

One court focused on the absence of the third party during the search in holding that the third party consent was invalid where the defendant was present and objecting to the search. In *In re D.A.G.,* 484 N.W.2d 787 (Minn.1992), police officers obtained consent to search a residence from a tenant who did not accompany the officers to the residence at the time of the search. During the search, a co-tenant was present and objected to the officer's actions. The court held that the police could not rely on the consent of an absent third party, over the objection of a co-tenant who is present at the house. The court stated that an absent party's rights to a jointly controlled area are subordinate to a present party's rights to the same area. According to the court, the rationale of "assumption of risk" underlying the third party consent doctrine is not persuasive when the person who is the target of the search is present and the consenting party is not.

b. Defendant's Prior Refusal

Some courts have held that the defendant's prior refusal to consent to a search does not invalidate subsequently obtained consent from a third party. For example, in *United States v. Baldwin,* 644 F.2d 381 (5th Cir.1981), the court held that the defendant's wife could consent to a search of an automobile where she possessed joint control over the car, despite the fact that the defendant had previously refused to consent to the search. The defendant was not present when the search occurred.

5.   **The Third Party Must Possess Actual or Apparent Authority**
     The Supreme Court has held that third party consent is valid if the third
     party possesses actual or apparent authority.

   a.   **Actual Authority: *United States v. Matlock***
        In *United States v. Matlock,* 415 U.S. 164, 94 S.Ct. 988, 39 L.Ed.2d 242
        (1974), the defendant was arrested in front of a house. A woman allowed
        the police to enter and search the house stating that she shared the
        house with the defendant. The Supreme Court held that the search was
        a valid consent search, because the woman had actual authority to
        consent to a search of the premises. The Court stated that "the consent
        of one who possesses common authority over [the] premises * * * is valid
        as against the absent nonconsenting person with whom that authority is
        shared." According to the Court, "the authority which justifies the
        third-party consent does not rest upon the law of property * * * but
        rests rather on mutual use of the property by persons generally having
        joint access or control for most purposes." See *United States v. Butler,*
        966 F.2d 559 (10th Cir.1992) (holding that third party had joint access
        to the searched premises, inasmuch as she had lived with the defendant
        and shared the same bedroom and was thus in a position to give
        effective consent to a search). The Court in *Matlock* found it unnecessary
        to determine whether a search is valid when based on the consent of a
        third party who has apparent but not actual authority over the premises.

   b.   **Apparent Authority: *Illinois v. Rodriguez***
        In *Illinois v. Rodriguez,* 497 U.S. 177, 110 S.Ct. 2793, 111 L.Ed.2d 148
        (1990), the Court considered the issue it left open in *United States v.
        Matlock.* The third party in *Rodriguez* was Rodriguez's woman friend,
        who had, unknown to the officers, moved out of his apartment a month
        before the search and retained a key without permission. Justice Scalia,
        writing for a six-person majority, agreed with the lower courts that the
        friend did not have actual authority to consent to a search of the
        apartment, as she had no joint access or control of the premises after
        moving out. According to the majority, however, the officers' *reasonable
        belief* that the friend had authority to consent (i.e. apparent authority)
        would validate the entry.

   c.   **Distinguishing Between Consent Searches and Waivers of Fourth
        Amendment Rights**
        Rodriguez argued that, if a reasonable belief of common authority could
        validate a search, the third party would in effect be making an
        unauthorized waiver of defendant's Fourth Amendment rights. But
        Justice Scalia responded that this argument confused the standard of
        waiver of constitutional rights with the standard for voluntary consent
        searches established by *Schneckloth v. Bustamonte.* See *Bustamonte,*
        discussed *supra,* (distinguishing between waiver of a constitutional right

and a consent search). Consent does not constitute a waiver of Fourth Amendment rights, but rather satisfies the Fourth Amendment requirement that a search be reasonable. Thus, *Rodriguez* reaffirms the principle established in *Bustamonte* that a consent search is not a waiver of Fourth Amendment rights but rather a reasonable search permitted by the Fourth Amendment.

d. **Reasonable Mistakes of Fact Are Allowed: Question of Authority Is Governed by the Standard of Reasonableness**

Because *Bustamonte* only requires that consent searches be reasonable, the officers who obtain consent from a third party are entitled to make reasonable mistakes concerning that party's authority to consent. Justice Scalia concluded in *Rodriguez* that the question of authority to consent should be governed by the same standard of reasonableness, and allowance for reasonable mistakes, as had been applied in other areas of Fourth Amendment jurisprudence, such as probable cause, the execution of a warrant, and the existence of exigent circumstances. See, e.g., *Hill v. California,* 401 U.S. 797, 91 S.Ct. 1106, 28 L.Ed.2d 484 (1971) (holding that probable cause can exist where there is a reasonable mistake of fact). According to the Court, it would be anomalous to allow for a reasonable mistake of fact to support probable cause or exigent circumstances, but not to allow for such a mistake to support a finding of third party consent. All these cases are governed by the Fourth Amendment's requirement that searches must be reasonable. Therefore, under *Rodriguez,* third party consent is valid where an officer would have possessed valid consent to search if the facts were as he reasonably believed them to be. The Court in *Rodriguez* remanded for a determination of whether the officers could have reasonably believed that Rodriguez's friend had actual authority to consent to a search of his apartment. See *United States v. Englebrecht,* 917 F.2d 376 (8th Cir.1990) (applying this standard and finding apparent authority for third party consent where "an individual who had been living in the same farmhouse with as well as working for Englebrecht consented to the search of the vehicles, which were parked near the farmhouse"). See also *United States v. McAlpine,* 919 F.2d 1461 (10th Cir.1990) (holding that police could have reasonably believed that woman who reported that she was being held against her will by two men who had been sexually assaulting her was qualified to give effective consent to search of entire trailer where she had been held for two months).

e. **Dissent in *Rodriguez***

Justice Marshall, joined by Justices Brennan and Stevens, dissented in *Rodriguez* contending that third party consent searches are permissible, not because they are reasonable, but because a person "may voluntarily limit his expectation of privacy by allowing others to exercise authority over his possessions" and thus they are not searches at all. Justice

Marshall concluded that if an individual did not actually voluntarily assume the risk of third party consent, there would then be a "search" and the consent of a third party would not make the search reasonable.

f.   **Police Officers Must Make Reasonable Inquiries to Determine Whether Third Party Possesses Apparent Authority**

The Court in *Rodriguez* stressed that the police could not presume third party consent merely upon the assertion of the third party that he has common authority. The surrounding circumstances could be such that a reasonable person would doubt the truth of such an assertion. See e.g. Weinreb, *Generalities of the Fourth Amendment,* 42 U.Chi.L.Rev. 47 (1974) (arguing that a babysitter's assertions that she has common authority over the premises are not deserving of unquestioned acceptance, since it is contrary to common understanding for a babysitter to be permitted to admit police for a search while the parents are out). *Rodriguez* does not change the presumption in the lower courts that police officers must make reasonable inquiries as to whether a third party has actual authority when they find themselves in ambiguous circumstances. If the facts demand further inquiry, and more facts will be relatively easy to ascertain, then a duty of inquiry will be imposed under the Fourth Amendment standard of reasonableness. Compare *United States v. Poole,* 307 F.Supp. 1185 (E.D.La.1969) (holding that where officers who obtained consent searched around a person in the bedroom, the police had a duty to inquire whether some of the property searched was owned by that person) with *People v. Adams,* 53 N.Y.2d 1, 439 N.Y.S.2d 877, 422 N.E.2d 537 (1981) (excusing duty of further inquiry given exigencies of situation in which consent was given and search was made).

Example: In *United States v. Rosario,* 962 F.2d 733 (7th Cir.1992), police officers responded to a call by a motel clerk that a marijuana odor was present outside of a motel room. The officers knocked on the door and claimed that a man, later identified as Rubin Vilaro, consented to their entry. The defendant argued that "compared to the police in *Rodriguez,* 'the officers in the instant case had no information regarding Vilaro's authority to consent to the search of [the defendants'] room.'" The court held that the police officers obtained enough information during their brief encounter with Vilaro to make a reasoned judgment about his authority to admit them into his room. "Nothing about Vilaro's speech or mannerism suggested that he needed to obtain someone else's approval to permit the entrance of the officers." In addition, the court found that "[b]y allowing Vilaro unfettered access to the door, the appellants also gave him discretion to decide whom to admit, thereby sacrificing some degree of their privacy." The court noted, however, that in the absence of sufficient facts, officers have a duty to seek further information to determine whether they may reasonably infer that the third party has actual authority to consent to the search or entry.

A case in which further inquiry was found necessary is *United States v. Salinas–Cano,* 959 F.2d 861 (10th Cir.1992). There, the police received consent from the defendant's girlfriend to search her apartment after informing her that they were particularly interested in the defendant's belongings. The girlfriend consented to the search of the defendant's unlocked suitcase which he had left at the apartment. According to the court, no evidence was shown that indicated that the girlfriend exercised mutual use or possessed joint interest and control over the suitcase. The court also rejected the Government's argument that the girlfriend possessed apparent authority under *Rodriguez* to consent to the search. The court stated that "[t]he information known to the officer was insufficient to support a reasonable belief in [the girlfriend's] authority."

g. **Third Party Consent May Be Based on Actual But Not Apparent Authority**

After *Rodriguez,* a third party consent search can be supported by *either* actual or apparent authority. Although the *Rodriguez* fact situation concerns apparent but not actual authority, a consent search would be equally reasonable if based upon actual but not apparent authority. See, e.g., *United States v. Chaidez,* 919 F.2d 1193, 1201–02 (7th Cir.1990) (holding that although it was unreasonable to infer authority when person consenting to search said that she did not live in the house and was there only to do laundry, the fact that she had actual authority from the owner justified the search).

h. **Difference Between Mistakes of Fact and Mistakes of Law**

In *Stoner v. California,* 376 U.S. 483, 84 S.Ct. 889, 11 L.Ed.2d 856 (1964), the Court held that a warrantless search of the defendant's hotel room could not be based on the consent of the desk clerk. Rejecting the Government's argument that the officers properly relied on the apparent authority of the clerk, the Court stated that "the rights protected by the Fourth Amendment are not to be eroded by unrealistic doctrines of apparent authority." Although the holding in *Rodriguez* seems to contradict *Stoner,* the cases can be distinguished because the error by the officers as to the third party's authority in *Rodriguez* was one of *fact,* while the error by the officers in *Stoner* was one of *law.*

The officers in *Stoner* knew that the third party was a desk clerk and that the room was rented. They could not have reasonably believed that the clerk had the authority to allow entry into the room, because, as a legal matter, a hotel clerk does not possess the authority to allow entry into the room of a paying tenant. A mistake of law does not come within the apparent authority doctrine, as the Court in both *Stoner* and *Rodriguez* recognized.

>   ***Example:***   In *United States v. Brown,* 961 F.2d 1039 (2d Cir.1992), the court held that the defendant's landlady did not possess apparent authority to consent to the search of the defendant's apartment. The defendant's landlady would frequently enter the defendant's apartment using her key, when he was not home, if the electrical power in the house would short-circuit due to the defendant's use of the electricity. The landlady would enter in such circumstances only to turn off electrical appliances in Brown's apartment. During one such occasion, the landlady noticed guns in the defendant's apartment, called the police, and subsequently directed the officers into the apartment. Rejecting the Government's argument that *Rodriguez* supported the search, the court noted that "*Rodriguez* would not validate * * * a search premised upon an erroneous view of the law." The court found that the officers' conclusion that the landlady could consent to a search of the premises because she was authorized to enter Brown's apartment to turn off electrical appliances was not a reasonable, although factually erroneous, belief. Rather, this conclusion was "a misapprehension of the applicable rule of law" pertaining to the rental of a premises.

C.   SCOPE OF CONSENT

Even if the consent is voluntary—whether from the defendant or from a third party with actual or apparent authority—the consenting party may place limitations on the scope of the consent. A search is not a valid consent search if a reasonable person would conclude that it exceeds the limitations established by the consenting party. See, e.g., *United States v. Towns,* 913 F.2d 434 (7th Cir.1990) (holding that consent for entry into an apartment to look at defendant's identification did not permit a thorough seven hour search of the apartment).

1.   Officer Must Reasonably Believe That the Defendant Consented to the Area Searched

In construing the scope of consent, the question is whether a reasonable police officer would believe that the defendant consented to the area searched.

a. *Florida v. Jimeno*

In *Florida v. Jimeno,* __ U.S. __, 111 S.Ct. 1801, 114 L.Ed.2d 297 (1991), the Court held that an officer could reasonably conclude that when a suspect gave general consent to a search of his car, he also consented to a search of a paper bag lying on the floor of the car. Chief Justice Rehnquist, writing for a seven person majority, stated that the scope of consent is determined by a standard of objective reasonableness. According to the Court, "the scope of a search is generally defined by its expressed object." In *Jimeno,* the officer told the defendant that he was looking for narcotics in the car. In addition, Jimeno did not explicitly limit the scope of the search. The officer thereupon searched the car and found a bag in the passenger compartment. He searched the bag and found narcotics. The Court found that "a reasonable person might be expected to know that narcotics are carried in some form of container" and therefore that the search of the bag was within the scope of the general consent to search the car.

b. Distinguishing Between the Bag Found in the Car and a Locked Briefcase

In *Jimeno,* the Court distinguished the facts of the case from a situation where an officer received consent to search a trunk and pried open a locked briefcase found inside. The Court noted that "it is very likely unreasonable to think that a suspect, by consenting to the search of his trunk, has agreed to the breaking open of a locked briefcase within the trunk, but it is otherwise with a paper bag."

c. Dissent in *Jimeno*

Dissenting in *Jimeno,* Justice Marshall, joined by Justice Stevens, argued that a person has distinct privacy expectations in a car and in containers which might be found therein. He concluded that because general consent is ambiguous, the police should ask permission to search the car and its contents, or should ask for additional permission to search a container when it is found in the car. Justice Marshall stated that "[t]he majority's real concern is that if the police were required to ask for additional consent to search a closed container * * * an individual who did not mean to authorize such additional searching would have an opportunity to say no."

2. Ambiguity Regarding the Scope of the Consent Is Construed Against the Citizen

The *Jimeno* decision generally establishes that any ambiguity in the scope of the consent is construed against the citizen. So long as the officer's interpretation of an ambiguous or general consent is at all reasonable, the resulting search will be deemed within the scope of the consent, even if the citizen did not intend the consent to reach that far. It is up to the suspect to clarify the scope of an ambiguous consent. This can be done by imposing specific limitations at the outset, or by terminating the search if it proceeds to areas which the suspect wishes to keep private.

Example: In *United States v. Berke,* 930 F.2d 1219 (7th Cir.1991), the defendant, when asked by the officer if he could "look" into his bag, said yes. The officer proceeded to search the bag thoroughly, and discovered narcotics hidden at the bottom of the bag. The defendant argued that consent to "look" did not permit the officers to rummage through the bag. The court rejected this argument and held that the defendant's consent permitted a thorough search of the bag because the officers could reasonably believe that "look" meant "search". The court noted that the defendant did not ask for clarification of what the officers meant when they said they wanted to "look" inside.

3. Consent to Search Does Not Permit the Destruction Or Mutilation of the Area Searched

Because *Jimeno* distinguished the officer's opening of a paper bag from a case where an officer pries open a locked briefcase, courts have held that a search which requires mutilation or destruction of property or premises is beyond the reasonable scope of a general consent. See, e.g., *United States v. Strickland,* 902 F.2d 937 (11th Cir.1990) (noting that the general consent to search a car did not permit the slashing of defendant's tire).

a. Removing Car Door Panels May Be Within the Scope of Consent

Some courts have upheld the removal of door panels by police officers pursuant to a general consent to search the car. See *United States v. Gutierrez–Mederos,* 965 F.2d 800 (9th Cir.1992) (holding that search was reasonable where the police officer opened a side panel compartment of a hatchback pursuant to consent to search the car as defendant did not limit consent, knew officer wished to search for weapons and narcotics, and officer did not pry open or break the panel). See also *People v. Crenshaw,* 9 Cal.App. 4th 1403, 12 Cal.Rptr.2d 172 (1992), (holding that the nondestructive opening of a door panel by police officers was within the scope of consent to search the car). The rationale is that such activity does not require mutilation or destruction of property.

4. Construing the Scope of Body Searches After *Jimeno*

Jimeno establishes that ambiguities regarding the scope of consent are construed against the suspect. The courts have reached differing results after *Jimeno* where an officer obtains a general consent to a search of the suspect's person, and proceeds to search private areas, such as the genital area, for drugs. Can the search of a "person" reasonably be construed to extend to such areas? After *Jimeno*, some courts have validated such searches unless the defendant specifically places a limitation on the scope of the search. See *United States v. Rodney,* 956 F.2d 295 (D.C.Cir.1992) (upholding the search of defendant's crotch area as within the scope of consent where defendant consented to a body search). Other courts have disagreed. See *Davis v. State,* 594 So.2d 264 (Fla.1992) (holding that voluntary consent to search of one's person did not encompass search of groin area). Note that the search in *Rodney* was essentially a frisk of the suspect's crotch. The court in *Rodney* stated in dicta that a general consent to a body search could *not* be reasonably construed to permit a body cavity search.

D. REVOKING CONSENT

Since the defendant has the right to refuse consent and to control the scope of consent, it follows that he has the right to *revoke* a consent once given. Of course, consent cannot be revoked retroactively after the officer has found incriminating information. But it is clear that the officer's right to engage in a consent search can be terminated by the defendant—or by a third party if the officer is relying on third party consent. See *United States v. Springs,* 936 F.2d 1330 (D.C.Cir.1991) ("even after consent to search is initially given, a person may subsequently limit or withdraw that consent").

1. Withdrawal or Limitation of Consent Cannot Be Considered in Determining Reasonable Suspicion or Probable Cause

Suppose that an officer obtains voluntary consent to search a home and then, when he is about to enter a closet, the defendant revokes consent and forbids entry to the closet. Can the officer consider the defendant's actions as proof that there is something incriminating in the closet? Courts have answered in the negative. As one court put it: "The constitutional right to withdraw one's consent would be of little value if the very fact of choosing to exercise that right could serve as any part of the basis for finding the reasonable suspicion that makes consent unnecessary." *United States v. Carter,* 985 F.2d 1095 (D.C.Cir.1993). See also *United States v. Wilson,* 953 F.2d 116 (4th Cir.1991) (refusal to allow search of coat, after consenting to search of luggage and person, should not have counted as a factor in the analysis of reasonable suspicion).

*

IV

EAVESDROPPING AND THE USE OF SECRET AGENTS

Analysis

I. THE LAW ON ELECTRONIC SURVEILLANCE PRIOR TO *KATZ*

Before the landmark case of *Katz v. United States,* 389 U.S. 347, 88 S.Ct. 507, 19 L.Ed.2d 576 (1967), the Court held that Fourth Amendment limitations on electronic and other surveillance were determined by whether officers physically invaded a private area.

A. *OLMSTEAD*

In *Olmstead v. United States,* 277 U.S. 438, 48 S.Ct. 564, 72 L.Ed. 944 (1928), the Court held that a wiretap placed on the telephone lines of a suspect's house was not a search or seizure within the confines of the Fourth Amendment. The 5–4 majority reasoned that, even though Federal agents violated a state wiretapping law, the officers did not actually *trespass* on the premises of the defendant. Thus, there was no constitutional violation, and the incriminating telephone conversations could be admitted at trial. The Court stated that conversations overheard by officers illegally upon the premises of a suspect would be suppressed; but this was because the premises were protected from an illegal entry, not because the communications themselves were protected. The Court concluded that verbal communications were not "persons, houses, papers, [or] effects" and thus their seizure was beyond the purview of the Fourth Amendment.

1. Dissent in *Olmstead*

The dissent strongly objected to the majority's "unduly literal construction" of the Fourth Amendment which excluded wiretapping from the Amendment's protection. Justice Brandeis urged "[t]hat the makers of our Constitution * * * conferred, as against the government, the right to be let alone—the most comprehensive of rights and the right most valued by civilized men," and so "every unjustifiable intrusion upon the privacy of the individual, by whatever means employed, must be deemed a violation of the Fourth Amendment." Justice Holmes noted in a separate dissent that "it is a less evil that some criminals should escape than that the government should play an ignoble part."

B. DEVELOPMENT OF TRESPASS DOCTRINE

The Court used the *Olmstead* trespass rationale to permit the use of various other types of electronic surveillance equipment. For example, in *Goldman v. United States,* 316 U.S. 129, 62 S.Ct. 993, 86 L.Ed. 1322 (1942), the Court upheld the use of evidence obtained from a detectaphone "bug" that Federal officers placed against the outer wall of a private office. There was no Fourth Amendment problem because the officers installed the bug without physically entering the private office. In *On Lee v. United States,* 343 U.S. 747, 72 S.Ct. 967, 96 L.Ed. 1270 (1952), the Court upheld the use of testimony obtained from a wired informer who transmitted through a hidden microphone his conversation with the defendant to a Government agent stationed outside the premises. In *On Lee,* the informant *had* physically entered the presence, but had done so with the permission of the defendant, so again there was no trespass.

1.   **Retreat From Trespass Doctrine**

In *Silverman v. United States,* 365 U.S. 505, 81 S.Ct. 679, 5 L.Ed.2d 734 (1961), the Court held that the police violated the Fourth Amendment when they intercepted communications through the use of a "spike mike" without a warrant. The Fourth Amendment was triggered because the "spike mike" was placed into the wall of a residence in such a way that it made contact with the home's interior heating duct. Although an actual physical trespass occurred, the Court stressed that its decision did "not turn upon the technicality of a trespass upon a party wall as a matter of local law. It is based upon the reality of an intrusion into a constitutionally protected area." Thus the Court in *Silverman* abandoned its rigid adherence to the trespass doctrine, though the case could have been decided the same way had the trespass rule been used.

II.   *KATZ* "REASONABLE EXPECTATION OF PRIVACY" DOCTRINE

In *Katz v. United States,* 389 U.S. 347, 88 S.Ct. 507, 19 L.Ed.2d 576 (1967), Federal agents, acting without a warrant, placed a listening bug on the outside of a public telephone booth which they suspected the defendant was using to conduct an illegal gambling operation. The Court suppressed the evidence obtained through the bug, holding that its use was a search which required a warrant.

A.   **REASONING IN** *KATZ*

Although there was no trespass upon private property, the Court held that the trespass "underpinnings" of *Olmstead* and *Goldman* were no longer controlling. Rather, the Court relied in part upon *Silverman* for the notion that "the Fourth Amendment governs not only the seizure of tangible items, but extends as well to the recording of oral statements, overheard without any 'technical trespass under * * * local property law'". The Court stressed that the prohibition against unreasonable searches and seizures was to protect "people, not places" and, thus, "the reach of th[e Fourth] Amendment cannot turn upon the presence or absence of a physical intrusion into any given enclosure."

1.   **Dissent in** *Katz*

Justice Black objected to what he considered the majority's rewriting of the Constitution in order to placate the general public's objections to sweeping investigative tools. Justice Black argued that the Fourth Amendment should be read literally, not to "bring it into harmony with the times." Echoing the sentiments of the *Olmstead* Court, he stated that the written language of the Amendment only prohibited unreasonable searches and seizures directed at specific tangible items. Conversations are not tangible items with "size, form, and weight," and cannot, therefore, be searched or seized. Justice Black further argued that, far from being an "unknown possibility" at the time the Constitution was written, eavesdropping was an "ancient practice * * * condemned [at common law] as a nuisance." Justice Black reasoned that the Framers could have included words prohibiting the use of eavesdropping techniques had they so desired.

2. Electronic Surveillance After *Katz*

After *Katz,* electronic surveillance, as a constitutional matter, is treated the same as any other police investigative technique. If the police, in conducting electronic surveillance, obtain information as to which a person has a legitimate expectation of privacy, then a warrant based upon probable cause is presumptively required. In addition, Title III of the Omnibus Crime Control and Safe Streets Act imposes substantial statutory limitations on electronic surveillance. The statute sets forth minimum standards for Federal and state surveillance. Its requirements for a wiretap authorization arguably provide more protection than that mandated by the Fourth Amendment. Most electronic surveillance litigation therefore concerns statutory rather than constitutional interpretation.

III. USE OF SECRET AGENTS

Some electronic surveillance cases involve the recording of conversations by law enforcement where neither party involved in the conversation was aware of police observation. *Olmstead, Goldman,* and *Katz* were such cases. Other cases involve use of secret informers and undercover agents such that one party to a dialogue is conscious that communications are being recorded. *On Lee* was such a case. The Supreme Court has held that the testimony of secret agents, whether wired or merely repeating the substance of certain conversations, does not fall within the protected boundaries of the Fourth Amendment.

A. PRE-*KATZ* TRESPASS DOCTRINE

As previously noted, the *On Lee* Court, prior to *Katz,* held that the evidence obtained through use of a wire was not a trespass by fraud, and was properly admitted at trial. In *On Lee,* the Government had an acquaintance of the defendant enter his workplace and engage the defendant in what turned out to be an incriminating conversation. The informer did not testify at trial. Instead, the Government agent who listened to the conversation outside the premises eventually testified to its substance. The Court held that neither informer nor agent was "trespassing" on the defendant's property. It concluded that the contention that the informer trespassed by fraud was "verging on the frivolous."

1. *Lopez*

In *Lopez v. United States,* 373 U.S. 427, 83 S.Ct. 1381, 10 L.Ed.2d 462 (1963), the Court upheld the use of recorded testimony obtained from an IRS agent who, after receiving an unsolicited bribe offer, recorded from his office any subsequent conversations with the defendant. The Court held that no trespass had occurred (since Lopez came to the IRS agent's office), and that the recording only revealed what the defendant willingly disclosed to the agent who was then perfectly within his rights to disclose such information to the Government. The 6–3 majority had no problems with the use of the tape recorder in court, rather than simply having the agent testify from memory as to the conversation, since "the device was used only to obtain the most reliable evidence possible," and "the risk that petitioner took in offering a bribe * * * fairly included the risk that the offer would be accurately reproduced in court, whether by faultless memory or mechanical recording."

B. ASSUMPTION OF RISK

More recently, the Court has shifted from the trespass theory to an analysis which focuses on whether the defendant can be found to have assumed the risk that a person or associate was operating as an undercover agent. In *Lewis v. United States*, 385 U.S. 206, 87 S.Ct. 424, 17 L.Ed.2d 312 (1966), an undercover narcotics agent posed as a buyer of drugs in order to gain entry to the defendant's home where suspected drug transactions were taking place. Lewis invited the agent inside to purchase drugs, though of course he did not know that the ostensible purchaser was in fact an undercover agent. The agent, upon entry, obtained substantial evidence of drug activity. The Court held that the agent's conduct did not violate the Fourth Amendment. It emphasized that the agent did not "see, hear, or take anything that was not contemplated and in fact intended by petitioner as a necessary part of his illegal business," and that there is no reasonable expectation of privacy in illegal activity. Justice Brennan, in a concurring opinion, also noted that "the agent, in the same manner as any private person, entered the premises for the very purpose contemplated by the occupant and took nothing away except what would be taken away by any willing purchaser." See also *Hoffa v. United States*, 385 U.S. 293, 87 S.Ct. 408, 17 L.Ed.2d 374 (1966) (use of informant does not violate the Fourth Amendment where defendant voluntarily gave informant access to incriminating information; the Fourth Amendment did not protect the defendant's "misplaced confidence that [the informer] would not reveal his wrongdoing"); *United States v. White*, 401 U.S. 745, 91 S.Ct. 1122, 28 L.Ed.2d 453 (1971) (statements made to wired Government informant were not illegally obtained; Fourth Amendment does not protect the defendant's mistaken assumption that "a person to whom he voluntarily confides his wrongdoing will not reveal it;" the plurality concludes that "one contemplating illegal activities must realize and risk that his companions may be reporting to the police").

1. Limitation on Assumption of Risk

The *Lewis* Court distinguished an earlier case, *Gouled v. United States*, 255 U.S. 298, 41 S.Ct. 261, 65 L.Ed. 647 (1921), in which a business associate of the defendant gained entry to a house by pretending to stop by on a social visit. The Court invalidated the informer's subsequent search of the defendant's office during the defendant's absence as it held that the search exceeded the scope of reasonable consent extended to the informer. Unlike the agent in *Gouled*, the agent in *Lewis* remained within the reasonable boundaries of consent as extended to any individual who entered the house in order to purchase narcotics. Put another way, Lewis assumed the risk that the undercover agent would have access to information that a real buyer of drugs would have. But Gouled, by merely inviting his "friend" into his home, did not assume the risk that the "friend" would rummage through his home in his absence. If the "friend" had seen incriminating information plainly visible upon entry to Gouled's house, there would have been no Fourth Amendment violation under *Lewis*.

V

REMEDIES FOR FOURTH AMENDMENT VIOLATIONS

Analysis

341

I. INTRODUCTION

The Fourth Amendment provides the right to be free from unreasonable searches and seizures, but it says nothing about what should happen if a person's right is violated. Courts and legislative bodies have crafted various remedies for a violation of Fourth Amendment rights. If no evidence is recovered in the illegal search or seizure, then the remedy most often employed is a civil action for a violation of the plaintiff's constitutional rights. See 42 U.S.C.A. § 1983; *Anderson v. Creighton,* 483 U.S. 635, 107 S.Ct. 3034, 97 L.Ed.2d 523 (1987) (Federal civil rights action for alleged violation of Fourth Amendment rights). Far more frequently, the illegal police activity uncovers evidence which is later offered in the criminal trial of the person whose rights were violated. The remedy sought by the defendant in these cases is *exclusion* of the evidence. For these situations, the courts have established an *exclusionary rule.* Broadly stated, the rule provides that evidence obtained in violation of the defendant's Fourth Amendment must be excluded from trial. The remainder of this section focuses on the exclusionary rule.

A. HISTORICAL DEVELOPMENT

The exclusionary rule was not born contemporaneously with the Fourth Amendment. For over a century after the adoption of the Fourth Amendment, virtually the only remedies available to victims of illegal searches were civil suits in trespass or in replevin for return of the goods seized. The replevin action had no chance of success, however, if the evidence seized was contraband or the fruits or instrumentalities of crime, since those items were considered forfeited to the state regardless of the legality of the seizure. The trespass remedy often provided very limited damages, because while an intrusion into privacy may have been great, the actual act of trespass may well have been minor. The trespass remedy was also limited by doctrines of complete or qualified immunity granted to Government officials.

1. The *Weeks* Rule

The Supreme Court created an exclusionary rule to operate in the Federal Courts in *Weeks v. United States,* 232 U.S. 383, 34 S.Ct. 341, 58 L.Ed. 652 (1914). The Court declared that, if illegally obtained evidence could be used against the defendant in his trial, "the protection of the Fourth Amendment declaring his right to be secure against such searches and seizures is of no value, and, so far as those thus placed are concerned, might as well be stricken from the Constitution." It concluded that to allow such evidence to be admitted "would be to affirm by judicial decision a manifest neglect if not an open defiance" of the Fourth Amendment.

a. Rationale

The Court in *Weeks* articulated two rationales for excluding illegally obtained evidence. One was that the exclusionary rule is the only meaningful way to assure that officials respect the Fourth Amendment rights of the people. The other was that the interest in judicial integrity requires that the courts not sanction illegal searches by admitting the fruits of illegality into evidence.

b. **Fruits**

In *Silverthorne Lumber Co. v. United States,* 251 U.S. 385, 40 S.Ct. 182, 64 L.Ed. 319 (1920), these dual considerations were held to prohibit the copying of illegally seized documents, and the use of the copies as the basis of a subpoena for the originals, which had been returned pursuant to a motion by the defendant. The Court stated that the exclusionary rule should apply not only to the illegally obtained evidence itself (i.e. the originals) but to the fruits of the illegally obtained evidence as well (i.e. the copies). It concluded that "the essence of a provision forbidding the acquisition of evidence is not merely that evidence so acquired will not be used before the court but that it shall not be used at all."

2. *Wolf v. Colorado*

The Court in *Weeks* specifically rejected the notion that the exclusionary rule should apply to violations by state or local police; indeed, at the time of *Weeks* it was established that the Fourth Amendment itself applied only to the actions of Federal officials. Subsequently, in *Wolf v. Colorado,* 338 U.S. 25, 69 S.Ct. 1359, 93 L.Ed. 1782 (1949), the Court confronted two questions: 1) whether the Fourth Amendment was such a fundamental right that it should be incorporated into the Fourteenth Amendment's Due Process Clause and hence be applicable against the states; and 2) whether the exclusionary rule should similarly be applicable to the states through the Fourteenth Amendment's Due Process Clause. The Court held that the security provided by the Fourth Amendment was "basic to a free society" and "implicit in the concept of ordered liberty" and as such was enforceable against the states through the Due Process Clause. However, the Court held that "the ways of enforcing such a basic right raise questions of a different order." It stated that the *Weeks* rule "was not derived from the explicit requirements of the Fourth Amendment" and therefore that the exclusionary rule was not a constitutional requirement. So while the Fourth Amendment was a fundamental right, the exclusionary remedy was not a fundamental guarantee.

a. **Dissent in *Wolf***

The dissenters in *Wolf* argued, as had the majority in *Weeks,* that without an exclusionary rule to deter Fourth Amendment violations, the Fourth Amendment "might as well be stricken from the Constitution." The dissenters thought it anomalous that the Fourth Amendment could be considered so fundamental as to apply to the states when, without the exclusionary rule, it was essentially denied the force of law.

b. Due Process Violations

Wolf provided that a state court could constitutionally admit evidence obtained in violation of the Fourth Amendment. However, the Due Process Clause itself, even before *Wolf,* provided protection against police activity which "shocked the conscience". In *Rochin v. California,* 342 U.S. 165, 72 S.Ct. 205, 96 L.Ed. 183 (1952), officers broke into the defendant's home and used force in an unsuccessful attempt to keep the defendant from swallowing capsules which he had placed in his mouth. They then took the defendant to a hospital and directed a doctor to pump his stomach, forcing the defendant to vomit up the capsules. The Supreme Court held that the capsules must be excluded because the conduct of the officers was so egregious that the defendant's right to due process was violated. Thus, after *Rochin,* the exclusionary rule is a constitutionally required remedy for evidence obtained in violation of the Due Process Clause, but not for violations of the Fourth Amendment only. See also *Irvine v. California,* 347 U.S. 128, 74 S.Ct. 381, 98 L.Ed. 561 (1954) (repeated entries into the defendant's home violated the Fourth Amendment, but exclusion was not constitutionally required under the Due Process Clause because there was no "coercion, violence or brutality to the person").

3. *Mapp v. Ohio*

In *Mapp v. Ohio,* 367 U.S. 643, 81 S.Ct. 1684, 6 L.Ed.2d 1081 (1961), the Court overruled *Wolf* in part and held that "all evidence obtained by searches and seizures in violation of the Constitution is, by that same authority, inadmissible in a state court." As the dissenters had in *Wolf,* the majority in *Mapp* reasoned that the Fourth Amendment would be little more than a "form of words", and deprived of the force of law, if illegally obtained evidence could be freely admitted in a criminal trial. The Court reasoned that things had changed since *Wolf* was decided: more states had adopted the *Weeks* rule in the interim, and therefore there was more unanimity on whether the exclusionary rule was implicit in the concept of ordered liberty. Also, experience since *Wolf* had shown to the Court that remedies other than the exclusionary rule had proved "worthless and futile."

a. Dissent in *Mapp*

The dissenters in *Mapp* argued that *Wolf* had been based on a "sensitive regard for our federal system and a sound recognition of this Court's remoteness from particular state problems" and that nothing had changed since *Wolf* to warrant imposing the exclusionary rule on the states.

B. THE EXCLUSIONARY RULE IS NOT REQUIRED BY THE FOURTH AMENDMENT

The Court in *Mapp* had stated that the exclusionary rule was "part and parcel of the Fourth Amendment's limitation upon governmental encroachment of individual privacy" and "an essential part of the Fourth And Fourteenth

Amendments." Recently, however, the Court has taken the position that the exclusionary rule is merely a *"court-made rule"* designed to deter violations of the Fourth Amendment, and that a court is *not constitutionally required* to exclude illegally obtained evidence. See *United States v. Calandra,* 414 U.S. 338, 94 S.Ct. 613, 38 L.Ed.2d 561 (1974) (the exclusionary rule is "a judicially-created remedy designed to safeguard Fourth Amendment rights generally through its deterrent effect, rather than a personal constitutional right of the party aggrieved").

1.   Rationale

The Court's most recent exposition of its rationale for concluding that the exclusionary rule has no constitutional basis is contained in *United States v. Leon,* 468 U.S. 897, 104 S.Ct. 3405, 82 L.Ed.2d 677 (1984). The Court gave the following reasons for its position:

—There is *nothing in the language* of the Fourth Amendment which refers to the exclusionary rule as a required remedy.

—An examination of the origin and purposes of the Fourth Amendment makes clear that the use of illegally obtained evidence at trial "works no new Fourth Amendment wrong." The Fourth Amendment is violated *when the illegal search or seizure is made*, not when the evidence is admitted at trial. Therefore the subsequent admission of the evidence cannot be part and parcel of the Fourth Amendment wrong. This is unlike a violation of the Due Process Clause, where the admission of unfairly obtained evidence *at trial* is the wrong that is addressed; in contrast to a Fourth Amendment violation, a Due Process violation occurs when the evidence is admitted at trial, and there is therefore a constitutional right to have it excluded. See *Mapp v. Ohio, supra* (Harlan, J., dissenting) (distinguishing a Fourth Amendment violation from a confession obtained in violation of the Due Process Clause: "That [the Due Process right] is a *procedural right,* and that its violation occurs at the time [the defendant's] improperly obtained statement is admitted at trial, is manifest.").

—Since the Fourth Amendment violation is fully complete upon the search or seizure, the exclusionary rule "is neither intended nor able to cure the invasion of the defendant's rights which he has already suffered."

—Therefore, the rule can only be justified as a judicially-created remedy designed to *deter future violations* of the Fourth Amendment.

2.   Response

In *Leon,* Justice Brennan's dissent attacks the majority's holding that the exclusionary rule is not constitutionally required. He makes the following points:

—The fact that the exclusionary rule is "court-made" is not dispositive, since "many of the Constitution's most vital imperatives are stated in general terms and the task of giving meaning to these precepts is therefore left to subsequent judicial decisionmaking." In fact, the Bill of *Rights* does not establish an explicit remedy for any of the rights set forth. But it cannot seriously be argued that the Framers intended that the Bill of Rights would be hortatory only. The Framers did not envision such a thing as a Bill of Rights without meaningful remedies.

—The argument separating the officer's wrong from the subsequent admission of the evidence at trial is an unacceptably narrow view of Government. According to Justice Brennan, the Fourth Amendment "restrains the power of the government as a whole," and "the judiciary is responsible, no less than the executive, for ensuring that constitutional rights are protected."

—The majority's separation of the search from the admission of evidence at trial also reflects an unduly narrow conception of the search and seizure process. As Justice Brennan put it: "Because seizures are executed principally to secure evidence, and because such evidence generally has utility in our legal system only in the context of a trial supervised by a judge, it is apparent that the admission of illegally obtained evidence implicates the same constitutional concerns as the initial seizure of that evidence."

—Without the exclusionary rule, the Government would be allowed to profit from its own wrong. Such a possibility would have been rejected by the Framers, because the very purpose of the Bill of Rights was to control Government wrongdoing.

3. Applicability to the States

If the Constitution does not require the exclusion of evidence obtained in violation of the Fourth Amendment, it may be difficult to justify the Supreme Court's ruling in *Mapp* that the state courts must apply the exclusionary rule. Unlike the Federal courts over which the Supreme Court has supervisory authority, the Supreme Court's power over state courts is limited to questions of Federal constitutional law and other Federal law. Yet the Court, while rejecting *Mapp's* assertion that the exclusionary rule is required by the Fourth Amendment, has never rejected *Mapp's* holding that state courts must apply the exclusionary rule whenever a Federal court must do so. The Court has not chosen to explain its source of authority over state courts as to an exclusionary rule without a constitutional basis.

C. THE COST–BENEFIT ANALYSIS OF THE EXCLUSIONARY RULE

Since the Court has held that the exclusionary rule is not required as a matter of constitutional law, the viability of the exclusionary rule depends upon weighing the costs of the rule against the benefits it provides by deterring Fourth Amendment violations. The application of the cost-benefit analysis has sparked considerable debate about the validity and usefulness of the exclusionary rule.

1.   **Arguments Against the Exclusionary Rule: The Costs Outweigh the Benefits**
     Those who oppose the exclusionary rule argue that the cost of the rule outweighs the benefits it provides by deterring Fourth Amendment violations. The following points are most frequently made against the exclusionary rule:

     —The cost of the rule is the loss of admittedly reliable evidence, such as narcotics illegally seized in the search of a car. The exclusion of reliable evidence is a substantial cost because it may allow "the guilty to go free because the constable blundered."

     —The exclusionary rule also imposes a cost in the loss of public respect for the criminal justice system. When guilty criminals are set free on what the public may view as a "technicality," the integrity of the criminal justice system may well decline in the eyes of the public. Given these substantial costs, opponents of the rule argue, there must be an especially compelling showing of benefits provided by the exclusionary rule.

     —In terms of benefits, the exclusionary rule only protects those who are by definition guilty, and provides no meaningful protection to those who are innocent. For example, if an officer wants to conduct an illegal search simply to harass an innocent person, and is neither seeking nor expecting to find evidence, the threat of exclusion provides no meaningful deterrent effect.

     —Even in the context of a criminal investigation, the exclusionary rule is not a meaningful deterrent in most cases. The rule "does not apply any direct sanction to the individual official whose illegal conduct results in the exclusion of evidence." *Bivens v. Six Unknown Named Agents,* 403 U.S. 388, 91 S.Ct. 1999, 29 L.Ed.2d 619 (1971) (Burger, C.J., concurring). The fact that evidence is excluded from a trial months and even years after the officer's misconduct will have no meaningful effect on the wrongdoing officer.

     —The Fourth Amendment, as applied by the courts, is not clear enough in most cases to warrant a sanction for its misapplication by officers in the field. In some cases, for example, evidence is excluded by a divided appellate court on a close question. Opponents of the exclusionary rule argue that deterrence is particularly attenuated in such circumstances.

2. Arguments in Favor of the Exclusionary Rule: The Benefits Outweigh the Costs

Those who favor the exclusionary rule generally make the following arguments in its support:

—The cost of the loss of illegally obtained but reliable evidence is not imposed by the exclusionary rule, but rather by the Fourth Amendment itself. It is the Fourth Amendment which renders the search illegal. Thus, if the officer had complied with the Fourth Amendment, the evidence would never have been obtained in the first place. The Fourth Amendment *does* allow some guilty people to go free, because an officer who follows the law may be prevented from conducting some searches and seizures which could uncover evidence against a guilty person. But, as Justice Traynor has stated, any argument about cost to society was rejected when the Fourth Amendment was adopted. *People v. Cahan,* 44 Cal.2d 434, 282 P.2d 905 (1955).

—Even if the cost is considered the loss of reliable evidence, that cost is overrated because the vast majority of suppression motions are denied. The fact that so few suppression motions are granted is testimony to the fact that the exclusionary rule has been effective in shaping police conduct and conforming it to the law.

—Even if evidence is illegally obtained, it does not follow that "the guilty go free." In many cases, the guilty defendant's conviction is upheld because the admission of the illegally obtained evidence was harmless error. Other rules such as independent source and inevitable discovery are often invoked to allow admission of the evidence even though the officers acted illegally.

—The exclusionary rule does not protect only the guilty any more than the Fourth Amendment itself protects only the guilty. The guilty defendant is allowed to invoke the exclusionary rule in order to protect innocent persons from unlawful police activity. See Loewy, *The Fourth Amendment as a Device for Protecting the Innocent,* 81 Mich.L.Rev. 907 (1983) (Fourth Amendment can be invoked by the guilty because it is necessary to protect the innocent); *Arizona v. Hicks,* 480 U.S. 321, 107 S.Ct. 1149, 94 L.Ed.2d 347 (1987) ("there is nothing new in the realization that the Constitution sometimes insulates the criminality of a few in order to protect the privacy of us all").

—The argument that the exclusionary rule imposes no meaningful punishment of the offending officer misperceives the nature of the deterrent effect provided by the exclusionary rule. The rule is calculated to prevent, not to repair. The rule is designed to destroy the practical value of illegally obtained evidence. If illegally obtained evidence is of no practical use, police officers (and police departments, which are unlikely to encourage officers to engage in futile activity) will have no incentive to engage in illegal activity; they would have such an incentive if not for the exclusionary rule. It is in this broader sense that the exclusionary rule can have, and does have, significant deterrent effect. As Justice Traynor stated: "The objective of the exclusionary rule is certainly not to compensate the defendant for the past wrong done to him any more than it is to penalize the officer for the past wrong he has done. The emphasis is forward." Traynor, *Mapp v. Ohio at Large in the Fifty States*, 1962 Duke L.J. 319.

—The evidence shows that the exclusionary rule has had a positive effect on law enforcement. Some indicators are: a significant increase in the amount of search warrant applications; more aggressive efforts to educate police on the laws of search and seizure; and increasing cooperation between police and prosecutors to ensure that evidence is legally obtained so that it can be used at trial. See Orfield, *Deterrence, Perjury, and the Heater Factor: An Exclusionary Rule in the Chicago Criminal Courts*, 63 U.Colo.L.Rev. 75 (1992).

—Even if the exclusionary rule has limited practical effect, it has significant symbolic effect. As Chief Justice Burger stated, in the absence of some "meaningful alternative", the exclusionary rule should not be abolished lest "law enforcement officials were suddenly to gain the impression, however erroneous, that all constitutional restraints on police had somehow been removed." *Bivens, supra.*

3. Current Supreme Court Position

The Court has refused to abandon the exclusionary rule, even though it has expressed doubts about its efficacy and has often alluded to the costs imposed by the rule. Part of the reason for its adherence is that the Court is of the view that there is currently no effective replacement for the rule. Nonetheless, the Court has often chosen to create exceptions to the exclusionary rule for situations in which the Court views the costs of the rule to significantly outweigh the deterrence benefits that the rule would provide. See *Stone v. Powell*, 428 U.S. 465, 96 S.Ct. 3037, 49 L.Ed.2d 1067 (1976) (adhering to the view that the exclusionary rule provides benefits in deterrence, but holding that the costs of the rule outweigh it benefits when applied to habeas corpus actions).

4. Alternatives to the Exclusionary Rule

The Court has indicated that it will not abolish the rule in the absence of a "meaningful alternative." The efficacy of proposed alternatives is as hotly debated as the exclusionary rule itself. Recall that the Court in *Mapp* applied the exclusionary rule to the states in the first place because it was convinced that other remedies "have been worthless and futile."

a. **Civil Damage Actions**
The civil damage action is the most frequently cited alternative to the exclusionary rule. Currently, a person whose Fourth Amendment rights have been violated has a civil cause of action under state tort laws, as well as a Federal cause of action under 42 U.S.C.A. § 1983 (if the violation is by a state or local official) or *Bivens, supra* (if the violation is by a Federal official). Plaintiffs in such actions generally have encountered three major, often insurmountable problems which may render the possibility of a civil action an ineffective deterrent. First, victims of illegal searches and seizures are often criminals, and thus are not sympathetic plaintiffs; also, current doctrines of immunity often preclude recovery. Second, even if a jury would grant recovery, the monetary award for most Fourth Amendment violations would probably be quite small—often too small to justify bringing the case. Third, under current law, the governmental entity is often not liable for the judgment even when it is determined that the police officer acted unconstitutionally. This means that plaintiffs are usually left to attempt recovery from individual officers, who are often unable to pay.

b. **"Fortified" Tort Remedy**
Some have argued that a "fortified" tort remedy would be an effective replacement to the exclusionary rule. Under this view, the Government would be made liable for an officer's illegal behavior; liquidated damages would be available in cases where actual damages are minimal; and evidentiary rules would be employed to protect the plaintiff from the jury's possible assumption that the plaintiff is unworthy of recovery. Currently, no American jurisdiction has adopted such a fortified tort remedy.

c. **Criminal Prosecution of Offending Officers**
Some have suggested that criminal prosecution of an officer who conducts an illegal search or seizure would be an effective replacement for the exclusionary rule. Proponents contend that this would impose a meaningful deterrent on police officers, rather than the more diffuse deterrent effect claimed by the exclusionary rule. Critics of this alternative argue that it will not be a meaningful alternative because juries would be unlikely to convict a policeman of a crime merely because the officer conducted an illegal search or seizure. Also, a criminal prosecution would require some showing of intent, which would mean that many violations of the Fourth Amendment standards of objective reasonableness would go unpunished and undeterred.

d. **Police Regulations and Departmental Discipline**
Another proposed alternative is to have police departments establish rules of conduct to comply with the Fourth Amendment, and to require the departments to sanction rule violators by way of internal discipline.

Critics of this proposal argue that it would be unwise to trust police departments with the job of self-regulation, and that the current proliferation of police department rulemaking and internal discipline is in response to the exclusionary rule. Critics contend that in the absence of the exclusionary rule, there would be no assurance that departments would meaningfully seek to comply with Fourth Amendment standards.

II. STANDING TO INVOKE THE EXCLUSIONARY RULE

When a criminal defendant invokes the exclusionary rule on the ground that evidence was obtained in violation of the Fourth Amendment, there may be a question of whether the defendant is a proper party to assert the illegality and to obtain exclusion. This question is one of whether the defendant has "standing" to assert a Fourth Amendment violation.

A. FOURTH AMENDMENT RIGHTS ARE PERSONAL
Fourth Amendment rights are personal rights, and the standing requirement assures that a defendant does not obtain exclusion of evidence unless his own personal Fourth Amendment rights were violated. As the Court pointed out in *Jones v. United States,* 362 U.S. 257, 80 S.Ct. 725, 4 L.Ed.2d 697 (1960), it is not sufficient for the defendant to claim that he was prejudiced "only through the use of evidence gathered as a consequence of a search or seizure directed at someone else."

1. Deterrent Effect
On several occasions, the Court has recognized that the exclusionary rule would have a greater deterrent effect if it were applied in all cases in which illegally obtained evidence is offered against a criminal defendant. Before the search, the officer would know that the evidence obtained would be inadmissible not only as to the person whose rights would be violated, but as to any other person against whom the evidence would be relevant. But the Court has rejected the notion that this incremental deterrent effect is worth the substantial cost of exclusion in cases where the defendant's personal rights have not been violated. For example, the Court in *Alderman v. United States,* 394 U.S. 165, 89 S.Ct. 961, 22 L.Ed.2d 176 (1969), held that the defendant could not object to evidence obtained from an illegal wiretap of another co-defendant's conversation. The Court declared that it was not convinced that "the additional benefits of extending the exclusionary rule to other defendants would justify further encroachment upon the public interest in prosecuting those accused of crime and having them acquitted or convicted on the basis of all the evidence which exposes the truth."

2. Supervisory Power
The Court held in *United States v. Payner,* 447 U.S. 727, 100 S.Ct. 2439, 65 L.Ed.2d 468 (1980), that Federal courts may not exercise their supervisory

power over the conduct of litigation to exclude evidence in situations where the standing requirement is not met. In *Payner*, IRS agents investigating Payner stole the briefcase of another person and photocopied hundreds of documents. These were all offered in Payner's trial. The district court invoked its supervisory authority to exclude the evidence even though Payner had no standing. The court relied on the blatant and intentional nature of the Fourth Amendment violation. But the Supreme Court reversed, concluding that the balance of deterrence and cost that was reached in establishing the standing requirement did not change simply "because the court has elected to analyze the question under the supervisory power instead of the Fourth Amendment. In either case, the need to deter the underlying conduct and the detrimental impact of excluding the evidence remains precisely the same."

B. REASONABLE EXPECTATION OF PRIVACY

In *Jones v. United States, supra,* the Court held that a defendant who is "legitimately on the premises" where a search occurs, had standing to challenge its legality. Later, however, in *Rakas v. Illinois,* 439 U.S. 128, 99 S.Ct. 421, 58 L.Ed.2d 387 (1978), the Court asked itself "whether it serves any useful analytical purpose" to consider the standing question "distinct from the merits of a Fourth Amendment claim." The Court concluded that "the better analysis forthrightly focuses on the extent of a particular defendant's rights under the Fourth Amendment, rather than on any theoretically separate, but invariably intertwined concept of standing." Accordingly, "standing" questions are now resolved by substantive principles of Fourth Amendment law. The question is no longer whether a person is legitimately on the premises, but whether a person has a legitimate expectation of privacy in the area or thing that was searched.

1. Two–Pronged Test

Under *Rakas,* there is a two-pronged test to determine whether the defendant's personal rights are violated, so that he has "standing" to invoke the exclusionary rule. The two requirements are identical to the requirements established under *Katz* and its progeny to determine whether a search has occurred at all. See the discussion of *Katz, supra.* First, the person challenging the search must demonstrate a *subjective expectation* of privacy in the place searched or a possessory interest in the thing seized. Second, the person must demonstrate that this subjective expectation is one that *society accepts as reasonable.*

2. Burden on Defendant

The defendant "bears the burden of proving that he had a legitimate expectation of privacy that was violated by the challenged search and seizure." *Rawlings v. Kentucky,* 448 U.S. 98, 100 S.Ct. 2556, 65 L.Ed.2d 633 (1980).

3. Different Application From *Katz* Test

While the *Rakas* test for "standing" is identical to that applied under *Katz* for whether a search has occurred, the analysis for the two questions will differ somewhat. The question traditionally labelled as standing—whether the defendant's personal rights were violated—is not identical to the question of whether any Fourth Amendment search or seizure has occurred at all. For example, the police may have violated a legitimate expectation of privacy (for instance by entering a house) and yet the defendant may not have standing to object if *he* had no legitimate expectation of privacy in the premises. In other cases, such as with an aerial overflight, there will be no search at all and therefore the court will never reach the question of "standing." It follows that the question of whether personal rights have been violated is still a separate question from whether a search has occurred, even though both questions are governed by the same two-pronged test.

4. "Legitimately on the Premises" Test Rejected

Applying its "legitimacy of expectation" test, the Court in *Rakas* rejected the rule in *Jones,* which had provided that a person had standing to object to a search so long as he was legitimately on the premises. *Rakas,* which is discussed in greater detail *infra,* denied standing to a passenger who attempted to challenge an automobile search. The Court reasoned that a person legitimately on the premises may well not have a legitimate expectation of privacy in the particular area that is searched. For example, the "premises" test would have permitted a "casual visitor who has never seen, or been permitted to visit the basement of another's house, to object to a search of the basement if the visitor happened to be in the kitchen of the house at the time of the search." Clearly such a person would not have the right to object to a search under the expectation test adopted by *Rakas,* since the visitor would have no legitimate expectation of privacy in an area where he had never even entered or had access. The Court concluded that the "legitimately on the premises" test was overbroad and inconsistent with the premise that Fourth Amendment rights are personal rights.

a. Dissent in *Rakas*

Justice White, writing for the four dissenters in *Rakas,* argued that the *Jones* "legitimately on the premises" rule was an easily applied rule that reasonably effectuated the deterrent purposes of the exclusionary rule. In contrast, he argued, the majority's "legitimate expectation of privacy" rule is vague and indeterminate, and "undercuts the force of the exclusionary rule." He concluded that the majority's rule "invites police to engage in patently unreasonable searches every time an automobile contains more than one occupant." In such a situation, officers could be fairly certain that the illegally obtained evidence could be used against at least one of the people in the car.

5. Target Theory Rejected

The problem of target standing arises in a variety of contexts. For example, if officers are searching for a suspect in someone else's home, the fact that the officer enters the home without a warrant will violate the Fourth Amendment rights of the homeowner, not the suspect. See *Steagald v. United States,* discussed in the section on arrests. Under a "target" theory of standing, the suspect would be allowed to vicariously assert the homeowner's Fourth Amendment rights, since the police entered the house in order to arrest the suspect—he was the target of their activity. But the Court in *Rakas* specifically *rejected* the notion that a person has standing to object to a search merely because he is the person against whom the search is directed. As shown in the *Steagald* situation, a person may be a target, and yet the illegal search does not violate the target's expectation of privacy, but rather the privacy interests of another.

a. Deterrent Effect

The defendants in *Rakas* argued that target standing is necessary to guarantee the deterrent effect of the exclusionary rule. They reasoned that, without target standing, officers may decide to engage in illegal searches of third parties, knowing that the evidence could be used against their target, and unconcerned about the fact that it could not be used against the third party whose rights were violated. But the Court in *Rakas* responded that sufficient deterrent effect remained because the third party whose rights are violated "may be able to recover damages for the violation of his Fourth Amendment rights." So while the exclusionary rule would not deter the misconduct, the threat of civil sanction would operate as a substitute deterrent. The Court also noted its reluctance to extend the "substantial social cost" of the exclusionary rule by allowing it to be invoked by an enlarged class of persons.

6. Application of Expectation Test to the Facts of *Rakas*

In *Rakas,* police stopped a car in which the defendants were riding as passengers. The officers suspected that the vehicle was connected with a recent robbery. The officers searched the passenger compartment of the car and found a sawed-off shotgun under the front passenger seat and a box of shotgun shells in the locked glove compartment. The defendants did not own the car, and they never asserted a property interest in the shotgun or shells. The Court held that a person does not have a legitimate expectation of privacy in areas underneath the seat or in the glove compartment merely on the basis of being a passenger in the car.

a. Result in *Jones* Remains Sound

While the Court rejected the rule from *Jones* that standing is automatically conferred on a person legitimately on the premises, the Court noted that the *result* in *Jones* was correct. This was because the defendant in *Jones* had a legitimate expectation of privacy in the premises, beyond merely being present. In *Jones,* the defendant was arrested in the apartment of an absent friend, and drugs were found in the apartment. The friend had given Jones the right to use the entire apartment, and Jones had a key with which he could come and go. Moreover, with the exception of his friend, Jones had "complete dominion and control over the apartment and could exclude others from it." As such, *Jones* involved "significantly different factual circumstances" from those presented by the passengers in *Rakas;* Jones had a legitimate expectation of privacy in the premises while the defendants in *Rakas* did not.

b.   **Standing to Contest the Seizure**

Defendants in *Rakas* sought to contest the legality of the search of the car. They did not contend that the *stop* of the car was illegal. Lower courts have made it clear that a passenger has standing to object to the stop of a vehicle, since every passenger suffers *personal* inconvenience when the vehicle is seized. See *United States v. Greer,* 939 F.2d 1076 (5th Cir.1991) (passengers in car had standing to object to stop of car, but not to a search, since they claimed no ownership interest in the car or in the property seized).

7.   **Owners**

Under *Rakas,* an owner of a car will generally have standing to object to a search of the car even if he is not present at the time. *United States v. Kiser,* 948 F.2d 418 (8th Cir.1991). But the same is not true with respect to a stop of a car. For example, in *United States v. Powell,* 929 F.2d 1190 (7th Cir.1991), a car owned by the defendant and containing drugs was being driven across country to the defendant's home in Illinois. The defendant was waiting for the car at home, but the car was stopped en route. The driver of the car consented to a search, and drugs were discovered. The court found that while the stop of the vehicle was illegal, the defendant lacked standing to object to it. The court held that standing to object to a stop of a car is generally limited to those who were actually stopped with the car. The fact that the defendant owned the car did not give him standing to object to the stop, since he was not at the scene and was not personally inconvenienced by the stop. The court reasoned that the intrusion of a vehicle stop is personal to those in the car when the stop occurs. The court noted that at some point, a detention of the vehicle may implicate the owner's right to use the property, whether or not he is at the scene—for example, if it was seized for an extended period of time while the defendant was waiting to use it. But this was not the case with a momentary stop when the defendant was 1000 miles away. The court therefore concluded that the owner of the car had standing to object to the search but not the seizure. However, since the *search* was legal due to valid consent, the evidence was properly admitted against the defendant.

8. Permissive Use

If property is used with the permission of the owner, then the user will ordinarily have an expectation of privacy in the areas for which permission is granted. See *United States v. Rubio–Rivera,* 917 F.2d 1271 (10th Cir.1990) ("Where the defendant offers sufficient evidence indicating that he has permission of the owner to use the vehicle, the defendant plainly has a reasonable expectation of privacy in the vehicle and standing to challenge the search of the vehicle."). The scope of the user's expectation of privacy will depend on the scope of permissive use granted by the owner. For example, in *United States v. Pena,* 961 F.2d 333 (2d Cir.1992) the defendant, who borrowed a car with the permission of the owner, challenged the search of the door panels of the car. The court remanded to determine whether the scope of the permitted use extended to the right to "lift off the door panel and slip items into the door cavity". If not, the defendant would have no standing to object to the search of that area. (Of course, on remand, it is unlikely that Pena could meet his burden of showing that the permissive use extended to the interior of the door panels).

9. Overnight Guests

The recent case of *Minnesota v. Olson,* 495 U.S. 91, 110 S.Ct. 1684, 109 L.Ed.2d 85 (1990), concerned a previously unresolved issue of standing: whether an overnight guest in a home has standing to object to his own warrantless arrest. Police had probable cause to arrest Olson, and probable cause to believe that Olson was located in the home of a friend where he had been staying. Without a warrant, the police entered the friend's home and found Olson and arrested him. Olson challenged the legality of the entry into the apartment to arrest him. The question for the Court was whether Olson had a legitimate expectation of privacy in the third party's home; the Court held that he did. Justice White, writing for the Court, stressed that a person's "status as an overnight guest is alone enough to show that he had an expectation of privacy in the home that society is prepared to accept as reasonable." He noted that overnight guests are unlikely to be confined to certain areas of the house, and are likely to have a measure of control over the premises. The Court specifically rejected the State's argument that a place must be one's home in order to have a legitimate expectation of privacy there.

10. Possessory Interest in Items Seized Is Insufficient

In *Rakas,* the Court mentioned in the course of its analysis that the defendants had not claimed a possessory interest in the gun and the shells. But it does not follow that a defendant has standing to contest the search of an area merely because the items *seized* in the search are owned by the defendant. This was made clear in *Rawlings v. Kentucky,* 448 U.S. 98, 100 S.Ct. 2556, 65 L.Ed.2d 633 (1980). In *Rawlings* police entered Marquess' home to arrest him. He was not there, but they saw and smelled indications of marijuana, so some officers went to obtain a search warrant, while others remained on the scene with the five persons present. These persons were told that they could leave if they submitted to a body search. Rawlings and Ms. Cox decided to remain on the premises. Later, the warrant arrived. The warrant did not cover the search of persons present, but the officers nonetheless forced Ms. Cox to empty her purse. The purse contained narcotics, which Rawlings claimed were his. Rawlings testified at the suppression hearing that shortly before the police arrived, Cox had agreed to carry the drugs for him in her purse. The Supreme Court held that Rawlings had no legitimate expectation of privacy in Cox' purse. The Court reasoned as follows: 1) prior to the "sudden bailment" Rawlings had never sought or received access to Cox' purse; 2) Rawlings had no right to exclude other persons from access to Cox' purse; 3) other individuals had in fact rummaged through the purse; and 4) the "precipitous nature of the transaction hardly supports a reasonable inference that petitioner took normal precautions to maintain his privacy." Thus, while ownership ordinarily justifies a reasonable expectation of privacy as to an area searched, it does not necessarily justify standing to object to a search merely because of ownership of the property ultimately *seized.* In *Rawlings,* the area searched was Cox' handbag—she would have standing to object to that search on the basis of ownership, but Rawlings did not.

a. Bailment Relationships

In *Rawlings,* the Court emphasized the "precipitous" nature of the bailment relationship, and the fact that others had access to the purse, as reasons to conclude that Rawlings lacked a legitimate expectation of privacy in the purse. *Rawlings* does not preclude a finding of a legitimate expectation of privacy for more ordinary bailment relationships. See *United States v. Alberts,* 721 F.2d 636 (8th Cir.1983) (defendant has standing where she stored her belongings in closed, opaque containers at the residence of another with that person's knowledge and permission, and there was no general access to the containers by other individuals); *United States v. Most,* 876 F.2d 191 (D.C.Cir.1989) (defendant had standing to object to the search of a bag he checked with a store clerk; the court states that *Rawlings* did not "establish any general rule that an individual forfeits his reasonable expectation of privacy in his belongings simply by entrusting them to the care of another").

Conversely, a bailee of property may be able to establish a legitimate expectation of privacy in the property, despite the lack of an ownership interest. Similar to the overnight guest in *Olson, supra,* a bailee has the right—and often the duty—to exclude others from property entrusted to him. See *United States v. Perea,* 986 F.2d 633 (2d Cir.1993) (defendant who was delivering another person's duffel bag had standing to object to its search: "a person transporting luggage as a bailee, or at least with the permission of the owner, has a reasonable expectation of privacy that society would recognize").

b. Objecting to the Seizure

While Rawlings had no right to object to the search of Cox' purse, he would have a right to object to the *seizure* of his property contained in the purse. A seizure would implicate Rawlings' *personal* Fourth Amendment possessory interest in the item seized. See Knox, *Some Thoughts on the Scope of the Fourth Amendment and Standing to Challenge Searches and Seizures,* 40 Mo.L.Rev. 1 (1975). So for example, if police seized Rawlings' diary, or knife, from Cox' purse in the absence of probable cause, Rawlings would have standing to object to the seizure and the items could be subject to exclusion. Under the facts of *Rawlings,* however, the defendant's right to object to the seizure did him little good, since the items seized were narcotics, and the officer clearly had probable cause to seize these items under the plain view doctrine.

11. Disassociation With the Object of the Search

Where a defendant disavows any knowledge of or interest in property that is being searched or seized, such an action is inconsistent with a reasonable expectation of privacy, and the defendant will not have standing to object to the police activity.

a. Express Disassociation

The defendant's disavowal of an interest may be express. For example, in *United States v. Rush,* 890 F.2d 45 (7th Cir.1989), the defendant met a traveler at a train station and carried the suitcase that the traveler brought with him. When approached by police officers, the defendant disclaimed ownership of the suitcase and the traveler admitted ownership. The court held that the defendant had no standing to object to the search of the suitcase.

b. Disavowal by Conduct

A defendant may by his conduct be deemed to have disavowed an expectation of privacy. An example of this proposition is *United States v. Boruff,* 909 F.2d 111 (5th Cir.1990). Boruff bought a truck for use in a drug-smuggling scheme. He put the title, registration and insurance in the name of his co-conspirator, Taylor. Boruff added improvements to the truck, and it was understood that, if the truck were sold, the proceeds would go to Boruff. Taylor drove the truck to Mexico, followed closely by Boruff, who was driving a rented car. A suspicious border patrol agent stopped the truck and searched it. Boruff kept driving and was apprehended shortly thereafter. Boruff sought to exclude the evidence obtained in the search of the truck, but the court held that Boruff had failed to establish an expectation of privacy in the truck. The court reasoned that despite his ownership of the truck, "Boruff did everything he could to disassociate himself from the truck in the event it was stopped by law enforcement officials." See also *United States v. Lehder–Rivas,* 955 F.2d 1510 (11th Cir.1992) (where defendant left a locked suitcase with another and promised to pick it up within three months, but had still not picked it up 14 months later, he no longer retained an expectation of privacy in the suitcase).

c.   Use of Aliases and Other Efforts at Concealment

If a package is sent by common carrier, it is clear in most circumstances that the addressee has an expectation of privacy in the package, and can object to any illegal search of it. *United States v. Jacobsen,* 466 U.S. 109, 104 S.Ct. 1652, 80 L.Ed.2d 85 (1984) ("letters and other sealed packages are in the general class of effects in which the public at large has a legitimate expectation of privacy"). But what if the addressee is a fictitious person—an alias for the defendant? If an officer opens the package illegally, has the defendant lost his expectation of privacy by hiding his identity? Is this tantamount to disavowal of an interest in the package? Most courts have held that the use of a fictitious name does not deprive the defendant of the right to assert an objection to the search of a package which the defendant is entitled to receive.

> ***Example:***   In *United States v. Villarreal,* 963 F.2d 770 (5th Cir.1992), the defendant had a receipt for a 55 gallon drum shipped by a common carrier. He objected to the search of the drum. The court held that he had a legitimate expectation of privacy in the drum, even though the receipt was made out to a fictitious name. The court noted that Villarreal retained possession of the receipt, "which was the only indication of ownership available" and that he took possession of the drum and drove off with it. Distinguishing the facts in *Boruff, supra,* where Boruff retained no formal indicia of ownership of the truck and was not present when the truck was searched, the court concluded that it "could hardly be said that [Villarreal] disassociated himself from the object of the search."

12.   Coconspirator Standing

The Ninth Circuit Court of Appeals carved out a "coconspirator exception" to the general *Rakas* rule against vicarious assertion of Fourth Amendment rights. Under the Ninth Circuit rule, a defendant had standing to challenge a search of an area in which one of his coconspirators had a legitimate expectation of privacy, so long as the conspirators exercised "joint control" over the area searched. For example, in *United States v. Padilla,* 960 F.2d 854 (9th Cir.1992), officers searched a car being driven by a drug courier for the conspiracy. Those conspirators who exercised a "supervisory role" in the transportation of the drugs were held to have demonstrated "joint control and supervision over the drugs and vehicle." Consequently they had standing under the Ninth Circuit rule.

a. Rejection of Coconspirator/Joint Venture Standing

The Supreme Court granted certiorari in *Padilla*. In a brief, unsigned, unanimous opinion, the Court reversed the Ninth Circuit and rejected the coconspirator standing rule. *United States v. Padilla,* __ U.S. __, 113 S.Ct. 1936, 123 L.Ed.2d 635 (1993). The Court reasoned that to permit standing merely because the defendant was a coconspirator with managerial responsibility for the venture would be inconsistent with the *Rakas* requirement that the defendant must have a personal expectation of privacy implicated by the search. A joint venture does not itself establish that each party to the venture has a legitimate expectation of privacy when another party, or another party's property, is searched.

C. AUTOMATIC STANDING

Up until the 1960's, a defendant attempting to establish standing at a suppression hearing was confronted with a dilemma. In order to establish standing, the defendant would often testify that he owned or possessed the item which he sought to have suppressed, or that he owned or controlled the area in which the item was found. But this suppression hearing testimony was itself an admission of guilt, which could thereafter be admitted against the defendant at the trial. To assert his Fourth Amendment rights, the defendant often found it necessary to incriminate himself. To rectify this problem, the Supreme Court developed the doctrine of *automatic standing* in *Jones v. United States,* 362 U.S. 257, 80 S.Ct. 725, 4 L.Ed.2d 697 (1960).

1. Rationale of *Jones*

The Court in *Jones* reasoned that "to hold that petitioner's failure to acknowledge interest in the narcotics or the premises prevented his attack upon the search, would be to permit the Government to have the advantage of contradictory positions as a basis for conviction." On the one hand, the Government could have the evidence admitted on the ground that the defendant did not prove a possessory or ownership interest. On the other hand, the Government could argue to the trier of fact that the defendant had a possessory or ownership interest in the drugs. The Court concluded that "the prosecution here thus subjected the defendant to the penalties meted out to one in lawless possession while refusing him the remedies designed for one in that situation." The Court therefore held that, if the Government sought to convict a defendant on the basis of possession or ownership, this would eliminate the defendant's obligation to prove standing.

2. *Simmons* Rule

After *Jones*, the Court decided *Simmons v. United States,* 390 U.S. 377, 88 S.Ct. 967, 19 L.Ed.2d 1247 (1968). The defendant in *Simmons* could not benefit from the *Jones* rule because he was charged with bank robbery, a non-possessory offense. But the Court recognized that the defendant had the same dilemma as one charged with a possessory offense: to establish standing, he had to admit possession of the incriminating evidence that was seized; and this testimony could be used against him at trial. In *Simmons,* the Court established a *general* rule that a defendant's suppression hearing testimony cannot be used against him at trial. The Court found it "intolerable" that in order to assert his Fourth Amendment rights, a defendant would have to surrender his Fifth Amendment right not to incriminate himself.

3. **Automatic Standing Doctrine Abolished**

In *United States v. Salvucci,* 448 U.S. 83, 100 S.Ct. 2547, 65 L.Ed.2d 619 (1980), the Court abolished the automatic standing doctrine. The Court concluded that in light of *Simmons,* the reason for the rule had been eliminated, because *Simmons* "grants a form of use immunity" to defendants who assert their Fourth Amendment rights at a suppression hearing.

a. **Prosecutorial Inconsistency**

The Court in *Jones* had been concerned about the fact that the Government could take contradictory positions at the suppression hearing (i.e. that the defendant did not have a possessory interest) and at trial (i.e. that the defendant did have a possessory interest). The Court in *Salvucci* stated that it did not need to decide whether this risk of self-contradiction was weighty enough to support an automatic standing rule in the absence (after *Simmons*) of any risk of self-incrimination by the defendant. Rather, the Court concluded that after *Rakas* and *Rawlings,* "a prosecutor may simultaneously maintain that a defendant criminally possessed the seized good, but was not subject to a Fourth Amendment deprivation, without legal contradiction." The Court explained that "a person in legal possession of a good seized during an illegal search has not necessarily been subject to a Fourth Amendment deprivation."

b. **Risk of Impeachment**

The defendant in *Salvucci* argued that an automatic standing rule was required even after *Simmons,* because *Simmons* did not necessarily prevent a defendant from being *impeached* with his suppression hearing testimony, should he decide to testify at trial. The Court responded that it had not been decided whether *Simmons* precludes the use of suppression testimony for impeachment purposes, but that the danger of impeachment was an issue "which more aptly relates to the proper breadth of the *Simmons* rule, and not to the need for retaining automatic standing." Subsequently, lower courts have held that *Simmons* does not prevent the use of suppression hearing testimony for impeachment purposes. *People v. Sturgis,* 58 Ill.2d 211, 317 N.E.2d 545 (1974). The Supreme Court has not specifically decided this question.

III. EXCLUSION OF "THE FRUIT OF THE POISONOUS TREE"

A. INTRODUCTION

In most cases in which the exclusionary rule is invoked, the defendant seeks exclusion of the very evidence that was found in the illegal search or seizure. For example, if the officer conducts an illegal search of a car and discovers narcotics, the defendant will invoke the exclusionary rule to exclude the narcotics. The narcotics are termed the "direct" or "primary" evidence of the illegal search. In many cases, however, the defendant challenges evidence which was *derived from* an initial illegality. For example, officers may conduct an illegal search of a car which uncovers a list of homes where drugs are stored. They proceed to those homes, and their surveillance indicates evidence of drug trafficking. They obtain warrants to search these homes and seize the drugs they find. In this case, the list seized from the car is the primary evidence in relationship to the illegal search, while the subsequently discovered drugs are the derivative evidence. In these situations, it must be decided whether the exclusionary rule should be applied to exclude derivative as well as primary evidence—or, as the Court has put it, whether the exclusionary rule should apply to the "fruit of the poisonous tree."

B. EXCLUSIONARY RULE APPLIES TO "TAINTED" EVIDENCE

In *Silverthorne Lumber Co. v. United States,* 251 U.S. 385, 40 S.Ct. 182, 64 L.Ed. 319 (1920), officers illegally seized some documents from the Silverthornes. A court ordered the documents returned, but before doing so, the prosecutor made copies, and then caused the grand jury to issue a subpoena for the very same documents that had been seized. The Court found that the subpoenas were invalid. It reasoned that "the essence of a provision forbidding the acquisition of evidence in a certain way is that not merely evidence so acquired shall not be used before the Court but that it shall not be used at all." In other words, the exclusionary rule applies not only to the evidence originally obtained in an illegal search, but also to all evidence derived from the evidence obtained in the illegal search. The derived evidence is "tainted". It is "fruit of the poisonous tree." In *Silverthorne,* the prosecutor clearly used information from the illegally seized documents (indeed, the information was a copy of the document) in order to obtain the subpoena.

1. Standing Requirement Must Be Met

A defendant can successfully challenge derivative, tainted evidence only if he has standing to object to the original illegal search. In the previous example, where officers conduct an illegal search of a car and discover a list of drug locations, those who live at the drug locations, but have no privacy interest in the car, cannot argue that the subsequent searches are tainted by the illegal search of the car. To allow this would mean that they could assert the Fourth Amendment rights of another (i.e. the owner of the car), and this is not permitted under *Rakas, supra.* If the subsequent search is *itself* illegal (e.g. if it is conducted without probable cause), then those who live at the location would have the right to challenge that search. But, in the example given, the subsequent searches satisfy the Fourth Amendment requirements of warrant and probable cause. Only those with standing to object to the initial search can contend that evidence found in an otherwise legal search must be excluded because it is tainted by an earlier illegal search.

C. ATTENUATION

In some cases, the link between the illegal search or seizure and the evidence obtained is so attenuated that the evidence can no longer be meaningfully considered "tainted" or the "fruit of the poisonous tree." As Justice Frankfurter put it in a case where the Government sought to use information obtained from illegal wiretaps: "Sophisticated argument may prove a causal connection between information obtained through illicit wire-tapping and the Government's proof. As a matter of good sense, however, such connection may have become so attenuated as to dissipate the taint." *Nardone v. United States,* 308 U.S. 338, 60 S.Ct. 266, 84 L.Ed. 307 (1939). When evidence is so attenuated from the illegality, courts reason that the deterrent effect of the exclusionary rule is equally attenuated and that therefore the cost of excluding reliable evidence outweighs the negligible benefit of deterrence in these circumstances.

1. *Wong Sun*

The Court's leading case on attenuation is *Wong Sun v. United States,* 371 U.S. 471, 83 S.Ct. 407, 9 L.Ed.2d 441 (1963). The facts of *Wong Sun* are complicated, because there are several pieces of evidence, and the attenuation doctrine applies with different results as to the various pieces. Federal narcotics agents broke into Toy's apartment without probable cause, and handcuffed him. Toy immediately made a statement implicating Yee in the sale of narcotics. The agents went immediately to Yee, who surrendered heroin to them upon the officers' order to do so. Yee stated that he had bought the drugs from Toy and Wong Sun. Wong Sun was then illegally arrested, and both he and Toy were arraigned and released pending trial. Several days later, Wong Sun came to the offices of the Bureau of Narcotics, and was interrogated there. He was warned of his right to remain silent and his right to have a lawyer. Wong Sun confessed.

a. Possible "Fruits" in *Wong Sun*

There were two illegal police actions in *Wong Sun:* the entry into Toy's apartment, and the arrest of Wong Sun. There were three pieces of evidence which Toy and/or Wong Sun sought to exclude as tainted: 1) Toy sought to exclude the statement he made immediately after the illegal entry of his house; 2) Toy and Wong Sun both sought to exclude the drugs obtained from Yee; 3) Wong Sun sought to exclude his confession.

b. Test of Causation

The test set forth by the *Wong Sun* Court to determine whether there is a sufficient connection between the illegality and the evidence to justify exclusion is as follows: "whether, granting establishment of the primary illegality, the evidence to which instant objection is made has been come at by exploitation of that illegality or instead by means sufficiently distinguishable to be purged of the primary taint." It is clear that the Court rejected a "but for" test of taint. For example, there was little doubt Wong Sun would never have come to the officers and confessed but for his prior illegal arrest. Nonetheless, the Court rejected the proposition that "all evidence is fruit of the poisonous tree simply because it would not have come to light but for the illegal actions of the police." Thus, the confession could not be excluded as tainted unless the prior illegality was *exploited* in some meaningful way. The Court was concerned that a "but for" test would provide an unacceptably expansive application of the tainted fruit doctrine; in other words, the Court felt that the cost of excluding all evidence which has even a minimal "but for" connection to an illegality would outweigh the benefit of deterrence that such a rule would provide.

c. Application to the Facts of *Wong Sun*—Toy's Statement

The Court found that Toy's statement was subject to exclusion as fruit of the poisonous tree. The statement was made right after the illegal entry into his house (and in fact it was made while the illegality was continuing), and the Court noted that the intrusion was a serious violation of the Fourth Amendment, one that was likely to have had a significant effect on Toy. The Court rejected the argument that the taint of the illegal entry was "purged" by Toy's voluntary decision to confess. Given the fact that the confession was made during the course of an egregious illegal intrusion, the Court concluded that it was "unreasonable to infer that Toy's response was sufficiently an act of free will to purge the primary taint of the unlawful invasion."

d. Use of Narcotics Against Toy

The Court also held that the drugs turned over by Yee could not be used against Toy. The seizure of the drugs was the direct result of Toy's statement, which had already been held tainted by the illegal entry of Toy's apartment. Since one event followed immediately upon the other, the Court found no break in the chain of causation between the illegal entry of Toy's apartment and the drugs turned over by Yee.

e. Use of Narcotics Against Wong Sun

Even though the narcotics were tainted by the illegal entry into Toy's apartment, the Court found that they were admissible against Wong Sun. This was because, as discussed previously, a defendant's Fourth Amendment rights must be violated by the initial illegal search before he can object to the introduction of derivative evidence. Wong Sun had no legitimate expectation of privacy in Toy's apartment, and thus lacked standing to object to the entry of that apartment. As the Court stated, "the seizure of this heroin invaded no right of privacy of person or premises which would entitle Wong Sun to object to its use at his trial."

f. Use of Confession Against *Wong Sun*
Even though Wong Sun had initially been arrested without probable cause, the Court found that his subsequent confession was attenuated from this illegality. The Court reasoned that Wong Sun had been released for several days, and had returned voluntarily to the officers to make his statement. The Court therefore concluded that "the connection between the arrest and the statement had become so attenuated as to dissipate the taint."

2. Confessions and *Miranda* Warnings
In *Wong Sun,* the Court discussed the relationship between a Fourth Amendment violation and a subsequent confession. In *Brown v. Illinois,* 422 U.S. 590, 95 S.Ct. 2254, 45 L.Ed.2d 416 (1975), the Court returned to the same question but under radically different facts. Brown came into his apartment and found two policemen pointing guns at him. He was informed that he was under arrest for murder, handcuffed, and driven down to the police station. While at the station, Brown was twice given *Miranda* warnings and twice confessed. The first confession occurred 90 minutes after the arrest, the second occurred seven hours after the arrest. The lower court found that Brown had been arrested without probable cause, but held that the *Miranda* warnings broke the causal chain so that any subsequent statement was admissible so long as it was itself legally obtained. Brown did not claim that his confessions were themselves involuntary or illegally obtained. Rather, he claimed that they were tainted by the illegal arrest and that the *Miranda* warnings did not purge the taint.

a. *Miranda* Warnings Do Not Per Se Break the Chain of Causation
The Court in *Brown* held that both confessions were the tainted fruit of the illegal arrest and thus were improperly admitted at Brown's trial. It rejected the assumption of the lower courts that recitation of the *Miranda* warnings, in and of itself, was sufficient to purge the taint of an illegal arrest. The Court reasoned that such a rule would substantially diminish the deterrent effect of the exclusionary rule: "Any incentive to avoid Fourth Amendment violations would be eviscerated by making the warnings, in effect, a cure-all, and the constitutional guarantee against unlawful searches and seizures could be said to be reduced to a form of words."

b. ***Miranda* Warnings Are Relevant**
While the Court in *Brown* held that *Miranda* warnings were not
dispositive in dissipating the taint of an illegal search or seizure, it did
hold that the giving of warnings would be relevant in assessing the
connection between the illegality and the subsequent confession. What is
required is a case-by-case approach. The Court stated that the *Miranda*
warnings are an "important factor, to be sure" but that other relevant
factors included "the temporal proximity of the arrest and confession,
the presence of intervening circumstances, and, particularly, the purpose
and flagrancy of the official misconduct."

c. **Application to the Facts in *Brown***
The Court held that both of Brown's confessions were tainted by the
illegal arrest. The first confession occurred less than two hours after the
arrest, and "there was no intervening event of significance whatsoever."
This was in marked contrast with Wong Sun's confession, which
occurred several days after he had been arrested *and released*. The Court
also relied on the fact that the illegal arrest was a serious violation of
the Fourth Amendment, and thus the taint could not be easily
dissipated. According to the Court, "the impropriety of the arrest was
obvious" and the detectives wilfully engaged in the illegal arrest in order
to frighten and confuse Brown so that he would confess. Accordingly, the
deterrent purpose of the exclusionary rule would be well-served by
excluding the subsequent confessions. As to Brown's second confession,
the Court concluded that it "was clearly the result and fruit of the
first." Again there were no intervening acts such as consultation with
counsel, release, or arraignment by a magistrate. Also, the effect of the
first, tainted confession on the second was obvious; since Brown had
already confessed, he thought he had nothing to lose by confessing again.

d. **Burden on Government**
The Court in *Brown* made it clear that once an illegal search or seizure
is established, the Government has the burden of proving that the causal
chain is sufficiently attenuated to dissipate the taint of the illegality. See
also *United States v. Brady,* 842 F.2d 1313 (D.C.Cir.1988) (prosecution
has burden of proving that defendant's abandonment of property was not
tainted by illegal seizure).

e. **Progeny of *Brown***
Brown was held controlling in *Dunaway v. New York,* 442 U.S. 200, 99
S.Ct. 2248, 60 L.Ed.2d 824 (1979), where the defendant was arrested
without probable cause, brought down to the station, and confessed after
receiving *Miranda* warnings and waiving his rights. Again, the Court
rejected the notion that officers could "violate the Fourth Amendment
with impunity, safe in the knowledge that they could wash their hands
in the procedural safeguards of the Fifth." The Court also rejected the

argument that the confession should be admitted because it was voluntary. The Court explained that the question of taint is *not whether the derivative evidence is itself illegally obtained*—if it were itself illegally obtained, the evidence would be clearly inadmissible and a fruit of the poisonous tree question would not arise. Rather, the question is whether the confession, though voluntary, was obtained by *exploitation* of the previous Fourth Amendment violation.

Subsequently, in *Taylor v. Alabama,* 457 U.S. 687, 102 S.Ct. 2664, 73 L.Ed.2d 314 (1982), the Court found *Brown* and *Dunaway* controlling where a defendant was arrested without probable cause and confessed six hours later. He was given *Miranda* warnings three times and was allowed to see his fiance and friend for a short period while he was in custody. The Court found these factors, even cumulatively, to have been insufficient to purge the taint of the illegal arrest. The Court also held that a confession could be tainted fruit even though the police had not engaged in "flagrant or purposeful" misconduct—though of course the taint will be more easily purged if the violation is minor rather than serious.

f.   *Rawlings*

In *Rawlings v. Kentucky,* 448 U.S. 98, 100 S.Ct. 2556, 65 L.Ed.2d 633 (1980), the Court distinguished *Brown* and found that a confession was not the fruit of an illegal arrest. This was so even though the time between the confession and the arrest was just 45 minutes. The Court emphasized that temporal proximity was only one factor in assessing the taint of an illegal arrest, and that a taint may be purged in a relatively short period of time if the circumstances of the detention are not severe. In *Rawlings,* the detention was at a residence and occurred without a show of force, and the statements were spontaneous reactions to the discovery of evidence rather than the product of the illegal detention.

3.   Confession Made Outside the Home Is Not the Fruit of a *Payton* Violation

The Court distinguished *Brown, Dunaway* and *Taylor* in *New York v. Harris,* 495 U.S. 14, 110 S.Ct. 1640, 109 L.Ed.2d 13 (1990). In *Brown, Dunaway,* and *Taylor,* the Court excluded confessions as the fruit of arrests unsupported by probable cause. In contrast to the prior cases of arrest without probable cause, Harris confessed after an arrest made with probable cause, but without a warrant. Since Harris was arrested in his home, the lack of an arrest warrant violated *Payton v. New York,* 445 U.S. 573, 100 S.Ct. 1371, 63 L.Ed.2d 639 (1980). The challenged confession was made at the station an hour after the illegal entry into Harris' home. Harris argued that, under the previous cases, the confession was not attenuated from the illegal arrest and therefore should be excluded as the fruit of the poisonous tree.

a. Analysis in *Harris*

Justice White, writing for five members of the Court, held that a confession made outside the home cannot be the fruit of a *Payton* violation, and thus that Harris' confession was not tainted. The majority reasoned that, unlike the prior cases, Harris was not unlawfully in custody when he made the confession. Justice White stated that "the rule in *Payton* was designed to protect the physical integrity of the home; it was not intended to grant criminal suspects * * * protection for statements made outside their premises where the police have probable cause to arrest the suspect * * *." Thus, the violation of *Payton* constitutes an illegal *search* of the home, but not an illegal arrest; and while evidence obtained in the search of the home is subject to exclusion, there is no necessary connection between that search and a subsequent confession outside the home.

b. Deterrence

The majority in *Harris* stated that exclusion of the confession made outside the home was not necessary to deter violations of the *Payton* rule. Justice White argued that sufficient deterrence flows from the exclusion of any evidence found in the home during the arrest. The Court reasoned that the incremental deterrent effect attendant to excluding the confession as well would be minimal, since police in this situation by definition have probable cause to arrest outside the home: police could easily wait until the defendant left his home, then arrest him without a warrant and obtain a confession. As the Court stated, "it is doubtful therefore that the desire to secure a statement from a criminal suspect would motivate the police to violate *Payton*." According to the Court, the police do not need to violate *Payton* in order to arrest and interrogate a suspect (so excluding the results of the interrogation would provide no deterrent effect), whereas they may "need" to violate *Payton* to obtain evidence in the home that they could not otherwise obtain (so there is need for deterrence by excluding any evidence found in the home).

c. Dissent

Justice Marshall dissented in *Harris* in an opinion joined by Justices Brennan, Blackmun and Stevens. Justice Marshall contended that the rule adopted by the majority would give the police an incentive to violate *Payton*. He reasoned that the officer might enter illegally to save time (so that he wouldn't have to wait for the suspect to come out of the home), and that the officer could in any case exploit the in-home nature of the arrest to rattle the suspect and increase the likelihood of a confession. The dissent argued that *Payton* violations would not be sufficiently deterred if exclusion of evidence is limited to that found in the house: such a limited suppression would make the officer no worse off than if he had waited outside to make the arrest. There would thus be no cost, and a possibility of a benefit, to a warrantless in-home arrest.

d. No Retreat From *Brown*

Harris does not in any way question the fruits analysis in *Brown, Dunaway,* and *Taylor.* In those cases, the arrest was itself illegal because it was made without probable cause. *Harris* merely makes the point that a *Payton* violation does not even result in an illegal arrest. Rather, it is an illegal *search* of the home which has no necessary connection with a confession which subsequently occurs outside the home.

e. Seizure of Evidence in the Home in the Course of a *Payton* Violation

It is important to remember that in *Harris* the *Payton* violation turned up no evidence. Where the *Payton* violation does produce evidence (seen by the officers in the course of entering the home without a warrant) and is followed by a stationhouse confession that is *influenced* by the seizure of the tainted evidence, then the fruit of the poisonous tree doctrine may be applicable. There is thus a distinction between a confession which is the product of the *Payton* arrest (because the arrest itself is not illegal) and one which is the product of the *Payton* search (which is illegal).

Example: In *United States v. Beltran,* 917 F.2d 641 (1st Cir.1990), police arrested Beltran in her home without a warrant or exigent circumstances. During the arrest the police seized cocaine in plain view. They took the defendant to the stationhouse where she made incriminating statements. The court stated that "whether or the extent to which *Harris* applies may turn on questions of fact such as when the police seized the items in question or what motivated Ms. Beltran's statements" and remanded the case to the district court for a factual determination. Thus, if Beltran was rattled into a confession, not by the arrest, but by the fact that the police saw the cocaine, *Harris* would not apply and the confession could be tainted by the *Payton* violation.

f. Confessions in the Home

Unlike the facts of *Harris,* there will be a connection between the *Payton* violation and the confession if the defendant makes the statement *in the home* during the arrest. For example, in *United States v. McCraw,* 920 F.2d 224 (4th Cir.1990), a warrantless arrest in a hotel room in violation of *Payton* was followed by incriminating statements and a consent to search, which defendant gave immediately after the arrest and while still in the hotel room. Distinguishing *Harris,* the court suppressed the statements and the evidence, stating that "[a]ssuming that the consent to search and hotel room statements were voluntary by fifth amendment standards, the proximity in time and place between the arrest and the search and the statements and the absence of intervening circumstances nevertheless require suppression of this evidence to protect the physical integrity of the home and to vindicate the purpose of the Fourth Amendment."

4. Abandonment During the Course of an Illegal Search or Seizure

A taint question which often arises is where a defendant, who is the subject of an illegal search or seizure, tries to surreptitiously dispose of evidence, which is subsequently retrieved by the officers. Of course, the mere fact of abandonment in these circumstances does not mean that the evidence is admissible, any more than the voluntariness of a confession following an illegal arrest guarantees admissibility. If the abandonment was tainted by the illegal search or seizure, then it is subject to exclusion as fruit of the poisonous tree. See *United States v. Wilson,* 953 F.2d 116 (4th Cir.1991) (where defendant runs away from an illegal stop and throws drugs away while being chased, the drugs are not admissible because "Wilson's action was clearly the direct result of the illegal seizure, and it follows that the recovered drugs were the fruit of the illegality and must be suppressed.").

a. Calculated or Spontaneous

The question of whether abandoned property is tainted by a prior illegal search or seizure depends on whether the defendant has had sufficient time and opportunity to make a calculated decision, or whether instead the decision to abandon the property was a spontaneous reaction to the illegal activity. For example, in *People v. Boodle,* 47 N.Y.2d 398, 418 N.Y.S.2d 352, 391 N.E.2d 1329 (1979), the defendant was illegally arrested when a police officer told him to get into the patrol car to answer some questions. During the long drive to the station, Boodle threw a gun out the window. The court held that the taint of the illegal seizure was dissipated because the defendant's attempt to discard the gun "was an independent act involving calculated risk." The court concluded that Boodle's independent decision broke the causal link between the illegality and the recovery of the gun, so the evidence was held admissible.

In contrast, in *United States v. Wood,* 981 F.2d 536 (D.C.Cir.1992), the defendant was followed into a dark passageway by two officers who ordered him to "halt right there." Wood froze in his tracks, and dropped a gun between his feet. The officers handcuffed Wood, and then picked up the gun. Wood said, "that's not mine; I was just carrying it." The officers had no reasonable suspicion to stop Wood, and so the stop was found illegal. But the Government argued that the gun was admissible because Wood's act of discarding the gun was wholly independent of the illegal stop. The court rejected this argument and held that Wood's abandonment of the gun was a "spontaneous reaction to a sudden and unexpected confrontation with the police." The court stated that "unlike the defendant in *Boodle,* for example, Wood did not attempt to hide the gun on his person and then throw it out of the car window on the way to the police station." The court noted that "no time elapsed and no intervening events occurred between the commencement of the seizure and the dropping of the gun." Accordingly, the court held that the abandonment and the gun itself were tainted by the illegal seizure, and that the gun and Wood's statement were improperly admitted at trial.

5.   Criteria for Attenuation

While the determination of attenuation is a case-by-case approach, there are several factors which have been deemed relevant by the courts. Many of these factors are derived from the Supreme Court cases discussed above.

a.   Impact of the Illegality on the Defendant

The greater the impact on the defendant, the more likely it is that subsequently discovered evidence—such as a confession or contraband found after consent—will be tainted. For example, in *Brown,* the Court found it relevant that the officers made the illegal arrest to surprise and upset Brown. The arrest thus clearly influenced Brown's subsequent confessions. In contrast, in *United States v. Sheppard,* 901 F.2d 1230 (5th Cir.1990), defendant was at a border checkpoint when the officer stuck his head into the interior of the passenger compartment and smelled marijuana. The officer did not inform the defendant that he smelled marijuana. Rather, he simply directed the defendant's car to a secondary inspection area, and asked for consent to search the trunk. Consent was granted and drugs were found. The court assumed that the officer had acted illegally when he stuck his head into the passenger compartment; but it held that the evidence found in the trunk was not tainted by the illegal search. The court reasoned that the illegality had little effect on the defendant's decision to consent, because the defendant was unaware that the officer had smelled marijuana.

b.   Intervening Circumstances

Circumstances such as *Miranda* warnings, change of location, deliberative acts by the defendant, and acts by third parties are relevant in determining whether the chain of causation has been broken. As *Brown* teaches, however, no single intervening factor can be deemed automatically to purge the taint of an illegal search or seizure.

c.   Temporal Proximity

Obviously, the shorter the time between the challenged conduct and the discovery of the evidence, the more likely it is that the evidence will be found tainted. In particular, if the illegality is continuing at the time the evidence is discovered, it is extremely unlikely that a court will find that the taint has been dissipated. See *Sheppard, supra* (evidence not tainted where "the intrusion had ended prior to the consent").

d. Purpose and Flagrancy of the Misconduct

The more serious the misconduct, the more likely it is that it will affect subsequently obtained evidence, and vice versa. Also, courts assume that applying the exclusionary rule to derivative evidence is more likely to deter serious misconduct than it is to deter marginal misconduct. See *Sheppard, supra* (where officer momentarily stuck his head into the passenger compartment of a car at a border checkpoint, this was a "minor and technical" violation whose taint was dissipated by the time that consent was obtained).

6. Testimony of Live Witnesses

An illegal search or seizure may in some cases lead to the discovery of a witness who can give testimony against the defendant. Generally, courts have held that the witness' decision to testify against the defendant purges the taint from the illegality. As discussed above, the testimony will not be tainted fruit simply because the police would not even have discovered the witness "but for" the illegality.

a. *Ceccolini*

The leading case on whether witness testimony is the fruit of the poisonous tree is *United States v. Ceccolini,* 435 U.S. 268, 98 S.Ct. 1054, 55 L.Ed.2d 268 (1978). In *Ceccolini,* an officer stopped to talk with a friend who happened to be in Ceccolini's flower shop. While there, the officer illegally picked up and opened an envelope, and he found money and gambling slips. He then learned from his friend, who did not know of his discovery, that the envelope belonged to Ceccolini. The officer relayed this information to detectives who eventually referred it to the F.B.I. Four months later, an FBI agent questioned the officer's friend who was in the flower shop, without mentioning the illegally discovered gambling slips. The friend expressed a willingness to testify, and did so at the grand jury and at Ceccolini's trial.

b. Willingness to Testify Is Likely to Purge the Taint

The Court in *Ceccolini* held that, even though the path from the illegal search of the envelope to the witness' testimony was "straight and uninterrupted," the testimony was nonetheless so attenuated from the illegality as to not warrant its exclusion as the fruit of the poisonous tree. The Court stated that the "exclusionary rule should be invoked with much greater reluctance where the claim is based on a causal relationship between a constitutional violation and the discovery of a live witness than when a similar claim is advanced to support suppression of an inanimate object." This is because a live witness often makes a willing decision to testify, which is very likely to break the chain of causation. The Court also noted the cost of excluding the testimony of a live witness as tainted fruit. It would mean that a witness would be perpetually disabled "from testifying about relevant and material facts, regardless of how unrelated such testimony might be to the purpose of the originally illegal search or the evidence discovered thereby." Against this cost, the deterrent effect of the exclusionary rule was found to be minimal in the ordinary case, because an officer would be very unlikely to conduct an illegal search in order to find witnesses. Accordingly, the Court concluded that the exclusionary rule should only apply if there was an extremely close and direct link between the illegality and the witness' testimony.

c. Application to the Facts of *Ceccolini*
The Court found that the link between the illegality and the testimony in *Ceccolini* was far from extremely close and direct. It relied on the following five factors: 1) the testimony of the witness was an act of free will and was not induced by official authority as a result of the illegal search; 2) the information in the envelope was not used in questioning the witness; 3) four months elapsed between the illegal search and the F.B.I.'s contact with the witness; 4) both the identity of the witness and her relationship with Ceccolini "were well known to those investigating the case"; and 5) there was no evidence to indicate that the officer initiated the search "with the intent of finding a willing and knowledgeable witness to testify against" Ceccolini.

d. No Per Se Rule
Despite its reluctance to find that an illegal search will taint the subsequent testimony of a witness, the Court in *Ceccolini* declined to adopt a rule that the testimony of a live witness could never be excluded as the fruit of an illegal search or seizure. After *Ceccolini*, some live witnesses have been excluded from trial when there is an extremely close relationship between the illegality and the testimony—especially where the officer *exploits* the illegality to obtain the testimony.

Example: In *United States v. Ramirez–Sandoval*, 872 F.2d 1392 (9th Cir.1989), an officer conducted an illegal search of the defendant's van, which uncovered a list of names and numbers. Defendant was driving the van. One name on the list belonged to a man in the back of the van. The officer asked him what the number next to his name meant, and the man replied that he was an illegal alien and the number was the amount of money he had paid the defendant to be illegally transported to the United States. Defendant was tried for offenses involving harboring and transporting illegal aliens, and sought to exclude the testimony obtained from interrogation of the alien. The court, citing *Ceccolini*, stated that "verbal evidence, including live witness testimony, may be no less the fruit of official illegality than is tangible, documentary evidence." The court recognized that the "attenuated basis" rule is applied "more generously when the challenged evidence is live-witness testimony than when it is documentary evidence." Nonetheless the court found that the testimony of the alien was tainted by the illegal search of the van. The court distinguished *Ceccolini* on four grounds: 1) the illegally obtained list was used by the officer to question the witness; 2) no time elapsed between the illegal search and the initial questioning of the witness; 3) "the identities of the witnesses were not known to those investigating the case"; and 4) while the testimony was not coerced, the witness did not come forward of his own volition and his testimony "was induced by official authority as a result of the illegal search." See also *United States v. Rubalcava–Montoya*, 597 F.2d 140 (9th Cir.1978) (questioning of five illegal aliens found in a trunk pursuant to an illegal search; testimony of aliens was tainted fruit where statements were made immediately after illegal search and witnesses did not make an independent decision to come forward to testify).

7. Identifications

In *United States v. Crews*, 445 U.S. 463, 100 S.Ct. 1244, 63 L.Ed.2d 537 (1980), a defendant was arrested without probable cause, brought down to the station and photographed. He was then released. One of the victims of the crime subsequently identified the defendant's picture in a photo array, and he was re-arrested. At the trial, the victim identified the defendant as the perpetrator, and he was convicted. The defendant argued that the in-court identification was tainted by the illegal arrest, but the Court rejected this argument. The Court reasoned that there are three distinct elements of a victim's in-court identification: 1) the presence of the victim to testify at trial; 2) the ability of the victim to reconstruct the crime in his or her mind; and 3) the physical presence of the defendant, so that the victim can compare the defendant's appearance to the "picture" of the perpetrator in the victim's mind. Five members of the Court in different opinions concluded that an in-court identification should never be excluded as the fruit of an illegal arrest. For these Justices, none of the elements of in-court identification are affected by the arrest itself. Therefore, a person brought to trial following an illegal arrest can be identified, so long as the identification itself is not tainted by impermissible police suggestiveness. In other words, the illegal arrest adds nothing to the legal standard applied to all identification evidence.

D. INDEPENDENT SOURCE

Evidence will not be excluded as the fruit of the poisonous tree if the Government can show that it was derived from an independent source. The independent source exception operates to admit the fruits of illegally obtained evidence, when such fruits are also found by *legal means unrelated to the original illegal conduct.* For example, suppose that officers conduct an illegal search of a car and uncover a list of names and addresses. They obtain a warrant to search the premises at one of these addresses through use of the illegally obtained information. But simultaneously, other officers involved in an independent investigation were conducting an undercover drug buy at the address. The undercover agent believes that his cover has been "blown" and signals the back-up officers to enter the premises. The information discovered in this search is admissible even though the officers with the "tainted" warrant may discover the same information. This is because a legal means independent of the car search was conducted.

1. Rationale

The Supreme Court's most recent explication of the independent source exception occurred in *Murray v. United States,* 487 U.S. 533, 108 S.Ct. 2529, 101 L.Ed.2d 472 (1988). The Court explained that the basis of the exclusionary rule is to *deter* police misconduct, and not to punish the police. Therefore, the exclusionary rule puts the police "in the same, not a *worse,* position than they would have been in if no police error or misconduct had occurred." Where the challenged evidence has an independent source, application of the exclusionary rule would place the officers in a worse position than they would have been absent any violation. If no violation had occurred, the evidence would have been admitted due to the operation of the independent legal source.

2. Search With a Warrant After an Illegal Entry

In *Segura v. United States,* 468 U.S. 796, 104 S.Ct. 3380, 82 L.Ed.2d 599 (1984), the Court found that an illegal search of a residence could be cured when the officers later obtained a warrant, and where the probable cause supporting the warrant was not derived from information obtained in the illegal search. In *Segura,* agents unlawfully entered the defendant's apartment and remained there until a search warrant was obtained. During the course of the illegal entry, the officers saw narcotics paraphernalia, but they did not include this information in the warrant application. When the warrant was finally obtained, the agents found and seized narcotics and other evidence, which they had not previously observed. The Court held that the subsequently discovered evidence could not be excluded as the fruit of the poisonous tree, because the search pursuant to a warrant constituted an independent legal source. The Court emphasized that, before the illegal entry, the police had enough information with which to obtain a search warrant, and that no information obtained in the illegal entry was used in the warrant application.

3. **Evidence Initially Discovered in the Illegal Search**

In *Segura,* the question of whether the evidence initially discovered in the illegal search should be excluded was not before the Court. The question of whether the independent source exception could apply to the evidence obtained as a *direct* result of an illegal search was presented in *Murray v. United States, supra.* In *Murray,* police made an initial, admittedly illegal entry into defendant's premises. In the course of this illegal search, the police saw incriminating evidence, which they left in place. The police then obtained a warrant to search the premises. The illegally obtained information was not included in the warrant application, and thus did not affect the magistrate's decision to issue the warrant. The police then searched the premises pursuant to the warrant and seized the very evidence that was originally discovered in the illegal search. The Government sought to introduce, and the defendant sought to exclude, the evidence discovered in the initial illegal search. The question in *Murray* was whether the independent source exception could apply to *primary evidence, directly obtained from the illegal search,* as well as to derivative evidence, indirectly obtained from the illegality. See *United States v. Pimentel,* 810 F.2d 366 (2d Cir.1987) (discussing the distinction between "the direct and the indirect product of the unlawful search").

a. **Rediscovered Evidence Can Be Admissible**

The Court in *Murray* held that the exclusionary rule did not prevent the admission at trial of *rediscovered* evidence obtained through independent legal means. As with derivative evidence, the exclusion of the evidence initially discovered in the illegal search would put the officers in a worse position than if the search had never been conducted. If the illegal search had not been conducted, the police officers would have *initially* discovered the evidence in the course of a lawful search pursuant to a warrant. So the fact that it was actually *rediscovered* through independent legal means did not make a difference. Of course, the same would not be true if the warrant was issued on the basis of illegally obtained information. In that situation the warrant would not provide an independent legal source for obtaining the evidence.

b. **Danger of Confirmatory Searches**

The Court in *Murray* held that the mere showing that the warrant was issued on independent, legally obtained information could not be enough to invoke the independent source exception for "rediscovered" evidence. The Court was concerned that a mere showing of independent information would not be sufficient to deter illegal "confirmatory" searches.

Example: The danger of a confirmatory search is shown by the following hypothetical. Suppose that officers have probable cause to believe that drugs are in a warehouse. This does not mean that the officers will actually *find* drugs in the warehouse, because the probable cause standard is only a fair probability, not a certainty. If there are actually no drugs in the warehouse, the warrant application would end up to be a waste of time for the officers. There is a possibility, therefore, that the officers might wish to conduct an illegal warrantless search to see whether it is worth it to obtain a warrant—to "confirm" whether there are any drugs in the warehouse. If the officers only had to show that probable cause pre-existed the illegal search, they would have nothing to lose and everything to gain by doing a "confirmatory search." If they found something, it would still be admissible due to the information the police had prior to the entry, and the obtaining of the subsequent warrant. If they found nothing, they could avoid the bother of obtaining a warrant—of course, in conducting the search, the police would have illegally invaded the privacy of an innocent person. See *People v. Cook,* 22 Cal.3d 67, 98, 148 Cal.Rptr. 605, 623, 583 P.2d 130 (1978) ("Every time an officer fails to find the suspected evidence, he has also invaded the privacy of a citizen innocent of any wrongdoing."). See also *People v. Burr,* 70 N.Y.2d 354, 520 N.Y.S.2d 739, 514 N.E.2d 1363 (1987) ("To permit the police to search first and obtain a warrant only if their search uncovers or 'confirms' that there is incriminating evidence would ordinarily violate the warrant requirement * * *. The police could safely engage in such conduct because, if evidence were found in the course of an illegal search, they would still be permitted to seize it in a second search under independent color of law and use it at trial. Obviously, such a practice undermines the very purpose of the warrant requirement and cannot be tolerated * * *. The presence of an independent source for a warrant and subsequent search therefore does not automatically immunize an initial warrantless search and insure the admissibility of evidence seized pursuant to the warrant.").

c. **Protection Provided by *Murray***

To protect against the danger of a confirmatory search, the Court in *Murray* stated that the Government has the "onerous burden of convincing a trial court that no information gained from the illegal entry affected * * * the law enforcement officers' decision to seek a warrant." This burden could not be met simply by showing that the *magistrate* was not presented with illegally obtained information. The officer's decision to obtain a warrant could still have been affected by information uncovered in the illegal search. The Court in *Murray* therefore mandated an inquiry into the subjective intent of the officer. See *United States v.*

Restrepo, 966 F.2d 964 (5th Cir.1992) ("unlike the objective test of whether the expurgated affidavit constitutes probable cause to issue the warrant, the core judicial inquiry * * * is a subjective one: whether information gained in the illegal search prompted the officers to seek a warrant").

d. Officer's Assurance Not Sufficient

The Court in *Murray* stated, however, that the officers' mere assurance that the original search was not confirmatory in nature would not be dispositive. It declared that "where the facts render those assurances implausible, the independent source doctrine will not apply." Thus, *Murray* imposes two requirements for applying the independent source exception to "rediscovered" evidence: 1) an officer must have a "plausible" explanation for why the original illegal search was conducted—other than that it was to confirm whether there was any evidence worth seizing; and 2) information obtained in the illegal entry cannot be any material part of the basis for the warrant.

e. Application to the Facts of *Murray*

In *Murray,* the district court credited the officers' explanation that they entered the premises in an effort to apprehend anyone who might have been inside, and to guard against the destruction of evidence. That explanation was accepted by the Supreme Court, which stated that, while the officers "may have misjudged the existence of sufficient exigent circumstances to justify the warrantless entry * * * there is nothing to suggest that they went in merely to see if there was anything worth getting a warrant for." In other words, the explanation for the search did not mean that it was *legal,* but it was sufficiently close that the explanation was not implausible. The officers were wrong as to exigent circumstances but not *so* wrong as to render their motivation suspect. The officers were guilty of misjudgment, not bad faith.

f. Dissent in *Murray*

Justice Marshall, joined by Justices Stevens and O'Connor, dissented in *Murray.* He contended that the majority had not done enough to deter officers from conducting confirmatory searches. He argued that in most cases the officers will be able to at least plausibly state that they always intended to obtain a warrant. According to Justice Marshall, it will be the rare case in which an explanation such as that accepted in *Murray* will be so far wrong as to be implausible. Circumstances showing some slight risk of destruction of evidence will almost always exist—especially in drug cases where contraband can be quickly destroyed. Such circumstances need not even rise to the already low level of exigency found permissible to excuse a warrant—since if they do rise to that level, the original warrantless search is legal in the first place. In other words, the police can say that they *thought* the original search was legal, even though it turned out not to be. So long as the police were not completely unreasonable, their explanation that they thought they were acting legally will be considered plausible. Justice Marshall concluded that "the litigation risk" that a court may find an illegal confirmatory search "seems hardly a risk at all; it does not significantly dampen the incentive to conduct the initial illegal search."

g.   Direct/Indirect Distinction Rejected

The defendant in *Murray* argued that it was inappropriate to apply the independent source exception to evidence discovered as a *direct* result of the illegality. According to the defendant, this was an impermissible expansion of the independent source exception, which had traditionally applied only to permit the introduction of evidence that would otherwise have been excluded as fruit of the poisonous tree—not to the evidence found as a direct result of the illegal search.

The Court in *Murray,* however, rejected any primary/derivative or direct/indirect distinction insofar as the independent source exception was concerned. The Court explained that "this strange distinction would produce results bearing no relation to the policies of the exclusionary rule." If exclusion of direct evidence would place the officers in a worse position than they would have been absent their misconduct, the Court found no reason to exclude such evidence merely because it could be labelled "direct".

h.   Mixed Affidavits

Suppose that in a case like *Murray,* the officers include information obtained in the illegal search in their warrant application. Under *Murray,* the independent source exception should not permit the introduction of the evidence obtained in the search pursuant to a warrant, if the magistrate relied upon tainted information when the warrant was issued. But what if the officers included enough legally obtained information so that probable cause existed to issue the warrant without consideration of the illegally obtained information? What if the tainted evidence is surplusage? Courts after *Murray* have held that the independent source exception can apply where the warrant application contains information *sufficient for probable cause apart from the illegally obtained information.* Otherwise, the police would be put in a worse position than if the illegal search had not occurred: if the illegal search had not occurred, the evidence would have been obtained with a warrant based upon legally obtained information sufficient to establish probable cause. See *United States v. Herrold,* 962 F.2d 1131 (3d Cir.1992) ("If the application contains probable cause apart from the improper information, then the warrant is lawful and the independent source doctrine applies, providing that the officers were not prompted to obtain the warrant by what they observed during the initial entry."). The question is whether a neutral magistrate would have issued the warrant even if not presented with information that had been obtained during an unlawful search.

E. INEVITABLE DISCOVERY

The inevitable discovery exception allows the fruits of illegal activity to be admitted at trial if the Government can show that the challenged evidence would inevitably have been discovered through means completely independent of the illegal activity. For example, suppose that at the time of a legal in-home arrest, the police illegally obtain a letter in a search of the defendant's apartment. The letter indicates that the defendant has a sawed-off shotgun stored in a closet, which is a few feet away from where the defendant has been arrested and is being detained. Operating on that information, the police enter the closet and seize the gun. While the gun is a fruit of the poisonous tree, it is nonetheless admissible if the Government can show that it would have been inevitably discovered anyway in a routine search incident to arrest. See *People v. Fitzpatrick,* 32 N.Y.2d 499, 346 N.Y.S.2d 793, 300 N.E.2d 139 (1973) (where the court on these facts held the gun admissible under the inevitable discovery exception). In essence, the inevitable discovery exception is a "hypothetical" independent source exception. The relationship of inevitable discovery and independent source is shown if, under the facts above, the police had actually conducted a valid search incident to arrest and found the gun. The independent source exception would apply in that circumstance. See *United States v. Herrold,* 962 F.2d 1131 (3d Cir.1992) (since the evidence "was seized at the second [legal] search, there is no need to speculate as to whether the officers would have obtained a search warrant and whether they would have discovered the contraband for they did so;" hence, an inevitable discovery analysis was "inappropriate").

1. Rationale

The Supreme Court adopted the inevitable discovery exception to the exclusionary rule in *Nix v. Williams,* 467 U.S. 431, 104 S.Ct. 2501, 81 L.Ed.2d 377 (1984). The Court's reasoning was identical to that employed in adopting the independent source exception in *Segura* and *Murray, supra:* the exclusionary rule is applied to deter police misconduct, and not to punish the officers by making them worse off than if the illegality had not occurred. If the challenged evidence would have been inevitably discovered in the course of legal police activity anyway, then exclusion would indeed place the officers in a worse situation than if the illegality had not occurred.

2. Inevitability Must Be Shown by a Preponderance

In *Williams* the Court held that the exception would be applicable if the Government could prove by a *preponderance of the evidence* that the discovery would have inevitably occurred through legal means. This standard was found to be met under the facts of *Williams*. Williams was arrested and charged with murder of a young girl. Her body had not been found. An officer illegally obtained a confession from Williams, which led them to the location of the body. Meanwhile, a search party had been organized to find the body, and searchers were systematically covering the area in which the body was found by the officers who interrogated Williams. The officers, acting upon the illegally obtained confession, got to the body before the search party. The court held that evidence from the body and its location were admissible under the inevitable discovery exception, because the state proved by a preponderance of the evidence that the search party would have found the body shortly thereafter.

a.   Dissent

Justice Brennan, joined by Justice Marshall, dissented in *Williams*. The dissenters agreed that there should be an inevitable discovery exception, but they argued that the exception should not apply unless the Government provided *clear and convincing* proof that the challenged evidence would have been inevitably discovered through legal means. They reasoned that the hypothetical nature of the exception required cautious application and a heightened standard of proof.

3.   Applies to Fourth Amendment Violations

The Court in *Williams* applied the inevitable discovery exception to evidence that was obtained as the result of a violation of the Sixth Amendment (a confession obtained after indictment in the absence of counsel). But it is clear that the inevitable discovery exception applies to evidence obtained from violations of the Fourth Amendment as well. See *Murray, supra* (discussing the inevitable discovery exception in the context of Fourth Amendment violations); *United States v. Jackson,* 901 F.2d 83 (7th Cir.1990) (evidence obtained as a result of search based on involuntary consent was admissible because it would have been inevitably discovered in a *Terry* frisk).

4.   Primary Evidence

In *Murray, supra,* the Court held that the independent source exception applied to primary evidence, i.e. the very evidence directly obtained in the illegal search or seizure. Thus, the independent source exception is not just an exception to the fruit of the poisonous tree doctrine, but rather a more general exception to the exclusionary rule, allowing the admission of *any* evidence if it was obtained from a source independent of the illegal activity. In contrast, where the state invokes the inevitable discovery exception, the courts are in conflict as to whether the very evidence uncovered by the police misconduct can be admitted. This question frequently arises when the police illegally search an automobile. For example suppose the police properly stop an automobile and arrest the driver for speeding. Then, without probable cause, the police search the trunk and find drugs and a drug ledger. This warrantless search is illegal, since it is beyond the scope of the search incident to arrest exception, (see *New York v. Belton,* 453 U.S. 454, 101 S.Ct. 2860, 69 L.Ed.2d 768 (1981) (incident search does not extend to trunk of car)) and it is unsupported by the probable cause necessary to invoke the automobile exception to the warrant requirement (see *United States v. Ross,* 456 U.S. 798, 102 S.Ct. 2157, 72 L.Ed.2d 572 (1982) (warrantless search of trunk of car permissible so long as probable cause to search exists)). Nonetheless, the Government argues that all of the evidence found in the trunk is admissible under the inevitable discovery exception since, after the arrest of the driver, the car would have been impounded, and the trunk would have been opened and searched pursuant to a standard inventory search.

If inevitable discovery can in fact be shown, then all courts would admit the evidence indirectly derived from the illegal search. In our example, this would include witnesses, locations and physical evidence obtained by following leads contained in the drug ledger. The question is whether the primary evidence of the illegal search, such as the drugs or the ledger itself, is equally admissible. On this question there is dispute.

a. **Open Question**

The Supreme Court has not yet explicitly decided whether the inevitable discovery exception applies to primary as well as secondary evidence. *Nix v. Williams* is not definitive on the application of the inevitable discovery exception to primary evidence, since evidence concerning the body in *Williams,* and which the Court held admissible, was clearly derivative evidence. The primary evidence, directly obtained from the officer's illegal questioning of Williams, was the confession, which the Government did not offer at trial.

b. **One View—*Williams* Analysis Requires Application of Inevitable Discovery Exception to Primary Evidence**

Many courts have held that after *Williams,* the inevitable discovery exception must apply equally to primary as well as derivative evidence. See *United States v. Andrade,* 784 F.2d 1431 (9th Cir.1986) (accepting the Government's argument that primary evidence—drugs found in the trunk of an automobile—was admissible under the inevitable discovery exception, since an inventory of the illegally searched automobile would have been conducted). These courts read *Williams* as prohibiting application of the exclusionary rule where it would place the officers in a worse position than if the illegal search or seizure had not occurred. With primary as well as secondary evidence, exclusion is punitive if the evidence would have been inevitably discovered through legal means—the officers are in either case put in a worse position for having conducted an illegal search or seizure. Consequently most lower courts have held that the inevitable discovery exception applies equally to primary and derivative evidence.

Example: In *United States v. Pimentel,* 810 F.2d 366 (2d Cir.1987), the
Government illegally seized letters which would have been
uncovered in a lawful government audit. The court stated
that the letters were admissible even though they were the
direct product of the illegal search. The court held that
under the inevitable discovery exception, there is no basis
for distinguishing between primary and secondary evidence.

c.   **Contrary View—Primary Evidence Must Be Excluded Even if It Would
Have Been Discovered Through Legal Means**
A contrary position is taken by some courts, which have excluded
evidence found during an illegal search or seizure even if it would have
been discovered through legal means. These courts limit the inevitable
discovery exception to *fruits* of the illegally obtained evidence, and refuse
to apply it to the illegally obtained evidence *itself.*

Example: In *People v. Stith,* 69 N.Y.2d 313, 514 N.Y.S.2d 201, 506
N.E.2d 911 (1987), the court squarely rejected the notion
that the inevitable discovery exception could apply to
primary evidence, the very evidence obtained in the illegal
search. In *Stith,* the State argued that a gun uncovered in
an illegal search of a truck would inevitably have been
discovered in a lawful inventory search, and thus was
admissible. The court held that the inevitable discovery
exception should be applicable only to secondary, derivative
evidence: "evidence obtained indirectly as a result of leads or
information gained from that primary evidence." According
to the court in *Stith,* if the exception were to apply to
primary evidence, it would rob the exclusionary rule of all
deterrent effect. For example, with respect to automobile
searches, the police would never have an incentive to comply
with the limitations imposed by the probable cause
requirement, or with the spatial and temporal limitations of
the search incident to arrest doctrine. They would know
that, even if they violate those limitations, the evidence
uncovered will nonetheless be admissible because they can
argue that they would have conducted an inventory search
pursuant to police department guidelines, and that such
inventory search would have been legal. The police would
never have to comply with constitutional standards, so long
as they could point to some legal activity which would have
uncovered the evidence—which they would have done if they
hadn't already obtained the evidence illegally. As the court
in *Stith* stated: "applying the inevitable discovery rule in
these circumstances, and effecting what would amount to a
post hoc rationalization of the initial wrong would be an

unacceptable dilution of the exclusionary rule. It would defeat the primary purpose of that rule, deterrence of police misconduct."

d. Distinction From Independent Source Exception

Those courts which refuse to apply the inevitable discovery exception to primary evidence find it necessary to distinguish the independent source exception, which after *Murray* clearly applies to admit the very evidence found during the illegal search or seizure. The distinction proffered is that with the independent source exception, a legal search is *actually conducted at some point*. Ordinarily this means that the police obtain a warrant. In contrast, no legal search is ever conducted when the inevitable discovery exception is applied. This means that no warrant is ever obtained. Thus, if the inevitable discovery exception applies to primary evidence, the police can argue that their illegality should be excused because they *would have obtained a warrant*. Courts which refuse to apply the inevitable discovery exception to primary evidence are thus concerned that application of the exception would lead to the demise of the warrant requirement. See *United States v. Griffin*, 502 F.2d 959 (6th Cir.1974) (admitting evidence found in illegal search because police "planned to get a search warrant and had sent an officer on such a mission, would * * * tend in actual practice to emasculate the search warrant requirement of the Fourth Amendment."); contra, *United States v. Levasseur*, 620 F.Supp. 624 (E.D.N.Y.1985) (holding that evidence obtained in an illegal warrantless search was admissible because the officers would have inevitably obtained a warrant). In contrast, the application of the independent source exception to primary evidence can at least be justified because, as in *Murray*, a warrant was in fact obtained.

5. Inevitability, Not Possibility

For the inevitable discovery exception to apply, the Government must show that the challenged evidence would have been inevitably discovered through legal means that would actually have been used. For example, where the Government argues that evidence obtained in an illegal automobile or container search would have been inevitably discovered in an inventory, the Government must show that an inventory search is a standard practice that is routinely conducted. The mere possibility that an officer may have conducted an inventory search is not enough. See *United States v. Gorski*, 852 F.2d 692 (2d Cir.1988) (Government's argument that evidence would have been inevitably discovered in an inventory search was rejected because the record "reveals no evidence that such searches were an invariable, routine procedure in the booking and detention of a suspect at the particular FBI office involved").

a. Focus on What Would Have Been Done

For the inevitable discovery exception, the question is not what the police could have done or should have done, but what they actually *would* have done to reach the evidence by independent legal means. As one court has stated: "An investigation conducted over an infinite time with infinite thoroughness will, of course, ultimately or inevitably turn up any and all pieces of evidence in the world." *United States v. Feldhacker*, 849 F.2d 293 (8th Cir.1988). The court in *Feldhacker* concluded that "while the hypothetical discovery by lawful means need not be reached as rapidly as that actually reached by unlawful means, the lawful discovery must be inevitable through means that would actually have been employed."

b. Subpoenas

Most courts have refused to apply the inevitable discovery exception to illegally seized documents, where the Government argues that they would have been inevitably discovered through the use of a subpoena. The courts find such a scenario speculative as opposed to inevitable. See *United States v. Roberts*, 852 F.2d 671 (2d Cir.1988); *United States v. Eng*, 971 F.2d 854 (2d Cir.1992) (refusing to adopt a per se rule, but stating that "special care" is required to assure that there is a "substantial degree of directness in the government's chain of discovery argument, rather than a hypothesized leapfrogging from one subpoena recipient to the next until the piece of evidence is reached").

6. Legal Means Must Derive From Facts Independent of Illegal Search or Seizure

Where the Government points to a hypothetical independent source which arises from facts learned in the illegal search or seizure, the inevitable discovery exception cannot apply.

Examples: In *United States v. Thomas*, 955 F.2d 207 (4th Cir.1992), a hotel clerk suspected that Thomas and Henry, who had checked into Room 416 of the Hotel Belvedere, were at the hotel to deal some drugs. The clerk called the police. Two officers came to the hotel and illegally entered Room 416. Nobody was there. They searched the room, and instead of drugs, they found a bag containing thousands of dollars in bank wrappers. They began surveillance of Room 416 from a room across the hall. Henry then entered Room 416 for ten minutes. As he exited the room, he was stopped and handcuffed by the officers, and taken to the room across the hall, where he was questioned. The officers confronted Henry with the fact that they found money in Room 416. Then Henry signed a consent to search form for Room 416. The officers again entered Room 416 and in this second search, they found a bag belonging to Thomas, which they did not open.

Thomas then returned to Room 416, where he was arrested and handcuffed. He signed a consent to search form. The officers then opened the bag and found clothes and tennis shoes which were connected to the bank robbery. The Government relied on the inevitable discovery exception, arguing that the officers would have conducted surveillance of Room 416 from across the hall even if they had not entered the room; that they would have stopped Henry for questioning anyway; that Henry would have consented to a search of the room anyway; and that Thomas would have consented to a search of his bag anyway.

The court rejected the Government's "string of conjecture" and held that the inevitable discovery exception did not apply. The court noted that Henry became cooperative *only after the officers questioned him about the money found in Room 416,* and stated that if the officers, suspecting drug dealing, had stopped Henry for questioning, "there is no reason to believe Henry would have connected Thomas to a bank robbery or given consent to search." The court stated that "the fact making discovery inevitable must arise from circumstances other than those disclosed by the illegal search itself," and that the Government had not satisfied that test because "the bank money found in the illegal search changed the whole nature of the investigation that followed." See also *United States v. Ibarra,* 955 F.2d 1405 (10th Cir.1992) (rejecting the argument that evidence found after an unlawful impoundment of a car would have been inevitably discovered in an inventory search: "no inventory of the contents of defendant's vehicle could have been conducted but for the unlawful impoundment of the vehicle"; the court notes that a different result would have been reached if the officers engaged in an illegal *search* of a car that would have been legally impounded and inventoried regardless of the search).

7. Active Pursuit

A few courts have imposed the requirement that, in order to invoke the inevitable discovery exception, the police must be *actively pursuing* the lawful means at the time the illegal search is conducted. For example, in *United States v. Khoury,* 901 F.2d 948 (11th Cir.1990), the court rejected the argument that evidence obtained in an illegal search of a car would have been inevitably discovered in an inventory. The court reasoned that at the time of the illegal search, an inventory had *not yet begun,* and therefore that the active pursuit requirement was not met. Compare *United States v. Lamas,* 930 F.2d 1099 (5th Cir.1991) (active pursuit requirement is met when an officer has left the premises searched in order to obtain a warrant, even though the officer returned to the premises when he heard that the suspect had given—subsequently invalidated—consent to search; there is no requirement that an affidavit have been drafted before active pursuit is found). Other courts have refused to apply an active pursuit requirement, so long as the Government can show by a preponderance of the evidence that the evidence would have been discovered through legal means. In these courts, active pursuit is one way, but not the only way, to meet the state's burden of proof on inevitability. See e.g. *United States v. Thomas,* 955 F.2d 207 (4th Cir.1992) ("a situation other than a second investigation might make discovery inevitable"). In *Nix v. Williams, supra,* there was an active pursuit of legal means—the search party was actively searching for the body at the time the interrogating officers arrived at the body. The Court did not impose or even mention an active pursuit requirement, though the active pursuit of an independent investigation was obviously important to establishing that the body would have been inevitably discovered through legal means. Justice Stevens, concurring in *Williams,* and Justices Brennan and Marshall in dissent, argued that the inevitable discovery exception should never apply unless there was an active pursuit of legal means at the time the challenged evidence was obtained.

IV. "COLLATERAL USE" EXCEPTIONS TO THE EXCLUSIONARY RULE

A. INTRODUCTION
Even if the prosecution is proscribed by the exclusionary rule from admitting illegally obtained evidence as part of its case-in-chief at trial, there are several other possible uses to which such evidence could be put. The Supreme Court has considered whether the exclusionary rule ought to apply to a wide variety of uses of illegal evidence outside the context of the prosecution's case-in-chief. With one notable exception, the Court has consistently held that illegally obtained evidence can be used for collateral purposes. The rationale generally given is that sufficient deterrence of illegal searches and seizures will flow from the exclusion of illegally obtained evidence from the prosecution's case-in-chief, and therefore that the minimal benefits of preventing collateral uses of such evidence are outweighed by the costs of exclusion.

B. GRAND JURY
In *United States v. Calandra,* 414 U.S. 338, 94 S.Ct. 613, 38 L.Ed.2d 561 (1974), agents illegally seized certain documents located at Calandra's place of business. The documents related to loansharking activities. A grand jury was convened to investigate these activities, and Calandra was subpoenaed to appear so that he might be questioned on the basis of the information obtained from the illegally seized documents. Calandra moved to suppress the documents and refused to answer the grand jury's questions. The Supreme Court held that Calandra had no right to refuse to answer the questions, because the exclusionary rule did not apply to grand jury proceedings.

1. Rationale

The Court in *Calandra* reasoned that exclusion would be especially costly because it would "seriously impede the grand jury" and "delay and disrupt grand jury hearings." Against this cost, the Court found that the benefits of deterrence from an "extension of the exclusionary rule" were "uncertain at best." The Court reasoned that the threat of exclusion of illegally obtained evidence from the criminal trial provided the principal deterrent effect of the exclusionary rule, and that it was "unrealistic to assume" that there would be a significant incremental deterrent effect from excluding evidence from consideration by the grand jury. According to the Court, an officer would be unlikely to violate the Fourth Amendment with the sole intent to obtain an indictment from the grand jury, because the evidence upon which the indictment was based would be eventually excluded from trial.

2. Dissent

Justices Brennan, Douglas and Marshall dissented in *Calandra*. They argued that the exclusionary rule was necessary to ensure that "the government would not profit from its lawless behavior" and that, under the majority's approach, the Government would be able to profit from its own wrong because the illegally obtained evidence would be of *some* use.

C. SENTENCING

The Supreme Court has not considered whether the exclusionary rule is applicable to sentencing proceedings. However, lower courts have consistently held that the exclusionary rule is generally inapplicable to the trial court's consideration of evidence for purposes of sentencing. See *United States v. Robins*, 978 F.2d 881 (5th Cir.1992). This view has been unchanged by the advent of the Federal Sentencing Guidelines. Federal courts have consistently held that a district court imposing sentence under the Guidelines *must* ordinarily consider relevant, illegally obtained evidence. This is so even though the Guidelines remove a great deal of judicial discretion from sentencing and, in drug cases, impose a sentence based in large part on the quantity of the drugs associated with the defendant. As a result, "consideration of illegally seized evidence at sentencing is likely to result in increased penalties." *United States v. Tejada*, 956 F.2d 1256 (2d Cir.1992) (refusing to apply the exclusionary rule despite the changes wrought by the Guidelines, and holding that to avoid disparities in sentencing, the district judge *must* consider relevant, illegally obtained evidence).

1. Rationale

The courts which have refused to apply the exclusionary rule in sentencing proceedings have reasoned much the way the Supreme Court did in *Calandra*. According to these courts, the principal deterrent effect of the exclusionary rule is attributable to exclusion of illegally obtained evidence from the prosecution's case-in-chief; and the incremental deterrent effect of excluding the evidence from consideration at sentencing would ordinarily be minimal. Against this limited benefit, the exclusionary rule would impose a substantial cost, by limiting the information that a judge could consider in assessing an appropriate sentence.

2. Search or Seizure for Express Purpose of Enhancing a Sentence

While illegally obtained evidence is not ordinarily excluded from consideration at sentencing, courts have acknowledged an exception to this principle where the defendant makes a showing "that officers obtained evidence expressly to enhance a sentence." *United States v. Tejada, supra.* Courts reason that where it appears that the evidence has been illegally obtained *for the purpose of using it at sentencing* (rather than in the case-in-chief), then the exclusion of the illegally obtained evidence would have a deterrent effect sufficiently strong to outweigh the costs of exclusion. For example, in *United States v. Gilmer,* 814 F.Supp. 44 (D.Colo.1993), the defendant was properly arrested for drunk driving, and indicted for weapons and drug offenses on the basis of the evidence properly seized during the course of his arrest. After the indictment, officers illegally searched Gilmer's residence; this search turned up more drugs and weapons. This evidence was excluded from trial, but the Government urged the court to consider the illegally obtained drugs and weapons for sentencing purposes. Under the Sentencing Guidelines, this would have resulted in a substantial sentence, even though the defendant's actual conviction was for a relatively minor possessory offense. Under the Guidelines, the court must consider all "relevant conduct" in assessing sentence, including in many cases the possession and distribution of drugs other than those for which the defendant was charged and tried.

The *Gilmer* court held that under the circumstances, exclusion of the illegally obtained evidence from the sentencing hearing was required. The court found it likely that the second search was conducted to find evidence with which to enhance the sentence, and not for use at trial. It reasoned that at the time of the second search, the agents knew that they had a solid case based on the grand jury indictment; they made no effort to undertake a legal search which would produce admissible evidence; and they were indifferent concerning the legality of the search. The court concluded that "the circumstances demonstrate an unacceptably high incentive for the officers to violate the Fourth Amendment."

D. PAROLE OR PROBATION REVOCATION

The Supreme Court has not decided whether the exclusionary rule is applicable in parole and probation revocation proceedings. But, as with sentencing proceedings, lower courts have consistently held that the exclusionary rule is ordinarily inapplicable in these circumstances. Again, the analysis is that sufficient deterrence flows from exclusion of the illegally obtained evidence at a criminal trial, and that the benefit of minimal incremental deterrence from exclusion in parole or probation revocation proceedings is outweighed by the substantial cost of excluding reliable evidence from these proceedings. See *United States v. Winsett,* 518 F.2d 51 (9th Cir.1975) ("Because violation of probation conditions may indicate that the probationer is not ready or is incapable of rehabilitation by integration into society, it is extremely important that all reliable evidence shedding light on the probationer's conduct be available during probation revocation proceedings."). See also *United States v. Bazzano,* 712 F.2d 826 (3d Cir.1983) ("When the police conduct a search, their aim generally is to convict the target of the search of a substantive offense, and they know that any unconstitutional conduct on their part incident to the search will be grounds for suppressing the evidence at the defendant's trial."). The same result has been reached as to "supervised release" revocation proceedings under Federal law. *United States v. Montez,* 952 F.2d 854 (5th Cir.1992).

1. Some Circumstances May Require Exclusion

Courts have found some special circumstances in which exclusion of illegally obtained evidence from a parole or probation revocation proceeding would provide sufficient deterrent effect to outweigh the costs of exclusion. For example, one court has stated that illegally obtained evidence will be excluded from these proceedings where it appears that the search or seizure was done for purposes of *"harassment"* of the probationer or parolee. *United States v. Montez,* 952 F.2d 854 (5th Cir.1992) (no harassment found on the facts of the case). Another court has stated that where the search appears to have been conducted *expressly for the purpose of obtaining evidence for a parole or probation revocation,* rather than for use at a criminal trial, then the exclusionary rule should apply. *United States v. Rea,* 678 F.2d 382 (2d Cir.1982).

E. FORFEITURE PROCEEDINGS

In a case decided before *Calandra,* the Supreme Court held that the exclusionary rule was applicable to forfeiture proceedings. *One 1958 Plymouth Sedan v. Pennsylvania,* 380 U.S. 693, 85 S.Ct. 1246, 14 L.Ed.2d 170 (1965). Under the *Calandra* balancing test, it may be questioned whether the minimal deterrent effect of exclusion outside the context of criminal prosecution justifies the costs of excluding reliable evidence from a forfeiture proceeding. However, the holding in *Plymouth Sedan* has never been revisited by the Supreme Court, and therefore the courts have applied the exclusionary rule to forfeiture proceedings even after *Calandra.* See *United States v. $277.000.00 U.S. Currency,* 941 F.2d 898 (9th Cir.1991) (exclusionary rule applied in civil forfeiture proceedings directed at illegally seized vehicle and the money found within).

1. Proof of Criminal Violation Through Other Means

Plymouth Sedan involved a case in which the illegally obtained evidence was used to prove a criminal violation, which was a predicate to the forfeiture of an automobile. If the forfeitable nature of the object seized can be proven through other, legally obtained evidence, it does not matter that the object came to the authorities by way of an illegal search or seizure; forfeiture proceedings are not terminated merely because the Government came by the property illegally, any more than criminal proceedings are terminated merely because the defendant was illegally arrested. See *United States v. United States Currency $31,828,* 760 F.2d 228 (8th Cir.1985).

2. Owner Not Entitled to Return of Contraband

Plymouth Sedan concerned the forfeiture of an automobile, which was not inherently contraband. If the objects illegally seized are *contraband per se* (such as narcotics), the exclusionary rule does not demand their return to the owner. According to the Court in *Plymouth Sedan,* the return of contraband per se, merely because it was illegally seized, would frustrate "the express public policy against the possession of such objects." The Court therefore held that the exclusionary rule is applicable only when the property is "not intrinsically illegal in character." See also *United States v. Bagley,* 899 F.2d 707 (8th Cir.1990) (convicted felon not entitled to return of guns illegally seized from him).

F. DEPORTATION PROCEEDINGS

In *I.N.S. v. Lopez–Mendoza,* 468 U.S. 1032, 104 S.Ct. 3479, 82 L.Ed.2d 778 (1984), officers illegally seized Lopez–Mendoza and obtained inculpatory statements concerning his status as an illegal alien. These statements were later used in civil deportation proceedings, and served as the basis for Lopez–Mendoza's deportation. He argued that the fruit of the illegal seizure should have been excluded, but the Supreme Court held that the exclusionary rule is inapplicable in a civil deportation hearing.

1. Rationale

In *Lopez–Mendoza,* the Supreme Court did not purport to use its ordinary analysis, i.e. that the exclusionary rule should not apply to a collateral proceeding because sufficient deterrence flowed from excluding the evidence from a criminal prosecution. The Court recognized that a deportation proceeding was not "collateral" in this sense, because INS law enforcement efforts are geared specifically toward deportation proceedings rather than toward criminal prosecutions. Nonetheless, the Court found that the benefits of deterrence were outweighed by the costs of exclusion. The benefits of deterrence were found minimal because "deportation will still be possible when evidence not derived directly from the arrest is sufficient to support deportation" and because "it is highly unlikely that any particular arrestee will end up challenging the lawfulness of his arrest." The Court also relied on the fact that "the INS has its own scheme" of training and discipline designed to deter Fourth Amendment violations, and that alternative remedies such as declarative relief are available to challenge systematic violations of the Fourth Amendment by the INS. On the other hand, the Court found the costs of excluding evidence in deportation proceedings to be particularly substantial. The Court emphasized that an illegal alien is engaged in an "ongoing violation of the law" and that it would be inappropriate for courts to "close their eyes" to such continuous violations by applying the exclusionary rule. This was in contrast to criminal trials, where the defendant is being tried for a past transgression.

2. Dissent

Justice White wrote a dissenting opinion, joined in substantial part by Justices Brennan, Marshall and Stevens. He argued that "the costs and benefits of applying the exclusionary rule in civil deportation proceedings do not differ in any significant way from the costs and benefits of applying the rule in ordinary criminal proceedings." This was because civil deportation proceedings were the prime objective of the INS officials who made the illegal seizure.

G. CIVIL TAX PROCEEDINGS

In *United States v. Janis,* 428 U.S. 433, 96 S.Ct. 3021, 49 L.Ed.2d 1046 (1976), Los Angeles police officers illegally obtained cash and betting records from Janis. This information was passed to the IRS, which made an assessment against Janis on the basis of betting income, and levied on the seized cash in partial satisfaction of the assessment. Janis sued in Federal court to recoup the illegally seized cash, and the Government counterclaimed for the remainder of the assessment. The Supreme Court held that the exclusionary rule could not operate against the Government in civil tax proceedings, and therefore that the cash could be levied upon and Janis could be assessed for the remainder.

1. Rationale

The Court found the deterrent effect of the exclusionary rule to be "attenuated" where evidence is illegally obtained by a state law enforcement officer and subsequently used in a proceeding "to enforce only the civil law of the other sovereign." Coupled with the fact that sufficient deterrence flows from excluding the evidence from a criminal prosecution, the Court concluded that exclusion in a Federal tax proceeding "is unlikely to provide significant, much less substantial, additional deterrence" because the tax proceeding "falls outside the offending officer's zone of primary interest." The minimal deterrent effect was found to be outweighed by the cost of excluding reliable evidence from the Federal civil tax proceeding.

2. Dissent

Justice Stewart, writing for three dissenters, pointed out that law enforcement officials at all levels regularly provide Federal tax officials with information. He concluded that if law enforcement officers can "crack down" on criminals "by the simple expedient of violating their constitutional rights and turning the illegally seized evidence over to Internal Revenue Service agents on the proverbial silver platter, then the deterrent purpose of the exclusionary rule is wholly frustrated."

3. Search by Same Sovereign

The search in *Janis* was conducted by local officials and the evidence was ultimately used in a Federal tax proceeding. In a footnote in *Janis,* the Court indicated that the exclusionary rule might have more deterrent effect if the search were conducted by officials of the same sovereign which ultimately used the evidence. However, the courts which have been confronted with this question have generally refused to apply the exclusionary rule even where the search and the subsequent civil tax proceeding are both conducted by the same sovereign. For example, in *Tirado v. Commissioner,* 689 F.2d 307 (2d Cir.1982), the court found it "unsound to invoke the exclusionary rule on the assumption that officers of one federal agency have such a strong motivating interest in all federal law enforcement concerns that broad application of the rule will achieve significant marginal deterrence." The court thus found the Federal tax proceeding to be outside the "zone of primary interest" of the Federal narcotics officer.

H. HABEAS CORPUS PROCEEDINGS

In the 1960's and 1970's, the Supreme Court decided several important Fourth Amendment issues in cases which were brought to the Court through collateral attack of a finalized state court conviction; the procedural device for such an attack is ordinarily a *habeas corpus* proceeding brought in Federal court to challenge the constitutionality of a finalized state conviction. See, e.g., *Adams v. Williams,* 407 U.S. 143, 92 S.Ct. 1921, 32 L.Ed.2d 612 (1972) (legality of stop and frisk considered in a habeas corpus proceeding). However, in *Stone v. Powell,* 428 U.S. 465, 96 S.Ct. 3037, 49 L.Ed.2d 1067 (1976), the Court held that a habeas petitioner could *not ordinarily invoke the exclusionary rule* to challenge evidence seized in violation of the Fourth Amendment.

1. Rationale

As in previously discussed cases, the Court in *Stone* employed a cost-benefit analysis and found that the costs of applying the exclusionary rule in habeas proceedings outweighed the benefits in deterrence that exclusion would provide. The Court found that sufficient deterrence existed from exclusion at trial or on direct review, and that officers would be unlikely to "fear that federal habeas review might reveal flaws in a search or seizure that went undetected at trial and on appeal." On the cost side, the Court emphasized that the costs of exclusion were more substantial in the context of collateral attack than they would be at trial or on direct review. Allowing a remedy on collateral attack would impose greater burdens on the Government in a retrial, since finalized convictions are generally older than those appealed on direct review. Thus a retrial may be significantly more difficult due to the possible loss of witnesses and proof. Moreover, a Federal court's invalidation of a finalized state conviction, through use of the exclusionary rule, raises Federalism concerns and creates the cost of uncertainty associated with lack of finality of judgments.

2. Dissent

The dissenters in *Stone* argued that the Court was rewriting the statutes applicable to collateral attack, and that it was for Congress to decide "what the most efficacious method is for enforcing federal constitutional rights." The dissenters found it anomalous that "the defendant's unconstitutional confinement obtains during the process of direct review, no matter how long that process takes, but that the unconstitutionality then suddenly dissipates at the moment the claim is asserted in a collateral attack on the conviction."

3. Full and Fair Opportunity

The Court in *Stone* declared that "where the State has provided an opportunity for full and fair litigation of a Fourth Amendment claim, a state prisoner may not be granted federal habeas relief on the ground that evidence obtained in an unconstitutional search or seizure was introduced at trial." It follows that the exclusionary rule *will* be applicable in habeas proceedings where the state has *not* provided a "full and fair opportunity" to litigate the Fourth Amendment claim.

a. Definition of Full and Fair Opportunity

The Court in *Stone* did not define what it meant by a "full and fair opportunity" sufficient to preclude application of the exclusionary rule. Subsequent lower court cases have set forth the following requirements that must be met by the state courts in order to preclude a collateral attack on Fourth Amendment grounds: 1) there must be a *procedural opportunity* to raise a Fourth Amendment claim, including an opportunity for meaningful appellate review; 2) where material facts are in dispute, they must be determined by a *fact-finding court*; and 3) the state courts must recognize and *cannot wilfully refuse to apply* the correct Fourth Amendment standards.

b. Narrow Exception

It certainly does not follow, however, that a Fourth Amendment claim can be brought on habeas merely because the state courts wrongly decided a Fourth Amendment question. The lack of "full and fair opportunity" exception to *Stone* is intended to be extremely narrow. See *Pierson v. O'Leary*, 959 F.2d 1385 (7th Cir.1992) (it was sufficient that the state court stated the appropriate standard and applied it to the facts).

c. Ineffective Assistance

If the defendant's Fourth Amendment claim is lost in the state courts because counsel was *ineffective* in presenting it, then the ineffective assistance of counsel is a separate constitutional violation. Unlike a violation of the Fourth Amendment, a violation of the standards of effective assistance is cognizable in habeas proceedings. See *Kimmelman v. Morrison*, 477 U.S. 365, 106 S.Ct. 2574, 91 L.Ed.2d 305 (1986) (rejecting the argument that *"Stone's* restriction on federal habeas review of Fourth Amendment claims should be extended to Sixth Amendment ineffective assistance of counsel claims which are founded primarily on incompetent representation with respect to a Fourth Amendment issue").

I.   IMPEACHMENT

In a series of cases, the Supreme Court has held that the exclusionary rule does not prevent the prosecution from using illegally obtained evidence to impeach the defendant's testimony. The first case to recognize an impeachment exception was *Walder v. United States,* 347 U.S. 62, 74 S.Ct. 354, 98 L.Ed. 503 (1954), where the defendant, charged with narcotics sales, testified on direct examination and again on cross-examination that he had never bought, sold, or possessed narcotics. The prosecution was allowed to question the defendant about heroin that was illegally obtained from his home two years earlier; the judge gave a limiting instruction that the evidence could only be considered in assessing the defendant's credibility as a witness. The Supreme Court held that the illegally obtained evidence was properly admitted for impeachment purposes, concluding that "there is hardly justification for letting the defendant affirmatively resort to perjurious testimony in reliance on the Government's disability to challenge his credibility."

1.   Rationale

In adopting the impeachment exception, the Supreme Court has applied the basic cost-benefit analysis which it has utilized to develop other exceptions. On the cost side, the Court has found that an application of the exclusionary rule to prevent impeachment would not only impose the substantial cost of excluding reliable evidence; it would also give the defendant a license to commit perjury. As the Court in *Walder* put it, the rule should not provide the defendant "with a shield against contradiction of his untruths." On the benefits side, the Court has concluded that the principal deterrent effect of the exclusionary rule lies in the exclusion of illegally obtained evidence proffered in the prosecution's case-in-chief, and that the incremental deterrent effect of exclusion for impeachment purposes as well would be minimal. See *Harris v. New York,* 401 U.S. 222, 91 S.Ct. 643, 28 L.Ed.2d 1 (1971) ("The impeachment process here undoubtedly provided valuable aid to the jury in assessing petitioner's credibility, and the benefits of this process should not be lost, in our view, because of the speculative possibility that impermissible police conduct would be encouraged thereby.").

2.   Impeachment of Testimony First Brought Out on Cross–Examination

The defendant in *Walder* made a statement on direct examination that was in flat contradiction with the illegally obtained evidence. He made no attempt to avoid this contradiction. In *United States v. Havens,* 446 U.S. 620, 100 S.Ct. 1912, 64 L.Ed.2d 559 (1980), the Supreme Court extended the impeachment exception to a situation where the defendant successfully *avoided* contradiction with the illegally obtained evidence on direct examination, but was nonetheless impeached with the evidence due to his answers on *cross-examination*.

a.   Facts of *Havens*

Officers stopped McLeroth and Havens coming off a flight. They illegally searched Havens' suitcase and found a shirt from which a pocket had been torn out. When McLeroth was searched, the officers found a pocket sewn into his clothing. This pocket matched the shirt found in Havens' suitcase. Cocaine was found in the makeshift pocket. McLeroth pleaded guilty and testified against Havens; he admitted to having cocaine on his person. Havens took the stand and after acknowledging that he heard McLeroth's testimony, was asked by his counsel whether he had ever "engaged in that kind of activity with Mr. McLeroth." Havens answered in the negative. On cross-examination, Havens was asked more pointed questions: whether he had anything to do with sewing pockets into McLeroth's clothing and whether he had a shirt in his suitcase with the pocket missing. He answered both questions in the negative, and was impeached by the shirt and by testimony about its discovery.

b.   Analysis in *Havens*

The lower court had reversed Havens' conviction on the ground that the impeached testimony was not given on direct examination, but the Supreme Court found no meaningful distinction from *Walder.* The Court stated that in terms of the impeachment exception, there is "no difference of constitutional magnitude between the defendant's statements on direct examination and his answers to questions put to him on cross-examination that are *plainly within the scope of the defendant's direct examination*." The Court found that the questions put to Havens were fairly within the scope of direct: they were simply more pointed questions intending to pin down Havens' general testimony that he had nothing to do with McLeroth's cocaine trafficking. The Court reaffirmed its previous "assessment of the competing interests" by which it had established the impeachment exception to the exclusionary rule.

c.   Dissent in *Havens*

The dissenters in *Havens* argued that the majority had inappropriately extended the impeachment exception so that it was now in the control of the Government. After *Havens,* "the prosecutor can lay the predicate for admitting otherwise suppressible evidence with his own questioning." The dissenters were unconvinced that the majority had provided a meaningful limitation when it stated that the cross-examination must be "reasonably suggested" by the testimony on direct. According to the dissent, "traditional evidentiary principles accord parties fairly considerable latitude in cross-examining opposing witnesses." The dissent concluded that the only way for a defendant to avoid impeachment with illegally obtained evidence after *Havens* would be to "forego testifying on his own behalf." This practical consequence would mean that the impeachment exception would give police officers an incentive to violate the Fourth Amendment, because officers would *know* that evidence which they obtained illegally would have a positive effect in litigation—it will either keep the defendant from testifying, or it will be used as powerful impeachment evidence should he decide to testify.

3. Exclusionary Rule Prevents Impeachment of Defendant's Witnesses With Illegally Obtained Evidence

In *James v. Illinois,* 493 U.S. 307, 110 S.Ct. 648, 107 L.Ed.2d 676 (1990), the Court refused to extend the impeachment exception to allow impeachment of the defendant's *witnesses* with illegally obtained evidence. Thus, while the defendant will be impeached if he testifies in contradiction with illegally obtained evidence, the defendant's witnesses will not.

a. Facts of *James*

James told police officers that he had changed his hair color and style on the day after taking part in a shooting. The trial court suppressed this statement because it was the fruit of an arrest without probable cause. Prosecution witnesses at trial identified James, though they admitted that his hair color and style at trial was different from that of the perpetrator at the time of the shooting. James called a family friend, who testified that just before the shooting, James' hair color and style was the same as it was at trial, thus creating an inference that James had never changed it. The trial court, relying on the impeachment exception to the exclusionary rule, allowed the prosecution to introduce James' suppressed statement, to the effect that he had changed his hair, in order to impeach the credibility of the defense witness.

b. Analysis in *James*

The majority in *James* reversed the lower court and refused to extend the impeachment exception to the exclusionary rule to allow impeachment of defense witnesses with illegally obtained evidence. Justice Brennan, writing for the Court, found a compelling distinction between impeachment of a defendant's own testimony and that of defense witnesses. Despite his prior dissents on the impeachment exception, Justice Brennan argued that, as applied to the defendant, the impeachment exception serves salutary purposes: It "penalizes defendants for committing perjury," and yet "leaves defendants free to testify truthfully on their own behalf." According to the Court, the impeachment exception keeps perjury out of the trial and allows truthful testimony in, thus furthering in both ways the search for truth. In contrast, the Court asserted that there would be a loss of truthful testimony if the prosecution could impeach defense witnesses with illegally obtained evidence.

Justice Brennan argued that the fear of impeachment of one's witnesses likely would chill some defendants from even presenting the testimony of others. Unlike the defendant, who could carefully tailor truthful testimony to avoid reference to illegally obtained evidence, the defendant's witnesses could not be so easily controlled: "Defendants might reasonably fear that one or more of their witnesses, in a position to offer truthful and favorable testimony, would also make some statement in sufficient tension with the tainted evidence to allow the prosecutor to introduce that evidence for impeachment." The Court concluded that "an expanded impeachment exception likely would chill some defendants from calling witnesses who would otherwise offer probative evidence," creating a deleterious effect on the search for truth.

Nor, according to the majority, was the impeachment exception necessary in these circumstances to deter defense witnesses from offering perjurious testimony. The Court asserted that the threat of a perjury conviction would sufficiently deter defense witnesses from lying on the stand: unlike the defendant, who may be facing a substantial sentence for the crime charged, and who may well decide that a perjury conviction is the lesser of two evils.

Applying a cost-benefit analysis, the Court stated that the deterrent effect of the exclusionary rule would be substantially diminished if illegally obtained evidence could be used to impeach not only the defendant but the defendant's witnesses. This is because "expanding the impeachment exception to *all* defense witnesses would significantly enhance the expected value to the prosecution of illegally obtained evidence." The court therefore concluded that the benefits of exclusion, in terms of deterrence, were substantial, and the cost of exclusion, in terms of the loss of reliable evidence, was minimal.

c. Dissent in *James*

The four dissenters in *James* complained that the majority had granted the defendant "broad immunity to introduce whatever false testimony it can produce from the mouth of a friendly witness." The dissent found no legitimate distinction, in terms of the policies of the exclusionary rule, between impeachment of the defendant and impeachment of defense witnesses. Justice Kennedy, who wrote the dissent, was particularly concerned with the costs to the truthseeking process if defense witnesses could testify without fear of impeachment with probative evidence. Justice Kennedy argued that impeachment is even more vital for attacking untruthful testimony of a defense witness than it is for attacking the defendant; the defendant's self-serving testimony will be given limited weight by the jury anyway, whereas "testimony by a witness said to be independent has the greater potential to deceive." Justice Kennedy also noted that the state would suffer a negative impact from the lack of impeachment evidence: "Jurors will assume that if the prosecution had any proof the statement was false, it would make the proof known."

Justice Kennedy advocated a rule that illegally obtained evidence could be used to impeach defense witnesses, but only where there was a direct conflict between the evidence and the witness' testimony. According to the dissent, the requirement of a direct conflict would alleviate the majority's concern that the defendant would not present truthful witnesses for fear they would be impeached in virtually all cases.

J. SUBSEQUENT PERJURY TRIALS

The Supreme Court impeachment cases hold that evidence obtained in violation of the Fourth Amendment may be used to impeach the defendant at trial. But the Supreme Court has not decided whether such evidence may be used against the defendant in a subsequent prosecution for perjury. However, the lower courts have relied on the impeachment cases and have consistently held that illegally obtained evidence may be admitted in a prosecution for perjury.

Example: In *United States v. Varela*, 968 F.2d 259 (2d Cir.1992), the defendant was suspected of drug trafficking. He was illegally arrested and made statements implicating himself and certain co-conspirators in drug activity. These statements were suppressed because they were tainted by the arrest, and Varela was never brought to trial. Subsequently, Varela was subpoenaed to testify before a grand jury investigating drug trafficking by some of the people whom Varela previously implicated in his illegally obtained statement. Varela invoked his Fifth Amendment privilege but was granted immunity. Testifying before the grand jury, he contradicted his previous statement and denied that he knew anything about drug activity. He was subsequently tried for perjury, his illegally obtained statements were admitted, and he was convicted. The court held that the exclusionary rule does not bar the use of illegally obtained evidence in a subsequent perjury conviction.

1. Rationale

The courts have concluded that "the marginal deterrence" of excluding illegally obtained evidence from a perjury trial is outweighed by the cost of excluding reliable evidence. *Varela, supra.* According to the courts, it is unlikely that an officer investigating one crime would violate the law in order to obtain evidence that could only be used in an unrelated prosecution for perjury—especially since the perjury prosecution would be contingent on the defendant's decision to contradict, under oath, the illegally obtained evidence. As the court stated in *Varela*: "We refuse to ascribe such clairvoyance to law enforcement officers; at the time of Varela's arrest, the possibility of subsequent perjurious testimony was too remote to serve as a motivating factor to * * * officers bent on breaking up a suspected cocaine importation scheme." On the cost side, the courts note that suppression of illegally obtained evidence from a perjury trial would "convert the exclusionary rule into a license to commit perjury."

2. Search Following the Perjured Testimony

The cases which refuse to apply the exclusionary rule to perjury trials have dealt with facts in which the illegal search *precedes* the perjured testimony. In these circumstances, the likelihood that an illegal search would be conducted to obtain evidence for a perjury trial is remote. The argument for deterrence is stronger, however, when the search occurs *after* the defendant gives perjured testimony. Then the contingency of the defendant's decision to lie under oath has been lifted, and the possible use of the evidence in a subsequent perjury trial is more easily predicted by the officer. Therefore, courts have stated that "if the unlawful arrest or seizure followed the perjured testimony—instead of preceding it—law enforcement officials would have the requisite incentive to engage in Fourth Amendment violations to obtain convictions of those suspected of perjury." *Varela, supra.* In this situation, the exclusionary rule *will* apply.

V. THE "GOOD FAITH" EXCEPTION TO THE EXCLUSIONARY RULE

A. THE *LEON* CASE

In the previous section on "collateral" uses of illegally obtained evidence, the courts assumed that the illegally obtained evidence would be excluded from the prosecution's case-in-chief. But in *United States v. Leon,* 468 U.S. 897, 104 S.Ct. 3405, 82 L.Ed.2d 677 (1984), the Supreme Court held that "the Fourth Amendment exclusionary rule should be modified so as not to bar the use in the prosecution's case-in-chief of evidence obtained by officers acting in reasonable reliance on a search warrant issued by a detached and neutral magistrate but ultimately found to be unsupported by probable cause." *Leon* was the first case in which the Supreme Court held that evidence could be illegally obtained and yet would not be excluded in any context. See Dripps, "Living With *Leon,*" 95 Yale L.J. 906 (1986). As Justice Stevens stated in his dissent in *Leon:* "Today, for the first time, this Court holds that although the Constitution has been violated, no court should do anything about it at any time and in any proceeding."

1. Facts of *Leon*

In *Leon,* a confidential informant of unproven reliability informed police officers of drug activity at 620 Price Drive. He stated that he had personally observed a sale of drugs at that residence five months earlier. The police investigated, and found that some of the cars parked at the Price Drive residence belonged to persons who had been arrested for drug offenses. Officers also witnessed people often going into the house and then exiting with small paper sacks. Further investigation indicated that the suspects were associates of Leon, who had also been previously arrested on drug charges. Leon's house was then put under surveillance, and officers witnessed comings and goings consistent with drug activity. Based on these and other observations summarized in an affidavit, officers prepared an application for a warrant for the Price Drive residence, Leon's house, and another house associated with the suspects. A facially valid search warrant was issued, and the searches uncovered drugs and other evidence at each of the locations. The lower courts, while recognizing that the case was close, concluded that the affidavit was insufficient to establish probable cause. They reasoned that some of the information was fatally stale; that the informant's credibility was not established; and that the corroboration was not sufficient to shore up the defects in the informant's tip. One judge on the court of appeals dissented.

a.   Pre–*Gates*

Note that the lower court opinions in *Leon,* finding no probable cause for a warrant, were written before the Supreme Court decided *Illinois v. Gates,* discussed *supra* in the section on probable cause. It is very likely that the warrant found defective in *Leon* would have been found valid under *Gates,* thus obviating any need to determine whether a ''good faith'' exception should apply. This is because, under the *Gates* totality of circumstances approach, the corroborative evidence need not rise to any particular level of suspiciousness in order to shore up a defective tip. Clearly, the corroborative evidence obtained by the police officers in *Leon* was equal to if not greater than that held sufficient in *Gates.* As Justice Stevens stated in his dissenting opinion in *Leon,* ''it is probable ✻ ✻ ✻ that the Court of Appeals would now conclude that the warrant in *Leon* satisfied the Fourth Amendment if it were given the opportunity to reconsider the issue in light of *Gates.*''

2.   Holding in *Leon*

The Court concluded that the exclusionary rule should not apply because ''the officers' reliance on the magistrate's determination of probable cause was objectively reasonable, and application of the extreme sanction of exclusion is inappropriate.'' The Court based its finding of objectively reasonable reliance on the fact that the officer's ''affidavit related the results of an extensive investigation and, as the opinions of the divided panel of the Court of Appeals make clear, provided evidence sufficient to create disagreement among thoughtful and competent judges as to the existence of probable cause.'' Thus, while probable cause did not *in fact* exist (under the pre-*Gates* test) the question was close enough that the officers could reasonably rely on the magistrate's determination that probable cause did exist.

3.   Rationale—Officer Who Did Nothing Wrong Cannot Be Deterred

The majority in *Leon* reasoned that the exclusionary rule would have no deterrent effect where an officer, ''acting in objective good faith, has obtained a search warrant from a judge or magistrate and acted within its scope." Where the warrant in these circumstances is issued without probable cause, it is the *magistrate*, and not the law enforcement officer, who is in error. It is the magistrate's responsibility to determine whether probable cause exists. In the ordinary case, if the magistrate issues an invalid warrant, "there is no police illegality and thus nothing to deter." As the Court put it: "Penalizing the officer for the magistrate's error, rather than his own, cannot logically contribute to the deterrence of Fourth Amendment violations."

a. Can the Magistrate Be Deterred From Issuing Invalid Warrants?

The majority's analysis in *Leon* focusses on who made the error, and whether the exclusionary rule could have a deterrent effect on the state actor who made the error. Where an officer relies on a facially valid warrant which lacks probable cause, the error is ordinarily exclusively that of the magistrate. The question then is whether application of the exclusionary rule would *deter magistrates* from issuing warrants in the absence of probable cause. The majority in *Leon* concluded that the exclusionary rule would have no "significant deterrent effect on the issuing judge or magistrate." According to the Court, the magistrate has no stake in the outcome of a particular criminal trial, since she is a neutral judicial official. Therefore there is no incentive for the magistrate to obtain evidence in violation of the Fourth Amendment; and the exclusionary rule cannot be an effective means of destroying an incentive (to violate the law) which does not exist. This is in contrast with the law enforcement officer, who does have an incentive to violate the Fourth Amendment in order to obtain evidence more easily, because he is in the "competitive enterprise of ferreting out crime" and thus has a significant stake in the outcome of a criminal trial; this incentive can be destroyed by application of the exclusionary rule. The majority asserted that magistrates could be more effectively deterred from erroneous decisions by simply informing them of their errors in the course of a written opinion; that is, the magistrate's "professional incentives" will assure future compliance with the Fourth Amendment when a reviewing judge declares the warrant invalid, whether or not the evidence is excluded.

4. Dissent in *Leon*

Much of the argument of the dissenting Justices in *Leon* was addressed to the majority's assertion, previously discussed, that the exclusionary rule is merely a "court-made" rule and not constitutionally required. But other arguments were directed specifically to the majority's adoption of a good faith exception for invalid warrants. For example, Justice Brennan argued that the majority had ignored the "considerable long-term deterrent effect" that would be provided by exclusion of evidence obtained through the use of an invalid warrant. He stated that "if evidence is consistently excluded in these circumstances, police departments will surely be prompted to instruct their officers to devote greater care and attention to providing sufficient information to establish probable cause when applying for a warrant, and to review with some attention the form of the warrant." In other words, the exclusionary rule would encourage officers to act more carefully in the warrant process, and would discourage officers from blind reliance on the act of a magistrate. Justice Brennan was concerned that "the good faith exception will encourage police to provide only the bare minimum of information in future warrant applications." That is, the police would know that they could take the path of least resistance to obtaining a warrant and yet remain protected from judicial review. In a separate dissent, Justice Stevens argued that "if the police cannot use evidence obtained through warrants issued on less than probable cause, they have less incentive to seek those warrants, and magistrates have less incentive to issue them." Justice Stevens was concerned that under the good faith exception, officers may submit a warrant application to the magistrate even if they know that probable cause is lacking, on the chance that the magistrate may "take the bait. No longer must they hesitate and seek additional evidence in doubtful cases."

B. OBJECTIVE REASONABLENESS

The term "good faith" exception is really a misnomer, because the Court in *Leon* does not purport to allow illegally obtained evidence to be admitted simply because the officer had a *subjective good faith* belief that what he did was legal. The *Leon* exception *does not depend on the subjective state of mind of the officer*. Rather, the Court stated that the test is *purely objective*: "the officer's reliance on the magistrate's probable cause determination and on the technical sufficiency of the warrant he issues must be *objectively reasonable*."

1. Reasonably Unreasonable?

Justice Stevens, dissenting in *Leon*, criticized the majority's assertion that an officer could ever "reasonably" rely on an invalid warrant. In Justice Stevens' view, a search pursuant to an invalid warrant is itself unreasonable under the terms of the Fourth Amendment. He concluded that "an official search and seizure cannot be both reasonable and unreasonable at the same time." However, this argument misapprehends the majority's definition of an officer's "reasonable" reliance on an invalid warrant. Reasonable minds can differ as to whether a particular warrant is valid; the questions are not cut and dried and there is certainly room for dispute—as was the case in *Leon*, where one judge on the Court of Appeals panel dissented on the probable cause question.

2. Room for Reasonable Minds to Differ

What the good faith exception means is that in cases where a warrant is found invalid, the good faith exception will apply so long as reasonable minds can differ on the validity of the warrant. Where no reasonable argument can be made that the warrant is valid, then the good faith exception will *not* apply. Thus, the good faith exception is similar to the standard used for reviewing jury verdicts in civil cases. The standard is not whether the jury was correct or whether the reviewing court would have decided the case another way; rather, a verdict is only reversed if *no reasonable person* could have decided the way the jury did. So long as there is room for argument, then, the good faith exception will apply.

3. Clearly Established Law

Another useful analogy to the good faith exception comes from the qualified immunity cases decided under the civil rights statute, 42 U.S.C.A. § 1983. Qualified immunity means that even if the plaintiff's constitutional rights are violated, there is no liability unless the officer violated *clearly established law;* if the law was not clearly established at the time of the conduct, then there is room for argument as to whether the officer's conduct was lawful. The Supreme Court has equated the standards of qualified immunity with the objective reasonableness standard of the good faith exception to the exclusionary rule. See *Anderson v. Creighton,* 483 U.S. 635, 107 S.Ct. 3034, 97 L.Ed.2d 523 (1987) (rejecting the argument that an officer may not reasonably act unreasonably). Consequently, in *Leon,* the officer could reasonably rely on the warrant even though it lacked probable cause; the probable cause question was close enough that reasonable minds could differ.

C. EXCEPTIONS TO THE GOOD FAITH EXCEPTION

The Court in *Leon* took pains to *reject* a broad holding that the exclusionary rule would never apply when the officer acts in reliance on a warrant. Rather, the Court stated that "the officer's reliance on the magistrate's probable cause determination and on the technical sufficiency of the warrant he issues must be *objectively reasonable,* and it is clear that in some circumstances the officer will have *no reasonable grounds* for believing that the warrant was properly issued." Where all reasonable people would agree that a warrant is invalid, then the officer will be in error in relying on that warrant; and because it is the officer (as well as the magistrate) who makes the error in relying on an obviously invalid warrant, the exclusionary rule is presumed to have some deterrent in assuring future compliance.

The Court in *Leon* set forth *four situations* in which an officer's reliance on a warrant would be unreasonable. These are the four exceptions to the good faith exception.

1. Misleading Information

If the magistrate who issued the warrant "was misled by information in an affidavit that the affiant knew was false or would have known was false except for his reckless disregard of the truth," then the error in issuing the warrant was that of the *officer,* not the magistrate. The presumption in *Leon* is that officers can be deterred by operation of the exclusionary rule, though magistrates cannot. Thus, the Court in *Leon* held that the exclusionary rule still applies to violations of the *Franks* doctrine, discussed in the section on

probable cause. See *Dolliver v. State,* 598 N.E.2d 525 (Ind.1992) (no good
faith exception where the officer's affidavit "flagrantly misrepresented" the
nature of the informant's knowledge).

2. Abandonment of Judicial Role

The Court in *Leon* stated that where the issuing magistrate "wholly
abandoned his judicial role," then "no reasonably well-trained officer should
rely on the warrant." Again, the officer has made an error which can be
deterred. In *Lo–Ji Sales, Inc. v. New York,* 442 U.S. 319, 99 S.Ct. 2319, 60
L.Ed.2d 920 (1979), the Court, in a pre-*Leon* case, found that a magistrate
had abandoned his neutral role when he issued the warrant and then
participated in the search. The Court in *Leon* cited *Lo–Ji* as an example of a
case in which the warrant could not reasonably be relied upon.

a. Abandonment Must Be Known by Police

Since *Leon* focusses on deterrence of *police* misconduct, it follows that
the officer's reliance on a warrant issued by a magistrate who has
abandoned his judicial role is not fatal unless the officer knew or had
reason to know of this abandonment. For example, in *United States v.
Breckenridge,* 782 F.2d 1317 (5th Cir.1986), a judge admitted that he
had issued a warrant without reading the warrant application; he stated,
however, that he made it *look like* he was reading the application to the
officer who was applying for it. The court held that the officer could
reasonably rely on the warrant even though it was invalid.

b. Abandonment Other Than by Participation in the Search

It is clear that the magistrate can be found to have abandoned his
judicial role other than by participating in the search. Thus, in
Breckenridge, supra, if the officer had reason to know that the
magistrate had not even read the warrant application, then the good
faith exception would not permit the officer's reliance on the warrant.

Example: In *United States v. Decker,* 956 F.2d 773 (8th Cir.1992),
agents subjected a suspicious-looking UPS package to a
canine-sniff, and the dog positively alerted to drugs. The
agents then made a controlled delivery, and followed the
package to Decker's house. Decker was arrested when he
received the package. A search of his person revealed a small
amount of narcotics. An agent prepared an affidavit setting
forth these facts and applying for permission to seize
narcotics at Decker's house. The judge issued a warrant to
search Decker's house, but the warrant issued by the judge
*did not list any items to be seized other than the UPS
package,* which was already in the possession of the agents.
The search warrant was a standard form relating to stolen
property, not to drugs, and referred to the UPS package as

"unlawfully stolen." The judge later admitted that the flaws in the warrant were his fault and attributed these errors "to the fact that he was intrigued by the manner in which Agent Hicks became suspicious of the package and the ensuing investigation and therefore did not focus on the language of the warrant." Pursuant to the warrant, the officers seized more than 300 items from Decker's house, including a clock radio, two lamps, a microwave oven, and a weed eater. The court found that the issuing judge signed the warrant without reading it and that the warrant did not purport to list the property to be seized. The court concluded that the issuing judge acted as "a rubber stamp" and therefore that the agents could not reasonably rely on the warrant. Thus, the evidence obtained pursuant to the warrant was properly suppressed.

3. Affidavit Clearly Insufficient to Establish Probable Cause

The Court in *Leon* stated that an officer could not reasonably rely on a warrant issued on the basis of an affidavit "so lacking in indicia of probable cause as to render official belief in its existence entirely unreasonable." In other words, if all reasonable minds would agree that the information set forth in the affidavit did not constitute probable cause, then the officer could not reasonably rely on the magistrate's issuance of a warrant based on such flimsy information.

Example: The Court in *Leon* gave the "barebones affidavit" as an example of an affidavit so lacking in probable cause that it cannot reasonably be relied upon. The Court cited *Nathanson v. United States,* 290 U.S. 41, 54 S.Ct. 11, 78 L.Ed. 159 (1933), as an example of an impermissible, barebones affidavit. In *Nathanson,* the affiant stated that he had "cause to suspect and does believe that" illegally imported liquor was located on certain premises. An officer cannot reasonably rely upon a warrant issued on the basis of such a conclusory tip. The Court noted that the warrant held defective in *Leon* "clearly was supported by much more than a barebones affidavit" and thus could reasonably be relied upon. The affidavit in *Leon* related the results of an extensive investigation, rather than a bald conclusion.

a. Interface With *Gates*

Justice Brennan, dissenting in *Leon,* argued that after *Gates* the good faith exception, as applied to warrants lacking in probable cause, was meaningless. Given the relaxed standards of *Gates,* Justice Brennan argued that "it is virtually inconceivable" that a reviewing court "could first find that a warrant was invalid under the new *Gates* standard, but then, at the same time, find that a police officer's reliance on such an invalid warrant was nevertheless objectively reasonable." He concluded that the good faith standard and the *Gates* standard for probable cause overlapped completely, so that if a warrant was invalid under *Gates* it could not possibly be reasonably relied upon. In Justice Brennan's view, then, if a warrant lacks probable cause under *Gates* it by definition must "clearly lack probable cause" and thus it is within the third exception set forth in *Leon*.

b. Lower Courts

Since *Leon* was decided, only a few cases have reached the result found "virtually inconceivable" by Justice Brennan—that the warrant was not based upon probable cause but that the officer was nonetheless objectively reasonable in relying upon it. In most of these cases it appears that the reviewing court thought that *Gates* was satisfied in the first place. See *United States v. Martin,* 833 F.2d 752 (8th Cir.1987) (upholding district court's finding of lack of probable cause as not clearly erroneous, but applying the good faith exception because, if exercising *de novo* review, the court would have found probable cause to exist). In a few cases, however, courts have found the good faith exception applicable because reasonable minds could differ about whether the *Gates* standards were satisfied. See *United States v. Gibson,* 928 F.2d 250 (8th Cir.1991) (*Gates* standard not satisfied because police only corroborated a few "innocent details," but *Leon* applies because reasonable minds could differ on whether *Gates* standard is satisfied on such minimal corroboration). A more common result is that a court which finds that probable cause is lacking under *Gates* will also find that the officer was not objectively reasonable in relying on the warrant. See *United States v. Baxter,* 889 F.2d 731 (6th Cir.1989) (affidavit describing a tip from an anonymous informant, with corroboration only of the defendant's address and prior conviction on drug charges, is a barebones affidavit, and the officer was not objectively reasonable in relying on the warrant).

4. Facially Deficient Warrant

The Court in *Leon* stated that the good faith exception would not apply if a warrant was so facially deficient in failing to particularize the place to be searched or the things to be seized that an officer could not reasonably think it to be valid. If the warrant is so egregiously deficient in its particularization that all reasonable people would find it invalid, then an officer who relies on it is in error; and the Court in *Leon* presumes that the exclusionary rule can deter the errors of police officers.

a. *Sheppard*

The mere fact that the warrant is lacking certain formalities is not enough to trigger the "facially deficient" exception to *Leon*. This is made clear by the Court's decision in *Massachusetts v. Sheppard,* 468 U.S. 981, 104 S.Ct. 3424, 82 L.Ed.2d 737 (1984), the companion case to *Leon*. In

Sheppard, the judge issued a warrant on a form which authorized a search for "controlled substances" but which was actually meant to enable a search for evidence of a murder. The judge attempted to modify the form, but failed to incorporate an affidavit stating the items that could be sought by the searching officers. The judge assured the officers, however, that all the necessary clerical corrections had been made. The Court held that the evidence was properly admitted despite the defect in the warrant. It reasoned that the officers had done everything that could reasonably be expected of them, and that an officer is not required "to disbelieve a judge who has just advised him, by word and by action, that the warrant he possesses authorized him to conduct the search he has requested." See also *United States v. Russell,* 960 F.2d 421 (5th Cir.1992) (where the warrant failed to include an attachment listing the items to be seized, this was a clerical error attributable to the judge and officers could reasonably rely on the warrant).

b. Lack of Particularity

Sheppard dealt with a situation in which the warrant would have been sufficiently particular as to the place to be searched or the thing to be seized if not for some clerical oversight. A more difficult question is whether a warrant which is ambiguous or overbroad in its description can be reasonably relied upon, or whether it is facially deficient and thus within the fourth *Leon* exception. It is clear that the mere existence of an overbroad description does not preclude an officer's objective good faith reliance on the warrant—because there may be room for reasonable argument as to whether the description is in fact overbroad. Thus, the "facially deficient" exception applies only where no reasonable argument can be made that the descriptions in the warrant are sufficiently particular.

Examples: In *United States v. Buck,* 813 F.2d 588 (2d Cir.1987), a warrant included a catch-all clause allowing the seizure of items related to suspected terrorism. The court found that the seizure of evidence pursuant to that clause violated the Fourth Amendment's particularity requirement because many items could be linked to "terrorism" in the broad sense. But the court stated that the evidence seized pursuant to the clause was nonetheless admissible under the good faith exception. The court explained that "what the officers failed to do was to anticipate our holding today that the particularity clause of the Fourth Amendment prohibits the use of a catch-all description in a search warrant, unaccompanied by any list of particular items or any other limiting language." The court noted however, that *subsequent* use of such catch-alls would not trigger the good faith exception, because the court had just *clearly established* the proposition that such language was insufficiently particular.

In contrast to *Buck,* the court in *United States v. Spilotro,* 800 F.2d 959 (9th Cir.1986), found the good faith exception inapplicable to an overbroad description in a warrant. The warrant authorized the search of a jewelry store for "stolen gemstones and other items of jewelry," and gave no indication that all the jewelry in the store was stolen. The court found the description in the warrant to be *so overbroad that no reasonable officer could think it was sufficiently particular.* Therefore, the warrant was facially deficient and the good faith exception could not apply.

D. UNREASONABLE EXECUTION OF THE WARRANT

The Court in *Leon* cautioned that application of the good faith exception "assumes, of course, that the officers properly executed the warrant and searched only those places for those objects that it was reasonable to believe were covered by the warrant." Improper execution of a valid warrant is an error properly attributed to the officer rather than to the magistrate; and the Court in *Leon* presumed that errors by law enforcement officers can be deterred by application of the exclusionary rule. So for example, if the warrant authorizes a search of a certain hotel room and the officers extend the search to an adjoining room, this error in execution is not excused by the good faith exception. See the discussion earlier in this outline on execution of warrants.

E. "FREEZING" THE LAW

The dissenters in *Leon* expressed concern that adoption of a good faith exception would essentially preclude judicial review of warrants, because there would be no reason for a court to pass on the validity of a warrant if the question was close enough that any evidence obtained would be admissible anyway under the good faith exception. If this is so, it impairs the force of the majority's assertion that the exclusionary rule is unnecessary to deter magistrate errors. The majority posited that magistrates would be more effectively deterred by the threat of a published judicial opinion discussing the error. Under the dissent's view, no such judicial opinion is likely to be forthcoming.

1. Majority Unconvinced

The majority in *Leon* was not persuaded "that application of a good-faith exception to searches conducted pursuant to warrants will preclude review of the constitutionality of the search or seizure, deny needed guidance for the courts, or freeze Fourth Amendment law in its present state." The Court emphasized that "if the resolution of a particular Fourth Amendment question is necessary to guide future action by law enforcement officers and magistrates, nothing will prevent reviewing courts from deciding that question before turning to the good-faith issue." The dissenters responded that "it is difficult to believe that busy courts faced with heavy dockets will take the time to render essentially advisory opinions concerning the constitutionality of the magistrate's decision before considering the officer's good faith."

2. Post–*Leon* Practice

There is some indication in the cases decided after *Leon* that courts will generally avoid the substantive Fourth Amendment question if the case can be decided on good faith grounds. One court has specifically set forth a two-step review of a Fourth Amendment question: first, the court decides whether the good faith exception to the exclusionary rule applies; *if not,* then the court proceeds to the substantive question of whether the Fourth Amendment has been violated. *United States v. Kleinebreil,* 966 F.2d 945 (5th Cir.1992). Other courts, while not as explicit, generally refuse to decide Fourth Amendment questions if the officer could have reasonably relied on the warrant. See *United States v. Henderson,* 746 F.2d 619 (9th Cir.1984) (no need to decide validity of warrant where officer could reasonably assume that it was valid). This practice is not universal, however. See *United States v. Brewer,* 841 F.2d 667 (6th Cir.1988) (no need to decide good faith question, because the warrant was based on probable cause).

F.   RELIANCE ON UNCONSTITUTIONAL LEGISLATION

In *Illinois v. Krull,* 480 U.S. 340, 107 S.Ct. 1160, 94 L.Ed.2d 364 (1987), an officer conducted a warrantless inspection of an automobile wrecking yard. The officer relied on an administrative inspection statute which was subsequently held to be unconstitutional. The Supreme Court held that the evidence obtained in the inspection was nonetheless admissible under the good faith exception.

1.   Rationale

The Court's reasoning in *Krull* was similar to that employed in *Leon*. The majority stated that where the officer reasonably relies on a statute which is subsequently held unconstitutional, the officer has not committed a wrong and thus cannot be deterred by the exclusionary rule. Rather, the wrongdoer is the *legislature,* which has passed an unconstitutional law. The Court reasoned that, like the magistrate in *Leon,* the legislature cannot be meaningfully deterred by an application of the exclusionary rule. The Court explained that legislators were not like law enforcement officers, who have a stake in a particular criminal prosecution and who can therefore be deterred from misconduct by a threatened exclusion of evidence.

2.   Dissent

Justice O'Connor wrote a dissent for four Justices. She argued that the reasoning of *Leon* did not apply because there was a distinction between judicial officers and legislators. She explained that the judicial role is "particularized, fact-specific and non-political," whereas legislators often have an incentive to further law enforcement on broad political grounds. She expressed concern that legislatures could pass laws authorizing unconstitutional searches, with the assurance that at least some of the evidence obtained by such searches would be admitted—exclusion would not occur until the unconstitutionality of the statute was clearly established by the courts. She concluded that "providing legislatures a grace period during which the police may freely perform unreasonable searches in order to convict those who might have otherwise escaped creates a positive incentive to promulgate unconstitutional laws."

3. **Unreasonable Reliance on Unconstitutional Legislation**

As in *Leon,* the Court in *Krull* posited certain limited situations in which it would be objectively unreasonable for an officer to rely on another party's determination that a search is legal. However, the exceptions to the good faith exception are more even more limited when applied to legislative action than they are when applied to a magistrate's decision.

a. **Abdicating the Legislative Role**

First, "a statute cannot support objectively reasonable reliance if, in passing the statute, the legislature wholly abandoned its responsibility to enact constitutional laws." The Court, however, could not cite an instance in which a legislature has "abdicated its legislative role."

b. **Statute Clearly Unconstitutional**

The Court in *Krull* stated that an officer's reliance on a statute would be objectively unreasonable if "its provisions are such that a reasonable officer should have known that the statute was unconstitutional." In other words, if the legislature passes a statute which is in violation of *clearly established Fourth Amendment law,* then an officer would not be reasonable in relying on the statute, and the resulting evidence would be excluded. For example, if a legislature passed a statute authorizing police officers to enter a person's house to arrest that person in the absence of exigent circumstances, the good faith exception would not apply to a search and arrest conducted in reliance on that statute. This is because the Court has clearly established in *Payton v. New York* that an arrest warrant is required for an in-home arrest in the absence of exigent circumstances. The error in relying on the statute would be that of the officer, and the presumption is that law enforcement officers can be deterred from wrongdoing by application of the exclusionary rule.

4. **Misinterpretation of Legislation**

The *Leon/Krull* good faith exception does not apply to a police officer's reasonable though mistaken interpretation of the scope of a statute permitting a search. Such a mistake is one that is made by the *officer,* not by the legislature, and *Leon* posits that officers can be deterred from illegal activity through application of the exclusionary rule. So if the statute does not in fact authorize a search but the officer reasonably thinks it does, the evidence obtained in the search will be excluded unless it independently satisfies Fourth Amendment standards. See *People v. Madison,* 121 Ill.2d 195, 117 Ill.Dec. 213, 520 N.E.2d 374 (1988) (application of *Krull* to misinterpretation of a statute by an officer would mean that "officers would be encouraged to defy the plain language of statutes as written in favor of their own interpretations in conducting searches and seizures;" such a consequence is "fundamentally at odds with the central purpose of deterring police misconduct which underlies the exclusionary rule").

G. THE GOOD FAITH EXCEPTION AND WARRANTLESS SEARCHES AND SEIZURES

By its terms, the *Leon* good faith exception applies only where the officer reasonably relies on an invalid warrant. The good faith exception was extended in *Krull,* but only to situations where the officer reasonably relies on a legislative act. Thus, *the good faith exception does not currently apply to searches conducted by a police officer without a warrant and without reliance on statutory authority.* So far, the Court has applied the good faith exception only where the officer is reasonably relying on an intermediary.

Example: Suppose that an officer enters a house and seizes narcotics. He had no warrant, but he claims that he had probable cause and exigent circumstances due to the imminent destruction of evidence. At the suppression hearing, the court finds that exigent circumstances did not in fact exist because, on the facts, it was unlikely that evidence would be destroyed in the time it would have taken to obtain a warrant. But the court acknowledges that reasonable minds could differ as to the existence of exigent circumstnaces, and that given the presence of readily-destructible narcotics in the house, the officer's conclusion as to exigency was not so far-fetched as to be completely unreasonable. Even after *Leon,* the evidence would be *excluded,* because the officer's "objectively reasonable" miscalculation does not qualify for the good faith exception. See *United States v. Curzi,* 867 F.2d 36 (1st Cir.1989) ("the good-faith exception is not available" where officer conducted a warrantless search on the reasonable but mistaken assumption that the search was consistent with the Fourth Amendment). But see *United States v. De Leon–Reyna,* 930 F.2d 396 (5th Cir.1991) (adhering to the circuit's pre-*Leon* view that the good faith exception applies to illegal warrantless searches).

1. Rationale of *Leon* May Preclude Extension to Warrantless Searches and Seizures

The Court's predominant rationale in both *Leon* and *Krull* is that the application of the exclusionary rule must focus on the wrongdoer, and on whether the wrongdoer can be deterred from misconduct by the threat of excluding evidence. In *Leon* and *Krull* the wrongdoers were the magistrate and the legislature, respectively, and the Court posited that these parties could not be deterred by the risk of exclusion. However, the Court assumed and stated that officers could be deterred from misconduct by the exclusionary rule. Indeed, the four exceptions set forth in *Leon* involve situations in which the officer *has* done wrong and therefore the good faith exception does not apply. Therefore, the rationale employed in *Leon* makes it unlikely that the Court would apply the good faith exception to reasonable but illegal activity of law enforcement officers.

2. Some Language in *Leon* May Be Applicable to Warrantless Search Situations

While the rationale of *Leon* would cut against an extension of the good faith exception to errors by police officers, there is some language in *Leon* which may support such an extension. Specifically, the Court stated that "when law enforcement officers have acted in objective good faith or their transgressions have been minor, the magnitude of the benefit conferred on * * * guilty defendants offends basic concepts of the criminal justice system." This language is not limited to situations where the officer has reasonably relied on an intermediary.

H. REASONABLE RELIANCE ON A WARRANT BASED ON ILLEGALLY OBTAINED INFORMATION

While the good faith exception is currently limited to situations where an officer relies on either a magistrate's decision or a legislative act, a difficulty in applying this limitation arises because officers often conduct a warrantless search in the hope of discovering information with which to obtain a warrant. Before *Leon*, if a search warrant was based upon illegally obtained evidence, then the warrant itself was considered tainted and the evidence obtained upon executing the warrant was excluded as fruit of the poisonous tree. See *Murray v. United States*, discussed in the section on the fruit of the poisonous tree doctrine. Courts after *Leon* have split as to whether the good faith exception should apply where officers reasonably rely on a warrant that is issued on the basis of evidence obtained in an illegal warrantless search.

Example: Suppose the police legally arrest a person, but then conduct a search which is somewhat beyond the spatial limitations of the incident search rule as set forth by *Chimel v. California, supra* (e.g. they search the room adjoining the room in which the defendant has been arrested). In this search they discover a receipt for a storage space, and an indication on the receipt that drugs are being kept in the space. The officers prepare an application for a warrant to search the storage space. They describe the arrest, other pertinent circumstances, and state that the receipt was found in the search incident to arrest. The magistrate issues the warrant and the officers search the storage space and seize drugs. If the good faith exception applies, then the evidence is admissible even though it is fruit of the poisonous tree—unless the warrant is clearly lacking in probable cause because the illegality of the initial search would be obvious to any reasonable person. If the good faith exception does not apply, the evidence would be inadmissible as the fruit of the poisonous tree.

1. Split in Courts

Some courts have held that the good faith exception applies where the officer reasonably relies on a warrant based on illegally obtained information. For example, in *United States v. Thomas,* 757 F.2d 1359 (2d Cir.1985), the court reasoned that in these circumstances "there is nothing more that the officer could have or should have done" to be sure that the initial search was legal. The court concluded that "the magistrate, whose duty it is to interpret the law, determined that the [illegal search] could form the basis for probable cause; it was reasonable for the officer to rely on this determination." In other words, the magistrate's issuance of the warrant is considered a tacit determination, on which the officer can reasonably rely, that there is sufficient *legally obtained* information in the warrant application to support probable cause. In issuing the warrant, the magistrate is considered to have determined that the evidence used in the warrant application was legally obtained. And unless the magistrate is clearly wrong in that determination, an officer can rely upon it in objective good faith.

Other courts have stated that the good faith exception does not apply when a warrant is issued on the basis of illegally obtained information. According to these courts, this would be an extension of the good faith exception to warrantless searches—i.e. the initial illegal search, which was warrantless, would be excused by the good faith exception. More importantly, these courts reason that a magistrate's issuance of a warrant rarely if ever is a determination that the information contained in the warrant was legally obtained; this is especially true because an officer's affidavit rarely gives enough background information as to the circumstances of the initial search so as to allow the magistrate to pass on the legality of that search. Thus, in the usual case, the magistrate merely assesses probable cause and *assumes,* but does not determine, that the supporting information is legally obtained. See *United States v. Vasey,* 834 F.2d 782 (9th Cir.1987) (holding *Leon* inapplicable to a search warrant based on illegally obtained information: "A magistrate evaluating a warrant application based in part on evidence seized in a warrantless search is simply not in a position to evaluate the legality of that search.").

*

VI

THE PRIVILEGE AGAINST SELF–INCRIMINATION

Analysis

I. INTRODUCTION

The privilege against self-incrimination, as expressed in the Fifth Amendment of the Constitution, provides that "[n]o person ∗ ∗ ∗ shall be compelled in any criminal case to be a witness against himself." This privilege prohibits the Government from compelling individuals to provide incriminating testimony. Although the exact origin of the privilege is unclear, the right against self-incrimination was unquestionably established in English common law by the end of the seventeenth century. A century later, this privilege was explicitly incorporated into the Constitution of the United States. See Leonard W. Levy, Origins of the Fifth Amendment Right Against Self–Incrimination 433 (2d ed. 1986) for a complete discussion of the history of the privilege.

A. HISTORY OF THE RIGHT AGAINST COMPELLED SELF–INCRIMINATION

1. The English History

The privilege against self-incrimination developed in the Middle Ages as a shield against the oath ex officio, which was administered during inquisitorial proceedings in the ecclesiastical courts and the Courts of the Star Chamber. The oath ex officio required individuals to supply truthful answers to all questions asked by these courts. The courts forced suspects to swear to this oath before they were informed of the charges against them, the identity of their accusers, or the nature of the evidence against them. With the abolition of the oath in the late seventeenth century, the notion developed that a defendant should not be forced to answer questions that would put his "life or limb" in jeopardy. As coercive practices were often used to procure confessions, the privilege against self-incrimination gradually developed to protect individuals against persecution by the Government.

2. The History in the Colonies

The American Revolution reflected the principle that the Crown had failed to safeguard the rights of Englishmen. Thus, the colonists believed that the unwritten principles of English common law now required the explicit protection of a written document.

a. Development in the States

The privilege against self-incrimination appeared in Virginia's Declaration of Rights and provided that in all capital or criminal prosecutions, a man could not "be compelled to give evidence against himself." Eight states followed Virginia's example and used similar language in writing the privilege against self-incrimination into their bills of rights. This language, however, was significantly more restrictive than the common law right.

b. The Fifth Amendment

The language of the Fifth Amendment privilege differs from the language used in these earlier state documents. As originally proposed by James

Madison, the phrasing and placement of the privilege was unique and suggested a very broad right. This proposal was then amended to confine the privilege to criminal cases. It is unclear whether the framers intended the Fifth Amendment right to retain the contours of the common law privilege. For a complete discussion of the development of the privilege against self-incrimination in the colonies, see Pittman, "The Colonial and Constitutional History of the Privilege Against Self–Incrimination in America," 21 Va.L.Rev. 763 (1935).

B. THE POLICIES OF THE PRIVILEGE AGAINST SELF–INCRIMINATION

Many policies support the privilege against self-incrimination. The following is a list of the most commonly offered justifications for this privilege.

1. Protection of the Innocent

The privilege against self-incrimination protects innocent defendants from convicting themselves by a bad performance on the witness stand. *Quinn v. United States,* 349 U.S. 155, 162, 75 S.Ct. 668, 673, 99 L.Ed. 964 (1955). Some commentators criticize this justification, arguing that the privilege historically protects only guilty individuals.

2. The Cruel Trilemma

The state should not subject individuals to the "cruel trilemma" of choosing among self-accusation, perjury and contempt of court. *Brown v. Walker,* 161 U.S. 591, 637, 16 S.Ct. 644, 655, 40 L.Ed. 819 (1896). Some commentators argue that this rationale only justifies the privilege at trial because contempt of court cannot be used against individuals who refuse to answer to police questioning.

3. Limiting Perjury

It has been argued that if there were no privilege, people who were forced to testify would perjure themselves in an attempt to avoid incrimination. Some commentators state, however, that perjury is prevalent despite the existence of the privilege.

4. Unreliability of Coerced Statements

Self-deprecatory statements are not trustworthy, especially when they are the product of coercion. *Murphy v. Waterfront Comm'n of N.Y. Harbor,* 378 U.S. 52, 55, 84 S.Ct. 1594, 1596, 12 L.Ed.2d 678 (1964). Commentators note, however, that coercion may be barred without resort to a privilege as broad as that found in the Fifth Amendment, and that untrustworthy statements could be excluded even absent a privilege.

5. Preference for Accusatorial System

The privilege against self-incrimination is needed to allow for an accusatorial, rather than an inquisitorial system of criminal justice. *Murphy,* 378 U.S. at

55, 84 S.Ct. at 1596. This justification is criticized as simply a restatement of the privilege itself.

6. Deter Improper Police Practices

As self-incriminating statements are likely to be elicited by improper practices, the privilege protects individuals from the risk of inhumane treatment and governmental abuse. *Murphy,* 378 U.S. at 55, 84 S.Ct. at 1596. Commentators argue that the due process clauses of the Fifth and Fourteenth Amendments afford adequate protection against objectionable police practices.

7. Fair State–Individual Balance

The privilege supports the individual's right to be free from governmental interference and it requires the government to "shoulder the entire load" during contests with the individual. See Wigmore, A Treatise on the Anglo–American System of Evidence in Trials at Common Law VIII, § 2251, at 317 (3d ed. 1940). Some commentators argue that the probable cause requirements for search and arrest provide adequate protection against governmental disturbance, and that the privilege is not essential to protect against overreaching by the Government.

8. Preservation of Official Morality

"Any system * * * which permits the prosecution to trust habitually to compulsory self-disclosure as a source of proof must itself suffer morally thereby." Wigmore, *supra,* § 2251. This rationale is criticized as being tautological; it assumes that self-disclosure is immoral. Justice Scalia, in his dissent in *Minnick v. Mississippi,* 498 U.S. 146, 111 S.Ct. 486, 112 L.Ed.2d 489 (1990), argued that self-disclosure is a positive good: "While every person is entitled to stand silent, it is more virtuous for the wrongdoer to admit his offense and accept the punishment he deserves, not only for society, but for the wrongdoer himself * * *. We should, then, rejoice at an honest confession, rather than pity the 'poor fool' who has made it * * *. To design our laws on premises contrary to these is to abandon belief in either personal responsibility or the moral claim of just government to obedience."

9. Privacy Rationale

The privilege protects the right of each individual to an enclave in which the individual may lead a private life. *Murphy,* 378 U.S. at 55, 84 S.Ct. at 1596. Commentators argue, however, that it is immoral to suggest that a murderer is justified in withholding his aid because he "prefers to remain in a private enclave." Friendly, "The Fifth Amendment Tomorrow: The Case for Constitutional Change," 37 U.Cin.L.Rev. 671, 689–90 (1968).

10. First Amendment Rationale

The privilege shelters individuals from governmental intrusion and oppression concerning political and religious beliefs. Friendly, *supra,* at 696. Some commentators view the First Amendment as the appropriate vehicle for addressing this problem.

C. SCOPE OF THE PRIVILEGE

There are three basic components to the privilege against self-incrimination. Each of these components must exist in order for a person to effectively claim the privilege.

1. Compulsion by the State

First, there must be compulsion by the state. An example of such compulsion is the threat of imprisonment for contempt.

2. Witness Against Himself

Second, state compulsion is only impermissible if it forces a person to be a witness against himself.

a. Testimonial or Communicative Act

An individual only becomes a witness against himself when the state compels the individual to perform a testimonial or communicative act. Other evidence, such as physical evidence of a crime, is not protected by the Fifth Amendment privilege.

b. Legitimate Risk of Harm

Since the privilege only protects the individual from answering questions that are against self-interest, the individual must demonstrate a legitimate risk of harm stemming from the testimony.

c. Must Be Personal

The Fifth Amendment uses the term "himself." Thus, the privilege is personal and only applies to individuals. It does not apply to business entities.

3. Use in a Criminal Case

Third, the state cannot compel self-incriminating testimony in a criminal case. The privilege, however, possesses a much broader scope than this language seems to suggest.

II. PROCEEDINGS IN WHICH THE PRIVILEGE APPLIES

A. COMPULSION IN ANY PROCEEDING WHERE TESTIMONY MAY BE USED IN A CRIMINAL CASE

The language of the Fifth Amendment seems to suggest that the right against self-incrimination only protects individuals from the compulsion of testimony in a criminal case. The Supreme Court has held, however, that the privilege protects individuals from answering questions in any proceeding if their answers might incriminate them in a future criminal proceeding. *Lefkowitz v. Turley,* 414 U.S. 70, 94 S.Ct. 316, 38 L.Ed.2d 274 (1973).

1. Ultimate Use in a Criminal Case

The privilege may be asserted in any proceeding and at any time the Government seeks to compel a person to disclose information, (e.g. on a tax return, see *Garner v. United States,* 424 U.S. 648, 96 S.Ct. 1178, 47 L.Ed.2d 370 (1976)). An individual can invoke the privilege against self-incrimination in civil proceedings, administrative proceedings, etc. if the statement could ultimately be *used* against him *in a criminal case.* See *McCarthy v. Arndstein,* 266 U.S. 34, 45 S.Ct. 16, 69 L.Ed. 158 (1924) (upholding Fifth Amendment claim asserted by a party in a bankruptcy case, where the statement could have been used as an admission in the criminal proceeding). It is the threat of future use in criminal proceedings that gives rise to the privilege.

2. The Use of Compelled Testimony Outside of a Criminal Case Does Not Implicate the Fifth Amendment

The state may compel disclosure of information, however, for use in civil or other non-criminal proceedings. The Fifth Amendment privilege does not apply to protect against use of a compelled statement outside of a criminal case. See *Piemonte v. United States,* 367 U.S. 556, 81 S.Ct. 1720, 6 L.Ed.2d 1028 (1961) (holding that privilege does not prevent use of compelled testimony for purposes of private retribution).

B. WHAT IS A CRIMINAL CASE?

Thus, the question arises as to whether the proceeding in which the testimony could be used is a "criminal case." Courts are likely to uphold a legislative determination that a proceeding is "civil" in nature. See *United States v. Ward,* 448 U.S. 242, 100 S.Ct. 2636, 65 L.Ed.2d 742 (1980) (holding that a statute imposing a "civil penalty" upon persons discharging hazardous material into navigable waters was not "quasi-criminal").

1. Sexually Dangerous Persons Act

In *Allen v. Illinois,* 478 U.S. 364, 106 S.Ct. 2988, 92 L.Ed.2d 296 (1986), defendant's coerced confession was used against him in a proceeding under the Illinois Sexually Dangerous Persons Act and he was incarcerated. The Court held, 5–4, that a proceeding under the Act was not a criminal case within the meaning of the Fifth Amendment, but rather was a civil commitment proceeding for treatment purposes. Therefore, the Fifth Amendment did not prevent the use of compelled testimony in such an action.

2. Legislative Intent Is Crucial

The Court in *Allen* stated that the determination of the nature of a proceeding for Fifth Amendment purposes is a question of statutory construction. In this case, the Illinois legislature expressly provided that proceedings under the Act would "be civil in nature."

3. Criminal Law Objectives

The Act in *Allen* provided that the state could not file a petition under the Act unless it had already filed criminal charges. In addition, proceedings under the Act required satisfaction of a "beyond a reasonable doubt" standard of proof and those adjudicated sexually dangerous persons were incarcerated in prisons (though they received psychological therapy). Yet, the Court held that these traditional indicators of criminal law objectives could not outweigh the fact that the legislature had characterized the Act as "civil" in nature.

4. Dissent

Justice Stevens dissented in *Allen,* arguing that the Court was "permitting a State to create a shadow criminal law without the fundamental protection of the Fifth Amendment."

C. FOREIGN PROSECUTIONS

A witness may be concerned not only with the risk of domestic prosecution, but also with the risk of foreign prosecution. The Supreme Court has not addressed whether a foreign prosecution constitutes a "criminal case" within the meaning of the Fifth Amendment. See *Zicarelli v. New Jersey State Comm'n of Investigation,* 406 U.S. 472, 480–81, 92 S.Ct. 1670, 1676, 32 L.Ed.2d 234 (1972) (stating that because individual did not show substantial risk of foreign prosecution, the applicability of the Fifth Amendment privilege to such situations need not be addressed). The lower courts addressing this question have reached conflicting results although most courts have held that the Fifth Amendment does not protect against the risk of foreign prosecution. Compare *Moses v. Allard,* 779 F.Supp. 857, 882–83 (E.D.Mich.1991) and *In re Cardassi,* 351 F.Supp. 1080, 1086 (D.Conn.1972) (each extending the Fifth Amendment to protect against the threat of foreign prosecution) with *United States v. (Under Seal),* 794 F.2d 920, 925 (4th Cir.1986) and *In re Parker,* 411 F.2d 1067, 1070 (10th Cir.1969) (each holding that the Fifth Amendment privilege does not apply when the risk of prosecution arises outside of the United States).

III. WHAT IS COMPULSION?

A. USE OF CONTEMPT POWER

The state's use of the contempt power is the classic form of compulsion because it imposes substantial punishment on a witness who claims the privilege and presents the witness with the classic "cruel" trilemma: choosing between self-accusation, contempt and perjury—each of which could lead to imprisonment.

B. OTHER STATE–IMPOSED SANCTIONS

The Supreme Court has extended the concept of compulsion to include a broader range of sanctions in addition to contempt power. For example, in *Miranda v. Arizona,* 384 U.S. 436, 86 S.Ct. 1602, 16 L.Ed.2d 694 (1966), the Court found compulsion in the setting of custodial interrogation. See the discussion of *Miranda* in the material on confessions.

1. Economic Sanctions for Invoking the Privilege

In *Lefkowitz v. Turley, supra,* the state sought to interrogate public contractors about their previous transactions and to require these contractors to possibly incriminate themselves by demanding that they waive immunity. In addition, the state planned to disqualify these individuals as public contractors if they refused to testify and waive immunity. The Court held that the threat of economic sanctions imposed by the state was tantamount to compulsion, because the state was attempting to impose a significant penalty for invoking the privilege.

a. The Fifth Amendment Does Not Protect Against the Use of Immunized Testimony Outside of a Criminal Case

If the state gave the contractor in *Lefkowitz* immunity from criminal prosecution for his testimony, however, the state could then deny the contractor public contracts for refusing to testify. This result can occur because, once the contractor is immunized, his statements cannot be used against him and could not tend to incriminate him. Thus, any invocation of the privilege would be improper because no privilege exists in this situation. While it is improper to punish a person for a valid exercise of the privilege, it is perfectly permissible to penalize a person who refuses to testify when he has no right to refuse.

b. Use in a Civil Case

If the witness in *Lefkowitz* had been granted immunity, the state could use his incriminating statements against him by denying him contracts based on his testimony. While these statements would be compelled, the privilege only protects individuals from the use of compelled statements in a criminal case.

2. Denial of Financial Aid

In *Selective Service System v. Minnesota Public Interest Research Group,* 468 U.S. 841, 104 S.Ct. 3348, 82 L.Ed.2d 632 (1984), students challenged a statute that denied Federal financial assistance to male students who failed to register for the draft. Because these students needed to apply for financial aid and had illegally failed to register for the draft, they claimed that the statute violated the Fifth Amendment.

a. Analysis

The Supreme Court stated that the students had not yet been confronted with a need to assert the privilege because the Government had not refused any request for immunity or threatened to impose penalties for invoking the privilege. Moreover, the State did not compel the registrants to incriminate themselves on financial aid forms, merely because there was a question on the form which asked whether the applicant had registered for the draft. The students were not compelled to answer that question truthfully, because if they had done so, they would have rendered themselves ineligible for financial aid. The State did not require them to fill in a form that would have done them no good.

b. Late Registration

Of course, there was the possibility that a student would try to register late for the draft in order to qualify for financial assistance. And Chief Justice Burger, writing for the Court, noted that "a late registrant must disclose that his action is untimely when he makes a late registration with the Selective Service; the draft registration card must be dated and contain the registrant's date of birth." Furthermore, it is a crime to wilfully register late for the draft. Thus, the student who registered late in order to obtain financial assistance would be incriminating himself in the course of the draft registration. The question then would be whether the student was *compelled* to incriminate himself in the draft registration process because of the need to obtain financial aid. Put another way, the question would be whether it is compulsion when the state conditions financial assistance on self-incrimination. But this question was left open by the *Selective Service* Court, because no students before the Court had registered late. Rather, they had not registered at all, and made the somewhat spurious argument that they were compelled to fill in the financial form and admit that they had not yet registered—when in fact to fill in the form in such circumstances would have been a futile act. The Court did not decide whether conditioning financial aid on self-incrimination to the draft board would constitute compulsion and violate the Fifth Amendment.

c. Mere Invocation of the Privilege May Spark Governmental Investigation

The *Selective Service* case illustrates that the mere invocation of the privilege is likely to cause the Government to investigate a person who claimed the privilege. The Court, however, has not prevented the Government from focusing prosecutorial or investigative resources on individuals who invoke the privilege.

3. Comment on the Invocation of the Privilege

A comment by the prosecutor or the judge on the defendant's failure to testify constitutes compulsion. *Griffin v. California,* 380 U.S. 609, 85 S.Ct. 1229, 14 L.Ed.2d 106 (1965). The Court in *Griffin* held that adverse comment to the jury on the defendant's election not to testify constituted punishment for the invocation of silence and thus violates the Fifth Amendment. The Court stated that "comment on the refusal to testify is a remnant of the 'inquisitorial system of criminal justice.' "

a. Adverse Comment on Prior Invocation of the Privilege
It is unclear whether evidence of a defendant's prior invocation of the privilege (e.g. preliminary hearing, grand jury, etc.) may be used against the defendant without violating the privilege against self-incrimination. In *Jenkins v. Anderson,* 447 U.S. 231, 100 S.Ct. 2124, 65 L.Ed.2d 86 (1980), the Court held that a defendant who testified and claimed self-defense could be impeached with evidence of pre-arrest silence. The Court distinguished *Doyle v. Ohio,* 426 U.S. 610, 96 S.Ct. 2240, 49 L.Ed.2d 91 (1976) (holding that no impeachment was permitted regarding silence after receiving *Miranda* warnings), as resting on the due process clause, not on the privilege against self-incrimination.

b. Argument That Evidence Is Uncontradicted May Be Compulsion
A problem arises if the prosecutor argues to the jury that the Government's evidence is uncontradicted. Whether such an argument constitutes adverse comment on the defendant's failure to testify, as opposed to the defendant's failure to call witnesses or offer proof, depends on the facts of the particular case. Compare *Lent v. Wells,* 861 F.2d 972 (6th Cir.1988) (holding that statement that evidence was uncontradicted violates *Griffin* where defendant was the only person who could rebut the complainant's assertion that a sexual attack occurred), with *Lindgren v. Lane,* 925 F.2d 198 (7th Cir.1991) (finding no *Griffin* violation where the prosecutor argued that the testimony of a prosecution witness was undisputed because the defense witness offered in contradiction was not believable).

c. Invited Comment
In *United States v. Robinson,* 485 U.S. 25, 108 S.Ct. 864, 99 L.Ed.2d 23 (1988), the Court held that a prosecutor may comment on a defendant's failure to testify in response to defense counsel's argument that the defendant had not been permitted to explain his side of the story. Thus, the defense may open the door to comment on the invocation of the privilege.

IV. IDENTIFYING THE HOLDER OF THE PRIVILEGE

A. THE PRIVILEGE IS PERSONAL
The privilege against self-incrimination belongs only to the person who has incriminated himself by his own testimony.

1.   **Attorneys May Not Claim Privilege for Their Client**
     Thus, an attorney may not invoke the privilege by claiming that his
     testimony might incriminate his client. This would not be a violation of the
     client's privilege.

2.   **Subpoena Served Upon Accountant to Produce Taxpayer's Records Does
     Not Violate the Fifth Amendment**
     In *Couch v. United States,* 409 U.S. 322, 93 S.Ct. 611, 34 L.Ed.2d 548 (1973),
     the Court held that the Fifth Amendment did not apply when a subpoena
     was served on an accountant to turn over a taxpayer's records, because the
     taxpayer was not forced to incriminate himself. Although the accountant was
     subject to compulsion, the compulsion would not incriminate the accountant
     because he was not the target of the investigation.

3.   **Subpoena Served Upon Attorney to Produce Client's Documents Does Not
     Violate the Fifth Amendment**
     Similarly, in *Fisher v. United States,* 425 U.S. 391, 96 S.Ct. 1569, 48 L.Ed.2d
     39 (1976), the Supreme Court relied on *Couch* to hold that the Fifth
     Amendment did not apply to attorneys who received summonses from the
     IRS to produce client records, where the records would incriminate the client
     but not the attorney. But the Court indicated that, because of the
     attorney-client privilege, the documents would be protected from disclosure if
     they were protected in the hands of the client.

B.   **BUSINESS ENTITIES**
     1.   **Collective Entity Rule**
          In *Bellis v. United States,* 417 U.S. 85, 94 S.Ct. 2179, 40 L.Ed.2d 678 (1974),
          the Court held that the Fifth Amendment does not protect partnerships. It
          reasoned that to allow a partnership to assert a Fifth Amendment privilege
          would be inconsistent with the traditional rule that the privilege is a personal
          one. The Court relied on the language of the Amendment which is cast in
          personal terms.

     2.   **No Matter What the Entity**
          The Court in *Bellis* stated broadly that "no artificial organization may utilize
          the personal privilege." The Court was unconcerned that the partnership in
          Bellis was a law firm with three partners and a handful of employees. It did
          not matter how small the entity was, only that it was an entity. The Court
          has subsequently held that the *Bellis* rule applies equally to corporations.
          Thus corporations, like partnerships, are not entitled to the protection of the
          Fifth Amendment. See *Braswell v. United States,* 487 U.S. 99, 108 S.Ct. 2284,
          101 L.Ed.2d 98 (1988) (corporation wholly owned and operated by a single
          individual was not itself entitled to Fifth Amendment protection).

3. **Personal Privilege**

While the entity has no privilege, the individuals who work for the entity still retain a personal privilege. However, whether this personal privilege can be asserted when the entity is a target of the governmental investigation is a difficult question, which ordinarily arises when the Government subpoenas an individual for documents which will incriminate the entity as well as the individual. This problem is discussed in the section on production of documents, *infra*.

C. **THE FIFTH AMENDMENT PROTECTS SOLE PROPRIETORSHIPS**

Although partnerships and corporations do not possess Fifth Amendment protection, the Court in *United States v. Doe,* 465 U.S. 605, 104 S.Ct. 1237, 79 L.Ed.2d 552 (1984), held that the Fifth Amendment protected a sole proprietorship. The Court reasoned that a sole proprietorship is not an entity that is legally separate from the individual.

V. INFORMATION PROTECTED BY THE PRIVILEGE

A. **EVIDENCE IS NOT PROTECTED UNLESS IT IS TESTIMONIAL**

The Fifth Amendment applies only if the subject of compulsion is testimonial. Thus, a person can be compelled to produce incriminating physical evidence, such as a blood sample, because in doing so, the person is not forced to become a "witness" against himself. To determine if evidence is testimonial, one should not look at the ultimate fact to be proved, but rather the method used in attempting to prove it. The issue is whether the fact will be proven through physical or testimonial evidence.

1. **The Cruel Trilemma**

The distinction between physical and testimonial evidence centers around the "cruel trilemma". Physical evidence cannot be true or false. Thus, in producing physical evidence (e.g. a blood sample), the defendant cannot commit perjury. Physical evidence, therefore, does not place an individual in a cruel trilemma. In contrast, testimonial assertions can be true or false and thus may subject an individual to the cruel trilemma of self-incrimination, contempt or perjury.

2. *Schmerber v. California*

In *Schmerber,* 384 U.S. 757, 86 S.Ct. 1826, 16 L.Ed.2d 908 (1966), the Court found that the state did not violate the defendant's Fifth Amendment rights by withdrawing a blood sample from the defendant and subjecting it to chemical analysis despite the defendant's refusal. The Court held that the privilege only protects an accused from the compulsion of testimonial or communicative evidence.

3. **Extending** *Schmerber*

    In several cases, the Court has reaffirmed and extended its holding in *Schmerber*. See *United States v. Dionisio,* 410 U.S. 1, 93 S.Ct. 764, 35 L.Ed.2d 67 (1973) (holding that state compulsion of voice-prints does not violate the Fifth Amendment); *United States v. Wade,* 388 U.S. 218, 87 S.Ct. 1926, 18 L.Ed.2d 1149 (1967) (holding that forced participation in a line-up does not violate the defendant's Fifth Amendment privilege because "compelling the accused merely to exhibit his person for observation by a prosecution witness prior to trial involves no compulsion of the accused to give evidence having testimonial significance); *Gilbert v. California,* 388 U.S. 263, 87 S.Ct. 1951, 18 L.Ed.2d 1178 (1967) (holding that handwriting exemplars may be compelled from an unwilling defendant). Although an individual's voice and handwriting are means of communication, the sample itself, in contrast to the content of the communication, merely identifies a physical characteristic and is thus not protected by the Fifth Amendment.

4. *Pennsylvania v. Muniz*

    In *Pennsylvania v. Muniz,* 496 U.S. 582, 110 S.Ct. 2638, 110 L.Ed.2d 528 (1990), the Court elaborated upon *Schmerber* and stated that the line between testimonial and non-testimonial evidence is determined by examining whether the witness faces a cruel trilemma in disclosing the evidence. Police officers arrested Muniz for drunk driving. During custodial interrogation the officers failed to give Muniz *Miranda* warnings. In response to police questioning, Muniz exhibited slurred speech, failed a sobriety test, and stated that he did not know the date of his sixth birthday. The issue in *Muniz* was whether these pieces of evidence were testimonial and thus protected by the Fifth Amendment. The compulsion aspect of the Fifth Amendment was presumed by the Court, since the Court had previously held in *Miranda* that custodial interrogation in the absence of warnings constitutes compulsion. (See the discussion of *Miranda* in the section on confessions).

    a. **The Slurred Speech**

        First, the Court held that Muniz's slurred speech was physical evidence and was not protected by the Fifth Amendment. The evidence of slurred speech did not involve the content of the words but focused on the way in which these words were formed.

    b. **The Sobriety Test**

        Muniz failed the physical performance components of his sobriety test, and this fact was admitted against him at his trial on drunk driving charges. The Court did not determine whether a person's performance on a sobriety test was testimonial because Muniz did not raise this issue on appeal. Many lower courts, however, have held that such evidence is non-testimonial under *Schmerber,* because it is offered to show only physical impairment, independent of any communication which could either be true or false.

c.　The Sixth Birthday Question

During custodial interrogation, Muniz was asked the date of his sixth birthday, and he admitted that he was too drunk to figure it out. His statement was admitted against him at trial. The Court held that the answer to the sixth birthday question was testimonial, rejecting the state's argument that the evidence was admitted only to show that the physiological functioning of Muniz's brain was impaired by alcohol. Although Muniz's physiological processes may have been the ultimate fact that the state wished to prove, it was trying to prove this fact *through the use of testimonial evidence*. This holding does not conflict with the principles set forth in *Schmerber*. If the police had compelled Schmerber to answer questions about the alcohol content in his blood, his responses would have been testimonial even though the fact proven would concern Schmerber's physical condition.

d.　The Sixth Birthday Question and the Cruel Trilemma

The Court held that Muniz faced the cruel trilemma when asked the sixth birthday question, and therefore the question called for testimonial evidence. The trilemma laid out as follows: 1) Muniz could not remain silent, due to the pressures of custodial interrogation, which are tantamount to contempt; 2) if he answered the question truthfully—that he did not know the date of his sixth birthday because he was too drunk—this answer would incriminate him, as in fact it did; and 3) if he tried to answer falsely, by making up the date, this answer would also have incriminated him because it would have been evidence of intoxication as well as evidence of consciousness of guilt.

5.　A Statement Must Be Capable of Being True or False in Order to Be Testimonial

A compelled statement must be an express or implied assertion of fact that can be true or false in order to be considered testimonial. If not, an individual does not face the risk of perjury because a statement cannot be false unless it contains an express or implied assertion of fact. For example, in *Doe v. United States*, 487 U.S. 201, 108 S.Ct. 2341, 101 L.Ed.2d 184 (1988), the Government compelled a person to sign a form authorizing the release of bank records in a Cayman Island Bank. The Court noted that if the form had stated "I authorize the release of all my banking records" then it would have called for testimonial evidence, because it would contain an implied assertion that there were in fact bank records to be released. This fact could either be true or false, thereby implicating the cruel trilemma of contempt, incrimination and perjury if the person were compelled to sign it. However, the form in *Doe* authorized the release of bank records, *if any*. This was not an assertion that bank records existed. It was merely a direction to another person to do an act. A direction in itself cannot be true or false, and therefore when the Government compels a person to issue a direction, the Fifth Amendment is not violated.

6. Refusal to Supply Physical Evidence

Because the compulsion of physical evidence is not protected by the Fifth Amendment, an individual's refusal to supply the state with physical evidence may be used against him. If a suspect refuses to supply physical evidence, the state may bring an action for contempt. Contempt is permissible because the production of physical evidence does not present the truth-falsity-silence trilemma that is the concern of the Fifth Amendment. Also, the defendant's refusal to cooperate may be introduced at trial as consciousness of guilt. In *South Dakota v. Neville,* 459 U.S. 553, 103 S.Ct. 916, 74 L.Ed.2d 748 (1983), the Court held that the defendant's refusal to take a blood-alcohol test was not protected by the privilege against self-incrimination and thus could be used as evidence against him. Since the test would not involve testimonial evidence, it did not implicate the privilege. Thus, the refusal to take the test was not protected by the privilege.

7. Psychiatric Examinations

Defendants interviewed by a Government psychiatrist have a right to be warned that what they say to the psychiatrist may be used against them. *Estelle v. Smith,* 451 U.S. 454, 101 S.Ct. 1866, 68 L.Ed.2d 359 (1981). However, when an insanity defense is raised, the state may compel a defendant to undergo an examination to determine mental state at the time of a crime or competency to stand trial; any statements made in the course of such an examination can be used against the defendant. The reasoning is that by raising the insanity defense, the defendant has waived his Fifth Amendment right with respect to his mental condition. See *Buchanan v. Kentucky,* 483 U.S. 402, 107 S.Ct. 2906, 97 L.Ed.2d 336 (1987) (holding that the state's use of a psychiatric evaluation of the defendant to rebut a psychiatric defense did not violate the Fifth Amendment).

B. DOCUMENTS

The Supreme Court held in *Boyd v. United States,* 116 U.S. 616, 6 S.Ct. 524, 29 L.Ed. 746 (1886), that a subpoena of an individual's private books violated the Fifth Amendment. However, the Court in *Fisher v. United States,* 425 U.S. 391, 96 S.Ct. 1569, 48 L.Ed.2d 39 (1976), stated that "[s]everal of *Boyd*'s express or implicit declarations have not stood the test of time." The *Fisher* Court stated that the contents of documents are not protected by the Fifth Amendment if they were prepared before a Government subpoena was ever served. This is because the *preparation* of such documents is "wholly voluntary" and an act completely independent from the compelled act of *producing* the documents for use by the Government. Thus, the contents of voluntarily prepared documents do not constitute compelled testimonial evidence at the time they are prepared, and the pre-existing testimony does not itself, retroactively, become compelled when the Government orders the document to be produced. See also *United States v. Doe,* 465 U.S. 605, 104 S.Ct. 1237, 79 L.Ed.2d 552 (1984) (contents of records voluntarily prepared by a taxpayer are not protected by the privilege, since the Government did not compel the taxpayer to prepare incriminating records).

1. **Types of Testimony Compelled by a Subpoena for Documents: Content of Documents and the Act of Production**

    In *Fisher,* the Court looked at the types of incriminating testimony that are compelled by a subpoena for documents, and determined whether the Fifth Amendment privilege protects such testimony.

    a. **Content of Documents**

        In *Fisher,* taxpayers who were under investigation for possible civil or criminal liability under Federal income tax laws transferred documents received from their accountants to their respective attorneys. Because the subpoena in *Fisher* was directed at a third party, the attorneys, the Court held that the subpoena did not itself violate the Fifth Amendment. The Court did recognize, however, that because of the attorney-client privilege, the attorney could not be forced to produce the documents if the Fifth Amendment protected the client from doing so. However, this was not the case, since, as discussed above, the documents in the attorney's hands were voluntarily prepared well before the subpoena was served. Although the papers may have incriminated the taxpayer, the preparation of the papers was voluntary and thus they did not contain compelled testimonial evidence. Thus, because the Court found that the taxpayers did not have a Fifth Amendment privilege with regard to the content of the pre-existing documents, the attorney-client privilege did not protect the contents of the documents.

    b. **Act of Production**

        When the Government serves a subpoena, it does not compel the preparation of a document, but it does compel the *production* of the document. The Court in *Fisher* recognized that the act of producing a document could have certain testimonial aspects, which would trigger Fifth Amendment protection if the testimony could incriminate the person producing the documents (or could incriminate the client if the production is made by the attorney, as in *Fisher*). See also *United States v. Doe,* 465 U.S. 605, 104 S.Ct. 1237, 79 L.Ed.2d 552 (1984) (privilege may be invoked where the act of production itself involves testimonial self-incrimination). The Court in *Fisher* stated, however, that whether the testimonial aspects of the act of production are in fact incriminatory depends on the facts of the case.

2. **What Does the Act of Production Communicate and When Is It Incriminating?**

    The act of production communicates that the documents *exist*; that they are under the *control and in the possession* of the person producing the documents; and that the documents are *authentic* (i.e. that they are in fact the documents described by the subpoena).

Example: A suspect could resist a subpoena demanding the production of "all records of illegal bets" by claiming the privilege against self-incrimination. To turn over these records would be tantamount to stating that "these are records of illegal bets." That is, the admission that such records exist is itself an incriminatory admission independent from the contents of the documents.

a. Admitting That the Documents Exist

The mere existence of documents is usually obvious and thus ordinarily is not incriminating. For example, there is nothing incriminating in the mere existence of business records or in the records of accounts receivable. In some cases, however, the fact that certain documents exist could be incriminating. For example, the mere volume of records may be an incriminating fact independent of the contents of the records. Thus, in *In re Doe,* 711 F.2d 1187 (2d Cir.1983), a doctor was suspected of dispensing drugs without a proper medical purpose. The court held that a subpoena for patient records compiled during a two-week period triggered the privilege, because the existence of the records could be incriminating: there was such an inordinate number of patient files for the period that the doctor could not have seen so many patients for any appreciable period of time. The volume of the records was found incriminating independent of the contents of the records, which indicated that drugs were in fact prescribed.

b. Admitting Possession and Control of Documents

Ordinarily, there is nothing incriminating in having possession and control of a document—e.g., there is nothing incriminating in the records custodian having control over the records of the business. However, in some cases the admission of control may show an incriminatory affiliation with another person or business. For example, in *In re Sealed Case,* 832 F.2d 1268 (D.C.Cir.1987), a person allegedly involved with the Iran–Contra scandal was served with a subpoena to produce the records of foreign companies involved in covert and illegal activity. The court found that producing the records would be an incriminating admission that he was intimately involved with those corporations.

c. Admitting That the Documents Are the Ones Demanded by the Government: Authentication

If a subpoena requires the production of an individual's own documents, the Government could use the act of production to authenticate the documents at trial. By turning the documents over in response to the subpoena, the person is admitting that the documents are what the Government says they are. See Federal Rule of Evidence 901.

3. Foregone Conclusion

Although the Fifth Amendment protects against compelled, incriminating acts of production, such acts will rarely be protected in practice. Even if the act of production is incriminating, the Fifth Amendment will not apply if existence, control and authentication can be proven through independent evidence, such as through the testimony of other witnesses. If the admissions that are made by the act of production are cumulative, the act of production does not create a substantial risk of incrimination. Thus, in *Fisher*, the Court held that the information communicated through the act of production (existence, control and authenticity) did not pose a realistic threat of incrimination to the taxpayer because the attorney had already admitted each of these facts, and therefore the information communicated through the act of production was a "foregone conclusion."

4. Content of Personal as Opposed to Business Documents

In *Fisher* and *Doe,* the Court found that the privilege against self-incrimination does not protect the content of pre-existing, voluntarily prepared business documents. Although *Fisher* and *Doe* involved subpoenaed business records, their rationale could logically apply to personal documents such as diaries and love letters. Such an application would overrule *Boyd*, which held that the Fifth Amendment protected the content of personal papers from compelled production. The Supreme Court has not decided whether voluntarily prepared private papers are protected from compelled production. In her concurring opinion in *Doe*, Justice O'Connor stated "that the Fifth Amendment provides absolutely no protection for the contents of private papers of any kind." Justice Marshall, joined by Justice Brennan, concurring in part and dissenting in part in *Doe*, disagreed with Justice O'Connor's statement, arguing that the Court had decided only that the contents of voluntarily prepared *business* records were not protected, and that the Court had not reached the question as to personal papers. Most courts after *Doe* have held that the Fifth Amendment privilege does not protect the contents of voluntarily prepared documents. See *In re Grand Jury Proceedings on February 4, 1982,* 759 F.2d 1418 (9th Cir.1985); *In re Steinberg,* 837 F.2d 527 (1st Cir.1988). These courts reason that the rationale of *Fisher* and *Doe,* which separates the voluntary preparation of a document from its compelled production, applies equally to business and personal records. Some courts, however, distinguish between business and personal documents and hold that the privilege against self-incrimination protects the contents of personal documents. See e.g., *United States v. (Under Seal),* 745 F.2d 834 (4th Cir.1984).

5. Compelling Agents of Business Entities to Produce Documents: The Collective Entity Rule

The Fifth Amendment does not apply to business entities. But because an agent of the entity must produce compelled documents, the act of production may incriminate the agent.

a.   ***Braswell***

In *Braswell v. United States,* 487 U.S. 99, 108 S.Ct. 2284, 101 L.Ed.2d 98 (1988), the Government served a subpoena on Braswell, who was the manager and sole owner of a corporation targeted for investigation by the grand jury. The subpoena was served on Braswell in his capacity as a corporate agent, and demanded the production of incriminating corporate records. Braswell argued that while the corporation had no privilege, his own act of production would incriminate him personally because by producing the records, he would be admitting that they existed, that he controlled them, and that they were authentic. (No argument was made that the *content* of the documents would incriminate Braswell, since the contents were voluntarily prepared, and thus not protected by the Fifth Amendment after *Fisher*). The Court denied Braswell's claim and held that he was required to produce the documents on behalf of the corporation.

b.   **Reasoning in *Braswell***

The Court reasoned that the custodian of corporate records holds these records in a representative capacity, and when served in that capacity, he produces the documents not as a person but as a representative of the corporation. Thus, the act of production is not "a personal act, but rather an act of the corporation." The Court found it to be inconsistent to apply a personal privilege to an act which was really done by the corporation, not by the person. The Court also noted that if the agent could invoke a personal privilege, the corporation would be indirectly protected by the Fifth Amendment, in violation of the traditional rule which holds that the Fifth Amendment protects individuals and not entities.

c.   **Nonconstitutional Agency Analysis**

Under the *Braswell* analysis, the production of the documents is an act of the corporation and not a personal act. It follows that if Braswell is subsequently brought to trial, the Government cannot introduce his act of production as an admission that Braswell knew of the existence of the documents, or that Braswell possessed them or authenticated them. This is because the act of production was not Braswell's act but the corporation's act. However, the prosecution *can* introduce the fact that the *corporation* produced the documents, and therefore that the corporation admitted existence, control and authenticity. It is then up to the Government to link the defendant to the corporate act of production through independent evidence. As the Court in *Braswell* put it: "the jury may draw from the corporation's act of production the conclusion that the records in question are authentic corporate records, which the corporation possessed, and which it produced in response to the subpoena, and if the defendant held a prominent position within the corporation that produced the records, the jury may, just as it would had someone else produced the documents, reasonably infer that he had possession of the documents or knowledge of their contents." The Court concluded in *Braswell* that the custodian was not incriminated by personal production of the documents, but only by corporate production, which is not protected by the Fifth Amendment.

d. Oral Testimony Distinguished

In *Curcio v. United States,* 354 U.S. 118, 77 S.Ct. 1145, 1 L.Ed.2d 1225 (1957), the Court held that the collective entity rule did not allow the Government to force a corporate agent to give *oral* testimony, where that testimony would personally incriminate the agent. The Court in *Braswell* adhered to the rule in *Curcio,* and distinguished between oral testimony and document production. The Court stated that a corporate custodian assumes the risk of producing documents as part of the job, even if the production could end up incriminating him, but that a corporate agent does not by taking the job assume the risk of having to give incriminating oral testimony.

C. REQUIRED RECORDS

If the Government requires documents to be kept for a legitimate administrative purpose, neither the content nor the act of production of these documents are protected by the Fifth Amendment. See *Shapiro v. United States,* 335 U.S. 1, 68 S.Ct. 1375, 92 L.Ed. 1787 (1948) (statute requiring the keeping of certain business records does not violate the Fifth Amendment even though the recordkeeping is compelled and could subject the defendant to a risk of incrimination). Thus, the Government can compel an individual to write down incriminating statements in the record, can penalize that individual for failing to keep these records, and can imprison that individual for lying on such records. Although this individual faces a "cruel trilemma", the required records doctrine is an exception to the self-incrimination privilege. See Stephen A. Saltzburg, "The Required Records Doctrine: Its Lessons for the Privilege Against Self–Incrimination," 53 U.Chi.L.Rev. 6 (1986), for general information on the required records exception.

1. Legitimate Administrative Purpose

The required records exception only applies if the records are required to be kept in accordance with a legitimate administrative recordkeeping interest. If the recordkeeping requirement is targeted solely to a class that is inherently suspected of committing criminal activity, then the required records exception does not apply. See *Marchetti v. United States,* 390 U.S. 39, 88 S.Ct. 697, 19 L.Ed.2d 889 (1968) (holding that required records exception does not apply to statute requiring individuals to provide information about illegal gambling activities). This limitation on the exception is required, because otherwise the state could use the exception as a surrogate for criminal law enforcement and as a means to end-run the limitations of the Fifth Amendment.

2. *California v. Byers*

In *California v. Byers,* 402 U.S. 424, 91 S.Ct. 1535, 29 L.Ed.2d 9 (1971), the applicability of the required records exception to California's hit and run statute was at issue. The statute required anyone involved in an accident to stop at the scene and to leave his name and address. Byers was convicted of a misdemeanor for failing to report as required by the statute, and he sought reversal on the ground that the statute violated the Fifth Amendment. The Court held that the statute was valid under the required records exception. It noted that the statutory scheme was essentially regulatory, designed to make it more efficient to process insurance claims and accident suits. As such, the statute was directed to the motoring public at large, rather than to "a highly selective group inherently suspect[ed] of criminal activities".

VI. PROCEDURAL ASPECTS OF SELF–INCRIMINATION CLAIMS

A. DETERMINING THE RISK OF INCRIMINATION

In order for the Fifth Amendment privilege against self-incrimination to apply, a judge must determine whether the information demanded from a witness might possibly tend to incriminate the witness in the future. *Hoffman v. United States,* 341 U.S. 479, 488, 71 S.Ct. 814, 819, 95 L.Ed. 1118 (1951). If the testimony could provide a link in a chain of evidence that might be incriminating, the Fifth Amendment privilege protects such testimony. *Malloy v. Hogan,* 378 U.S. 1, 84 S.Ct. 1489, 12 L.Ed.2d 653 (1964). If an admission is purely cumulative, however, the admission does not present a realistic threat of incrimination and thus the privilege does not protect against such testimony. See *Fisher v. United States,* 425 U.S. 391, 96 S.Ct. 1569, 48 L.Ed.2d 39 (1976), discussed *supra.*

1. Possibility, Not Likelihood of Criminal Sanction

A statement can tend to incriminate even if the offense admitted is rarely if ever prosecuted. For example, if a person is forced to admit to buying a small amount of narcotics from a certain person, the state may be tempted to argue that the statement does not really incriminate the witness because the state would not prosecute such a small-scale drug purchaser. But this argument would fail, because the offense admitted to is a criminal offense, and the question is not whether it is routinely prosecuted but whether it could be prosecuted.

B. ASSERTION OF THE PRIVILEGE

Whenever a person is compelled to answer questions that might tend to incriminate him, he has the right to refuse to answer. If he does answer, however, the privilege is lost with respect to the answer and it can be used as evidence. See *Garner v. United States,* 424 U.S. 648, 96 S.Ct. 1178, 47 L.Ed.2d 370 (1976) (holding that a person who answered questions on his tax return, rather than invoking the privilege, had not been compelled to testify against himself).

C. IMMUNITY

Even assuming the testimony tends to incriminate a witness, the Government may compel testimony when the witness has received immunity. This is because, when immunity is granted, the witness' testimony can no longer incriminate him, and therefore he no longer faces the truth-falsity-silence trilemma that is the concern of the Fifth Amendment—the truth "prong" of the trilemma provides no risk of incarceration in these circumstances. There are two types of immunity: transactional immunity and use immunity.

1. Transactional Immunity

If an individual receives transactional immunity, the Government guarantees that it will not prosecute him for any transaction described in the testimony. Transactional immunity is the broadest form of immunity. At one time, the court appeared to require transactional immunity to supplant the privilege against self-incrimination. *Counselman v. Hitchcock,* 142 U.S. 547, 12 S.Ct. 195, 35 L.Ed. 1110 (1892). But in *Kastigar v. United States,* 406 U.S. 441, 92 S.Ct. 1653, 32 L.Ed.2d 212 (1972), the Court held that use and derivative use immunity was coextensive with the privilege and sufficed to supplant it. Thus, transactional immunity gives greater protection than is constitutionally required.

2. Use and Derivative Use Immunity

Use and derivative use immunity prevents the use of testimony or other information obtained from a person "or any information directly or indirectly derived from such testimony or other information." The Supreme Court held in *Kastigar v. United States,* 406 U.S. 441, 92 S.Ct. 1653, 32 L.Ed.2d 212 (1972), that a grant of use and derivative use immunity is coextensive with the Fifth Amendment privilege, and therefore that a person who receives such immunity has no right to refuse to testify.

a. Prosecution Is Still Possible

The Government may grant use immunity and yet still prosecute the witness for the transaction admitted to, if there is evidence independent of such testimony and the fruits of such testimony.

b. Government's Burden

To subsequently prosecute a person who has received use immunity, the burden is on the Government to prove that the evidence it proposes to offer against the witness at trial is derived from a legitimate independent source. The Government may show that this evidence is free from taint and thus not fruit of the immunized testimony by establishing a "Chinese Wall" between the prosecutors exposed to the testimony and the prosecutors who will bring the case against the witness.

c.   Witnesses Should Not Have Access to Immunized Testimony

In *United States v. North,* 920 F.2d 940 (D.C.Cir.1990), the court held that despite the use of a "Chinese Wall," the prosecution did not fulfill its burden of showing that its evidence was free from taint, where Government witnesses had seen the defendant's immunized testimony on national television. A majority of the panel concluded that, if witnesses have memories refreshed by immunized testimony, their refreshed testimony is tainted, even though the prosecution was not responsible for the taint.

D.   WAIVER OF THE PRIVILEGE

Individuals can waive their privilege against self-incrimination. In addition to explicitly waiving the privilege, an individual can waive the privilege by giving testimony that is inconsistent with the retention of the privilege.

1.   Subject Matter Test

If a witness testifies or supplies information as to part of a story, he cannot, under a claim of the privilege, refuse to testify about related subject matter. Testimony, whether complete or incomplete, does not however waive the privilege as to an unrelated topic. For example, in *United States v. Hearst,* 563 F.2d 1331 (9th Cir.1977), the defendant testified that she was under duress from members of the Symbionese Liberation Army at the time of the bank robbery with which she was charged. The court found that these comments served as a waiver of the privilege as to cross examination questions concerning a later period in which she allegedly lived with SLA members voluntarily. The court reasoned that the conditions of the defendant's confinement at two separate points in time were really part of the same subject matter—i.e. the impact of these conditions on her state of mind. Compare *Lesko v. Lehman,* 925 F.2d 1527 (3d Cir.1991) (defendant who testifies at capital sentencing hearing concerning biographical information does not waive the privilege with respect to circumstances surrounding the crime).

VII

SELF–INCRIMINATION AND CONFESSIONS

441

I. CONFESSIONS AND DUE PROCESS

A. THE REQUIREMENT THAT A CONFESSION BE "VOLUNTARY" IN ORDER TO BE ADMISSIBLE AT A STATE TRIAL

In 1936, the Court took its first step toward creating constitutional protection against the use of coerced confessions at state trials. Earlier holdings concerning confessions in Federal cases were grounded in the common law of evidence and the Fifth Amendment privilege against self-incrimination. See *Bram v. United States,* 168 U.S. 532, 18 S.Ct. 183, 42 L.Ed. 568 (1897). These grounds were not available in state cases, because the Court lacked the "supervisory power" to create state rules of evidence, and because the Fifth Amendment privilege was not binding on the states in this era. See *Twining v. New Jersey,* 211 U.S. 78, 29 S.Ct. 14, 53 L.Ed. 97 (1908) (the privilege is not a "fundamental right"); *Malloy v. Hogan,* 378 U.S. 1, 84 S.Ct. 1489, 12 L.Ed.2d 653 (1964) (overruling *Twining*). Therefore the Court turned to Due Process as the source for its ruling that only "voluntary" confessions would be admissible in state trials. *Brown v. Mississippi,* 297 U.S. 278, 56 S.Ct. 461, 80 L.Ed. 682 (1936).

1. Three Possible Protections

The doctrinal evolution of the "voluntariness" standard took place between 1936 and 1964, when Due Process was the sole constitutional basis for challenging confessions in state cases. In 1964, the Court established the Sixth Amendment as a source of rights for defendants whose confessions were elicited after indictment, and in 1966 the Court relied on the Fifth Amendment to create rights for all suspects facing custodial interrogation. See *Miranda v. Arizona,* 384 U.S. 436, 86 S.Ct. 1602, 16 L.Ed.2d 694 (1966) (Fifth Amendment rights), and *Massiah v. United States,* 377 U.S. 201, 84 S.Ct. 1199, 12 L.Ed.2d 246 (1964) (Sixth Amendment rights). Today, defendants may be eligible for one or both of these sources of protection, and all defendants are entitled to rely on Due Process to challenge their confessions.

2. Evolution of Due Process

The Court decided 35 Due Process cases during the pre–1964 era, but it is possible to understand the "voluntariness" standard by studying only one or two representative opinions. The Court first relied on Due Process to ban the courtroom use of confessions obtained by *physical torture,* and then enlarged this ban to prohibit the use of confessions obtained by *psychological coercion.* The Court focused on *three factors* in determining the voluntariness of a confession: the *actions of the police;* the *characteristics of the defendant;* and the *circumstances surrounding the confession.* The Court was most likely to find a confession to be involuntary when all three factors strongly suggested the presence of psychological coercion. For example, a confession might well be involuntary if an illiterate defendant with limited mental abilities was denied contact with friends, family, or counsel, and was continuously interrogated, by a large number of police officers, for many hours, without sleep or food.

3. **Little Precedential Value**

The Court usually cited a large number of factual details to support a finding of involuntariness under the "totality of circumstances." Thus each precedent provided only a negative example of what police conduct was improper in a unique situation; similar conduct might produce a "voluntary" confession from a more competent defendant in somewhat less stressful circumstances. Not surprisingly, lower courts had difficulty applying Due Process precedents to many new factual settings, because the definition of voluntariness was a question of "degrees," and it was hard to find any bright line that separated higher degrees of coercion from lower degrees. This was especially true with psychological tactics, which were regarded as being much more ambiguous and case specific than physical torture or coercion.

4. **Reliability Is Not the Only Concern**

A few core principles did emerge from the Due Process precedents. The Court's rationale for excluding involuntary confessions originally derived from its concern about the *reliability* of this evidence. Yet it is clear that even a confession obtained by physical torture can be reliable—i.e. the person tortured may be truthfully, if involuntarily, admitting to a crime that he actually committed. Accordingly, the Court's rationale for excluding involuntary confessions expanded into a commitment to deter "inquisitorial" police methods that were incompatible with an "accusatorial" system of justice. This led the Court to invalidate confessions even when independent evidence supported the reliability of the conviction. The Court often disapproved of specific kinds of police conduct, such as significant promises of benefit or threats of harm, extreme forms of deception, and physical or psychological deprivations that reduced a defendant's capacity to exercise the "free will" to speak or remain silent.

5. **Continuing Viability of the Due Process Test**

Ultimately, the Court decided that lower courts and police needed more positive guidance about acceptable interrogation practices, and it established some *per se* rules for confessions in *Massiah* and *Miranda*. Most confession cases today are argued on these grounds. Recently, however, the Court reaffirmed the current vitality of the Due Process doctrine established in the pre–1964 era. See *Arizona v. Fulminante,* 499 U.S. 279, 111 S.Ct. 1246, 113 L.Ed.2d 302 (1991). Today, Due Process usually is invoked by defendants who confess after "waiving" their *Miranda* or *Massiah* rights, and by defendants who are not eligible for such rights.

The Due Process "voluntariness" doctrine of the 1990s remains focused on the three factors of police conduct, the defendant's character, and the circumstances surrounding the confession. However, the current law differs in two respects from that of the pre–1964 era. The Court now allows the "harmless error" doctrine to be applied to involuntary confession cases. The Court also requires that an element of "police overreaching," and not simply the defendant's lack of "free will," must be established in order to show a Due Process violation.

B. THE PROHIBITION AGAINST ADMISSION OF A CONFESSION THAT IS EXTRACTED BY PHYSICAL COERCION

In *Brown v. Mississippi,* 297 U.S. 278, 56 S.Ct. 461, 80 L.Ed. 682 (1936), the Court held that admission into evidence of a confession extracted by "brutality and violence" violated Due Process.

1. Rationale

A unanimous Court condemned two aspects of the police use of torture to procure a confession for purposes of conviction. First, the use of physical coercion made a mockery of the right to a fair trial, and second, it was "revolting" to a sense of justice. Therefore, the use of a coerced confession at trial violated the fundamental right to fair trial procedures. The Court acknowledged that a state has broad discretion to establish procedural rules in criminal cases, but observed that it may not substitute the "rack and torture chamber" for the witness stand. In effect, the state police and prosecutor had accomplished this in *Brown,* where it was undisputed that two defendants were whipped repeatedly, and another was strung up in a mock lynching and repeatedly choked. The Court found the trial was only a "mere pretense" because the state "contrived a conviction resting solely on confessions obtained by violence."

2. Perspective

The evidence of coercion in *Brown* was overwhelming. The defendants' physical injuries were obvious when their confessions were taken by police, as one defendant had a rope burn on his neck and another could not sit down because he had been whipped so severely. Evidence of official bad faith was also strong: the police officers who abused the defendants admitted their acts, and one deputy even testified that he had whipped one defendant, but not "too much for a Negro." The jury was instructed not to rely on the confessions if there was a "reasonable doubt" about their reliability because of any coercion. Yet the jurors convicted the defendants and sentenced them to death. In short, *Brown* was the ideal case for announcing a new Due Process safeguard against the use of involuntary confessions. However, two important problems soon emerged concerning *Brown* 's application to cases that involved less dramatic evidence of coercion.

C. PSYCHOLOGICAL COERCION

Soon after *Brown,* the Court decided to expand the Due Process concept of "involuntariness" to include some forms of psychological coercion. In doing so, however, the Court confronted the difficult line-drawing problem of defining "how much" coercion was "too much." *Brown*'s rule against physical torture provided no assistance here, as psychological coercion was so much harder to define than physical coercion. The former could be created in intangible ways, with many different combinations of coercive factors existing in different cases. As long as the Court was not prepared to ban police interrogations entirely, it was forced to rely on some kind of case-by-case approach to measuring voluntariness in cases involving psychological coercion. Not surprisingly, the Court chose to create such a doctrine by resorting to the traditional Due Process practice of identifying a number of "relevant" factors, and making a judgment about their collective contribution to a constitutional violation in the "totality of the circumstances." This doctrine vested trial and appellate courts with a large amount of discretion to make subjective determinations about the existence of coercion in every case where a confession was challenged.

1. **Incommunicado Interrogation**
    As was evident in *Brown,* the Court's ability to measure the "voluntariness" of a confession depended upon the defendant's ability to produce evidence of coercion during interrogation. Yet when interrogation was *incommunicado,* no independent eyewitnesses were likely to be available to support a defendant's version of the events surrounding the confession. In *Brown,* the police provided this support, but in a typical case the facts were more likely to be disputed. Thus, judicial assessment of coercion usually depended upon the credibility of the parties to the "swearing contest," namely the police and the defendant. Even careful and objective trial judges might distrust the testimony of the accused, and judges who favored the police were likely to uphold confessions as "voluntary" on the basis of police testimony.

2. **Subjective Enforcement**
    In short, the voluntariness standard was dependent for its enforcement on the attitudes of the lower courts toward the testimony of police officers concerning their own use of coercion. Coerced confessions might be accepted as "voluntary" by these courts, either because the police officers lied or because they interpreted their own actions as non-coercive ones. Moreover, lower courts were free to decide "close cases" in favor of the police whenever the "totality" of circumstances in the Court's precedents could be distinguished from the "totality" in the particular cases before them.

3. **Case-by-Case Approach**
    In the era between *Brown* and *Massiah* the Court condemned various methods of police interrogation of defendants. Some convictions were reversed when forms of physical abuse helped to produce psychological coercion. For example, the Court reversed convictions where confessions were produced by 36 hours of continuous questioning, or by forcing the defendant to remain naked in jail. See *Ashcraft v. Tennessee,* 322 U.S. 143, 64 S.Ct. 921, 88 L.Ed. 1192 (1944) (continuous questioning); *Malinski v. New York,* 324 U.S. 401, 65 S.Ct. 781, 89 L.Ed. 1029 (1945) (naked defendant). Other convictions were

reversed when threats, promises, or tricks were used to create psychological pressure on a defendant. For example, the Court condemned the state's use of a psychiatrist who pretended to be a doctor who promised pain relief to a defendant, and then used suggestive interrogation to obtain a confession. See *Leyra v. Denno,* 347 U.S. 556, 74 S.Ct. 716, 98 L.Ed. 948 (1954). The Court also reversed a conviction where the police promised the defendant that only his confession would guarantee his protection from a mob of angry people outside the jailhouse door. See *Payne v. Arkansas,* 356 U.S. 560, 78 S.Ct. 844, 2 L.Ed.2d 975 (1958). Yet the Court also upheld convictions during this era when a defendant was not abnormally vulnerable to coercion, and was treated with some consideration by the police. See, e.g., *Crooker v. California,* 357 U.S. 433, 78 S.Ct. 1287, 2 L.Ed.2d 1448 (1958) (well-educated defendant was given food and allowed to smoke). More than 20 years after *Brown,* some members of the Court finally proposed to create an alternative to the "voluntariness" standard, in order to create more definitive limitations upon coercive police interrogations.

4. *Spano v. New York*

In *Spano v. New York,* 360 U.S. 315, 79 S.Ct. 1202, 3 L.Ed.2d 1265 (1959), a unanimous Court held that a "massive" overnight interrogation of an indicted defendant violated Due Process, when police ignored the defendant's repeated requests for his lawyer, and used a "false friend" of the defendant's to tell him that his failure to confess would cause the friend to lose his job, and thereby endanger the friend's young family.

a. Rationale

The Court examined the totality of circumstances and concluded that the defendant's will was "overborne by official pressure, fatigue, and sympathy falsely aroused" by the manipulation of his friendship with the police cadet who obtained his confession. The Court cited numerous factors to support its holding. Three aspects of the defendant's vulnerability to coercion were deemed relevant: he was foreign born, and had limited education and a history of emotional instability. Seven aspects of the police conduct were cited with disapproval. The police questioned the defendant continuously for eight hours, during the night, using a total of 14 officers, and asking leading questions. The police also ignored the defendant's repeated refusals to talk, and his repeated requests to consult his lawyer, who had advised him to remain silent when he was arrested. The police repeatedly used the "false friend" to tell the defendant that his failure to confess would endanger the friend's job and his support of his young family. Finally, two aspects of the surrounding circumstances were identified as significant. The defendant was indicted, and the police had an eyewitness, and thus had no need to solve the crime by procuring a confession. Given all of these facts, the Court concluded that the confession was not voluntary. The Court also emphasized that the inadmissibility of a coerced confession was based not only on its inherent "untrustworthiness," but also on the principle that "police must obey the law while enforcing the law," because life and liberty can be "as much endangered" by illegal police actions as by the acts of criminals themselves.

b. A Proposed Right to Counsel

Four Justices in *Spano* argued that the conviction should also be reversed on an alternative Due Process ground. These Justices argued that Due Process was violated because the defendant was deprived of his right to *consult with counsel* anytime after his indictment on a capital charge. By secretly interrogating the defendant and denying his requests to consult with counsel, the police used a "kangaroo court" procedure that denied him effective representation by counsel at trial. Another concurring opinion reasoned that since the Constitution guaranteed the right to counsel at a capital trial, it could "vouchsafe no less to the same man under midnight inquisition in the squad room of a police station."

c. Debate Over Right to Counsel

The analysis of the concurring Justices in *Spano* was an attempt to limit the inherent indeterminacy of the "voluntariness" standard by ignoring each defendant's unique perspective, and focusing on a few, clear-cut variables, such as the indicted status of a defendant, and the refusal of the police to allow a defendant to consult with counsel. Not all members of the Court approved of this approach to reformulating confession law, however. For it was forseeable that once a right to counsel was created in the "secret trial of the police precinct," this right would be sought by unindicted suspects undergoing custodial interrogation. Such an expansion of this right might interfere with the ability of the police to investigate unsolved crimes and gather evidence to support convictions in many cases. Thus, the *Spano* plurality's proposed rule ultimately cracked open a debate about how to reconcile the interests of the police in obtaining confessions with the interests of suspects in consulting with counsel, who were likely to advise them to remain silent. Once *Massiah* and *Miranda* were decided, this debate became quite complicated, and it has continued unabated in opinions establishing Fifth and Sixth Amendment doctrines for confessions.

D. THE MODERN DUE PROCESS STANDARD—DISAGREEMENTS ABOUT JUDICIAL INTERPRETATIONS OF "VOLUNTARINESS" AND "COERCION"

1. Threats of Violence

In *Arizona v. Fulminante,* 499 U.S. 279, 111 S.Ct. 1246, 113 L.Ed.2d 302 (1991), the Court held that a credible threat of physical violence created sufficient coercion to render a confession involuntary. Fulminante made a statement implicating himself in a murder of a child, while he was imprisoned on another charge. The statement was made to an undercover informant. Fulminante had been threatened by other inmates who suspected him of being a child-murderer. The undercover informant offered to protect Fulminante from these threats, on the condition that Fulminante would tell him the truth about what happened.

2. Rationale

The *Fulminante* Court relied on the totality of the circumstances to find that the state supreme court made a "permissible" finding of coercion in a "close case." This finding was based on the threat of physical violence, the defendant's reaction to it, and surrounding circumstances that enhanced the coercive nature of the threat. In addition, the Court found that the defendant's vulnerability to coercion supported its conclusion.

3. Relevant Factors

Four aspects of the circumstances rendered the confession involuntary: 1) The defendant was a prison inmate who was in danger of physical harm from fellow inmates who suspected he was a child murderer. 2) The informant became a Government agent while in prison serving time for extortion, and he was instructed to find out about the defendant's knowledge of the murder. 3) The informant "masqueraded as an organized crime figure," told the defendant he knew about the murder rumors, and offered the defendant his "protection" only if he would confess. In making this offer, the informant relied on the fact that other inmates had been giving the defendant "rough treatment." 4) The defendant confessed immediately in response to the threat, "in the belief that [his] life was in jeopardy" if he did not. Thus, the confession was the product of coercion produced by a "credible threat of physical violence" under the circumstances.

a. Defendant's Characteristics

The Court noted that certain characteristics of the defendant supported its judgment. For example, the defendant had little education, and was short and slight in build. Also, he had requested protective custody during an earlier stay in prison, and then had been admitted to a psychiatric hospital when he was unable to cope with the isolation imposed by this custody.

b. Actual Violence Not Required

The Court in *Fulminante,* relying on prior cases, emphasized that actual violence by Government agents was unnecessary to support a finding of coercion. The "credible threat of physical violence" was enough to produce the "mental" coercion to confess. Specifically, the Court held that coercion could be established when a Government agent offered protection from violence in exchange for a confession. See *Payne v. Arkansas,* 356 U.S. 560, 78 S.Ct. 844, 2 L.Ed.2d 975 (1958) (where a police officer promised protection from "an angry mob outside the jailhouse door"). Thus, the defendant in *Fulminante* was coerced because he feared physical violence from other inmates, absent protection from the "mobster" informant.

4. Dissent

Chief Justice Rehnquist authored a dissenting opinion for four Justices. The Chief Justice argued that the confession was "the product of an essentially free and unconstrained choice," and that the defendant's will had not been "overborne" by the informant's conduct. Specifically, he found that there was not sufficient evidence that a credible threat of physical violence produced the confession, and that the majority's ruling created "a more expansive definition" of voluntariness than was warranted under Due Process precedents. The dissenters noted that the defendant never told the informant or others that he was "in fear of other inmates," nor did he solicit "protection" from the informant. They also noted that the defendant was "an experienced habitué of prisons, and presumably able to fend for himself." Further, the dissenters argued that the defendant's lack of awareness that he was talking to an informant created "none of the danger of coercion" that results from more typical interrogations by police officers.

5. Perspective

Fulminante was a closely divided case, and it illustrates how difficult it is for a defendant to prove that his confession was "coerced." The Court was divided over the question whether the informer's conduct was inherently coercive under the circumstances. The majority inferred that the defendant believed his "mobster" friend was capable of encouraging other inmates to attack him if he did not confess. This made the mobster's "promise" into a threat, like the implicit threat of the police officer in *Payne* to let the angry mob attack the defendant. Given the circumstances, the threat was "credible"—the defendant had received "rough treatment" already, he was vulnerable to future retaliation in prison, and the informant behaved like an "organized crime figure" by making an offer the defendant could not refuse.

Yet the dissenters did not believe that the average inmate would be coerced by the informant's behavior. They found the "mobster" to be non-threatening—he "simply requested" that the defendant "speak the truth" about his crime, and the defendant was free to ignore his request. Thus, the informant's gambit was a "legitimate investigatory procedure," and the defendant was an unlucky man who confided in a false friend. Even the majority justices found *Fulminante* to be a "close case," which suggests that police practices may not be held inherently coercive when they fall short of threats of violence.

6. Some Police Coercion Required

In *Colorado v. Connelly*, 479 U.S. 157, 107 S.Ct. 515, 93 L.Ed.2d 473 (1986), the Court held that Due Process was not violated by the admission into evidence of a confession prompted by the auditory hallucinations of a psychotic defendant. Where the police were unaware of the defendant's mental illness at the time he confessed, the subsequent interrogation of the defendant was not "coercive police activity." Thus, the defendant's confession was "voluntary."

a. **Rationale**

The Court declared that even when the "free will" of a defendant is overborne by a mental illness which causes him to confess, Due Process is not violated absent police conduct "causally related to the confession." This holding was supported by the Court's interpretation of Due Process precedents, and by its view that the Due Process "exclusionary rule" for confessions is justified only when exclusion will deter coercive police activity.

The Court observed that "coercive government misconduct" was the focus of its Due Process doctrine in *Brown,* and that all subsequent confession cases "contained a substantial element of coercive police conduct." While cases like *Spano* found that the defendant's mental condition could be a "significant factor" in the "voluntariness calculus," this factor alone never was held to be controlling. Instead, Due Process precedents revealed that there must be a "link between coercive activity of the State" and "a resulting confession." Without this limitation, the "voluntariness" inquiry would become too difficult for judges to make, as they would often be unable to "divine a defendant's motivation for speaking".

b. **Deterrence**

The Court in *Connelly* declared that the Due Process "exclusionary rule" for confessions has the same purpose as the Fourth Amendment exclusionary rule, namely, the deterrence of future constitutional violations by police officers. Like its Fourth Amendment counterpart, the Due Process rule imposes "a substantial cost" on law enforcement because it proscribes the admission of "relevant evidence." The Court determined that exclusion of the confession in *Connelly* could not deter coercive police conduct in future cases (because the police had not engaged in such tactics in *Connelly*). Instead, the Court concluded that state rules of evidence should govern the question whether the confession of a mentally ill defendant is sufficiently reliable to be admitted at trial.

c. **Dissent**

Justices Brennan and Marshall dissented. Justice Brennan declared that the confession of a mentally ill defendant does not reflect the exercise of "free will," and therefore is "coerced" and inadmissible. He criticized the *Connelly* majority for failing "to recognize all forms of involuntariness or coercion as antithetical to Due Process," and failing "to acknowledge free will as a value of constitutional consequence." In order to preserve the Due Process values of "private conscience and human dignity," Justice Brennan proposed that a confession should be treated as "involuntary" where the source of coercion is the mental condition of the defendant, the actions of third parties, police misconduct, or some combination of these factors. Justice Brennan noted that judges routinely inquire into "the motivation and competence of the defendant" in any "voluntariness inquiry," and could follow the same approach if the defendant's mental condition were the sole basis for a finding of coercion.

Justice Brennan also disagreed with the Court's observation that deterrence of police misconduct was the only rationale for the Due Process exclusionary rule. He argued that the rule also creates a safeguard for "the integrity of our adversary system," and that the judicial action of admitting the confession into evidence was "state action" that violated Due Process in *Connelly*. Finally, Justice Brennan argued that Due Process should require a trial court to find "substantial indicia of reliability" of a confession of a mentally ill person in order to admit it into evidence. He derived this requirement from two aspects of Due Process precedents—the Court's historic preference for "accusatorial practices," and its distrust of confessions because of "their decisive impact upon the adversarial process" and potential for "profoundly prejudicial" consequences. In *Connelly*, Justice Brennan found that "not a shred" of evidence linked the defendant to the crime, except his confession. He decried the Court's willingness to have the defendant tried, imprisoned and possibly executed "based solely" upon a confession obtained when he was in a delusional state.

d. Perspective

The *Connelly* majority was clearly concerned about the inherent difficulty of distinguishing among types of "internal" coercion, and of creating a "competency" standard for judicial findings of coercion. The *Connelly* Court also might have been influenced by the Court's many decisions concerning the meaning of "compulsion" under *Miranda* and its progeny. No Fifth Amendment "compulsion" exists when police are following all the *Miranda* rules properly. See, e.g., *Moran v. Burbine*, 475 U.S. 412, 106 S.Ct. 1135, 89 L.Ed.2d 410 (1986). In *Connelly*, the police did follow all the rules. Yet the dissenters proposed that police officers should be penalized for interrogating a suspect who happens to be mentally ill. This clashed with the spirit of the Court's modern interpretations of *Miranda*, and its focus on the need to deter deliberate police violations of *Miranda* rules.

7. The Harmless Error Doctrine and Involuntary Confessions

In *Arizona v. Fulminante,* 499 U.S. 279, 111 S.Ct. 1246, 113 L.Ed.2d 302 (1991), the Court held that the erroneous admission of an involuntary confession may be held to be "harmless error" under *Chapman v. California,* 386 U.S. 18, 87 S.Ct. 824, 17 L.Ed.2d 705 (1967). The state must prove that the admission of such a confession was "harmless beyond a reasonable doubt." A reviewing court must exercise "extreme caution" before holding that the admission of a confession is harmless, because of the risk that a coerced confession is unreliable, and because of the "profound impact" that a confession has upon the jury. However, the erroneous admission of an involuntary confession is *not* per se reversible error.

8. An Involuntary Confession Is Not Admissible at Trial for Any Purpose

In *Mincey v. Arizona,* 437 U.S. 385, 98 S.Ct. 2408, 57 L.Ed.2d 290 (1978), the Court held that a coerced confession may not be admitted either in the state's case-in-chief, or during the state's cross-examination of a defendant whom the state wishes to impeach when she takes the stand. The *Mincey* Court rejected the state's argument that coerced confessions should be treated the same way as confessions that violate *Miranda,* which are admissible to impeach a defendant who takes the stand. See *Harris v. New York,* 401 U.S. 222, 91 S.Ct. 643, 28 L.Ed.2d 1 (1971).

II. CONFESSIONS AND FEDERAL SUPERVISORY POWERS

A. THE *McNABB–MALLORY* RULE

During the same era that the Court was developing the case-by-case "voluntariness doctrine" under Due Process, it took a step towards creating a *per se* "exclusionary rule" for confessions obtained by Federal agents during the improper detention of suspects following arrest. This rule was derived from a Federal statute that required agents to bring a suspect to the "nearest judicial officer" for a preliminary hearing following arrest. In *McNabb v. United States,* 318 U.S. 332, 63 S.Ct. 608, 87 L.Ed. 819 (1943), the Court held that confessions obtained from Federal defendants convicted of murder were improperly admitted because the defendants were detained for three days of interrogation, instead of being taken to a judicial officer.

1. Rationale

The *McNabb* Court invoked its "supervisory authority" over Federal courts in order to justify its exclusionary rule, and explained that admission of confessions obtained during illegal detention "would stultify the policy which Congress enacted into law." This policy was the need to require a prompt judicial appearance in order to guard "against the misuse of the law enforcement process."

2. Nature of Delay
The *McNabb* rule required the Court to decide what sort of delay in making a prompt appearance would be improper. In *Mallory v. United States*, 354 U.S. 449, 77 S.Ct. 1356, 1 L.Ed.2d 1479 (1957), the Court relied on Rule 5(a) of the Federal Rules of Criminal Procedure to require that Federal agents take arrested suspects to court "without unnecessary delay." In *Mallory*, the confession was held to be inadmissible because agents delayed the rape suspect's court appearance from the time of arrest in the early afternoon until the next morning. The *McNabb–Mallory* rule did allow for "necessary" delays, of course, so that lower courts could accept confessions that were obtained during a time when no magistrate was available, or when other special justifications existed.

B. DEMISE OF *McNABB–MALLORY* RULE
The Court never elevated the *McNabb–Mallory* rule to the status of constitutional doctrine, and only a few state courts chose to emulate it by creating similar rules based on "prompt appearance" requirements in state statutes. Most states have such statutes, but most state courts preferred to treat a delayed detention as only one factor in a voluntariness inquiry. In 1968, Congress moved to abolish the *McNabb–Mallory* rule by enacting 18 U.S.C.A. § 3501(c). This statute provides that a confession should not be excluded from evidence *per se* because of a delay of up to six hours after arrest, and that any delay "need not be conclusive" on the issue of the voluntariness of the confession.

1. Relationship to *Miranda*
In its time, the *McNabb–Mallory* rule served the function of allowing the Court to invalidate Federal confessions based on clear-cut police failure to follow a procedure designed to reduce the risk of police coercion of arrested suspects. In this way, the rule foreshadowed the Court's later adoption of the *Miranda* rules, which were animated by a similar search for clear-cut safeguards to protect suspects from the coercive pressures of interrogation. Perhaps because the Court found the *Miranda* rules to be superior safeguards, it has not chosen to employ the *McNabb–Mallory* rule since 1968, or to address the issue whether Congress had the authority to abolish it. Thus, the rule is largely a relic in the museum of confession doctrines, although it remains alive and well in the few states that continue to adhere to it as a matter of state law.

III. CONFESSIONS AND THE SIXTH AMENDMENT BEFORE MIRANDA

In 1964, a majority of the Court seized upon two opportunities to establish the Sixth Amendment as a source for confession law. First, the Court created a rule prohibiting the "deliberate elicitation" of a confession from an indicted defendant by secret Government agents. Next, the Court turned to the more difficult case of the unindicted suspect undergoing custodial interrogation by police. Here, the Court held back from creating broad rules concerning all suspects. It did, however, require the police to honor a suspect's request to consult her retained lawyer during interrogation, and to warn such a suspect of her right to remain silent.

The Court's dramatic extension of the Sixth Amendment into the pre-indictment context was soon discredited by other precedent restricting the attachment of the right to counsel to events occuring at or after the initiation of "adversary judicial proceedings." See *Kirby v. Illinois,* 406 U.S. 682, 92 S.Ct. 1877, 32 L.Ed.2d 411 (1972). By this time, the Court's creation of Sixth Amendment protections for unindicted suspects had become superfluous because of equivalent Fifth Amendment protections established in *Miranda v. Arizona,* 384 U.S. 436, 86 S.Ct. 1602, 16 L.Ed.2d 694 (1966). Today, the Sixth Amendment law of confessions exists in the form for which it was first created, namely, as a source of safeguards for indicted defendants, who are interrogated either by the police or by secret government agents.

A. THE PROHIBITION ON "DELIBERATE ELICITATION" OF INCRIMINATING STATEMENTS FROM INDICTED DEFENDANTS BY SECRET GOVERNMENT AGENTS

In *Massiah v. United States,* 377 U.S. 201, 84 S.Ct. 1199, 12 L.Ed.2d 246 (1964), the Court held that the Sixth Amendment was violated in a narcotics case, when the Government used an informant, who had been indicted along with Massiah, to elicit incriminating statements from him while the two were free on bail and awaiting trial. The Government relied on this evidence to obtain Massiah's conviction, and the Court reversed.

1. Rationale

The Court borrowed the rationale of the concurring opinions in *Spano v. New York,* 360 U.S. 315, 79 S.Ct. 1202, 3 L.Ed.2d 1265 (1959), and held that all indicted defendants possess a Sixth Amendment right to consult with counsel upon request during interrogation by police. The Court then extended this rule to defendants who were interrogated by secret agents, because "if such a rule is to have any efficacy, it must apply to indirect and surreptitious interrogations" as well as those conducted by police.

a. Critical Stage

The *Massiah* Court reasoned that after indictment, a defendant is "entitled to a lawyer's help," and to a trial in an "orderly courtroom" protected by "all the procedural safeguards of the law." Therefore, such a defendant must be given the aid of counsel in the "extrajudicial proceeding" of police interrogation, or he will be denied effective representation "at the only stage when legal aid and advice would help him."

2. Deliberate Elicitation

The Court in *Massiah* held that the Sixth Amendment right to consult counsel during interrogation could not be circumvented through "deliberate elicitation" of a confession by secret Government agents after indictment. This practice was even "more" of a serious imposition on a defendant than a stationhouse interrogation, because the defendant in *Massiah* did "not even know" that he was being interrogated. In response to the Government's argument that it needed to use secret agents to conduct continuing investigations of indicted defendants, the Court declared that "it was entirely proper" to investigate a defendant's criminal activities. But, the Court insisted, the defendant's own incriminating statements could not be used against him at his trial. Implicitly, the Court suggested, such statements could be used to convict others.

3. Dissent

Justice White dissented, in an opinion for three Justices, arguing that the Court's interpretation of the Sixth Amendment was unsupportable, and that indicted defendants should be required to face the risk that their trusted confederates might be Government informants in disguise. He argued that no Sixth Amendment violation existed in *Massiah,* because the defendant was not "prevented" from consulting with counsel, because no meetings with counsel were "disturbed or spied on," and because the defendant's preparation for trial "was in no way obstructed." He found no compelling reason to extend the Sixth Amendment "to out-of-court conversations" obtained "without counsel's consent or presence." He accused the *Massiah* majority of requiring counsel's presence in order to ensure that counsel "would foreclose any admissions at all." To Justice White, this rule was "nothing more than a thinly disguised" preference for prohibiting the use of out-of-court confessions entirely, which policy would have "a severe and unfortunate impact" upon most criminal cases. Justice White concluded that the Court's new exclusionary rule was "peculiarly inappropriate" in the context of secret agents, because of the lack of "official coercion" created by such surreptitious interrogators.

4. Open Question

One question left open in *Massiah* was the scope of the Court's prohibition on the use of informants to obtain confessions from indicted defendants. The *Massiah* dissenters argued that the Court's new rule completely foreclosed the use of informants "at any time after the right of counsel attaches." The language of the Court was ambiguous, however, as it prohibited only the "deliberate elicitation" of incriminating statements. In *Massiah,* the defendant was free on bail, and agreed to meet with his co-defendant, who had become a Government informant after being indicted. During their meeting in the co-defendant's car, which was wired to broadcast any statements to a nearby agent, the defendant and his confederate had a "lengthy conversation." This, then, was sufficient evidence of "deliberate elicitation" of the confession.

What was left unclear in *Massiah* was whether more passive conduct by an informant might be acceptable; for example, an informant might be approached by a defendant who makes incriminating statements without prompting. In such a case, the Court would have to decide whether the Government's role in creating the informant's desire to report the defendant's admissions was an unacceptable "circumvention" of the defendant's Sixth Amendment rights. Ultimately, Justice White's view that even indicted defendants should be required to suffer the risks of exposure from "false friends" won the allegiance of a majority of the Court, at least where an informant is more an "ear" (i.e., a listener) than a "mouth" (i.e., a speaker). See *Kuhlmann v. Wilson,* 477 U.S. 436, 106 S.Ct. 2616, 91 L.Ed.2d 364 (1986).

5. Limited Facts

The facts of *Massiah* did not provide the Court with an opportunity to flesh out the implications of its rule that indicted defendants had a right to consult counsel during police interrogation. The Court's language implied that this right applied to all such defendants, including those who did not ask to speak to counsel. So, several open questions remained after *Massiah*. Should indicted defendants receive a *"Massiah* warning," informing them of their Sixth Amendment right to counsel, and of the right to remain silent in counsel's absence? Should similar rights be given to unindicted suspects, and to indigents who would need to consult appointed counsel? Should a defendant or suspect be allowed to waive her rights, and if so, under what circumstances?

When *Massiah* was decided, the Court was considering the Sixth Amendment answers to some of these questions in *Escobedo v. Illinois,* 378 U.S. 478, 84 S.Ct. 1758, 12 L.Ed.2d 977 (1964). After its decision in *Escobedo,* however, the Court turned to the Fifth Amendment as the basis for answering all these questions in *Miranda.* Not until many years later would the Court rely again on the Sixth Amendment as a source of rights for indicted defendants undergoing custodial interrogation. See *Brewer v. Williams,* 430 U.S. 387, 97 S.Ct. 1232, 51 L.Ed.2d 424 (1977).

B. "DELIBERATE ELICITATION" OF A CONFESSION FROM AN UNINDICTED SUSPECT WHO ASKS TO SEE HIS RETAINED COUNSEL

In *Escobedo v. Illinois,* 378 U.S. 478, 84 S.Ct. 1758, 12 L.Ed.2d 977 (1964), the Court extended the Sixth Amendment right to counsel to an unindicted suspect in custody. It held his confession to be inadmissible because he had been denied an opportunity to consult with his retained counsel during interrogation, and had not been warned of his right to remain silent.

1. Rationale

The Court relied on Massiah's rationale, and found that the interrogation of the suspect in *Escobedo* was the functional equivalent of the post-indictment stage, because the suspect had become the "accused" when the purpose of the interrogation was not to investigate an unsolved crime, but rather was designed to obtain a confession from a targeted suspect. The Court stated that it would "exalt form over substance" to make the right to counsel depend on the formality of an indictment. It further noted that, without the right to consult counsel, the suspect's ultimate trial would become "no more than an appeal from the interrogation," and the right to counsel at trial would be "a very hollow thing."

In response to the state's argument that the creation of a new right to consult counsel would cause a decrease in the number of confessions, the Court criticized the police practice of reliance on confessions, declaring that this leads to "incomplete" investigations, and a "readiness to resort to bullying and to physical force and torture." The Court concluded that if a suspect's reliance on the constitutional right to "absolute silence" would "thwart the effectiveness" of our system of law enforcement, then "there is something very wrong with that system."

2. Dissent

Four Justices dissented in *Escobedo,* and three filed opinions objecting to the Court's extension of the Sixth Amendment into the pre-indictment stage. Justice Harlan predicted that the *Escobedo* rule would "seriously and unjustifiably" restrict "perfectly legitimate methods" of law enforcement. Justice Stewart agreed, and argued that only the "institution of formal, meaningful judicial proceedings" marks the point where "adversary proceedings" commence and constitutional guarantees attach. Justice White declared that the *Escobedo* majority transformed the right to counsel into "an impenetrable barrier to any interrogation once the accused has become a suspect." He objected to the Court's creation of this barrier in a setting where "no compelled statements" were obtained in violation of the Fifth Amendment privilege. He also decried the Court's criticisms of confessions, as reflecting an unjustifiable "distrust of law enforcement officers everywhere."

3. Perspective

Within two years, *Escobedo*'s Sixth Amendment rule was superceded by *Miranda* 's Fifth Amendment rules, which granted suspects all the rights provided by *Escobedo,* and more. Within another six years, *Escobedo*'s holding that a pre-indictment event could be a "critical stage" was erased by the Court's adoption of Justice Stewart's standard requiring the initiation of "adversary judicial proceedings" for attachment of the Sixth Amendment right to counsel. See *Kirby v. Illinois,* 406 U.S. 682, 92 S.Ct. 1877, 32 L.Ed.2d 411 (1972) (holding that a pre-indictment lineup is not a "critical stage"). Finally, *Escobedo*'s substance lost all its Sixth Amendment content when the Court reinterpreted it as a "Fifth Amendment" case. See *Moran v. Burbine,* 475 U.S. 412, 106 S.Ct. 1135, 89 L.Ed.2d 410 (1986).

Escobedo is noteworthy today because it illustrates the Court's readiness before *Miranda* to require police to warn suspects of their right to remain silent, and to honor a suspect's request to consult with counsel during interrogation. The *Miranda* right to consult counsel on request is the right most consistently honored by the Court today. See, e.g., *Minnick v. Mississippi,* 498 U.S. 146, 111 S.Ct. 486, 112 L.Ed.2d 489 (1990); *Arizona v. Roberson,* 486 U.S. 675, 108 S.Ct. 2093, 100 L.Ed.2d 704 (1988). What *Escobedo* left unresolved were questions that the Court took up in *Miranda,* namely the scope of "warnings" needed by an interrogated suspect, the conditions upon which a "waiver" of rights could be secured by police, and the applicability of the rights to silence and counsel to indigent suspects.

IV. CONFESSIONS AND THE FIFTH AMENDMENT

A. *MIRANDA v. ARIZONA*

In *Miranda v. Arizona,* 384 U.S. 436, 86 S.Ct. 1602, 16 L.Ed.2d 694 (1966), the Court held that a police officer may not interrogate a suspect in custody until she gives the suspect four "warnings" describing his rights, and then seeks a "knowing, intelligent and voluntary" waiver of these rights from the suspect. A police officer also must cut off questioning if a suspect invokes his right to silence or his right to consult counsel, even if this invocation follows a waiver of rights.

1. Rationale

The Court reasoned that the *Miranda* rules were required in order to safeguard a suspect's Fifth Amendment right to remain silent from the *inherently coercive pressures of custodial interrogation* by police in the absence of such safeguards. The Court's opinion first explained its rationale and holding in four parts. Then it applied its new rules to the facts of four cases, and found the confessions in all of them to be inadmissible.

a. Custodial Interrogation Constitutes Fifth Amendment Compulsion

The *Miranda* Court expressed its disapproval of the "police-dominated" atmosphere of modern custodial interrogations, and the "evils" it can bring. The Court noted that "third degree" techniques of physical abuse by interrogators were "sufficiently widespread to be the object of concern." Likewise, psychologically-oriented techniques were viewed as creating "intimidation" of suspects that was "equally destructive of human dignity." Thus, judicially-created "protective devices" were necessary in order to "dispel the compulsion inherent in custodial surroundings."

b. **Interrogation Techniques**

The Court relied on police manuals on interrogation techniques to describe modern practices used by police to undermine a suspect's will to remain silent. These techniques included the following: placing the suspect in isolated and unfamiliar surroundings, displaying an air of confidence in his guilt, minimizing the seriousness of the offense, interrogating persistently in order to "overwhelm" the suspect, using the "Mutt and Jeff" routine where one officer acts friendly and the other hostile, placing the suspect in a fraudulent lineup where he is identified as the wrongdoer, telling the suspect that his silence indicates he has something to hide, and advising the suspect to save himself and his family the expense of a lawyer and "handle this" by himself.

c. **Not Involuntary Under the Due Process Clause, but Presumptively Compelled Under the Fifth Amendment**

The Court noted that such intimidating police techniques may produce a confession that is not "involuntary" under Due Process standards. Nonetheless, the Court found such techniques to be "menacing" and full of "potentiality for compulsion." Even without police use of such techniques, the "very fact" of custodial interrogation "exacts a heavy toll on individual liberty and trades on the weakness" of suspects. Therefore, the Court found the practice of *incommunicado* interrogation to be "at odds" with the Fifth Amendment privilege against self-incrimination. Without "safeguards" to dispel the compulsion inherent in this practice, the Court declared that *no confession* "can truly be the product" of a suspect's "free choice." Thus, the *Miranda* Court established a bright-line rule that a confession made in response to custodial interrogation was compelled self-incrimination and inadmissible.

d. **The Fifth Amendment Privilege Against Self–Incrimination Applies to Custodial Interrogation**

The Court declared that the "foundation" underlying the Fifth Amendment privilege is the requirement that Government must accord "dignity and integrity" to its citizens. The privilege is "fulfilled" only when a person is guaranteed the right to remain silent, not only at trial, but also during custodial interrogation.

The Court determined that the policies underlying the existence of the privilege at trial include the need to maintain a "fair state-individual balance" by requiring the Government to prove its case by its own "independent labors." This form of proof, rather than the use of compelled confessions, establishes "respect for the inviolability of the human personality." The privilege is part of an individual's "right to a private enclave where he may lead a private life," and it is a "mainstay" of the adversary system. The Court concluded that the "principles embodied in the privilege" apply equally to both the formal compulsion of testifying unwillingly against oneself at trial, and to the "informal compulsion" of custodial interrogation by police.

e. Precedent

In applying the Fifth Amendment to custodial interrogation (and thus outside the formal processes of subpoena and trial), the *Miranda* Court cited precedents, including *Bram v. United States,* 168 U.S. 532, 18 S.Ct. 183, 42 L.Ed. 568 (1897), and *Escobedo.* In *Bram,* the Court relied on the privilege in creating a "compulsion" standard for Federal interrogations, and emphasized that an accused may not be subjected to "improper influences" by interrogators seeking a confession. In *Escobedo v. Illinois,* 378 U.S. 478, 84 S.Ct. 1758, 12 L.Ed.2d 977 (1964), the Court found that it was the "compelling atmosphere" of custodial interrogation that caused the suspect to speak, in the absence of the "protective" devices of the right to consult counsel, and a warning about the right to remain silent. Thus, *Escobedo* established that "the presence of counsel" would make the process of interrogation "conform to the dictates of the privilege."

2. The *Miranda* Safeguards

The Court established two objectives for its safeguards. The first was to "adequately and effectively" apprise a suspect of her rights. The second was to insure that "the exercise of those rights" was "fully honored" by police. The Court held that the event of "custodial interrogation" requires the police to comply with *Miranda* safeguards, in the absence of "equally effective" procedures that may be devised by Congress or the states.

a. The Warnings

A suspect must be apprised of her rights through warnings of the right to remain silent, and of the fact that anything she says "can and will be used" against her in court. The suspect must also be informed that she has the right to "consult with a lawyer and to have the lawyer" with her during interrogation, and that if she is indigent "a lawyer will be appointed to represent" her. The warnings about the rights to silence and counsel are *"absolute prerequisites to interrogation."* The warning about the appointment of counsel must be given "when there is any doubt at all" about a suspect's ability to retain counsel.

b. Functions of the Warnings

The Court declared that the warnings would help to overcome the "inherent pressures of the interrogation atmosphere." First, they inform the suspect of her rights and thus make an "intelligent decision" as to the exercise of these rights possible. Also, the warnings would "show the suspect" that the police were prepared to honor her rights. They also would make her "acutely aware" that she was "not in the presence of persons acting solely" in her interest.

c. Second–Tier Safeguards

The *Miranda* Court declared that the warnings alone would be insufficient to protect a suspect's exercise of the Fifth Amendment privilege. In addition, a suspect needed an opportunity to consult with counsel, because the atmosphere of custodial interrogation could "operate very quickly to overbear" her will, even after warnings were given. The procedural requirements imposed by *Miranda* in addition to the warnings are known as the second-tier safeguards, and are essentially designed to guarantee that the rights described in the warnings will be respected if the suspect decides to invoke them.

d. Honoring the Suspect's Rights: The Right to Silence

Under *Miranda,* a suspect may invoke her right to silence "in any manner, at any time prior to or during questioning." When she does, "the interrogation must cease." If police obtain an incriminating statement after invocation, it "cannot be other than the product of compulsion."

e. Honoring the Suspect's Rights: The Right to Consult Counsel

If a suspect says that she "wants an attorney," the interrogation *"must cease* until an attorney is present." When the attorney is present, the suspect "must have an opportunity to confer" with counsel, and to have counsel *"present during any subsequent interrogation."* If police want to interrogate an indigent suspect, they "must make known" to her that "a lawyer will be provided" for her "prior to any interrogation." If a suspect asks for counsel, a lawyer need not be provided for "a reasonable period of time" while police continue to investigate. However, police may not question the suspect during this time.

f. The *Miranda* Right to Counsel Distinguished From the Sixth Amendment Right to Counsel

The right to counsel provided by *Miranda* must be distinguished from the Sixth Amendment right to counsel in interrogations established by the Court in *Massiah.* The *Miranda* right to counsel is not constitutionally guaranteed. Rather, it is a procedural safeguard designed to provide protection for the defendant's right to remain silent in the fact of custodial interrogation—provided, however, that the suspect decides that he needs this protection and *invokes* the right to counsel. In contrast, the Sixth Amendment right to counsel applies *automatically,* whenever an *indicted* defendant is subject to deliberate elicitation by a Government agent. The indicted defendant does not have to invoke his Sixth Amendment right—as shown by the facts in *Massiah,* who did not even know that he was speaking to a Government agent and hence had no reason to invoke his right to counsel. However, while the *Miranda* right to counsel is not automatic and must be invoked, it is in one sense broader than the automatic Sixth Amendment right to counsel: it applies *before indictment*, in any situation of custodial interrogation.

3. **Waiver of *Miranda* Rights**
The *Miranda* Court stated that police must seek a waiver of rights before interrogating a suspect in the absence of an attorney. The state must bear the "heavy burden" of meeting the "high standard" of proving that a suspect "voluntarily, knowingly and intelligently" waived her rights to silence and counsel.

   a. **Sufficient Proof of Waiver**
   The *Miranda* Court noted that an express statement that the suspect "is willing" to talk and "does not want an attorney," followed closely by an incriminating statement, "could" constitute a valid waiver.

   b. **Insufficient Proof of Waiver**
   Under *Miranda,* a waiver may not be presumed from a suspect's silence after warnings. Nor may a waiver be presumed from the "fact that a confession was in fact eventually obtained." There must be evidence in the record that the suspect "understandingly rejected the offer" of counsel. A suspect may invoke her rights after answering some questions, and thereby withdraw any waiver given at the outset.

   c. **Evidence That Negates Waiver**
   The Court in *Miranda* mentioned certain circumstances which would clearly cut against a finding of waiver. These include "lengthy interrogation or incommunicado incarceration," or "any evidence" the suspect was "threatened, tricked or cajoled" into a waiver.

4. **Attachment of the Privilege**
The *Miranda* safeguards attach when a suspect is subjected to custodial interrogation at the police station, or "otherwise deprived" of her "freedom of action in any significant way." The warnings and waiver requirements are "prerequisites to the admissibility of any statement" made when the privilege attaches, including both "inculpatory" and "exculpatory" admissions that may prove guilt by implication. *Miranda* does not apply, however, to general "on-the-scene questioning as to facts surrounding a crime" or other "general questioning of citizens in the fact-finding process."

5. ***Miranda* Is Not a "Constitutional Straightjacket"**
The Court recognized that Congress and the states may create "alternatives for protecting the privilege" that are as effective as the *Miranda* rules. The Court emphasized that it did not want to "handicap sound efforts at reform" by creating a "constitutional straightjacket" that would hamper the creation of these alternatives. It also noted that the Constitution does not require "adherence to any particular solution" for dispelling the inherent compulsion

of custodial interrogation "as it is presently conducted." But in the absence of "equally effective" procedures for protecting the rights of suspects, *Miranda* safeguards "must be observed."

6. The *Miranda* Requirements and Law Enforcement Goals

The *Miranda* Court rejected arguments that its rules would result in harm to law enforcement. The Court refused to find that "the end" of obtaining confessions justified "the means" of ignoring the suspect's rights, because this was "pernicious doctrine" that would allow the Government to be a "lawbreaker." The Court acknowledged that confessions "may play an important role in some convictions," but noted that in other cases this role was overstated. In the four cases under review "considerable" evidence of guilt had been acquired independently of the confession. The Court also rejected the argument that "unfettered" police discretion to detain suspects would be beneficial to innocent people, who could "clear themselves" by talking. Such a person would be "better able" to do so "after warnings and with counsel present," declared the Court.

a. F.B.I. Practice

The *Miranda* Court relied on the F.B.I.'s use of warnings and waiver practices, similar to those created in *Miranda,* to support its prediction that "effective law enforcement" would not be hampered by requiring such practices in state and local law enforcement agencies. The Court also relied on the "experience of other countries," including England, Scotland, India and Ceylon, to illustrate how the danger to effective law enforcement from *Miranda*-type requirements was "overplayed."

7. Dissent

Four Justices dissented in *Miranda,* and three filed dissenting opinions.

a. Justice Clark's Dissent

Justice Clark advocated a compromise, somewhere between the positions of the majority and three other dissenting colleagues. He proposed that the Court rely on Due Process to require the police to give the *Miranda* warnings, and to prove waiver under the "totality" of the circumstances. Under Justice Clark's "voluntariness inquiry," the failure to give warnings would be only one relevant factor in determining whether Due Process was violated.

Justice Clark proposed his compromise because he argued the majority's doctrine was going "too far too fast," in the absence of empirical knowledge about "the practical operation" of the *Miranda* requirements.

Justice Clark believed that custodial interrogation was "an essential tool" in law enforcement, and feared that doctrinaire rules "inserted at the nerve center of crime detection may well kill the patient." He also disagreed with the Court's criticism of police practices, because the "police manuals" cited in *Miranda* were not "shown by the record" to be officially in use, and because incidents of police brutality were "rare" exceptions.

b. Justice Harlan's Dissent

Justice Harlan was joined in his dissent by Justices Stewart and White. Justice Harlan argued that the *Miranda* majority's new rules were unsupported by precedent, and were unwise and dangerous as a matter of policy.

First, Justice Harlan voiced disapproval of the *Miranda* majority's extension of the Fifth Amendment to the interrogation process. He advocated that the Due Process doctrine should remain the sole standard for judging confessions, as neither Fifth nor Sixth Amendment precedents supported the Court's ruling. Justice Harlan praised the case-by-case Due Process doctrine as "elaborate," sophisticated," "sensitive," "judicial," and "flexible." He saw nothing wrong with its lack of predictability, and found that disagreements about its interpretation were "usually confined to that borderland of close cases where it matters least." He found that Due Process precedents gave proper recognition to the value of confessions as a tool of law enforcement.

Justice Harlan acknowledged that the Fifth Amendment privilege embodied "basic principles always capable of expansion," but he found the Court's expansion of the privilege in *Miranda* to be unwarranted for several reasons. First, the Due Process standard already incorporated a "protective concern" for suspects and an emphasis on "adversarial values." Second, Fifth Amendment precedents never condemned "all pressure" to incriminate oneself, and Justice Harlan found no reason for the Fifth Amendment to prohibit "the relatively mild pressure" that the Due Process doctrine permitted. Finally, he argued that no precedent required "precise knowledge of one's rights" as a prerequisite to the loss of Fifth Amendment protections.

Justice Harlan argued that the precedential "linchpin" of *Miranda* was the law interpreting the Sixth Amendment right to counsel. He found the roles of counsel at trial and at an interrogation to be "vastly different," and so rejected the Court's reliance on Sixth Amendment precedents in *Miranda*. For Justice Harlan, counsel's role at trial was to protect an untrained defendant in a confrontation with an expert prosecutor; at the police station, a lawyer would be merely "an obstacle to truth-finding."

Justice Harlan also criticized the *Miranda* decision on policy grounds. He predicted that the *Miranda* rules would achieve nothing positive, and would have negative consequences. The rules would not deter "blatant" coercion, because police could lie about warnings and waivers as readily as they could lie about brutality, and get away with it. Moreover, the rules would "markedly decrease" the number of confessions. Justice Harlan viewed confessions as important for "crime control," and found that the social costs of crime were "too great" to justify the Court's "hazardous experimentation" with society's welfare.

Justice Harlan also predicted that the Court's rules would meet with "widespread objection," as the majority's conception of "fairness" for suspects was not shared by "many thinking citizens." In Justice Harlan's view, society had "always paid a stiff price for law and order," and the cost of "mild" coercion of suspects was "worth the price paid for it."

Finally, Justice Harlan objected to the Court's "heavy-handed," "one-sided," and "precipitous" action of "criminal law reform," because it was untimely, given the reform studies in progress by the A.B.A., the A.L.I., a Presidential Commission, and other groups and state legislatures. Justice Harlan predicted that *Miranda* would "handicap" these efforts at reform. By contrast, if the majority would only be "more patient," better results and more "just" compromises could be achieved by these other groups, and the "initiative" in reform would be restored "to those forums where it truly belongs."

c. **Justice White's Dissent**

Justice White was joined in his dissent by Justices Harlan and Stewart. Justice White argued that the *Miranda* requirements were unsupported by the Fifth Amendment precedents, had no "rational" factual foundation, and improperly weakened the "ability of the criminal law" to provide for public safety. Justice White argued that the text of the Fifth Amendment required "simply that nobody shall be compelled" to testify at trial against himself.

Next, Justice White argued that the *Miranda* doctrine was both unnecessary and full of inherent contradictions. He concluded that the *Miranda* Court's goal was not to reduce "coercion" in any rational way, but simply to prevent police from obtaining confessions in most cases.

First, Justice White found that the Court's factual basis for its holding was "patently inadequate." This was because *Miranda*'s premise that custodial interrogation is inherently coercive was based only on the Court's "extrapolation" from outdated police manuals. In fact, Justice White observed, the level of coercion varies from one interrogation to the next. Justice White argued that even if some new doctrine were needed in order to dispel "indiscernible" coercion more effectively, mechanisms such as transcripts, observers, or time limits could be imposed on police interrogations to achieve this goal.

Justice White argued that *Miranda*'s logic also violated "common sense," because it required confessions elicited by a *single question* to be treated as "compelled," but allowed spontaneous confessions with the same custodial pressures to be treated as voluntary. Justice White found it "irrational" to believe that either the *Miranda* warnings, or the presence of counsel could make coercion "disappear"; he also found it paradoxical that the defendant's *waiver* of rights could be accepted as voluntary under *Miranda,* even though it occurred in the "inherently coercive" setting of interrogation.

In Justice White's view the *Miranda* majority had three goals: to give suspects a right to silence that would be invoked in most cases, to give the state "a severe, if not impossible" burden of proof of waiver, and to forbid interrogation except in the presence of counsel "for all practical purposes." Therefore, *Miranda* was not confined to protecting the Fifth Amendment privilege, but focused on creating a "Fifth Amendment right to counsel." Justice White found "no warrant in the Fifth Amendment" for "installing counsel as the arbiter of the privilege."

Finally, Justice White determined that *Miranda*'s possible advantages over the Due Process doctrine for confessions were "far outweighed by its likely undesirable impact" on public safety. In addition to the deleterious effect on law enforcement, Justice White predicted that the ambiguity of certain *Miranda* rules would impose a cost of "judicial time and effort" in interpreting these rules in future litigation. He identified four open questions that would require case-by-case definition: whether a suspect is "in custody," whether she is under "interrogation," whether she has "waived" her rights, and whether particular evidence is an inadmissible "fruit" of a *Miranda* violation. Given the uncertainties concerning *Miranda*'s application, Justice White rejected the notion that its rules would provide a "bright line" for police to determine whether interrogation "may be safely pursued."

8. Perspective

Miranda was a closely-divided case, and *Miranda* issues are hotly debated both within and outside the Court today. Before examining the major areas of law-making under *Miranda,* it is useful to consider how the *Miranda* opinions created the foundation for the modern debate about its meaning.

a. **The "Non-constitutional" Status of the *Miranda* Rules**

The *Miranda* Court conceded that its "safeguards" were not constitutionally required. This concession set the stage for a debate about the significance of the "non-constitutional" status of the *Miranda* rules. Ultimately, a majority of the Court would rely on this status to justify restrictive interpretations of the scope of the rules, at least in some doctrinal areas. See, e.g., *Oregon v. Elstad,* 470 U.S. 298, 105 S.Ct. 1285, 84 L.Ed.2d 222 (1985) (holding that when police violate *Miranda* during an initial interrogation, a confession following a subsequent proper interrogation is not an inadmissible "fruit" of the initial violation); *New York v. Quarles,* 467 U.S. 649, 104 S.Ct. 2626, 81 L.Ed.2d 550 (1984) (establishing a "public safety exception" to the requirement that police give *Miranda* warnings).

b. ***Miranda* as the Definitive Solution for the Problems Presented by Custodial Interrogation**

The *Miranda* rules established a new regime for judicial review of confessions, yet the Court's opinion was ambiguous concerning the evolution of that regime in the future. Some critics argue that the Court did not go far enough in *Miranda,* because the warnings alone could not "dispel" much of the coercion created by interrogation, and because the right to consult counsel would not protect suspects who "waived" their rights before consulting a lawyer. These critics complain that *Miranda* incorrectly rejected the argument that a person subject to custodial interrogation "needs a lawyer to waive the right to a lawyer." They argue, as did Justice White, that *Miranda* is inherently contradictory because it presumes that a person is coerced in the milieu of custodial interrogation, but then permits the person to "voluntarily" waive the rights that would protect him in that very situation.

Arguably, the *Miranda* Court left the door open to imposing further restrictions on custodial interrogations, and in later cases the Court was faced with claims that *Miranda* should be extended to create new rules that would effectuate its policies. See, e.g., *Colorado v. Spring,* 479 U.S. 564, 107 S.Ct. 851, 93 L.Ed.2d 954 (1987) (claim that suspect should be informed of the subject of the interrogation prior to waiver); *Moran v. Burbine,* 475 U.S. 412, 106 S.Ct. 1135, 89 L.Ed.2d 410 (1986) (claim that suspect should be informed, prior to waiver, that an attorney wants to talk to him). In resolving these and other claims, however, a majority of the Court usually chose to treat *Miranda* as the definitive solution for dispelling the "coercion" of the interrogation process, and to reject the need to expand the requirements established in *Miranda* itself.

c. **The Need for Further Judicial Definition of *Miranda* Concepts, and for Case-by-Case Application of These Definitions**

Justice White's dissent identified four open questions after *Miranda*, namely, the meaning of "custody," "interrogation," "waiver," and "fruits." Four other major issues would require the Court's attention in later cases as well: the propriety of impeaching a defendant with evidence obtained in violation of *Miranda,* the scope of permissible ambiguity in the *Miranda* warnings, the propriety of the resumption of interrogation after invocation of rights, and the need for a "public safety" exception to the suspect's right to receive warnings. Two other issues would also be resolved—the relevance of the nature of the offense to the *Miranda* requirements, and the role of *Miranda* in undercover activity by police.

Some "black letter" definitions of *Miranda* concepts would emerge from the Court's debates about these issues. Usually, the application of each *Miranda* concept to a given factual setting was held to require consideration of a "totality" of factors. The Court's own applications of its *Miranda* concepts to the facts of given cases often signaled to lower courts that restrictive interpretations of the scope of *Miranda* rights were acceptable, in light of the vital role confessions play in the system of law enforcement. Thus, the spirit of the *Miranda* dissents came to occupy a place of prominence in post-*Miranda* jurisprudence.

d. **The *Miranda* Compromise**

If the *Miranda* Court had followed through on its premise that custodial interrogation was inherently coercive, and that counsel was a necessary safeguard in dispelling this coercion, it would have reached the logical conclusion that all confessions made in the absence of counsel (which is to say, almost all confessions) are inadmissible. The Court, however, rejected this radical proposal, because it was not prepared to rule that confessions had no place in law enforcement. So the Court compromised. *Miranda* provides a right to silence and to counsel, but the decision whether to invoke these rights (and conversely whether to waive them) are made in the same coercive atmosphere that the Court was so concerned about. In subsequent cases, the Court has held steady to this "compromise" which is designed to provide some protection to suspects, without severely impinging on law enforcement interests.

B. **IMPEACHING THE DEFENDANT–WITNESS AT TRIAL**

The *Miranda* Court reasoned that both "exculpatory" and "inculpatory" statements should be covered by its holding, because "exculpatory" ones were "often used to impeach" the defendant's testimony at trial, and thus "to prove guilt by implication." Some lower courts assumed that this reasoning implied that a confession obtained in violation of *Miranda* would be inadmissible at the defendant's trial for any purpose, including impeachment. However, five years after *Miranda* was decided, a majority of the Court rejected such a broad view of its holding, and held that a prosecutor may use statements obtained in violation of *Miranda* to impeach a defendant's "credibility" on cross-examination.

This "impeachment exception" to *Miranda* led to further litigation concerning the prosecution's right to cross-examine the defendant about *Miranda*-related events. At first, the Court restricted the state's impeachment powers, and held that Due Process barred the prosecution from referring to the defendant's silence after receiving *Miranda* warnings. This ruling proved to be a narrow restriction, however. Later, the Court found no constitutional bar to the prosecution's reference on cross-examination to a defendant's pre-arrest or post-arrest silence before receiving warnings. In these cases, no governmental action "implicitly induced" the defendant to remain silent, because no *Miranda* warning "implicitly assured" the defendant that silence could not be held against him.

The Court's holdings concerning the "impeachment exception" reflected a preference for exposing a defendant to the traditional process of cross-examination, in order to reveal any potential perjury to the jury, and thereby to increase the reliability of verdicts. In the Court's judgment, the value of enhancing the "truth-finding" potential of a trial outweighed the need to create any further deterrence of police violations of *Miranda*. As it turned out, this judicial philosophy was not limited to impeachment cases. Later the Court's reasoning in these cases would be used to justify further restrictive interpretations of *Miranda* doctrine, such as the ruling that *Miranda* violations are not "constitutional violations," as well as rulings permitting the admission of certain evidentiary "fruits" of *Miranda* violations at trial.

1. *Miranda*–Defective Statements May Be Used to Impeach a Defendant Who Takes the Stand at Trial
In *Harris v. New York,* 401 U.S. 222, 91 S.Ct. 643, 28 L.Ed.2d 1 (1971), the Court held that a defendant could be asked on cross-examination about incriminating post-arrest statements he made to police which were inconsistent with his trial testimony, even though the police failed to inform him of his right to counsel before the statements were made. At trial, the defendant testified that he sold baking powder, not heroin, to an undercover agent. In his post-arrest statements he claimed to have acted for the agent in buying heroin from others; when he was cross-examined, he could not remember making these statements. The Court determined that the *Miranda*-defective statements could be used to impeach the defendant, where the jury was instructed that the post-arrest statements could be considered in judging the defendant's "credibility," but not as evidence of guilt.

2. Rationale
The Court valued the benefits of the impeachment process in *Harris* over the benefits to be obtained by excluding *Miranda*-defective statements on cross-examination. This was because the Court found that the defendant's

right to testify did not "include the right to commit perjury," and that sufficient deterrence of police misconduct could be achieved by exclusion of statements obtained in violation of *Miranda* from the state's case-in-chief. The "possibility" of further deterrence was found to be no justification for shielding the defendant from exposure to cross-examination about his prior inconsistent statements.

3. Dissent

Four Justices dissented in *Harris,* and Justice Brennan filed an opinion, in which Justices Douglas and Marshall joined. Justice Brennan argued that *Miranda* proscribed any use of the fruits of a *Miranda* violation, and that the *Harris* rule was wrong because it abandoned two of *Miranda* 's goals—the deterrence of police misconduct, and the safeguarding of the integrity of the adversary system. Justice Brennan declared that it was "monstrous" for courts to "abet the law-breaking officer" by sanctioning the use of illegally obtained evidence at trial. He predicted that the *Harris* rule would go "far toward undoing much of the progress made in conforming police methods" to the Constitution.

4. Perspective

Harris was the first case which signalled that a new consensus concerning *Miranda* was emerging among members of the Court. By the time *Harris* was decided, the Court had acquired three new members: Chief Justice Burger and Justices Blackmun and Marshall. Of these, only Justice Marshall signed the dissent in *Harris;* thus, the *Miranda* consensus of five Justices was replaced with the *Harris* consensus of five Justices opposed to expanding *Miranda*. Soon after *Harris* was decided, Justices Rehnquist and Powell joined the Court, and neither of these Justices became enthusiastic supporters of *Miranda*. It appears, then, that the *Miranda* doctrine was launched shortly before judicial support for its creation collapsed on the Court. In hindsight, some retrenchment concerning its application can be seen as inevitable.

5. Consequences of Analysis in *Harris*

It is useful to highlight the main elements of the *Harris* majority's thinking, as its analysis created a tradition of restrictive interpretation of the *Miranda* opinion. First, the Court treated the truth-finding function of the trial as superior to the Fifth Amendment values protected by the *Miranda* safeguards. Second, the Court did not value the need for a powerful remedy to prevent the "inherent coercion" of police interrogation without safeguards; the coercion presumed by *Miranda* was deemed inadequate to justify the exclusion of illegal statements during the impeachment process. Third, the Court embraced a rule that permitted the erosion of *Miranda* 's rights in practice. For, even though *Harris* prohibited the use of illegal statements to "prove guilt" during cross-examination, the jurors' awareness of these statements could lead them to infer guilt when rejecting the defendant's "credibility." Finally, the Court assumed that exclusion of *Miranda*-defective confessions from the case-in-chief would sufficiently deter *Miranda* violations, and therefore that application of an exclusionary rule in any context beyond the case-in-chief would provide a benefit too minimal to justify the cost of excluding reliable evidence.

6.   Continued Affirmation of the *Harris* Rule

In *Oregon v. Hass,* 420 U.S. 714, 95 S.Ct. 1215, 43 L.Ed.2d 570 (1975), the Court held that the *Harris* rule applied to statements obtained where a police officer violated *Miranda* by interrogating a defendant after he received warnings and invoked the right to counsel. At trial, the defendant testified to a minor role in a burglary, but in post-arrest statements (after invoking and being denied the right to counsel) he had admitted taking the property himself. The Court held that it was proper for the prosecutor to cross-examine him about the inconsistencies between his two versions of the crime.

a.   Rationale

The Court held that the reasoning of *Harris* justified the prosecutor's use of the illegal statements in *Hass* to impeach the defendant, even though the nature of the *Miranda* violation was different—i.e. *Harris* involved a failure to give warnings while *Hass* involved a failure to abide by them. Justice Blackmun conceded that a police officer who gave accurate warnings might be tempted to interrogate a defendant improperly after the defendant made the decision that he would not talk. After *Harris* a police officer had an incentive to abide by *Miranda* by giving warnings, in order to make any statement that might be made, admissible in the prosecution's case-in-chief. In *Hass,* however, where the police officer had given warnings already, and the suspect was unwilling to talk, he arguably had no incentive to abide by *Miranda* and refrain from interrogation; the worst that could happen was that the defendant would confess and the statements could be used to impeach him at trial. But the Court concluded that whatever difference might exist between the "incentive" to seek impeachment evidence in *Harris* and *Hass,* "the balance was struck in *Harris,* and we are not disposed to change it now."

b.   Dissent

Justice Brennan dissented, in an opinion joined by Justice Marshall. Justice Brennan argued that the *Hass* Court went "beyond *Harris* in undermining *Miranda*." He concluded that *Hass* left police with "almost no incentive" to abide by *Miranda* by honoring a suspect's invocation of his rights.

7.   *Miranda*–Defective Confessions Cannot Be Used to Impeach Defense Witnesses

In *James v. Illinois,* 493 U.S. 307, 110 S.Ct. 648, 107 L.Ed.2d 676 (1990), the Court held that the fruits of a Fourth Amendment violation may not be used to impeach a defendant's witnesses, even though they may be used to impeach the defendant. Presumably, this means that the illegal fruits of a *Miranda* violation cannot be used to impeach a defendant's witnesses. This is because the Court now treats the "impeachment exception" for both Fourth Amendment and *Miranda* violations as being governed by the same principles. For further treatment of *James,* see the discussion of the impeachment exception to the Fourth Amendment, *supra.*

8. **When a Suspect Invokes the Right to Silence After Receiving** *Miranda* **Warnings, the Prosecution May Not Use the Evidence of That Silence for Any Purpose at Trial**
In *Doyle v. Ohio,* 426 U.S. 610, 96 S.Ct. 2240, 49 L.Ed.2d 91 (1976), the Court held that a prosecutor may not impeach a defendant's testimony at trial by asking about his failure to provide the same explanation to the police, immediately after his arrest and receipt of *Miranda* warnings. At trial, the defendants testified that they had been "framed" by another participant in a drug sale, but they did not mention this to police after their arrest. The Court held that the warnings implicitly assure a suspect that "silence will carry no penalty," and so the prosecutor's reference to a defendant's post-warning silence at trial violated the defendants' right to Due Process.

a. **Rationale**
The Court reasoned that it would be unfair to penalize a defendant for relying on the assurance in the warnings that he has "the right to remain silent," by allowing the prosecutor to use his silence for impeachment purposes. The Court found that while the *Miranda* warnings "contain no express assurance that silence will carry no penalty," this assurance is implicit. A suspect is not informed that "his silence, as well as his words" can be used against him at trial, and it would be "reasonable" for anyone to assume that the "right to remain silent" means that silence cannot be penalized. Thus, the *Doyle* rule rests on "the fundamental unfairness of implicitly assuring a suspect that his silence will not be used against him and then using his silence to impeach an explanation subsequently offered at trial."

b. **Due Process, Not Fifth Amendment**
The Court did not rely on the Fifth Amendment to prohibit the prosecutor's use of the defendant's silence in *Doyle.* The Court simply noted that the *Miranda* warnings were a "prophylactic means of safeguarding Fifth Amendment rights," according to *Michigan v. Tucker,* 417 U.S. 433, 94 S.Ct. 2357, 41 L.Ed.2d 182 (1974), and relied on Due Process for its holding. Under the Due Process Clause, it was fundamentally unfair to provide an assurance in the *Miranda* warnings, and then to renege on that assurance at trial.

c.   **Dissent**

The three *Doyle* dissenters argued that the majority erroneously created a "presumption" that any defendant's post-warning silence "was the product of reliance on the *Miranda* warning." They began with the premise that a defendant's pre-trial silence would be admissible for impeachment purposes if he was not entitled to receive *Miranda* warnings. The purpose of the impeachment would be to show that the defendant's testimony was contradicted by his "prior inconsistent silence." The dissenters saw no reason to treat a defendant differently when his silence was preceded by the warnings. The dissent conceded that a defendant's post-arrest silence might be a response to the *Miranda* warnings, at least in some cases. But if that were the case, a defendant could explain this to the jury, in response to the prosecution's attempt to impeach him. In this way, the warnings would "salvage the defendant's credibility." The dissent concluded that "the risk that a truthful defendant will be deceived by the *Miranda* warning" and be unable to explain his "honest misunderstanding" at trial, was "much less" than the risk that the *Doyle* rule "will merely provide a shield for perjury."

d.   **Perspective**

To the *Doyle* majority, a suspect's possible exercise of *Miranda* rights was worthy of protection, even when a suspect did not formally invoke the right to silence. The Court assumed that when police gave a suspect the *Miranda* warnings, it was likely that her failure to make exculpatory statements was motivated by reliance on the privilege. Given this likelihood, the impeachment process posed too great a danger that her reliance on the privilege would be penalized in every case where she wished to testify at trial. By contrast, the *Doyle* dissenters were unwilling to infer "implicit" reliance on the privilege based on a suspect's silence. They were more concerned with a defendant's reliance on *Miranda* as a "shield" for perjury, than with the need to protect a defendant from the whipsaw effect of the *Miranda* warnings and the use of post-warning silence at trial.

e.   **Limitations of Due Process Analysis**

The Due Process rationale employed in *Doyle* made the Court's decision restrictive in a certain way. It limited the precedential effect of the *Doyle* analysis, by making it inapplicable to cases evaluating the parameters of *Miranda*. As *Doyle* was not grounded in *Miranda* doctrine, it could not be used to justify broad interpretations of the need to give "accurate" warnings to suspects, or to protect a suspect's implicit reliance on the privilege in other cases. Also, the Court's Due Process analysis focussed on the implied guarantees in the *Miranda* warnings, and on the unfairness of withdrawing those guarantees at trial. This analysis has no application where *Miranda* warnings have not even been given.

f. Reasons for Due Process Analysis

There are several factors that may explain the Court's reliance on Due Process. First, the votes of Justices White and Stewart were necessary to create a majority in *Doyle*. Both justices dissented in *Miranda*, and they may have preferred to use a Due Process rationale in *Doyle* in order to avoid an "expansion" of *Miranda* rights. Second, the Due Process holding helped to accentuate the Court's commitment to its earlier holding in *Tucker* that *Miranda* rights were not Fifth Amendment rights, but were instead merely prophylactic rules not required by the Constitution. (See the discussion on this point *infra*). Finally, the Court's reliance on Due Process relieved it from the need to devote much energy to reconciling the *Doyle* rule with *Harris*, whose "impeachment exception" was grounded in *Miranda* doctrine.

g. Continued Affirmation of *Doyle*

In *Brecht v. Abrahamson*, ___ U.S. ___, 113 S.Ct. 1710, 123 L.Ed.2d 353 (1993), the Court affirmed the vitality of the *Doyle* rule. The Court distinguished between the *Miranda* safeguards, which are not required by the Constitution but which are merely prophylactic safeguards, from the *Doyle* rule which is grounded in Due Process and fundamental fairness. The Court stated that "*Doyle* was not simply a further extension of the *Miranda* prophylactic rule. Rather * * * it is rooted in fundamental fairness and due process concerns. However real these concerns, *Doyle* does not overprotect them." The Court concluded that "due process is violated whenever the prosecution uses for impeachment purposes a defendant's post-*Miranda* silence" and that *Doyle* "does not bear the hallmarks of a prophylactic rule."

h. *Doyle* and the Insanity Defense

In *Wainwright v. Greenfield*, 474 U.S. 284, 106 S.Ct. 634, 88 L.Ed.2d 623 (1986), the Court held that under *Doyle* a prosecutor may not use the defendant's post-warning silence in order to rebut an insanity defense at trial. In *Wainwright*, the prosecutor sought to introduce evidence of the defendant's silence in order to prove that the defendant engaged in rational behavior upon arrest, which was inconsistent with his insanity defense to the charge of sexual battery. The Court held that *Doyle* barred the use of post-warning silence in insanity cases because "the implied assurance contained in the *Miranda* warning" is that silence will not be used for any purpose, including impeachment at trial. The Court noted that the state could introduce evidence of the defendant's rational "behavior" during arrest, as long as the prosecutor carefully "avoided any mention of the defendant's exercise of his constitutional rights."

i. Waiver of *Miranda* Rights and Post–Warning Silence

In *Anderson v. Charles*, 447 U.S. 404, 100 S.Ct. 2180, 65 L.Ed.2d 222 (1980), the Court held that *Doyle* did not apply to a case where a defendant waived his rights following the *Miranda* warnings, and gave police a statement before trial. In such a case, a prosecutor can cross-examine a defendant concerning inconsistencies between omissions in his pre-trial statement and his trial testimony. The defendant in *Anderson* did not exercise his right to remain silent, because the omissions in his post-waiver statement did not constitute "silences." So it was not unfair to use the statement (and its omissions) against him because the warnings specifically informed him of that possibility. *Doyle* bars only the use of "silence maintained after receipt of governmental assurances" contained in the warnings.

j.   **No Evidence of Silence**
In *Greer v. Miller*, 483 U.S. 756, 107 S.Ct. 3102, 97 L.Ed.2d 618 (1987), the Court held that no *Doyle* violation occurred when a prosecutor's attempt to inquire about post-arrest silence was cut short by a defense objection, and the jury was instructed to "ignore" the prosecutor's question. On these facts, no evidence concerning silence was heard by the jury, and no further question or argument about silence was heard. Thus, *Doyle* was not violated.

9.   **When a Defendant Is Silent Before *Miranda* Warnings Are Given, the Prosecution May Use Evidence of That Silence for Impeachment Purposes**
a.   **Silence Before Arrest**
In *Jenkins v. Anderson,* 447 U.S. 231, 100 S.Ct. 2124, 65 L.Ed.2d 86 (1980), the Court held that the use of pre-arrest silence to impeach a defendant violated neither the Fifth Amendment nor the *Doyle* rule embodied in the Due Process Clause. Therefore, the prosecutor in *Jenkins* was allowed to impeach the defendant's testimony concerning his claim of self-defense to a murder charge, by asking him why he failed to report the homicide to anyone for two weeks before he turned himself in.

b.   **Rationale**
As to the Fifth Amendment, the Court conceded that the *Jenkins* defendant might feel compelled to forgo the privilege before arrest "if his failure to speak later can be used to impeach him." But this form of compulsion did not violate the Fifth Amendment because it did not impair "to an appreciable extent" the policies behind the privilege. The Court observed that its interpretation of the Fifth Amendment was supported by *Harris v. New York*, 401 U.S. 222, 91 S.Ct. 643, 28 L.Ed.2d 1 (1971). *Harris* held that a defendant could be impeached with the illegal fruits of a *Miranda* violation, because he was "under an obligation to speak truthfully" on the witness stand, and could be subjected to "the traditional truth-testing device" of impeachment by questioning about prior inconsistent statements or acts.

As to the Due Process Clause and *Doyle,* the *Jenkins* Court found that Due Process is violated only when "governmental action" induces a defendant to remain silent. In *Jenkins,* the defendant's silence occurred before *Miranda* warnings were given, and so his silence was not caused by the implicit assurance that his silence would not be penalized. Since the Government had given Jenkins no promises, it had not reneged on any promises by using his silence against him at trial.

c.   Dissent

Justice Marshall dissented, in an opinion joined by Justice Brennan. Justice Marshall argued that the *Jenkins* rule violated Due Process because the defendant's failure to report the crime "was not probative of the falsity of his testimony at trial." Thus, it was "fundamentally unfair" to allow the jury to draw the inference of falsity from his silence. Justice Marshall also argued that the *Jenkins* rule violated the Fifth Amendment, because it replaced the privilege against self-incrimination "with a duty to incriminate oneself," and thus created a "substantial" burden on both the privilege and the decision "to exercise the right to testify in one's own defense."

d.   Silence After Arrest

In *Fletcher v. Weir,* 455 U.S. 603, 102 S.Ct. 1309, 71 L.Ed.2d 490 (1982), the Court held that *Doyle* did not apply to a defendant who had remained silent after arrest, but before receiving *Miranda* warnings. The Court reasoned that the event of arrest is not "governmental action which implicitly induces" a defendant to remain silent. *Doyle* applies only when the Government induces silence "by implicitly assuring the defendant that his silence would not be used against him"—i.e. by giving the *Miranda* warnings. Thus, the prosecutor in *Fletcher* could impeach the defendant by asking him about his failure to tell the police about his claim of self-defense before he received *Miranda* warnings.

C.   THE FRUIT OF THE POISONOUS TREE, AND THE NON-CONSTITUTIONAL NATURE OF THE *MIRANDA* SAFEGUARDS

The *Miranda* Court held that a defendant's confession was inadmissible if police violated the *Miranda* rules, but did not determine whether "fruits" of confessions were inadmissible as well. For example, a defendant's inadmissible confession can lead police to a witness who incriminates the defendant, or to incriminating physical evidence. Or, a defendant's inadmissible confession may lead police to question him further; even if police observed the *Miranda* rules during the second interrogation, it is possible to view a second confession as the "fruit" of the first one.

Before *Miranda,* the problem of such derivative evidence was addressed in Fourth Amendment law by the use of the "fruit of the poisonous tree" doctrine, which required the exclusion of fruits of Fourth Amendment violations that were the products of police exploitation of the original violation. However, the fruit of the poisonous tree doctrine has been applied by the Court only to violations of the Constitution. It is only constitutional violations which are so serious as to mandate exclusion not only of the evidence discovered by the illegal act but also the fruits derived from that evidence.

Soon after the Court established the "impeachment exception" to *Miranda* in *Harris,* it created a "fruits" doctrine for *Miranda* that allowed prosecutors to use the testimony of a witness whose identity was the "fruit" of a defendant's inadmissible confession. The Court ruled that the fruit of the poisonous tree doctrine did not apply to the fruits of a *Miranda* violation, because the *Miranda* "safeguards" were not "constitutional rights."

1. **When Police Learn the Identity of a Witness From a Defendant's Inadmissible Confession, the Testimony of That Witness Is Not an Inadmissible "Fruit" of the Confession**
    In *Michigan v. Tucker,* 417 U.S. 433, 94 S.Ct. 2357, 41 L.Ed.2d 182 (1974), the Court held that police violation of *Miranda* does not constitute a violation of the Fifth Amendment. The Court also held that a witness's testimony should be admissible at trial, even when the identity of the witness is the "fruit" of a confession obtained after police fail to inform a defendant of his right to have counsel appointed under *Miranda.* In *Tucker,* the defendant identified a witness who would support his alibi to a rape charge, during an interrogation that violated *Miranda.* When the police contacted the witness, he provided information that incriminated the defendant. At trial, Tucker's statement about the alibi witness was excluded as a statement obtained in violation of *Miranda.* But the witness' statements implicating Tucker were not obtained by violating *Miranda* because the witness gave them voluntarily. If these statements were to be excluded, it would have to be as "fruits" of the "poisonous" *Miranda*-defective confession. But the Court refused to apply the fruits doctrine, held that the witness' testimony at trial was properly admitted, and affirmed the defendant's conviction for rape.

    a. **Rationale**
        The Court had two reasons for its conclusion that the "fruits" doctrine for constitutional violations was not controlling in *Tucker.* First, Justice Rehnquist observed that the *Miranda* opinion recognized that a violation of its "procedural safeguards" did not constitute a Fifth Amendment violation. For the *Miranda* Court stated that the Constitution did not "necessarily require any particular solution" for the protection of Fifth Amendment rights during custodial interrogation. Second, a "comparison of the facts" of *Tucker* with the "historical circumstances underlying the privilege" showed that no Fifth Amendment violation occurred when police merely failed to properly give Tucker all of his *Miranda* warnings. He was not subjected to "Star Chamber proceedings"; nor was there any "legal sanction, such as contempt," which his silence would have

incurred. As no constitutional violation occurred in *Tucker*, the fruits doctrine was not applicable.

b. **Balancing Approach**

Because the fruit of the poisonous tree doctrine did not *mandate* exclusion for the fruit of a *Miranda* violation, the *Tucker* Court proceeded to undertake a balancing of costs and benefits to determine whether exclusion, while not mandated, was nonetheless *appropriate*. The Court began its balancing analysis by identifying the possible benefits of excluding the "fruit" of the *Miranda* violation in *Tucker*. It found that those benefits were outweighed by the cost of excluding the independent witness's testimony.

First, the Court observed that the benefit of the *Miranda* exclusionary rule is the deterrence of future police illegality. The Court believed that the exclusion of *Tucker*'s confession provided all the deterrence necessary to safeguard Fifth Amendment rights, and that exclusion of the witness's testimony would have little "extra" deterrent effect. Thus, the benefits of exclusion were minimal.

The Court next observed that the witness's testimony in *Tucker* was reliable evidence; thus, the traditional justification of employing an exclusionary rule in order to protect courts from "untrustworthy evidence" was inapplicable. Unlike the defendant, the witness was subject to no custodial pressures; his evidence was also reliable because it was "subject to the normal testing process of an adversary trial."

The Court found that all of the justifications for excluding the witness's testimony were outweighed by the "strong" interests in providing the jury with "all concededly relevant and trustworthy evidence," and in the "effective prosecution of criminals." Moreover, the Court noted that *Harris*'s "impeachment exception" established the principle that inadmissible *Miranda* evidence is not inadmissible "for all purposes."

c. **Dissent**

Justice Douglas dissented, in an opinion that disputed the majority's conclusion that a *Miranda* violation does not constitute a violation of the Fifth Amendment. He declared that *Miranda*, by its terms, established a "constitutional standard for protection of the privilege." Without a "constitutional basis" for its safeguards, he noted, the Court would have been powerless to reverse *Miranda*'s conviction, or to prescribe "preferred modes of interrogation." He argued that *Miranda*'s language was misinterpreted by the *Tucker* majority. For when the *Miranda* Court stated that "adherence to any particular solution" was not required by the Constitution, this meant only that "police need not mouth the precise words contained in the Court's opinion." Justice Douglas emphasized that the *Miranda* Court held that its safeguards were required "in the absence of equally effective" measures, and that no such measures were observed in *Tucker.* Since *Miranda* violations were "constitutional violations," Justice Douglas found that the fruits doctrine applied to *Tucker,* and concluded that the testimony of the witness who was discovered by unconstitutional police action should have been excluded at trial.

d. Perspective

The Court's reasoning in *Tucker* implied that the "fruit of the poisonous tree" doctrine was not appropriate generally for *Miranda* violations, as this doctrine was required only for "constitutional rights." However, some lower courts interpreted *Tucker* as a narrow decision, in light of several of its features. First, the *Tucker* Court relied on the fact that the interrogation at issue took place before the *Miranda* decision, when it determined that the police action "was pursued in complete good faith," and that the "deterrence rationale" for excluding the witness's testimony had little force. Second, the Court expressly reserved the question whether the fruit of a *Miranda* violation should be excluded "regardless of when the interrogation took place." Of course, much of *Tucker*'s reasoning would support the admission of a witness's testimony in a case where an interrogation occurred after *Miranda* was decided. Finally, however, *Tucker* did not specifically address whether the fruits doctrine could be used where the "fruit" involved was not an independent witness, but a defendant's own admissions, or physical evidence.

2. When Police Violate *Miranda* in Obtaining an Initial Confession, This Does Not Necessarily "Taint" a Subsequent Statement Obtained During a Proper Interrogation

In *Oregon v. Elstad,* 470 U.S. 298, 105 S.Ct. 1285, 84 L.Ed.2d 222 (1985), the Court held that an initial failure to administer *Miranda* warnings to a suspect in custody did not "taint" a subsequent confession that occurred after warnings were given and a waiver obtained. Therefore this second confession was admissible at trial, and the defendant's burglary conviction was affirmed. Where no "deliberately coercive or improper tactics" accompanied the initial *Miranda* violation, a subsequent administration of the warnings was held to "cure" any lingering compulsion from the first interrogation.

a. Rationale

The Court extended *Tucker*'s reasoning to allow a defendant's "voluntary" testimony to be admitted at trial, even when it was a "fruit" of a prior unwarned admission. The Court determined that only fruits which are the product of "compulsion" must be excluded at trial, and that all of the "surrounding circumstances and the entire course of police conduct" are relevant in determining the existence of compulsion.

However, it is irrelevant to the "compulsion" inquiry that a defendant may have made a second confession because he erroneously believed that he had "nothing to lose" because his first unwarned admission would be used to convict him anyway. Therefore, while the first unwarned admission in *Elstad* was inadmissible, the second confession at the stationhouse was admissible, because the defendant received warnings and waived his rights, and because no "actual coercion" took place during either interrogation.

b. Non-constitutional Safeguards

The *Elstad* Court found that *Tucker* established the non-constitutional status of the *Miranda* safeguards and therefore held that the fruit of the poisonous tree doctrine does not mandate exclusion of the fruits of a *Miranda*-defective confession. Justice O'Connor noted that the *Miranda* exclusionary rule "sweeps more broadly than the Fifth Amendment itself," and requires the exclusion of voluntary statements which are "presumed" to be compelled. Further, cases decided after *Miranda* supported the conclusion that statements obtained in violation of *Miranda,* but which in fact were voluntarily made, should not be excluded for all purposes. *Harris,* for example, held that statements obtained from *Miranda* violations are admissible for impeachment purposes. *Tucker* likewise limited *Miranda*'s exclusionary rule, and held that neither the goal of deterrence of *Miranda* violations nor the goal of suppression of untrustworthy evidence would be served by excluding the "fruit" of an independent witness's testimony at trial. This reasoning applied "with equal force" in *Elstad,* where the fruit was "the accused's own voluntary testimony," which occurred after warnings were given and a valid waiver obtained.

c. The Fruits of Involuntary Confessions Are Excluded

The Court in *Elstad* found that there were two circumstances in which a second confession must be excluded even though the officers properly give *Miranda* warnings before that confession. One situation is where the first confession is *involuntary,* in the sense that it was obtained against the defendant's free will. Officers who have obtained an involuntary confession have violated the Constitution (specifically the Due Process Clause), and not merely a prophylactic safeguard; and the fruit of the poisonous tree doctrine is fully applicable to constitutional violations. So if the first confession is involuntary, the second confession must be excluded if derived from the first under the principles established in *Wong Sun.* (See the discussion of the fruit of the poisonous tree doctrine in the section on the Fourth Amendment exclusionary rule, *supra*). On the facts in *Elstad,* however, the Court determined that although the defendant's first unwarned confession was *Miranda*-defective, the failure to give warnings did not mean that this admission "was actually coerced."

d.   Subsequent Confession Excluded if It Is Obtained Involuntarily

The second situation in which a subsequent confession may be excluded after *Elstad*, even though the officers gave *Miranda* warnings, is where the second confession is *itself* involuntarily obtained. The giving of *Miranda* warnings does not foreclose the possibility that a subsequent confession may be involuntary. The police officers may use coercive tactics to force a defendant to waive his *Miranda* rights and confess. If that is the case, the confession is inadmissible. Similarly, the police may deceive the defendant in such a way as to unfairly overcome his will to remain silent. For example, the police may incorrectly tell the defendant that he has already "let the cat out of the bag" by confessing, and that a subsequent confession is a mere formality, where in fact the initial confession is inadmissible because it is *Miranda*-defective. While a single bit of misinformation may not be enough to render the confession involuntary, it may contribute to other circumstances to support a finding that the defendant's confession was coerced.

e.   Second Confession Not Involuntary in *Elstad*

In *Elstad*, the Court found that the defendant's second confession was not involuntarily obtained, because the officers did not deceive Elstad into thinking that he had let the "cat out of the bag." If Elstad was under the misimpression that he had done so, then that was a mistake of his own making, and the Due Process Clause does not provide for exclusion of confessions which are not attributable to affirmative police misconduct. See *Colorado v. Connelly* in the discussion on confessions and Due Process. In *Elstad*, the administration of the *Miranda* warnings at the stationhouse served to "cure" the defendant's inability to exercise the privilege intelligently, and to make the second confession "an act of free will." The Court found that whatever subtle form of pressure might exist in the defendant's mind from the revelation of his "guilty secret" was very different from traditional "official coercion" flowing from "physical violence or other deliberate means calculated to break the suspect's will."

f.   "Cat Out of the Bag" Warning Not Required

The Court in *Elstad* rejected the proposal that police inform suspects that their prior admissions may not be admissible evidence, and that they have not let the "cat out of the bag" where they might mistakenly believe that they had. The Court found that such a warning requirement would be likely to decrease the number of confessions; thus, it would impose a "high cost" on "legitimate law enforcement activity," and permit "highly probative evidence" to be "irretrievably lost" to the fact-finder at trial.

g. **Balancing Approach**

As in *Tucker,* the *Elstad* Court, after finding that the fruit of the poisonous tree doctrine did not mandate exclusion, applied a balancing of interests test to determine whether it was appropriate to exclude a properly warned second confession which was obtained after the defendant had already confessed without warnings. The Court found that the benefit of deterring *Miranda* violations by applying the exclusionary rule was attenuated in these circumstances, because an officer would already be deterred from violating *Miranda* because of the fact that the first confession would be excluded. Against the minimal deterrent effect resulting from exclusion of the subsequent confession, the Court weighed the cost of excluding a reliable confession, obtained voluntarily after *Miranda* warnings; the Court concluded that the costs of exclusion outweighed the benefits.

h. **Dissent**

Justice Brennan dissented in *Elstad,* in an opinion joined by Justice Marshall; Justice Stevens filed a separate dissent. Justice Brennan argued that the *Wong Sun* fruits doctrine should be used in *Miranda* cases, and that a confession obtained in violation of *Miranda* should be presumed to taint "a subsequent confession unless the prosecution can show" that the taint is "attenuated." He predicted that *Elstad*'s departure from this rule would deal a "crippling blow" to the efficacy of *Miranda*'s protections. He criticized the *Elstad* majority's belief that warnings can "break any causal connection" between an illegal confession and a legal one, because it contradicted the Court's precedents, and demonstrated "a startling unawareness of the realities of police interrogation." He disagreed with the Court's finding that a first confession created merely a "speculative and attenuated disadvantage" for a suspect, particularly when separate interviews "are often but stages of one overall interrogation."

Justice Brennan rejected the Court's finding that exclusion of the unwarned admission alone in *Elstad* would "provide meaningful deterrence" of police misconduct. He argued that *Elstad* gave officers an incentive to obtain an unwarned confession, due to the likelihood that a suspect would then confess a second time after being given *pro forma* warnings.

Justice Stevens disagreed with the *Elstad* majority's view that two distinct types of coercion should be treated differently in the interrogation context—the "irrebuttably presumed coercion" that exists when no warnings are given, and "actual coercion" that involves physical violence or "means calculated to break the suspect's will." He argued that it was "not faithful to the holding of *Miranda*" to create such a distinction, and that a "major purpose of treating the presumption of coercion" from a lack of warnings as "irrebuttable" was to "avoid the kind of fact-bound inquiry" that *Elstad* requires.

Justice Stevens also disagreed with the Court's "characterization of the police misconduct" in *Elstad,* which appeared to imply that "there was no constitutional violation." He argued that "the same constitutional analysis" should apply, whether an interrogation was "actually coercive or irrebuttably presumed to be coercive." He noted that by rejecting that premise, the *Elstad* majority treated *Miranda* and its progeny "as nothing more than an illegitimate exercise of raw judicial power." Justice Stevens believed that *Miranda* was grounded on the Fifth Amendment, and that the "Federal Constitution" protected the defendant from enduring custodial interrogation "without first being advised of his right to remain silent."

i.   Other Types of *Miranda* Violations

A question raised by *Elstad* is whether its rationale can be applied to *Miranda* violations other than a failure to warn a suspect in custody. For example, suppose that police fail to obtain a valid waiver before continuing an interrogation, and obtain an inadmissible statement; or, suppose that police persist in interrogating a suspect who has invoked the right to silence or counsel, and obtain an inadmissible statement. If *Elstad*'s reasoning were applied to these cases, police would need only to give fresh warnings and secure a waiver, in order to make a subsequent statement a "voluntary" and admissible fruit. Under current *Miranda* doctrine concerning waiver and invocation of rights, such police practices would be unacceptable. Thus, *Elstad*'s rationale has the power to restrict *Miranda* rights significantly, if it is extended by the Court in the future to other types of *Miranda* violations. Some lower courts have extended *Elstad*'s reasoning in this way. See *Greenawalt v. Ricketts*, 943 F.2d 1020 (9th Cir.1991) (applying *Elstad* where police improperly obtained a waiver of *Miranda* rights).

3.   Physical Evidence as the Fruit of a *Miranda* Violation

In *Elstad,* the Court held that a confession obtained as the fruit of a *Miranda*-defective confession was admissible, so long as the second confession was itself legally obtained. The lower courts have applied similar reasoning to allow the admission of physical evidence obtained as a fruit of a *Miranda* violation. According to these courts, the fruit of the poisonous tree doctrine does not apply to exclude such evidence, since that doctrine only applies to constitutional violations, and the *Miranda* safeguards are not constitutionally required. See *United States v. Gonzalez–Sandoval*, 894 F.2d 1043 (9th Cir.1990) (reasoning of *Tucker* and *Elstad* "applies as well to non-testimonial physical evidence obtained as a result of a *Miranda* violation").

D. THE "VOLUNTARY, KNOWING, AND INTELLIGENT" WAIVER OF *MIRANDA* RIGHTS

The *Miranda* Court required the state to prove that a suspect "waived" his rights before police obtained a statement during custodial interrogation. But the *Miranda* opinion gave only one example of a case where a waiver "could" be found, and several examples of cases where positive evidence of waiver was "insufficient." These examples could not provide much guidance for resolving the large variety of waiver "encounters" that police would have with suspects, which could be rife with ambiguity concerning the suspect's understanding of the warnings and willingness to waive his rights.

Twenty years after *Miranda,* the Court provided a definition of the critical elements of a "voluntary, knowing, and intelligent" waiver:

> First the relinquishment of the right must have been voluntary in the sense that it was the product of a *free and deliberate choice* rather than intimidation, coercion, or deception. Second, the waiver must have been made with a *full awareness* both of the nature of the right being abandoned and the consequences of the decision to abandon it. No waiver can be considered knowing and intelligent in the absence of *Miranda* warnings.

Moran v. Burbine, 475 U.S. 412, 106 S.Ct. 1135, 89 L.Ed.2d 410 (1986). More specific rules concerning waiver have been provided by a handful of holdings where the Court has made judgments about waivers on the facts of particular cases.

The Court's waiver rulings establish the *Miranda* warnings as the definitive solution for the problem of inherent coercion and lack of information during custodial interrogation. Therefore, the police *do not need to provide additional information* that would help the suspect decide whether to exercise the privilege, such as information concerning the subjects of the interrogation, the inadmissibility of prior admissions, or an attorney's desire to consult with the suspect.

1. A Waiver Need Not Be "Express"

In *North Carolina v. Butler,* 441 U.S. 369, 99 S.Ct. 1755, 60 L.Ed.2d 286 (1979), the Court rejected a defendant's claim that his waiver of *Miranda* rights was invalid because he did not explicitly state that he waived his right to assistance of counsel. The defendant received written warnings, and was asked to sign a waiver form. He replied, "I will talk to you but I am not signing any form." He then made incriminating statements, and was convicted of kidnapping, armed robbery, and assault. The Court held that an express written or oral waiver of his right to counsel was not an absolute requirement for a valid waiver, and remanded the case to the state court for resolution of the waiver issue.

a. Rationale

The Court determined that *Miranda* did not hold that an "express written or oral statement" was indispensable to a waiver, and that such an "inflexible" *per se* requirement did not accord with the policy behind the *Miranda* safeguards. The *Butler* Court interpreted *Miranda* as holding only that waiver could not be "presumed" from silence. However, silence "coupled with a course of conduct" consistent with abandonment of *Miranda* rights would support a finding of waiver.

b. Dissent

The three dissenters in *Butler* argued that *Miranda* held that no effective waiver could be recognized "unless specifically made." On the facts of *Butler,* no "affirmative" waiver could be shown, because the defendant refused to sign the form and "said nothing" when advised of his right to a lawyer. The dissenters criticized a rule which would allow "courts to construct inferences from ambiguous words and gestures." They also argued that the *Butler* rule would lead lower courts to reach inconsistent results when faced with difficult cases where a defendant's words and actions had "uncertain meaning." By contrast, an express waiver rule would eliminate "these difficulties" and would impose no significant burden on the police.

2. It Cannot Be Presumed That a Suspect Has the Capacity to Understand the *Miranda* Warnings, Because the State Has the Burden of Proving Waiver

a. Insufficient Proof of Suspect's Understanding of Warnings

In *Tague v. Louisiana,* 444 U.S. 469, 100 S.Ct. 652, 62 L.Ed.2d 622 (1980), the Court summarily reversed a conviction for armed robbery, because the state had not proven that the defendant's statement following *Miranda* warnings was taken after a valid waiver of rights. The Court found that the state court erred in finding waiver where the police officer claimed at trial to have recited the *Miranda* warnings, but could not remember the rights himself, "could not recall" whether he asked the suspect whether he understood the rights, and "couldn't say yes or no" whether the suspect was literate or capable of understanding the rights. The *Tague* Court held that the state court erred in holding that a suspect can be presumed to understand the *Miranda* warnings. *Miranda* held that a waiver "may not be presumed," and both *Miranda* and *Butler* emphasized that the state bears the "great" burden of proving waiver; in *Tague,* "no evidence at all" supported a finding of waiver.

b. Sufficient Proof of Suspect's Understanding of Warnings

In *Colorado v. Connelly,* 479 U.S. 157, 107 S.Ct. 515, 93 L.Ed.2d 473 (1986), the Court held that mental illness did not negate a defendant's ability to "voluntarily" waive his rights. The Court remanded the case on the issue whether the defendant's waiver was "intelligent." If the waiver were valid, the defendant's confession would be admissible in his trial for murder.

c.   Voluntariness Aspect of Waiver Is the Same as the Due Process Test for Confessions

The *Connelly* Court determined that the voluntariness inquiry "in the *Miranda* waiver context" should be the same as the voluntariness inquiry in the Due Process context. Therefore, the "voluntariness" of a waiver depended "on the absence of police overreaching," especially since the sole concern of the Fifth Amendment is "governmental coercion." In *Connelly,* where police did not know of defendant's severe mental illness at the time he waived his rights, the defendant's waiver was voluntary because there was no "overreaching." It was irrelevant that experts later found that the defendant would have been unable, at the time of waiver, either "to make free and rational choices" or "use the information" about his *Miranda* rights because of his mental illness.

d.   The Mentally Ill Defendant's Ability to Make an "Intelligent" Waiver After *Connelly*

Lower courts after *Connelly* have held that a mentally ill defendant cannot "knowingly and intelligently" waive her *Miranda* rights. See, e.g., *Smith v. Zant,* 887 F.2d 1407 (11th Cir.1989) (en banc). Unlike the voluntariness aspect of waiver, which is dependent on a finding of police misconduct, the knowledge component of waiver requires a capacity on the part of the suspect to understand the import of the *Miranda* warnings. The suspect's capacity for understanding is a factor independent from police wrongdoing; thus, if the suspect fails to understand the warnings, a waiver cannot be found even if the police have properly given the warnings.

3.   A "Conditional" Waiver May Be "Knowing and Intelligent"

In *Connecticut v. Barrett,* 479 U.S. 523, 107 S.Ct. 828, 93 L.Ed.2d 920 (1987), the Court held that if, after receiving the warnings, a defendant makes a conditional waiver of *Miranda* rights, a subsequent confession is admissible so long as police comply with the suspect's condition. In *Barrett* the defendant, after receiving the warnings, stated that he was willing to "talk" to police, but that he would not make a written statement. The police let him talk, and his statement was admitted at trial by the testimony of the officers who heard the confession. The Court held that where the suspect made his intentions "clear" and the police honored them, his statements made after the "conditional waiver" were admissible.

a.   Rationale

The *Barrett* Court found that the defendant understood his *Miranda* rights sufficiently to make a valid waiver. He received warnings on three separate occasions, and waived his rights each time before he made two separate statements. Before his first statement, he told police he understood his rights. Before each waiver was given, he stated that he would not make a written statement without an attorney, but would "talk" about the crime. Thus, both waivers that led to oral admissions were voluntary. The Court next found that "nothing in *Miranda*" required the police to disregard the suspect's willingness to talk because of his limited request for counsel. As long as the police refrained from obtaining a written statement without counsel, the suspect's limited request was "honored" under *Miranda*. Chief Justice Rehnquist noted that if the suspect's request for counsel had been more "ambiguous," it might have been appropriate to construe it broadly as a general request for the presence of counsel. However, no "interpretation" of the request was required, because the suspect "made clear his intentions," and did not attempt to invoke the right to counsel "for all purposes."

b. Justice Brennan's Concurrence

Justice Brennan found that the defendant's waiver was valid because he testified at trial that he did understand that he did not have to talk to police without a lawyer present. Thus, while his "limited" waiver suggested that he may not have understood his right to remain silent (i.e. that he might have mistakenly thought that oral as opposed to written confessions could not be used against him), the defendant's own testimony belied any such inference, and therefore the state satisfied its burden of proving a "knowing and intelligent" waiver.

4. A Waiver Is Valid Even When a Suspect Is Not Informed of Matters That Would Be Useful in Making an Informed Decision About Exercising the Privilege

In a series of three cases, the defendants each argued that their waivers, made after the warnings were given, were not sufficiently "knowing and intelligent" because the warnings did not contain certain information that the defendants thought to be critical to the waiver decision. In each case, the Court rejected this argument and held that the *Miranda* warnings, as a matter of law, impart information sufficient to establish a knowing and intelligent waiver on the part of a person with the capacity to understand the warnings. The fact that it might be helpful for the suspect to know other facts and circumstances has been held irrelevant to the waiver question, since *Miranda* does not require that the waiver be "brilliant" or "made with a knowledge of all possibly relevant information." All that is required is that the defendant know and understand that he has the right to silence and to the assistance of counsel, as well as the consequences of waiving those rights.

5. **A Suspect Need Not Be Informed of All the Subjects of the Interrogation Before Making a Waiver**

In *Colorado v. Spring*, 479 U.S. 564, 107 S.Ct. 851, 93 L.Ed.2d 954 (1987), the Court held that police could obtain a valid waiver from a suspect without telling him that the subject of the interrogation would concern both the firearms crime for which he was arrested, and an unrelated murder. The defendant claimed that his confession concerning the murder was not admissible, because he had not "knowingly and intelligently" waived his rights concerning that crime when he signed the waiver after his firearms arrest. The Court found that the suspect was warned that "anything" he said could be used against him, and that this warning adequately conveyed "the consequences of abandoning the privilege." Therefore, the Court found that the defendant's waiver was valid, and his confession admissible; his murder conviction was affirmed.

   a. **Rationale**

   The Court found that *Miranda* did not require that a suspect "know and understand every possible consequence" of a waiver. The defendant was given his *Miranda* warnings, and he understood them; thus, his waiver was "knowing and intelligent." The police "silence" about their intention to ask the defendant about an unrelated crime was not "trickery" that negated the voluntariness of the waiver. Such silence could not "cause a suspect to misunderstand" his right to refuse to answer "any question which might incriminate him." As *Miranda* does not require police to provide a suspect with all "useful" information that might affect his decision to confess, the police in *Spring* were not obliged to inform the defendant of all subjects of the interrogation.

   b. **Dissent**

   Justice Marshall dissented, in an opinion joined by Justice Brennan. He argued that the federal agents in *Spring* used an effective "ploy" by failing to inform the defendant that they would ask him about an unrelated state crime that he "could not have expected" to be a subject of questioning. The coercive aspects of this ploy could easily "rise to a level of deception," and could not be justified in light of *Miranda*'s strict waiver requirements. Justice Marshall believed it was reasonable to conclude that the defendant would not have waived his rights during an arrest for the firearms violation if he had known that he would be questioned about the murder. Therefore, he determined that the state did not meet its "heavy burden" of proving waiver.

6. **A Suspect Need Not Be Informed That a Prior Unwarned Confession Would Be Inadmissible at Trial**

In *Oregon v. Elstad*, 470 U.S. 298, 105 S.Ct. 1285, 84 L.Ed.2d 222 (1985), the Court held that a suspect was able to make a "knowing" and "intelligent" waiver, even though he was unaware that his incriminating statement during a prior interrogation was inadmissible at trial. The defendant in *Elstad* admitted his involvement in a burglary during brief questioning in his home, and argued that his later waiver preceding a stationhouse interrogation, and after receiving the *Miranda* warnings, was based on his belief that he had nothing to gain by silence, because "his fate was sealed" by his first admission. The Court rejected his claim that the police should have given him "an additional warning" at the stationhouse concerning the inadmissibility of his earlier statement, because such a requirement was "neither practicable nor constitutionally necessary."

a. Rationale

The Court found that the requirement of additional warnings concerning possible violations of *Miranda* during an initial interrogation was not "practicable," because such violations might not be identified by police until after a second confession was obtained during a later interrogation. Justice O'Connor noted that definitions of custody and other *Miranda* issues involve "murky and difficult" determinations that police are "ill-equipped" to make on behalf of a suspect during an ongoing investigation. The Court concluded that a waiver should be valid even if a suspect lacks "a full and complete appreciation of all the consequences" that may result from "the quality of evidence" in his case.

b. Dissent

Justice Brennan dissented, in an opinion joined by Justices Marshall and Stevens. Justice Brennan argued that a warning which stated that a prior unwarned statement *may* be inadmissible, would help to dispel the coercion of custodial interrogation, and would ensure that a waiver was not influenced by a defendant's erroneous belief in the hopelessness of exercising *Miranda* rights after an initial confession.

7. **A Suspect Need Not Be Informed That an Attorney Is Trying to Consult With Him**

In *Moran v. Burbine,* 475 U.S. 412, 106 S.Ct. 1135, 89 L.Ed.2d 410 (1986), the Court held that the defendant's waiver was valid, even though police deliberately failed to inform him that an attorney retained by his sister was calling the police station, and asking to be present during his interrogation. In *Moran,* the police also told the attorney that the defendant would not be interrogated, and then proceeded to interrogate him in her absence. The Court found no reason to interpret *Miranda* as either prohibiting police from deliberately deceiving counsel concerning the ongoing interrogation of a suspect, or prohibiting police from denying counsel's request to see a suspect. Therefore, the Court held that the defendant's three written confessions were admissible because of valid waivers, and affirmed his murder conviction.

a. Rationale

First, the Court found that the waiver was "voluntary," because no "coercion" resulted from police conduct. The waiver was also "knowing and intelligent," because the defendant received warnings, and signed a written waiver form during three separate interviews, stating that he understood his rights and did not want to consult with counsel. The Court rejected the claim that an event "occurring outside the presence of the suspect" could be relevant to his "capacity to comprehend and knowingly relinquish a constitutional right." Justice O'Connor conceded that it would have been "useful" for the defendant to know that a lawyer was trying to gain access to the defendant while he was in custody. But as *Elstad* held, *Miranda* did not require the police to supply such "useful" information that might affect a suspect's decision to exercise the privilege. Once the defendant had received *Miranda* warnings, he had all the information required by *Miranda* to produce a valid waiver.

b. Upsetting the *Miranda* Compromise

The *Burbine* Court rejected any requirement that the police inform a suspect that his lawyer was looking for him on a more fundamental ground as well: such an obligation would impose an unfair "handicap" on the investigatory process, and cause an increase in the number of suspects who would invoke the privilege. This, in turn, would impose a "substantial cost" on society's "compelling interest" in securing confessions and punishing criminals. The Court found that *Miranda* had struck a fair compromise between the interest of citizens to be free from coercion, and the interest of the state in obtaining reliable evidence. This delicate balance would be upset if police were required to give a suspect more warnings than required by *Miranda*.

c. Deliberate Failure to Notify the Suspect

Justice O'Connor acknowledged that the police may have deliberately failed to tell the defendant about the lawyer's efforts to consult with him. Even so, the "state of mind of the police" was "irrelevant" to the validity of the waiver. Police silence could not constitute "trickery" under *Miranda* that would "vitiate" the voluntariness of a waiver, because it could not deprive a suspect of the "knowledge essential to his ability to understand" his rights.

d. Affirmative Misrepresentation

The Court in *Burbine* distinguished between an officer's deliberate *failure* to impart information that the suspect might find useful from an officer's *affirmative misrepresentation* which gives the suspect mistaken information. Affirmative deception makes it less likely that the suspect knowingly and voluntarily waived his rights. So for example, if the officers had stated to Moran that his counsel had called and left a message that he was not coming by and that Moran ought to just confess, then the Court might have found a subsequent confession to be involuntary. However, it must be noted that police deception does not *automatically* render a subsequent confession involuntary. Deception is only one relevant factor in a totality of circumstances inquiry. See *Green v. Scully,* 850 F.2d 894 (2d Cir.1988) (confession voluntary even though police deceive the defendant into thinking that his palm print was found at the crime scene). In contrast, an officer's mere nondisclosure of information which the suspect might find helpful is not relevant *at all* to the waiver inquiry after *Burbine.*

e. Deceiving the Attorney, and the Attorney's Role in *Miranda*

The *Burbine* Court rejected the claim that *Miranda* should be "extended" to invalidate a confession where the police deceive an attorney concerning a suspect's ongoing interrogation. The Court concluded that this proposed Fifth Amendment doctrine would ignore the "underlying purposes" of *Miranda,* and upset the "proper balance" between law enforcement needs and the protection of a suspect's rights. The Court noted that *Miranda* rights were merely "prophylactic safeguards" and not constitutional rights, according to *Tucker.* Their only "legitimacy" came from their "mission" of dispelling coercion during interrogation, not from any potential role in molding police conduct. Thus, they could not serve as a basis for regulating police deception of attorneys, because this kind of police action had "no relevance" to the degree of compulsion experienced by a suspect during interrogation.

The *Burbine* Court noted that *Miranda* had rejected the position "that the actual presence of a lawyer was necessary to dispel the coercion" of an interrogation. Instead, the Court declared that *Miranda* opted only for giving the suspect "the power to exert some control" over the interrogation. Thus, *Miranda* did not support the defendant's proposed rule. Again, the *Miranda* Court had created a compromise between the interests of citizens and the state. The compromise was struck by granting citizens safeguards from custodial interrogation, but with the proviso that it is *up to the suspect* to invoke the rights provided. This delicate balance would be upset if an attorney were given the right, independent of the suspect's wishes, to be kept informed and to consult with the suspect. Consequently, the attorney has *no role to play* under *Miranda* until the suspect decides to invoke the right to counsel.

f. Dissent

Justice Stevens dissented, in an opinion joined by Justices Brennan and Marshall. He argued that there could be no "constitutional distinction" between police silence concerning counsel's proffered assistance and a "deceptive misstatement" on this subject. Therefore, he advocated a rule that would require the police to inform a suspect of an attorney's desire to consult with him, in order to further "dispel" the inherent compulsion of custodial interrogation.

Justice Stevens interpreted the *Moran* Court's holding as a finding that a state has a "compelling interest" in "lawyer-free, incomunicado custodial interrogation," which justifies deliberate police interference with an attorney's access to a client. He found this position to be inconsistent with the Court's traditional "strictest scrutiny" of incommunicado interrogation.

Justice Stevens rejected the *Moran* majority's finding that the police deception through "silence" could have no "bearing" on the knowing and intelligent waiver of rights. He found that "omission of a critically important fact" by police was similar to "deception by means of a misleading statement," as both police acts deprived a suspect "of knowledge essential to his ability to understand" his rights, and thus, to waive them knowingly and intelligently.

8. **The State Must Prove a Waiver Was "Voluntary, Knowing and Intelligent" by a Preponderance of the Evidence**
    In *Colorado v. Connelly*, 479 U.S. 157, 107 S.Ct. 515, 93 L.Ed.2d 473 (1986), the Court held that a state did not have to prove a waiver by "clear and convincing evidence," but only by a "preponderance" of the evidence. It determined that the state should have the same burden for proving waiver as for proving that a confession is "voluntary."

    a. **Rationale**
        The Court concluded that the determination of a waiver, like the voluntariness determination, had "nothing to do with the reliability" of verdicts. Therefore, the Court borrowed the rationale of *Lego v. Twomey*, 404 U.S. 477, 92 S.Ct. 619, 30 L.Ed.2d 618 (1972), where it adopted a "preponderance" standard for the state's burden of proving the voluntariness of a confession. The Court found it was "doubtful" that a "clear and convincing evidence" standard would increase the deterrent effect of *Miranda*'s exclusionary rule, compared to the "preponderance" standard. Moreover, whatever increase might occur would be outweighed by "the public interest in placing probative evidence before juries" for the purpose of reaching accurate verdicts. Chief Justice Rehnquist noted that if constitutional Due Process protections could be enforced through a "preponderance" standard (as is the case under *Lego*), then a waiver of the "auxiliary protections" of *Miranda* "should require no higher burden of proof."

b. Dissent

Justice Brennan dissented, in an opinion joined by Justice Marshall, and argued that the Court's adoption of the "preponderance" standard ignored "the explicit command" of *Miranda:* the state has a "heavy burden" to prove waiver, as "high standards" of proof must be required for the waiver of constitutional rights. He reasoned that police control over interrogations in the *Miranda* context made it "appropriate to place a higher burden of proof" on the state to demonstrate waiver of *Miranda* rights.

E. WAIVER AND THE RESUMPTION OF QUESTIONING AFTER INVOCATION OF RIGHTS

The waiver cases just discussed all dealt with fact situations in which the suspect was given warnings and then made a decision to speak to the police. More difficult questions arise where the suspect receives warnings, decides to invoke his right to silence or to counsel, and then *changes his mind* and decides to speak to the police. Obviously, it is more difficult for the state to prove that the suspect waived his rights after invoking them than it is when the suspect simply confessed without ever invoking his rights. Something must account for the suspect's change of heart—something other than police coercion or an official disrespect of the suspect's invocation of his rights.

Miranda required that police must "cut off questioning" when a suspect invokes her rights. Presumably, this meant that police must stop seeking a waiver if a suspect invokes her rights before waiving them; if she invokes her rights in the middle of interrogation, the interrogation "must cease." Yet a suspect sometimes continues to talk to the police after invocation, and this may create some ambiguity about the status of her decision to remain silent and to wait for counsel before making a statement. Even if a suspect does remain silent, police often wish to find out whether she has changed her mind about her invocation, so that they can renew the attempt to seek a waiver. If *Miranda*'s command to "cut off questioning" were taken literally, police would be denied the power to resume questioning after invocation under any circumstances, except perhaps where a suspect explicitly "revoked" her invocation.

Nine years after *Miranda* was decided, the Court announced that it was appropriate under some circumstances to allow police to obtain a waiver from a suspect who invoked her right to remain silent. This was permissible so long as the police "scrupulously honored" the suspect's right to remain silent. However, the Court refused to extend its reinterrogation rule concerning invocation of the right to silence to a suspect's invocation of the right to counsel. The Court also held that no waiver may be sought from a suspect who actually consults with counsel following invocation; police may not reinitiate interrogation of such a suspect without counsel present. Yet the Court agreed that police could seek a waiver if a suspect invoked the right to counsel, but later "initiated" a "generalized discussion" of the investigation.

1. **Police May Obtain a Waiver From a Suspect Following His Invocation of the Right to Remain Silent**

    In *Michigan v. Mosley,* 423 U.S. 96, 96 S.Ct. 321, 46 L.Ed.2d 313 (1975), the Court held that *Miranda* did not create a *"per se* proscription of indefinite duration" upon police interrogation following a suspect's invocation of the right to remain silent. Instead, *Miranda* requires only that the "right to cut off questioning" must be "scrupulously honored." Police complied with this requirement in *Mosley,* by ceasing the interrogation concerning the robberies for which the defendant was arrested, following his invocation. It was permissible for police to seek a waiver from the defendant two hours later, concerning a crime "different in nature and in time and place" from the crime for which the suspect was arrested. Therefore his confession, made after again receiving the warnings and voluntarily waiving his rights, was admissible, and his murder conviction was affirmed.

    a. **Rationale**

        The Court found that *Miranda*'s mandate concerning the right to "cut off questioning" was ambiguous, and interpreted it to mean that "interrogation after a momentary cessation" would be impermissible. However, on the facts of *Mosley,* the police neither refused to discontinue the interrogation, nor persisted in "repeated efforts to wear down [the suspect's] resistance and make him change his mind." Therefore, the defendant's initial invocation was "scrupulously honored," and police were entitled to seek a waiver for interrogation about a different crime.

        The Court noted that it was "absurd" to interpret *Miranda*'s "right to cut off questioning" as a "blanket prohibition" against the "taking of voluntary statements" after invocation, or as a "permanent immunity" from interrogation. Justice Stewart declared that this would create "wholly irrational obstacles" to police investigations and "deprive suspects" of the opportunity to make "informed and intelligent assessments" of their interests. The goal of *Miranda* was to require police to respect a suspect's invocation, and to give the suspect control over the time of the interrogation, its subject, and its duration. A resumption of interrogation after invocation does not necessarily undermine these goals.

    b. **Momentary Cessation**

        The Court in *Mosley* cautioned that the continuation of interrogation "after a momentary cessation" would "frustrate the purposes of *Miranda,*" because it would allow "repeated rounds of questioning to undermine the will" of the suspect. See *Charles v. Smith,* 894 F.2d 718 (5th Cir.1990) (no waiver where interrogation resumed two minutes after right to silence invoked). Compare *Grooms v. Keeney,* 826 F.2d 883 (9th Cir.1987) (officers scrupulously honored the suspect's invocation of the right to silence where interrogation was resumed after a four-hour "cooling off" period).

c. Applied to Facts of *Mosley*

On the facts, the Court found that the defendant's invocation was "scrupulously honored." When he refused to answer any questions about the robberies, a police officer reasonably could interpret this invocation as being limited to those crimes. Thus, the attempt to seek a waiver in order to interrogate about a different crime was proper, when it was undertaken by a different police officer who gave the defendant a new set of *Miranda* warnings, and when it occurred two hours after the initial cut off of questioning.

d. Justice White's Concurrence

Justice White objected to the *Mosley* majority's condemnation of continued interrogation after only "a momentary cessation" following invocation, because he did not want to make all confessions inadmissible *per se* under these circumstances. He found the *Mosley* test to be too strict, because it would "rob the accused of the choice to answer questions voluntarily" for some time following "his own previous contrary decision." Instead, he argued that courts should assess whether a waiver following invocation was "voluntary." If the continued questioning undermined the will of the suspect on the facts of a given case, then courts could find the waiver to be "involuntary."

e. Dissent

Justice Brennan dissented, in an opinion joined by Justice Marshall, and argued that the *Mosley* rule failed to "assure with reasonable certainty" that a confession would not be obtained "under the influence" of the inherent compulsion of the interrogation process. He contended that *Miranda* established "a virtually irrebuttable presumption of compulsion" concerning statements which are "the product of renewed questioning." In order to rebut such a presumption, "adequate procedural safeguards" would be necessary, because *Miranda* found that "renewed questioning itself" is part of the process that creates coercion and undermines the suspect's free will. He concluded that the *Mosley* majority's "safeguards" would not protect a suspect's right to invoke the privilege, because they were "vague and ineffective." He preferred that a suspect either be arraigned before reinterrogation, or that "resumption of questioning should await appointment and arrival of counsel." By contrast, the *Mosley* procedures would encourage police to stop the interrogation "until the police station's coercive atmosphere does its work," and makes the suspect likely to respond to resumed questioning.

f.   *Mosley*'s Application to Different Factual Settings

Mosley's holding emphasized a number of factors: the fresh warnings, the two-hour break between interrogations, the different subject of the second interrogation, the different identity of the officer, and the immediate cessation of interrogation following the original invocation. The Court has not provided further guidance concerning *Mosley*'s application to cases where one or more of these factors are absent. Lower courts have sometimes disapproved the extension of *Mosley* to cases where the break between interrogations was very short, or where multiple reinterrogations occurred. See, e.g., *Charles v. Smith,* 894 F.2d 718 (5th Cir.1990) (reinterrogation impermissible after two-minute break); *Vujosevic v. Rafferty,* 844 F.2d 1023 (3d Cir.1988) (reinterrogation impermissible after four attempts to renew questioning). In theory, however, *Mosley*'s application is potentially flexible, as long as there is evidence that the invocation was "honored," and the suspect's will was not "undermined."

g.   Knowing and Voluntary Waiver Must Still Be Found

The *Mosley* Court made clear that the "scrupulous honor" requirement which arises after the suspect has invoked his right to silence is a requirement in *addition* to that which applies to any *Miranda* waiver question, i.e. that the suspect knowingly and voluntarily waived his *Miranda* rights. The state makes a stronger case on the general waiver issue if the officer gave a fresh set of warnings upon reinterrogation. Otherwise the state is subject to an argument that the defendant forgot about the warnings or forgot about the consequences of waiving *Miranda* rights during the cooling off period.

2.   The Definition of "Invocation" of the Right to Silence

What if the suspect's statement in response to the warnings is so ambiguous as to be reasonably construed as either an invocation of the right to silence or as a willingness to talk. For example, what if the suspect says, "I probably shouldn't tell you anything, my brother will be mad." The Court has not defined what must be said for a suspect to invoke the right to silence, although it has held that the right to counsel may be invoked in a brief statement that is "neither indecisive nor ambiguous." See *Smith v. Illinois,* 469 U.S. 91, 105 S.Ct. 490, 83 L.Ed.2d 488 (1984) (valid invocation where suspect is informed of the right to counsel and says, "Uh, yeah, I'd like that"). Nor has the Court provided guidance concerning the action that police must take when an invocation is ambiguous. Most lower courts have prohibited police from continuing interrogation after an ambiguous invocation of silence, but have allowed police to ask *"clarifying" questions* until it is clear whether an invocation was actually made. So in the majority of courts, a question such as "Are you telling me that you don't want to talk?" will be permissible after an ambiguous invocation, whereas a question such as "Are you telling me that you don't want to tell my why you did it?" will not. See, e.g., *United States v. Pena,* 897 F.2d 1075 (11th Cir.1990) (reinterrogation impermissible because police failed to clarify ambiguity in invocation before obtaining waiver).

a. Request to See a Third Party Is Not an Invocation of the Right to Silence

In *Fare v. Michael C.,* 442 U.S. 707, 99 S.Ct. 2560, 61 L.Ed.2d 197 (1979), the Court held that a juvenile's request to have his probation officer present during the interrogation was not the equivalent of an invocation of the right to silence. The Court found that the juvenile's request "might well be consistent with a desire to speak to the police." Justice Blackmun noted that the request was relevant in evaluating whether the juvenile had waived his rights, however. In the absence of further evidence of the juvenile's intent to invoke the right to silence, the Court held that no invocation occurred. The juvenile's waiver was found to be valid, and his confession was held to be admissible in his murder trial.

3. Police May Not Obtain a Waiver From a Suspect Following the Invocation of the Right to Counsel, Absent the Suspect's "Initiation" of Further Communications With the Police

In *Edwards v. Arizona,* 451 U.S. 477, 101 S.Ct. 1880, 68 L.Ed.2d 378 (1981), the Court held that once a suspect invokes the right to counsel, a "valid waiver of that right cannot be established by showing only that he responded" to renewed police-initiated interrogation, even if that interrogation follows new *Miranda* warnings. Thus, the mere fact that the suspect's waiver could be found knowing and voluntary under the circumstances is not enough, if the suspect has invoked the right to counsel and the police, as opposed to the suspect, have initiated interrogation. In *Edwards,* the defendant had invoked his right to counsel by saying, "I want an attorney before making a deal." The police ceased interrogation, and then returned in the morning to renew interrogation; the defendant was told that he "had" to talk to them. The police gave the defendant new *Miranda* warnings, told him they wanted to talk to him, and ultimately obtained a confession. The defendant's subsequent waiver was held invalid because of the police-initiated reinterrogation, and his confession was held inadmissible.

a. Rationale

The Court relied on *Miranda*'s mandate that "the interrogation must cease until an attorney is present," once a suspect invokes the right to counsel. The Court began by noting that a suspect could waive his rights before invocation under *Butler,* but that when police claimed that a suspect waived after invocation of the right to counsel (i.e. that the suspect changed his mind for some reason), "additional safeguards" were necessary beyond the giving of new *Miranda* warnings prior to reinterrogation. Therefore, the Court determined that police cannot obtain a valid waiver from a suspect who invokes his right to counsel, unless the suspect "initiates further communication, exchanges, or conversations with the police" or unless counsel is provided.

b. **Distinction From *Mosley***

The Court in *Edwards* emphasized that different "procedural safeguards" were triggered by the invocation of the right to counsel than by the invocation of the right to silence. The reason was that if the suspect invokes only the right to silence, he may later decide on his own that it is in his interest to talk to the police; presumably, then, there is no harm in approaching him after a while and asking him if he has changed his mind. But if the suspect invokes his right to counsel, this indicates that he feels overmatched and is unwilling to deal with the police without legal assistance. It is unlikely that such a person would then unilaterally change his mind and decide that he was fully capable of dealing with the police without any assistance. Therefore, stricter procedural safeguards are required—no interrogation, ever, until the suspect initiates it—where counsel is invoked.

c. **Applied to the Facts of *Edwards***

On the facts, the Court found that the defendant made a "sufficient invocation" of his right to counsel, and that the police returned the next day and informed him that they wanted to talk to him, after advising him again of his *Miranda* rights. While it was "not clear" what prompted him to agree to talk to the police, it was clear that he was "interrogated" when the police played a tape of an accomplice's statement at his request. As the defendant's subsequent confession was made "without having had access to counsel," there was no valid waiver.

d. **Contrast With Totality of Circumstances Approach**

Justice Powell, concurring in the judgment in *Edwards,* agreed with the result because the defendant was "subjected to renewed interrogation" against his will, which was "incompatible with a voluntary waiver." However, Justice Powell disapproved of the new and "unclear" *per se* rule that a valid waiver cannot be obtained after invocation of the right to counsel, unless the suspect "initiates" communication. He argued that the suspect's "initiation" of a conversation should be only one factor in the inquiry into the "totality" of circumstances concerning waiver. He believed that police should be able to "inquire whether a suspect has changed his mind" after invocation, as well as engage in "routine conversations" about "unrelated matters."

e. **Bright Line Rule**

The *Edwards* "no reinterrogation until the suspect initiates" rule is a per se, bright line rule. A confession is automatically excluded under *Edwards* if the police initiate reinterrogation of the suspect after he has invoked his right to counsel—even if the state can make a convincing argument that the defendant knew his rights and voluntarily waived them. So for example, if the defendant invokes the right to counsel and, two hours later an officer approaches him politely and asks him if he has changed his mind, and gives fresh warnings, the subsequent confession is inadmissible even if the suspect, when approached, says "I have changed my mind; I was just about to tell you about it when you came to me." The *Edwards* Court adopted a bright-line rule for ease of administration and to give police clear guidance, and also to *overprotect* the rights of a person who has invoked the right to counsel. The Court determined that a prophylactic safeguard was necessary to protect a person in such a vulnerable position from being badgered by police into confessing without counsel.

f. Two–Step Approach

The *Edwards* Court made clear that the bright-line initiation requirement is in addition to the general requirement that all *Miranda* waivers must be knowing and voluntary. Thus, even if the suspect initiates renewed interrogation, the state must show that the suspect understood his *Miranda* rights and voluntarily waived them. The state will find it easier to prove a knowing and voluntary waiver if the officer gives fresh warnings at the time of the reinterrogation.

4. The Definition of a Suspect's "Initiation" That Must Occur Before a Waiver Can Be Sought Following Invocation of the Right to Counsel

The *Edwards* Court did not define what it meant by "initiation." Subsequent cases have provided some guidance, but there is still dispute as to whether certain suspect-initiated contacts constitute an initiation of reinterrogation as opposed to communication on some other matter.

a. A Suspect's Request for a Polygraph Examination Constitutes Initiation

In *Wyrick v. Fields,* 459 U.S. 42, 103 S.Ct. 394, 74 L.Ed.2d 214 (1982), the Court held that a soldier's waiver of rights was valid when it was made prior to a polygraph examination which he requested, after consultation with counsel. As the defendant "initiated" the polygraph examination, it was proper for the polygraph examiner to seek a waiver of rights, which the defendant signed. This waiver indicated that the defendant did not want counsel during the examination, and the Court found that he also implicitly waived his right to counsel during "post-test" questioning by the examiner. Thus, statements made during this questioning were admissible, as well as later statements to police, and the defendant's conviction for rape was affirmed.

b. Change of Circumstances

In *Fields,* the Court found a valid waiver of the right to counsel during post-test questioning under the "totality" of circumstances. That is, the waiver extended not only to the questions asked during the polygraph examination, but also to follow-up questions by which the questioner asked the defendant to elaborate upon or explain his answers. The Court reasoned that by requesting the polygraph, the defendant waived both his right to counsel, and his right to be "free of interrogation." The Court rejected the claim that the "post-test" questioning was a separate interrogation, and treated it as part of the whole "meeting" for which rights were waived.

The Court concluded that a suspect's waiver for the polygraph examination would constitute a waiver as to post-test questioning as well "unless the circumstances *changed so seriously* that his answers were no longer voluntary," or no longer based on a knowing and intelligent relinquishment of his rights. Thus, the Court left open the possibility that post-test questioning would be impermissible where it goes beyond the scope of the subject matter of the polygraph examination, or where the circumstances of the post-test questioning were radically different from those of the polygraph examination itself. See *United States v. Gillyard,* 726 F.2d 1426 (9th Cir.1984) (no waiver as to post-test questioning where two agents entered and subjected the defendant to an hour of questioning without *Miranda* warnings).

c. **Dissent**

Justice Marshall dissented in *Fields,* and argued that the "totality" of the circumstances showed that no valid waiver was obtained for post-test questioning. The defendant agreed "only to submit to a polygraph," and was not explicitly informed that he would be questioned after the test. He thus rejected the majority's assertion that by permitting the polygraph, the defendant could reasonably assume that he would also be subject to follow-up questions. He contended that a suspect who takes a polygraph test expects it to be a "discrete test," with a "readily identifiable beginning and end." Thus, the scope of the defendant's "initiation" was limited, and police should not have been able to use evidence of his pre-test waiver to prove that a waiver existed for his post-test statements.

5. **Suspect's Desire for Generalized Discussion About the Crime**

In *Oregon v. Bradshaw,* 462 U.S. 1039, 103 S.Ct. 2830, 77 L.Ed.2d 405 (1983), a plurality of the Court defined "initiation" as an inquiry or statement evidencing a "desire" to "open up a more generalized discussion relating directly or indirectly to the investigation." An inquiry or statement that merely relates "to routine incidents of the custodial relationship" does not constitute "initiation." In *Bradshaw,* the defendant invoked the right to counsel, and then in the course of being transported from the police station to the jail, asked an officer: "Well, what is going to happen to me now?" This made it possible for the officer to discuss the investigation, and later obtain a valid waiver when the defendant received fresh warnings and agreed to take a polygraph examination, and made incriminating statements during post-test questioning. The Court found the defendant's statements to be admissible, and affirmed his manslaughter conviction.

a. Rationale

The *Bradshaw* plurality reiterated the *Edwards* two-step test, stating that a court must first determine whether "initiation" occurred; if it did, then a court must decide whether a knowing and voluntary waiver was obtained. If it did not, then a knowing and voluntary waiver is not possible. Justice Rehnquist found that the fact of initiation itself is not *per se* proof of waiver, and that the "totality" of circumstances must be examined. On the facts of *Bradshaw,* the plurality decided that the police officer did not violate *Edwards* because the defendant's question "reasonably could have been interpreted" by the officer as relating to the investigation.

Justice Rehnquist found that some inquiries by suspects are "so routine that they cannot" be assumed to represent a desire to discuss the investigation. Such inquiries would include a request "for a drink of water," or a request "to use the telephone." However, the inquiry in *Bradshaw* was reasonably interpreted as a request for generalized discussion of the investigation, as evidenced by the police officer's response. The suspect invoked his right to counsel at the police station; he was being taken on a trip to the county jail when he asked what was going to happen. The police officer responded by saying, "You do not have to talk to me," and "You have requested an attorney and I don't want you talking to me unless you so desire," and "since you have requested an attorney, you know, it has to be at your own free will." Justice Rehnquist noted that generalized discussion ensued only after the defendant told the officer he "understood." Thus there was no *Edwards* violation.

b. Knowing and Voluntary Waiver

After finding that the first, "initiation" step of *Edwards* was satisfied, the Court in *Bradshaw* found the defendant's written waiver to be valid under the totality of the circumstances. The waiver occurred the day after the initiation when the defendant agreed to take a polygraph test, at the suggestion of the officer who discussed the case with him the day before. As there was no evidence of "threats, promises or inducements to talk," and the defendant changed his mind about his invocation "without any impropriety on the part of the police," the waiver was voluntary. It was also knowing and intelligent, because the defendant had been informed of his rights with fresh warnings and understood them.

c.	**Justice Powell's Concurrence**

Justice Powell concurred in the judgment, but objected to the two-step approach to the inquiries concerning "initiation" and waiver. He acknowledged that all the other Justices supported a two-step approach, although they were evenly divided over the proper definition of an "initiation." He argued that courts should "engage in more substantive inquiries than 'who said what first'." Notwithstanding these views, he agreed with the plurality's finding that the defendant's waiver was valid under the totality of the circumstances.

d.	**Dissent**

Justice Marshall dissented, in an opinion joined by Justices Brennan, Blackmun, and Stevens, and argued that an "initiation" occurs only when the suspect communicates *explicitly* about the "subject matter of the criminal investigation." He argued that, unless the statement or inquiry invites "further interrogation," police cannot obtain a valid waiver. In Justice Marshall's view, the defendant's question sought only "to find out where police were going to take him." This conclusion could be drawn from several circumstances: the defendant had invoked his rights only minutes earlier, he was put in a police car, and he had the "normal reaction" of wanting to know where he was going. Justice Marshall complained that the plurality's interpretation of "initiation" allowed police to "capitalize on the custodial setting," and to reinterrogate based on responses that suspects typically have to a "loss of control over their freedom of movement."

e.	**Perspective**

In effect, the *Bradshaw* Court defined the scope of the right to invoke counsel as follows: if a suspect wants to consult with counsel before making a statement, she can preserve this right, with certainty, only by invoking it and remaining silent thereafter. As Justice Rehnquist's opinion reveals, the resolution of an "initiation" question is primarily a method for determining whether police have violated *Edwards* by badgering a suspect impermissibly. It is not primarily an inquiry concerning the suspect's possible intent to revoke her invocation. The plurality's "initiation" finding in *Bradshaw* was based on the police officer's interpretation of the suspect's inquiry, and on the officer's quick attempt to warn the suspect that he did not "have to talk" and should not talk unless it was his "desire" to do so at his own "free will." The officer's speech and acts convinced the plurality that the suspect was not "badgered" in *Bradshaw,* and thus, that *Edwards* was not violated.

f.	**Post-*Bradshaw* Applications of the "Initiation" Rule**

While neither the broad nor the limited definition of "initiation" commanded a majority of the Court in *Bradshaw,* the lower courts have followed the plurality's broader definition, meaning that more inquiries from suspects will be considered initiation rather than fewer. See *United States v. Velasquez,* 885 F.2d 1076 (3d Cir.1989) ("initiation" was communicated when suspect asked, "What is going to happen?"). These courts reason that the plurality's test is a reasonable compromise between individual and state interests and that Justice Marshall's test "might convert the prophylactic value of the initiation requirement into an overly stringent substantive hurdle." The courts also point out that the suspect is not bereft of protection under the plurality test: questions which are clearly attendant to custodial issues will not be considered initiation, and even if initiation is found, the state must still prove that the defendant's waiver was knowing and voluntary.

6.   **Ambiguous "Invocation" of the Right to Counsel**
In *Smith v. Illinois,* 469 U.S. 91, 105 S.Ct. 490, 83 L.Ed.2d 488 (1984), the Court held that a suspect's post-invocation "responses to further interrogation may not be used to cast doubt on the clarity of his initial request for counsel." Therefore the police violated *Edwards* when they ignored the defendant's statement, "Uh, yeah, I'd like to do that," made in response to the warning that he had a right to "consult with a lawyer and have a lawyer present during the interrogation." Statements made after continued interrogation were inadmissible under the *Edwards* per se rule.

a.   **Rationale**
The Court rejected the state's argument that the defendant's "clear and unequivocal" request was only an "indecisive inquiry," when viewed together with his later responses to questioning, when he stated, "I don't know what's what, really," and then agreed to talk. It would be "unprecedented and untenable" to permit post-invocation statements to cast "retrospective" doubt upon a request for counsel, where nothing was ambiguous about either the request itself or the statements that preceded it. The Court declared that it would be improper to allow police to proceed "as if the defendant had requested nothing, in the hope that" later statements might create ambiguity concerning the invocation.

b.   **Open Question**
The *Smith* Court found that the suspect's invocation of counsel was not ambiguous merely because it was preceded by an "uh". The Court, however, declined to address the question of how an "ambiguous or equivocal" invocation should be defined, or of what consequences should follow from such an invocation.

c.   **Dissent**
Justice Rehnquist dissented, in an opinion joined by Justice Powell. He saw "no reason why the entire flavor of the colloquy" could not be considered by the courts that must make factual determinations concerning the ambiguity of an invocation. He believed that the police

"were faithfully attempting to follow" *Miranda,* and that the facts of *Smith* did not "fit the mold" of either *Edwards* or *Bradshaw,* where clear invocations were given, with no subsequent ambiguities in the record.

7. **The Consequences of an "Ambiguous or Equivocal" Invocation of Counsel**
The *Smith* Court noted that lower courts have used three different approaches to ambiguous invocations of the right to counsel. Some have held that police must cease all questioning when an ambiguous invocation is made, while others require some degree of "clarity" in an invocation before questioning must be "cut off." Most lower courts have allowed police to ask only "clarifying" questions after an ambiguous invocation, in order to determine whether the suspect does want to invoke her rights. Under this view, the police can ask "Are you asking for counsel?" but they can not say "We found your gun at the scene." See, e.g., *United States v. Gotay,* 844 F.2d 971 (2d Cir.1988). For an example of a case where the court did not recognize a defendant's act as an invocation because it was too vague to be even "ambiguous," see *Quadrini v. Clusen,* 864 F.2d 577 (7th Cir.1989) (showing the police a lawyer's business card is not an invocation of counsel).

8. **A Request to See a Third Party Is Not an Invocation of the Right to Counsel**
In *Fare v. Michael C.,* 442 U.S. 707, 99 S.Ct. 2560, 61 L.Ed.2d 197 (1979), the Court held that a juvenile's request to have his probation officer present during the interrogation did not constitute an invocation of the right to counsel.

   a. **Rationale**
   The Court reasoned that it is the "pivotal role of legal counsel" in protecting the privilege that justified *Miranda*'s *per se* rule that police must honor the invocation of the right to counsel. No such justification existed for honoring a suspect's request for "a probation officer, a clergyman, or a close friend." Moreover, the Court found that a probation officer was not sufficiently similar to a lawyer to justify an "extension" of *Miranda*'s *per se* rule in *Fare.* The Court stated that a probation officer often is not trained in the law, and is not a trained advocate. Nor is a probation officer able to offer "independent advice," because he is an employee of the state, and his duty "may conflict sharply" with the interests of the juvenile. Further, a probation officer's communications with a juvenile are not protected by law. For these reasons, a probation officer is not able to offer "the type of legal assistance necessary" to protect a suspect's privilege during interrogation.

   The Court also rejected the argument that the "close relationship" and "trust" between a juvenile and his probation officer justified an extension of *Miranda* in *Fare*. This rationale would cut the *Miranda* holding "completely loose from its own explicitly stated rationale," which was the need to provide legal assistance to suspects. Further, such an extension of *Miranda* could be used to justify a juvenile's right to cut off questioning after invocation of the desire to consult with any trustworthy person.

b. Dissent
Justice Marshall dissented, in an opinion joined by Justices Brennan and Stevens. Justice Powell dissented separately. Justice Marshall argued that *Miranda* should be interpreted to require that "interrogation cease whenever a juvenile requests an adult who is obligated to represent his interests." He believed such a request should be treated as an invocation of the right to counsel, because it is an obvious attempt to obtain advice by a person who cannot "be compared to an adult in full possession of his senses and knowledgeable of the consequences of his admissions." Further, a juvenile is unlikely either to trust his own ability to secure counsel, or to trust the police to do so; he will be likely to "turn to his parents, or another adult responsible for his welfare, as the only means" of obtaining counsel.

Justice Powell argued that waivers by juveniles should be examined with "special care." He found that the defendant in *Fare* was "immature, emotional, and uneducated," and therefore especially vulnerable to the "skillful, two-on-one, repetitive style of interrogation" conducted by the police. He also had a "limited understanding" of how to conduct himself with the police, according to his probation officer. Therefore, on the facts of *Fare*, Justice Powell concluded that no "fair interrogation" had been conducted.

9. The *Edwards* Rule Applies When Police Seek to Obtain a Waiver in Order to Interrogate Concerning a Crime That Is Different From the One for Which the Suspect Invoked His Right to Counsel
In *Arizona v. Roberson*, 486 U.S. 675, 108 S.Ct. 2093, 100 L.Ed.2d 704 (1988), the Court held that when a suspect invokes the right to counsel, the *Edwards* rule bars police from initiating an interrogation about a crime different from the one for which he was arrested and invoked his right. Thus, a suspect's Fifth Amendment invocation of the right to counsel is *not "offense-specific."* When the police officer in *Roberson* sought to interrogate Roberson in custody concerning a burglary, the officer did not know that Roberson had invoked his right to counsel three days earlier during his arrest for an unrelated burglary. Roberson was given new warnings, waived his rights and confessed to the unrelated burglary. But he had not initiated the interrogation. The Court found that *Edwards* "focuses on the state of mind of the suspect and not of the police," and so the police officer's unawareness of the earlier invocation was irrelevant. The defendant's statements made

during the second interrogation were held to be inadmissible in the absence of initiation by the suspect, and his conviction for the second burglary was reversed.

a. Rationale

The Court held that the benefits of a "bright line" application of *Edwards* to all interrogations after the invocation of counsel outweighed the burdens imposed on the police by the requirement that they honor a suspect's invocation of counsel. A suspect's request for counsel expressed "his own view that he is not competent to deal with the authorities without legal advice." Nothing about the context of custodial interrogation supports the idea that a suspect's invocation of counsel is "investigation-specific." Nor does the mere existence of a separate police investigation justify the creation of an exception to the *Edwards* rule to allow "police-initiated" interrogation concerning that investigation.

The Court noted that its precedents "repeatedly emphasized the virtues of a bright-line rule" in cases interpreting *Edwards*. This approach informs both police and prosecutors "with specificity" of the rules that must be followed during custodial interrogations; it also informs lower courts clearly as to what kinds of statements are inadmissible. The Court found nothing "ambiguous" about the *Edwards* rule, which is a "corollary" to *Miranda*'s requirement that "interrogation must cease" after an invocation of the right to counsel.

b. *Mosley* and *Barrett* Inapposite

The *Roberson* Court acknowledged that *Mosley* permitted interrogation about a different crime after invocation of the right to silence, but noted that such an invocation "does not raise the presumption" that the suspect "is unable to proceed without a lawyer's advice." Such a presumption existed in *Roberson,* and so *Mosley* was inapposite. The Court also acknowledged that *Barrett* allowed police to interrogate a suspect who had made a "limited" invocation of the right to counsel, but noted that this was only because the suspect made an explicitly limited invocation. In *Roberson,* the defendant made no "limited" invocation of his right to counsel, and the "presumption" that he wanted to consult with counsel did not "disappear simply because the police approached the suspect" about a different investigation.

c. Analogy to *Spring*

The *Roberson* Court observed that *Miranda* requires police to inform a suspect that "anything" he says may be used against him, and that under *Spring,* a suspect's willingness to talk after such a warning is considered to be "unqualified." Similarly, when a suspect expresses his unwillingness to talk without counsel, this unwillingness should be presumed to be "unqualified" as well, so that it applies to all offenses.

As the *Spring* Court determined, "there is no reason to assume that a suspect's state of mind is in any way investigation-specific."

d. Policy Arguments

The Court in *Roberson* rejected the state's proposed exception to *Edwards* on policy grounds. First, it rejected the state's assurances that police officers concerned with a separate investigation would be unlikely to "badger" a suspect, by questioning her "so repeatedly and in such quick succession" that it would undermine her will. To the contrary, the majority found no reason to believe that such officers would "be any less eager" than usual to question a suspect. More specifically, when a suspect is unable to "cope" without counsel (as evidenced by the fact that the right to counsel has been invoked), further interrogation would "surely exacerbate" the pressure to speak. "Mere repetition" of the *Miranda* warnings would not overcome this pressure, especially in a case like *Roberson* where the suspect's invocation was followed by three days in custody without any provision of counsel.

e. Information Permissible

The state in *Roberson* complained that an initiation requirement would be anomalous as applied to unrelated investigations, because there would be no reason for a suspect to know that such an investigation was even being conducted; the state argued that initiation would therefore rarely if ever occur with respect to unrelated crimes. But the Court noted that a suspect could rely on counsel to help her deal with separate investigations, and had no need to speak to police in order to learn about the existence of such investigations. The police could simply inform counsel. Moreover, the Court observed that when the police have decided "temporarily not to provide counsel," they are free "to inform" the suspect about a separate investigation, so long as this "communication does not constitute interrogation."

f. Dissent

Justice Kennedy dissented, in an opinion joined by Chief Justice Rehnquist, and argued that "the problems to which *Edwards* was addressed" were not present in *Roberson*. Therefore, he advocated that police should have been allowed to seek a waiver of rights from the defendant in *Roberson* concerning an interrogation about the different crime. Justice Kennedy argued that when a subsequent interrogation "is confined to an entirely independent investigation," it creates "little risk" of badgering. He believed that a suspect's rights would be sufficiently protected by requiring the police to readvise him of his *Miranda* rights and seek his consent to the interrogation concerning the different crime. He found no reason to believe that a suspect would believe his rights "are fictitious if he must assert them a second time." Instead, a suspect would believe that his invocation was, indeed, efficacious, because he could observe that questioning concerning the crime for which he was arrested had terminated. If he were told that further questioning could not relate to that crime, he would "understand that he may invoke his rights again" concerning the new investigation.

Justice Kennedy argued that most suspects who invoke their rights "will want the opportunity" to learn about the existence of a separate investigation, and to calculate their interests anew "to decide to speak" to police "with or without representation." He predicted that the *Roberson* rule would deprive the "nationwide law enforcement network" of a valuable tool "now routinely used to solve major crimes." Typically, the police will check the name and fingerprints of a suspect in custody "against master files," and will often discover that the suspect is wanted for questioning on an unrelated offense. Under *Roberson,* such questioning would be barred whenever a suspect invokes the right to counsel. Justice Kennedy believed that this result did not strike "an appropriate balance" between the need to protect a suspect's freedom from coercion, and the need to avoid "disruption of legitimate law enforcement efforts."

10. Request for Counsel at an Initial Appearance in Court Is a "Sixth Amendment Invocation" That Does Not Constitute an Invocation of *Miranda* Rights

In *McNeil v. Wisconsin,* ___ U.S. ___, 111 S.Ct. 2204, 115 L.Ed.2d 158 (1991), the Court held that a defendant's request for counsel at "an initial appearance on a charged offense" was not an "implied" invocation of the *Miranda* right to counsel under the Fifth Amendment. In *McNeil,* the defendant asked for counsel at his initial appearance in court on an armed robbery charge, and was given appointed counsel. He was interviewed later that night by police concerning crimes unrelated to that with which he had been charged. He was given the *Miranda* warnings, he waived his rights at this interview and during three further interviews, and confessed to these unrelated crimes. The Court found that the *Roberson* rule did not apply, and therefore that McNeil's confessions to unrelated crimes were admissible at the trial for those crimes.

a. Rationale

The Court reasoned that in order for a suspect to invoke his *Miranda* right to counsel, both *Miranda* and *Edwards* require, "at a minimum, some statement that can reasonably be construed" as a request for counsel's assistance "in dealing with custodial interrogation by the police." The "ordinary meaning" of a request for counsel at an initial appearance does not satisfy this definition. The Court refused to interpret a defendant's Sixth Amendment invocation of counsel as implying a Fifth Amendment invocation of counsel, because this would "seriously impede law enforcement."

Justice Scalia, writing for the majority, declared that under *Edwards,* the purpose of invoking the Fifth Amendment right to counsel is to protect "the desire to deal with the police only through counsel." By contrast, the purpose of invoking the Sixth Amendment guarantee is to receive protection at "critical confrontations" with the "expert adversary" at or after the commencement of adversary judicial proceedings. Thus when the defendant in *McNeil* invoked the "Sixth Amendment interest," he did not necessarily invoke "the *Miranda–Edwards* interest." Even if it were "likely" that the defendant would want to invoke his Fifth Amendment interest as well, such "likelihood" is "not the test for applicability of *Edwards.*" Thus, because the defendant in *McNeil* did not explicitly invoke his *Miranda* right to counsel, the *Edwards* and *Roberson* rules did not apply to his interrogations by police on charges different from that for which he was arrested and charged.

b. **Too Costly**

Justice Scalia rejected the defendant's proposal that the definition of an invocation under *Edwards* should be expanded to encompass the act of asking for counsel's assistance at arraignment. He found that no significant "advantages" would be obtained from such a rule, because a defendant is already empowered to exercise his *Miranda* rights explicitly during post-appearance interviews with police. Moreover, the proposed rule would "do much more harm than good," because it would make "most persons in pretrial custody for serious offenses" immune to any approach by police for questioning about other crimes. This immunity would be detrimental to society's welfare, because the "ready ability" to obtain "uncoerced" confessions is "an unmitigated good," and confessions "are essential to society's compelling interest in finding, convicting, and punishing" criminals. See *Moran v. Burbine,* 475 U.S. 412, 106 S.Ct. 1135, 89 L.Ed.2d 410 (1986).

c. **Dissent**

Justice Stevens dissented, in an opinion joined by Justices Marshall and Blackmun, and argued that the Court's decision would "have only a slight impact on custodial procedures," because competent counsel could circumvent *McNeil* by having their clients invoke the *Miranda* right to counsel at arraignment. Nonetheless, Justice Stevens disapproved of the Court's reasoning in principle, because it would cause "confusion" and "undermine the protections" of the adversarial system. He argued that the Court's fears of impeding law enforcement were "grossly exaggerated." He also found that there is a danger of compulsion when a defendant is interrogated by police, despite his invocation of counsel in court. Therefore, he argued that *Edwards'* protection should not depend upon the location of the defendant, or upon the identity of the official from whom counsel is sought.

d. **Anticipatory Invocation of the *Miranda–Edwards* Right to Counsel**
The *McNeil* Court did not resolve the question whether a defendant could invoke her *Miranda* right to counsel by specifically referring to *Miranda* during a first court appearance. As discussed above, Justice Stevens in dissent argued that this would be possible and that it would therefore provide an easy evasion of the Court's restrictive interpretation of the Sixth Amendment right to counsel. In dicta, however, the Court rebutted the claim by the *McNeil* dissenters that such a strategy would be an adequate invocation under *Edwards*. Justice Scalia noted that most rights "must be asserted when the government seeks to take the action they protect against." Implicitly, this would mean that *Miranda* rights cannot be invoked "anticipatorily, in a context other than custodial interrogation." Justice Scalia also declared that even though a *Miranda* right may be invoked prospectively by a suspect in custody, this "does not necessarily mean" that the Court "will allow it to be asserted" prospectively by a defendant in court.

11. **Police May Not Initiate Interrogation of a Suspect Following the Invocation of the Right to Counsel Under *Edwards*, Even After the Suspect Has Consulted With Counsel**
In *Minnick v. Mississippi*, 498 U.S. 146, 111 S.Ct. 486, 112 L.Ed.2d 489 (1990), the Court held that *Edwards* prohibits police from initiating an interrogation with a suspect who has invoked his right to counsel, unless counsel is present. This rule applies "whether or not" the suspect "has consulted with counsel." In *Minnick*, the defendant was sentenced to death for murder, and his conviction was based on a confession obtained by police after he consulted with counsel several times, following an invocation of his *Edwards* right. Even though his attorney told the defendant not to talk to anyone or sign any waivers, Minnick did confess when a police officer visited him in jail, and talked to him first about "how everybody was" back home, and then about the crime. The Court held the defendant's confession to be inadmissible and reversed his murder conviction.

a. **Rationale**
The Court found that the protection of *Edwards* should not be "terminated or suspended by consultation with counsel," because the prohibition of police-initiated questioning protects suspects from police "badgering," and provides the "clarity and certainty" of a "bright-line rule" for police and lower courts. The Court rejected the state's proposal that a suspect's consultation with counsel should terminate the protection of *Edwards*, because a "consultation is not a precise concept," and because contacts with counsel do not "remove the suspect" from the "coercive pressures" of custody.

b. Bright–Line Rule

Justice Kennedy, writing for the majority, declared that the "presence of counsel" requirement would be beneficial in preserving the "bright-line" quality of the *Edwards* rule, which conserves judicial resources and "implements *Miranda* protections" in "straightforward terms." By contrast, the state's proposal to allow interrogation after consultation with counsel would have undesirable effects. It would require lower courts to define the "imprecise" concept of "consultation," which would inject ambiguity into the application of *Edwards*. It would require police to determine whether adequate consultation had taken place before initiating interrogation, which could interfere with the attorney-client privilege. It would cause a suspect "whose counsel is prompt" in consulting him to "lose the protection of *Edwards,*" and create an incentive for counsel to be "dilatory" in order to preserve a client's rights. Therefore, the Court declined to "adopt a regime in which *Edwards'* protection could pass in and out of existence multiple times" during custody, with every invocation creating its protection, and every consultation destroying it.

c. Dissent

Justice Scalia dissented, in an opinion joined by Chief Justice Rehnquist. Justice Scalia criticized the *Edwards* rule, and argued that even if *Edwards* was justified, the Court's "extension" of *Edwards* in *Minnick* was not. He also argued that the Court's waiver rules had "gone far beyond any genuine concern" for a suspect's understanding of her rights, and erected inappropriate barriers to protect suspects against the "folly" of confessing. Justice Scalia considered *Edwards* "a solitary exception" to the Court's waiver jurisprudence, because of its *per se* prohibition on police-initiated interrogation after invocation. By contrast, waiver holdings in *Mosley, Butler,* and *Fare* rejected such a *per se* approach, and required case-by-case scrutiny of police attempts to obtain a waiver. Justice Scalia acknowledged that the "prophylactic" *Edwards* rule created certain benefits, but argued that "so would a rule that simply excludes all confessions" by all suspects in custody. He declared that the Court's other waiver precedents treated these "benefits" appropriately, as outweighed by "the need for police questioning as a tool for effective enforcement of the criminal laws."

Justice Scalia distinguished *Edwards* as a case where the Court assumed that a suspect without counsel is "likely to be ignorant of his rights and to feel isolated in a hostile environment." However, once a suspect consults with counsel, he "knows that he has an advocate on his side," and that the police "will permit him to consult that advocate." He also should have a "heightened awareness" of his right to remain silent, based on counsel's advice. Therefore *Edwards* should have no application to a case like *Minnick,* because the situation of the suspect has changed;

an "irrebuttable presumption" that his confession is based on ignorance or "coercion" at this point has "no genuine basis in fact."

Justice Scalia contended that the *Minnick* rule would significantly "constrict" law enforcement, by creating a "perpetual irrebuttable presumption" that prevents police from initiating waiver discussions about any crime, or even asking whether a suspect has "changed his mind" about his invocation. He argued that *Edwards* protection should "cease to apply, permanently" once consultation occurs, and that "any discussion" with an attorney should suffice to establish a consultation. Under his proposal, police would not be required to determine the adequacy of a consultation, and the *Edwards* rule would not "pass in and out of existence" during custody.

F.   INCOMPLETE OR AMBIGUOUS *MIRANDA* WARNINGS

The *Miranda* opinion gave three descriptions of the "warnings" to be given to suspects. The first two warnings were stated in consistent terms: the suspect must be told she has the right to remain silent, and that "anything" she says may be used against her. The third and fourth warning were not described as clearly, however.

First, at the outset of the opinion, the Court stated that a suspect must be warned that "he has a right to the presence of an attorney, either retained or appointed." Later, the Court stated that a suspect must be warned "that he has the right to consult with a lawyer and to have the lawyer with him during interrogation." A suspect must also be told "not only that he has the right to consult with an attorney, but also that if he is indigent a lawyer will be appointed to represent him." During a final summary of the third and fourth warning, the Court stated that a suspect must be told that "he has the right to the presence of an attorney, and that if he cannot afford an attorney one will be appointed for him prior to any questioning if he so desires."

What is missing from the Court's three formulations was an explanation, in non-legalistic terms, of three propositions that may not be obvious to a layperson. That is, if a suspect is indigent, she has: 1) the right to have counsel appointed for her prior to an interrogation; 2) the right to consult with such counsel before interrogation; and 3) the right to have such counsel present at any interrogation. After *Miranda* was decided, lower courts sometimes came to different conclusions concerning the degree of permissible ambiguity in the warnings, especially concerning the suspect's right to receive and consult with appointed counsel before questioning. Ultimately, the Court's rulings established the principles that no "talismanic incantation" of the warnings was necessary, and that some ambiguity in the warnings was acceptable.

1. **The *Miranda* Warnings Need Not Inform a Suspect Explicitly of the Right to Have an Attorney Appointed Before Further Questioning**
    In *California v. Prysock,* 451 U.S. 1301, 101 S.Ct. 1773, 68 L.Ed.2d 185 (1981), the Court held that a defendant was adequately apprised of his "right to appointed counsel before questioning" when police told him, in separate warnings, that he had the "right to talk to a lawyer before you are questioned, have him present with you while you are being questioned, and all during the questioning," and that he also had the "right to have a lawyer appointed to represent you at no cost to yourself." In *Prysock,* the juvenile defendant's statements, made after these warnings and in the presence of his parents, were held to be admissible, and his convictions for murder, robbery, burglary, and other crimes were upheld.

    a. **Rationale**
        The Court held that *Miranda* stated only that the warnings described in the Court's opinion, or their "equivalent," should be given to suspects. Thus, no particular "talismanic incantation" is required to satisfy *Miranda.* Most lower courts did not require a "verbatim recital" of the warnings from the *Miranda* opinion; they only required that the warnings not link a reference to appointed counsel to "a future point in time after police interrogation." In *Prysock,* no such link occurred. While the two warnings at issue were not given in succession, but were separated by the recitation of two other warnings, this fact did not make the warnings "inadequate" under *Miranda* since there is no requirement that the warnings be given in any precise order.

    b. **Dissent**
        Justice Stevens dissented, in an opinion joined by Justices Brennan and Marshall. Justice Stevens observed that *Miranda*'s final summary of the warnings expressly required a suspect to be told "that if he cannot afford an attorney one will be appointed for him prior to any questioning if he so desires." In *Prysock,* the defendant was not "adequately" informed of his right, because he was not given the "crucial information that the services of the free attorney were available *prior to* the impending questioning." Further, the warnings that were given were "ambiguous" on their face, and susceptible to different interpretations. The last warning was particularly unclear, because "lawyers are normally appointed by judges, and not by law enforcement officers," and so the reference to "appointed" counsel "could have been understood to refer to trial counsel." The dissenters concluded that *Miranda* was violated because the words used by the officer in *Prysock* did not adequately convey the existence of a "right to appointed counsel before questioning."

2. **Warnings Which State That "We Have No Way of Giving You a Lawyer, But One Will Be Appointed for You, if You Wish, if and When You Go to Court"**
    In *Duckworth v. Eagan,* 492 U.S. 195, 109 S.Ct. 2875, 106 L.Ed.2d 166 (1989), the Court held that *Miranda* warnings need only "reasonably convey" the *Miranda* rights to a suspect, and that under this standard it was acceptable for the police to use the "if and when you go to court" language in the warnings given in *Duckworth.* The warnings, in their totality, apprised the defendant of his right "to have an attorney present if he chose to answer questions." Therefore, his statements were held to be admissible, and his attempted murder conviction was affirmed.

    a. **Rationale**
        The Court found that the "if and when you go to court" language accurately described the procedure for appointment of counsel, and anticipated the "commonplace" question of a suspect as to when counsel would be appointed.

    b. **Prophylactic Rules**
        The Court in *Duckworth* emphasized that the warnings "are not themselves rights protected by the Constitution." Therefore, the Court declared that reviewing courts need not scrutinize *Miranda* warnings "as if construing a will or defining the terms of an easement."

    c. **Totality of Warnings**
        The Court found that the warnings in *Duckworth* did not impermissibly link the reference to appointed counsel to a "future point in time after the police interrogation," because other statements in these warnings made reference to the suspect's right to counsel "before" he is interrogated, and to the right to stop answering questions until he talks to a lawyer. Thus, "in their totality" the warnings adequately apprised the defendant of his rights.

    d. **Dissent**
        Justice Marshall dissented in an opinion joined by Justices Brennan, Blackmun, and Stevens. Justice Marshall argued that the "if and when you go to court" language was inconsistent with *Miranda*'s requirement that a warning must "clearly inform" a suspect that an attorney can be appointed for him "prior to any questioning." He contended that the placement of the "if and when" language in the eight-sentence warning could lead a suspect to believe that he had a right to counsel "before and during" questioning, but that if he were indigent, one would be appointed only "if and when" he went to court. The phrasing of the warning contained an important omission—it did not tell a suspect that if he so chose the "questioning would be delayed until a lawyer was appointed," if and when he did actually go to court. Justice Marshall noted that a "frightened suspect, unlettered in the law," could not be

expected to interpret the "if and when" language as the *Duckworth* majority did, like "lawyers or judges or others schooled in interpreting legal or semantic nuance."

Justice Marshall also argued that the "if and when you go to court" language had one further defect. Most suspects would interpret this to mean "if and when you go to trial." The "negative implication" of this idea is that a suspect will never get an attorney, unless he is taken to court. This implication creates coercive pressure on a suspect, who may be afraid to invoke a right to counsel because it means he will remain in custody without one until he goes to trial. Therefore, the *Duckworth* warning created a "threat of indefinite deferral of interrogation," which may provoke a suspect to talk to the police "for that reason alone." To Justice Marshall, the cure for the *Miranda* violation in *Duckworth* was simple. Deleting the "if and when" language would solve the problem, and pose "no great burden on law enforcement officers to eradicate the confusion" produced by the warning.

e. **Implying That Appointed Counsel Is Optional With the Authorities**
In *United States v. Connell,* 869 F.2d 1349 (9th Cir.1989), the officer's oral warning to the suspect was that "if you cannot afford a lawyer, one may be appointed for you." He also received written warnings which stated that if he could not afford a lawyer, "arrangements will be made to obtain one for you in accordance with the law." The court held these warnings to be misleading and therefore found that the resulting confession was obtained in violation of *Miranda.* While the court recognized that a flexible approach to the warnings was permissible after *Prysock,* it stated that the oral warning was affirmatively misleading because it implied that the right to appointed counsel was in fact optional with the authorities. Nor did the written warning sufficiently cure this misinformation, because it provided for a right to counsel in accordance with the law, and a suspect "is not required to know what the requirements of the law are." The court reasoned that the whole purpose of the warnings was to convey the requirements of the law, and this the warning did not do. Thus, the court drew a line between a merely *ambiguous* warning, as in *Prysock,* and an *affirmatively misleading* warning.

G. THE MEANING OF "CUSTODY"
The *Miranda* Court held that its safeguards were required when *two conditions were present simultaneously* —custody and interrogation. Thus, *Miranda* does not apply to a suspect who is interrogated outside of custody, or to a suspect who is in custody but is not interrogated. The *Miranda* Court stated that "by custodial interrogation, we mean questioning initiated by police officers after a person has been taken into custody or otherwise deprived of his freedom of action in any significant way." On its face, this definition was potentially quite broad, and was

certainly broad enough to encompass various forms of police contact with a suspect outside the stationhouse. However, this definition, by itself, did not provide much guidance to lower courts as to whether custodial events should be defined in a categorical way, or according to the "totality" of circumstances on a case-by-case basis. Ultimately, no hard and fast rules emerged from most of the Court's custody cases after *Miranda*. Findings of custody outside the stationhouse were both upheld and rejected, as were findings of custody at the stationhouse.

Eleven years after *Miranda* was decided, the Court came to endorse a definition of custody that required either formal arrest, or "restraint on freedom of movement of the degree associated with arrest." The Court stated that in determining whether a person is in custody, a court must employ a totality of circumstances approach.

Not surprisingly, lower courts have come to identify a large variety of factors as "influencing" the custody inquiry in the Court's diverse precedents. These factors include: 1) the *purpose* of the police investigation; 2) the *place and length* of the interrogation; 3) the suspect's *awareness of her freedom to leave*; 4) the suspect's *actual freedom from restraint*; 5) the *source of initiation* of the contact with the suspect; 6) the use of *"coercive stratagems"* by the police; and 7) the similarity of the setting to the *"police-dominated"* atmosphere of the stationhouse. The lower courts have stated that these factors must be applied *objectively* rather than subjectively. That is, the question is whether the totality of circumstances would indicate to a reasonable person that the police activity was so coercive as to constitute an arrest. Essentially, the courts have equated the test for custody with the test for whether a defendant is under arrest for Fourth Amendment purposes. See *California v. Beheler*, 463 U.S. 1121, 103 S.Ct. 3517, 77 L.Ed.2d 1275 (1983) (custody is determined by whether there is a "formal arrest or restraint on freedom of movement of the degree associated with a formal arrest"). Thus, it is useful to refer to the section on *Terry, supra*, where the distinction between stops and arrests is discussed.

1. Custody Outside the Stationhouse

In *Orozco v. Texas*, 394 U.S. 324, 89 S.Ct. 1095, 22 L.Ed.2d 311 (1969), the Court held that a defendant was effectively "in custody," when he was awakened at 4:00 a.m. and questioned in his bedroom by four officers. One of the officers testified that the suspect was not free to go, but was "under arrest," even though there was no evidence that the defendant was so informed. The police questioned the defendant as to his name, his presence earlier that night at a restaurant where a homicide was committed, whether he owned a gun, and the location of the gun. As the defendant was not given *Miranda* warnings, his statements were held to be inadmissible, and his murder conviction was reversed.

a. Rationale

The Court held that it was not necessary to "extend" *Miranda* to find custody in *Orozco,* because *Miranda* held that warnings were required when a person was "deprived of his freedom in any significant way." The Court rejected the state's argument that a custodial situation could not be found because the defendant was "in his own bed, in familiar surroundings." Justice Black emphasized that in the eyes of the police the defendant was "under arrest and not free to leave," as established by an officer's testimony.

b. Dissent

Justice White dissented, in an opinion joined by Justice Stewart, and argued that *Miranda*'s safeguards were justified only at the stationhouse, where the "conditions and practices" of coercive interrogations pose a unique threat to a suspect's exercise of the privilege. Justice White found that as the defendant was in "familiar quarters, the questioning was brief, and no admissions were made which were not backed up by other evidence." Thus, there was no basis for applying *Miranda,* according to its own rationale.

c. When Custody Does Not Exist Outside the Stationhouse

In *Beckwith v. United States,* 425 U.S. 341, 96 S.Ct. 1612, 48 L.Ed.2d 1 (1976), the Court held that agents of the Internal Revenue Service were not required to give warnings to a defendant who consented to a three-hour interview with them, in his private home, concerning his Federal income tax liability over a five-year period. The agents told him that one of their functions was to investigate the possibility of criminal tax fraud. The defendant made statements and gave them records relating to his tax liability. Later he argued that he had misapprehended the nature of the agents' inquiry, even though he had been advised by the agents that he could consult with counsel before responding, and that anything he said could be used against him in a criminal prosecution. The Court held that an "interview with a government agent" possessed none of the "inherently coercive" elements of the stationhouse interrogations at issue in *Miranda;* therefore, the Court found that the defendant's statements were admissible, and affirmed his conviction. See also *United States v. Hurtado,* 899 F.2d 371 (5th Cir.1990) (interrogation not custodial where defendant invited officers into her home, officers never brandished weapons, did not threaten her or restrict her movement, and she was not told she was under arrest; the psychological pressure that defendant experienced because she feared her illegal activity might be discovered is irrelevant to the determination of custody, which focusses on objective factors of police coercion).

d. "Focus" on the Suspect Does Not Equal Custody

The Court in *Beckwith* rejected the defendant's argument that because he was the "focus" of an investigation, he was under "psychological restraints" during his confrontation with the I.R.S. agents, which constituted the "functional equivalent" of custody. The Court explained that *Miranda*'s rationale was grounded entirely in concerns with "custodial" interrogation and its "compulsive" atmosphere, not with the "strength or content of the government's suspicions" at the time the questioning was conducted. Compare *United States v. Griffin,* 922 F.2d 1343 (8th Cir.1990) (custody found where two officers were waiting for the defendant when he came home, told defendant's parents to leave, interviewed him for two hours, and told defendant that he could not leave the room unless an officer accompanied him).

2. Custody in Prison

In *Mathis v. United States,* 391 U.S. 1, 88 S.Ct. 1503, 20 L.Ed.2d 381 (1968), the Court held that a person who was interrogated while in jail serving a sentence on a charge that was unrelated to the interrogation, was in custody for *Miranda* purposes.

a. Rationale

The Court held that the "whole purpose" of *Miranda* was to protect the Fifth Amendment rights of a person in custody, and that the reason for a defendant's custody was irrelevant to his need for *Miranda* protection.

b. Dissent

Justice White dissented, in an opinion in which Justices Harlan and Stewart joined. Justice White argued that *Miranda*'s requirements were intended to apply to situations where "pressure" to answer questions "flows from a certain type of custody," namely stationhouse interrogations of those "charged with or suspected of a crime." By contrast, the defendant in *Mathis* was "in familiar surroundings" in state prison, and was not "coerced" by his interview with the Federal agent anymore "than is the citizen interviewed at home."

c. No Automatic Rule

The Court in *Mathis* did not hold that every interrogation of a prisoner would trigger *Miranda*. Rather, the prison environment was one factor in the totality of circumstances which indicated that the defendant in *Mathis* was in custody while he was being interrogated. So for example, in *United States v. Conley,* 779 F.2d 970 (4th Cir.1985), the defendant was suspected of involvement in a knife fight in prison. He was escorted to a conference room in the prison control center to await transfer to the infirmary for treatment of his wound. He was handcuffed, and when a correction officer asked him in a friendly manner what had happened, Conley gave an incriminating statement. The court noted that, if the custody rule were applied literally, "every question directed to a prison inmate in connection with what ultimately may prove to be criminal activity" would trigger *Miranda*. The court rejected the notion that *Mathis* established such a per se rule, reasoning that such a position "would seriously disrupt prison administration by requiring, as a prudential measure, formal warnings prior to many of the myriad informal conversations between inmates and prison guards." The court was unwilling to "torture *Miranda* to the illogical position of providing greater protection to a prisoner than to his nonimprisoned counterpart." See also *Cervantes v. Walker*, 589 F.2d 424 (9th Cir.1978) (refusing to read *Mathis* as a per se rule that a prisoner is automatically in custody for *Miranda* purposes).

d. More Than Usual Restraint

When a prisoner is subject to interrogation, the court, in assessing whether the circumstances were custodial, determines "whether the inmate was subjected to more than the usual restraint on a prisoner's liberty." *Conley, supra*. The court in *Conley* found that the defendant was not in custody for *Miranda* purposes, because the questioning was brief, and it was standard procedure to handcuff prisoners who were being transported to the infirmary in the maximum security facility in which Conley was incarcerated. The court concluded that "Conley's freedom of movement cannot be characterized as more restricted than that of other prisoners to and from the facility, either by virtue of his confinement or the nature of the questioning by prison personnel." Therefore, *Miranda* warnings were not required.

3. Custody May Not Exist in the Stationhouse

In *Oregon v. Mathiason,* 429 U.S. 492, 97 S.Ct. 711, 50 L.Ed.2d 714 (1977), the Court held that a suspect at the stationhouse was not in custody when he came to the station voluntarily, and was told that he was not under arrest, and was allowed to leave after his confession. Thus, police did not need to give warnings to the parolee defendant, who was given a message to call a police officer, and then asked to meet with the officer at the stationhouse in order to "discuss something." After the suspect arrived, he was interviewed about a burglary, told that he was a suspect and that his truthfulness would "possibly be considered" by a judge or prosecutor, and falsely told that his fingerprints were found at the scene. A few minutes later, the defendant confessed, received warnings, and confessed again. The Court held that the "coercive environment" of the stationhouse and the circumstances of the interview did not suffice to create "custody" under *Miranda*.

a. Rationale

The Court found that *Miranda* was intended to be limited to cases where a restriction exists on a person's freedom. Such a restriction does not necessarily exist "simply because the questioning takes place in the stationhouse, or because the questioned person is one whom the police suspect." The Court rejected the idea that a "coercive environment" alone could trigger the need for *Miranda* warnings, because "any interview" with the police will have "coercive aspects," and because police should not be required to administer warnings "to everyone they question." The Court found it most important that Mathiason came of his own accord to the stationhouse to be interviewed. Compare *Dunaway v. New York*, 442 U.S. 200, 99 S.Ct. 2248, 60 L.Ed.2d 824 (1979) (suspect was under arrest when he was put in a police car and brought to the stationhouse against his will, and then interrogated at the stationhouse).

b. Dissent

The three dissenters in *Mathiason* argued that the defendant could have had "an objectively reasonable belief" that he was not free to leave during questioning, because he was told that he was a suspect and told about his "fingerprints" at the scene. They argued that the Court had given insufficient attention to the coercive environment of the stationhouse, and to the fact that the defendant was a parolee, whose presence at the station at police request could hardly be deemed voluntary.

c. When a Suspect Is Asked to Accompany Police to the Stationhouse

In *California v. Beheler*, 463 U.S. 1121, 103 S.Ct. 3517, 77 L.Ed.2d 1275 (1983), the Court held that under *Mathiason,* no *Miranda* warnings were required when a defendant was interviewed at the stationhouse, after he "voluntarily agreed to accompany the police" there. The defendant initially called the police to report a murder, and then consented to a search of his yard, where police found the suspected murder weapon. Later in the evening, the police returned and asked him to accompany them to the stationhouse, while advising him that "he was not under arrest." After he confessed during his interview, he was released. On these facts, *Mathiason* was held to be controlling, so that no finding of custody was justified. Therefore, the defendant's confession was held to be admissible, and his conviction for aiding and abetting murder was affirmed. The Court found it irrelevant that Mathiason had driven himself to the station while Beheler had been driven by officers. In each case, the defendant voluntarily consented to come to the station. This factor was significant in dispelling the coercive atmosphere that the stationhouse might otherwise provide.

d. Perspective

In *Mathiason* and *Beheler,* the Court relied primarily on two objective factors—that the suspects chose to come to the stationhouse, and that they were told that they were not under arrest. By ignoring the subjective perspectives of the suspects in these cases, such as Mathiason's feelings and beliefs as a parolee, the Court signalled to lower courts that they may infer a suspect's belief in a lack of restraint, without inquiring into a suspect's actual beliefs concerning a "deprivation" of his freedom. That is, the lower courts have been instructed to take an objective rather than a subjective approach to the question of custody. See *United States v. Bengivenga*, 845 F.2d 593 (5th Cir.1988) ("A suspect is in custody for *Miranda* purposes when placed under formal arrest or when a reasonable person in the suspect's position would have understood the situation to constitute a restraint on freedom of movement of the degree which the law associates with formal arrest. The reasonable person through whom we view the situation must be neutral to the environment and to the purposes of the investigation— that is, neither guilty of criminal conduct and thus overly apprehensive nor insensitive to the seriousness of the circumstances.").

4.   **Custody Does Not Exist Simply Because a Suspect Is Required to Meet With a Government Official or Body**
In *Minnesota v. Murphy,* 465 U.S. 420, 104 S.Ct. 1136, 79 L.Ed.2d 409 (1984), the Court held that a defendant on probation was not in custody when he was summoned to the office of his probation officer, to discuss a "treatment plan" for his probationary term. The probation officer had uncovered evidence of Murphy's admissions to crimes committed seven years earlier, and she planned to relay any incriminating statements he made in the meeting to the police. When Murphy arrived at her office, the officer told him that he needed a treatment program because of these crimes, and the defendant admitted his guilt. As a probationer, he was required to be truthful with the probation officer "in all matters," upon penalty of probation revocation. The Court held that the defendant was not in custody during his interview, and therefore that the probation officer was not required to give him *Miranda* warnings.

a.   **Rationale**
The Court held that any "compulsion" a probationer feels in an interview cannot be compared to the "compulsion" condemned by *Miranda.* Even though the probation officer could compel the defendant's "attendance and truthful answers" at the interview, this did not subject him to any more pressure than is faced, for example, by a witness who is called to testify before a grand jury. Such a witness is not entitled to *Miranda* warnings. See, e.g., *United States v. Mandujano,* 425 U.S. 564, 96 S.Ct. 1768, 48 L.Ed.2d 212 (1976). Further, while the probation officer in *Murphy* may have sought to elicit incriminating evidence during the interview, this was insufficient to trigger the need for *Miranda* warnings under *Beckwith.* The defendant's lack of awareness of the "scope" of the probation officer's investigation did not distinguish

him from defendants in other non-custodial settings who are subjected to questioning.

b. Three Distinguishing Factors

The Court observed that three factors served to distinguish the probationer's interview from stationhouse interrogation. First, an interview would not convey the message that the defendant had "no choice but to submit" to the will of the probation officer, and confess. Second, it would not thrust the defendant into an "unfamiliar atmosphere" created for the purpose of "subjugating his will." Third, no compulsion was created in the defendant's interview by suggestions that the interrogation would "continue until a confession" was obtained. The only pressure the defendant "might have felt" was based on his awareness that if he left, his probation status might be jeopardized. The Court explained that this pressure was not "comparable" to the coercion of custodial interrogation where a suspect "literally cannot escape a persistent" examiner.

5. Custody Does Not Exist When a Person Is Called to Testify Before a Grand Jury

In *United States v. Mandujano,* 425 U.S. 564, 96 S.Ct. 1768, 48 L.Ed.2d 212 (1976), a plurality of the Court held that a prosecutor did not have to give *Miranda* warnings to a suspect who was called to testify before a grand jury, and interrogated concerning his involvement in narcotics traffic. Chief Justice Burger noted that *Miranda*'s rationale was based on the need to negate the "compulsion" inherent in stationhouse interrogation where police may abuse their powers. Such a rationale could not be extended to questioning "under the guidance of a judge" before a grand jury. He also noted that *Miranda* emphasized that the "compulsion to speak in the isolated setting" of the stationhouse could be greater than "in courts or other official investigations, where there are often impartial observers to guard against intimidation or trickery." Thus, the "marked contrasts" between the grand jury setting and the stationhouse justified a finding that grand jury witnesses were not entitled to *Miranda* warnings.

6. Custody Does Not Exist During a Normal Traffic Stop

In *Berkemer v. McCarty,* 468 U.S. 420, 104 S.Ct. 3138, 82 L.Ed.2d 317 (1984), the Court held that the roadside detention of a motorist pursuant to a traffic stop does not constitute "custody" under *Miranda*. The police officer who stopped the driver in *Berkemer* intended to arrest him because of his intoxicated behavior after the stop, but the Court concluded that no custody existed because the officer did not subject the defendant to "restraints comparable to a formal arrest." The seizure was a *Terry* stop as opposed to an arrest. Therefore, the officer was not required to give warnings before questioning the driver as to whether he had been "using intoxicants," or before administering a "field sobriety" test. Both the results of the test, and the driver's unwarned admission that he had consumed drugs and alcohol, were held to be admissible, and his conviction for "driving while intoxicated" was affirmed.

a. Rationale

While a motorist is not "free to leave" a roadside detention, the Court decided that *Miranda* should be enforced "only in those types of situations in which the concerns that powered the decision are implicated." The Court found that the "pressures" of detention inherent in a *Terry* stop do not approach the "inherent coercion" of stationhouse interrogation, because a driver expects a traffic stop to be brief, temporary, and conducted in the safety of the public eye.

b. Stop/Arrest Distinction

The Court rejected the defendant's argument that *Miranda* warnings should be given to all motorists during traffic stops, for three reasons. First, traffic stops do not resemble a stationhouse interrogation, which "frequently is prolonged," and in which a suspect "often is aware that questioning will continue" until he answers all his interrogator's questions. Justice Marshall, writing for the Court, noted that a motorist, by contrast, expects "to be allowed to continue on his way" after a brief detention and, perhaps, a citation. Second, a traffic stop does not make a motorist feel "completely at the mercy of the police," because it typically takes place in public view, and involves "only one or at most two officers." Thus, a traffic stop is not "police-dominated" in the same way as a stationhouse interrogation. Finally, Justice Marshall observed that the "nonthreatening" character of *Terry* stops explained why none of the Court's Fourth Amendment precedents suggested that they were "subject to the dictates of *Miranda.*"

c. Probable Cause Test Rejected

The Court in *Berkemer* rejected the defendant's alternative argument that *Miranda* warnings should be given to a detained driver whenever a police officer has probable cause to make an arrest. *Miranda* was designed to "neutralize" coercion, and coercion has "little to do with the strength" of a police officer's suspicions. Moreover, such a proposal would be too difficult for the police to administer. It would require them to constantly "monitor the information available" to them while conversing with a motorist, and to make a difficult prediction concerning the earliest possible moment that probable cause might arise for arrest.

d. More Coercive Activity May Lead to a Finding of Custody

The Court in *Berkemer* did not purport to hold that all detentions and interrogations made in the course of a traffic stop would be free from *Miranda* constraints. If police, in the course of effectuating a detention for a traffic violation, engage in coercive activity associated with a formal arrest, then any interrogation will trigger *Miranda* protections. Justice Marshall acknowledged that this custody definition is not a "bright-line" rule, but found that it was preferable to a *per se* requirement that warnings be given to all motorists. That requirement would "substantially impede the enforcement" of traffic laws, and do "little to protect citizens' Fifth Amendment rights."

e. Applied to the Facts

On the facts of *Berkemer,* the Court concluded that no custodial "restraint" existed, based on several factors. The time between the stop and arrest was "short," the driver was not informed that his detention was for the long term, or that the officer had decided to arrest him, and the police officer only asked a "modest" number of questions. The defendant was only asked to perform a "simple" test within view of passing motorists. This treatment was "not the functional equivalent of formal arrest."

H. THE MEANING OF "INTERROGATION"

The concept of interrogation is a critical one in *Miranda* doctrine. Even if a suspect is in custody, police do not need to give warnings, unless they interrogate him. It is the combination of custody and interrogation that triggers the inherent coercion that requires the *Miranda* safeguards. After warnings are given, interrogation cannot continue in the absence of a valid waiver, and "must cease" when invocation occurs. Police often try to lay a foundation for waiver by asking the suspect whether he understands his rights, and is willing to waive them. However, their efforts to seek a waiver and to interrogate may become blurred together during the questioning that follows the warnings. Thus, police interrogation may violate *Miranda* in three ways. Police may interrogate improperly without giving warnings when custody exists; they may interrogate improperly after warnings without a waiver; and they may interrogate improperly after a suspect's invocation of *Miranda* rights, in cases where they fail to comply with the waiver-after-invocation standards of *Mosley* or *Edwards.*

Fourteen years after *Miranda* was decided, the Court created a definition of "interrogation" that was designed to be broad enough to cover police actions as well as words. The Court decided to assess the event of "interrogation" from the point of view of the reasonable police officer, and to prohibit not only intentional interrogations, but also any activity by police who "should have known" that what they were doing was "reasonably likely to elicit an incriminating response." The Court also required that "the perceptions of the suspect" be considered in making assessments concerning the existence of "interrogation."

1. **Interrogation Includes Express Questioning, and Any "Words or Actions on the Part of the Police" That They "Should Know Are Reasonably Likely to Elicit an Incriminating Response"**

    In *Rhode Island v. Innis,* 446 U.S. 291, 100 S.Ct. 1682, 64 L.Ed.2d 297 (1980), the Court held that police officers did not interrogate a defendant who had invoked his right to silence, when a brief dialogue ensued between two officers concerning the whereabouts of the murder weapon. The defendant was arrested for the shotgun murder of a cab driver at 4:30 a.m., and placed in custody in a police car for the drive to the station. One of the officers said to another, within the defendant's hearing, that "there's a lot of handicapped children running around in this area [because of a nearby school], and God forbid one of them might find a weapon with shells and might hurt themselves." The other officer said they should continue to search for the weapon. At this point, the defendant interrupted them, and offered to show them where the shotgun was, near the scene of the arrest. The Court found that his statements concerning the shotgun, as well as the gun itself, were admissible evidence, and affirmed his murder conviction.

    a. **Definition of Interrogation**

        The Court held that "interrogation" by police under *Miranda* should be interpreted as "express questioning or its functional equivalent." This includes words or actions that police "should have known were reasonably likely to elicit an incriminating response" from an *average suspect.* On the facts of *Innis,* the Court determined that no "interrogation" occurred. The police dialogue was brief and not "evocative," and the police had no reason to think the suspect was "peculiarly susceptible" to their statements.

    b. **More Than Express Questioning**

        The *Innis* Court rejected a narrow interpretation of *Miranda* that would limit "interrogation" to express questioning, as this would create an incentive for police to devise indirect methods of interrogation in order to obtain admissible statements. Justice Stewart, writing for the majority, noted that the "concern" of the *Miranda* Court was not limited to the need to protect a suspect from the coercion of express questioning. For example, the use of fraudulent line-ups and other psychological ploys was condemned in *Miranda,* because these are coercive forms of interrogation.

    c. **Relevance of Police Intent**

        The Court decided that *Miranda* safeguards were designed to protect suspects from "coercive police practices, without regard to objective proof of the underlying intent of the police." Therefore, a definition of interrogation should focus "primarily upon the perceptions of the suspect," and include acts that are likely to "elicit an incriminating response from the suspect." The intent of the police is relevant, of course, because an officer who intends to elicit information is more likely to elicit a response than an officer who has no such intent. But intent itself is not dispositive—the question is whether the police activity was reasonably likely to elicit an incriminating response.

d. The Average Suspect and Peculiar Susceptibility

The Court in *Innis* stressed that police "cannot be held accountable for the unforeseeable results" of their actions; thus, interrogation should include only behavior that police "should have known" would be *"reasonably likely"* to elicit a response from an *average suspect.* The police activity must be assessed by its effect on an average suspect, because police are not required to predict an individual, idiosyncratic, subjective response. On the other hand, if police know or have reason to know that the suspect has a "peculiar susceptibility" to a certain tactic, ploy, or statement, then an officer must be held accountable for using a tactic which is reasonably likely to play on that susceptibility. For example, if the officer knows that the suspect is a religious fanatic, then statements concerning religion may be found to have an effect on such a suspect where they would not have the same effect on an average suspect. Cf. *Brewer v. Williams,* 430 U.S. 387, 97 S.Ct. 1232, 51 L.Ed.2d 424 (1977) (where the defendant was suspected of murdering a young child and hiding the body, the officer's statements that the child deserved a "Christian burial" were impermissible where the officer knew that the defendant was a religious fanatic).

e. Applied to the Facts

On the facts of *Innis,* Justice Stewart found that the police dialogue was not the "functional equivalent" of interrogation, for four reasons. First, the officers had no indication that the suspect was *"peculiarly susceptible"* to an appeal to his conscience concerning the safety of handicapped children. Second, the Court noted that it was "understandable" that police should share their concerns about the children with each other; thus, there was no indication of an intent to elicit incriminating information, which would have made it more likely to have done so. Third, the dialogue consisted of "a few offhand remarks," not a "lengthy harangue." Finally, the police comments were not "particularly evocative," even though they happened to "strike a responsive chord" in the defendant. Essentially, the Court found that the officer's statement was *not* reasonably likely to elicit incriminating information from the *average suspect.* That Innis actually did respond was therefore an unforeseeable event that did not warrant exclusion under *Miranda.*

f. Justice Marshall's Dissent in *Innis*

Justice Marshall agreed with the Court's definition of interrogation, but declared that he was "utterly at a loss to understand" its application of this definition to the facts of *Innis*. The defendant was in handcuffs in a patrol car with three officers, driving away from the scene of the arrest, when one officer began "almost immediately to talk about the search for the shotgun." Justice Marshall identified the officer's speech as a "classic interrogation technique" of appealing to a suspect to confess "for the sake of others," in order to "display some decency and honor." Justice Marshall declared that it verged on "the ludicrous" to conclude that an appeal to protect the lives of handicapped children would not be expected to have an effect on the defendant, "in the absence of some special interest" in this subject. Moreover, Justice Marshall noted that the officers knew the defendant "would hear and attend to their conversation" because of the close quarters of the police car; they also knew that they would travel past "the very place where they believed the weapon was located." Given all these circumstances, he concluded that interrogation occurred even though the officer's remarks "were nominally addressed" to another police officer. Justice Marshall expressed concern that the Court's vision of an "average" suspect was of a person who was impervious to appeals to conscience or decency; therefore any such appeal could never be interrogation because it was not reasonably likely to elicit an incriminating response from an "average suspect."

g.   **Justice Stevens' Dissent in *Innis***

Justice Stevens argued that a proper definition of "interrogation" should include any police conduct that "has the same purpose or effect as a direct question." He also argued that the *Innis* test afforded suspects "considerably less protection" than his test, because it would allow police to make statements that "call for a response" from the suspect—so long as a court would determine, in hindsight, that the statement was not reasonably likely to elicit a response from an average suspect. He predicted that the Court's standard would "exclude every statement that is not punctuated with a question mark" from the definition of interrogation.

Justice Stevens disagreed with the Court's application of its new interrogation test to the facts of *Innis*. He found that the Court's assumption that suspects "are not susceptible to appeals to conscience" was "directly contrary to the teachings of police interrogation manuals." Justice Stevens also thought it was suspicious that the officer who made the remarks about the handicapped child was not usually assigned to the "caged" patrol car. He doubted that the "true purpose" of the officer's remarks was to voice a concern over handicapped children, as the chances of anyone finding the weapon at 4:30 a.m. were "slim." Moreover, he found the remarks to be evocative, and pointed out that the officer used "emotionally charged" words: "God forbid" a "little girl" should find the gun and hurt herself.

2.   Mere Possibility That the Suspect Might Incriminate Himself Does Not Mandate a Finding of Interrogation

In *Arizona v. Mauro,* 481 U.S. 520, 107 S.Ct. 1931, 95 L.Ed.2d 458 (1987), the Court held that the police decision to allow a wife to talk to her husband in custody was not the kind of "psychological ploy" that was the "functional equivalent" of interrogation. In *Mauro,* the defendant had confessed to killing his son, and then invoked his right to counsel. His wife was "adamant" in insisting on speaking to him, and no secure interview room was available. Therefore, the police allowed the two to meet in an office, and told them that their conversation would be recorded by an officer in the room. The tape recorder was in plain view. The defendant, in attempting to console his wife, made incriminating statements. The Court held that the police action did not rise to the level of "interrogation" under *Innis;* therefore, the defendant's recorded statements were held to be admissible, and his murder conviction was affirmed.

a.   Rationale

The Court held that the purpose of *Miranda* was to prevent police from "using the coercive nature of confinement to extract confessions" that would not be given in "an unrestrained environment." The police actions in *Mauro* did not meet this description. As the defendant was not subjected to "compelling influences, psychological ploys, or direct questioning," no interrogation occurred. Justice Powell, writing for the Court, observed that police do not interrogate a suspect "simply by hoping that he will incriminate himself." Thus, although the officers in *Mauro* admitted that they knew that it was possible the defendant would incriminate himself, this was insufficient to create "interrogation."

b.   Relevant Factors

Justice Powell relied on several aspects of the facts in *Mauro* for his conclusion that the police acted "reasonably and lawfully" by allowing Mauro's wife to meet with him. First, the officer who was present during the meeting asked the defendant "no questions about the crime or his conduct." Second, there was "no evidence that the officers sent Mrs. Mauro in" for the purpose of "eliciting incriminating statements." The police testified that they advised the wife not to talk to her husband, but that she was "adamant" about doing so. Third, there were legitimate security reasons for taping the meeting and for having a police officer present, which were "not related to securing incriminating statements." The police testified that they were concerned for the wife's safety, and concerned whether she might smuggle in a weapon for an escape attempt from the non-secure office. They also were concerned that the two spouses "might cook up a lie or swap statements with each other." Finally, Justice Powell examined the situation from the defendant's perspective. He doubted that a suspect would feel "that he was being coerced to incriminate himself in any way," simply by being told that his wife would be allowed to speak with him. The defendant was "fully informed" at the time the meeting began that an officer would be present, and would tape record the conversation. He was not forced to talk to his wife, because he "could have chosen not to speak," given his knowledge that the police were listening.

c. Dissent

Justice Stevens dissented, in an opinion joined by Justices Brennan, Marshall and Blackmun. Justice Stevens argued that interrogation occurred, as the police "allowed" the defendant's conversation "to commence at a time when they knew it was reasonably likely to produce an incriminating statement." Justice Stevens argued that the Court had not applied *Innis* properly, because it was not "unforeseeable" to the police that their words or actions would provoke incriminating statements. He believed the Court's holding was erroneously based on the implicit assumption that the "mere lack of explicit police subterfuge" could preclude a finding of interrogation. Justice Stevens concluded that, even though the defendant's wife requested the meeting, it was the police who "exploited" the situation, and exercised exclusive and unilateral control over the conditions of the meeting.

d. Perspective

Mauro's holding takes on a potentially narrow character in light of the combination of facts that the Court relied on to uphold the police action as "lawful." Thus, lower courts can distinguish *Mauro* in cases where police surreptitiously record a suspect's conversations during stationhouse interviews, or deceive suspects into believing that their conversations will go unheard, or take steps to initiate a meeting between the suspect and others.

On the other hand *Mauro* does contribute new criteria for the interrogation inquiry under *Innis,* and thus its reasoning may be more important than its narrow factual circumstances. For example, it helps to consider how *Mauro* would have been decided on the *Innis* criteria alone, if the wife were treated as a police "agent." The conversation between the husband and wife was more than "few offhand remarks." It concerned the evocative subject of the killing of their son. The wife's comments were directly addressed to the husband. In essence, the *Mauro* majority establish a more permissive standard for cases where police do not personally provoke the suspect to speak, as in *Innis,* but rely instead on a "situation" where a third person creates the impetus for self-incrimination.

3. Confrontation With Incriminating Evidence as a Form of Interrogation

In *Edwards v. Arizona,* 451 U.S. 477, 101 S.Ct. 1880, 68 L.Ed.2d 378 (1981), the Court found that interrogation occurred when the police offered to play a tape of an accomplice's confession to a suspect who invoked his right to counsel. The suspect asked them to play it, and made an incriminating statement after listening to it. The Court cited the *Innis* test without discussion. One reading of this result is that an average suspect who is confronted with incriminating evidence is likely to make a statement; and even an explanatory statement intended by the suspect to exculpate himself is excluded under *Miranda* where offered against the defendant at trial to show consciousness of guilt. See *Michigan v. Tucker, supra.*

a. Distinction From the Ploy in *Innis*

In *Innis,* the Court held that an appeal to a person's conscience or decency is not reasonably likely to elicit a response, in the absence of some peculiar susceptibility to such a ploy. In contrast, *Edwards* held, without discussion, that confronting a person with incriminating evidence is likely to elicit an incriminating response from the average suspect. The difference in result can be explained by the Court's apparent view of an average suspect as a person who is impervious to appeals to the welfare of others, but who is very sensitive to his own situation in a criminal investigation. See also *People v. Ferro,* 63 N.Y.2d 316, 482 N.Y.S.2d 237, 472 N.E.2d 13 (1984) (interrogation found where officers placed the fruits of Ferro's crime in front of his jail cell).

b. Not a Universal Rule

Perhaps because the Court in *Edwards* concluded without discussion that Edwards had been interrogated, the lower courts do not always find that confronting a suspect with incriminating evidence constitutes interrogation *per se.* See, e.g., *Shedelbower v. Estelle,* 885 F.2d 570 (9th Cir.1989) (telling the defendant that he was identified by eyewitness, which was false, was not interrogation).

4. Routine Booking Questions Are an Exception

The Court in *Innis* held that express questioning constitutes interrogation, but provided an exception for necessary questions that are merely "attendant to custody." In *Pennsylvania v. Muniz,* 496 U.S. 582, 110 S.Ct. 2638, 110 L.Ed.2d 528 (1990), the Court held that a defendant may be interrogated concerning "biographical data necessary to complete booking or pretrial services." When a suspect is arrested, police typically ask her name, address, age, and other such questions during the booking process. The Court determined that these questions do constitute "interrogation," even though they are not intended "to elicit information for investigatory purposes." However, the Court created an exception to *Miranda* for such "routine booking questions."

a. Rationale

Four Justices in *Muniz* endorsed the proposition that where questions are "requested for record-keeping purposes only," and are "reasonably related to the police's administrative concerns," they should fall within a "routine booking exception" to *Miranda*. Four other Justices found it unnecessary to reach the question of whether there is a booking questions exception to *Miranda*, but these Justices were nonetheless clearly in favor of such an exception. In *Muniz*, the defendant was arrested for drunken driving, and taken to a booking center, where police asked his "name, address, height, weight, eye color, date of birth, and current age." He did not receive *Miranda* warnings before giving answers, which were incriminating because he stumbled over the answers and gave incorrect information on some points; his answers were offered as evidence of drunkenness at trial. The Court decided that police did not need to give *Miranda* warnings before interrogating a defendant concerning the subjects involved in the seven questions asked in *Muniz*. Thus, the defendant's statements were held to be admissible at trial.

b. A Question That Is "Designed to Elicit Incriminatory Admissions" Is Not a "Routine Booking Question"

The *Muniz* Court stated that a question will not come within the "booking questions exception," if it is "designed to elicit incriminatory admissions." In *Muniz* the police asked an "eighth question" during the booking process, which concerned the date of the defendant's "sixth birthday." The state did not argue that this question fell within the booking questions exception. If the state had made this argument, a majority of the Court implicitly would have treated the sixth birthday question as one "designed to elicit incriminatory admissions." The Court found that the defendant was asked this question because the state had "an investigatory interest" in the answer. In *Muniz*, the defendant could not remember the date of his sixth birthday, and this evidence was used to prove his intoxication at trial. See *United States v. Hinckley*, 672 F.2d 115 (D.C.Cir.1982) (questions about defendant's recent addresses are not within the booking exception where they were made with the clear investigative purpose of learning about the defendant's recent movements, and where the interrogation was conducted by officers who did not ordinarily book suspects).

c. Chief Justice Rehnquist's Concurrence

The Chief Justice filed a concurring opinion in *Muniz*, and was joined by Justices White, Blackmun and Stevens. He acknowledged that there should be a "booking questions exception" to *Miranda*, but found it unnecessary to consider whether this exception applied to *Muniz*. Instead, he concluded that the defendant's responses to all eight questions were "non-testimonial," and therefore not protected under the Fifth Amendment.

d. Dissent

Justice Marshall dissented on the question of whether there should be a booking questions exception to *Miranda*. He argued that the Court's new exception would require "difficult time-consuming litigation" to determine its application and scope. He also believed that the exception would only "undermine" the clarity of the *Miranda* doctrine.

5. Interrogation Does Not Include Statements and Instructions Necessary for Custodial Procedures

In *Pennsylvania v. Muniz,* 496 U.S. 582, 110 S.Ct. 2638, 110 L.Ed.2d 528 (1990), the Court held that police did not "interrogate" the defendant under *Innis* when they gave him "carefully scripted police instructions" concerning how he should perform physical sobriety tests after the booking process. In *Muniz,* the defendant was asked to perform three tests after his arrest for drunken driving. The officers and the defendant had a short discussion concerning how the tests were to be conducted. In the course of these discussions, Muniz made incriminating statements concerning his intoxicated state. The Court held that these statements were not the product of interrogation, and therefore, that no *Miranda* warnings were required as part of the police instructions. Thus, the defendant's statements were held to be admissible at trial.

a. Rationale

The Court found that the police words and actions directing the defendant in the performance of the sobriety tests "were not likely to be perceived as calling for any verbal response." The police statements were "limited and carefully worded inquiries" as to whether the defendant understood their instructions. Thus, they were necessarily "attendant to" a legitimate police procedure, and did not fall within the *Innis* definition of interrogation.

b. Dissent

Justice Marshall dissented, and argued that the police knew that the defendant was intoxicated, and therefore "reasonably likely" to have trouble understanding their instructions.

I. THE APPLICATION OF *MIRANDA* TO UNDERCOVER POLICE ACTIVITY

In *Illinois v. Perkins,* 496 U.S. 292, 110 S.Ct. 2394, 110 L.Ed.2d 243 (1990), the Court held that *Miranda* warnings are not required "when the suspect is unaware that he is speaking to a law enforcement officer." Therefore, an undercover agent posing as a fellow prisoner may elicit incriminating statements from an incarcerated suspect without violating *Miranda*. In *Perkins,* two informants posed as inmates, in order to uncover evidence of the defendant's involvement in a murder. They invited him to help plan a jail break, and one of them directly asked him if he had ever "done" anybody. The defendant then supplied them with the details of his involvement with the murder; the Court held that his unwarned confession was admissible at trial, and affirmed his murder conviction.

1. Rationale

The Court held that when a suspect is talking to "someone whom he believes to be a fellow inmate," the "coercive atmosphere" of police interrogation is missing. Therefore, questioning by undercover agents does not "implicate the concerns underlying *Miranda.*" The Court reasoned that *Miranda* should be enforced only "in those types of situations in which the concerns that powered the decision are implicated." Moreover, coercion is determined "from the perspective of the suspect," and a suspect who is speaking to cellmates, whom he assumes are not police officers, will not feel "compelled to speak" by the traditional pressures of police interrogation. Although the defendant in *Perkins* was in "custody," this fact alone did not mandate *Miranda* warnings. Justice Kennedy, writing for the Court, observed that there must be "interplay" between custody and police interrogation, before it can be presumed under *Miranda* that a suspect's statements are "coerced" during the process of an interrogation without warnings. Where an incarcerated suspect is motivated to speak "solely by the desire to impress" fellow inmates, he must assume the risk that those inmates may be police officers.

2. Justice Brennan's Concurrence

Justice Brennan concurred in the Court's judgment concerning *Miranda,* but argued that "the deception" practiced upon the defendant raised "a substantial claim" of a Due Process violation that was not before the Court. Justice Brennan believed that the "police method" used in *Perkins* deserved close scrutiny, because the pressures of custody make an inmate vulnerable to the need to confide in others, and because the state could exploit this vulnerability by ensuring that an inmate is "barraged with questions" from undercover agents. Justice Brennan observed that the deliberate "manipulation" of the defendant by the police in *Perkins* raised "serious concerns" that his will may have been overborne. See *Arizona v. Fulminante* in the discussion of Due Process and confessions, *supra.*

3. Dissent

Justice Marshall dissented, and argued that the Court's new "exception" to *Miranda* improperly interpreted that decision as being concerned solely with police "coercion." Instead, he argued that *Miranda's* concern was with "any police tactics that may operate to compel a suspect in custody" to make incriminating statements; he believed that undercover activity was one such tactic.

J. MISDEMEANORS AND *MIRANDA*

In *Berkemer v. McCarty,* 468 U.S. 420, 104 S.Ct. 3138, 82 L.Ed.2d 317 (1984), the Court held that *Miranda* protections apply to suspects who are arrested for misdemeanor traffic offenses, as well as to those arrested for more serious crimes.

Once the defendant in *Berkemer* was in custody for drunken driving, the police could not interrogate him at the stationhouse without giving him *Miranda* warnings. Therefore his unwarned answers to police questions as to whether he had been drinking or using drugs were inadmissible at his trial.

1. Rationale

The Court unanimously endorsed the rule that *Miranda* warnings should be given to all suspects before custodial interrogation. This "bright-line" rule informs police explicitly as to their duties, and informs lower courts clearly as to the circumstances that make confessions inadmissible. The Court rejected the state's argument that an "exception" to *Miranda* should be "carved out" for misdemeanor traffic offenses. It concluded that a "misdemeanor exception" would "impair the simplicity and clarity" of police enforcement of *Miranda*. In order to invoke such an exception, police would be required to "guess as to the nature of the criminal conduct at issue" before interrogating a suspect. For example, it might turn out that a collision was the result of a misdemeanor, such as drunk driving, or a felony, such as negligent homicide, or both. At the time of an arrest, the crimes involved in some accidents might be unknown or unknowable.

2. No Good Reason to Reject a Bright–Line Rule

The Court in *Berkemer* found that neither of the state's justifications for a "misdemeanor exception" were compelling enough to justify the costs that would be incurred by undermining the "clarity" of *Miranda's* application. First, the Court rejected the state's argument that the dangers of inherent coercion do not exist when a suspect is questioned about a misdemeanor traffic offense. Justice Marshall, writing for the Court, observed that the need for *Miranda* safeguards exists in all arrests, whether suspects are in custody for felony offenses, or for misdemeanor offenses. The *Miranda* requirements are meant, in all cases, to ensure that police do not trick suspects into confessing, to relieve the coercive pressures of the custodial setting, and to free courts from case-by-case scrutiny of the "voluntariness" of confessions. Second, the Court rejected the state's argument that law enforcement would be "more effective" if *Miranda* warnings were not required for misdemeanor traffic offenses. Justice Marshall expressed doubt that the *Miranda* warnings "hamper" the investigation of such offenses, and noted that the occasions where a motorist is suspected "only of a misdemeanor" are rare.

K. THE "PUBLIC SAFETY EXCEPTION" TO *MIRANDA*

In *New York v. Quarles*, 467 U.S. 649, 104 S.Ct. 2626, 81 L.Ed.2d 550 (1984), the Court held that police may ask questions "reasonably prompted by a concern for public safety" without first advising a suspect in custody of the *Miranda* warnings. In *Quarles,* the police arrested and handcuffed a rape suspect at 12:30 a.m. in a supermarket, based on a tip from a victim who described the suspect and said he was armed. Before the arrest, a police officer chased the defendant to the back of the store, and lost sight of him briefly before he caught him, frisked him, and discovered that he was wearing an empty shoulder holster. The Court held that it was proper for the officer to refrain from giving the *Miranda* warnings, and to ask the defendant, "Where is the gun?" When the suspect said, "The gun is over there," it was also proper for the officer to retrieve it from an empty carton. Both the defendant's statement concerning the location of the gun, and the gun itself, were held to be admissible in the prosecution's case-in-chief.

1.   Rationale

The Court determined that the "doctrinal underpinnings" of *Miranda* did not require its application in a case where police questions were "reasonably prompted by a concern for public safety." The warnings might "deter" a suspect from answering such questions, and the Court found that the "need for answers" to these questions outweighed the "need" for *Miranda's* "prophylactic" protection of the privilege.

a.   Cost–Benefit Analysis

The *Quarles* Court interpreted *Miranda* as holding that the "possibility of fewer convictions" was an acceptable price to pay for the benefit of protecting the Fifth Amendment privilege through the requirement of the prophylactic *Miranda* warnings. Justice Rehnquist reasoned that the cost-benefit calculus of *Miranda* should be different, however, in a case where there is "danger to the public", and where the warnings may deter a suspect from giving information to the police that is necessary to protect the public in an emergency circumstance. In this situation, the costs of the *Miranda* rule of exclusion are more significant—not only will there be fewer convictions because of the warnings, but there will also be an imminent risk of harm to the public. This added cost led the Court to conclude that, where public safety is at stake, the costs of the *Miranda* exclusionary rule outweighed the benefits in deterrence that the rule would provide.

b.   No Bright–Line Rule

The Court in *Quarles* conceded that its new "exception" would "lessen the degree of clarity" of *Miranda*'s application. However, Justice Rehnquist predicted that the *Quarles* rule "would not be difficult for police officers to apply" because they "can and will distinguish almost instinctively" between permissible "public safety" questions and impermissible interrogation.

c.   Applied to the Facts

On the facts of *Quarles,* the Court found that the situation and the police questioning came within the scope of the "public safety exception." The police were confronted with "the immediate necessity" of ascertaining the whereabouts of the gun, which they "had every reason to believe" had been removed from the empty holster and discarded in the supermarket. If the gun were not located, it posed several dangers to the public safety: "an accomplice might make use of it," or a customer or employee might find it. Finally, the police officer asked "only the question necessary to locate the missing gun" before giving the defendant the *Miranda* warnings.

2. Justice O'Connor's Opinion

Justice O'Connor disagreed with the majority's adoption of a public safety exception to *Miranda*. She argued that the "public safety exception" was unjustifiable because it would blur "the clear strictures" of *Miranda;* therefore, she determined that the defendant's statement, "The gun is over there," should not be admissible evidence. She noted that "the Court has repeatedly refused to bend the literal terms" of *Miranda,* at least when a suspect is subjected to custodial interrogation without warnings. She predicted that the *Quarles* rule would make *Miranda* "more difficult to understand," and that some police would rely on the rule, only to have such reliance rejected by reviewing courts. Given the ambiguity of the "public safety exception" as defined by the *Quarles* majority, Justice O'Connor feared that litigation over the rule would create "a finespun new doctrine," complete with "hair-splitting distinctions" about the "exigencies" necessary to trigger the exception. Justice O'Connor agreed with the result as to the admissibility of the gun itself, however. In her view, the gun was a "fruit" of the *Miranda* -defective confession, and she argued that the exclusionary rule does not apply to physical evidence which is the fruit of a *Miranda* -defective confession. (See the discussion of the fruit of the poisonous tree, *supra.*)

3. Dissent

Justice Marshall dissented, in an opinion joined by Justices Brennan and Stevens, and argued that the *Quarles* holding was unjustified because there was convincing evidence to support the finding that the missing gun posed no threat to public safety. He noted that the police "could easily have cordoned off the store" and searched for the gun. The defendant was not believed to have an accomplice, and the store was deserted, "except for the clerks at the checkout counter." The defendant had been reduced "to powerlessness," and the police were confident enough of their safety to "put away their guns." Thus, there was no danger to the police, to the employees of the store, to customers, or to the public generally, that justified the need to ask, "Where's the gun?"

Justice Marshall also agreed with Justice O'Connor's criticisms of the *Quarles* rule, and declared that the Court had destroyed "forever the clarity of *Miranda* " for police and lower courts. He believed that it would be difficult for police to apply the *Quarles* rule without making mistakes, because they would "have to decide" whether an unwarned interrogation was justified in a "public safety" case, and to "remember to interrupt the interrogation" and provide warnings "once the focus of the inquiry shifts from protecting the public's safety to ascertaining the suspect's guilt."

4. Exigent Circumstances

In *Quarles,* there was dispute among the Justices as to how grave the threat to public security was under the facts of the case. The majority found a sufficient public safety problem from a loose gun accessible to the public. The Court pointedly did not require more imminent circumstances (e.g. a bomb that is about to go off within minutes), nor did it require more grave consequences. The courts after *Quarles* have generally equated the *Miranda* "public safety" exception with the exigent circumstances exception to the Fourth Amendment warrant requirement. That is, if the circumstances present a sufficiently imminent risk to excuse a warrant, they also pose a sufficient risk to excuse the *Miranda* warnings. See *United States v. Simpson,* 974 F.2d 845 (7th Cir.1992) (warnings not required before asking about the location of a gun in an apartment where officers are responding to a domestic disturbance). See the discussion of exigent circumstances, *supra.*

5. Subject Matter Limitation on Questioning

The Court in *Quarles* held that the officer's questioning was sufficiently within the public safety exception because he asked the suspect only about where the gun was, and did not ask him about the rape for which he was suspected. Presumably, then, if the officer had asked about the rape without giving the warnings, then any statement made by the defendant about the rape would not have fallen within the public safety question and would have been excluded. Sometimes, however, it is difficult to determine which questions fall within the subject matter of public safety and which fall outside the scope of the exception. Courts after *Quarles* have allowed officers considerable leeway to ask questions which could be construed as either addressing the public safety problem or as addressing the underlying crime.

Example: In *Fleming v. Collins,* 954 F.2d 1109 (5th Cir.1992), officers were responding to a bank robbery, when they came upon a person whom they knew to be a local used car salesman; the salesman had a person later determined to be Fleming pinned to the ground, and he was holding a gun to Fleming's head. Fleming had already been shot. The officers intervened, picked Fleming up, and asked him three questions, none of which were proceeded by the *Miranda* warnings. The first question was, "Who shot you?" to which Fleming replied, "The man at the bank." The second question was "Where is your gun?" to which Fleming replied, "I dropped it." The third question was, "Who was with you in the robbery?" to which Fleming replied, "Nobody. I did not get any money, either."

The Fifth Circuit Court of Appeals panel held that the first two questions were permissible as within the scope of the *Quarles* public safety exception, but that the third question was beyond the scope of the exception, because it dealt more with the bank robbery than with the confrontation that the officers came upon or with the loose gun that they learned about. But the Fifth Circuit then took the case en banc and held that all three questions were permissible under the public safety exception. The majority of the en banc court reasoned that *Quarles* provided flexibility to officers and authorized officers to rely on their instincts in applying the public safety exception. It concluded that it was not the role of a court to carefully parse out each question asked by the officers in an emergency situation. Thus, unless the officer's questioning went clearly and exclusively to the substantive crime rather than to a public safety matter, it would be permissible in the absence of warnings under *Quarles*. The third question in *Fleming* was permissible because the officers may have been concerned about armed and dangerous accomplices in the area, and because the questioning was related closely enough to the gun left somewhere by Fleming.

6. Involuntary Confessions Not Admitted

The confession obtained in *Quarles* was *Miranda*-defective: the defendant gave incriminating information without having received *Miranda* warnings. It was for this reason that the Court could balance the costs and benefits of applying the exclusionary rule where the public safety was at stake; the linchpin of the Court's analysis was that exclusion of the confession was not *constitutionally* required because it was merely *Miranda*-defective. It follows that if the confession were *involuntary,* it would have been inadmissible even if it were obtained in response to a public safety problem. This is because if a confession is obtained involuntarily, the Due Process Clause is violated, and exclusion of the confession is constitutionally required. See *Mincey v. Arizona, supra* (impeachment exception to *Miranda* exclusionary rule does not apply where the confession was obtained in violation of the Due Process Clause).

V. CONFESSIONS AND THE SIXTH AMENDMENT AFTER *MIRANDA*

After *Miranda* was decided, the Court did not revisit its doctrine concerning the Sixth Amendment right to counsel under *Massiah* for many years. The occasion for the Court's return to the doctrine came in a case where a fugitive turned himself in, after the police promised his attorney that he would not be interrogated after arraignment until he consulted in person with the attorney. The police did not honor this promise, and obtained incriminating statements from the defendant. While the defendant's *Miranda* rights may have been violated, the case involved difficult questions under the *Miranda* precedents in 1977, and the Court declined to address these questions. Instead, a closely divided Court invalidated the confession on Sixth Amendment grounds, and held that *Massiah* prohibited the police from "deliberate elicitation" of incriminating statements from the defendant, in the absence of counsel, after arraignment. See *Brewer v. Williams,* 430 U.S. 387, 97 S.Ct. 1232, 51 L.Ed.2d 424 (1977).

After *Brewer,* the Court was called upon to delineate the scope of the Sixth Amendment right to counsel, and the shadow of the *Miranda* doctrine hung over every Sixth Amendment interpretation of the rights of indicted defendants faced with custodial interrogation. In some cases, the Court borrowed from *Miranda* doctrine to create a parallel right under *Massiah,* as when it held that the protection of *Edwards* applied to defendants who invoked the Sixth Amendment right to counsel at arraignment. In other cases, the Court rejected the *Miranda* analogy, as when it held that a *Massiah* invocation did not encompass an "unqualified" request for the assistance of counsel in dealing with the police during an interrogation that concerned "different" crimes.

Ultimately, the picture of *Massiah* rights that emerged from the Court's post-*Brewer* decisions closely resembled the doctrinal landscape of *Miranda.* The Court found that *Miranda* warnings sufficed to notify a defendant of the *Massiah* right to counsel. The Court employed the same language for its waiver standard for *Miranda* rights and *Massiah* rights. The Court prohibited "deliberate elicitation" of admissions under *Massiah* in terms that resembled its prohibition of "interrogation" under *Miranda.* In sum, *Massiah* provided distinctive protections primarily for defendants faced with surreptitious interrogation, not for those facing police interrogators. It remains an open question whether *Massiah*'s exclusionary rule is merely a "prophylactic safeguard" like its *Miranda* counterpart, or is instead a full-fledged constitutional right.

A. *BREWER V. WILLIAMS: Massiah* Applies to Police Efforts to "Deliberately Elicit" Incriminating Statements From a Suspect Whose Sixth Amendment Right to Counsel Has Attached

In *Brewer v. Williams,* 430 U.S. 387, 97 S.Ct. 1232, 51 L.Ed.2d 424 (1977), the Court held that the Sixth Amendment right to counsel was violated when police deliberately elicited incriminating statements from a defendant who had been arraigned on an arrest warrant for murder. This violated *Massiah v. United States,* 377 U.S. 201, 84 S.Ct. 1199, 12 L.Ed.2d 246 (1964), because the defendant had not waived his Sixth Amendment right to counsel by "intentionally relinquishing" it before police obtained his statements.

1. Facts of *Brewer*
The defendant was suspected of murder, and he fled from Des Moines to Davenport; he surrendered to the police in Davenport on advice of counsel in Des Moines. He was arraigned in Davenport. The Des Moines police promised his counsel that the officers who were sent to Davenport to pick up the defendant would not question him during the drive back to Des Moines. Counsel told the defendant of this promise, and advised him not to talk to the police until after consultation with him. At his arraignment in Davenport,

the defendant conferred with another attorney, who also advised him not to talk to the police until he saw his counsel in Des Moines. When the Des Moines police arrived in Davenport, the local attorney urged them to carry out their promise not to interrogate the defendant, but the police expressed "reservations," and they refused to allow the attorney to accompany them back to Des Moines.

The defendant was given *Miranda* warnings upon arrest, at arraignment, and then again by the Des Moines detectives before they embarked on their 160–mile journey. During the ride, the defendant informed the police repeatedly that he would talk to them after he saw his lawyer. However, one police officer knew that the defendant was deeply religious, and was a former mental patient. Not long after leaving Davenport, he made a speech to the defendant concerning the importance of finding the body of the murder victim, in order to give her a "Christian burial." He then told the defendant, "I don't want you to answer me. I don't want to discuss it any further. Just think about it as we're riding down the road." After the police car had traveled another 100 miles or so, the defendant made incriminating statements about the location of evidence, and led the police to the body. He was convicted of murder. The Court declined to consider whether the police violated *Miranda*. Instead, the Court reversed the murder conviction on Sixth Amendment grounds, because the police violated *Massiah*. The defendant's statements, as well as the fact that he showed the police to the body, were held to be inadmissible at trial.

2. Rationale

The Court held that the Sixth Amendment right to counsel attached at the initiation of the "judicial proceedings" at arraignment, and was not "intentionally relinquished" by the defendant before the police "deliberately elicited" statements from him in violation of *Massiah*.

a. Deliberate Elicitation After a Formal Charge

Relying on *Massiah,* the Court in *Brewer* held that the Sixth Amendment prohibits police from *deliberately eliciting* information in the absence of counsel, when a suspect has been formally charged. The police officer in *Brewer* violated *Massiah* by making the "Christian burial speech," because it was a case of deliberate elicitation. The officer knew that the defendant was being represented by two lawyers, and yet "purposely sought" to "obtain as much incriminating evidence as possible" during the defendant's imposed isolation in the police car on the way to Des Moines.

b. No Waiver

The Court found "no reasonable basis" for finding a waiver of the right to counsel on the facts of *Brewer.* In the absence of evidence of waiver, the state did not meet its heavy burden of proving the defendant's "intentional relinquishment or abandonment" of this right. The Court noted that Williams had secured attorneys "at both ends" of the trip, and they acted as his agents in telling the police that no interrogation would be allowed on the journey. Second, he consulted with these attorneys four times, and was assured by them that the police would not question him. Finally, he clearly expressed his desire for the presence of counsel before interrogation by stating that he would talk to police after he met with counsel in Des Moines. Thus, the defendant both expressly and implicitly asserted his right to counsel repeatedly throughout his encounter with the police.

3. **Unethical Behavior as the Touchstone of Sixth Amendment Analysis**

In a concurring opinion, Justice Stevens used a somewhat different approach to the problem of deliberate elicitation of statements from an accused (one who has been formally charged with a crime). Justice Stevens noted that the defendant's "experienced" lawyer trusted the police to "honor a commitment" made during negotiations for the defendant's surrender. In order for the Court to express its concern about the need for effective representation of counsel, the state in *Brewer* "could not be permitted to dishonor its promise" to the defendant's lawyer. Thus, in his view, the confession was properly excluded because the officers acted unethically.

Indeed, in the later case of *Rhode Island v. Innis, supra,* the Court distinguished the Sixth Amendment from *Miranda* on ethical grounds. According to the Court in *Innis, Miranda* protects the suspect from the compulsion that is inherent in custodial interrogation. Thus, its focus is on whether the suspect has been *pressured* by police activity, rather than on whether such activity is unethical or in bad faith. In contrast, the Sixth Amendment focusses on whether the state has acted unethically by deliberately approaching a defendant for information, in the absence of his counsel, after a formal charge has been filed. See Code of Professional Responsibility DR 7–104, which prohibits a lawyer in the course of a matter from contacting an opposing party in the absence of counsel. (Rule 4.2 of the Model Rules of Professional Conduct is to the same effect). In *Brewer,* the Court (and especially Justice Stevens) reasoned that when a formal charge has been filed, litigation has begun, and it is inappropriate for the state to approach the adversary for information in the absence of counsel. See also *United States v. Johnson,* 954 F.2d 1015 (5th Cir.1992) ("Once the government has brought formal charges against an individual the adversary relationship between the parties is cemented * * *. The government may not try to circumvent the protection afforded by the presence of counsel during questioning. The vice is not deprivation of privacy, but interference with the parity required by the Sixth Amendment.").

4. Dissent

Four Justices dissented in *Brewer* in three separate opinions. The dissenters argued that there was sufficient positive evidence of waiver in the record: Williams had been given warnings, consulted with counsel, and confessed freely, knowing the consequences. They contended that waiver should not be a "formalistic" concept, and that an implied waiver should be found in *Brewer,* because the defendant "knew" of his right and intended to "relinquish it."

Justice Blackmun's dissenting opinion stressed that *Brewer* was distinguishable from *Massiah,* for two reasons. First, he found that the police did not interrogate the defendant in *Brewer.* He inferred this from the fact that the goal of the police was "not solely" to obtain incriminating evidence, but also to do their "duty" by locating the body. Justice Blackmun argued that the *Brewer* majority appeared to define "deliberate elicitation" under *Massiah* as any police conduct that is motivated by the desire to obtain information from a suspect. He found this definition to be "far too broad." Second, Justice Blackmun observed that the defendant in *Massiah* was "imposed upon" because he did not know the identity of his informant-interrogator; in *Brewer,* the defendant knew he was talking to the police, and had been warned not to do so.

5. Why Not Use *Miranda?*

Miranda applies to all custodial interrogation, whether it occurs before or after a formal charge has been brought. So a question raised by *Brewer* was why the Court found it necessary to rely on the *Massiah* doctrine. A possible explanation is that *Brewer* was decided before the Court created the *Miranda* protections articulated in *Edwards* and its progeny. It is notable that the Christian burial speech did not produce incriminating statements until roughly two hours later. Thus, in order to find a *Miranda* violation in *Brewer,* the Court would have been required to hold that the single act of interrogation tainted the later confession and disabled the police from seeking a waiver. The Court's *Miranda* decisions before 1977 did not endorse such a limitation on the police, and some observers have suggested that the *Brewer* Court's reliance on *Massiah* indicated that a majority of the Court was not willing to find that the waiver in *Brewer* was "involuntary" under *Miranda.*

As *Miranda*'s protections became limited in scope by the Court's decisions of the 1980s, some commentators and lower courts perceived that the Court might be prepared to provide "stronger" protections across the board for "Sixth Amendment" defendants than for *Miranda* defendants. For example, the language the Court used to describe waiver was different, at first, for Fifth and Sixth Amendment rights. *Miranda* required only that a waiver must be "voluntary, knowing and intelligent," but *Brewer* required that a waiver must be the "intentional relinquishment or abandonment of a known right or privilege." In theory, it would have been possible for the Court to require "Sixth Amendment" defendants to receive "greater" rights than *Miranda* defendants. Ultimately, however, the Court nipped this possibility in the bud. See, e.g., *Patterson v. Illinois,* 487 U.S. 285, 108 S.Ct. 2389, 101 L.Ed.2d 261 (1988) (*Miranda* warnings suffice to notify an indicted defendant of the Sixth Amendment right to counsel); *Moran v. Burbine,* 475 U.S. 412, 106 S.Ct. 1135, 89 L.Ed.2d 410 (1986) (treating the *Brewer* and *Miranda* definitions of waiver as interchangeable equivalents).

6.   Affirmation of the *Brewer–Massiah* Rule

In several cases after *Brewer,* the Court affirmed the validity of the *Brewer–Massiah* rule. For example, the Court held that a state psychiatrist may not interview an indicted defendant in order to discover information to be used against him at a capital sentencing hearing. See *Estelle v. Smith,* 451 U.S. 454, 101 S.Ct. 1866, 68 L.Ed.2d 359 (1981) (no interview without a waiver of the defendant's right to consult with counsel). See also *Satterwhite v. Texas,* 486 U.S. 249, 108 S.Ct. 1792, 100 L.Ed.2d 284 (1988) (*Estelle* violation); *Powell v. Texas,* 492 U.S. 680, 109 S.Ct. 3146, 106 L.Ed.2d 551 (1989) (defendant may not be subjected to a psychiatric examination and examined on the issue of future dangerousness without notice to counsel).

7.   Must Be Formally Charged; Having Counsel Is Not Enough

The Court in *Moran v. Burbine,* 475 U.S. 412, 106 S.Ct. 1135, 89 L.Ed.2d 410 (1986), declined to expand the attachment of the *Brewer–Massiah* right to a defendant who had not been indicted, but whose family had retained counsel on his behalf during his custodial interrogation. According to the Court, Sixth Amendment rights are triggered by a formal charge (such as arraignment or indictment), rather than a formal relationship with counsel. Thus, merely having a retained counsel does not trigger Sixth Amendment rights prior to a formal charge. Conversely, if the defendant has been formally charged, his right to counsel is violated if the state engages in deliberate elicitation, even if the defendant has not established a formal relationship with a lawyer. See *United States v. Henry,* 447 U.S. 264, 100 S.Ct. 2183, 65 L.Ed.2d 115 (1980) (right to counsel applies automatically when officers engage in deliberate elicitation after a formal charge).

B.   SIXTH AMENDMENT WAIVER

The Court in *Brewer* held that a waiver of Sixth Amendment rights could not be found merely because a defendant was warned of his rights and subsequently confessed. The same is true for *Miranda* rights. See *Tague v. Louisiana, supra.* The Court in *Brewer* did not purport to decide all Sixth Amendment waiver questions, however—the most important question being whether waiver under the Sixth Amendment should be decided under the same standards applied to determine waiver of *Miranda* rights.

1. **If an Accused Invokes the Sixth Amendment Right to Counsel at Arraignment, Police May Seek a Waiver of Sixth Amendment Rights Only if the Accused "Initiates" Contact With the Police**

   In *Michigan v. Jackson,* 475 U.S. 625, 106 S.Ct. 1404, 89 L.Ed.2d 631 (1986), the Court held that the *Edwards* rule applied to a defendant who requested the assistance of counsel at arraignment. Defendants in two cases challenged the admissibility of statements made during post-arraignment questioning by police. At arraignment, each defendant had asked that counsel be appointed to assist him. After arraignment, police approached each defendant, gave them *Miranda* warnings, and obtained voluntary waivers and incriminating statements. The Court held that the purported waivers of Sixth Amendment rights to counsel were invalid, because the defendants did not "initiate" contact with the police after invoking their rights. Thus, the Court concluded that the bright-line "intitiation" rule of *Edwards* was applicable to an invocation of Sixth Amendment rights, and so it did not matter that the waivers may actually have been voluntary under the totality of the circumstances.

   a. **Rationale**

      The Court reasoned that *Edwards* should be applied to an invocation of a Sixth Amendment right to counsel, because this right required "at least as much protection as the *Miranda* right to counsel." The Court concluded that when a request for counsel is made at arraignment, the assertion of the Sixth Amendment right is "no less significant, and the need for additional safeguards no less clear" than when the Fifth Amendment right to counsel is asserted during custodial interrogation. Justice Stevens, writing for the Court, observed that after the initiation of adversary judicial proceedings, a defendant has a right to rely on counsel as an exclusive "medium" for communication with the police. The Sixth Amendment right is so important that, once it attaches, police are prohibited from certain investigatory techniques that are permissible in the pre-attachment stage. See, e.g., *Massiah v. United States,* 377 U.S. 201, 84 S.Ct. 1199, 12 L.Ed.2d 246 (1964). Therefore, the Court concluded that the "legal differences" between the Fifth and Sixth Amendment contexts only strengthen the justification for requiring the protection of the *Edwards* rule in the post-arraignment setting.

   b. **Invocation at Arraignment Applies for All Subsequent Critical Stages**

      The Court in *Jackson* rejected the state's argument that a request for counsel at arraignment does not necessarily "encompass" a request for counsel's assistance when dealing with the police. The Court held that it was required to "give a broad, rather than a narrow, interpretation to a defendant's request for counsel." Justice Stevens relied on the Court's policy of indulging in "every reasonable presumption against waiver" of "fundamental" constitutional rights, and determined that the defendants' requests in *Jackson* encompassed an implicit request for a "lawyer's services at every critical stage of the prosecution." And the Court had already held in *Massiah* that deliberate elicitation by the state after a charge represented a "critical stage" in the criminal prosecution because of the potential that damaging evidence would be obtained for use against the defendant at trial. Thus, the defendant's invocation encompassed this later stage.

c. Lack of Police Knowledge Irrelevant

The Court in *Jackson* also rejected the state's argument that *Edwards* should not apply to the requests in *Jackson* because police may not know of such requests made during arraignment. Once the Sixth Amendment right attaches, the state must honor it; this requirement disables the police from claiming ignorance of requests made to a judge.

d. Dissent

Justice Rehnquist dissented, joined by Justices Powell and O'Connor, and argued that the *Edwards* rule did not "make sense" in the context of the Sixth Amendment. Justice Rehnquist observed that the *Jackson* holding applied *Edwards* only to defendants who expressly invoked the right to counsel. He argued that this aspect of *Jackson*'s holding contradicted Sixth Amendment precedents which held that the right to counsel *does not depend upon its invocation,* but upon the initiation of adversary judicial proceedings. Justice Rehnquist attributed this "glaring inconsistency" to the absence of a "coherent, analytically sound basis" for the *Jackson* decision.

2. *Jackson* Applies Only if the Accused Invokes the Right to Counsel

In *Patterson v. Illinois,* 487 U.S. 285, 108 S.Ct. 2389, 101 L.Ed.2d 261 (1988), the Court held that *Jackson* implicitly held that invocation of the right to counsel was necessary to trigger the protection of *Edwards*. If this were not so, the *Jackson* decision to borrow the *Edwards* rationale would have been "unnecessary," because the police would have been barred *per se* from initiating interrogation after arraignment. Like the Fifth Amendment right to counsel, which exists during custody, but is not protected by the *Edwards* rule until invocation, the Sixth Amendment right to counsel exists upon attachment, but is not protected by the *Jackson* rule until invocation. See also *Montoya v. Collins,* 955 F.2d 279 (5th Cir.1992) (*Jackson* does not apply where the magistrate told the defendant that counsel was being appointed for him, and defendant said nothing; while not rejecting counsel, defendant never sought to consult with counsel).

3. Sixth Amendment Right to Counsel Is Offense–Specific. Police May Seek a Waiver, in the Absence of Initiation by the Accused, With Respect to a Crime Unrelated to the Formal Charge

In *McNeil v. Wisconsin,* __ U.S. __, 111 S.Ct. 2204, 115 L.Ed.2d 158 (1991), the Court held that a defendant's request for the assistance of counsel at a "first appearance" encompassed only a request for assistance *concerning the offense with which he was charged.* Therefore, the police could approach him to seek a waiver of *Miranda* rights as to a crime unrelated to the charge. The defendant in *McNeil* was charged with armed robbery; he requested counsel, and was represented at his initial appearance by an attorney from the Public Defender's Office. Later that evening, the police interviewed the defendant in jail concerning their separate investigation of a murder, attempted murder and armed burglary. The defendant was given *Miranda* warnings and signed a waiver; then he made statements about these crimes. These actions were repeated at two subsequent interviews. If the *Jackson–Edwards* rule were applicable, the confession would have been inadmissible, because McNeil had not initiated the contact with the police after invoking his rights. But the Court declined to extend the *Jackson* rule to cover police interrogation concerning different crimes. And the *Edwards–Roberson* rule was inapplicable because McNeil had invoked only his Sixth Amendment rights and not his *Miranda* rights in his initial appearance. (This aspect of the opinion is discussed in the section on *Miranda, supra*). Therefore, the defendant's statements were held to be admissible, and his convictions for these other crimes were affirmed.

a. Rationale

The Court held that a defendant's invocation of the right to counsel cannot embrace a request for assistance in future unrelated investigations, because "adversary judicial proceedings" have not been initiated for such prosecutions. As the Sixth Amendment right is "offense-specific," the *Jackson* "effect" must be "offense-specific," too. Thus, the *Edwards* rule, which was adopted in *Jackson,* could not be applied in *McNeil.* The "offense-specific" nature of Sixth Amendment rights has been well-established since *Massiah,* where the Court stated that it was permissible for officers to obtain information from a charged defendant concerning uncharged crimes, and to use such statements in later trials on those unrelated charges.

b. Dissent

Justice Stevens dissented, joined by Justices Marshall and Blackmun, and argued that *Jackson* established the importance of giving "a broad, rather than a narrow, interpretation" to a defendant's request for counsel at arraignment. Therefore, the defendant's request for counsel in *McNeil* should be read to encompass a desire to deal with the police only through counsel, for interrogation on any subject. Justice Stevens feared that the *McNeil* rule would generate confusion in the law, as lower courts would be required to "flesh out the precise boundaries" of the new "offense-specific" limitation on the Sixth Amendment. He also feared that *McNeil* might encourage lower courts to tolerate police decisions to file charges selectively, "in order to preserve opportunities for custodial interrogation."

4.   **The *Miranda* Warnings Adequately Inform an Indicted Defendant of the Sixth Amendment Right to Counsel. Therefore, Police May Obtain a Valid Waiver of the Sixth Amendment Right to Counsel After Giving Only These Warnings**

In *Patterson v. Illinois,* 487 U.S. 285, 108 S.Ct. 2389, 101 L.Ed.2d 261 (1988), the Court held that the *Miranda* rights provide the "sum and substance" of the rights provided by the Sixth Amendment; no extra warnings were required to establish a knowing and voluntary waiver of Sixth Amendment rights. The defendant in *Patterson* was indicted, but did not invoke his right to counsel at arraignment, and thus did not qualify for *Jackson*'s protection from police-initiated questioning. Police gave him *Miranda* warnings in custody, and sought and obtained a waiver, as well as incriminating statements. Later that day, a prosecutor repeated this procedure, and further statements were obtained. Patterson did not deny that he understood the warnings, but he argued that the warnings were insufficient to inform him of his Sixth Amendment right to counsel, as opposed to his rights under *Miranda*. The Court decided that the value and function of counsel was the same during pre-indictment and post-indictment custodial interrogation, and therefore, that no "extra" information about the Sixth Amendment right to counsel was needed for an indicted defendant to be adequately apprised of this right. The Court held the defendant's statements to be admissible under *Massiah,* and affirmed his murder conviction.

a.   **Rationale**

Justice White began by stating that the test for waiver of both the Fifth and Sixth Amendment rights to counsel focused on the same pragmatic question: Was the defendant aware of his right, and of the possible consequences of waiver? In order to give a "knowing" waiver, a defendant must be made aware of the "usefulness of counsel" and the "dangers" of proceeding without counsel. It was evident to the Court that the *Miranda* warnings sufficed to communicate these aspects of the Sixth Amendment right to counsel to a defendant. The Court noted that the state's decision to begin formal "adversarial judicial proceedings" against a defendant did not "substantially increase the value of counsel" at questioning, or "expand the limited purpose" that counsel served at questioning. Therefore, no different warnings, and no "more searching inquiry" was needed for a Sixth Amendment waiver than for a Fifth Amendment waiver.

b.   **Distinction From Waiver of Counsel at Trial**

Justice White acknowledged that a "more searching inquiry" was needed for the waiver of the Sixth Amendment right to counsel at trial. See *Faretta v. California,* 422 U.S. 806, 95 S.Ct. 2525, 45 L.Ed.2d 562 (1975) (valid waiver requires a searching examination of the defendant and extensive warnings concerning the value of counsel at trial). But he attributed this requirement to the fact that the "dangers and disadvantages of self-representation" at trial are more substantial, and less obvious to the accused than the comparable dangers and disadvantages of self-representation during interrogation. Put another way, the consequences of a waiver of counsel at trial were more complex, more wide-ranging, and less obvious than the consequences of a waiver of counsel for police questioning. At trial, counsel has a variety of important functions, whereas at questioning, counsel's sole and obvious function is to protect the defendant from saying anything which could incriminate him.

c.   Dissent

Justice Stevens dissented, joined by Justices Brennan, Marshall, and Blackmun. He found that the situation of the post-indictment defendant differed from that of the pre-indictment suspect, because the adversary position of the state becomes clear only after indictment. Also, after indictment, any interrogation cannot be justified by the state as an attempt to solve a crime, but only as an extra effort to "buttress the government's case." Consequently, counsel's role becomes more crucial in post-charge questioning than it is in pre-charge questioning, and therefore the waiver standards should be more stringent at this later stage.

Justice Stevens argued that *Miranda* warnings alone were insufficient to make an indicted defendant aware of the disadvantages of waiving the right to counsel at that point. For example, such disadvantages included the defendant's limited ability, without counsel, to examine the indictment before submitting to interrogation, and to negotiate a plea bargain skillfully before interrogation. Justice Stevens argued that "at least minimal advice is necessary" concerning these disadvantages, and determined that it must include advice that goes beyond the *Miranda* warnings.

Finally, Justice Stevens disagreed with the majority's holding that the necessary advice for a waiver of Sixth Amendment rights could be provided by "an adversary party," such as a police officer or a prosecutor. First, the offering of advice by such an adversary "may lead an accused to underestimate" the "true adversary posture" of the interrogator. Second, the "adversary posture" of the interrogator will "inevitably tend to color the advice offered." Third, advice offered by those with a conflict of interest "cannot help but create a public perception of unfairness and unethical conduct."

d.   Indictment Warning

The defendant in *Patterson* knew of his indictment before he waived his right to counsel, and so the Court did not reach the issue whether a suspect should be told of his indictment before a Sixth Amendment waiver can be sought by police. Some lower courts have relied on the broad rationale of *Patterson* to find that it is not necessary for police to provide such information before seeking a waiver. See, e.g., *Riddick v. Edmiston,* 894 F.2d 586 (3d Cir.1990).

5. **Two Exceptions Where Waiver Standards May Differ**
The Court in *Patterson* held that where a defendant has been charged and has not invoked his Sixth Amendment right to counsel, the waiver of Sixth Amendment rights is governed by essentially the same principles as the waiver of *Miranda* rights. The Court, however, described two exceptions where an accused would not have waived his Sixth Amendment rights, "even though the challenged practices would pass constitutional muster under *Miranda.*"

a. **Lawyer Trying to Reach an Indicted Defendant**
The Court in *Patterson* stated that where police know that an indicted defendant's lawyer is trying to reach him, the police must inform the defendant of that fact before there can be a knowing waiver of Sixth Amendment rights. This is in contrast to *Miranda,* where a knowing waiver can be made if the defendant is unaware that his lawyer is trying to reach him. See *Moran v. Burbine, supra.* The reason for the distinction is that *Miranda* rights are concerned with pressure on the suspect, and no pressure can be created by information about which the defendant is unaware. In contrast, the Sixth Amendment is concerned with preventing Government officials from engaging in the unethical activity of intruding upon the attorney-client relationship once formal litigation has begun. Thus, in the Sixth Amendment situation, a defendant who is waiving the right to an attorney-client relationship is entitled to know an important factor of that relationship—that counsel is seeking him out.

b. **Undercover Activity**
Another difference between the Fifth and Sixth Amendment arises where the state employs an undercover informant to obtain information. *Miranda* does not apply to undercover activity (see *Illinois v. Perkins, supra*) whereas the Sixth Amendment does (see *United States v. Henry, infra*). The Court in *Patterson* pointed out that the standard waiver rules cannot apply in the undercover context. That is, a defendant could never be found to have waived his Sixth Amendment rights when questioned by an undercover agent, because by definition he does not even know that he is talking to a Government official. See *United States v. Johnson,* 954 F.2d 1015 (5th Cir.1992) (accused must "know he is being questioned by the government before he can knowingly waive his right not to be interrogated by the government without his lawyer").

C. "DELIBERATE ELICITATION" AND THE PASSIVE EAR

The Sixth Amendment obviously does not prohibit all contact between a state official and an indicted defendant in the absence of counsel. For example, the Sixth Amendment does not require the state to provide a bunk for counsel next to an incarcerated defendant who is awaiting trial, on the off-chance that the defendant might say something incriminating during the course of the day. It is only when the state "deliberately elicits" information from the accused in the absence of counsel that the Sixth Amendment is triggered. In these instances, the state is acting unethically by interposing itself between the accused and his counsel during the course of litigation. In several cases, the Court has sought to define the parameters of "deliberate elicitation."

1. *Massiah* Is Violated When a Government Informant Seeks to Obtain Incriminating Statements From an Indicted Defendant by Having "Conversations" With Him, Even if the Informant Does Not Directly Question the Defendant

In *United States v. Henry,* 447 U.S. 264, 100 S.Ct. 2183, 65 L.Ed.2d 115 (1980), the Court held that "deliberate elicitation" of incriminating statements can occur when an incarcerated Government informant leads a defendant to believe that he is a fellow inmate, and talks with the defendant about the crime for which the defendant is indicted. In *Henry,* the defendant was indicted for armed robbery, and refused to talk to police while in custody. A Government agent learned that a paid informant was housed in the same cellblock as the defendant, and told him to "be alert" to any statements Henry made about the armed robbery. The agent also warned the informant "not to initiate any conversation with or question" Henry about the crime. The informant testified at trial that he had "an opportunity to have some conversations" with the defendant, where incriminating statements were made. The Court found that the informant was not a "passive listener," and that under *Massiah* it was not necessary to determine whether the informant raised the "subject of the crime under investigation" with the defendant. Therefore, the defendant's statements were held to be inadmissible, and his conviction for armed robbery was reversed.

a. Rationale

The Court determined that *Massiah* applied in *Henry* because of three factors. The jail inmate acted *"under instructions as a paid informant,"* pretended to be nothing more than a "fellow inmate," and *engaged* an incarcerated defendant in conversation *about his crime* after he was indicted. This "combination of circumstances" constituted *deliberate elicitation* which required exclusion of incriminating statements obtained from the conversation. The Court reaffirmed *Massiah*'s mandate that the Sixth Amendment "must apply to indirect and surreptitious interrogations as well as those conducted in the jailhouse."

b. **Conduct Likely to Elicit Incriminating Information Is Deemed Deliberate**

Chief Justice Burger, writing for the Court, reasoned that the informant's conduct was "attributable" to the Government. The Government argued that its agent "did not intend" that the informant would take "affirmative steps to secure incriminating information," though that is in fact what happened. The Court responded that even if the agent lacked specific intent to have the informant elicit information, the agent "must have known" that the "propinquity" of the informant and the defendant in the same cellblock, and the fact that the informant would be paid for any information provided, would be "likely" to lead to the result in *Henry*. Thus, where the informant's own testimony revealed that he was not a "passive listener," but an active participant in "conversations" with the defendant, this conduct was sufficient to satisfy *Massiah*'s deliberate elicitation requirement. Thus, after *Henry,* "deliberate" elicitation does not focus on the subjective intent of the officer but rather on whether a *reasonable person would find it likely* that a planned course of conduct would lead to the elicitation of incriminating information from a formally charged defendant.

c. **Undercover Activity; Distinction From *Miranda***

The Court in *Henry* rejected the Government's argument that "a less rigorous standard" should be used to assess a Sixth Amendment violation where a defendant is speaking to an undercover agent, than in a case where the defendant is knowingly speaking to the police, as in *Brewer.* Chief Justice Burger reasoned that the Court should not "infuse" inapposite Fifth Amendment concerns about compelled self-incrimination into *Massiah*'s doctrine concerning the protection of the Sixth Amendment right to counsel. *Miranda* focuses on the pressure imposed on suspects in the course of custodial interrogation. It is thus important to consider whether the defendant knew that the questioning party was a police officer; if not, there is no pressure on suspects created by the interplay between custody and police interrogation that is the concern of *Miranda*. See *Illinois v. Perkins, supra* (*Miranda* does not apply to undercover activity). In contrast, the Sixth Amendment focuses on whether the Government has unethically interposed itself between the defendant and his counsel during the course of litigation (i.e. after a formal charge has been filed). That intrusion is unethical whether it occurs through police questioning or through undercover activity. It is for this reason that the Sixth Amendment is applicable to post-charge undercover activity, but *Miranda* is not. See the concurring opinion of Justice Powell in *Henry* (emphasizing that *Massiah* serves the "salutary purpose" of "preventing police interference" with the attorney-client relationship after the initiation of formal adversary proceedings).

d. Dissent

Justice Blackmun dissented, in an opinion joined by Justice White. Justice Rehnquist dissented separately. Justice Blackmun argued that *Massiah*'s rule encompassed only "action undertaken with the specific intent to evoke an inculpatory disclosure." He disapproved of the Court's "expansion" of *Massiah* in *Henry*, to cover "even a 'negligent' triggering of events resulting in reception of disclosures." By contrast with *Massiah* and *Brewer*, the *Henry* Court created a "likely to induce" test for elicitation that required exclusion of a defendant's statements even when an agent engaged in no "overreaching," and believed his "actions to be wholly innocent and passive." Justice Blackmun argued that the *Henry* expansion was misguided because it punished police conduct that was not "culpable." For example, the Government agent in *Henry* was careful to tell the informant, in effect, "Don't ask questions, just keep your ears open." Justice Blackmun saw no "good reason" to expand Sixth Amendment protections beyond "their outermost point" as established in *Massiah*.

Justice Rehnquist argued that the "doctrinal underpinnings" of *Massiah* were "difficult to reconcile with the traditional notions of the role of an attorney." He agreed with Justice White's argument in his *Massiah* dissent, that the existence of a right to counsel at trial did not justify the creation of a right to counsel's presence at "out-of-court conversations" with police or other state agents. Justice Rehnquist argued that the Court's Sixth Amendment precedents recognized that the "theoretical foundation" of the right to counsel is based on "the traditional role of an attorney as a legal expert and strategist." Justice Rehnquist asserted that there was "no constitutional or historical support" for concluding that counsel should "serve as a sort of guru who must be present" whenever a defendant may feel inclined to give incriminating statements to an agent of the prosecution. He declared that "nothing in the Sixth Amendment" or the "Framers' intent" suggested that the commencement of the adversary process disempowered the Government from seeking evidence from the defendant.

2. *Massiah* Is Violated When the Government Records an Informant's Meeting With an Indicted Defendant, Even When the Defendant Initiates the Meeting

In *Maine v. Moulton*, 474 U.S. 159, 106 S.Ct. 477, 88 L.Ed.2d 481 (1985), the Court held that the Sixth Amendment guarantees an indicted defendant the right to "rely on counsel as a medium between" the defendant and the state. Both *Massiah* and *Henry* established the state's "affirmative obligation not to act in a manner that circumvents" the right to counsel; neither precedent turned on the identity of the actor who "initiated" the encounter between the informant and the defendant. Therefore, the Court found that the Government's recording of a co-defendant informant's conversation in

(S., C. & H.) Crim.Proc. BLS—20

Moulton was a "knowing exploitation" of "an opportunity to confront the accused without counsel being present," even though the defendant initiated their meeting. In *Moulton,* the Government agent asked the co-defendant informant to wear a "body wire transmitter" to a meeting with the defendant, where the two men planned to discuss their defenses for the upcoming trial. The Court held that this Government act provided sufficient proof under *Henry* that the agent "must have known" that the informant was "likely to obtain incriminating statements" from the defendant in the absence of counsel. Therefore, the defendant's statements were held to be inadmissible, and his theft convictions were reversed. As in *Henry,* the Court ruled that "deliberate elicitation" could be found even though the officer had no specific intent to elicit information from the defendant. The officer is deemed to have intended the natural consequences of his planned activity.

3. **Use of a "Listening Post" Does Not Constitute Deliberate Elicitation**
In *Kuhlmann v. Wilson,* 477 U.S. 436, 106 S.Ct. 2616, 91 L.Ed.2d 364 (1986), the Court held that the Government does not violate *Massiah* when a jailhouse informant makes no effort to "stimulate conversations" about the crimes with which an incarcerated defendant is charged. In these circumstances, there is no "elicitation" barred by the Sixth Amendment. In *Kuhlmann,* the defendant was arraigned for robbery and murder, and the Government "planted" an informant in his cell to listen to his conversations. The defendant initiated a conversation where he admitted his presence at the robbery, but denied knowing the robbers. The informant responded by telling him that this explanation "didn't sound too good." Later the defendant changed the details of his story, and ultimately admitted guilt to the informant. The Court held that the informant's single remark did not suffice to change his "passive" posture, and that *Henry* was not violated. Therefore, the defendant's statements were held to be admissible, and his convictions for robbery and murder were affirmed.

a. **Rationale**
The Court reasoned that the primary concern of *Massiah* and its progeny is to prohibit attempts to extract information from defendants who have been formally charged, in the absence of counsel. Such activity constitutes an affirmative intrusion into the attorney-client relationship. However, when an informant takes no action, besides "merely listening," his activity may be "deliberate" but there is no "elicitation" of a confession, and no affirmative evasion of the defendant's right to the assistance of counsel. Justice Powell noted that a Sixth Amendment violation does not occur where the Government obtains a defendant's statements "by luck or happenstance" after the right to counsel has attached. Thus, the mere "reporting" of statements by an informant is not barred by the Sixth Amendment, whether the informant does so voluntarily, or because of a "prior arrangement" with the Government. Under *Henry,* the defendant must prove that "the police and their

informant took some action" that was deliberately designed to *elicit* incriminating statements.

b.   Applied to the Facts

On the facts of *Kuhlmann,* the Court found that no *Massiah* violation occurred. The agent instructed the informant to "listen" to the defendant, and to refrain from asking questions. The informant asked no questions, and listened to the defendant's "spontaneous" and "unsolicited" remarks. The informant's one remark, reacting to the defendant's initial story, did not transform their interaction into a situation where the "action" of the informant was designed to elicit further incriminating remarks. See also *United States v. York,* 933 F.2d 1343 (7th Cir.1991) (there was no elicitation of incriminating statements by the informant, and therefore no Sixth Amendment violation, where the informant simply responded with neutral comments when incriminating topics were brought up by the defendant; informants are not required to reveal their status by refusing to participate in the natural flow of prison conversation).

c.   Dissent

The three dissenters argued that *Kuhlmann* did not present the issue whether an informant could behave like a "listening post" without violating *Massiah.* They found *Kuhlmann* to be "virtually indistinguishable" from *Henry,* because the Government "intentionally created a situation in which it was foreseeable" that the defendant "would make incriminating statements without the assistance of counsel." They noted that *Henry* prohibited the circumvention of the right to counsel through "deliberate elicitation" of statements, and that under *Henry* it was irrelevant whether the informant asked "pointed questions" about the crime, or merely engaged in "general conversation" about it. It was also irrelevant in *Henry* that the Government agent told the informant not to ask questions, given the actual conduct of the informant. The dissenters concluded that the informant in *Kuhlmann* behaved like the one in *Henry,* because he "encouraged" the defendant to talk about the crime, by "conversing with him on the subject" over the course of several days. The informant even explicitly commented on the defendant's first exculpatory story, and told him that he had better come up with a better explanation. The Government's "intentional creation" of a *Henry* situation in *Kuhlmann* was also evidenced by the fact that the defendant was assigned to a cell that overlooked the scene of the crime, and the fact that the informant developed a "relationship of cellmate camaraderie" with the defendant. Based on all these circumstances, the dissenters maintained that the state's actions "had a sufficient nexus" with the defendant's confession to justify a finding of "deliberate elicitation."

4.   Defining the Scope of the Government's Agency Relationship With an Informant

If a private individual obtains information from an indicted defendant, and then unilaterally refers it to the Government, there is no Sixth Amendment violation. This is because there is no impermissible state action in obtaining the information. (See the analogous discussion of private searches in the section on the Fourth Amendment). However, if the private individual is acting as a state agent in obtaining information (such as the informant was in *Henry*), then the agent's activity is attributable to the Government. The Court in *Henry* and *Kuhlmann* did not describe the kind of Government relationship with an informant that makes it "accountable" for the informant's acts. In both cases, no question concerning the informant's status arose, because both informants entered into express agreements with a Government agent concerning their surveillance of the defendants.

Lower courts have found that an agency relationship may exist when an informant "at large" has been promised a reward for information about any inmate. See, e.g., *United States v. York*, 933 F.2d 1343 (7th Cir.1991) (jailhouse plant was a state agent as a matter of law when he conversed with the defendant; the mere fact that the state creates a market for information does not make every informant a state actor; however, if the state agrees in advance, implicitly or explicitly, that the informant will obtain information, then the informant is a state agent; it does not matter that the agency is not targeted toward a specific individual but rather to the prison population at large; nor does it matter that the state leaves it to the informant to decide how to proceed; the question is whether there is a prior agreement between the state and the informant; here there was, because the informant had been promised a reward for suitable information obtained from any source, and the informant was motivated by a concern to obtain that reward). Compare *United States v. Watson*, 894 F.2d 1345 (D.C.Cir.1990) (no agency relationship existed even though informant was in regular contact with the DEA, because he was only a private "entrepreneur"; therefore the fact that the informant was paid for his information *after* giving it does not indicate that he was acting as a state agent while obtaining the information).

D.   DELIBERATE ELICITATION AND CONTINUING INVESTIGATIONS

In *Maine v. Moulton*, 474 U.S. 159, 106 S.Ct. 477, 88 L.Ed.2d 481 (1985), the Court held that the Sixth Amendment was violated under *Massiah* when the Government asked an informant to record a meeting with his co-defendant, where the meeting was for the "express purpose" of discussing the charges pending against them. The Court rejected the Government's claim that because its investigation concerned "new" crimes that the defendant might be planning (i.e., killing witnesses to the charged crime), any statements that were obtained during such an investigation should be admissible in the trial for the crime with which he was originally charged. The Court found that *Massiah* prohibited the use of any statements that concerned the pending charges, and reversed the defendant's convictions for theft, because such statements were improperly admitted at his trial.

1. Rationale

The Court reasoned that it could not create an exception to the *Massiah* rule "whenever the police assert an alternative, legitimate reason for their surveillance" of an indicted defendant. Such an exception would invite police abuse in the form of "fabricated investigations" and create a risk of "evisceration" of *Massiah* rights. Justice Brennan, writing for the Court, observed that *Massiah* established a "sensible solution" for the problem of the Government's need to continue to investigate "the suspected criminal activities" of indicted defendants. That solution was to allow the evidence gained in these investigations to be used at a subsequent trial on the crimes that were uncharged at the time the statements were made. Statements pertaining to pending charges, however, are inadmissible when they are obtained in violation of *Massiah*—even if the purpose of the investigation was to obtain information about uncharged crimes.

2. Deliberate Elicitation Found From Likely Consequences

The State in *Moulton* argued that there was no Sixth Amendment violation, because the informant was instructed to obtain information only about crimes for which Moulton had not yet been charged. Moulton was charged with theft and the state received information of his intent to kill a witness. Officers sent Colson, Moulton's co-defendant who agreed to cooperate with the Government, to meet with Moulton and obtain information about the plan to kill witnesses. They instructed Colson only to talk about eliminating witnesses, not about the underlying theft charges. In the course of the conversation about eliminating witnesses, Colson led Moulton into talking about their theft activities, and it was these statements that were offered at Moulton's theft trial. The *Moulton* Court rejected the argument that deliberate elicitation could not be found because the officer instructed Colson to talk only about witnesses. The Court reasoned that the agents *should have known* that despite their instructions, a conversation between co-defendants about killing witnesses was likely to touch upon the underlying crime on which the witnesses were to testify. Justice Brennan noted that "direct proof of the State's knowledge will seldom be available," but that "proof that the State must have known that its agent was likely to obtain incriminating statements" suffices to establish a Sixth Amendment violation. Thus, as in *Henry*, the Court held that deliberate elicitation can be found even if there is no showing that officers affirmatively intended to obtain incriminating information; officers are deemed to intend the natural consequences of a plan that they deliberately set into motion.

3. Dissent

Chief Justice Burger dissented, in an opinion joined by Justices White and Rehnquist, and in part by Justice O'Connor. He argued that *Massiah*'s "deliberate elicitation" rule was intended to prohibit only "elicitation for the purpose of using" statements "against the defendant in connection with charges for which the Sixth Amendment right" had attached. In *Moulton*, by contrast, there was no "deliberate elicitation" in this sense, but only tape recording for "legitimate purposes not related to the gathering of evidence concerning the crime" for which the defendant had been indicted. Therefore, it could not be said that the officers in *Moulton* "planned an impermissible interference with the right to the assistance of counsel" under *Henry*.

E.   THE SIXTH AMENDMENT EXCLUSIONARY RULE

As previously discussed, the Fourth Amendment exclusionary rule is not constitutionally-mandated, and therefore its application is dependent on a cost/benefit analysis assessing the deterrent effect of the rule and the costs of exclusion. Similarly, the *Miranda* exclusionary rule is not constitutionally required, because the *Miranda* rules are considered prophylactic safeguards designed to overprotect the Fifth Amendment right. In contrast, if police activity violates the Due Process Clause, exclusion *is* constitutionally required, because Due Process limitations are clearly part of the Constitution, and because a violation of Due Process occurs *when the evidence is admitted at trial*. This distinguishes a Due Process violation from a Fourth Amendment violation, which occurs when the illegal search or seizure is conducted, and is thus completely separate from the later act of exclusion or admission of the evidence at trial.

The Supreme Court has not decided the constitutional status of the Sixth Amendment exclusionary rule, which operated to exclude the illegally obtained confessions in *Brewer, Henry,* and *Moulton*. This question is of some importance because if the Constitution requires the exclusion of evidence obtained in violation of the Sixth Amendment, then certain exceptions that have been applied to *Miranda*-defective confessions would not be applicable in the Sixth Amendment context. For example, there could be no "public safety" exception to the Sixth Amendment; nor could there be an impeachment exception; nor could there be an exception which would allow the fruits of Sixth Amendment violations to be admitted. Each of these exceptions to *Miranda* is based on the non-constitutional source of the *Miranda* exclusionary rule.

1.   **A Statement Obtained in Violation of *Michigan v. Jackson* May Be Used to Impeach a Defendant's Credibility at Trial**
In *Michigan v. Harvey,* 494 U.S. 344, 110 S.Ct. 1176, 108 L.Ed.2d 293 (1990), the Court held that the rule of *Harris v. New York*, 401 U.S. 222, 91 S.Ct. 643, 28 L.Ed.2d 1 (1971) (allowing the use of *Miranda*-defective statements to impeach the defendant at trial), should apply to evidence obtained in violation of *Michigan v. Jackson*, 475 U.S. 625, 106 S.Ct. 1404, 89 L.Ed.2d 631 (1986). The defendant in *Harvey* invoked his right to counsel at arraignment, thereby triggering the protection of *Jackson*. The police then violated *Jackson* by initiating an interview with him, where he received *Miranda* warnings, waived his rights, and made incriminating statements. His waiver may well

have been knowing and voluntary, but his statements were nonetheless excluded from the case-in-chief because they were obtained in violation of the bright-line *Edwards–Jackson* initiation requirement. But the Court held that while the *Jackson*-defective statements could not be used in the case-in-chief, they were nonetheless admissible to impeach the defendant when he testified at trial. The Court held that the *Jackson* rule was derived directly from *Edwards,* and represented only a transposition of the "prophylactic standards" of the *Miranda* doctrine into the Sixth Amendment context. Therefore, the *Harris* rule should also be transposed from the same *Miranda* template, and impeachment of the defendant's credibility with *Jackson*-defective statements should be allowed in *Harvey.*

a. Rationale

The Court reasoned that *Jackson's* "prophylactic rule" is no different from that of *Edwards,* for it is designed to ensure that only "voluntary, knowing, and intelligent" waivers of the Sixth Amendment right to counsel are made by defendants. The commencement of the adversarial process does not affect the purpose of the *Jackson* rule, so the rule does not implicate the "constitutional guarantee of the Sixth Amendment itself." Chief Justice Rehnquist asserted that the "roots" of *Jackson* "lie" in the *Miranda* decisions, and that *Jackson* "simply superimposed the Fifth Amendment analysis of *Edwards* onto the Sixth Amendment." The *Harris* rule held that the "prophylactic" *Miranda* protections were inapplicable in the impeachment process, because of the need to prevent the defendant's perjury. The Chief Justice observed that "there is no reason" for treating the "prophylactic" rule of *Jackson* any differently than other *Miranda*-based rules. He reasoned that there was only a "speculative possibility" that the prohibition of a prosecutor's use of a *Jackson*-defective statement for impeachment purposes would increase the deterrence of future *Jackson* violations by police. Sufficient deterrence would, as in *Harris,* be provided by exclusion of such a statement from the state's case-in-chief.

The Court rejected the defendant's argument that "postarraignment interrogations" necessarily implicate the Sixth Amendment. After the Sixth Amendment right to counsel attaches, a defendant is free to waive it under *Patterson v. Illinois,* 487 U.S. 285, 108 S.Ct. 2389, 101 L.Ed.2d 261 (1988). *Jackson's* rule required only that the "analysis" of the waiver issue should change after invocation, and that an *Edwards*-style prohibition on police-initiated questioning should attach. Like *Edwards, Jackson* renders "some otherwise valid waivers of constitutional rights invalid" after invocation; in neither case should the "shield" of this rule be "converted into a license for perjury."

b. Constitutional Status of Sixth Amendment Exclusionary Rule Left Open
The Court did not address the defendant's argument that the police conduct in *Harvey* violated the "core values" of the Sixth Amendment, or his argument that such a violation would make his statements inadmissible for impeachment purposes. The record concerning the defendant's waiver was insufficient for the Court to make an independent determination whether it was knowing and voluntary. Thus the Court decided that it could not "consider the admissibility for impeachment purposes of a voluntary statement obtained in the absence of a knowing and voluntary waiver of the right to counsel."

c. Dissent
Justice Stevens dissented, in an opinion joined by Justices Brennan, Marshall and Blackmun. Justice Stevens criticized the *Harvey* majority's characterization of *Jackson* as a "prophylactic" rule, and argued that it ignored the reasons behind the Sixth Amendment exclusionary rule's application in *Jackson.* Unlike the Fourth Amendment and *Miranda* exclusionary rules, the Sixth Amendment rule operates "as a necessary incident of the constitutional right itself." According to *Massiah,* a defendant's Sixth Amendment right is violated when statements that were "deliberately elicited" in counsel's absence are "used against him at his trial." Justice Stevens disagreed with the *Harvey* Court's supposition that no significant increase in deterrence of *Jackson* violations would be achieved by prohibiting a prosecutor's use of *Jackson*-defective statements for impeachment purposes. Once a charge is filed, an investigation "is often virtually complete," and police have no incentive to abide by *Jackson* in order to preserve the use of statements for a prosecution's case-in-chief. Thus, they have "everything to gain and nothing to lose" by violating *Jackson* in order to obtain impeachment material.

2. Does the Constitution Require Exclusion of a Confession Obtained in Violation of the Sixth Amendment?
In *Harvey,* the Court discussed, but did not decide whether the Sixth Amendment exclusionary rule is grounded in the Constitution. *Harvey* dealt with a prophylactic rule that was not itself required by the Sixth Amendment. Some lower courts have held that a confession obtained in violation of *Massiah* cannot be used for impeachment purposes, because the Sixth Amendment's exclusionary rule is constitutionally based. See, e.g., *United States v. Brown,* 699 F.2d 585 (2d Cir.1983). In the view of these courts, the violation of the Sixth Amendment occurs when the incriminating information is admitted at trial. It is at that point that the right to counsel is effectively vitiated, because it is at that point that counsel's role in effectively defending the defendant is impaired. This is in contrast to the Fourth Amendment, where the violation occurs at the time of the illegal search, not at the time the evidence is admitted at trial. See *Withrow v.*

Williams, __ U.S. __, 113 S.Ct. 1745, 123 L.Ed.2d 407 (1993) (distinguishing Fourth Amendment violations from violations of fundamental trial rights, on the ground that "the exclusion of evidence at trial can do nothing to remedy the completed and wholly extrajudicial Fourth Amendment violation").

Other courts also have required exclusion of the fruits of a Sixth Amendment-defective confession at trial. See, e.g., *United States v. Kimball,* 884 F.2d 1274 (9th Cir.1989). These courts distinguish Sixth Amendment violations from *Miranda* violations, as to which the fruit of the poisonous tree doctrine does not apply, on the ground that the *Miranda* safeguards are not constitutionally required.

VI. PROCEDURES REGARDING CONFESSIONS

A. PROCEDURES AT TRIAL

1. The Judge, Not the Jury, Must Determine the "Voluntariness" of a Confession

In *Jackson v. Denno,* 378 U.S. 368, 84 S.Ct. 1774, 12 L.Ed.2d 908 (1964), the Court held that a jury could not be permitted to determine the legality of a confession under the "voluntariness" standard. Instead, a defendant is entitled to a ruling from a judge that a confession is "voluntary," before that confession may be admitted at trial.

a. Rationale

The Court held that jury determinations of voluntariness suffer from two defects, and that the only correction for these defects is to require that such determinations must be made by a judge. First, when a jury makes an assessment of voluntariness, the evidence of the confession will inject "irrelevant and impermissible" consideration of the potential truthfulness of the confession into the jury's legal judgment. This will happen because laypeople are likely to have difficulty separating the issue of the confession's "voluntariness" from the issue of its truthfulness. Second, even if a jury determines that a confession was involuntary, it may be influenced by the confession in its determination of guilt or innocence.

b. *Jackson* Hearing

The Court in *Jackson* determined that a defendant is entitled to request a hearing to determine the voluntariness of a confession before trial. The Court observed that at this hearing, the judge must rule on the voluntariness of the confession, and must not consider the "reliability" of the confession in making a legal judgment concerning its admissibility under Due Process doctrine. This is because a confession which was obtained involuntarily must be excluded under the Due Process Clause, even if it is reliable. See *Doby v. South Carolina Department of*

Corrections, 741 F.2d 76 (4th Cir.1984) (trial court impermissibly relied upon the truth of the confession in deciding whether it was voluntary). Also, the defendant who testifies at a *Jackson* hearing does so without prejudice to his privilege not to take the stand at trial. *United States v. Dollard,* 780 F.2d 1118 (4th Cir.1985).

2. Due Process Requires That a Defendant Be Allowed to Offer Evidence at Trial That Attacks the Weight of a Confession That Is Admitted as Voluntary

In *Crane v. Kentucky,* 476 U.S. 683, 106 S.Ct. 2142, 90 L.Ed.2d 636 (1986), the Court held that "elementary notions of Due Process" require that a defendant be allowed to attack the weight of his confession at trial, if it is held to be voluntary and admitted at trial. To prohibit the defendant from doing so would deny him the right to be heard concerning the probative value of the Government's evidence. Thus, the voluntariness of the confession is a question distinct from the weight which the jury ought to give it.

3. The Government Must Prove the Voluntariness of a Confession by a Preponderance of the Evidence

In *Lego v. Twomey,* 404 U.S. 477, 92 S.Ct. 619, 30 L.Ed.2d 618 (1972), the Court rejected the argument that the prosecution should have to prove that a confession was voluntary "beyond a reasonable doubt" in order for it to be admissible at trial. Instead, the Court endorsed the "preponderance of the evidence" standard as the appropriate one for determining the voluntariness of a confession.

a. Rationale

The Court reasoned that the "beyond a reasonable doubt" standard was not a necessary element of a "voluntariness" inquiry, because the question of the voluntariness of a confession is independent from the defendant's guilt. See *In re Winship,* 397 U.S. 358, 90 S.Ct. 1068, 25 L.Ed.2d 368 (1970) (requiring that proof "of every fact necessary to constitute the crime" with which a defendant is charged must be demonstrated "beyond a reasonable doubt"). Justice White noted that the beyond a reasonable doubt standard mandated by *Winship* as to the elements of a crime was required in order to "ensure against unjust convictions by giving substance to the presumption of innocence." Unlike the factual issue of guilt in *Winship,* the issue of "voluntariness" is unrelated to the reliability of a verdict, as the "reliability" of a confession is not part of the "voluntariness" inquiry. Therefore, a guilty verdict is not "less reliable" simply because "the admissibility of a confession is determined by a less stringent standard."

b. Dissent

Justice Brennan dissented, in an opinion joined by Justices Douglas and Marshall, and argued that the Court's adoption of the "preponderance" standard did not provide sufficient protection to ensure that "involuntary" confessions were excluded from criminal trials.

4. **Waiver of *Miranda* Rights Determined by Preponderance Standard**
In *Colorado v. Connelly,* 479 U.S. 157, 107 S.Ct. 515, 93 L.Ed.2d 473 (1986), the Court adopted the *Lego* standard as the appropriate burden for the state in cases where the prosecution must show that a proper waiver of *Miranda* rights was obtained. See discussion of *Connelly, supra.*

B. CONFESSIONS AND HABEAS CORPUS

1. **The Doctrine of *Stone v. Powell* Does Not Apply to Federal Habeas Review of *Miranda* Violations**
In *Withrow v. Williams,* ___ U.S. ___, 113 S.Ct. 1745, 123 L.Ed.2d 407 (1993), the Court held that a defendant is entitled to habeas relief when a violation of *Miranda* is found, and rejected the state's argument that the existence of a "full and fair" opportunity to litigate the *Miranda* claim in state courts should limit Federal court review. The Court found that *Miranda* violations differ in crucial respects from Fourth Amendment violations, and held that the *Stone* doctrine is inapplicable in *Miranda* cases. See *Stone v. Powell,* 428 U.S. 465, 96 S.Ct. 3037, 49 L.Ed.2d 1067 (1976). See the discussion of *Stone* in the section on the Fourth Amendment exclusionary rule.

*

VIII

CONSTITUTIONAL LIMITS ON IDENTIFICATION EVIDENCE

Analysis

I. INTRODUCTION

This chapter examines the dangers associated with identification evidence, and the safeguards that the Supreme Court has fashioned to assure that witness error will not irreparably taint criminal litigation. Although both courts and commentators believe eyewitness testimony to be frequently questionable and susceptible to "post-experience suggestion", juries often find the probative value of such evidence at trial to be extremely high. In order to protect a suspect's right to a fair trial, the Supreme Court has imposed constitutional limitations on admissibility of identifications by witnesses.

II. POST–INDICTMENT IDENTIFICATIONS

The Court decided in 1967 that identification after indictment, or an equivalent formal proceeding, triggers a defendant's Sixth Amendment right to counsel. *United States v. Wade,* 388 U.S. 218, 87 S.Ct. 1926, 18 L.Ed.2d 1149 (1967); see also *Gilbert v. California,* 388 U.S. 263, 87 S.Ct. 1951, 18 L.Ed.2d 1178 (1967).

A. THE *WADE–GILBERT* RULE

In *Wade,* the defendant was identified in court by two bank employees present during a bank robbery. The witnesses had picked out Wade in a line-up absent counsel seven months following the incident. The Court found that a post-indictment line-up conducted without notice to and in the absence of defense counsel, and without a valid waiver of such counsel, was unconstitutional.

1. Critical Pre-trial Stage

Although the post-indictment line-up at issue in *Wade* and *Gilbert* took place before trial, the Court held that in light of modern criminal procedures, the Sixth Amendment right to counsel applies to *critical pre-trial stages* as well as at trial. "Critical stage" analysis developed in earlier cases such as *Massiah v. United States,* 377 U.S. 201, 84 S.Ct. 1199, 12 L.Ed.2d 246 (1964), where the suspect, after being arraigned and released on bail, was surreptitiously monitored in conversation with an accomplice who was working with the police. The Court held that post-indictment conversation of the defendant deliberately elicited by the police in absence of counsel violated the Sixth Amendment guarantee, and must be excluded from trial. In both *Massiah* and *Wade,* the Court was concerned that a defendant's right to a fair trial would be compromised if the prosecution could bring forward such evidence obtained absent counsel. The Court reasoned that the right to counsel at trial means the right to *effective* counsel. In order to guarantee that counsel is effective at trial, the Court decided that counsel must be present at these critical pre-trial stages to avoid any prejudice arising from particular confrontations during the prosecution's gathering of evidence. Although the Government characterized the line-up as a "mere preparatory step" in the gathering of evidence—similar to analyzing blood and clothing found at a crime scene—the Court found identification evidence to be "pecularily riddled with innumerable dangers and variable factors which might seriously, even crucially, derogate from a fair trial." The Court noted that "once a witness has picked out the accused at [a] lineup, he is not likely to go back on his word later on, so that in practice the issue of identity may * * * for all practical purposes be determined there and then, before the trial."

2. Observer Status of Counsel

While the *Wade* Court held that the presence of defense counsel was required at post-indictment line-ups, it was inspecific about the role that counsel would play at the line-up. Subsequent cases, however, have held that counsel is present in a "passive" observer status. Although "passive", the role of counsel is considered critical in reconstructing the line-up at trial. The defendant's presence and observations during this process are only minimally helpful in determining whether prejudicial or suggestive procedures were used during his line-up. The defendant is undergoing an emotionally charged experience, possibly behind bright lights or a one-way mirror, without any schooling in the detection of suggestive influences by the police. Furthermore, the jury is apt to regard defendant's statements about the pre-trial line-up as self-serving, if, indeed, the defendant chooses to take the stand and possibly open himself up to cross-examination regarding prior convictions. The attorney, on the other hand, is generally more skilled in the detection of suggestive influences, both through experience and familiarity with case law. The attorney observes the questioning of witnesses by police during the line-up. Notes and observations of the proceedings allow the attorney to *effectively cross-examine the identification witnesses* at trial, and to demonstrate any prejudicial or suggestive conduct, intentional or not, present during the pre-trial line-up.

3. Substitute Counsel

The *Wade* majority mentioned in dictum that substitute counsel could satisfy the requirement of counsel's presence at the line-up. However, counsel is not a sufficient "substitute" if he is at the line-up representing the defendant's accomplice. See *United States ex rel. Burton v. Cuyler*, 439 F.Supp. 1173 (E.D.Pa.1977).

B. "PER SE" EXCLUSION

In *Wade,* the prosecutor had not elicited the pretrial identification in the Government's case-in-chief. It was brought out by defense counsel. Thus, the *Wade* decision only involved the question of whether the in-court identification upon which the Government relied was tainted by the line-up. In *Gilbert,* a companion case, the Court faced the question of whether a post-indictment, pre-trial identification in the absence of counsel could be used as evidence in the prosecution's case-in-chief. The Court adopted a "per se" rule of exclusion as a remedy for post-indictment out-of-court identifications that take place absent counsel: exclusion was required even if the state could show that the identification was in fact reliable. The Court, concerned about the consequences at trial of improper identification procedures, held that only the extreme sanction of per se exclusion would effectively deter police violations of the defendant's constitutional rights during a critical pre-trial stage. As a result, this exclusion applies even if the line-up was conducted so scrupulously that counsel's presence would be (theoretically) meaningless. The evidence from such line-ups is excluded whether or not there is a question of improper police procedure. See *Frisco v. Blackburn*, 782 F.2d 1353 (5th Cir.1986) (if counsel was not present at a line-up conducted after a preliminary hearing, then evidence of the identification is automatically excluded and "the state is not entitled to an opportunity to show that the testimony had an independent source").

1. In–Court Identification and Independent Source

However, although evidence regarding the out-of-court identification at a line-up conducted without counsel is excluded from trial, it does not automatically follow that an *in-court identification* by the same witness is excluded as well. The *Wade* Court held that the in-court identification would be excluded as well if it was *tainted* by the previous, illegal line-up. The Court reasoned that the mere exclusion of an illegal pre-trial identification would be an insufficient protection of the right to counsel if the prosecution could merely call the witness to the stand to make an in-court identification which was derived from the illegal line-up. The Court noted that witnesses rarely change their mind once they have identified a suspect. On the other hand, it is not *necessarily* true that the in-court identification stems directly from the excluded out-of-court line-up or, in other words, that the in-court identification is "fruit" of the "poisonous" pre-trial procedure. The Court held that the in-court identification would be admissible if it stemmed not from exploitation of the out-of-court identification but, instead, from an independent source "sufficiently distinguishable to be purged of the primary taint." Thus, the prosecution must prove that, under the totality of circumstances, the in-court identification was not a result of the improper pre-trial line-up. See *McKinon v. Wainwright*, 705 F.2d 419 (11th Cir.1983) (where the illegal pre-trial identification is not itself admitted at trial, "the at-trial identification constitutes reversible error only if it is based on, influenced by, or tainted from the earlier unconstitutional identification").

2. Relevant Factors

Certain factors are relevant to determine whether an in-court identification is based on a source independent from an illegal pre-trial identification. The independent source would of course be the witness' view of the suspect at the time of the crime, or at some time other than during the illegal line-up. The question, then, is whether the witness' in-court identification stems from a different opportunity to view the suspect, or rather whether it stems from the illegal line-up. Some relevant factors considered under the Court's test are: the extent of the *prior opportunity to view* the defendant other than at the illegal line-up; discrepancies, if any, between the witness' description of the suspect before the line-up was conducted, and the defendant's actual appearance; the *certainty* of the witness' identification at the line-up or, conversely, the witness' failure to identify the defendant on prior occasions; the *lapse of time* between the initial opportunity to view the perpetrator and the line-up identification; and the *degree of suggestiveness* employed in the tainted pre-trial line-up.

Example: Suppose that a kidnap victim escapes from his captor after three months in captivity. The captor is placed in a line-up, where the victim identifies him certainly and immediately as the perpetrator. However, defense counsel was not present at the line-up. This means that the pre-trial identification is excluded. However, the victim may permissibly identify the captor at trial, because the identification stems from a source clearly independent from the illegal line-up; the identification is based on the long-term, close-quarters captivity. See *McKinon v. Wainwright,* 705 F.2d 419 (11th Cir.1983) (at-trial identification admissible where the witness had known the defendant long before the crime and had spent several hours with him on the day of the crime).

3. Dissent
The judges dissenting in both *Wade* and *Gilbert* were concerned with the far-reaching effects of such a broad prophylactic rule of per se exclusion. Without concrete proof of widespread, improper police practices, the dissent believed the majority was basing its exclusion of relevant identification evidence on "pure speculation". The dissenters argued that the constitutional right to counsel should not be "dependent on judges' vague and transitory notions of fairness and their equally transitory * * * assessment of the risk that * * * counsel's absence might derogate from [a defendant's] right to a fair trial." They contended that the risk of unreliable identifications could be adequately regulated by allowing the defense to introduce the facts and circumstances of pre-trial line-ups in order to impeach the credibility of in-court identifications.

III. PRE–INDICTMENT IDENTIFICATIONS

The line-ups that took place in *Wade* and *Gilbert* were post-indictment procedures. Although the Court did not emphasize the timing of the line-ups in these cases, in subsequent cases it refused to extend the *Wade–Gilbert* exclusionary rule to counsel-free out-of-court identifications that occur prior to indictment or formal charge. The Court drew the line between pre- and post-formal charges in *Kirby v. Illinois,* 406 U.S. 682, 92 S.Ct. 1877, 32 L.Ed.2d 411 (1972).

A. *KIRBY*
In *Kirby,* a witness identified two suspects at a police station show-up. The show-up occurred before the suspects had been formally charged with the crime;

counsel was not present during the identification. The witness then testified at trial both to the station house show-up and to identify the men in-court. The Court held the testimony admissible, declaring that the Sixth Amendment right to counsel applied only to "criminal prosecutions" and thus was triggered only after formal adversarial proceedings had begun against the defendant.

1. Rationale

The Court stated that it would not transform a "routine police investigation" into an "absolute constitutional guarantee", reasoning that the "initiation of judicial criminal proceedings is far from a mere formalism. It is only then that the government has committed itself to prosecute, and only then that the adverse positions of government and defendant have solidified." Since the Sixth Amendment by its terms applies only to "criminal prosecutions," it follows that the Sixth Amendment right to counsel applied in *Wade* and *Gilbert* could only apply after a criminal prosecution has begun; and it is only when a formal charge has been filed that the adversary process—as opposed to the investigatory process—can be deemed to have begun.

2. Adversarial Proceedings

The Court in *Kirby* distinguished investigatorial proceedings from adversarial proceedings. It is only after the adversary process has begun that there is a criminal prosecution at which the right of counsel can apply. Such proceedings are begun when the state formally accuses the defendant of having committed the crime. This is generally done through *indictment, arraignment, preliminary hearing, or information*. Thus, if a line-up is conducted after these events, *Wade* will apply. For criminal proceedings brought by the states, the Court looks to state law to determine when criminal proceedings have commenced. See *Meadows v. Kuhlmann*, 812 F.2d 72 (2d Cir.1987) (line-up held after filing of formal complaint in New York is governed by *Wade* rule).

3. Dissent

The dissenting judges in *Kirby* stressed that while the identifications in *Wade* and *Gilbert* occurred after the filing of formal charges, neither decision relied on this fact as in any way relevant. Rather, the dissent saw those holdings as protections for the basic right to a fair trial from the inherent suggestibility of pre-trial identifications—regardless of when those identifications might have been made. The dissenters argued that the "initiation of adversary judicial criminal proceedings" was "completely irrelevant" to the question of whether a defendant would be afforded effective assistance of counsel at his trial.

B. APPLICATION OF THE SIXTH AMENDMENT RIGHT TO COUNSEL AFTER *KIRBY*

The *Kirby* Court was concerned about extending the *Wade* rationale into "routine police investigations". Many identifications are made on the street only minutes after the event. Application of the *Wade* rule in these circumstances would obviously create problems; the delay resulting from waiting for counsel to arrive may perversely decrease the reliability of the identification due to the fading memory of witnesses.

It should be noted that the vast majority of identification procedures are conducted before a formal charge has been filed. Indeed, most are conducted to obtain evidence with which to bring a formal charge. Thus, the *Kirby* decision significantly reduced the number of cases to which *Wade's* exclusionary rule would apply.

1.   Delaying Indictment

Although the *Kirby* Court stated that *Wade* would apply only after formal proceedings had been instigated against the defendant, courts have held that if adversary proceedings, such as the filing of an indictment, are *"deliberately delayed"* in order to evade the *Wade* rule, the resulting identification will be invalidated. See *United States ex rel. Burbank v. Warden,* 535 F.2d 361 (7th Cir.1976). However, it is quite difficult to prove that an indictment was deliberately delayed. See *United States ex rel. Hall v. Lane,* 804 F.2d 79 (7th Cir.1986) (no evidence that delay was caused by bad faith).

2.   Charge–Specific

Even after a defendant has been formerly charged, the *Wade* exclusionary rule only applies to charges included in the formal charge. It is permissible to hold a counsel-free line-up for an indicted defendant as to a different charge, since being indicted on one charge is not a "criminal prosecution" as to any other. See e.g., *United States ex rel. Hall v. Lane,* 804 F.2d 79 (7th Cir.1986) ("The fact that appellant was in custody for an unrelated offense at the time of the line-up has no bearing on [the right to counsel] since the government had not committed itself to prosecute appellant for this offense at the time of the line-up.").

C.   PHOTOGRAPHIC IDENTIFICATION

In *United States v. Ash,* 413 U.S. 300, 93 S.Ct. 2568, 37 L.Ed.2d 619 (1973), the Court further restricted the *Wade* exclusionary rule, and held that a defendant has *no right to counsel at a photographic identification* conducted either pre- or post-indictment.

1.   Rationale

The Court distinguished *Wade* by noting that photo displays do not require the actual presence of the defendant, and concluded that the presence of counsel was unnecessary to protect the defendant from an adversarial confrontation. The Court saw photo displays as a mere preparatory step in the gathering of evidence where the defense counsel had an "equal ability * * * to seek and interview witnesses himself." Justice Stewart, concurring in the result, concluded that "a photographic identification is quite different from a line-up, for there are substantially fewer possibilities of impermissible suggestion when photographs are used, and those unfair influences can be readily reconstructed at trial."

2. Dissent

The three dissenting judges argued that the right to counsel issue should not turn on whether photographic identifications included the corporeal presence of the defendant but, instead, whether exclusion of defense counsel at such displays could result in a denial of effective assistance of counsel for the defendant at trial. The dissenters believed that the same "inherent suggestibility" of pre-trial line-ups existed in photographic identifications, and as both the defendant and defense counsel were not present during the displays, there was even "less likelihood that irregularities in the procedure [would] ever come to light."

3. Video Identifications

The lower courts have held that *Ash* and not *Wade* applies to post-charge video identifications. They reason that the identification of a suspect on a video tape is more like a photo display than an actual line-up, and that, as in *Ash,* the defendant is not physically present, so there is no adversarial confrontation requiring counsel's assistance. See *United States v. Amrine,* 724 F.2d 84 (8th Cir.1983).

IV. DUE PROCESS LIMITATIONS ON SUGGESTIVE IDENTIFICATIONS

The Court in *Kirby* took pains to note that, by holding that the right to counsel was inapplicable to pre-charge identifications, it had not freed such identifications from all constitutional scrutiny. Where the Sixth Amendment right to counsel does not apply to an identification procedure, the identification must still satisfy the requirements of the Due Process Clause. The Court has held that the Due Process Clause requires exclusion of evidence of an identification if *police suggestiveness created a substantial risk of mistaken identification*. See *Stovall v. Denno,* 388 U.S. 293, 87 S.Ct. 1967, 18 L.Ed.2d 1199 (1967) (applying Due Process standards to an identification not controlled by *Wade*). The Court has reasoned that it is fundamentally unfair to convict a defendant on the basis of unreliable identifications that are manufactured by police suggestiveness.

A. TWO–FACTOR TEST

The Court has stressed that the defendant has the burden of proving a due process violation. This burden is satisfied only if the defendant can prove two independent factors. First, the defendant must show that the identification procedure was *impermissibly suggestive*. If so, the defendant must then show the identification was *unreliable* under the *totality of circumstances*. See *Foster v. California,* 394 U.S. 440, 89 S.Ct. 1127, 22 L.Ed.2d 402 (1969) (one-on-one show-up combined with unduly suggestive line-ups render Government's identification procedures so impermissibly suggestive as to create a substantial risk of mistaken identification; witness was uncertain about the identification and only got a fleeting glimpse of the perpetrator at the time of the crime).

1. Exigent Circumstances

The Supreme Court has held that exigent or extraordinary circumstances allow for "permissible" suggestiveness. In other words, the Court has held that certain circumstances could make suggestive police procedures necessary and, thus, permissible. One example of such a case is *Stovall v. Denno,* 388 U.S. 293, 87 S.Ct. 1967, 18 L.Ed.2d 1199 (1967). In *Stovall,* a vicious attack upon a married couple resulted in the death of the husband, and the hospitalization of the wife who had been stabbed eleven times. Due to the witness' serious injuries and proposed surgical procedure, a suspect in the attack was brought to the hospital for a one-on-one show-up. The Court held that the show-up procedure, while suggestive, was permissible due to the near-death condition of the witness. Indeed, the Court opinion called attention to the flip-side of such suggestive confrontations by pointing out that the witness "was the only person in the world who could possibly *exonerate* Stovall."

a. Rarely Applied Exception

Although the Government occasionally argues that there is a legitimate excuse for employing a suggestive procedure, the courts rarely find the circumstances so exigent as to allow the state to conduct a suggestive identification. See *Neil v. Biggers,* 409 U.S. 188, 93 S.Ct. 375, 34 L.Ed.2d 401 (1972) (argument that one-on-one show-up was necessary due to defendant's "unusual physical description" was rejected; but evidence ultimately found admissible as reliable under the totality of circumstances).

2. The Linchpin of Reliability

Even if the police have employed unnecessarily suggestive police procedures, it does not necessarily follow that the resulting identification is unreliable. The identification may be reliable *despite* police suggestiveness. See *Manson v. Brathwaite,* 432 U.S. 98, 97 S.Ct. 2243, 53 L.Ed.2d 140 (1977) (identification of a photo, without an array of similar photos, was impermissibly suggestive and yet the identification was reliable because the witness would have made the same identification even if there had been an array). Thus, *suggestive procedures*—one-on-one show-ups, distinctively standing out in line-ups (i.e. tallest, heaviest, only black defendant in line), individual or repetitive pictures—are considered in light of all the circumstances in determining whether an independent source exists for a reliable identification.

**B.   RELEVANT FACTORS IN DETERMINING THE RELIABILITY OF AN
IDENTIFICATION**

Where impermissibly suggestive police practices have been used, an identification
will still be admissible if it would have been made *despite* the police
suggestiveness. See *Manson v. Brathwaite,* 432 U.S. 98, 97 S.Ct. 2243, 53 L.Ed.2d
140 (1977) (rejecting the argument that an identification should be automatically
excluded where the police have employed impermissibly suggestive procedures). An
identification will be made despite police suggestiveness where the witness had a
"picture" of the perpetrator in his mind *before* the identification, and this picture
was so firmly established that it was unaffected by the attempts of the police to
put their own "picture" of the perpetrator in the witness' mind, through the use
of suggestive tactics. In other words, if the witness has an *independent source* for
the identification outside the suggestive police tactics, then these tactics have not
caused an unreliable identification, and exclusion is unwarranted. See *Manson* (in
cases where the identification is reliable despite an unnecessarily suggestive
identification procedure, exclusion of the identification is "a Draconian sanction").

Thus, the test for whether an identification is admissible despite police
suggestiveness is the same as the test applied for whether an in-court
identification is admissible despite the fact that the police have conducted a
post-indictment line-up without the presence of counsel. In either case, *if the
illegal police activity had no effect on the proffered identification, then the
identification is admissible.* The factors used to determine whether impermissible
suggestiveness affected the resulting identification were set forth by the Court in
Manson:

1.   Degree of Police Suggestiveness

The more suggestive the police procedure, the more likely it is to have an
effect on the resulting identification. For example, a one-on-one show-up is
much more likely to have an effect on the witness than is a photo array
where the photos may be dissimilar, but where the witness is at least
presented with more than a single option.

2.   Opportunity to View

If the witness had a substantial opportunity to view the suspect before the
identification—for example by getting a good look at the perpetrator when
the crime was committed—then the witness will have a stronger picture in
his mind; and this picture will be less subject to change through police
suggestiveness than would a vague picture obtained with a poor opportunity
to view the suspect. For example, if the witness was the store clerk in a
robbery, and looked straight at the robber for five minutes in a well-lighted
store, then the witness' identification is less likely to be affected by police
suggestiveness than if she had been outside the store and got a fleeting
glimpse of the robber from 40 feet away in an unlighted parking lot.

3.   Degree of Attention

The opportunity to view the perpetrator before the identification means little if the witness made little of that opportunity because her attention was focussed on other matters. If the witness paid little attention to the perpetrator, then the picture of that person in her mind is a vague one, subject to the effects of police suggestiveness.

4.   Accuracy of the Description

Ordinarily, a witness describes the perpetrator before an identification is made. The correlation between the description and the ultimate identification, or the lack thereof, can tend to show the effect of police suggestiveness on the identification. For example, if the witness describes the perpetrator as six feet tall, 200 pounds, and then picks a person 5' 6" and 150 pounds after a one-on-one show-up, there is strong evidence that the witness was affected by police suggestiveness. Conversely, if the witness describes a unique physical characteristic before the identification (e.g. a facial scar), and the witness picks a person with that characteristic in a one-on-one show-up, then there is strong evidence that the police suggestiveness had no effect on the identification. Finally, if the pre-identification description is overly general (e.g. a tall man with light complexion), then there is ample room for the police to fill in the details of that picture through police suggestiveness; but this is not as strong a possibility if the pre-identification description of the witness is finely detailed.

5.   Level of Certainty

The Supreme Court has indulged the presumption that the more certain the witness is when making the identification, the more likely it is that the identification proceeds from a source independent from the police suggestiveness. Compare *Manson* (witness' "positive assurance" that the photo was that of the perpetrator indicated that the identification was unaffected by police suggestiveness), with *Foster v. California,* 394 U.S. 440, 89 S.Ct. 1127, 22 L.Ed.2d 402 (1969) (Due Process violated where the witness remained uncertain that the defendant was the perpetrator even after a one-on-one show-up). Some courts are not as confident that the witness' certainty is an indication that the identification is unaffected by police suggestiveness. See *Rodriguez v. Young,* 906 F.2d 1153 (7th Cir.1990) (court views reliability of "certainty" factor with skepticism as it might simply reflect the "corrupting effect of the suggestive procedures themselves").

6.   The Time Between the Pre-identification Opportunity to View and the Identification Itself

It is well-accepted that memory of a person or event fades over time. Thus, the witness' mental "picture" of the perpetrator becomes more vague and fuzzy as time passes—and more susceptible to suggestive police influences. Therefore, an identification made shortly after the witness' original opportunity to view the suspect is more likely to be free from the taint of police suggestiveness than an identification made a long time thereafter. See *Manson* (photographic identification made two days after the crime is unaffected by police suggestiveness: "We do not have here the passage of weeks or months between the crime and the viewing of the photograph.").

C. TOTALITY OF THE CIRCUMSTANCES

The determinative question under the Due Process Clause is whether unnecessary police suggestiveness has created a substantial risk of mistaken identification. Thus, as the Court in *Manson* stated, "reliability is the linchpin in determining the admissibility of identification testimony." Reliability of the identification is determined by a totality of circumstances test, in which all of the above factors are relevant, and *none are dispositive*.

Example: In *Neil v. Biggers,* 409 U.S. 188, 93 S.Ct. 375, 34 L.Ed.2d 401 (1972), the victim of a rape identified the defendant in a one-on-one show-up conducted more than seven months after the crime. Obviously, the time between the crime and the identification, as well as the inherently suggestive nature of a one-on-one show-up, were factors which cut against the reliability of the identification. But the Court concluded that "the identification was reliable even though the confrontation procedure was suggestive." The Court relied on the following factors: the witness had refused to identify others who had been placed before her in show-ups and line-ups, which indicated that she was not very susceptible to police suggestiveness; she was with her assailant for a half-hour at the time of the crime; she faced him directly and intimately at that time in a well-lighted environment; she was "no casual observer" but rather quite attendant to the circumstances; her description of the perpetrator before the identification "might not have satisfied Proust but was more than ordinarily thorough"; she had no doubt at the time of identification that the defendant was the perpetrator; and the problem of faded memory was alleviated to some extent by the fact that she stated that there was something about the perpetrator's face that she could never forget.

1. If Pre-trial Identification Is Excluded, At–Trial Identification Is Excluded as Well

If the pre-trial identification is unreliable because it is caused by police suggestiveness, then the Due Process Clause requires that it be excluded from trial. *Foster v. California, supra.* It also follows that the taint of police suggestiveness extends to any at-trial identification. If the prior identification was caused by police suggestiveness, there can by definition be no independent legal source for the in-court identification. If there were such a source, it would have served to admit the pre-trial identification as well. See *Dispensa v. Lynaugh,* 847 F.2d 211 (5th Cir.1988) (identification caused by police suggestiveness requires exclusion of both pre-trial and at-trial identifications).

D. EXAMPLES OF DUE PROCESS IDENTIFICATION CASES
1. Identifications Excluded

It is the rare instance where an identification evidence will be excluded on the ground that it is tainted by impermissible police suggestiveness. One example is *Foster v. California,* 394 U.S. 440, 89 S.Ct. 1127, 22 L.Ed.2d 402 (1969). In *Foster,* an eyewitness was shown a three person line-up where the defendant, standing in the middle and the only person dressed similarly to the alleged perpetrator, was approximately half a foot taller than the two other men. The witness was unable to positively identify the defendant. Foster was then brought into an office for a one-on-one show-up with the witness, who still could not make a positive identification. One week later, the witness was brought in for a second line-up where Foster was the only suspect that remained from the previous week. At this point, the witness positively identified Foster. At trial, the witness testified to his pre-trial identification and also made an in-court identification. However, the Supreme Court found the "suggestive elements in this identification procedure made it all but inevitable that [the witness] would identify petitioner whether or not he was in fact the man," and that the procedure "so undermined the reliability of the eyewitness identification as to violate due process."

Another rare instance is *United States v. Watkins,* 741 F.2d 692 (5th Cir.1984), where the court held that the witness' opportunity to view the suspect was too minimal to support a source for the identification independent from the impermissible police suggestiveness. In *Watkins,* a witness to a post office robbery identified the defendant at trial based on a show-up where the defendant was displayed to witnesses while handcuffed in a patrol car. Although the show-up occurred shortly after the robbery, the witness had very little basis for identifying the defendant. Through much of the robbery, the witness was lying face down with a gun pointed at her head by an assailant wearing a ski mask. The court held that under the totality of the circumstances, there was a substantial likelihood of misidentification.

2. Identifications Found Reliable Under the Totality of Circumstances

United States ex rel. Hudson v. Brierton, 699 F.2d 917 (7th Cir.1983), provides a typical approach to admitting identification testimony under the Due Process Clause. In *Hudson,* a witness engaged armed bank robbers in a high speed automobile chase, at one point coming within about half a foot of the robbers' car. Although the witness eventually lost the robbers, he was subsequently called down to the police station and identified the defendant, who was handcuffed and locked in a jail cell. In assessing the reliability of this identification, the court balanced factors such as the witness' close proximity to the robbers' car versus the distraction of being fired upon at close range while speeding along a highway. While noting the highly suggestive identification procedure, the court concluded that the character of the witness was such as to make it extremely unlikely he "would be affected * * * in light of his serious attitude and diligence with respect to the episode." Like the witness in *Biggers,* the witness in *Hudson* had demonstrated that he was not the type of person to be affected by police suggestiveness.

IX

THE RIGHT TO COUNSEL

Analysis

I. TWO SOURCES FOR COUNSEL RIGHTS: THE SIXTH AMENDMENT AND THE FOURTEENTH AMENDMENT

The Sixth Amendment provides that "[i]n all criminal prosecutions, the accused shall enjoy the right * * * to have the Assistance of Counsel for his defence." The Sixth Amendment applies directly to the Federal Government, and applies to the states through the incorporation doctrine of the Fourteenth Amendment. See *Gideon v. Wainwright,* 372 U.S. 335, 83 S.Ct. 792, 9 L.Ed.2d 799 (1963). However, the scope of the right to counsel is more limited in state courts than in Federal courts. Compare *Johnson v. Zerbst,* 304 U.S. 458, 58 S.Ct. 1019, 82 L.Ed. 1461 (1938) (providing for the right to counsel in all Federal criminal trials) with *Scott v. Illinois,* 440 U.S. 367, 99 S.Ct. 1158, 59 L.Ed.2d 383 (1979) (applying the right to counsel in state trials only where defendants receive jail sentences).

The Fourteenth Amendment plays an important role as a source of rights to counsel in cases where the Sixth Amendment does not apply. The Due Process Clause of this Amendment provides that states shall not "deprive any person of life, liberty, or property, without due process of law." A parallel provision in the Fifth Amendment binds the Federal Government to observe the Due Process guarantee. One prominent example of a Due Process right is the right to counsel on appeal. See *Douglas v. California,* 372 U.S. 353, 83 S.Ct. 814, 9 L.Ed.2d 811 (1963) (counsel for the first appeal only).

There are other rights that are usually studied in connection with the right to counsel. One is the right to self-representation, which is held to be an implicit provision of the Sixth Amendment. See *Faretta v. California,* 422 U.S. 806, 95 S.Ct. 2525, 45 L.Ed.2d 562 (1975). Another is the Due Process right to the basic tools of a defense at trial, which includes the right to obtain expert witnesses. See *Ake v. Oklahoma,* 470 U.S. 68, 105 S.Ct. 1087, 84 L.Ed.2d 53 (1985). Due Process is also a source of rights of access to the appellate process, such as the right to obtain a trial transcript. See *Griffin v. Illinois,* 351 U.S. 12, 76 S.Ct. 585, 100 L.Ed. 891 (1956).

The Equal Protection Clause of the Fourteenth Amendment is a third source of rights to counsel and related rights. This clause holds that states cannot "deny to any person * * * the equal protection of the laws." This guarantee is used to give extra support to Due Process rights concerning access to the appellate process, such as the rights to appellate counsel and transcripts. See *Douglas v. California,* 372 U.S. 353, 83 S.Ct. 814, 9 L.Ed.2d 811 (1963) (counsel); *Griffin v. Illinois,* 351 U.S. 12, 76 S.Ct. 585, 100 L.Ed. 891 (1956) (transcripts).

The Supreme Court's reliance on varying sources for counsel rights is best understood by studying the historical evolution of these rights. So this outline follows the typical casebook format, and begins with a detailed analysis of the early development of the right to counsel at trial. First, however, some basic points about the right to counsel are presented, with the elements of Sixth and Fourteenth Amendment rights summarized separately.

A. BASICS OF THE SIXTH AMENDMENT RIGHT TO COUNSEL

The text of the Sixth Amendment contains two ambiguities. First, what sort of assistance is meant by "assistance of counsel"? Second, what kind of a proceeding qualifies as a "criminal prosecution"? It is now settled that the assistance of counsel encompasses the right of indigent defendants to receive appointed counsel, as well as the right to use retained counsel of choice. Counsel must provide "effective" assistance, and generally must not have conflicts of interest. The right to assistance of counsel and to "effective" assistance may be waived, and the right to self-representation invoked in its stead. These rights apply only to particular stages of a criminal case, as a "criminal prosecution" is limited to the trial and certain other "critical stages."

1. The Right to "Assistance of Counsel" Encompasses the Right to Retained Counsel of Choice

The intent of the Sixth Amendment's Framers was to insure that criminal defendants could be represented at trial by their retained counsel. Under English law, attorneys were prohibited from appearing on behalf of defendants in felony cases. The Sixth Amendment reversed this rule, and made counsel's assistance available to all who could afford to hire a lawyer.

a. Qualified Right

The Court recognizes a Sixth Amendment right to retained counsel of choice, but holds that it must sometimes yield to particular state interests. One such interest is the state's use of forfeiture statutes to restrain a defendant from spending potentially forfeitable assets before trial. *Caplin & Drysdale, Chartered v. United States,* 491 U.S. 617, 109 S.Ct. 2646, 105 L.Ed.2d 528 (1989) (upholding federal forfeiture statute against Sixth Amendment attack). The Court in *Caplin* held that the forfeiture provision was constitutional, even though it might render a client destitute and thus without funds to pay his counsel of choice. The right to retained counsel of choice is a qualified right, and one major qualification is that it is dependent on the ability to pay. The Court held that a defendant subject to forfeiture had no right to pay counsel with assets that were the fruits of illegal activity. Another interest that can override the qualified right to chosen counsel is the prosecutor's right to object to defendant's use of counsel who has potential conflicts of interest. *Wheat v. United States,* 486 U.S. 153, 108 S.Ct. 1692, 100 L.Ed.2d 140 (1988) (upholding trial judge's discretion to disallow representation in such cases, even if the defendant wants to proceed with conflict-laden retained counsel of choice).

2. The Right to Appointed Counsel for Indigent Defendants

Indigent defendants have the right to appointed counsel in *all Federal prosecutions. Johnson v. Zerbst,* 304 U.S. 458, 58 S.Ct. 1019, 82 L.Ed. 1461 (1936). Indigent defendants also have the right to appointed counsel in all *state felony* prosecutions. *Gideon v. Wainwright,* 372 U.S. 335, 83 S.Ct. 792,

9 L.Ed.2d 799 (1963). In *misdemeanor* or petty offense cases, counsel must be provided only if the defendant receives an actual *jail sentence.* See *Argersinger v. Hamlin,* 407 U.S. 25, 92 S.Ct. 2006, 32 L.Ed.2d 530 (1972) (extending the right to counsel to these defendants) and *Scott v. Illinois,* 440 U.S. 367, 99 S.Ct. 1158, 59 L.Ed.2d 383 (1979) (limiting the right to these defendants). The defendants who are thus excluded from Sixth Amendment protection include those who are charged with a minor crime for which jail is not an "authorized" penalty, and those charged with a minor crime for which jail is authorized but who receive only a fine as the actual penalty.

    a.   The Definition of "Indigency"
        The Court has not prescribed a constitutional standard for indigency. It has left the definition to the state and Federal courts. These courts base their decisions to appoint counsel on indigency standards that vary among jurisdictions.

    b.   No Constitutional Right to Appointed Counsel of Choice
        The Court allows state and Federal courts to decide whether to take the defendant's preferred choice of counsel into account when making appointments. Trial judges have broad discretion in this field, and a defendant's request for particular counsel may be rejected without inquiring into the merits of the request. The Supreme Court rejects the idea that a defendant has a Sixth Amendment right to a "meaningful attorney-client relationship" with appointed counsel who represents him in the pre-trial stages of a case. See *Morris v. Slappy,* 461 U.S. 1, 103 S.Ct. 1610, 75 L.Ed.2d 610 (1983) (upholding trial judge's refusal to grant a continuance which would have allowed original counsel to represent defendant at trial instead of appointed replacement).

3.   The Definition of a "Criminal Prosecution" Where Counsel Rights Apply
    The Court has adopted a two-part test for identifying those events that are part of a "criminal prosecution" where counsel's assistance is needed. First, the event must occur after "adversarial judicial proceedings" have begun, and second, the event must be a "critical stage" in the trial process. *United States v. Wade,* 388 U.S. 218, 87 S.Ct. 1926, 18 L.Ed.2d 1149 (1967).

    a.   When "Adversarial Judicial Proceedings" Begin
        The formal commencement of a criminal prosecution is usually marked by the appearance of a prosecutor and a judge. A prosecutor may either file a charging document (a complaint or information) in court, or file a grand jury's indictment in court. *Massiah v. United States,* 377 U.S. 201, 84 S.Ct. 1199, 12 L.Ed.2d 246 (1964). Or, a defendant may be brought to court for arraignment or a first appearance. *Brewer v. Williams,* 430 U.S. 387, 97 S.Ct. 1232, 51 L.Ed.2d 424 (1977). It is unclear whether the issuance of an arrest warrant by a magistrate marks the formal commencement of an adversarial proceeding. An event must occur at or

after the commencement of adversarial proceedings in order to be part of a criminal prosecution. Compare *United States v. Wade,* 388 U.S. 218, 87 S.Ct. 1926, 18 L.Ed.2d 1149 (1967) (Sixth Amendment right to counsel attaches at post-indictment lineup) with *Kirby v. Illinois,* 406 U.S. 682, 92 S.Ct. 1877, 32 L.Ed.2d 411 (1972) (Sixth Amendment does not attach at pre-indictment lineup).

b.   **The Definition of "Critical Stage"**
A proceeding qualifies as a critical stage if it is a trial-like event, where an accused is confronted by "the procedural system" or the prosecutor, or both, in a situation where the results, without the presence of counsel, might "reduce the trial itself to a mere formality." *United States v. Gouveia,* 467 U.S. 180, 104 S.Ct. 2292, 81 L.Ed.2d 146 (1984). Critical stages include a preliminary hearing, a post-indictment lineup, and a sentencing hearing. See *Coleman v. Alabama,* 399 U.S. 1, 90 S.Ct. 1999, 26 L.Ed.2d 387 (1970) (preliminary hearing); *United States v. Wade,* 388 U.S. 218, 87 S.Ct. 1926, 18 L.Ed.2d 1149 (1967) (post-indictment lineup); *Mempa v. Rhay,* 389 U.S. 128, 88 S.Ct. 254, 19 L.Ed.2d 336 (1967) (deferred sentencing hearing). Events that are not critical stages include photographic identification procedures, handwriting exemplar procedures, probation revocation hearings, and administrative detention of inmates. See *United States v. Ash,* 413 U.S. 300, 93 S.Ct. 2568, 37 L.Ed.2d 619 (1973) (photographic identification); *Gilbert v. California,* 388 U.S. 263, 87 S.Ct. 1951, 18 L.Ed.2d 1178 (1967) (handwriting exemplars); *Gagnon v. Scarpelli,* 411 U.S. 778, 93 S.Ct. 1756, 36 L.Ed.2d 656 (1973) (probation revocation); *United States v. Gouveia,* 467 U.S. 180, 104 S.Ct. 2292, 81 L.Ed.2d 146 (1984) (administrative detention).

c.   **Confessions and the Right to Counsel**
Some confessions are obtained under circumstances that violate the Sixth Amendment right to counsel. The doctrine on this subject is discussed *supra* in the section on confessions. See *United States v. Massiah,* 377 U.S. 201, 84 S.Ct. 1199, 12 L.Ed.2d 246 (1964); *Brewer v. Williams,* 430 U.S. 387, 97 S.Ct. 1232, 5 L.Ed.2d 424 (1977); *Michigan v. Jackson,* 475 U.S. 625, 106 S.Ct. 1404, 89 L.Ed.2d 631 (1986). Most often, confessions are obtained during post-arrest, *pre-charge* custodial interrogation, which is considered part of the investigatorial, rather than adversarial, process, and thus not covered by the Sixth Amendment. See *Moran v. Burbine,* 475 U.S. 412, 106 S.Ct. 1135, 89 L.Ed.2d 410 (1986).

B.   BASICS OF THE FOURTEENTH AMENDMENT
Most Fourteenth Amendment rights to counsel and related rights are based on the Due Process Clause. There are Due Process rights to counsel at trials and other stages that are not covered by the Sixth Amendment. There is a Due Process right to counsel on the first appeal, which includes a right to effective

assistance of counsel. There are rights to tools for an adequate defense at trial and on appeal, such as expert witnesses and trial transcripts.

1. Due Process Rights to Counsel at Trial

Defendants in state misdemeanor and lesser offense cases do not have a Sixth Amendment right to appointed counsel, unless they receive a sentence of imprisonment. See *Scott v. Illinois,* 440 U.S. 367, 99 S.Ct. 1158, 59 L.Ed.2d 383 (1979). Such defendants may, however, have a right to appointed counsel under the Due Process Clause if they can show that a totality of special circumstances establishes the need for counsel.

2. Counsel for Non-critical Stages

The Due Process Clause sometimes requires counsel to be appointed on a case-by-case basis at non-critical stages. For example, counsel may be required for some defendants in probation revocation proceedings. See *Gagnon v. Scarpelli,* 411 U.S. 778, 93 S.Ct. 1756, 36 L.Ed.2d 656 (1973) (when substantial reasons make revocation inappropriate and when the reasons are complex or difficult to present without counsel).

3. The Right to Counsel on Appeal

There is a *per se* Due Process right to counsel on the first appeal. *Douglas v. California,* 372 U.S. 353, 83 S.Ct. 814, 9 L.Ed.2d 811 (1963). But there is no such right for later appeals, for the certiorari process, or for collateral attack. See *Ross v. Moffitt,* 417 U.S. 600, 94 S.Ct. 2437, 41 L.Ed.2d 341 (1974) (later appeals and certiorari); *Pennsylvania v. Finley,* 481 U.S. 551, 107 S.Ct. 1990, 95 L.Ed.2d 539 (1987) (state habeas); *Murray v. Giarratano,* 492 U.S. 1, 109 S.Ct. 2765, 106 L.Ed.2d 1 (1989) (state habeas for capital cases).

a. The Right to Effective Assistance of Counsel on Appeal

Due Process requires that counsel provide effective assistance on the first appeal. *Evitts v. Lucey,* 469 U.S. 387, 105 S.Ct. 830, 83 L.Ed.2d 821 (1985). Appellate counsel has no duty to argue every colorable issue, simply because the defendant wants the issues argued. *Jones v. Barnes,* 463 U.S. 745, 103 S.Ct. 3308, 77 L.Ed.2d 987 (1983) (counsel may winnow out weaker issues using reasonable professional judgment). If there is no underlying Due Process right to counsel then there is no Due Process right to effective assistance of counsel, even if counsel is representing the defendant. See *Wainwright v. Torna,* 455 U.S. 586, 102 S.Ct. 1300, 71 L.Ed.2d 475 (1982) (no right to effective assistance of retained counsel in second appeal).

b. The Role of Appellate Counsel Who Feels That the Appeal Has No Merit

If counsel believes an appeal is frivolous, counsel must request permission to withdraw and file a brief referring "to anything in the record that might arguably support the appeal." *Anders v. California,* 386 U.S. 738, 87 S.Ct. 1396, 18 L.Ed.2d 493 (1967). A state may require counsel to discuss why the appeal lacks merit. *McCoy v. Court of Appeals of Wisconsin,* 486 U.S. 429, 108 S.Ct. 1895, 100 L.Ed.2d 440 (1988). The Due Process requirement of filing an *Anders* brief applies only when there is an underlying Due Process right to counsel. *Pennsylvania v. Finley,* 481 U.S. 551, 107 S.Ct. 1990, 95 L.Ed.2d 539 (1987) (state habeas counsel need not file *Anders* brief).

4. Due Process Right to Tools With Which to Prepare an Effective Case at Trial and on Appeal

Besides the right to counsel, the Court has held that in some circumstances the state must provide technical support for counsel, so that an effective case can be prepared.

a. The Right to a Trial Transcript

In order for an indigent defendant to have adequate access to the appellate process, a trial transcript must be provided by the state. *Griffin v. Illinois,* 351 U.S. 12, 76 S.Ct. 585, 100 L.Ed. 891 (1956) (state must pay for a transcript even though the right to appeal is not a constitutional right).

b. The Right to Obtain Expert Witnesses for Trial

Due Process requires that indigent defendants receive the basic tools of an adequate defense at trial, and this includes expert witnesses where they are necessary for an effective presentation of the case. *Ake v. Oklahoma,* 470 U.S. 68, 105 S.Ct. 1087, 84 L.Ed.2d 53 (1985) (an appointed psychiatrist is required when defendant demonstrates that sanity is to be a significant factor at trial).

c. The Rights of Indigent Prisoners to Tools for Appeal in Lieu of Counsel

Although indigent defendants have no right to counsel beyond the first appeal, they have rights to substitute forms of assistance for use in subsequent appeals and collateral attack.

i. Jailhouse Lawyers

Inmates must be allowed to have access to the assistance of other inmates who are "jailhouse lawyers." *Johnson v. Avery,* 393 U.S. 483, 89 S.Ct. 747, 21 L.Ed.2d 718 (1969) (inmates may assist others in preparing habeas corpus petitions).

ii. Prison Libraries

Prison authorities must provide meaningful access to the courts for inmates by furnishing "adequate law libraries or adequate assistance from persons trained in the law." *Bounds v. Smith,* 430 U.S. 817, 97 S.Ct. 1491, 52 L.Ed.2d 72 (1977).

5. **Equal Protection Rights of Indigents in the Appellate Process**
States cannot grant appellate review "in a way that discriminates" against defendants "on account of their poverty." *Griffin v. Illinois,* 351 U.S. 12, 76 S.Ct. 585, 100 L.Ed. 189 (1956). This means that states must give indigents "meaningful access" to the appellate process. *Ross v. Moffitt,* 417 U.S. 600, 94 S.Ct. 2437, 41 L.Ed.2d 341 (1974). This prohibition gives rise to various rights for indigent defendants.

a. **The Right to Counsel on Appeal**
The right to counsel for the first appeal is supported by the Equal Protection Clause, as well as the Due Process Clause. *Douglas v. California,* 372 U.S. 353, 83 S.Ct. 814, 9 L.Ed.2d 811 (1963). However, neither Clause supports a right to counsel on later appeals. *Ross v. Moffitt,* 417 U.S. 600, 94 S.Ct. 2437, 41 L.Ed.2d 341 (1974).

b. **The Right to Transcripts and Filing Fee Waivers**
Defendants have a right to receive trial transcripts from all state trials, as a matter of Equal Protection and Due Process. *Mayer v. City of Chicago,* 404 U.S. 189, 92 S.Ct. 410, 30 L.Ed.2d 372 (1971) (state must pay for an indigent defendant's transcript, even when no Sixth Amendment right to counsel existed at trial). Transcripts of state habeas hearings must also be provided. *Gardner v. California,* 393 U.S. 367, 89 S.Ct. 580, 21 L.Ed.2d 601 (1969). Indigent defendants cannot be required to pay filing fees for appeals or post-conviction proceedings. *Burns v. Ohio,* 360 U.S. 252, 79 S.Ct. 1164, 3 L.Ed.2d 1209 (1959) (appeals); *Smith v. Bennett,* 365 U.S. 708, 81 S.Ct. 895, 6 L.Ed.2d 39 (1961) (post-conviction proceedings).

c. **The Right to Be Free From Special Penalties Resulting From Indigency**
Indigents who are unable to pay fines cannot be incarcerated beyond statutory maximum terms, or incarcerated at all when a statute prescribes only a fine as a penalty. *Williams v. Illinois,* 399 U.S. 235, 90 S.Ct. 2018, 26 L.Ed.2d 586 (1970) (no incarceration beyond maximum); *Tate v. Short,* 401 U.S. 395, 91 S.Ct. 668, 28 L.Ed.2d 130 (1971) (no incarceration under fine-only statute). Nor may such indigents be subjected to the automatic revocation of probation. *Bearden v. Georgia,* 461 U.S. 660, 103 S.Ct. 2064, 76 L.Ed.2d 221 (1983) (hearing must be granted to determine whether payment of fines over time may be arranged).

II. THE EVOLUTION OF THE RIGHT TO APPOINTED COUNSEL AT TRIAL

The Supreme Court first granted a Due Process right to capital defendants to have appointed counsel in state trials on a case-by-case basis. Shortly thereafter, the Court held that appointed counsel is required in *all* Federal criminal trials. Thus a double standard was created, and the logic of this standard came under repeated attack. Yet the double standard withstood attack for over thirty years, and state defendants received appointed counsel only when they could demonstrate special circumstances requiring an appointment. The first major blow to the standard came when the Court applied the Sixth Amendment to the states through the incorporation doctrine of the Fourteenth Amendment. Ultimately, however, the Court declined to abolish the double standard entirely, and held that a Sixth Amendment right to counsel does not exist for state defendants charged with misdemeanors or lesser crimes, unless they receive jail sentences. This scope limitation was established in 1979, and seems unlikely to change in the near future. While the doctrinal evolution of Sixth Amendment rights to trial counsel may be over, Due Process remains a potential source of rights for those who are unprotected by the Sixth Amendment.

A. THE RIGHT TO APPOINTED COUNSEL IN CAPITAL CASES
The evolution of the right to counsel at trial began with the Supreme Court's assessment of the value of appointed counsel in capital cases. Ultimately the Court came to treat the capital status of the crime as sufficient justification *per se* for the appointment of counsel. This Due Process right became settled long before the Sixth Amendment became a source of rights for state defendants.

1. The Due Process Right to Appointed Counsel in Capital Cases
In *Powell v. Alabama,* 287 U.S. 45, 53 S.Ct. 55, 77 L.Ed. 158 (1932) the Court held that counsel must be appointed in order to satisfy Due Process in some capital trials in state courts. *Powell*'s reasoning is subject to competing interpretations.

a. The Broad Rationale
The *Powell* Court found that the right to counsel is fundamental because the right to a hearing is a fundamental requirement of Due Process. A lack of counsel impairs the right to a hearing, because the right to be heard is useless to a layperson who cannot communicate without a lawyer at a legal hearing like a criminal trial. For example, a defendant may be convicted upon improper charges or through the use of inadmissible evidence, as she lacks a lawyer's knowledge of rules of evidence and procedure.

b. Required Before Trial
The Court in *Powell* stated that counsel's skills are needed not only at trial, but also before trial in order to prepare a defense. The defendants in *Powell* were given appointed counsel formally on the day of trial,

which violated Due Process because it precluded "the giving of effective aid in the preparation and trial of the case."

c. Implications of the Broad Rationale

Powell's reasoning was not confined to establishing a right to counsel in capital cases. It implied that counsel is necessary in all criminal cases, as it emphasized every layperson's lack of legal skills, and every defendant's need for assistance in preparing a defense and exercising legal rights. If the right to counsel is "fundamental," this would imply that the right has an absolute value that does not fluctuate on a case-by-case basis.

d. The Narrow Rationale

A more narrow view of *Powell* is that the Court found that the Due Process violation was particularly "clear" because of four factual circumstances: "[the defendants'] youth, the circumstances of public hostility, the imprisonment and the close surveillance * * * by the military forces, [and] the fact that their friends and families were all in other states and communication with them [was] necessarily difficult."

e. Implications of the Narrow Rationale

The *Powell* Court expressly reserved judgment as to whether the failure to appoint counsel would violate Due Process "in other criminal prosecutions, or under other circumstances." This reasoning implied that Due Process rights are most appropriately decided on a case-by-case basis. The facts of *Powell* presented truly egregious circumstances, and it was unclear how the standards set forth would apply to other cases.

f. Post–*Powell* Debate

Powell's two rationales set forth the arguments for the debate about the proper scope of the right to counsel, which debate occupied the Court for almost fifty years. Each rationale has its strengths and weaknesses. The broad rationale is realistic about the needs of laypersons. But it does not consider whether counsel might be unnecessary in some petty criminal cases, such as traffic violations penalized only by fines. Adherence to the broad rationale also would seem to require a *per se* right to counsel, which remedy is inconsistent with the typical Due Process remedy that focuses on a "totality of circumstances" and requires case-by-case application.

The narrow rationale is consistent with the typical analysis for Due Process. However, it is unrealistic about the needs of laypersons, and it does not create clear guidelines for lower courts because of the subjectivity inherent in applying the case-by-case test. Trial courts cannot accurately predict how appellate courts will define the concept of a "vital and imperative" need for counsel. Thus, defendants who are similarly situated may not be treated in a uniform way.

g. **Case-by-Case Approach Applied**
The narrow rationale was accepted by lower courts as the governing approach for appointing counsel after *Powell*. But the weaknesses of this approach created the pressure to find a better alternative. For that, courts needed to look no further than the *Powell* opinion's broad rationale.

h. **What About the Sixth Amendment?**
When *Powell* was decided, the Sixth Amendment right to counsel was not applicable to the states. See *Gideon v. Wainwright,* 372 U.S. 335, 83 S.Ct. 792, 9 L.Ed.2d 799 (1963); *Betts v. Brady,* 316 U.S. 455 (1942).

i. **What About Equal Protection?**
Modern observers regard the prosecution of the *Powell* defendants as a case of grave racial injustice. See Dan T. Carter, Scottsboro: A Tragedy of the American South (1969). But Equal Protection precedent provided no basis for addressing the unfairness of the trial in the *Powell* era. By creating a ground-breaking Due Process rule, the Court went beyond the racial context of the case to create rights for all capital defendants.

2. **A *Per Se* Right to Counsel in Capital Cases**
The disadvantages of *Powell*'s narrow rationale requiring case-by-case inquiry became apparent to the Supreme Court over time. Yet rather than admit these disadvantages, the Court simply announced that all capital defendants needed appointed counsel. See *Bute v. Illinois,* 333 U.S. 640, 68 S.Ct. 763, 92 L.Ed. 986 (1948) ("if these charges had been capital charges, the court would have been required * * * by the Fourteenth Amendment" to assign counsel "in the event of the inability of the accused to procure counsel"); *Hamilton v. Alabama,* 368 U.S. 52, 82 S.Ct. 157, 7 L.Ed.2d 114 (1961) (*Bute* dicta becomes Court holding). Thus, the Court expanded the application of the *Powell* right without choosing to explain why the case-by-case approach was workable for non-capital cases but not for capital ones.

B. THE RIGHT TO APPOINTED COUNSEL IN FEDERAL CASES
In *Johnson v. Zerbst,* 304 U.S. 458, 58 S.Ct. 1019, 82 L.Ed. 1461 (1938) the Court held that the Sixth Amendment embodies a right to appointed counsel for defendants in all Federal criminal prosecutions.

1. **Rationale**
Justice Black's opinion in *Johnson* held that the broad rationale of *Powell* is embodied in the Sixth Amendment right to counsel. The Court emphasized that all laypersons need counsel because they lack legal skills to put on a defense. It reasoned that defendants need a lawyer to act as an adversary in a trial where the "prosecution is presented by experienced and learned counsel." Moreover, even when a case seems simple, a lawyer's skills are

needed. For what is simple to a lawyer is "intricate, complex and mysterious" to laypeople.

2. All Criminal Prosecutions
The Sixth Amendment, by its terms, applies to all criminal prosecutions. The *Johnson* Court read the right to appointed counsel into that amendment, and applied it to all defendants.

3. Expansive Analysis
Justice Black made no reference to the history of the Sixth Amendment and its application in Federal court. Before *Johnson,* it was assumed that the Sixth Amendment's Framers only intended to guarantee the right to be heard by retained counsel. See *Powell v. Alabama,* 287 U.S. 45, 53 S.Ct. 55, 77 L.Ed. 158 (1932). Justice Black also ignored the narrow rationale of *Powell,* thus implicitly repudiating it. *Johnson*'s *per se* right to counsel set the stage for an inevitable challenge to *Powell* 's formula of case-by-case adjudication of rights to counsel in state court.

C. THE RIGHT TO APPOINTED COUNSEL IN NON-CAPITAL CASES IN STATE COURT
While the Court ultimately held that the Due Process Clause required appointed counsel in state capital cases, there was considerable dispute as to whether a similar right applied in non-capital cases.

1. The Initial Refusal to Apply the Sixth Amendment Right to Counsel to the States
In *Betts v. Brady,* 316 U.S. 455, 62 S.Ct. 1252, 86 L.Ed. 1595 (1942), the Court rejected the argument that the Sixth Amendment right to counsel should be incorporated through the Fourteenth Amendment and applied to the states. It held that in a non-capital case, the right to appointed counsel derives from Due Process and requires a showing of special circumstances under *Powell. Betts* gave a ringing endorsement to the narrow rationale of *Powell,* and absolutely rejected the broad rationale. The Court reasoned that a *per se* right to counsel would create an unnecessary "straightjacket" for the states, and force them to appoint counsel for even petty cases like traffic crimes. The Court expressed confidence that appellate courts could use *Powell* 's case-by-case formula to reverse convictions whenever a defendant without counsel was "at a serious disadvantage" at trial.

a. Application of Totality of Circumstances Test
The Court held that there was no Due Process violation in *Betts,* where the indigent defendant was convicted of robbery and sentenced to eight years in prison. The defendant waived a jury, so his trial was informal and the judge could "see impartial justice done" without counsel. His case involved a "simple issue of veracity" of witnesses. The defendant was middle-aged and of ordinary intelligence, and not "wholly unfamiliar

with criminal procedure," thanks to a prior guilty plea and conviction. He was thus at no "serious disadvantage" without counsel.

b. Dissent

Justice Black dissented in an opinion for three justices, on the ground that the broad rationale of *Powell* should be used to expand the Due Process right to counsel to cover all defendants charged with serious felonies, like the defendant in *Betts*. Justice Black found this right to be "fundamental" based on the legislative and judicial practices of a large majority of states supporting a right to counsel in serious felony cases.

2. The Sixth Amendment Right to Counsel Applies to the States

In *Gideon v. Wainwright,* 372 U.S. 335, 83 S.Ct. 792, 9 L.Ed.2d 799 (1963) the Court held that the right to counsel should be incorporated into Due Process and applied to the states through the Fourteenth Amendment. *Gideon* overruled *Betts* and created a *per se* right to appointed counsel for indigent defendants charged with felonies.

a. Rationale

Justice Black relied on the broad rationale of *Powell* to overrule *Betts*. Indigent defendants without counsel do not receive "fair trials" where they stand "equal before the law." Lawyers are "not luxuries, but necessities," as shown by the use of retained counsel by defendants who can afford it, and the use of prosecutors by state criminal justice systems. Thus, the Sixth Amendment right to counsel is "fundamental" and must be incorporated into Due Process under the Fourteenth Amendment and applied to the states. The Court concluded that at least for felony cases, *Betts* must be overruled, because it was wrong when decided, and because only three states favored its preservation.

b. Justice Harlan's Opinion

Justice Harlan concurred in an opinion that sheds further light on the demise of the *Betts* rule. He stated that after 1950, the Court paid only "lip service" to *Betts,* and granted all claims for counsel in felony cases. It relied on the "complexity" of even "routine" legal issues, in order to find "special circumstances" as required by *Betts*. The "mere existence of a serious charge" became reason enough for creating a *de facto* right to counsel that was absolute. For Justice Harlan, the *Gideon* rule was necessary so that "state courts with front-line responsibility" would conform their practices to the Court's tradition of granting counsel in felony cases.

c. Perspective

Justices Harlan and Black agreed on the need for changing the *Betts* rule, but disagreed about the proper interpretation of *Powell, Johnson* and *Betts*. Justice Black preferred to minimize the significance of

Powell's narrow rationale in order to find *Betts* to be an "abrupt break" from *Powell* and *Johnson*. Justice Harlan preferred to defend *Betts* as a reasonable extension of *Powell*'s narrow rationale. This quarrel is rooted in differing philosophies about the "incorporation" of various provisions of the Bill of Rights into Due Process under the Fourteenth Amendment. Justice Harlan did not want to "carry over" the "whole body of federal law" and "apply it in full sweep to the States," as Justice Black would have it. In *Gideon,* however, Justice Black followed the tradition of expanding the right to counsel only far enough to cover individuals who are similarly situated to the defendant before the Court. Thus, his opinion left open the question whether a defendant charged with only a misdemeanor would have a right to appointed counsel in a state case.

3.   Right to Appointed Counsel for Defendants Who Receive a Jail Sentence for Misdemeanors and Petty Offenses

In *Argersinger v. Hamlin,* 407 U.S. 25, 92 S.Ct. 2006, 32 L.Ed.2d 530 (1972) the Court expanded the right to appointed counsel in state cases beyond felony crimes and held that a jail sentence cannot be imposed on any indigent defendant who was not given appointed counsel at trial.

a.   Rationale

The *Argersinger* Court relied on the broad rationales of *Powell* and *Gideon* to extend the Sixth Amendment right to counsel to state defendants who are sentenced to jail for misdemeanors or "petty offenses." The defendant in *Argersinger* was denied counsel by the lower court because the maximum penalty authorized for his crime was less than six months in jail. The Court rejected this petty crime boundary as a proper limit on the right to counsel, because it lacked support in history and practice, and because it appeared to be arbitrary and unrelated to a defendant's likely need for counsel. The Court found that constitutional and legal questions may be "no less complex" in cases like *Argersinger* than in cases like *Gideon*.

b.   Jail Time

The Court determined that it "need not consider" whether to extend the right to appointed counsel to misdemeanor defendants who do not receive a jail sentence, because the defendant in *Argersinger* received one. It reasoned that jail is never "petty" from a defendant's point of view, "and may well result in quite serious repercussions affecting his career and reputation."

c.   Case-by-Case Alternative

Justices Powell and Rehnquist concurred in *Argersinger* in an opinion that advocates a case-by-case formula for assigning counsel in state petty crime cases. This formula resembles *Betts,* as it directs trial judges to consider three factors, including the "complexity" of the task of defense, the seriousness of the likely sentence, and "individual" factors such as the defendant's capabilities. Justice Powell argued that his formula was superior to the *Argersinger* majority's rule, which he thought to be "mechanistic" and overbroad in providing counsel in the absence of proof of need. He reasoned that even where a defendant receives a jail sentence, a case may be so "simple" that the aid of counsel is unnecessary. He concluded that a case-by-case formula gives trial judges the discretion to determine whether the costs of counsel exceed the benefits in petty cases.

d. Perspective
The *Argersinger* Court splits down the same fault line observed in earlier cases. While the majority endorsed the broad reasoning of *Powell, Johnson,* and *Gideon,* the concurring Justices plainly shared the views of Justice Harlan as expressed in his *Gideon* concurrence. They rejected the application of a single Sixth Amendment standard to both Federal and state courts, and embraced the philosophy of *Betts* and the narrow rationale of *Powell*. As Justice Powell revealingly put it, Due Process "embodies principles of fairness rather than immutable line drawing."

4. Right to Appointed Counsel Conditioned Upon Actual Imprisonment for State Misdemeanors and Petty Offenses
In *Scott v. Illinois,* 440 U.S. 367, 99 S.Ct. 1158, 59 L.Ed.2d 383 (1979) the Court held that the Sixth Amendment's *per se* right to counsel in state misdemeanor and petty offense cases is limited to defendants who actually receive a jail sentence. Where imprisonment is authorized by statute, but the defendant receives only a fine, the *Argersinger* right does not attach. Thus, while the defendant in *Scott* faced an authorized penalty of up to one year in jail, he received only a $50 fine for his shoplifting crime; therefore the state was not required to appoint counsel for him. Recall, however, that in state *felony* cases, there is an absolute right to appointed counsel regardless of whether the defendant receives a jail sentence. *Gideon, supra.*

a. Rationale
The *Scott* Court identified the "central premise" of *Argersinger* as the idea "that actual imprisonment is a penalty different in kind from fines or the mere threat of imprisonment." The Court refused to extend *Argersinger*'s rule to defendants facing only "authorized" imprisonment, because this would "create confusion" and "impose unpredictable, but necessarily substantial, costs" on all states. By contrast, the Court found the *Argersinger* rule itself to be "workable" and a suitable stopping point for the right to counsel. The Court pointed out that state criminal laws regulate a broad range and variety of petty crimes, compared to the narrower field of petty Federal crimes. Thus, imposition of the Federal

Johnson absolute right to counsel on the states might create "special difficulties."

b. Dissent

Justices Brennan, Marshall, and Stevens dissented. Justice Brennan defended the application of a right to counsel to all defendants facing "authorized imprisonment." He argued that it is more fair, efficient, and uniform than the *Scott* rule, and he dismissed the majority's concern with costs as "irrelevant" and "speculative," given the ability of most states to provide free counsel under various forms of the authorized imprisonment standard. Justice Blackmun, in a separate dissent, would have held that a defendant is entitled to counsel for any misdemeanor punishable by more than six months' imprisonment—making the right contiguous to the right to a jury trial.

c. Practical Application

The majority's rule is somewhat awkward in practice. It requires trial judges to decide *before* trial what sentence will be imposed *after* trial. The judge at the outset of the case must appoint counsel for an indigent whenever she wishes to preserve the option of giving a jail sentence. In effect, the majority imposes a Sixth Amendment bargain upon judges— "no jail, no counsel; no counsel, no jail." See *Moore v. Jarvis,* 885 F.2d 1565 (11th Cir.1989) ("In essence, the *Scott* holding set up a trade-off whereby states could choose between providing indigent defendants with appointed counsel and foregoing jail time for convictions obtained without appointed counsel. *Scott* holds that, if the state wants to incarcerate an indigent defendant, the state must provide appointed counsel.").

d. Due Process Arguments After *Scott*

In the pre-*Gideon* era, state defendants who lacked Sixth Amendment rights were required to argue that "special circumstances" justified the appointment of counsel on Due Process grounds. Presumably, these arguments remain available in the post-*Scott* era. A claim for a Due Process right could be made by a defendant sentenced to pay a very large fine, or to sentences such as the loss of a license or community service. Each defendant would need to claim that the lack of counsel caused her some special and serious detriment, considering the totality of circumstances of her case. Compare *Lassiter v. Department of Social Services,* 452 U.S. 18, 101 S.Ct. 2153, 68 L.Ed.2d 640 (1981) (Due Process does not require appointed counsel for parental status termination, as no liberty interest is at stake).

e. *Scott* Is an "Anomaly" in the Context of Other Rights to Counsel

Justice Brennan's *Scott* dissent labeled the majority's denial of counsel an "anomalous result." He noted that a defendant will have a Sixth

Amendment right to a jury trial where there is no right to counsel. See *Baldwin v. New York,* 399 U.S. 66, 90 S.Ct. 1886, 26 L.Ed.2d 437 (1970) (jury trial right attaches to crimes for which more than six months imprisonment is authorized). *Scott* is an anomaly in other ways. A *Scott* defendant can be denied the right to appointed counsel at trial but not on appeal. See *Douglas v. California,* 372 U.S. 353, 83 S.Ct. 814, 9 L.Ed.2d 811 (1963). Likewise a *Scott* defendant may not be denied the right to counsel during custodial interrogation or at arraignment. See *Miranda v. Arizona,* 384 U.S. 436, 86 S.Ct. 1602, 16 L.Ed.2d 694 (1966); *Brewer v. Williams,* 430 U.S. 387, 97 S.Ct. 1232, 51 L.Ed.2d 424 (1977). The same *Scott* defendant may also enjoy the right to counsel at "critical stages" such as post-indictment lineups and preliminary hearings, but not at trial. See *United States v. Wade,* 388 U.S. 218, 87 S.Ct. 1926, 18 L.Ed.2d 1149 (1967); *Coleman v. Alabama,* 399 U.S. 1, 90 S.Ct. 1999, 26 L.Ed.2d 387 (1970).

f.   Suspended Sentence Impermissible

After *Scott,* it is impermissible to imprison a defendant on the basis of an uncounselled conviction. Courts after *Scott* have held that it is equally impermissible to impose a suspended sentence on the basis of an uncounselled conviction. See *United States v. Reilley,* 948 F.2d 648 (10th Cir.1991) ("Since the Court's conditional threat to imprison Reilley could never be carried out, the threat itself is hollow and should be considered a nullity.").

g.   Collateral Consequences of Uncounselled Convictions

In *Baldasar v. Illinois,* 446 U.S. 222, 100 S.Ct. 1585, 64 L.Ed.2d 169 (1980) the Court, without a majority opinion, held that a valid uncounselled misdemeanor conviction could not be used to elevate Baldasar's second conviction from a misdemeanor to a felony. Four Justices concluded that an enhanced penalty, on the basis of an uncounselled previous conviction, was tantamount to imprisonment on that prior conviction, in violation of *Scott.* Four Justices found no problem in using the prior uncounselled conviction for enhancement purposes, because Baldasar received no jail time at the time of his first conviction, and he received counsel at the time of his second conviction. Justice Blackmun cast the deciding vote, reiterating his dissenting view in *Scott* that a defendant has the right to counsel for any misdemeanor punishable by more than six months' imprisonment. Justice Blackmun asserted that Baldasar was entitled to counsel at the time of his *first* conviction on a charge for which imprisonment for more than six months was authorized (though he received no actual jail time); he therefore concluded that a subsequent enhancement on the basis of the uncounselled conviction was a fortiori impermissible. Looking at the votes in *Baldasar,* it appears that five Justices at the time would have permitted some enhancement of a subsequent offense on the basis of a prior uncounselled conviction. Lower courts have read *Baldasar* to mean that a valid uncounselled misdemeanor conviction can be used for enhancement, *unless all three of the following factors are present:* 1) a subsequent misdemeanor is *automatically* converted by statute, 2) into a *felony,* and 3) the defendant receives a jail term which he would not otherwise receive, solely *because* of the prior uncounselled conviction. See *United States v. Peagler,* 847 F.2d 756 (11th Cir.1988) (no *Baldasar* violation where "defendant's sentence was not automatically increased by statute from a non-jail offense to a jail offense because he had a criminal record"); *United States v. Castro–Vega,* 945 F.2d 496 (2d Cir.1991) (uncounselled misdemeanor conviction can be used to determine the appropriate criminal history category under the Sentencing Guidelines, for a crime that was already a felony).

D. THE RIGHT TO COUNSEL AT CRITICAL STAGES OF A CRIMINAL PROSECUTION

The Sixth Amendment guarantees the assistance of counsel in "all criminal prosecutions." This language implies that the right to counsel attaches at some pre-trial stages of a case, as counsel must prepare a defense before trial begins. See *Powell v. Alabama,* 287 U.S. 45, 53 S.Ct. 55, 77 L.Ed. 158 (1932) (defendant must have the "guiding hand of counsel at every step in the proceedings").

After *Gideon,* the Court took up the task of identifying the stages of a criminal proceeding where counsel is necessary to assist a defendant. At first, the Court created a broad definition of "critical stages" where counsel would be needed to provide a "meaningful" defense and assure that a defendant's "interests" would be protected. Ultimately, the Court settled upon a narrower definition, requiring counsel only at trial-like events where a defendant confronts "the procedural system," or the prosecutor, or both. The Court also chose to limit the right to counsel to those critical stages that occur at or after "the initiation of adversary judicial proceedings" against a defendant.

1. Post–Indictment Line-up Is a Critical Stage

In *United States v. Wade,* 388 U.S. 218, 87 S.Ct. 1926, 18 L.Ed.2d 1149 (1967) the Court held that a post-indictment lineup is a "critical stage" where the Sixth Amendment requires the presence of appointed counsel. The Court found the principles of *Powell* required a two-part analysis to determine whether a particular stage is critical. This test is: 1) whether "substantial potential prejudice to a defendant's rights" inheres in a confrontation; and 2) whether the presence of counsel may "help to avoid that prejudice." The Court held that the circumstances of post-indictment lineups met these standards, and therefore that counsel was required to be present at such line-ups. See also *Gilbert v. California,* 388 U.S. 263, 87 S.Ct. 1951, 18 L.Ed.2d 1178 (1967) (post-indictment lineup identifications are inadmissible when counsel is absent).

a. **Rationale**
The Court noted that modern pre-trial procedures, unlike those of 1791, involve investigative police techniques that "can settle a defendant's fate and reduce the trial to a mere formality." Both the text of the Sixth Amendment and the *Powell* opinion were invoked to establish the goal that counsel be appointed to assure a meaningful defense "at any stage where counsel's absence might derogate from the right to a fair trial." Counsel's role was defined broadly: "to assure that the defendant's interests will be protected consistently with the adversary theory of prosecution." The Court concluded that pre-trial confrontations must be scrutinized to determine whether counsel is needed "to preserve the defendant's right to a fair trial as affected by the right meaningfully to cross-examine and to have effective assistance of counsel." As to line-ups, the Court concluded that the presence of counsel was necessary because counsel could observe the line-up and be prepared to offer relevant evidence and perform effective cross-examination of eyewitnesses at trial to suggest the unreliability of their identifications.

2. **Preliminary Hearing Is a Critical Stage**
In *Coleman v. Alabama,* 399 U.S. 1, 90 S.Ct. 1999, 26 L.Ed.2d 387 (1970) the Court held that a preliminary hearing preceding indictment is a "critical stage" where counsel is required, because this stage meets *Wade*'s two-part test. The Court implicitly found the "prejudice" component of *Wade* to consist of a defendant's loss of opportunities to be protected "against an erroneous or improper prosecution."

a. **Helpfulness of Counsel**
The Court noted four ways in which "counsel's help" may provide benefits at a preliminary hearing before indictment. Counsel's skills may lead to a rejection of the charge at the hearing, to the discovery of the state's case, to the making of a record for use at trial to impeach state witnesses or to preserve testimony of defense witnesses, and to the granting of bail or psychiatric examination.

b. **Other Opinions**
Justice Brennan's majority opinion applying his own *Wade* doctrine was hit from both sides. In a concurring opinion, Justice Black faulted the Court for tying the critical stage concept not so much to the Sixth Amendment as to the "right to a fair trial as conceived by judges." Chief Justice Burger declared in dissent that the Court "amended the Sixth Amendment" in *Wade* by inventing the critical stage concept.

3. **Revising the Critical Stage Test to Require a Trial–Like Confrontation**
In *United States v. Ash,* 413 U.S. 300, 93 S.Ct. 2568, 37 L.Ed.2d 619 (1973) the Court held that a post-indictment photographic identification is not a critical stage. *Wade*'s two-part test was effectively abandoned, in favor of a

"historical" test limiting the appointment of counsel to trial-like events where the defendant needs "aid in coping with legal problems or assistance in meeting his adversary."

a.   Rationale

The Court reasoned that since a defendant is absent when a photographic identification occurs, there is no need for counsel at this event. The *Ash* Court relied on Sixth Amendment history and caselaw, as well as critical-stage precedents, to determine that counsel's only role at a critical stage is to advise or assist a defendant *in person*. The Court declared that the "core purpose" of the Sixth Amendment is to guarantee assistance at trial, where the defendant is confronted by "the intricacies of the law and advocacy of public prosecutor." Cases from *Powell* to *Argersinger* endorsed the idea that counsel is needed to compensate for the lay defendant's "deficiencies" in legal skills. *Wade* and *Coleman* then extended a right to counsel to pre-trial stages where counsel functioned in a trial-like setting. Therefore, a "historical" test evolved for the concept of a critical stage, confining it to *trial-like confrontations* where the defendant is present.

b.   Limits on Critical Stage Theory

The Court in *Ash* declared that *Wade* could not have held that counsel attaches at any stage where police activity may prejudice the defendant later at trial. Such a broad interpretation would mandate the presence of defense counsel at all prosecution interviews with witnesses, as suggestiveness may inhere in these events; and it would also extend to virtually any form of prosecutorial investigation.

c.   Dissent

The three dissenters in *Ash* argued that the majority had rewritten *Wade*, and ignored all its general rationales as well as its two-part test. They found that the same prejudice existed in *Ash* as existed in *Wade*, because the difficulties of reconstructing the circumstances of a photographic display are "at least equal to, and possibly greater than" those involving lineups. The dissenters concluded that counsel has many tasks to perform in providing a meaningful defense, and that the *Ash* Court improperly limited counsel's Sixth Amendment role to that of a personal legal advisor and trial performer.

d.   Continued Affirmation of *Ash*'s "Trial–Like Confrontation" Critical Stage Test

In *United States v. Gouveia*, 467 U.S. 180, 104 S.Ct. 2292, 81 L.Ed.2d 146 (1984) the Court cited *Ash* approvingly for its assessment of the "core purpose" of the Sixth Amendment, and for its definition of the critical stage test as one where "the accused [is] confronted, just as at trial, by the procedural system, or by his expert adversary, or by both."

The Court in *Gouveia* held that the defendants had no right to counsel when they were placed in administrative detention prior to their being indicted.

4. Right to Counsel Limited to Critical Stages Occurring at or After the "Initiation of Adversary Judicial Proceedings"

In *Kirby v. Illinois,* 406 U.S. 682, 92 S.Ct. 1877, 32 L.Ed.2d 411 (1972) the Court held that a post-arrest identification conducted before indictment is not a stage where the Sixth Amendment right to counsel attaches. This is because the onset of a "criminal prosecution" occurs only at or after "the initiation of adversary judicial proceedings—whether by way of formal charge, preliminary hearing, indictment, information or arraignment."

a. Rationale

The Court chose the moment of formal "prosecutorial proceedings" as the only rational "starting point" for the attachment of the right to counsel. Only then is the Government "committed to prosecute" and the defendant faced with "the prosecutorial forces" and "the intricacies of the law." The Court relied on the language of the Sixth Amendment which limits its protection to "criminal prosecutions" and reasoned that a prosecution cannot be considered to have begun until the state formally accuses the defendant of a crime. Such a formal accusation distinguishes the preliminary, investigatory stage from the adversary proceeding of a criminal prosecution.

b. Dissent

Justices Brennan, Marshall and Douglas dissented in an opinion declaring that the moment of arrest is a more realistic starting point for the provision of counsel. Justice Brennan noted that counsel is needed in a pre-charge line-up for the same reasons as in *Wade,* and accused the Court of limiting Sixth Amendment protection without justification beyond "mere formalism."

c. Inconsistent With Speedy Trial Rights

Justice Brennan also argued that the *Kirby* interpretation of a "criminal prosecution" was inconsistent with other Sixth Amendment precedent, for the same term in which the Court decided *Kirby,* it held that the Sixth Amendment right to speedy trial begins with an arrest. *United States v. Marion,* 404 U.S. 307, 92 S.Ct. 455, 30 L.Ed.2d 468 (1971).

d. Continued Affirmation of *Kirby*

In *United States v. Gouveia,* 467 U.S. 180, 104 S.Ct. 2292, 81 L.Ed.2d 146 (1984) the Court held that the right to counsel does not attach for prison inmates in administrative detention who are awaiting prosecution for prison crimes. *Kirby*'s rule was affirmed, and found to be supported by the reasoning of *Ash* concerning the proper role of counsel. The Court found no reason to expand the Sixth Amendment role of counsel to that of a pre-indictment investigator. Justices Brennan and Marshall dissented, relying on the reasoning of their *Kirby* dissents. Justice Marshall would have found the detention in *Gouveia* to be a critical stage where defendants need counsel to preserve their abilities to prepare a defense during long government delays in filing charges.

E.   THE SIXTH AMENDMENT RIGHT TO APPOINTED COUNSEL IN POST–TRIAL STAGES

1.   The Right to Counsel at Sentencing

In *Mempa v. Rhay,* 389 U.S. 128, 88 S.Ct. 254, 19 L.Ed.2d 336 (1967) a unanimous Court held that a right to counsel exists at sentencing hearings, because of the "critical nature" of this event. Implicitly, the Court treated a sentencing hearing as part of a "criminal prosecution."

a.   Rationale

The Court found that the "substantial rights of a criminal accused may be affected" at a sentencing hearing, and that counsel is needed to protect these rights. The defendant in *Mempa* was placed on probation following a guilty plea, but not formally sentenced until a probation violation triggered a "probation revocation" hearing. The Court held that counsel was required at this hearing, because the judge not only determined whether probation was violated, but also sentenced the defendant for his original crime.

b.   Role of Counsel

The Court found that the "critical nature" of the *Mempa* hearing derived from the sentencing activity performed by the judge. Counsel was required so that the defendant could have an effective defense at this stage. Counsel's role is to produce mitigating evidence and present sentencing arguments to influence the judge's recommendation to the sentencing authorities as to the sentence for the original crime. Also, the right to appeal and withdrawal of the plea could be preserved effectively at this stage only by counsel.

2.   What Specific Sentencing Procedures, Aside From a Hearing, Are Covered by the Sixth Amendment?

It is not clear whether *Mempa*'s holding applies to all sentencing-related events. For example, the Federal Sentencing Guidelines provide for pre-hearing interviews between defendants and probation officers who make sentencing recommendations to the judge. At least one lower court held that such an interview is not a "critical stage" because it is non-adversarial. See *United States v. Johnson,* 935 F.2d 47 (4th Cir.1991).

3. A "Criminal Prosecution" Ends After Sentencing

In *Gagnon v. Scarpelli,* 411 U.S. 778, 93 S.Ct. 1756, 36 L.Ed.2d 656 (1973) the Court held that *Mempa* does not apply to a traditional parole revocation hearing. The Court relied on *Morrissey v. Brewer,* 408 U.S. 471, 92 S.Ct. 2593, 33 L.Ed.2d 484 (1972), which held that revocation of parole is not part of a criminal prosecution. In *Gagnon,* the defendant was sentenced to parole and a suspended jail term, and then faced with a parole revocation hearing when parole was violated. The defendant in *Gagnon* enjoyed no Sixth Amendment right to counsel at his hearing because the sentence to parole for his original crime was imposed at trial. There was no deferred sentencing as in *Mempa.* The Court concluded that after sentencing, a defendant's criminal prosecution is over.

4. Due Process Rights to Counsel at Stages That Are Not Part of a "Criminal Prosecution"

Defendants who are ineligible for Sixth Amendment rights to counsel may be eligible for a Due Process right to counsel. For example, *Gagnon v. Scarpelli,* 411 U.S. 778, 93 S.Ct. 1756, 36 L.Ed.2d 656 (1973) endorsed a *Betts*-style right to counsel for parole revocation hearings. See discussion *infra.* Also, *Douglas v. California,* 372 U.S. 353, 83 S.Ct. 814, 9 L.Ed.2d 811 (1963) mandated a right to counsel on the first appeal of a conviction. See discussion *infra.*

F. CONFESSIONS AND SIXTH AMENDMENT RIGHTS TO COUNSEL

Custodial interrogations by police, or non-custodial elicitation of confessions by Government agents, may take place after the onset of "adversarial judicial proceedings" (i.e. after the Government has filed a formal charge). If so, the Sixth Amendment right to counsel applies. See *Massiah v. United States,* 377 U.S. 201, 84 S.Ct. 1199, 12 L.Ed.2d 246 (1964) (elicitation by government informant after indictment); *Brewer v. Williams,* 430 U.S. 387, 97 S.Ct. 1232, 51 L.Ed.2d 424 (1977) (custodial interrogation after arraignment).

1. Deliberate Elicitation After Indictment or Formal Charge

Although *Massiah* predated *Wade,* the *Ash* Court characterized it, in retrospect, as a "critical stage" case. See *United States v. Ash,* 413 U.S. 300, 93 S.Ct. 2568, 37 L.Ed.2d 619 (1973). Under the *Ash* standard, the *Massiah* defendant needed counsel for "aid in coping with legal problems." Presumably, this aid is the advice not to incriminate oneself when talking to a potential Government informant. The same *Ash* rationale applies to a *Brewer*-type of defendant who is openly interrogated by police. For further discussion of these confession cases, see the Chapter on confessions.

2. Confessions Before Indictment or Formal Charge

Before *Miranda v. Arizona,* 384 U.S. 436, 86 S.Ct. 1602, 16 L.Ed.2d 694 (1966), the Court toyed with the idea of relying on the Sixth Amendment to regulate confessions produced by custodial interrogations that precede the onset of adversarial judicial proceedings. See *Escobedo v. Illinois,* 378 U.S. 478, 84 S.Ct. 1758, 12 L.Ed.2d 977 (1964) (Sixth Amendment violated on the facts of a pre-indictment custodial interrogation). *Escobedo* was decided, however, before the Court adopted its bright-line rule that the Sixth Amendment attaches only after formal charge or indictment. See *Kirby v. Illinois,* 406 U.S. 682, 92 S.Ct. 1877, 32 L.Ed.2d 411 (1972). Once *Miranda* was decided, the Court embarked on the course of relying on Fifth Amendment doctrine to provide counsel rights for pre-indictment defendants in custody. While the procedure of custodial interrogation may satisfy the "trial-like" criteria for a "critical stage," this alone is insufficient to establish a Sixth Amendment right, because a criminal prosecution, in Sixth Amendment terms, does not arise until a formal charge has been filed against the accused. After *Kirby,* the large bulk of confessions are immune from Sixth Amendment scrutiny, because they occur in the pre-indictment time zone. See also *Moran v. Burbine,* 475 U.S. 412, 106 S.Ct. 1135, 89 L.Ed.2d 410 (1986) (reinterpreting *Escobedo* as a Fifth Amendment holding and holding that there is no Sixth Amendment right to counsel in a pre-charge setting, even if the defendant has retained counsel).

G. THE RIGHT TO COUNSEL AND RELATED RIGHTS ON APPEAL

The right to appeal has a different history from the right to trial, and so the evolution of the right to counsel on appeal is different from the story of the Sixth Amendment's evolution from *Powell* to *Scott.* First, the right to appeal is not expressly guaranteed in the Constitution. Second, neither the English common law nor colonial practice required appeals of right in all criminal cases. Not surprisingly, the Sixth Amendment speaks only of a right to counsel in a "criminal prosecution," and not about counsel on appeal. Even when statutory rights to appeal became widespread among the states, the Court found that an appeal was not "at common law * * * a necessary element of due process of law." *McKane v. Durston,* 153 U.S. 684, 14 S.Ct. 913, 38 L.Ed. 867 (1894). Thus, the *McKane* Court declared that "whether an appeal should be allowed, and if so, under what circumstances" is a matter for the states to determine.

By the 1950s all states granted appeals of right as a matter of state law, and Federal defendants enjoyed a statutory right of appeal. Thus, it was a moot question whether *McKane* should be reconsidered. The lively debate that divided the states was whether indigents should be afforded the means to pursue a meaningful appeal, through the waiver of filing fees, and the provision of tools for appeal, such as free transcripts and appointed counsel.

For its first foray into this debate, the Court chose to address the question whether a state could deny an effective appeal to indigents who could not pay for a transcript. The most difficult problem was finding a constitutional basis for establishing an indigent's right of access to appeal. Due Process alone was a weak basis in the 1950s. *McKane* stood in the way, and *Betts* implied that Due Process was not a source of *per se* rights for indigents, but only case-by-case assessment of their needs. Therefore, the Court chose to intertwine Due Process with Equal Protection, in order to create a blended doctrinal basis for a right to non-discriminatory treatment for indigents seeking access to the appellate courts.

This non-discrimination principle came to encompass both the right to fee waivers for indigents and the right to appointed counsel on the first appeal of right. Ultimately, in the 1970s, the Court halted the expansion of this principle by declining to grant rights to counsel for indigents seeking access to discretionary appeals and to the certiorari process. Nonetheless, the Court's initial precedents created a backdoor around *McKane*. Looking back, the Court declared that its blended Due Process and Equal Protection doctrine created "the fundamental constitutional right of access to the courts." *Bounds v. Smith,* 430 U.S. 817, 97 S.Ct. 1491, 52 L.Ed.2d 72 (1977). Using this foundation, the Court later came to create rights based on Due Process alone. See, e.g., *Evitts v. Lucey,* 469 U.S. 387, 105 S.Ct. 830, 83 L.Ed.2d 821 (1985) (effective assistance of appellate counsel required by Due Process).

1. The Right to a Transcript on the First Appeal

In *Griffin v. Illinois,* 351 U.S. 12, 76 S.Ct. 585, 100 L.Ed. 891 (1956), the Court held unconstitutional a state rule that effectively denied appellate review to defendants who could not afford to pay for a transcript. The rule required that defendants file a bill of exceptions in order to appeal. Such a bill could not be prepared so as to include claims of trial error without a transcript. The Court held that a state must provide a free transcript to indigents in order to insure "adequate and effective" appellate review on a first appeal of right.

a. Rationale

Justice Black's plurality opinion referred repeatedly to Equal Protection and Due Process as requiring the result in *Griffin*. He noted that the aim of Equal Protection and Due Process in the judicial system is "equal justice," and declared that the state cannot enforce rules that are neutral on their face but "invidiously discriminatory" in application. Nor can a state discriminate on the grounds of poverty any more "than on account of religion, race or color." Denial of a free transcript to indigents was found invidious because "ability to pay costs in advance bears no rational relationship to a defendant's guilt or innocence."

b. Adequate Review Required

The Court in *Griffin* stated that Equal Protection and Due Process protect defendants at trial and at "all stages of the proceedings." Thus, even though *McKane* found that an appeal is not constitutionally required, states must conform to Equal Protection and Due Process requirements when they decide to provide for appeals. There is no requirement that a state have a system of appeal, but if it has one, it must be run fairly and without discrimination. The Court concluded that "there can be no equal justice where the kind of trial" or appeal a defendant gets "depends on the amount of money" he or she has.

c. Justice Frankfurter's Concurrence

Justice Frankfurter did not find it necessary to intertwine Equal Protection and Due Process in order to approve a right to free transcripts. He preferred to rely on Equal Protection alone, out of deference to *McKane*'s holding that an appeal is not a Due Process right. In *Griffin* he found that the state had "shut off" appellate review to indigents in a way that has no "relationship to a rational policy of criminal appeal."

d. Dissent

Justice Harlan dissented in an opinion for four Justices. He argued that it was inappropriate to mesh Due Process analysis with Equal Protection analysis. He concluded that neither protection was a sufficient source for establishing a right to free transcripts for indigents. Justice Harlan found that Equal Protection was not violated in *Griffin* because the state does not create invidious discrimination by providing privileges that indigents cannot afford. According to Justice Harlan, Equal Protection does not impose "an affirmative duty to lift the handicaps flowing from differences in economic circumstances." As to the Due Process Clause, Justice Harlan found that it only requires that appeals should not be denied for "arbitrary or capricious reasons." He concluded that the state's desire to economize by requiring defendants to pay for transcripts is not "capricious." He found no necessary analogy between the right to defend oneself at trial and on appeal, because there is a right to a trial, but no right to an appeal under *McKane*.

e. Perspective

Some modern observers categorize *Griffin* as an Equal Protection case, both because Justice Frankfurter's vote relying on Equal Protection was essential to create a majority, and because terms like "equal justice," and "invidious discrimination" are familiar mainstays of equal protection rhetoric. Yet the Court itself persisted in treating *Griffin* as a case resting on a blend of Equal Protection and Due Process law. See, e.g., *Mayer v. City of Chicago*, 404 U.S. 189, 92 S.Ct. 410, 30 L.Ed.2d 372 (1971); *Ross v. Moffitt*, 417 U.S. 600, 94 S.Ct. 2437, 41 L.Ed.2d 341 (1974). To understand *Griffin*'s reliance on this doctrinal blend, it helps to remember that such a rationale achieved two goals in 1956. First, by blending equality notions into a Due Process analysis, Justice Black sidestepped the limitations of pure Due Process law under *McKane* and *Betts*, and simultaneously summoned the authority of "strict scrutiny" analysis from civil cases like *Brown v. Board of Education*, 347 U.S. 483, 74 S.Ct. 686, 98 L.Ed. 873 (1954). Certainly, the state's interest in "saving money" would not survive strict scrutiny, and this is why the

Griffin plurality was able to condemn the state's rule by simply citing the "invidious discrimination" concept.

Second, by blending Due Process concerns about fair judicial procedure into its equal protection analysis, the Court limited the precedential value of *Griffin* to the context of an indigent's access to the courts. Without the Due Process element in *Griffin,* the Court would have been hard pressed to explain why its treatment of indigents as a suspect class did not necessarily apply to civil cases involving pure Equal Protection law—such as wealth discrimination in education, services and the like.

f. Limitations on *Griffin* Analysis

The success of the *Griffin* Court's blending of two constitutional sources depends on the willingness of observers to refrain from separating these sources into their more familiar identities, for the whole was intended to be greater than the sum of the parts. Justice Harlan insisted that the blend was not legitimate, and that Due Process and Equal Protection questions required independent analysis. Later, a majority of the Court reinterpreted *Griffin*'s novel formulation and broke its two sources apart, in order to find that neither sufficed to protect indigents at every level of the appellate process.

2. The Right to a Transcript in Any State Proceeding

In *Mayer v. City of Chicago,* 404 U.S. 189, 92 S.Ct. 410, 30 L.Ed.2d 372 (1971) a unanimous Court effectively extended *Griffin* to create a right to a free transcript for indigents in any state criminal proceeding. Specifically, the *Mayer* Court required a transcript for a defendant who was convicted of a petty offense that was punishable by a fine only. *Mayer* was the culmination of *Griffin*'s progeny of nine transcript cases, decided between 1958 and 1970, which covered state proceedings that include appeal, habeas and collateral attack. See, e.g., *Roberts v. LaVallee,* 389 U.S. 40, 88 S.Ct. 194, 19 L.Ed.2d 41 (1967) (*Griffin* requires provision of preliminary hearing transcript to indigents).

a. Rationale

The *Mayer* Court reaffirmed *Griffin*'s doctrine as resting on both Equal Protection and Due Process, and as allowing "no invidious discrimination" against indigents. The Court reasoned that the denial of a transcript in a non-felony case is invidious, because a defendant's poverty "bears no more relationship to guilt or innocence" than in a felony case. The Court rejected the state's argument that its interests in economy and in "not burdening the appellate process" outweighed an indigent's interest in a transcript. It found that *Griffin*'s principle "does not represent a balance" between competing interests, but rather was "a flat prohibition against pricing indigent defendants out of" effective appeals that are available to defendants of means. Thus, the invidiousness of the discrimination exists no matter what sentence is imposed, and the state's fiscal interests are "irrelevant."

3. **The Right to a Fee Waiver on Appeal**
    In *Burns v. Ohio,* 360 U.S. 252, 79 S.Ct. 1164, 3 L.Ed.2d 1209 (1959) the Court held unconstitutional a state rule denying leave to appeal to a defendant who could not afford to pay the docket fee. The Court relied on *Griffin*'s rationale to hold that a state must waive fees for indigents seeking access to a discretionary appeal that follows an unsuccessful first appeal of right.

    a. **Rationale**
        The *Burns* Court rejected the idea that *Griffin*'s "equal justice" doctrine is limited to a first appeal of right. Once a state establishes appellate review, "*Griffin* holds ∗ ∗ ∗ it may not foreclose indigents from access to any phase of that procedure because of their poverty." The Court also rejected the notion that the discretionary nature of a state supreme court's jurisdiction is relevant to application of the "equal justice" doctrine. It held that as long as defendants with means could seek leave to appeal, indigent defendants could not be "denied that opportunity" on grounds of poverty. According to *Griffin*'s logic, the ability to pay the costs of a docket fee bears no "rational" relationship to the potential merit of an indigent's appeal.

    b. **The Right to a Fee Waiver in Other State Proceedings**
        Implicitly, the Court's logic in *Burns* could be used to extend the right to fee waivers to other stages of state criminal proceedings. In later cases, the Court followed through with this logic. See *Smith v. Bennett,* 365 U.S. 708, 81 S.Ct. 895, 6 L.Ed.2d 39 (1961) (right to fee waiver for state habeas application).

4. **The Right to Appointed Counsel on the First Appeal of Right**
    In *Douglas v. California,* 372 U.S. 353, 83 S.Ct. 814, 9 L.Ed.2d 811 (1963) the Court extended *Griffin*'s rationale to require the appointment of counsel for indigents on the first appeal of right. The Court held unconstitutional a state rule that required indigents to seek the appointment of counsel from an appellate court, which would review the trial record and determine whether counsel "would be of advantage to the defendant or helpful to the court." Such a procedure was held to be an "invidious discrimination" against indigents under *Griffin.*

    a. **Rationale**
        The Court found that every element of *Griffin*'s rationale applied to the issue of appointment of counsel on appeal. The state's rule discriminated unfairly because it provided ineffective access to appeal for indigents who lack counsel. Justice Douglas found that the state rule in *Douglas*

discriminated against indigent defendants, because such defendants were forced to rely on the discretion of an appellate judge to find error in "a barren record," while defendants with means could rely on retained counsel to do so. Only indigents were forced to run "the gantlet of a preliminary showing of merit," which was difficult to do based on the record alone.

b. Open Question

In language reminiscent of *Argersinger,* Justice Douglas noted that the Court "need not now decide" whether counsel must be appointed for later discretionary appeals, because it was concerned "only with the first appeal." He also noted that "absolute equality is not required," as long as there is no invidious discrimination. Here, however, the state gave the poor only the right to a "meaningless ritual" while the rich enjoyed the right to a "meaningful appeal."

c. Dissent

Justices Harlan and Stewart dissented, in an opinion that resembled Harlan's dissent in *Griffin.* Once again, Justice Harlan rejected the idea that Equal Protection and Due Process could be blended together, and he concluded that appointed counsel on appeal could not be justified under either doctrine. Justice Harlan argued that Equal Protection does not require the state to affirmatively "lift the handicaps" of poverty by providing counsel to the indigent. As to Due Process, Justice Harlan argued that there was no violation because adequate appellate review was possible without counsel. To Justice Harlan, the state provision at issue in *Douglas* provided indigents with an adequate appeal, because they received the benefits of "expert legal appraisal" of the record by a judge, and "full consideration" of a *pro se* appeal even if counsel was denied.

d. Perspective

The Court in *Douglas* stressed that counsel was required for indigents because "the merits of the one and only appeal an indigent has of right" were being decided. This brief comment, together with his conciliatory dicta that "absolute equality is not required," would be read by a later Court as a justification to limit the *Douglas* rationale to a first appeal. This limitation, in turn, would permit the Court to ignore all the transcript and fee waiver precedents that held *Griffin*'s rationale to be applicable to *all* stages of a state criminal proceeding.

5. No Right to Appointed Counsel in Discretionary Appeals

In *Ross v. Moffitt,* 417 U.S. 600, 94 S.Ct. 2437, 41 L.Ed.2d 341 (1974), the Court held that an indigent has no constitutional right to appointed counsel for discretionary appeals, such as to the state supreme court or to the Supreme Court itself. The *Ross* Court relied on Justice Harlan's reasoning in

Douglas and *Griffin,* and insisted that Equal Protection and Due Process doctrines should be treated as separate tools of analysis. By doing so, the Court was able to modify the elements of the "equal justice" rationale, and to find a denial of counsel to be neither "unfair" nor a denial of "meaningful access" to indigents seeking to bring discretionary appeals.

a.   Rationale

Justice Rehnquist concluded that neither Equal Protection nor Due Process provided an "entirely satisfactory basis" for the *Griffin* and *Douglas* holdings. Therefore, he chose to address each constitutional doctrine separately in *Ross,* as each depends "on a different inquiry emphasizing different factors."

b.   Due Process

Justice Rehnquist found that a state does not deny Due Process "by refusing to provide a lawyer at every stage" of an appeal. He reasoned that a Due Process inquiry must focus on "fairness between the state and the individual," and not on how the state treats "other individuals in the same situation." Justice Rehnquist concluded that defendants without counsel have "meaningful access" to a discretionary appeal, and thus the Due Process Clause was not violated in *Ross.* The *Ross* defendant had an "adequate opportunity to present his claims" through the medium of counsel's brief from the first appeal, the defendant's *pro se* brief for the discretionary appeal, and the record of the first appeal, including the appellate court's judgment. Justice Rehnquist emphasized that the function of discretionary appeals is to provide a vehicle for courts to address important issues and correct errors of law, not to provide review of determinations of guilt. The Supreme Court's longstanding practice of denying counsel to indigent certiorari petitioners provided further support for his conclusion that counsel is not necessary for indigents to have "meaningful access" to discretionary appeals.

c.   Equal Protection

As to Equal Protection, Justice Rehnquist concluded that it did not add significantly to the Due Process analysis already employed. He stated that the Equal Protection inquiry must focus on the nature of the "disparity in treatment" between indigent defendants and others, but that some disparity is acceptable as long as an indigent does not receive a "meaningless ritual" on appeal. He reasoned that while a defendant may be "somewhat handicapped" without counsel on a discretionary appeal, this handicap is "far less" than that suffered by the *Douglas* defendant. The Court concluded that an indigent defendant has adequate access to a discretionary appeal due to the existence of a record and a brief from the first appeal of right, and held that there was no Equal Protection violation in *Ross.* The fact that a lawyer would be helpful to the indigent did not mean that the state was constitutionally required to appoint one.

d. Dissent

Justices Douglas, Brennan and Marshall dissented in an opinion which found that *Douglas*'s "equal justice" principle dictated that counsel should be appointed for discretionary appeals. Justice Douglas declared that discretionary review is a "substantial right," and that counsel can be of "significant assistance" by writing a brief addressed to the specialized legal issues that arise in a second appeal. He contended that indigents will be at a "substantial disadvantage" without counsel, because their first appellate brief is not likely to address such issues. The dissenters concluded that the "same concepts of fairness and equality" that mandated the appointment of counsel in *Douglas* should mandate it in *Ross*.

e. The End of Equal Protection Analysis

Justice Rehnquist's interpretation of *Griffin* and *Douglas* created an Equal Protection boundary for the rights of indigents that proved to be quite enduring. Even the *Ross* dissenters recognized that *Griffin*'s "invidious discrimination" formula had to be replaced with another Equal Protection standard. By the time *Ross* was decided, *Griffin*'s reliance on this formula had been undermined by the Court's holding that wealth discrimination does not require strict scrutiny. See *San Antonio Independent School District v. Rodriguez*, 411 U.S. 1, 93 S.Ct. 1278, 36 L.Ed.2d 16 (1973). Thus, the formula dropped out of sight in *Ross*, because the Court chose to reinterpret *Griffin* and *Douglas* to make them consistent with Equal Protection doctrine concerning indigents in civil cases. As Justice Rehnquist put it, there are limits "beyond which the equal protection analysis may not be pressed without doing violence to principles recognized in other decisions of this Court." After *Ross*, the usefulness of Equal Protection as an analytical tool was diminished. It was considered to be essentially equivalent to the Due Process inquiry of *adequate access* to the criminal justice system. Thus the Court turned away from its earlier reliance on Equal Protection doctrine as a source of rights for indigents in the criminal process, in favor of sole reliance on the Due Process Clause. Yet the Court has never explicitly abandoned the *holdings* of *Griffin*, *Douglas*, and the transcript line of cases.

6. Postscript to *Ross:* No Absolute Right to a Transcript for Federal Prisoners in a Habeas Proceeding

In *United States v. MacCollom*, 426 U.S. 317, 96 S.Ct. 2086, 48 L.Ed.2d 666 (1976) the Court refused to hold unconstitutional a Federal statute that provided a free transcript to prisoners seeking habeas relief only if the "judge certifies the suit is not frivolous and that the transcript is needed to decide the issue presented." See 28 U.S.C.A. § 753(f).

a. Rationale

The Court relied on the *Ross* interpretation of *Douglas* and *Griffin* to approve the use of a "necessity" standard when granting transcripts to habeas defendants. The Court found that the statutory standard comported with "fair procedure" under *Douglas,* because Due Process established no right to appeal or to collateral attack, and because the standard was neither "arbitrary" nor "unreasonable." It also concluded that the statutory condition did not violate Equal Protection, because "absolute equality is not required" under *Ross.* The central question under both Equal Protection and Due Process is whether a defendant has "adequate access" to pursue an appeal, and this must be decided in light of the avenues which the defendant "chose not to follow." The Court determined that the habeas petitioner had no right to a "delayed duplicate" transcript when he had failed to invoke his well-established right to a transcript in an initial appeal.

b. Dissent

Justices Brennan and Marshall dissented in an opinion that found the *MacCollom* holding to be a "plain departure" from *Griffin* and from post-*Griffin* precedents granting absolute rights to a transcript to state prisoners pursuing collateral attack. Justice Brennan labelled the court's decision as "egregious" because a claim of ineffective assistance is "virtually impossible to substantiate without a transcript." Justice Brennan concluded that the Court's reliance on *Ross* was misplaced, and that the defendant's actions in forgoing an initial appeal and transcript were irrelevant to his Equal Protection right to a transcript on habeas.

c. Perspective

MacCollom made it clear that the Court's *Ross*-based reasoning would be used for all indigent claims of access to the processes of appeal and collateral attack. The post-*Griffin* transcript cases were all decided before *Ross* abandoned the "invidious discrimination" formula upon which they were based. While the literal reasoning of these cases supported the *MacCollom* dissenters, the Court made it clear that the analysis in those cases was outmoded, in light of the reasoning of *Ross*—though the Court did not purport to upset the previous holdings on access to transcripts.

H. THE RIGHT TO COUNSEL IN PROCEEDINGS THAT ARE NOT PART OF A CRIMINAL PROSECUTION

Soon after *Gideon* was decided, the Court faced the question whether a right to counsel should be provided to indigents in a proceeding that was not a "criminal prosecution" under the Sixth Amendment. Due Process precedents established the right to a hearing and fair procedures whenever a person's "liberty" was at stake.

A jail sentence was only one kind of liberty loss faced by indigents, as physical confinement in state institutions could result from determinations made at hearings in a variety of "civil" proceedings. The question was, and is, whether appointed counsel is a fundamental right in such non-criminal proceedings.

1. The Right to Counsel in Juvenile Delinquency Proceedings
The Court held that the Constitution provides a right to counsel for juveniles when it decided *In re Gault,* 387 U.S. 1, 87 S.Ct. 1428, 18 L.Ed.2d 527 (1967). The Court found that a civil delinquency proceeding carried with it "the awesome prospect of incarceration" in a state juvenile institution. The Court relied on *Gideon*'s reasoning to find that a juvenile needed "the guiding hand of counsel" to prepare a defense and protect her interests.

a. Rationale
The Court identified two important similarities between a delinquency hearing and a criminal trial. First, a juvenile could be subjected "to the loss of liberty for years," and so this hearing was "comparable in seriousness to a felony prosecution." Second, an attorney was needed to perform the tasks required for an effective defense at the hearing, such as fact investigation, and the presentation of evidence and cross-examination of witnesses. The Court rejected the state's argument that either the judge or the probation officer could protect a juvenile's interests adequately. *Powell* and *Gideon* foreclosed the possibility that the judge could adequately represent the juvenile. Nor could the probation officer fairly do so while playing the roles of arresting officer and state witness against the juvenile.

b. Special Nature of Juvenile Proceedings Found Irrelevant
The Court rejected the state's argument that counsel would interfere with the rehabilitative mission of a delinquency hearing, or alter its character in undesirable ways. It noted that counsel "can play an important role" in rehabilitation. Further, if the presence of counsel made the proceedings more adversarial, this was desirable because the juvenile courts "deal with cases in which facts are disputed" so that "adversary procedures are called for."

c. Other Protections
The *Gault* Court further mandated that the state provide notice of the hearing to the juvenile, and honor the juvenile's rights to confront and cross-examine witnesses, and to invoke the privilege against self-incrimination. The state was also required to provide a transcript of the hearing, as well as appellate review of the juvenile court's decision.

d. Justice Harlan's Opinion
Justice Harlan agreed with the Court's extension of *Gideon* to delinquency proceedings, and provided additional justifications for a right

to counsel in this context. He noted that precedents dating back to *Powell v. Alabama,* 287 U.S. 45, 53 S.Ct. 55, 77 L.Ed. 158 (1932) suggested that the importance of counsel has "special force" for "those who are commonly inexperienced and immature," such as juveniles.

However, Justice Harlan objected to the provision of other safeguards in a juvenile proceeding, such as the privilege against self-incrimination and the rights of confrontation and cross-examination. He argued that counsel's use of these safeguards might affect the informal character and the rehabilitative mission of a delinquency proceeding. Justice Harlan envisioned counsel as a helpful advocate even in a forum that lacked "the atmosphere" of a criminal trial.

2. The Right to Counsel in Probation Revocation Proceedings

In *Gagnon v. Scarpelli,* 411 U.S. 778, 93 S.Ct. 1756, 36 L.Ed.2d 656 (1973), the Court rejected a claim for a right to counsel for all convicted indigents facing probation or parole revocation proceedings, and endorsed a case-by-case rule for provision of counsel.

a. Rationale

The *Gagnon* Court endorsed a presumption that counsel should be provided for probationers who raised either a "colorable claim of innocence" on the facts, or who possessed mitigation arguments that were "complex" or "difficult to present." The abilities of the probationer also were held to be relevant because "the unskilled or uneducated" might have difficulty presenting evidence and conducting cross-examination. In doubtful cases the Court directed the hearing body to appoint counsel if the probationer was not "capable of speaking for himself." The claim for a *per se* right to counsel, however, was rejected. The Court declared that a *per se* right to counsel would produce "direct costs and serious collateral disadvantages." First, it would delay the hearing process and impose financial costs. Second, it would provoke the state to start using prosecutors instead of probation officers at the hearings. These prosecutors, in turn, would argue more vigorously for reincarceration, and cause the hearing body to become "less attuned to the rehabilitative needs" of probationers. These costs could be justified when a probationer's "version of a disputed issue can fairly be represented only by a trained advocate." But in the ordinary case, the existence of a probation violation is usually undisputed—the only dispute in most cases is over the consequences of the violation, an issue on which counsel is not required.

b. Not Like a Criminal Trial

The Court in *Gagnon* found that "there are critical differences" between criminal trials and probation revocation hearings, and that it was in the interest of "both society and the probationer" to preserve these differences. In a revocation hearing, there are no rules of evidence, and there is no prosecutor or lay jury. Thus, the need for counsel derived "not from the invariable attributes" of the hearing, but from the existence of *disputed facts* in occasional cases. Therefore a *Betts*, case-by-case, special circumstances standard was the appropriate one to use to identify probationers who actually needed counsel.

c. **Distinction From *Gault***

Essentially, the state arguments that were accepted in *Gagnon* were rejected in *Gault*. For example, the state claimed in *Gault* that a delinquency proceeding needed to be "informal" and "flexible," because the hearing involved no prosecutor, or rules of evidence, or lay jury, but only an "expert" judge concerned with the mission of "rehabilitation." The *Gagnon* Court distinguished *Gault* on several grounds. It noted that an unconvicted juvenile was more deserving of counsel than a convicted probationer, and that a juvenile needed counsel more because a delinquency hearing was the functional equivalent of an adult's criminal trial. Also, the *Gagnon* Court accepted the idea that counsel could not benefit either the probationer or the hearing body in most cases. By contrast, the *Gault* Court presumed that the facts would be disputed in a typical delinquency case. Therefore, counsel was likely to help both the juvenile and the judge. Thus, the state's interest in denying a *per se* right to counsel in *Gault* was not supported by the argument that it was a needless expense. Finally, the *Gagnon* Court assumed that the presence of counsel would injure the interests of a probationer, because prosecutors would influence the hearing body to exchange its rehabilitative priorities for a more punitive perspective. In *Gault,* however, the Court rejected the idea that counsel would interfere with the rehabilitative mission of the juvenile court.

d. **Perspective**

Gagnon and *Gault* reflected different views concerning the value of a state's interests in "informality, flexibility and economy." The Court had many reasons to find the state interests to be weightier in *Gagnon* than in *Gault,* but it did not choose to explain the *Gagnon* holding solely in these terms. Instead, the Court's reasoning laid the foundation for future rejections of a right to counsel in proceedings that lacked the formal trappings of prosecutor and jury. Indeed, after *Gagnon,* no Court majority endorsed a *per se* right to counsel in a civil case again. *Gagnon* became the Court's compass, and *Gault* became its distinguishable precedent.

3. **No Right to Counsel in Prison Disciplinary Proceedings**

In *Wolff v. McDonnell,* 418 U.S. 539, 94 S.Ct. 2963, 41 L.Ed.2d 935 (1974) the Court held that the Constitution does not provide a right to counsel for inmates facing disciplinary proceedings. The Court held that where the inmate is illiterate or where the issue is complex, the inmate "should be free to seek the aid" of a fellow inmate or a prison staff member.

a.   Rationale
The Court recognized that the prisoner had a Due Process liberty interest at stake in disciplinary hearings, because serious misconduct in prison could be punished by a loss of "good-time" credits toward a shorter sentence. But in light of *Gagnon,* this did not mean that a right to counsel was required. The Court found that the state's interests in denying a right to counsel were even stronger in *Wolff* than they were in *Gagnon.* Not only would the presence of counsel give the hearings "an adversary cast," and reduce their "utility as a means to further correctional goals." The Court also found that it would be very difficult for the state to provide counsel "in sufficient numbers at the time and place" of the prison hearings. Thus, even a case-by-case right to counsel was *too much of a burden* to impose on the state. The Court concluded that the right to consult a *non-lawyer assistant* was adequate to meet the needs of particular inmates who were incapable of presenting evidence in their defense.

b.   Dissent
Justices Marshall and Brennan dissented, in an opinion advocating the creation of a *per se* right to a non-lawyer assistant. Justice Marshall explained that a "high percentage" of inmates are illiterate, or have only limited education or intelligence. Justice Marshall conceded, however, that "counsel on either side would be out of place," and that the practical problems of providing counsel might be "insurmountable" for such hearings.

c.   Proceedings to Transfer a Prisoner to a State Mental Institution
In *Vitek v. Jones,* 445 U.S. 480, 100 S.Ct. 1254, 63 L.Ed.2d 552 (1980), the Court held that Due Process required the state to appoint a mental health professional to assist a prisoner in a hearing to decide whether the prisoner should be involuntarily committed to a mental hospital. The Court determined that the issue of an inmate's mental health would be decided based on expert testimony that is "relatively incomprehensible" to lay people and that most inmates would not "possess the competence or training" to protect their own interests. Accordingly, the Court adopted a *per se* rule that the prisoner was entitled to assistance. Four members of the Court were of the opinion that a prisoner in these circumstances had an absolute right to counsel, but the narrower holding of *Vitek* is that Due Process is satisfied if the state appoints a mental health professional, rather than counsel, to assist the prisoner.

d.   Perspective

The state's interest in denying counsel was weaker in *Vitek* than in *Wolff,* and both the inmate's liberty interest and need for assistance was stronger in *Vitek* as well. The state's interest in "informal and flexible" procedures in disciplinary hearings was strong in *Wolff,* because the Court assumed that a significant number of inmates would be subjected to such hearings, and that the hearings would be held frequently in order to maintain order and discipline in the prison population. In contrast, the *Vitek* Court assumed that comparatively few inmates would be subjected to a mental health hearing.

The liberty interest of the inmates in *Wolff* was a "conditional" one like those of the probationers in *Gagnon.* It was dependent upon the agreement of an inmate to abide by prison rules, and its potential loss was caused by an inmate's violation of that agreement. By contrast, the liberty interest in *Vitek* was closer to the "absolute" interest of the juvenile in *Gault.* The *Vitek* Court declared that inmates are entitled to expect that a criminal conviction will be punished by incarceration in prison, not by confinement in a mental hospital, accompanied by involuntary treatment for mental illness. The liberty interest in *Vitek* was not dependent on the agreement of an inmate, nor was its potential loss caused by any action of an inmate. According to *Gagnon,* it was justifiable to give "less" Due Process to persons with a conditional liberty interest, and "more" Due Process to those with an absolute interest. Moreover, the mental condition of the *Vitek* inmate, like the immature character of the *Gault* juvenile, created a special need for a *per se* right to some assistance, though not necessarily to the assistance of counsel.

e.   Different Procedural Protections

Further evidence of the weight given to the inmate's interest in *Vitek* is shown by the Court's decision to impose other procedural safeguards in mental health hearings. For example, the Court required the decisionmaker in such hearings to be independent, and gave the inmate the right to confront and cross-examine witnesses, except for good cause. By contrast, the *Wolff* Court allowed the decisionmaker at a disciplinary hearing to be a committee of prison staff, and declined to give inmates a right to confront and cross-examine witnesses. Even the inmate's right to present evidence was limited by the discretion of the prison staff to restrict the right if it endangered "correctional goals."

4.   No Absolute Right to Counsel in Summary Court–Martial Proceedings

In *Middendorf v. Henry,* 425 U.S. 25, 96 S.Ct. 1281, 47 L.Ed.2d 556 (1976) the Court held that neither the Sixth Amendment nor Due Process guaranteed a right to counsel for enlisted men and women facing summary courts-martial proceedings.

a. No Sixth Amendment Right to Counsel
The Court held that a summary court-martial is not a "criminal prosecution" under the Sixth Amendment. It acknowledged that charges of criminal violations of military law were adjudicated at such hearings, and that enlisted personnel could receive sentences of up to 30 days confinement or 45 days of hard labor. While this was sufficient to create a "liberty interest," the Court noted that not every hearing where a loss of liberty is threatened is *"ipso facto"* a criminal prosecution.

The Court found that *Gault* and *Gagnon* identified *two qualities* as being characteristic of a non-criminal proceeding. The first was the lack of adversary procedural trappings, such as prosecutor, lay jury, trial judge, and rules of evidence. The second was the existence of some function that went beyond criminal law enforcement, such as the rehabilitative function of the hearings in *Gault* and *Gagnon.* The Court concluded that a summary court-martial possessed both non-criminal characteristics. In this summary proceeding, the presiding officer served as judge, prosecutor, jury, and defense counsel. The hearing also served the special function of regulating the life of the military community. Many military offenses had no civilian counterparts, and the hearings determined only military punishments meted out to military personnel.

b. No Due Process Right to Counsel
The Court found that as in *Wolff,* the Government interests in denying counsel outweighed the interests of the individuals seeking counsel, so that no Due Process right to counsel should exist. The Court reasoned that as in *Gagnon,* the presence of counsel would interfere with the non-criminal goals of the hearing. It would turn a "brief, informal" proceeding concerning petty offenses into one that unjustifiably consumed military resources.

c. Dissent
Justice Marshall wrote a dissent joined by Justice Brennan. He argued that a summary court-martial should be treated as a "criminal prosecution" because of the criminal nature of the charges brought against enlisted defendants. Justice Marshall determined that the goal of a summary court-martial was a traditionally punitive one, and that counsel was necessary because the decisionmaker could not protect the defendant's interests. Justice Marshall also argued that the *Middendorf* majority gave too much weight to military interests in the Due Process calculus.

5. No Absolute Right to Counsel for Indigents in Proceedings to Terminate Parental Rights
In *Lassiter v. Department of Social Services,* 452 U.S. 18, 101 S.Ct. 2153, 68 L.Ed.2d 640 (1981), the Court held that the Constitution does not provide a

per se right to counsel to an indigent facing a hearing to terminate her status as a parent.

a. Rationale

The Court determined that precedents such as *Gideon, Gault,* and *Vitek* established that a right to counsel exists only "where the litigant may lose his physical liberty if he loses the litigation." Thus, the Court established a presumption that no right to counsel exists unless an "interest in personal freedom" is at stake.

b. Balance of Interests

The Court in *Lassiter* held that an indigent's liberty interest in parental status did not qualify as an interest in "personal freedom," and therefore determined that the governing Due Process analysis was that of *Mathews v. Eldridge,* 424 U.S. 319, 96 S.Ct. 893, 47 L.Ed.2d 18 (1976) (involving a property interest). *Mathews* required the Court to weigh the parent's liberty interest, the state's interest in denying counsel, and the "risk of an erroneous decision" without counsel, and then "to set their net weight in the scales against the presumption" that a right to counsel did not exist. In striking this balance, the Court found that the *Mathews* factors would favor a right to counsel in some cases and not in others. The parent's interest was always "commanding," and the state's interest in economy and expediency usually would be less significant. But the risk of error would vary, because the complexity of the facts and evidence would vary from case to case. The Court concluded that Due Process did not require a *per se* right to counsel, for such an absolute requirement would sacrifice the state's interests in "informality, flexibility, and economy" unnecessarily. On the facts of *Lassiter,* the Court found that there was no evidence that counsel could have made a "difference" in the result, and that there was no error in denying counsel.

c. Dissent

Justice Blackmun dissented in an opinion for three Justices. He rejected the Court's formulation of a "presumption" against a right to counsel in cases where an interest in physical liberty is not at stake. He argued that the *Lassiter* hearing qualified for a *per se* right to counsel because the interest in parenthood was fundamental, and the hearing involved a trial-type of proceeding, complete with judge, prosecutor, and rules of evidence.

d. Perspective

Lassiter is important because it clarified the law, and signalled the end of the development of counsel rights in cases where an indigent's physical liberty is not at stake.

The *Lassiter* dissenters provided a helpful framework for organizing the family of precedents from *Gault* to *Middendorf*, and the *Lassiter* majority did not dispute the legitimacy of this framework. According to the dissenters, the precedents could be arranged upon a Due Process spectrum, with *Gault* at one end (absolute right to counsel), and *Wolff* at the other (no right to any assistance in any case). Each case involved a different combination of three variables: the state interest, the liberty interest, and the type of hearing procedures. At the *Gault* end, counsel was required because the state interests in denying counsel were weak, the liberty interest was strong, and adversary trappings were present in a delinquency hearing. At the *Wolff* end, counsel was not required because the state interests were strong, the liberty interest was weak, and adversary trappings were lacking in the prison disciplinary hearing. *Gagnon* fell in the middle of the spectrum, *Vitek* was located closer to *Gault,* and *Middendorf* was very close to *Wolff.*

e.   Need for Limitation

If this framework was an accurate way of portraying the Due Process rationales of the prior cases, why did the Court decline to use it in *Lassiter?* Most likely, it is because the *Lassiter* majority viewed the indigent parent's claim for counsel as the first of many such claims that could be made in future civil cases. Any civil hearing with adversary trappings would qualify for the *Gault* end of the spectrum, unless the Court could find that the state interests outweighed the individual interest. Such weighing could be a difficult and debatable exercise, as the Court's divided opinions in *Middendorf* revealed.

Thus, if the Court wanted a more predictable way to limit counsel rights in civil cases, it needed to break away from the Due Process framework as envisioned by the *Lassiter* dissenters. It made this break by declaring that a "physical" liberty interest was weightier *per se* than other interests, so that the *Gault*-to-*Wolff* formulations could be discarded as inapposite to the *Lassiter* problem. See also *Medina v. California,* ___U.S. ___, 112 S.Ct. 2572, 120 L.Ed.2d 353 (1992) (*Mathews* balancing test is inapplicable to Due Process questions arising in criminal cases).

f.   Case-by-Case Approach

The *Lassiter* Court indicated that counsel would be required in some civil cases, if the balance of interests strongly favored the appointment of counsel. However, the Court's approval of a denial of counsel on the facts of *Lassiter* sent a "hands-off" signal to lower courts. No specific guidelines were proffered by the Court, and a denial of counsel was held to be appropriate if there was no strong evidence that the lack of counsel affected the outcome.

I.   THE RIGHT TO COUNSEL AND RELATED RIGHTS IN COLLATERAL ATTACK PROCEEDINGS

After *Ross* was decided, it appeared unlikely that the Court would be prepared to grant a right to counsel in collateral attack proceedings, which were even more remote from the trial than the discretionary appeal stage where no counsel was required. Yet before *Ross,* prisoners seeking access to habeas remedies had been granted protection from state "impairment" of their access to the courts. One such protection was the right to receive assistance from fellow inmates who were "jailhouse lawyers," and this right was grounded both on references to *Griffin*'s doctrine and on the statutory right of access to federal habeas corpus. Even after *Ross,* the Court expanded this right of "access to the courts" into a full-blown constitutional doctrine that required a right of access to prison law libraries for inmates pursuing habeas remedies. Ultimately, however, this doctrine did not prevent the Court from applying *Ross*'s reasoning to the context of collateral attack, where indigents could rely on legal materials from their first appeal to draft habeas petitions and present their claims "adequately."

1.   A Prisoner's Right of Access to the Courts: Assistance From Other Inmates
In *Johnson v. Avery,* 393 U.S. 483, 89 S.Ct. 747, 21 L.Ed.2d 718 (1969) the Court struck down a state prison regulation that barred inmates from assisting other prisoners in preparing petitions for habeas relief. The Court found that this ban denied illiterate and poorly educated prisoners their rightful access to the courts.

a.   Rationale
The Court determined that prison authorities could impose "reasonable regulations" on the activities of prison "writ writers" in the interests of "disciplinary administration." However, the Court held that a total ban on the activities of these inmates was reasonable only if the state could show that illiterate inmates were provided with *adequate access to the courts through alternative methods*. As the prison authorities could make no such showing in *Johnson,* the Court found that the prison's regulation denied a prisoner the ability to receive adequate access to habeas proceedings. The Court relied on the *Griffin* line of cases and on the habeas statutes to conclude that prison inmates had a right to adequate access to habeas relief. See *Ex Parte Hull,* 312 U.S. 546, 61 S.Ct. 640, 85 L.Ed. 1034 (1941) (prison authorities may not screen habeas petitions, because this "impairs" a prisoner's right to apply to a Federal court for habeas relief, and thus violates statutory rights granted by Congress). The Court observed that the state could not ban illiterate or poorly educated prisoners from filing collateral attack petitions, and yet the effect of the prison ban on writ writers "does just that."

b.   Dissent
Justices White and Black dissented, in an opinion that expressed skepticism as to whether inmate writ writers would provide "adequate"

access to the courts. Justice White argued that such untrained inmates would draft "inadequate and misconceived" petitions, thereby burdening the courts and prejudicing their prisoner "clients." He considered the prison's ban to be necessary, because of "severe" disciplinary problems caused by the power of jailhouse lawyers to influence other inmates.

c.   Statutory or Constitutional Right

It may not be obvious why the *Johnson* Court could not ground its holding more explicitly in the Due Process and Equal Protection doctrine, or why the Court found it necessary to rely on the Federal habeas statute to justify its holding. Traditionally, the Court gave great deference to the power of prison authorities to regulate the life of prisoners. See e.g., *Wolff v. McDonnell,* 418 U.S. 539, 94 S.Ct. 2963, 41 L.Ed.2d 935 (1974) (citing examples of limitations on the rights of inmates). No Due Process precedent gave indigent prisoners the same rights as other indigents, or held that prison regulations were subject to close scrutiny by courts. Therefore, the *Johnson* Court needed to characterize the right of "access to the courts" as a unique right of prisoners that could be protected without unsettling other "prison" precedents. *Hull* provided a useful source for the *Johnson* holding, because the statutory right to federal habeas corpus was expressly designed for the use of prisoners. Later, various members of the Court would quarrel about whether *Johnson* actually established a "constitutional" right of access to courts, or only enlarged a statutory one. At the time, however, *Johnson*'s statutory rationale served to justify the Court's abandonment of deference to the actions of prison authorities, whenever they impaired a prisoner's ability to seek state or Federal relief from unconstitutional confinement.

2.   The Right of Access to a Prison Law Library for Preparing Habeas Petitions

In *Bounds v. Smith,* 430 U.S. 817, 97 S.Ct. 1491, 52 L.Ed.2d 72 (1977), the Court held that prisoners have a constitutional right of access to the courts that encompasses the right of access to a law library to prepare petitions for habeas proceedings. The Court also held that in the absence of library facilities, "adequate assistance from persons trained in the law" would be an acceptable "alternative means" to achieve the goal of "meaningful access" to collateral attack remedies.

a.   Rationale

The Court relied on two lines of authority to support its holding that the state had an affirmative duty to provide a prison library as a "remedial measure" to insure that an inmate's access to courts was "adequate, effective, and meaningful." First, the *Bounds* Court traced the origins of the right of "access to the courts" to *Hull*'s principle that the state may not abridge or impair a prisoner's right of access to Federal habeas corpus. Justice Marshall, writing for the Court, declared that *Griffin* and its progeny moved beyond *Hull* to require the state to undertake remedial measures in order to insure that prisoners and others received adequate access to the courts. *Johnson* applied "essentially the same standards" in requiring the state to provide inmates with access to the services of writ writers. Later, *Ross* validated *Griffin*'s principles by requiring "adequate opportunities to present claims fairly." Thus, "meaningful access" to the courts was the "touchstone" of both the *Hull–Johnson* and *Griffin–Ross* lines of precedent.

The Court rejected the state's arguments that a prison law library was unnecessary to assure prisoners meaningful access to the habeas process. It explained that the *Johnson* right of access to writ writers did not make a library unnecessary, because habeas was not so "simple" that inmates could prepare adequate petitions without reference to legal authorities. The Court also pointed out that without a library, an inmate would be unable to respond to arguments based on legal authorities in the state's briefs. The Court found that inmates could not rely exclusively on briefs and transcripts from their trials and first appeals, because state and Federal habeas actions are "original" ones requiring new research. Unlike the discretionary appeals involved in *Ross,* collateral attack proceedings functioned as an avenue for judicial correction of errors, in the "first line of defense against constitutional violations."

b.   Dissent

The dissenters argued that law libraries would be of little use to "untutored inmates," and questioned the existence of a constitutional right of access to the courts. They also found it unjustifiable to require a state to "subsidize" access to the exercise of a Federal statutory right. The dissenting Justices declared that the *Hull–Johnson* and *Griffin–Ross* precedents supported only a right of "physical access" to the courts. In *Bounds,* the state's failure to fund libraries did not actually block inmates from filing petitions, as happened in *Hull.* Nor did the state "limit contacts" that would aid inmates in doing so, as in *Johnson.* Under *Ross,* indigent prisoners had no valid claim, because they had an "adequate opportunity" to present their claims *pro se.* The dissenters objected to the *Bounds* ruling because it conflicted with *Ross,* and because the "logical destination" of a right of "access to the courts" must be a future ruling that counsel would be required for prisoners pursuing collateral attack remedies.

3.   No Right to Appointed Counsel in Habeas Proceedings

In *Pennsylvania v. Finley,* 481 U.S. 551, 107 S.Ct. 1990, 95 L.Ed.2d 539 (1987) the Court held that the constitutional standard of "effectiveness" for appellate counsel was not applicable to habeas proceedings. As no "underlying constitutional right" to counsel existed in such proceedings, no right to "effective" counsel existed either. Thus, no constitutional violation occurred when counsel withdrew from representation and informed the trial court that the habeas petition had "no merit." See *Anders v. California,* 386 U.S. 738, 87 S.Ct. 1396, 18 L.Ed.2d 493 (1967) (holding that such conduct by appellate counsel on the first appeal violates Due Process).

a. Rationale

The Court relied on the reasoning in *Ross.* Under *Ross,* an indigent who is attacking a conviction after the first appeal is entitled merely to an *adequate* opportunity for fair presentation of his claims. If counsel is not necessary for an adequate presentation in these contexts, then appointment of counsel is not constitutionally required. As in *Ross,* an adequate opportunity to pursue a habeas claim was provided despite the absence of counsel. The petitioner had access to a trial transcript, appellate brief, and judicial opinion from his first appeal.

Finally, Justice Rehnquist noted that a right to "effective" assistance of counsel existed on appeal only because there was an underlying constitutional right to counsel on appeal. See *Evitts v. Lucey,* 469 U.S. 387, 105 S.Ct. 830, 83 L.Ed.2d 821 (1985) (holding that states may not "cut off" the right to appeal because of appellate counsel's ineffectiveness in failing to file a timely appeal).

b. Dissent

Justices Brennan and Marshall dissented in an opinion which argued that counsel's withdrawal from the case violated Equal Protection and Due Process on the facts of *Finley,* and that it was unnecessary to reach the broad question addressed by the majority's ruling. Justice Brennan argued that Finley was denied an opportunity to present claims fairly because counsel performed no meaningful review of the record.

4. No Right to Counsel in Habeas Proceedings, Even in Capital Cases

In *Murray v. Giarratano,* 492 U.S. 1, 109 S.Ct. 2765, 106 L.Ed.2d 1 (1989) the Court held that death row inmates seeking access to habeas proceedings have no constitutional right to appointed counsel.

a. Rationale

A plurality of the Court relied on *Finley* and found no reason to distinguish capital cases from non-capital cases, insofar as access to a habeas remedy was concerned. The plurality rejected the claim that *Bounds* supported the creation of a right to counsel in *Giarratano* to insure a right of "access to the courts." Justice Rehnquist observed that the *Bounds* right was grounded "on a constitutional theory considered in *Finley.*" Therefore, *Finley* limited *Bounds,* and was held to govern *Giarratano.*

b. Justice Kennedy's Concurrence

Justices Kennedy and O'Connor concurred in an opinion that gave more weight to the relevance of *Bounds* than did the plurality. Justice Kennedy agreed with the *Giarratano* dissenters' assessment that habeas review was a "central part" of the review process in capital cases. He acknowledged that a large percentage of death row inmates received habeas relief, and that the complexity of capital habeas law made it impossible for petitioners to succeed without assistance. However, Justice Kennedy was reluctant to impose a "categorical" solution of a *per se* right to counsel, and relied on *Bounds* to argue that "meaningful access" to the courts could be provided in alternative ways. He pointed out that no Virginia death row inmate had ever been unable to obtain counsel to assist in preparing a state habeas petition, and he preferred to honor *Bounds* by entrusting further development of habeas counsel rights to the state and Federal legislatures.

c. Dissent

Justices Stevens, Brennan, and Marshall dissented, in an opinion arguing that *Powell, Gideon, Griffin, Douglas, Ross, Finley,* and *Bounds* supported a right to counsel for death row inmates. Both the "right to counsel" and the right of "access to the courts" cases justified the provision of counsel because the state habeas process in Virginia was the "key" to meaningful appellate review in capital cases, as the state appellate process did not provide a sufficient safeguard against miscarriages of justice. The dissenters pointed out that the success rate of capital habeas petitioners showed that there was a "high incidence of uncorrected error" in capital trials and appeals. Therefore, the state habeas process served as a *de facto* extension of the appellate review process; indeed, some kinds of errors could be argued or discovered only at the habeas stage.

J. THE RIGHT OF ACCESS TO AN APPOINTED EXPERT AT TRIAL

In *Ake v. Oklahoma,* 470 U.S. 68, 105 S.Ct. 1087, 84 L.Ed.2d 53 (1985), the Court held that when sanity is likely to be a "significant factor" at trial, a defendant is entitled to access to a psychiatrist's assistance in "evaluation, preparation, and presentation" of a defense. The Court also held that when sanity was likely to be a significant factor at a capital sentencing hearing, a defendant was similarly entitled to such assistance. These rights were derived from the principle that Due Process requires that indigents must be provided with the "raw materials integral to building an effective defense."

1. Rationale

The Court stated that "meaningful access to justice" was the theme of cases such as *Gideon, Griffin, Douglas,* and *Ross.* It declared that the Fourteenth Amendment's guarantee of "fundamental fairness" required that indigent defendants have an "opportunity to participate meaningfully" in criminal trials. This meant that they must be given a "fair opportunity" to present a defense," which, in turn, requires that a state must provide an indigent with the "raw materials" and "basic tools" for building an effective defense. The Court concluded that a defendant's interest in life or liberty was "uniquely compelling," and that a state's interest in avoiding the expense of funding experts was "not substantial." Both the state and the defendant had "compelling interests" in the accurate disposition of the case.

The Court found that access to an expert in some cases "may well be crucial" to a defendant's ability to "marshall a defense." Where the defendant's mental state is an issue, the Court noted that a psychiatrist can contribute to a defense in many ways—by gathering relevant facts, explaining behavior, preparing defense counsel to cross-examine a prosecutor's expert and make sense of her answers, and translating "complex and foreign" information for the jury. These skills made a psychiatrist's testimony a "virtual necessity" for any chance of success in proving insanity.

2. Applied to the Facts

The Court held that the defendant in *Ake* made an adequate showing that insanity was likely to be a "significant factor" at the trial. This finding was based on several aspects of *Ake*, including the filing of the insanity plea, the trial court's decision to have the defendant evaluated for competency to stand trial, the finding by the prosecution's expert that the defendant was competent only when given large doses of medication, as well as his opinion that the defendant's severe mental impairment after the crime could have existed earlier.

3. Dissent

Justice Rehnquist dissented and argued that the evidence in *Ake* did not show that insanity was likely to be a "significant factor," either at the trial stage or at the sentencing phase. Justice Rehnquist objected to the idea that an appointed expert would assist in "evaluation, preparation, and presentation" of a defense, because he believed that doctors should be "fact" witnesses, not "advocates."

a. Application Beyond Psychiatric Experts

Under the analysis in *Ake*, the state may have an obligation to appoint a defense expert other than a psychiatrist, if the defendant can show that the expert's assistance is likely to be especially valuable, and that deprivation of that assistance will create a high risk of error. However, two features of *Ake*'s rationale make it possible for lower courts to apply the "right to an expert" narrowly. First, a trial judge may deny an expert to a defendant whose showing is weaker than the strong showing made in *Ake*. Second, a judge may determine that a particular kind of expert is not a "virtual necessity" for presenting a defense. Not surprisingly, lower court interpretations of *Ake* sometimes reflect a narrow reading of its scope. These interpretations often cite *Caldwell v. Mississippi*, 472 U.S. 320, 105 S.Ct. 2633, 86 L.Ed.2d 231 (1985), where the Court held that "undeveloped assertions" that an expert will be beneficial are insufficient to entitle a defendant to appointment of an expert under *Ake*. Still, there are several lower court cases which have reversed convictions for failure to provide expert assistance deemed necessary under the circumstances. See *Dunn v. Roberts*, 963 F.2d 308 (10th Cir.1992) (denial of funds to retain expert to explain nature of battered spouse syndrome precluded the defendant from presenting an effective defense in prosecution for aiding and abetting felony-murder; specific intent was an essential element of aiding and abetting, and an expert could have aided the defense by supporting the defendant's assertion that her presence at the scene of the crime was the result of repeated battering, and not the result of an intent to assist in criminal conduct).

III. EFFECTIVE ASSISTANCE OF COUNSEL

A. INTRODUCTION

The Supreme Court has held that the right to counsel means more than merely being represented at trial by a member of the bar. Rather, the right to counsel means the right to *effective assistance* of counsel. The difficulty is in determining whether counsel's performance has breached minimum standards of effectiveness and whether, assuming counsel was ineffective, the defendant was prejudiced in some way which warrants a retrial.

1. Applies to Appointed and Retained Counsel

Both appointed and retained counsel are subject to review for ineffectiveness. Thus, the defendant does not in any way "waive" his right to effective assistance of counsel merely by choosing a lawyer who acts ineffectively. See *Cuyler v. Sullivan*, 446 U.S. 335, 100 S.Ct. 1708, 64 L.Ed.2d 333 (1980) ("Since the State's conduct of a criminal trial itself implicates the State in the defendant's conviction, we see no basis for drawing a distinction between retained and appointed counsel that would deny equal justice to defendants who must choose their own lawyers.").

2. Applies to Trial, Sentencing, and Other Critical Stages

Wherever the Sixth Amendment right to counsel applies, the right to effective assistance of counsel applies as well. Thus, the defendant has a right to effective assistance in sentencing, guilty pleas, and the first appeal of right, as well as at trial. See *Strickland v. Washington, infra* (effectiveness standards applied at capital sentencing); *Hill v. Lockhart*, 474 U.S. 52, 106 S.Ct. 366, 88 L.Ed.2d 203 (1985) (ineffective assistance in advising defendant improperly as to guilty plea); *Evitts v. Lucey*, 469 U.S. 387, 105 S.Ct. 830, 83 L.Ed.2d 821 (1985) (ineffective assistance on first appeal of right).

3. Inapplicable Where Right to Counsel Does Not Apply

Conversely, if there is no right to counsel, there is no right to effective assistance of counsel. As previously discussed in this outline, the Supreme Court has held that there is no right to counsel for appellate review or for collateral attack beyond the first appeal of right. As a result, if counsel acts ineffectively at these stages, there is no constitutional claim of ineffective assistance. See *Pennsylvania v. Finley*, 481 U.S. 551, 107 S.Ct. 1990, 95 L.Ed.2d 539 (1987) (no claim of ineffective assistance is cognizable where counsel's mistakes occurred on collateral attack); *Wainwright v. Torna*, 455 U.S. 586, 102 S.Ct. 1300, 71 L.Ed.2d 475 (1982) (no right to counsel at certiorari stage, therefore no claim of ineffective assistance can be asserted).

B. *STRICKLAND*

In *Strickland v. Washington*, 466 U.S. 668, 104 S.Ct. 2052, 80 L.Ed.2d 674 (1984), the Supreme Court held that the defendant must make two showings in order to obtain a reversal for ineffective assistance of counsel.

1. Deficient Performance

First, defendant must show that counsel made errors so serious that his "representation fell below an objective standard of reasonableness" and was not "within the range of competence demanded of attorneys in criminal cases."

2. Prejudice

Second, the defendant must show that counsel's incompetent representation prejudiced him. The standard for prejudice is whether "there is a *reasonable probability* that, but for counsel's unprofessional errors, the result of the proceeding would have been different." The Court defined a reasonable probability as "a probability sufficient to undermine confidence in the outcome."

3. Strict Test

The Court in *Strickland* recognized that its two-pronged test was "rigorous" and "highly demanding," and that it imposed a significant burden on the defendant challenging counsel's performance. The *Strickland* test makes it unlikely that many claims of ineffective assistance will be successful. The Court justified its test by stating that "it is all too tempting for a defendant to second-guess counsel's decision after conviction or adverse sentence, and it is all too easy for a court, examining counsel's defense after it has proved unsuccessful, to conclude that a particular act or omission of counsel was unreasonable." The Court was concerned that "intrusive post-trial inquiry into attorney performance" would chill vigorous advocacy by making counsel reluctant to make decisions that might later be found ineffective.

C. ELEMENTS OF COMPETENCE

The Court in *Strickland* noted that effective representation entails both a reasonably thorough *investigation* and a reasonably competent *presentation* of the defendant's case.

1. Investigation

In order to make strategic choices, the defense counsel must be informed of pertinent information. Ordinarily this requires defense counsel to question witnesses, investigate crime locations, interview family members, etc. Thus, courts after *Strickland* have found that a complete failure to conduct an investigation is ordinarily ineffective, since a counsel who has done no investigation will not have enough information with which to make strategic decisions such as which witnesses to call or which defense to bring. See *United States v. Gray,* 878 F.2d 702 (3d Cir.1989) (counsel ineffective where he fails to contact 25 neutral eyewitnesses listed by the defendant, in a case in which the jury would have to make a credibility determination between the defendant and the complainant); *Thomas v. Lockhart,* 738 F.2d 304 (8th Cir.1984) (counsel's investigation was deficient where he did nothing beyond reading the police file).

a. Information Provided by the Defendant

The Court in *Strickland* stated that the reasonableness of counsel's investigative efforts "depends critically" on information supplied by the defendant. For example, when a defendant informs counsel that a certain line of investigation would be fruitless or harmful, then counsel's failure to pursue that line cannot later be found unreasonable. See *Hance v. Zant,* 981 F.2d 1180 (11th Cir.1993) (failure to investigate defendant's background held not ineffective where defendant instructed counsel not to contact and involve the members of his family, and counsel complied with his client's instructions "because he feared that if he did not, he would lose Hance's cooperation in the defense strategy").

b. Reasonable Limitations on Investigation

The Court in *Strickland* noted that at some point, an attorney's decision to end an investigation will be a reasonable professional judgment. For example, in *Burger v. Kemp,* 483 U.S. 776, 107 S.Ct. 3114, 97 L.Ed.2d 638 (1987), the defendant argued that counsel was ineffective in deciding to conclude an unsuccessful search for witnesses to testify to the defendant's good character at his capital sentencing proceeding. The defendant had given counsel a list of possible character witnesses, counsel had contacted the first several on the list, and each had negative things to say about the defendant. The Court concluded that under the circumstances, "counsel's decision not to mount an all-out investigation was supported by reasonable professional judgment." See also *Wilkins v. Iowa,* 957 F.2d 537 (8th Cir.1992) ("A less than exhaustive investigation is adequate for constitutional purposes if reasonable professional judgments limit its scope.'').

2. Presentation

Presentation of a defense is a function of decisionmaking by defense counsel. Decisions include which witnesses to call, which arguments and objections to make, whether to ask for a certain jury instruction, etc. The Court in *Strickland* stated that a reviewing court must be ''highly deferential'' in reviewing counsel's decisions, and that ''*strategic choices* made after through investigation of law and facts relevant to plausible options are *virtually unchallengeable*.'' Thus, if counsel's decision, though mistaken, can be fairly considered a strategic choice, it is extremely unlikely that a court will find that counsel provided ineffective assistance. Moreover, the court must assess counsel's performance from the point of view of the circumstances known or reasonably knowable *at the time the decision was made*. The Court in *Strickland* cautioned that ''every effort must be made to eliminate the distorting effects of hindsight, to reconstruct the circumstances of counsel's challenged conduct, and to evaluate the conduct from counsel's perspective at the time.''

Example: In *Wilkins v. Iowa,* 957 F.2d 537 (8th Cir.1992), the defendant entered a bar with a gun in his waistband under his jacket. He struck up a conversation with an ex-girlfriend, to the consternation of her fiancé. Words were exchanged, and the fiance started moving toward Wilkins, who drew the gun from his waistband and shot the fiancé twice, killing him. A blood alcohol test showed that Wilkins had a blood alcohol content of .219. Wilkins had been depressed and was taking a depressant, although it was not clear that he took it on the day of the shooting. Wilkins had been seeing a psychiatrist. Wilkins' defense counsel, Walter, interviewed the psychiatrist and some of the eyewitnesses called at trial. Walter decided to focus on a defense of justification or self-defense and place less emphasis on the theories of diminished capacity or intoxication. The victim was a large man with a history of violence. At trial, Walter did not argue diminished capacity during opening or closing arguments, he did not introduce into evidence the results of Wilkins' blood alcohol test, and he did not call the psychiatrist to testify. He did, however, elicit testimony concerning the degree of Wilkins' intoxication. The trial court instructed the jury on both self-defense and diminished capacity. The jury returned a verdict of first-degree murder.

Attacking his conviction on grounds of ineffective assistance, Wilkins argued that Walter had inadequately presented the diminished capacity claim. The court, however, concluded that Walter's decision ''was a valid exercise of professional judgment in formulating trial strategy, which we will not second-guess on appeal." The court found that Walter's decision to essentially forego the diminished capacity defense was reasonable, even if mistaken, on the following grounds: 1) it was appropriate to "go for broke" with the complete defense of self-defense rather than the partial defense of diminished capacity, because Wilkins was extremely reluctant to go to jail for any time at all; 2) it was appropriate to pick one defense instead of two, since Walter made a reasonable (if arguable) judgment that diminished capacity and justification are inconsistent defenses—if a jury believes the defendant was impaired, it would not find his justification defense credible, and if he could think clearly enough to respond to a threat, his diminished capacity defense would lose credibility; 3) the justification defense was a reasonable defense to pick of the two available, since it was not only a complete defense but it was also supported to some degree by the evidence. The fact that Walter's decisions backfired was irrelevant to whether they were reasonable strategy *at the time they were made.*

3. Decisions Based on Errors of Law

If counsel makes a decision based on an incorrect assumption of relevant legal standards, then the decision cannot be justified as strategic and will consequently be found ineffective. For example, in *Cave v. Singletary*, 971 F.2d 1513 (11th Cir.1992), the defendant was charged with felony murder arising from an armed robbery. Defense counsel throughout the trial *emphasized* that Cave had committed the robbery, but that he was not guilty of murder because he had not been the shooter. These statements amounted to a concession by defense counsel to the jury that the State had proven its case, because under the felony murder statute, commission of the robbery was sufficient: it was irrelevant that the defendant had not been the shooter. At the hearing after the conviction on the ineffectiveness claim, defense counsel argued that "she understood the concept of felony murder, but deliberately misstated the law throughout the trial in an attempt to confuse the jury." Her stated strategy "was to attempt to separate in the jurors' minds the robbery and the murder, then confuse the jury about the elements of felony murder so that they would acquit Cave of the murder charge."

The court found that counsel had rendered ineffective assistance. It stated that "the mere incantation of the word strategy does not insulate attorney behavior from review." The court was convinced that counsel "completely misunderstood the law of felony murder, which is a concept that often confuses laypeople, but should be within the grasp of lawyers." Thus, the court disbelieved counsel's post-hoc explanation of strategy. But the court pointed out that "even if counsel's misstatements of the law were strategic in nature, we would not consider such a strategy to be reasonable under the circumstances because defense counsel may not encourage the jurors to ignore the court's instruction and apply the law at their caprice." So even if counsel understood and misstated the law of felony murder, she made a mistake of law (which could not be deemed strategic) as to the jury's duty to follow the judge's instructions. See also *Kimmelman v. Morrison,* 477 U.S. 365, 106 S.Ct. 2574, 91 L.Ed.2d 305 (1986) (counsel was ineffective for failure to file a timely suppression motion because he had conducted no discovery, laboring under the mistaken notion that the State was required to turn over all inculpatory evidence to the defense).

D.   PREJUDICE

The prejudice standard is designed to assess whether it is worthwhile to retry a case in which ineffectiveness occurred. As such, it performs the same function as the "harmless error" test applied to constitutional violations.

1.   Strength of the Government's Case

To apply the prejudice standard the reviewing court must assess the strength of the prosecution's case and the significance of defense counsel's error. It is obvious that, no matter how fundamental counsel's error, a conviction would still be reasonably probable if the prosecution's evidence is overwhelming. For example, in *Cave v. Singletary, supra,* the court found that defense counsel was ineffective for arguing to the jury, in a felony murder case, that her client was clearly guilty of robbery but not of murder. Nonetheless, the court refused to reverse the conviction because the evidence that Cave had actually committed the robbery was overwhelming. Cave had confessed to the robbery and other witnesses to the crime had identified him. Thus the court concluded that "in this case, Cave has not demonstrated that there is a reasonable probability that, but for counsel's incompetence, the result of the trial would have been different.

2.   Weakness of the Government's Case

Conversely, the weaker the Government's case, the more likely it is that defense counsel's unprofessional conduct will have an effect on the outcome. Thus, in *Atkins v. Attorney General of Alabama,* 932 F.2d 1430 (11th Cir.1991), defense counsel failed to object to the introduction of a fingerprint card which was offered at trial to make a comparison between Atkins' fingerprints and those found at the scene of the crime. The card included a printed notation of a prior arrest that would not have been admissible against Atkins. The court found that the failure to object to clearly inadmissible evidence constituted ineffectiveness, and that without the error there was a reasonable probability that the outcome of the proceeding would have been different. The court stressed that the evidence against Atkins was barely sufficient to support the jury's verdict. While Atkins' fingerprints were found at the scene, this was explainable because the victim testified that Atkins had worked for him at the house two days prior to the crime. Also, there was no other physical evidence to tie Atkins to the crime. Under these circumstances, the court found that the evidence of the prior arrest could have had "an almost irreversible impact on the minds of the jurors." See also *United States v. Gray,* 878 F.2d 702 (3d Cir.1989) (where the trial was basically a credibility determination between defendant and complainant, the failure to call disinterested eyewitnesses who would support the defendant's testimony constituted prejudice under *Strickland*).

3. **No Right to a Lawless or Improper Verdict**
The defendant cannot be "prejudiced" from defense counsel's refusal to persuade the jury to decide the case in an improper manner; nor can he be prejudiced if defense counsel decides to make an improper argument but does so ineffectively. Thus, in *Nix v. Whiteside,* 475 U.S. 157, 106 S.Ct. 988, 89 L.Ed.2d 123 (1986), the defendant complained that he was denied effective assistance of counsel because his lawyer threatened that if Whiteside lied on the stand, the lawyer would disclose the perjury to the trial court. The Court noted that under *Strickland,* the defendant must prove prejudice, and that Whiteside had "no valid claim that confidence in the result of his trial has been diminished by his desisting from the contemplated perjury." The Court reasoned that even if the jury had been persuaded by the perjury, "a defendant has no entitlement to the luck of a lawless decisionmaker." See also *Lockhart v. Fretwell,* ___ U.S. ___, 113 S.Ct. 838, 122 L.Ed.2d 180 (1993) (no prejudice where counsel fails to make argument at trial on basis of then existing law, where the law had been changed by the time of review; question of prejudice is not solely one of result-orientation).

4. **Per Se Prejudice**
In *United States v. Cronic,* 466 U.S. 648, 104 S.Ct. 2039, 80 L.Ed.2d 657 (1984), the Supreme Court declared that there are certain limited circumstances in which ineffectiveness and prejudice are *presumed,* because "the likelihood that any lawyer, even a fully competent one, could provide effective assistance of counsel is so small that a presumption of prejudice is appropriate *without inquiry into the actual conduct of the trial.*"

   a. **Limited Exception**
   The Court in *Cronic* stressed that the "per se reversal" exception to the two-pronged *Strickland* test was extremely limited, to egregious circumstances in which ineffective representation and prejudice were all but a certainty—i.e. where misconduct and prejudice is so likely that the "cost of litigating" the question would be unjustified. The limited nature of this exception is shown by the facts of *Cronic,* where the court *refused* to presume ineffectiveness and prejudice despite the following factors: 1) Cronic was charged in a complex fraud involving a check-kiting scheme; 2) Cronic was given a young lawyer with a real estate practice and with no prior trial experience; 3) the court allowed counsel only 25 days to prepare the defense, even though it had taken the Government over four years to investigate and prepare its case. Despite these factors, the Court found that a presumption of ineffectiveness and prejudice was unjustified. Among other things, the Court noted that "every experienced

THE RIGHT TO COUNSEL

criminal defense attorney once tried his first criminal case," and that the underlying historical facts to be proven at trial were not in dispute. The Court concluded that "when there is no reason to dispute the underlying historical facts, the period of 25 days to consider the question whether those facts justify an inference of criminal intent is not so short that it even arguably justifies a presumption that no lawyer could provide the respondent with the effective assistance of counsel required by the Constitution." See also *Paradis v. Arave,* 954 F.2d 1483 (9th Cir.1992) (no presumption of ineffectiveness and prejudice where defense counsel appointed in a capital murder case had passed the bar only six months prior to trial, and had not taken any classes in criminal law, criminal procedure or trial advocacy in law school).

b. Total Denial of "Counsel"

The *Cronic* per se reversal exception to the general *Strickland* test has generally been limited to cases in which counsel was not even a lawyer properly admitted to the bar, or was subject to some other incapacity by which he could not function as "counsel" within the meaning of the Sixth Amendment. See *Solina v. United States,* 709 F.2d 160 (2d Cir.1983) (per se reversal where defendant's trial counsel held himself out as an attorney but had never passed a bar exam; counsel cannot be "counsel" as that term is defined in the Sixth Amendment where he was "engaging in a crime" during the representation of the defendant). See also *United States v. Novak,* 903 F.2d 883 (2d Cir.1990) (per se reversal where defense counsel had obtained admission to the bar by fraud); *Pilchak v. Camper,* 935 F.2d 145 (8th Cir.1991) (per se reversal where defense counsel was suffering from Alzheimer's disease during the course of the trial). On the other hand, if defense counsel was disbarred, suspended or incapacitated *subsequent* to the representation, or if defense counsel's failure to maintain a license to practice is merely a ministerial oversight, then a presumption of ineffectiveness and prejudice is unwarranted. See *United States v. Rosnow,* 981 F.2d 970 (8th Cir.1992) (no per se reversal where counsel was suspended subsequent to most of the material representation of the defendant, and defendant was represented by co-counsel as well); *Reese v. Peters,* 926 F.2d 668 (7th Cir.1991) (no per se reversal where defense counsel's license was suspended for failure to pay dues).

c. Ineffectiveness and Prejudice May Still Be Found on the Facts

If a court holds that a presumption of ineffectiveness and prejudice is unwarranted, it has not held that defendant received the Sixth Amendment right to effective assistance of counsel. Rather it has held that the defendant has the burden of showing ineffectiveness and prejudice *on the record.* For example, on remand in *Cronic, supra,* the court of appeals held that Cronic's counsel had performed ineffectively, and that counsel's errors were prejudicial to Cronic. The court found that counsel's stated strategy of "clouding the issues" could not be a satisfactory explanation for the selection of a defense, and that counsel failed to object to inadmissible evidence due to a misunderstanding of the statute under which Cronic was tried. These errors were found prejudicial given the weakness of the case against Cronic.

E. MULTIPLE REPRESENTATION

The standards for ineffectiveness and prejudice are different when the defendant's claim is that defense counsel labored under a conflict of interest arising from multiple representation of clients in related matters. Multiple representation may create a conflict because defendants may have different interests at stake, so that the attorney cannot zealously represent both or all the clients. For example, one client may be more blameworthy than another; an attempt to shift blame from a less culpable client to a more culpable client would obviously present a conflict of interest. See *Holloway v. Arkansas,* 435 U.S. 475, 98 S.Ct. 1173, 55 L.Ed.2d 426 (1978) (multiple representation may "prevent an attorney from challenging the admission of evidence prejudicial to one client but perhaps favorable to another, or from arguing at the sentencing hearing the relative involvement and culpability of his clients in order to minimize the culpability of one by emphasizing that of another").

1. No Per Se Rule

The Court in *Holloway v. Arkansas,* 435 U.S. 475, 98 S.Ct. 1173, 55 L.Ed.2d 426 (1978), made it clear that multiple representation of criminal defendants is not a per se violation of the right to effective assistance. The Court reasoned that in some cases, a common defense by a single counsel may be the most appropriate and vigorous defense.

2. Limited Presumption

In *Cuyler v. Sullivan,* 446 U.S. 335, 100 S.Ct. 1708, 64 L.Ed.2d 333 (1980), the Court stated that "trial courts may assume that multiple representation entails no conflict or that the lawyer and his clients knowingly accept such risk of conflict as may exist." However, because of the potential risk of ineffective assistance arising from multiple representation, the Court held that a defendant would be entitled to a reversal if he could demonstrate that "an *actual conflict of interest adversely affected his lawyer's performance."* Thus, the Court created a *limited and conditional presumption of prejudice.* Prejudice is presumed, but only if the defendant establishes that counsel "actively represented conflicting interests" *and* that "an actual conflict of interest adversely affected his lawyer's performance." If the defendant can show that counsel acted in conflict to the defendant's detriment, he need not make the further *Strickland* showing that counsel's error had some reasonably probable effect on the outcome. See *United States v. Winkle,* 722 F.2d 605 (10th Cir.1983) ("A defendant who shows that a conflict of interest actually affected the adequacy of his representation need not demonstrate prejudice in order to obtain relief."). Thus, even if the prosecution's case is overwhelming, the defendant is entitled to a retrial if defense counsel had an actual conflict and harmed the defendant's case in some way as a result of the conflict. See *Strickland, supra* (discussing the limited presumption of prejudice where counsel is burdened by a conflict of interest, and noting that "it is difficult to measure the precise effect on the defense of representation corrupted by conflicting interests").

Example: In *Nealy v. Cabana,* 782 F.2d 1362 (5th Cir.1986), defense counsel represented both Nealy and his brother, who were being tried separately for the same crime. The evidence against Nealy was overwhelming, but Nealy wanted to call his brother to the stand to testify to some mitigating factors. Defense counsel decided not to call the brother, and testified later that he was motivated by the fact that the testimony could be used against the brother in his trial. The court reversed Nealy's conviction, finding that defense counsel had labored under an actual conflict of interest, and that the decision not to call the brother adversely affected the lawyer's performance. Consequently, the strength of the Government's case against Nealy was irrelevant. See also *United States v. Martin,* 965 F.2d 839 (10th Cir.1992) (reversal required where counsel employed "united we stand, divided we fall" theory of defense in a drug conspiracy case, claiming that no conspiracy existed, and vehemently opposed the defendant's wish to testify that he had withdrawn from the conspiracy and thus was less culpable: "Defendant has presented the classic conflict situation in which, in order to reduce the degree of his own culpability, he would have to testify in contravention of his co-defendants' theory of the defense.").

3. Conflict May Be Waived

A defendant may waive his right to conflict-free counsel by choosing to proceed to trial with an attorney who has an actual conflict of interest. *United States v. Rodriguez,* 982 F.2d 474 (11th Cir.1993). This waiver must, however, be knowing, intelligent and voluntary, and must be established by clear and unequivocal language. See *United States v. Petz,* 764 F.2d 1390 (11th Cir.1985) (waiver ineffective where defendant was never expressly informed of his right to separate, conflict-free counsel); *United States v. Rodriguez,* 982 F.2d 474 (11th Cir.1993) (waiver valid where the defendants were informed of their right to separate counsel, were asked whether they believed that there was or could be a conflict of interest, were informed that the Government had more evidence against one of the defendants than against the other two, and were made aware that counsel could not, because of the multiple representation, employ a shifting blame strategy).

4. Waiver Does Not Bind the Court
If the defendant validly waives the right to conflict-free counsel, the trial court may constitutionally permit the multiple representation. However, the trial court is not *required* to permit multiple representation when there is, or may be, an active conflict of interest. The client's waiver does not bind the trial court because the court may consider the actual or potential conflict to have a negative impact on the integrity of the trial. In *Wheat v. United States*, 486 U.S. 153, 108 S.Ct. 1692, 100 L.Ed.2d 140 (1988), the defendant argued that the trial court violated his constitutional right to chosen counsel when the court disqualified defense counsel against the defendant's wishes. The trial court reasoned that counsel's multiple representation could create an active conflict of interest and refused to abide by the waiver. The Supreme Court held that the trial court did not err. It concluded that the Sixth Amendment right to chosen counsel is "circumscribed" by the "independent interest in ensuring that criminal trials are conducted within the ethical standards of the profession and that legal proceedings appear fair to all who observe them."

a. Judicial Discretion
The Court concluded that the trial court "must be allowed substantial latitude in refusing waivers of conflicts of interest," even if it ultimately turns out that multiple representation would not have actually created an active conflict. The question is whether, at the time the decision to disqualify is made, there is an *indication of "a serious potential for conflict."* If so, the court will not be in error in disqualifying defense counsel even though the defendant has waived his right to conflict-free counsel.

F. INEFFECTIVE ASSISTANCE THROUGH NO FAULT OF DEFENSE COUNSEL
In some cases, the defense counsel may perform ineffectively not because of his own malfeasance, but rather because of some state-imposed limitation. Thus, in *Herring v. New York,* 422 U.S. 853, 95 S.Ct. 2550, 45 L.Ed.2d 593 (1975), the Court stated that the right to effective assistance of counsel "has been understood to mean that there can be no restrictions upon the function of counsel in defending a criminal prosecution in accord with the traditions of the adversary factfinding process." In *Herring,* the Court invalidated a statute which gave the judge in a non-jury trial the power to deny defense counsel the opportunity to make a closing argument. Likewise, in *Geders v. United States,* 425 U.S. 80, 96 S.Ct. 1330, 47 L.Ed.2d 592 (1976), the trial court prohibited defense counsel from consulting with the defendant during a 17-hour overnight recess between the defendant's direct and cross-examination. While recognizing that the trial court had a legitimate concern that the defendant would be "coached," the Court decided that this draconian method of preventing coaching violated the defendant's right to the effective assistance of counsel.

1. Per Se Reversal

The Court in *Herring* stated that if state interference deprives counsel of "the opportunity to participate fully and fairly in the adversary factfinding process," then the defendant's right to effective assistance is violated, and reversal is *automatic*. The Court does not inquire into whether counsel's performance absent the interference was adequate, and no actual prejudice need be shown. Even a single instance of interference can result in per se reversal, as indicated by both *Herring* and *Geders*.

2. Line–Drawing

Not every state interference with defense counsel is so fundamental as to deprive counsel of the opportunity to participate fully and fairly in the adversary proceeding. Thus, in *Perry v. Leeke,* 488 U.S. 272, 109 S.Ct. 594, 102 L.Ed.2d 624 (1989), a state trial judge refused to allow the defendant to consult with counsel during a 15–minute recess between his direct and cross-examination. The Court held that this interference was not so fundamental as to deprive the defendant of effective assistance of counsel, and distinguished the interference from that in *Geders,* where the trial court refused to allow counsel to confer with the defendant during an overnight recess. As the dissenters in *Perry* pointed out, the difference between state-imposed interference during a 15–minute recess and state-imposed interference during an overnight recess is one of degree rather than kind.

IV. THE RIGHT TO SELF–REPRESENTATION

A. *FARETTA*

In *Faretta v. California,* 422 U.S. 806, 95 S.Ct. 2525, 45 L.Ed.2d 562 (1975), the Court held that a criminal defendant has a right to represent himself, which is guaranteed by the Sixth Amendment. The Court recognized that the Sixth Amendment's guarantee of a right to counsel did not plainly state that there is also a right to waive counsel. However, the Court reasoned that the Sixth Amendment "grants to the accused personally the right to make his defense" and that it is the defendant who "suffers the consequences if the defense fails." The Court concluded that "the right to self-representation—to make one's own defense personally—is thus necessarily implied by the structure of the Amendment."

1. Policy Arguments Supporting *Faretta*

The Court in *Faretta* was clearly aware that it is usually a mistake to proceed without a lawyer. However, the Court set forth two policy arguments which it felt outweighed the negative consequences of self-representation.

a. Right of Free Choice

First and most importantly, the option of self-representation respects the personal autonomy of the defendant. As the Court stated, those who wrote the Bill of Rights "understood the inestimable worth of free choice." Imposing counsel against the defendant's plain desire to represent himself renders the right to free choice in this context a nullity. The Court concluded that "to force a lawyer on a defendant can only lead him to believe that the law contrives against him," and that although the defendant "may conduct his own defense ultimately to his own detriment, his choice must be honored out of that respect for the individual which is the lifeblood of the law."

b. **Strategic Benefit**
The *Faretta* Court stated that "in some rare instances, the defendant might in fact present his case more effectively by conducting his own defense." This could occur where forced representation by counsel may render the defendant disillusioned and uncooperative, or where the defendant representing himself may receive some sympathy from the jury in being matched against overwhelming prosecutorial forces.

2. **Dissent**
The three dissenters in *Faretta* complained that the majority had found a right to self-representation "tucked between the lines of the Sixth Amendment." The dissenters were also concerned about the effects of self-representation on the criminal justice system. They stated that a widespread exercise of the "newly discovered" right of self-representation would result in added congestion for the courts and would have a negative impact on the quality of justice.

B. **SELF–REPRESENTATION REQUIRES KNOWING WAIVER OF RIGHT TO COUNSEL**
After *Faretta,* a defendant simultaneously has a right to counsel and a right to self-representation. Obviously, one of these mutually exclusive rights must be elected and the other waived before a trial can proceed. Thus, the defendant must be fully advised of the consequences of proceeding without counsel before he can be found to have invoked his right to self-representation. See *United States v. Robinson,* 913 F.2d 712 (9th Cir.1990) (for a knowing and intelligent waiver, "a criminal defendant must be aware of the nature of the charges against him, the possible penalties, and the dangers and disadvantages of self-representation").

1. **Invocation of Right to Self–Representation Must Be Unequivocal**
Most courts have held that in addition to being informed about the consequences of self-representation, the defendant must "unequivocally" waive his right to counsel and invoke his right to represent himself. Thus, any ambiguity in the defendant's statements about his willingness to forego counsel will be construed against the invocation of his right of self-representation. See *Meeks v. Craven,* 482 F.2d 465 (9th Cir.1973) (defendant, when asked whether he wanted to represent himself, said "yes, I think I will"; held, not an unequivocal demand for self-representation because "I think I will hardly meets the constitutional criteria for waiver of counsel").

2. Tension Between Rights to Counsel and Self–Representation Requires an Unequivocal Waiver of Counsel

The "unequivocal request" requirement has been developed by the courts to resolve the tension between the mutually exclusive rights to counsel and to self-representation. Requiring that the request for self-representation be unequivocal ensures that the defendant does not inadvertently waive the right to counsel "through occasional musings on the benefits of self-representation." *Adams v. Carroll,* 875 F.2d 1441 (9th Cir.1989). Also, the requirement protects the courts by preventing the defendant from taking advantage of the mutual exclusivity of the rights of counsel and self-representation. As the court in *Adams v. Carroll* put it: "A defendant who vacillates at trial between wishing to be represented by counsel and wishing to represent himself could place the trial court in a difficult position." This is because if counsel is appointed, the defendant could argue on appeal that he really wanted to represent himself; but if he does represent himself, he could argue that he really wanted counsel. The requirement of unequivocality "resolves this dilemma by forcing the defendant to make an explicit choice. If he equivocates, he is presumed to have requested the assistance of counsel." Id. See *Meeks v. Craven, supra* ("An unequivocal demand to proceed pro se should be, at the very least, sufficiently clear that if it is granted the defendant should not be able to turn about and urge that he was improperly denied counsel.").

3. Need Not Know Rules of Evidence and Trial Practice

In *Faretta,* the trial judge, after questioning Faretta about the hearsay rule and state law governing the challenge of prospective jurors, ruled that Faretta had not made "an intelligent and knowing" waiver of the right to counsel. The Supreme Court held that this was error, and concluded that Faretta's "technical legal knowledge, as such, was not relevant to an assessment of his knowing exercise of the right to defend himself." Rather, the question is whether the defendant 1) was warned of the consequences of a waiver of counsel, 2) made a voluntary decision, 3) was competent and understood his rights, and 4) unequivocally stated that he wished to represent himself.

C. LIMITATIONS ON THE RIGHT OF SELF–REPRESENTATION

The right of self-representation is not absolute. In *Faretta* and later cases, the courts have recognized that certain conditions can be imposed on the defendant's right to proceed pro se, where such conditions are necessary to further legitimate and countervailing state interests.

1. Disruption of the Trial

The Court in *Faretta* recognized that "the right of self-representation is not a license to abuse the dignity of the courtroom." Thus, if the defendant is disrupting courtroom proceedings, using the courtroom as a "soapbox," or in some other way imposing a substantial burden on the proceedings through self-representation, then the court may appoint counsel even against the defendant's wishes. See *Savage v. Estelle,* 924 F.2d 1459 (9th Cir.1990) (defendant with a severe speech impediment was found unable to "abide by rules of procedure and courtroom protocol"; therefore, the right to self-representation was properly denied).

2. Treated Like a Lawyer

The Court in *Faretta* cautioned that if the defendant opts to represent himself, he can be held to the same standards as would apply to a lawyer handling the case. The Court stated that the pro se defendant was subject to all "relevant rules of procedural and substantive law."

3. Standby Counsel

While the pro se defendant is subject to all pertinent courtroom rules, it is obvious that many such defendants are unfamiliar with those rules and that this unfamiliarity may impair the progress of the trial. Also, it could happen that the pro se defendant becomes disruptive or simply gives up in the middle of trial and asks for counsel; it would clearly present a problem of trial management for counsel to be appointed at that juncture. The Court in *Faretta* therefore stated that a court can appoint standby counsel "to aid the accused if and when the accused requests help, and to be available to represent the accused in the event that termination of the defendant's self-representation is necessary." The Court made it clear that standby counsel could be appointed "even over objection by the accused."

a. Limits of Standby Counsel

The limits on standby counsel were explored by the Court in *McKaskle v. Wiggins,* 465 U.S. 168, 104 S.Ct. 944, 79 L.Ed.2d 122 (1984). Wiggins contended that his standby counsel violated his right to self-representation by essentially taking over the case. Counsel argued with Wiggins over his choice of strategy, made objections to the judge at sidebar concerning Wiggins' handling of his defense, openly assisted Wiggins in handling courtroom rules, and occasionally interjected objections and comments while witnesses were testifying. The Court in *Wiggins* stated that standby counsel must act within the limits of the two policy arguments supporting *Faretta*: that the defendant has a personal right to make his own decisions, and that the defendant may have a strategic interest in obtaining jury sympathy through self-representation. Accordingly, standby counsel cannot seize *actual control* over the defendant's case, or else the right of personal autonomy would be violated. Nor can standby counsel *appear to the jury* to be running the case, or else the strategic interest supporting *Faretta* would be undermined. The Court noted that "participation by standby counsel outside the presence of the jury engages only the first of these limitations," and that the personal autonomy aspect of *Faretta* was satisfied so long as the defendant is allowed to "address the court freely" and "all disagreements between counsel and the pro se defendant are resolved in the defendant's favor whenever the matter is one that would normally be left to the discretion of counsel." Thus, standby counsel can press any arguments he wishes to the judge, so long as the defendant has the final say.

b. Procedural Problems
The Court in *Wiggins* held that standby counsel may assist the defendant in overcoming routine procedural and evidentiary problems, even against the defendant's wishes, without undermining the defendant's appearance to the jury as a person defending himself. On the facts of *Wiggins,* the Court concluded that "counsel's unsolicited involvement was held within reasonable limits" and that Wiggins had made the key strategic decisions and generally appeared to the jury to be representing himself.

c. No Right to Standby Counsel
Faretta recognizes that the trial court *may* appoint standby counsel, as a procedural device to protect the integrity of the trial. But it is clear that the defendant has no *right* to standby counsel should he decide to represent himself. It is evident from cases like *Wiggins* that some courts may be reluctant to appoint standby counsel, lest they by doing so give the defendant a possible argument on appeal that the standby counsel rendered ineffective assistance. While the defendant has no right to claim ineffective assistance if he represents himself, he does have the right to claim that standby counsel was ineffective. See *Wiggins*.

4. Election Must Be Timely
Another qualification on the right of self-representation is that the defendant must make the decision to represent himself sufficiently *before* trial so that the court can adjust accordingly. See *Horton v. Dugger,* 895 F.2d 714 (11th Cir.1990) (request for self-representation, made on the first day of trial, held untimely).

D. *FARETTA* VIOLATION CANNOT BE HARMLESS
Suppose the defendant is denied the right to self-representation after an unequivocal invocation of that right, and he is convicted. Can the Government argue on appeal that the defendant was actually well-represented by defense counsel and that counsel did a far better job than the defendant would have done had he represented himself? In other words, can a *Faretta* violation constitute harmless error? The Supreme Court in *Wiggins* answered in the negative. The Court reasoned that a violation of *Faretta* means that the defendant has been deprived of his *choice* to represent himself, regardless of the probable negative consequences to his case. It is therefore no answer to say that the counsel imposed upon the defendant against his will did a better job than the defendant could have done. The Court in *Wiggins* concluded that the right to self-representation "is either respected or denied; its deprivation cannot be harmless."

*

APPENDIX A

CRIMINAL PROCEDURE— SAMPLE EXAMINATION

Marilyn and Tipper are students at State University, the largest state controlled university in the State. Both are computer whizzes and often refer to themselves and their friends as "hackers." They take great pride in being able to find ways around security protections which computer owners install to protect confidential information. On one occasion, they used a small personal computer and a modem (a device which permits one computer to speak to another over telephone lines much the way a Lexis or Westlaw terminal can communicate with a database) to circumvent the security codes in the University President's computer system and left him a happy birthday message on his screen which he saw when he arrived at the office on his birthday.

The State has become alarmed in recent years about the activity of some computer hackers. In some instances, hackers have been responsible for viruses which have destroyed computer data. In other instances, hackers have been blamed for pranks, like changing the grades in the registrar's office at a community college. And, in one widely reported case, hackers found their way into computerized data at a military base and leaked confidential information contained in the database to the press. As a result, the State has adopted a law, the Computer Protection Act, which reads as follows:

> It shall be a class 5 felony, punishable by up to two years in prison and a $10,000 fine, for any person to knowingly intercept, receive, record, copy, or examine any data stored in a computer database or network if it would appear to a reasonable person that the person or persons who control such database or network have

sought to exclude by means of passwords, codes or other mechanisms persons not expressly authorized to use the database or network from access to it.

The statute has not discouraged all hackers, and it certainly has not discouraged Marilyn and Tipper.

In fact, Marilyn and Tipper have vowed to each other and to their friends that they will demonstrate the folly of the statute and show the State that it cannot and should not attempt to use the criminal law to deal with a minor irritant like hackers. After considerable thought about how best to get the attention of lawmakers, Marilyn told Tipper that they should use their computer to tap into the judicial database of the state and to erase all of the computer records relating to persons convicted of criminal acts. Tipper expressed some concern about the plan and suggested that it might be more of a demonstration than was needed, and also that it might be difficult to carry out the plan. After some discussion, Tipper agreed that they would see how difficult it would be to tap into the database and then decide whether to carry out the plan.

Marilyn and Tipper have two friends, Barbara and Hillary, who are law clerks for a state court of appeals judge. In the course of general conversations, Marilyn and Tipper obtain sufficient information from Barbara and Hillary to tap into the state judicial system computer. They find that access to the judicial database requires use of a password and an identification number. To the surprise of Marilyn (and to the relief of Tipper), it is not easy to crack the security system and to obtain access to the data and their efforts fail.

Unbeknownst to Marilyn and Tipper, the administrator of the judicial database has installed an innovative device called "telephone number identification." This device identifies and records the telephone number used by anyone seeking access to the judicial database. The device works well, and each of the efforts which Marilyn and Tipper have made to contact the database have resulted in their telephone number being recorded. Each morning the administrator examines the telephone numbers which have been recorded in order to determine how the database is being used, who are the most frequent users, and whether the security of the system is intact. For two mornings in a row, the administrator has seen several contacts with the database from a number which she does not recognize. Her records show that a number of calls have been made from the same number and that the database indicates that in each instance "entry was refused." Concerned about the possible invasion of the security of the database, she calls the state police and asks if they can contact the telephone company and find out some information about the number. The state police make a visit to the offices of the phone company and learn that the telephone number is listed to Marilyn Bird, at 16 Massachusetts Ave., on the campus of State University.

The state police report what they have learned to the administrator who asks that the police continue to conduct an investigation. Two officers, Cagney and Lacey, arrange a meeting with the President of State University. They tell him about what the court administrator discovered and that they have learned that a telephone listed to Marilyn

Bird was used to contact the judicial database. They ask whether the President can help them in their investigation. The President tells them about the happy birthday greeting that he found on his computer and telephones the Dean of Students to ask the Dean to speak with the officers. The Dean of Students knows Marilyn and Tipper well and tells the officers that Tipper is Marilyn's roommate. The Dean then provides the officers with class schedules for Marilyn and Tipper and goes with the officers to one of the classes to point out Marilyn and Tipper. The Dean also tells the officers that Marilyn and Tipper belong to the University's computer club which meets that afternoon and every Wednesday afternoon. The two officers, dressed in casual clothes, decide that they will attend the meeting and pretend that they are college students interested in computers. The meeting begins on time and is attended by approximately 40 people, including Marilyn and Tipper. The discussion is confined to how "Windows" can be used with Lexis and Nexis, and the officers have no understanding of what is being discussed.

When the meeting ends, Cagney strikes up a conversation with Tipper, and Cagney pretends to be interested in buying a personal computer. Cagney asks Tipper what she uses, and Tipper offers to show her the IBM clone she and her roommate use. Cagney walks with Tipper to 16 Massachusetts Ave. and enters a two bedroom apartment. Tipper shows her a computer which sits on a desk in the living room which the two entered as they walked through the front door. The two talk for a while, until Tipper excuses herself to use the restroom. As she begins to exit the living room, Cagney asks "Can I try the computer?" Hearing a "yes, help yourself," Cagney sits down at the desk and turns the computer on. As it warms up and runs some programs which set forth a menu, Cagney leafs through some papers on the desk and comes upon a note that reads, "court database, 333–3275." Recognizing the number as the number of the judicial database, Cagney puts the papers back as they were. On the menu, Cagney recognizes some files that can be used in connection with a modem to communicate with other computers. When Tipper comes back, Cagney asks whether the computer has a modem, and Tipper indicates that an internal modem is contained inside the computer.

Cagney decides to ask to use the restroom in order to be able to look around the apartment. After obtaining Tipper's permission, Cagney walks to the restroom which is located between two bedrooms. Looking left and right, Cagney is able to see into both bedrooms. She notices a bunch of computer paper on the bed in one room. When she returns from the restroom, Cagney asks whether she can use a mirror in one of the bedrooms in order to fix her hair. Tipper agrees, and Cagney walks into the bedroom with the computer paper, picks up the paper and sees a printout of a list of words, including the following: judge, justice, court, clerk.

While Cagney deals with Tipper, Lacey is on the campus talking with Marilyn. Lacey asks Marilyn whether anyone in the club ever engages in computer pranks, and Marilyn states "some of us do, and we have a monster job that Tipper and I are working on." Although Marilyn does not know it, Lacey is secretly taping the conversation with a small recording device that she has hidden in her bag.

Cagney leaves the apartment and meets up with Lacey, and the two exchange the information they have obtained. They agree that Cagney will seek a warrant to search the apartment and that Lacey will seek the help of the University President in gathering evidence. But, before they seek the warrant, the officers decide to do some further investigation. They go to an electronics store and purchase a box of diskettes and they hide a small voice transmitter in the diskette box. They drive over to the apartment where Tipper had taken Cagney and Cagney goes to the door. She knocks and Tipper answers. Cagney tells Tipper that she just bought some new diskettes and asks whether Tipper would be willing to format them for her. Tipper agrees, Cagney leaves the box, and agrees to return that morning. Later that day, Cagney and Lacey overhear Tipper and Marilyn having a discussion in which Tipper says, "Well, why don't we try the database again tomorrow night."

Early the next morning, Cagney submits to a State Magistrate–Judge an affidavit which reads as follows:

"My name is Sharon Cagney. I am a State Police officer and have served in the State Police for seven years. During this time I have had occasion to investigate all manner of crime, including computer crimes. I submit this affidavit under penalty of perjury.

"Earlier this week, the Administrator of the judicial database informed myself and my fellow officer, Janet Lacey, that someone had been seeking entry into the database. This person or persons had no way of knowing that the database is protected with an identification system that identifies and records all numbers from which calls are made into the system. Lacey and I followed up on this information and visited the phone company. We learned that the telephone number is listed to Marilyn Bird at 16 Massachusetts Ave. on the campus of State University. We visited the University, spoke to the President, met Marilyn Bird and her roommate, Tipper. I personally visited the apartment in which the two live. In that apartment I saw a computer with a modem, and I also saw a piece of paper that contained the telephone number of the judicial database. I also saw a computer printout with various words on it, including 'judge,' 'justice', 'court,' and 'clerk.' While I was in the apartment, Officer Lacey had a conversation with Tipper in which she stated that she and Marilyn were in fact trying to break into the database. Furthermore, Officer Lacey and I overheard a conversation in which Tipper stated to Marilyn that they should try again to break into the database tomorrow night.

"On the basis of the facts set forth above, I believe that Marilyn and Tipper have violated the statute protecting the confidentiality of computerized information, known as the Computer Protection Act, which is a class 5 felony and that they are in possession of relevant evidence that would demonstrate their violation of the statute. Based on these facts, I seek a search warrant for the apartment at 16 Massachusetts Ave. to search for and seize all computers, computer paper, disks, and any other records that might relate to the crime identified herein."

The State Magistrate–Judge issues a search warrant which contains the following language: "This warrant commands the State Police to search the apartment at 16 Massachusetts Ave. belonging to Marilyn Bird and her roommate, Tipper, and to locate and seize all computers, computer paper, disks, and any other records that might relate to the Computer Protection Act." Cagney and Lacey take the warrant to the apartment. They knock, and when Tipper answers, they state that they are police officers with a search warrant. Tipper opens the door, the officers enter, and they begin their search. They examine every closet, drawer, file, and space in the apartment and seize the computer on the desk and a printer, all diskettes (both the 5¼" floppies and the 3½" floppies which are near the computer). They also take checkbooks, calendars, phone bills, and papers found on the desk near the computer.

When the search is over, Cagney tells Tipper she is under arrest. Tipper asks why, and Cagney tells her she is charged with violating the Computer Protection Act. Cagney handcuffs Tipper and searches the handbag which she had near her. In the handbag she finds some additional computer disks, another checkbook and a handwritten note containing the telephone number of the judicial database. She shows the note to Lacey, and Tipper, seeing the two reading the note, states, "It was a stupid idea, a really stupid idea. I'm sorry." "Sorry about what," Lacey asks. "You know, the judicial records. I'm sorry," Tipper answers. "Where's your roommate?" Lacey asks. Tipper says she is not sure, but she might be at school. Lacey asks whether Marilyn has a car, and Tipper answers that Marilyn drives a black Honda Accord with the license plate "Hack."

Cagney telephones the President of the University to inform the President that Tipper is arrested and to ask for help in locating Marilyn. The President promises help, asks the Dean of Students to find Marilyn, and waits for the Dean to look for her. The Dean finds Marilyn and brings her to the President, who says, "Marilyn, this is awful. Tipper has been arrested. The police are looking for you. The University is embarrassed. Now, I demand that you tell me exactly what you two have been up to. You can consider yourself suspended, and depending on how much you cooperate, you might or might not be expelled." Marilyn answers, "Well, we were going to break into the judicial database and erase some records. It was really Tipper's idea." The President responds, "Well, the police are on their way."

Marilyn runs from the President's office, gets her car, and drives off. Cagney and Lacey, with Tipper in the car, see Marilyn driving toward them, turn on their lights, and stop Marilyn's car. With gun in hand, Lacey places Marilyn under arrest, handcuffs her and places her in the patrol car with Tipper. Lacey drives Marilyn's car to the State Police station while Cagney drives Marilyn and Tipper in the patrol car. The officers book the two arrestees and take them before a Magistrate–Judge. The Magistrate–Judge tells them that they are charged with violating the Computer Protection Act and that each must post $10,000 bond in order to be released. Neither has that much money, but Marilyn calls her parents who agree to post bond for the two the next day. Marilyn and Tipper spend the night in jail waiting. After the appearance before the Magistrate–Judge, Lacey does a complete search of the car and in the trunk finds a briefcase. Inside is a piece of paper with the words, "Destroy the records!" written on it in large type.

Before Marilyn's parents arrive, Cagney takes Marilyn from her cell and says, "I got a call from the President. He told me what you said and that you claim it was all Tipper's fault. If that is true and you cooperate, things might go better for you. It's up to you." Marilyn responds, "It was all her fault, and I will cooperate, but I want to talk to a lawyer first. Is that alright?" "Sure!" responds Cagney.

When Marilyn's parents arrive, Cagney tells them about his conversation with Marilyn and says that "any information you can find out will help us and your daughter." As they are leaving the station, Marilyn's mother says to Cagney that "Marilyn told me that they were going to erase all the records of people convicted. I hope that helps."

Two days later, the grand jury indicts Marilyn and Tipper for violating the Computer Protection Act. After hearing of the indictment, Tipper calls Cagney on the phone and states, "I never wanted to break into the database. Can't you help me?" Cagney responds by saying, "I'll do what I can, but I'm not sure that I can help at this point. But, if you want me to try, come on down and we can talk." Tipper arrives at the station, tells Cagney everything that happened, and asks for a break.

YOUR LAW FIRM HAS BEEN RETAINED BY BOTH MARILYN AND TIPPER. ALTHOUGH YOU HAVE INFORMED THEM ABOUT THE CLEAR POSSIBILITY OF A CONFLICT OF INTEREST, THEY HAVE DECIDED THAT IT WOULD BE USEFUL AT THE OUTSET TO HAVE ONE FIRM GIVE THEM A PRELIMINARY ANALYSIS OF WHETHER ANY OF THE EVIDENCE OBTAINED AGAINST THEM MIGHT BE SUPPRESSED. YOUR FIRM HAS BEEN GRANTED COMPLETE ACCESS TO THE INVESTIGATORY FILE, AND YOU HAVE INTERVIEWED YOUR CLIENTS, THE STATE POLICE OFFICERS, THE COURT ADMINISTRATOR AND THE UNIVERSITY PRESIDENT. YOU KNOW ABOUT ALL THE STATEMENTS MADE BY EITHER TIPPER OR MARILYN AND ABOUT THE EVIDENCE SEIZED FROM THEM. YOUR TASK IS TO WRITE A MEMORANDUM DISCUSSING ALL REASONABLE MOTIONS TO SUPPRESS, THE RESPONSE THE STATE WILL MAKE TO THE MOTIONS, AND THE LIKELY RESOLUTION OF EACH MOTION.

Remember that clarity is important. Your answer should make clear each motion to suppress you believe is reasonably available to Marilyn and/or Tipper, the arguments in support of and against these motions, and the most probable resolution. The "most probable resolution" is the least important part of your answer. If your analysis of the strengths and weaknesses of each motion is adequate, the "most probable resolution" is likely to emerge almost automatically. You may use the names of important and familiar cases without full citations or even full titles. For example, if you are relying on Mapp, *you can just use this shorthand reference to the case.*

CRIMINAL PROCEDURE— SAMPLE ANSWER

I. PROBABLE CAUSE

It is probably true that—despite all of the evidence that the police have gathered—Tipper and Marilyn are innocent of any criminal act. The statute provides that it is a felony for any person "to knowingly intercept, receive, record, copy or examine any data" stored in a computer under circumstances in which a reasonable person should know that the person who controls the database is trying to exclude everyone except those who are specifically authorized to examine the data. It is clear from the totality of the facts that neither Tipper nor Marilyn actually decided that they would intercept, receive, record, copy or examine anything in the database. They agreed to examine the difficulty of tapping into the database and *then and only then* to decide whether to go forward with a plan of erasing criminal records.

It is difficult to argue that Tipper and Marilyn have conspired with each other or done anything amounting to an attempt. They have, at most, decided to explore whether or not they will engage in acts which, if undertaken, would be criminal. It is not a crime under the statute to use a modem to contact a database. It is not a crime to experiment. Thus, when all is said and done, it appears that, when all the facts are known, Marilyn and Tipper are not guilty of violating the statute. Indeed, if the police had all the facts at the time they obtained the warrant, they would not have had probable cause for an arrest or search.

But, the question is not whether Marilyn and Tipper are actually guilty. Rather, the question is whether there was probable cause to believe them to be guilty at the time that the police and the magistrate judge engaged in their official acts. It is, after all, possible to have a valid arrest and valid search of people who, in hindsight, are determined to be innocent. Probable cause is not certainty. It is assessed on the basis of information in the hands of governmental actors at the time they act, not afterward.

II. REASONABLE EXPECTATIONS OF PRIVACY

Marilyn and Tipper may argue that the "telephone number identification" violates the reasonable expectation of a caller that she is not being recorded. The Government's response surely will be that caller i.d. is widely enough known that there can be no reasonable expectation of privacy. Moreover, the Government will further argue that any security precautions which the Government takes with respect to its own database cannot be unreasonable when imposed upon outsiders. It will be difficult for Marilyn and Tipper to prevail on this argument.

Similarly, Marilyn and Tipper may seek to challenge the use of undercover officers who lie about their true motives and their identities, especially when they use falsity to obtain entrance into a house (which is as we know neither a database nor a car). But, the Government's response that people have no expectation that others with whom they deal are not cooperating with the Government is surely likely to prevail. The Supreme Court's decisions in *Lopez* and other cases indicate that the Court does not protect people from misplaced confidence in others.

Tipper and Marilyn may consider a challenge to the obtaining of their telephone number by the police from the telephone company. But, cases involving bank records (*Schultz*) suggest that Government agents may obtain information from third parties who possess it without violating any expectations of privacy on the part of persons to whom the information relates.

Another claim that has little chance of success is Marilyn's challenge to Lacey's secret recording of their initial conversation. The Government can argue that people assume the risk that those with whom they speak might be recording the conversation. In view of the Supreme Court's recent expectation of privacy cases, the Government is likely to win.

III. THE SNOOPING BY CAGNEY

Although Cagney's entrance into the apartment was consented to by Tipper, who cannot successfully make a reasonable expectation of privacy argument based on Cagney's undercover status, Cagney's actions inside the apartment cause problems. Cagney has consent to use the computer. Thus, what she finds when she uses it is in plain view. Her question to Tipper about the modem is valid, as is Tipper's answer. Any challenge to the question based on *Miranda* will lose because this is not custodial interrogation and Tipper does not know she is talking to a police officer. (*Perkins*)

When Cagney "leafs through some papers" on the desk without consent, she invites an Arizona v. Hicks challenge, because she goes beyond the scope of her invitation. One question is who has standing to raise the challenge. Marilyn is not home. It might turn on whether the papers belong to both women, or only to one. Assuming that both have standing to make a challenge, the Government will argue that there was consent or that the papers were in plain view. The Government will likely lose, just as it did in *Hicks*. This may be a small search, but *Hicks* indicates that a small search is still a search. Thus, there might be a chance to suppress evidence of the telephone number of the judicial database.

Similarly, when Cagney asks to use a mirror to fix her hair, she engages in questionable conduct. Here too, standing is a question. It might be that only the person whose room was examined has standing. We don't have enough facts to offer a definitive opinion. Tipper will urge that Cagney was feigning having to use the bathroom and to fix her hair. The fact is, however, that the Government will win any challenge to the observations that Cagney made on the way to the bathroom and while standing in the bedroom. Anything observed was in plain view in places which Tipper had consented to have Cagney present. The fact that Cagney had an ulterior motive is not disqualifying. When Cagney picked up the computer paper off the bed, arguably she violated *Hicks* again. This too looks like a little search, but a search nonetheless. It is possible that Tipper and Marilyn may manage to suppress the evidence of the words appearing on the computer paper.

IV. THE DISKETTES

Under *Knotts* and *Karo,* it seems that the police may buy a box of diskettes and place anything that they want in the box. They own it, and they can do with it as they please. A problem arises, however, when they offer the box to Tipper in what is the equivalent of her home. This raises a question whether the special privacy interests of the home are violated. In the "beeper" case, the Court refused to approve the warrantless monitoring of beepers inside a house. This might suggest that electronic surveillance of conversations would be even more likely to be condemned because it is more intrusive. However, the Government will argue that Tipper never purchased the diskettes and at all times understood that she was receiving the property of another. Having chosen to receive it, may Tipper still claim she had a reasonable expectation of privacy that it did not contain anything but diskettes? This is a tough issue based on the few precedents that exist. If Marilyn and Tipper prevail, their statement will be suppressed. If not, the statement will be admissible evidence.

V. THE WARRANT

Marilyn and Tipper will argue that the warrant is the fruit of illegal searches and that there was no probable cause to support it. On the probable cause point, the Government will argue that a magistrate could have concluded that there was an apparent attempt to violate the law. Given the identification system employed by the judicial database and the other evidence obtained by the police, it certainly could have appeared to a reasonable magistrate that the suspects were involved in a conspiracy to violate the Computer Protection Act. There was probable cause on the face of the affidavit.

But, Tipper and Marilyn will be able to raise serious fruit of the poisonous tree questions. Assuming that the two *Hicks* violations discussed above taint the information in the affidavit that Cagney saw the judicial database telephone number in the apartment and saw a computer printout with various words upon it, Tipper and Marilyn will have an argument that, if this evidence were excluded, the warrant would not have issued. The Government will respond that there was sufficient remaining evidence to establish probable cause.

The Government's response will trigger a claim by Tipper and Marilyn that two of the statements contained in the affidavit were false, and on this point they are correct. Cagney's affidavit is absolutely false to the extent that she claims that Tipper told Lacey that she and Marilyn were trying to break into the database. This statement is not only false, but it is also difficult to find any reasonable explanation for it. One problem with the alleged statement is that Lacey was talking to Marilyn while Cagney was with Tipper. Thus, the reference to Lacey's talking to Tipper was certainly wrong. It is possible, however, that this is a typo and that Cagney meant to put "Marilyn" in place of "Tipper." The fact remains, however, that the conversation that is described did not occur. Cagney does not fairly summarize what Marilyn told Lacey. The other statement that is false is Cagney's statement that she and Lacey overheard a conversation in which Tipper stated to Marilyn that they should try to break into the database tomorrow night. There was no such conversation. Instead, the officers overheard Tipper say, "why don't we try the database again tomorrow night." Tipper did not say that the two should try to break in. We know from the facts that Tipper and Marilyn agreed not to decide whether to break in until they were sure that they would be able to do so if they wanted to.

Thus, Tipper and Marilyn have a Franks v. Delaware issue. The Court will disregard all statements made perjuriously or with reckless disregard of the truth. The first false statement appears to be of this type. It creates a conversation that never occurred. It is difficult to know how this can be deemed to be an honest error. The second statement is more problematic. Cagney will assert that she believed she heard the statement she reported, and that she reported it as she remembered it. This might well be a case of negligence, and negligently included information is not disregarded in the warrant application. Thus, the issue is whether, assuming the first statement cannot be relied upon but the second can be, there is sufficient evidence remaining to establish probable cause. If the *Hicks* violations exclude the evidence of the telephone number and the computer paper, and if the first *Franks* statement is excluded, Tipper and Marilyn's chances of success in having the warrant invalidated improve. Moreover, if the hidden mike in the diskette box is deemed to have been an intrusion into a reasonable expectation of privacy, the second *Franks* statement would be suppressed and the warrant application would have little left to support it.

Of course, the Government will argue good faith and cite *Leon*. *Leon* will excuse police who rely on a warrant issued by a magistrate when the warrant is not bad on its face. The Courts are divided on whether *Leon* applies to a warrant based on information obtained in violation of the Fourth Amendment. If the evidence discussed in the several paragraphs immediately preceding is suppressed, the only remaining evidence will be the identification of Marilyn's telephone number by the secret identification system, the fact that the telephone number is listed to Marilyn, the observation of the computer and the knowledge of a modem. Is this enough to establish probable cause? Marilyn and Tipper will argue that it is not, and the Government will argue that it is. The Government's argument will not be strong at this point.

If the warrant is invalid, and not excused by the good faith exception, the search conducted pursuant to it will be invalid. If the warrant is valid, or excused by the good faith exception, the search is valid, up to a point. The point is the overbreadth of the warrant. Marilyn and Tipper will cite *Andresen* and claim that the language "any other records" is overbroad. The Government will cite the same case and argue that the language is similar to that approved by the Court. Marilyn and Tipper have the stronger argument. In *Andresen* the warrant was limited, according to the Supreme Court, to documents involving Lot 13T in a particular subdivision. The officers' discretion was therefore limited. No such limitation exists in the warrant described here. Many lower court decisions condemn such broad language. However, under the good faith exception, the warrant must be so overboard that no reasonable person could rely on it.

Assuming that the language is that overbroad, Marilyn and Tipper might be able to suppress the checkbooks, calendars, phone bills and other papers seized. Standing will rear its head again, however. Each can only suppress the items as to which she had a reasonable expectation of privacy.

VI. THE ARREST OF TIPPER

If the warrant is invalid as lacking in probable cause when all of the fruits of the poisonous tree are excluded, the arrest of Tipper is invalid for two reasons. First, the entry into the home would be pursuant to an invalid warrant, making the arrest of Tipper in the home invalid under *Payton*. Second, if there was no probable cause to search, there would appear to be no probable cause to arrest; the bulk of the evidence would be tainted.

If the arrest is invalid, the search incident thereto is invalid, and the fruits thereof would be suppressed. The fruits would include the statement made by Tipper. The Government might argue that an invalid arrest in the home does not require suppression of evidence (*Harris*), but it would lose as to evidence obtained in the home as a result of an illegal search and arrest.

VII. TIPPER'S STATEMENT

If Tipper was validly arrested, she will nevertheless claim that the statement she made to the officers should be suppressed because she was in custody. The Government will argue that she volunteered the statement and that like *Connelly* the Government does not have to stop a person from volunteering. The Government will likely prevail. Tipper may argue that the question, "Sorry about what?" amounted to interrogation. But, the Government will claim that Tipper initiated the entire conversation. At some point, the Government must administer *Miranda* warnings but probably not at the time a person is confessing.

It might be that the question about the whereabouts of Marilyn is Government-initiated. But, it is difficult to find anything incriminating in the answer. Tipper might have a decent *Miranda* issue, but her statement is not likely to help the Government very much. Marilyn lacks standing to complain.

VIII. MARILYN'S STATEMENT TO THE PRESIDENT

The President of a state university is a Government official. When he confronts Marilyn and tells her she is suspended and might be expelled, Marilyn will rely on *Lefkowitz* to argue that any statement she made was compelled in violation of the privilege against self-incrimination. The Government will respond that the threat was less substantial than in *Lefkowitz* and that this was not custodial interrogation. Marilyn will win. Any threat that compels testimony is prohibited, and *Lefkowitz* is not dependent on the existence of custody. Thus, Marilyn will be able to suppress her statement. Tipper has no standing.

IX. THE ARREST OF MARILYN AND SEARCH OF HER CAR

Marilyn can challenge her arrest on the basis of the absence of probable cause. No warrant is required under *Watson* for a felony arrest. If the evidence discussed in connection with Tipper's arrest and the search warrant is suppressed, it is possible that Marilyn's arrest will be invalidated and that all of the evidence that flows from it will be deemed fruit of the poisonous tree.

Even if Marilyn's arrest is valid, she will challenge the search of her car on the ground that it was warrantless. The Government will rely on *Belton* and *Acevedo*. The

Government will lose. *Belton* does not abolish the requirement that a search incident to arrest be relatively contemporaneous, and Belton does not allow the search of a trunk. And *Acevedo* does not excuse probable cause as the minimum standard for an auto search. There is nothing in the facts presented to demonstrate probable cause to search the car. The paper seized in the trunk of the car will be suppressed, unless the search can be deemed to be a valid inventory search. The police would have to show that they routinely search cars, look in the trunk and examine papers. If the police can show a routine practice, the evidence can be admitted in some courts under the inevitable discovery exception, even if the actual search conducted was not an inventory search.

X. MARILYN'S STATEMENTS

Once Marilyn and Tipper are informed of the charges against them by a magistrate-judge, their *Massiah* rights, as defined in Brewer v. Williams, kick in. Any attempt to deliberately elicit statements from either, absent a valid waiver of the *Massiah* right, will be condemned. Thus, Marilyn will move to suppress her statement to Cagney. It appears that the statement is obtained in violation of both *Massiah* and *Miranda*, since it involves custodial questioning of a person after a formal charge has been leveled and without a valid waiver under *Patterson*. This is not an *Edwards* or *Jackson* situation because there is no indication that Marilyn mentioned the word "lawyer" until after she made a statement. Under *Miranda* her statement can be used for impeachment. Whether it can be so used under *Massiah* is still open. Because this is not a *Jackson* case, the *Harvey* rationale is not directly applicable.

Apparently, the police have sought to enlist Marilyn's parents to assist them. Marilyn's parents become agents of the police under *Massiah* (but not *Miranda* because of *Perkins*) when they obtain a statement from Marilyn and relay it to the police. Marilyn will move to suppress under *Massiah*. The Government will cite *Mauro* and claim that they did not force the parents to ask any questions or Marilyn to answer any. But, *Mauro* is not on point. It is a *Miranda* case in which the Mauros were permitted to talk with each other only if a police officer was present. The officer put a tape recorder in plain view. The instant case is a *Massiah* case, and the facts presented are akin to *Massiah* itself, since Marilyn did not know she was dealing with parents who had been directed by the Government to seek information. Her motion to suppress her statement is likely to be granted.

XI. TIPPER'S STATEMENT

Tipper will move to suppress the contents of her telephone conversation with Cagney. She will urge that her *Massiah* rights were violated. But, she volunteered the first part of the statement. It is difficult to say that Cagney deliberately elicited anything. When Cagney suggests that Tipper come to the station, the situation may change.

Tipper will argue that this is deliberate elicitation. The government will respond that it is all part of what Tipper initiated. This is a close question.

XII. THE INDICTMENT

Tipper and Marilyn might move to dismiss the indictment on the ground that it is the fruit of the various illegalities set forth above. Should they prevail on many of their claims, little admissible evidence would exist. Yet, the *Calandra* case indicates that challenges to grand jury action on the basis of illegally seized evidence are not likely to succeed.

APPENDIX C

GLOSSARY

A

Administrative Search: As there is a reduced expectation of privacy in commercial property (as opposed to an individual's private residence), the Court allows for warrantless administrative inspections of pervasively/closely regulated industries if the warrantless inspection necessarily furthers a substantial governmental interest, and statutes provide constitutionally adequate substitutes for a warrant (i.e. notification, scope, limitation of inspector's discretion.) SEE SPECIAL NEEDS ANALYSIS

Arrest: To deprive a person of his liberty by legal authority based on probable cause for the purpose of holding or detaining him to answer a criminal charge. All that is required for an "arrest" is some act by an officer indicating his intention to detain or take a person into custody and thereby subject that person to the actual control and will of the officer; no formal declaration of arrest is required. SEE CUSTODIAL INTERROGATION, MIRANDA RIGHTS

Arrest Warrant: A written order of the court which is made on behalf of the state, or United States, and is based upon a complaint, or the filing, and is issued pursuant to statute and/or court rule and which commands a law enforcement officer to arrest a person and bring him before a magistrate. The warrant is issued by a "neutral and detached magistrate"—as opposed to police officers who are engaged in the often competitive enterprise of ferreting out crime—who is capable of determining whether probable cause exists. The warrant must be signed by the magistrate and must contain the name of the defendant or, if his name is unknown, any name or description by which he can be identified with reasonable certainty. Although an arrest warrant is not necessary for arrests made in public, an arrest warrant must be issued for an in-home arrest in the absence of exigent circumstances, as it is presumptively unreasonable to make a search or seizure in a home without a warrant. For Fourth Amendment purposes, an arrest warrant founded on probable cause implicitly carries with it the limited authority to enter a dwelling in which the suspect lives when there is reason to believe the suspect is within. However, it is important to note that a warrantless in-home arrest *itself* is not illegal, but merely constitutes an illegal *search* of the home. Also, a *search* warrant is necessary when looking for a suspect in a third party's home absent exigent circumstances or consent. Otherwise, an arrest warrant for a suspect could be used as a "general warrant" to search an entire neighborhood. COMPARE SEARCH WARRANT

Attenuation: Under the totality of circumstances, if "fruit" from an illegal search or seizure did not come through the exploitation of that illegality, but instead, by means sufficiently distinguishable to be purged of the primary taint, then the evidence is admissible at trial and is not subject to the exclusionary rule. The egregiousness or flagrancy of the initial violation will be an important factor in the court's determination of whether or not the fruit is tainted. SEE FRUIT OF THE POISONOUS TREE DOCTRINE

Automobile exception: An automobile can ordinarily be searched without a warrant, so long as there is probable cause to believe that evidence or contraband is located in the area to be searched. This exception does not require that the car actually be in motion at the time the officers obtain such probable cause. If the police do not perform an immediate search, the car may be seized and held without a warrant, and a subsequent warrantless search is ordinarily valid.

B

Border search: Search conducted by immigration or customs officials at borders of the country to prevent and to detect illegal entry, whether or not there is any suspicion of illegality directed to the particular person or thing to be searched. The border search is a longstanding, historically recognized exception to the warrant requirement that validates the Government's strong interest in protecting American borders and regulating goods flowing into the country (i.e. narcotics, explosives,

illegal aliens, communicable diseases.) "Routine" border searches—any search at a level below a body cavity or full strip search—require no suspicion at all; non-routine border searches require reasonable suspicion. To qualify as a "border search" a search must occur at the border or its functional equivalent. SEE SEARCH

C

Consent search: A warrantless search made by police after the subject of the search has "freely and voluntarily" consented as determined by the totality of the circumstances. "Voluntary" consent means that it was not the result of duress or coercion, express or implied, or any other form of undue influence exercised against the defendant. As consenting to a search is not considered a *waiver* of a right, the test is merely whether consent was voluntary. There is no requirement that the suspect be informed of the right to refuse consent. The state has the burden to prove "voluntariness" by a preponderance of the evidence. Furthermore, it is up to the suspect to limit and define any ambiguities regarding the scope of the consent. COMPARE WAIVER

Custodial Interrogation: Custodial interrogation, within the *Miranda* rule requiring that the suspect be advised of his constitutional rights, means questioning initiated by law enforcement officers after a person has been taken into custody or otherwise deprived of his freedom in any significant way. Custody can occur without the formality of arrest and in areas other than in a police station; basically it is a question of whether the police officers are controlling the situation in a manner that would lead a reasonable person to believe that he is in custody. SEE INTERROGATION

D

Deliberate Elicitation: After the suspect has been formally charged, a police officer may not "deliberately elicit" a response from a defendant without an attorney present, or a valid waiver of counsel. In the context of Sixth Amendment Right to Counsel, "deliberation" can be shown when the officer's statements are reasonably likely to elicit a response. "Eliciting" a response can be accomplished in ways more subtle than simply questioning the defendant. "Elicitation" occurs when the officer causes information to be drawn out of the defendant; this requires an affirmative effort, an active attempt, by the officer or Government agent. Simply listening to the defendant speak is not enough to trigger the "elicitation" element in the Sixth Amendment right to counsel. The court's focus in determining whether information was "deliberately elicited" from the defendant is on the intent of the officer as he converses or speaks with the suspect.

E

Encounter: An encounter occurs when the contact between police officers and citizens is at a level where a reasonable, innocent person, in view of all the circumstances surrounding the incident, would believe he was free to decline the officers' requests or otherwise terminate the encounter. As an encounter is not defined for Fourth Amendment purposes as a "seizure" of a citizen and, indeed, is considered totally consensual, it does not need to be justified by any standard of proof (i.e. the police officer need not *justify* his contact with that citizen.) COMPARE STOP AND FRISK, ARREST

Exclusionary Rule: Where evidence has been obtained in violation of the search and seizure protections guaranteed by the Fourth Amendment of the Constitution, the illegally obtained evidence cannot be used in the case-in-chief against the defendant, and this rule has been held to be applicable to the States. However, since this remedy is a court-created rule, and not explicitly required by the Constitution, the illegally obtained evidence *can* be used at the trial to impeach the credibility of the defendant, as well as in numerous other proceedings—i.e. civil litigation, sentencing, and parole and probation revocation hearings. SEE GOOD FAITH EXCEPTION, FRUIT OF THE POISONOUS TREE DOCTRINE

Exigent Circumstances: Emergency conditions which excuse the warrant requirement.

F

Fruit of the Poisonous Tree doctrine: Evidence which is spawned by or directly derived from an illegal search or illegal interrogation is generally inadmissible against the defendant because of its original taint, although knowledge of facts gained independently of the original and tainted search is admissible.

G

"Good Faith" exception to the exclusionary rule: Provides that evidence is not to be suppressed where it was discovered by officers acting in good faith and in reasonable, though mistaken, belief that they were authorized by a magistrate or by the legislature to take those actions.

H

Habeas Corpus: A collateral proceeding instituted to determine whether a defendant is being unlawfully deprived of his or her liberty; a means by which to challenge the constitutionality of a decision after all appeals have elapsed. It is not an appropriate proceeding for appeal-like review of discretionary decisions of a lower court; it tests the state court's application of the law *at the time* of the case. Thus, new rules of law are not generally retroactive on habeas, except for two very limited exceptions.

I

Independent Source: An exception to the exclusionary rule which allows evidence to be introduced if it can be traced to a source independent from an illegal search or arrest.

Inevitable Discovery: A "hypothetical" independent source exception to the exclusionary rule, which permits evidence to be admitted in a criminal case, even though it was obtained unlawfully, when the Government can show by a preponderance of the evidence that discovery of the evidence by lawful means was inevitable. This rule applies even if police officers act in bad faith (i.e. deliberate violation of defendant's Fourth Amendment rights) because the exclusionary rule is not designed to place police officers in a worse position than if the violation had never happened. A minority of courts have limited the inevitable discovery exception by requiring the police to be "actively pursuing" lawful means at the time that the illegal search is being conducted. COMPARE INDEPENDENT SOURCE, FRUIT OF THE POISONOUS TREE DOCTRINE

Interrogation: Questions asked by an officer as well as any comments or ploys which are "reasonably likely to evoke an incriminating response" from the average suspect. SEE CUSTODIAL INTERROGATION

Inventory search: An inventory search is an administrative step following arrest and preceding incarceration, or following the valid seizure of property. This community caretaking function requires regulations and police procedures to be in place in order to control discretion of the officers. "Inventory" is a detailed list of articles of property, containing a designation or description of each specific article.

Invocation: For Fifth Amendment purposes, a defendant must affirmatively invoke his Miranda rights to silence and counsel (as opposed to his Sixth Amendment right to counsel which is triggered merely by the arraignment process or a similar formal proceeding). If a defendant waives his right to silence after an invocation, the Government can prove the "voluntary" waiver prong by showing they "scrupulously honored" defendant's rights by giving defendant a cooling off period after he cut off questioning, as well as proving the defendant knowingly and intelligently waived his rights. If a defendant invokes his right to counsel, the police officers are not allowed to interrogate or re-approach the defendant unless his counsel is there or the defendant himself initiates the interrogation. SEE WAIVER

L

Legitimate expectation of privacy: "What a person knowingly exposes to the public, even in his own home or office, is not subject to Fourth Amendment protection. But what he seeks to preserve as private, even in an area accessible to the public, may be constitutionally protected." Police activity does not constitute a search unless it intrudes upon a legitimate expectation of privacy.

M

Miranda rights: Prior to any custodial interrogation (that is, questioning initiated by law enforcement officers after a person is taken into custody or otherwise deprived of his freedom in any significant way) the person must be warned: 1) that he has a right to remain silent; 2) that any statement he does make may be used as evidence against him; 3) that he has a right to the presence of an attorney; 4) that if he cannot afford an attorney, one will be appointed for him prior to any questioning if he so desires. Unless and until these warnings and a waiver of these rights are demonstrated at the trial, no evidence obtained in the interrogation may be used against the accused. However, as the *Miranda* warnings are simply prophylactic measures designed to ensure the constitutional right against self-incrimination, evidence from a Miranda violation *is* permitted at trial to impeach the credibility of the defendant, as well as in numerous other proceedings. SEE PROPHYLACTIC RULE

N

"New" rule: "New rules" are generally inapplicable to habeas cases. The Supreme Court defines a "new rule" as one not dictated by existing precedent. SEE HABEAS CORPUS

O

Open field doctrine: This doctrine permits police officers to enter and search a field without a warrant as there is no legitimate expectation of privacy: "Open fields do not provide the setting for those intimate activities that the Amendment is intended to shelter from government interference or surveillance." The term "open fields" may include any unoccupied or undeveloped area outside of the curtilage. COMPARE PLAIN VIEW

P

Plain View: Objects within the plain view of an officer engaged in legal activity are subject to seizure without a warrant and may be introduced in evidence.

Probable Cause: A fair probability of criminal activity under the totality of circumstances. It is a fluid concept turning on the assessment of probabilities in particular factual contexts—not readily, or even usefully, reduced to a neat set of rules. Probable cause to arrest exists where facts and circumstances within officers' knowledge and of which they had reasonably trustworthy information are sufficient in themselves to warrant a person of reasonable caution in the belief that an offense has been or is being committed; it is not necessary that the officer possess knowledge of facts sufficient to establish guilt, but more than mere suspicion is required.

Prophylactic Rule: Prophylactic rules are court-made safeguards or practical reinforcements of rights protected by the Constitution.

Protective Sweep: When police officers have a legal right to enter premises they are allowed to conduct a quick and limited search of the premises if they have reasonable suspicion to believe that such an inspection is necessary to protect themselves and others from potential harm.

R

Reasonable Suspicion: The standard of proof necessary to justify a *Terry* stop. Police officers must have a particularized and objective basis—based on specific and articulable facts—for suspecting the defendant of criminal activity. The relevant inquiry is not whether particular conduct is innocent or guilty but the degree of suspicion that attaches to particular types of non-criminal acts. COMPARE PROBABLE CAUSE, ENCOUNTER

S

Search: Visual observation or physical intrusion which infringes upon a person's reasonable expectation of privacy constitutes a "search" in the constitutional sense.

Search Incident to Arrest: A police officer who has the right to arrest a person either with or without a warrant may search his person and the immediate area of the arrest for weapons and to prevent the destruction of evidence. Often, a search incident to arrest results in exigent circumstances which allows for a wider, more thorough search for hidden evidence or dangerous compatriots. However, exigent circumstances must be proven by the facts of each case, and the fact of arrest, while pertinent, is not dispositive of whether there is a risk of destruction of evidence or harm to police officers. The Supreme Court has held that when a person is arrested in a car, police can automatically search the passenger compartment. SEE EXIGENT CIRCUMSTANCES

Search Warrant: The Fourth Amendment provides that "no warrants shall issue, but upon probable cause, supported by oath or affirmation, and particularly describing the place to be searched, and the persons or things to be seized." A search warrant is an order in writing, issued by a justice or other magistrate, in the name of the state, directed to a sheriff, constable, or other officer, authorizing him to search for and seize any property that constitutes evidence of the commission of a crime, contraband, the fruits of crime, or things otherwise criminally possessed; or, property designed or intended for use or which is or has been used as the means of committing a crime. A warrant may be issued upon an affidavit or sworn oral testimony.

Seizure: A "seizure" of property under the Fourth Amendment occurs when there is some meaningful interference with an individual's possessory interest in that property. "Seizure" of an individual, within the Fourth Amendment, connotes the taking of one physically or constructively into custody and detaining him, thus causing a deprivation of his freedom in a significant way, with real interruption of his liberty of movement. An officer's actual physical touching or grasping of a suspect is always defined as a seizure whether or not the suspect submits to being detained. However, if an officer engages in a non-physical show of authority, a seizure occurs only if a reasonable person would not feel free to leave *and* actually submits to authority.

Special Needs Analysis: When a search is conducted for a "special need" beyond criminal law enforcement, the Supreme Court has reasoned that the traditional requirement of a warrant based on probable cause is ill-suited to such searches. Special needs searches and seizures are permitted if they are reasonable. This "reasonableness" analysis balances the need for a particular search against the degree of invasion upon personal rights which the search entails. Special needs analysis has been applied to administrative, civil-based, and public safety searches. SEE ADMINISTRATIVE SEARCH

Standing Requirement: For Fourth Amendment purposes, an individual must show that he personally had a legitimate expectation of privacy in the area searched in order to establish standing to object to the evidence obtained.

Stop and Frisk: Reasonable suspicion allows a police officer to stop a person suspected of criminal activity. Attendant to a stop, a frisk may be conducted if the officer has reasonable suspicion that the suspect is armed and dangerous. A frisk is conducted to protect an officer's safety, is limited to removal of possible weapons, and is not an evidentiary search. COMPARE ENCOUNTER, ARREST

T

Totality of Circumstances test: Test used to determine the constitutionality of various search and seizure procedures, including the issuance of a search warrant. The test focuses on all the circumstances of a particular case, rather than any one factor.

U

Unnecessarily suggestive: The Due Process Clause prohibits the admission of identifications where unnecessary suggestiveness has created a substantial likelihood of irreparable mistaken identification. However, an unnecessarily suggestive procedure will not always taint a line-up or other identification procedure.

V

Voluntariness: Under the Due Process Clause, involuntary confessions by a suspect will not be allowed as evidence at trial. Whether a confession is "voluntary" is determined by the amount of coercive police activity involved (rather than on the defendant's state of mind), and is reviewed on a case-by-case, totality of the circumstances basis. Police officers are allowed to play on a suspect's ignorance, anxieties, fears, and uncertainties; but they are not allowed to magnify them to the point where rational decision becomes impossible.

W

Waiver: The knowing and voluntary relinquishment—express or implied—of a legal right.

APPENDIX D

TEXT CORRELATION CHART

	Saltzburg & Capra (4th Edition)	Kamisar, LaFave, & Israel (2nd Edition)	Allen & Kuhns (2nd Edition)	Scarboro & White	Johnson	Weinreb (5th Edition)	White & Tomkovicz
ELEMENTS OF THE FOURTH AMENDMENT							
Legitimate Expectation of Privacy	23–35	148–51	421–512	1–47	18–23		1–8
Probable Cause	67–101	173–98	565–99	118–77	175–94	42–43, 265–76	51–86
Warrant and Particulars	55–67, 101–136, 157–61	164–73, 198–208	599–608, 811–19	178–92, 288–89, 400–02	104–28, 153–58, 160–74, 194–99	43–44, 77–84, 86–90, 250–53, 267–77, 324–35, 356–66	86–125
Arrests —In House	151–57, 383–84	232–40	650–65	322–24	109–116	43–58	155–72
—Out of House	136–51	208–19	647–50	304–12	635–42	24–43, 62–76, 84–85, 94–109	90–101
SEARCHES NOT COVERED BY THE FOURTH AMENDMENT							
Open Fields	36–39	156–57	521–29		68–69	405–7	22–30
Public Access	35–36, 39–45, 343–46	151–56, 157–59	512–21, 529–44		65–71, 89–96	397–405	15–22, 31–49
Only Illegal Activity	45–48	160–62			78–80	136	45, 334–40
Sensory Enhancement Devices	48–52	162–64			80–89	396	8–14
EXCEPTIONS TO WARRANT AND PROBABLE CAUSE							
Plain View	211–212, 238–43	225–27	638–47, 794–98	388–400	118–19	286–94	269–85
Exigent Circumstances	155–56, 219–20, 265–82	227–32, 238–39	609–14		142–53	287–88, 300–04, 321–24	176–84
Inventory Search	313–19	263–69	747–55	359–82	136–42	334–42	225–45

	Saltzburg & Capra (4th Edition)	Kamisar, LaFave, & Israel (2nd Edition)	Allen & Kuhns (2nd Edition)	Scarboro & White	Johnson	Weinreb (5th Edition)	White & Tomkovicz
Search Incident to Arrest —General	213–30	219–225, 295–308	720–39	289–304, 313–22, 325–51, 382–88	104–115	297–307	126–47, 172–76
—Automobile	230–37	257–63	739–47		155	307–9	147–54
Car Exception —General	244–53	240–46	614–25	193–98, 209–11, 351–59		325–34	184–202
—Movable Property (Luggage/Containers)	253–64	246–57	625–38	346	128–36	305–7	202–225
Consent	330–41	321–35	829–43	430–51	97–103	231–62	246–69
Stop & Frisk, and the Boundaries of Reasonable Suspicion	161–213	269–95	684–720, 769–93, 810–28	193–245	200–241	116–67	286–373, 398–419
—Roadblocking (*Sitz*)	309–313	315–16	759–69		255–60	167–78	388–95
SPECIAL NEEDS							
Administrative Search	282–93	308–12	665–83	245–61	158–59	346–7	397
Civil Based (School/Prison)	52–55, 294	159–60, 316–19	798–804		2–18, 71–78	260–2	374–88
Public Safety (Airport/Railroads)	294–309	319–21	804–810	261–64		395	395–97
Border	319–330	312–15	755–59	265–87	242–55	394–5	332–33
REMEDIES							
Exclusionary Rule	27–28, 356–69, 372–77	118–24, 141–48	544–64	47–117	24–64, 261–69	179–85	693–709
Good Faith Exception	410–34	124–41	891–906		286–320	185–218	791–817
Standing	395–404	728–47	847–66	403–29	273–82	359–84	709–739

	Saltzburg & Capra (4th Edition)	Kamisar, LaFave, & Israel (2nd Edition)	Allen & Kuhns (2nd Edition)	Scarboro & White	Johnson	Weinreb (5th Edition)	White & Tomkovicz
Fruit of the Poisonous Tree							
—Independent Source	384–90	753–56	884–87			275	740–48
—Inevitable Source	390–93	757–62	1358–65			218–28	748–59
—Attenuation	377–84	747–52	867–72	451–63	271	95–98	759–75
—Identification of Live Witness	394–95	752–53, 756–57	872–84		269–73	97	773–74
Impeachment	404–410	773–81	888–90, 1329–58		282–86	184–5	817–37
RETROACTIVITY	15–22	38–43, 1516–59	98–116	840–68		1408	
SELECTIVE INCORPORATION	5–15	28–38	67–98	78–82			
ELEMENTS OF THE FIFTH AMENDMENT							
Fifth Amendment Right against Self-Incrimination (*Miranda*)	440–88, 508–25, 552–53	441–75, 539–59	1105–1156, 1207–08	464–87, 544–57	346–59, 412–28, 540–50	523–27	479–98
—Public Safety Exception (*Quarles*)	571–74	471, 498–505, 763	1281–1296		462–67	595–8	498–507
Waiver	533–41	475–81, 505–09	1208–1224	557–59	485–95	545–9	538–51
—after Invocation of the Right to Silence	541–42	509–11	1224–26	559	484–85	537–8	551–59
—after Invocation of the Right to Counsel	542–52	511–39	1227–1243		482–85	549–51	559–77
Custody (defined)	553–60	481–87	1181–1207	559–61	456–67	573–81	508–20
Interrogation (defined)	561–70	487–98	1156–1181	561–64	468–73, 481–82	539–45	520–38
Prophylactic Rule	525–33	470–73, 552–4, 763–64	1230–31, 1296–1313	564–81	495–502	599–604	775–91
Voluntariness	488–504	412–31, 559–75	1084–96, 1277–1328	509–26	397–405, 502–40	503–8	447–77

ELEMENTS OF THE SIXTH AMENDMENT	Saltzburg & Capra (4th Edition)	Kamisar, LaFave, & Israel (2nd Edition)	Allen & Kuhns (2nd Edition)	Scarboro & White	Johnson	Weinreb (5th Edition)	White & Tomkovicz
Sixth Amendment Right to Counsel (*Massiah & Brewer*)	504-08, 574-84	431-41, 575-84	1096-1105	526-42	405-12	508-516	579-600
Waiver	584-87	585-88	1270-77		485	514	600-01
Deliberate Elicitation (defined)	587-93	584-85, 588-95	1243-70		473-82	511-3	601-24
Identification —General (*Wade/Gilbert*)	596-605	596-612	331-59	625-26, 628	429-53	471-81	625-42
—Limits (*Kirby/Ash*)	605-08	612-21	359-93	628	453-54	481-8	643-665
Due Process—Unnecessary Suggestiveness	608-27	621-33	393-420	628-29	439-44, 454-55	481	667-91
Right to Counsel —Indigents	628-50	54-103, 1121-26	123-208	539-42	360-78	681-4	
—Counsel of Choice	1067-84	1060-73, 1100-21	267-83, 316-330			687	
Right to Self-Representation (*Faretta*)	1084-98	1048-60	283-316	539	390-96	1214-24	
Ineffective Assistance of Counsel	1023-67	1073-1100	208-267	542-44	378-90	1196-1211	

APPENDIX E

TABLE OF CASES

†